NO LONGER T
UNIVERSITY OF

D0780336

THE YALE EDITIONS OF
The Private Papers of James Boswell
(Research Edition)

FREDERICK W. HILLES (1900–1975)

The Editorial Committee of the Yale Editions of the Private Papers of James Boswell records with deep sense of loss the death on 10 December 1975 of Frederick W. Hilles, Ph.D., L.H.D., O.B.E., Bodman Professor of English Emeritus, Yale University. He was an active and much valued member of the Editorial Committee from the inception of the Yale Editions in 1949. An authority in everything pertaining to the great painter to whom the *Life of Johnson* is dedicated, he edited the third volume of Yale's Reading Edition of the Boswell Papers, *Portraits, by Sir Joshua Reynolds*. He served from 1949 as General Editor of Yale's Research Edition of Boswell's Correspondence, of which the present volume is the third. His quiet but generous benefactions over many years were crucial to the continued publication of the Yale Boswell Editions.

Boswell's Correspondence, Volume 3
General Editor: Frederick W. Hilles

THE CORRESPONDENCE OF JAMES BOSWELL
WITH CERTAIN MEMBERS OF THE CLUB

THE CORRESPONDENCE

OF

James Boswell

WITH

Certain Members
of The Club

including Oliver Goldsmith, Bishops Percy and Barnard,
Sir Joshua Reynolds, Topham Beauclerk,
and Bennet Langton

EDITED WITH AN INTRODUCTION AND NOTES BY
CHARLES N. FIFER

PROFESSOR OF ENGLISH
STANFORD UNIVERSITY

McGRAW-HILL BOOK COMPANY
NEW YORK   TORONTO

First published in 1976 in Great Britain by William Heinemann Ltd. Copyright © 1976 by Yale University. Simultaneously published in the United States by McGraw-Hill Book Company. All rights reserved by Yale University. No part of this publication may be reproduced, stored in a retrieval system, or transmitted, in any form or by any means, electronic, mechanical, photocopying, recording, or otherwise, without the prior written permission of the publisher.

Library of Congress Cataloguing in Publication Data

Boswell, James, 1740–1795.
The correspondence of James Boswell with certain members of The Club, including Oliver Goldsmith, Bishops Percy and Barnard, Sir Joshua Reynolds, Topham Beauclerk and Bennet Langton.

(His Correspondence, v. 3) (The Yale editions of the private papers of James Boswell)
Includes bibliographical references.
1. Boswell, James, 1740–1795. I. Fifer, Charles N., 1922–   ed. II. Title. III. Series: The Yale editions of the private papers of James Boswell.
PR3325.A94   vol. 3   828'.6'09 [B]   73–18260
ISBN 0–07–020750–x

PR
3325
A94
V.3

PRINTED IN GREAT BRITAIN

EDITORIAL COMMITTEE

FREDERICK A. POTTLE, Ph.D., Litt.D., L.H.D., LL.D., Sterling Professor of English Emeritus, Yale University; *Chairman.*

FRANK BRADY, Ph.D., Professor of English, Graduate School and Hunter College, City University of New York.

FREDERICK W. HILLES, Ph.D., L.H.D., O.B.E., Bodman Professor of English Emeritus, Yale University.

HERMAN W. LIEBERT, Librarian Emeritus, Beinecke Rare Book and Manuscript Library, Yale University.

DAN LACY, M.A., Litt.D., Senior Vice President, McGraw-Hill Book Company.

ADVISORY COMMITTEE

WALTER JACKSON BATE, Ph.D., Abbott Lawrence Lowell Professor of the Humanities, Harvard University.

WILLIAM BEATTIE, C.B.E., M.A., LL.D., Litt.D., Honorary Professor of the University of Edinburgh, Sometime Librarian of the National Library of Scotland.

THOMAS G. BERGIN, Ph.D., Litt.D., L.H.D., O.B.E., Sterling Professor of Romance Languages Emeritus, Yale University.

PAUL S. BREUNING, Litt.D., Sometime Deputy Librarian of the University of Utrecht.

CLEANTH BROOKS, B.Litt., D.Litt., L.H.D., Gray Professor of Rhetoric, Yale University.

JAMES L. CLIFFORD, Ph.D., Litt.D., L.H.D., F.R.S.L., William Peterfield Trent Professor of English Emeritus, Columbia University.

THE RIGHT HONOURABLE THE EARL OF CRAWFORD AND BALCARRES, K.T., G.B.E., Litt.D., D.C.L., LL.D., Chairman of the Board of Trustees, National Library of Scotland.

L. P. CURTIS, Ph.D., Colgate Professor of History Emeritus, Yale University.

SIR JAMES FERGUSSON OF KILKERRAN, Bart., LL.D., F.R.S.E., Sometime Keeper of the Records of Scotland.

ARTHUR A. HOUGHTON, Jr., L.H.D., LL.D., Litt.D., Lit.D., D.Sc., New York City.

MARY HYDE, Ph.D., D.Litt., Four Oaks Farm, Somerville, New Jersey.

RONALD IRELAND, Q.C., Sheriff of the Lothians and Peebles.

W. S. LEWIS, Litt.D., L.H.D., LL.D., F.R.S.L., F.S.A., Fellow Emeritus of Yale University and Editor of the Yale Edition of Horace Walpole's Correspondence.

HENRI PEYRE, Dr. ès L., Sterling Professor of French Emeritus, Yale University.

L. F. POWELL, M.A., D.Litt., F.R.S.L., F.L.A., Sometime Librarian of the Taylor Institution, Reviser of Hill's Edition of Boswell's *Life of Johnson.*

UNDERGRADUATE

76 - 135980

NOV 11 1976

UNIVERSITY OF WASHINGTON LIBRARY
CONCORDIA UNIVERSITY LIBRARY
PORTLAND. OR 97211

GENERAL EDITORIAL NOTE

THE research edition of the Private Papers of James Boswell will consist of at least three co-ordinated series: Boswell's journal in all its varieties, his correspondence, and the *Life of Johnson* in an arrangement which will show the method and progress of its composition. The undertaking is a co-operative one involving many scholars, and publication will proceed in the order in which the volumes are completed for the press. It is expected that the whole edition will consist of not fewer than thirty volumes.

In the parallel "reading" or "trade" edition, which began publication in 1950 and has now reached its tenth volume, those portions of the papers have been selected which appeared likely to interest the general reading public, and the object of the annotation has been to illuminate the documents themselves as compositions. The annotation in that series may be said to be turned in towards the text.

The annotation of the research edition, on the contrary, is turned out from the text, and is intended to relate the documents to the various areas of scholarship which they are capable of illuminating: history in many of its varieties (literary, linguistic, legal, medical, political, social, local), biography, bibliography, and genealogy. The comprehensiveness and coherence of the papers that Boswell chose to preserve make them almost uniquely useful for such exploitation.

The journal and its related notes and memoranda will be presented in one chronological sequence, but the correspondence will appear in three different kinds of volumes: *subject* volumes, which will select letters relatable to a topic or theme, of which the present volume is an illustration, *single-correspondence* volumes (for example, Boswell's correspondence with John Johnston of Grange); and *miscellaneous-correspondence* volumes, which will collect the remaining letters in chronological sequence. Since, with all its gaps, the journal provides a more continuous and detailed record of Boswell's life than the correspondence does, it has been taken as the primary document for the annotation of his daily activities and the identification of the persons he met or mentioned. In particular, the volumes of the journal will contain, in alphabetized Biographical Supplements, condensed biographical accounts of all the contemporaries of Boswell whom he mentions in those volumes in more than an allusive way. The correspondence volumes will deal in a more summary fashion with matters that are to receive systematic "depth" annotation in the journal volumes, but will themselves provide "depth" annotation on their own special topics and on persons and events not mentioned in the journal.

FRANK BRADY
FREDERICK W. HILLES
HERMAN W. LIEBERT
DAN LACY

FREDERICK A. POTTLE
Chairman

ACKNOWLEDGEMENTS

IT is, of course, impossible to acknowledge the assistance of everyone who has helped me to prepare this edition or to indicate specifically the nature of their contributions. I can, however, list the names of those, not always mentioned in the notes, to whom I am particularly indebted for their co-operation and generosity. I am especially grateful to F. W. Hilles, F. A. Pottle (for whose help no acknowledgement is adequate), Marion S. Pottle, R. F. Metzdorf, B. F. Houston, Helen Cooper, and Harriet Chidester, all of whom at one time or another have read this book, or portions of it, and have provided an immense amount of help.

Deserving of special thanks are J. C. P. Langton and John Montgomery-Massingberd, descendants of Bennet Langton, for their generosity in providing me with unlimited access to their family records and for their continued friendly interest in the progress of this edition.

For other acts of literary and sometimes even social kindness I am greatly obliged to the following, some of whom are no longer living: Eva S. Balogh, F. W. Bateson, William Beattie, A. S. Bell, Frank Brady, Cleanth Brooks, W. A. Clebsch, J. L. Clifford, R. C. Cole, T. W. Copeland, Mr. and Mrs. Roger Coxon, the Earl of Crawford and Balcarres, T. R. Davis, N. P. Dawnay, W. Enderby, Joseph Ewan, Nesta Ewan, A. F. Falconer, F. G. Fassett, J. D. Fleeman, D. C. Gallup, E. R. Hardy, Donald Hyde, Mary Hyde, J. F. Kermode, Mary E. Knapp, H. W. Liebert, David Levin, E. L. McAdam, Jr., Angus McIntosh, Sir Owen Morshead, D. D. Murison, J. M. Osborn, R. M. Schmitz, Edmund T. Silk, D. Nichol Smith, Joan Varley, Marshall Waingrow, Eugene Waith, R. S. Walker, and David Yerkes.

I am grateful to the American Council of Learned Societies, the American Philosophical Society, the National Endowment for the Humanities, the National Trust, and Yale University for their support, financial and moral, of this volume.

And, finally, acknowledgements are due the staffs of the Yale and Stanford libraries.

C. N. F.

CONTENTS

CONTENTS

ALPHABETICAL TABLE OF
BOSWELL'S CORRESPONDENTS

[1] Letters marked with a dagger are known from various sources of evidence to have existed, but the manuscripts are untraced and no printed texts of them have been found.

TABLE OF BOSWELL'S CORRESPONDENTS

TABLE OF BOSWELL'S CORRESPONDENTS

ALPHABETICAL TABLE OF LANGTON'S CORRESPONDENTS

CORRESPONDENTS OF OTHER
MEMBERS OF THE CLUB

PREFACE

THIS edition of letters contains the known correspondence of James Boswell with the following twenty-four members of The Club, more than half the membership from the year of its founding (1764) to the year of his death (1795): Sir Joshua Reynolds; Bennet Langton; Topham Beauclerk; Oliver Goldsmith; Sir John Hawkins (original members); Thomas Percy, later Bishop of Dromore (1768); Charles James Fox (1774); George Steevens (1774); Thomas Barnard, later Bishop of Killaloe and of Limerick (1775); Adam Smith (1775); Joseph Warton (1777); John Fitzpatrick, second Earl of Upper Ossory (1777); Richard Marlay, later Bishop of Clonfert and of Waterford (1777); William Windham (1778); William Scott, later knighted, and created first Baron Stowell (1778); Edward Craggs-Eliot, first Baron Eliot of St. Germans (1782); Thomas Warton (1782); Richard Burke (1782); Charles Burney (1784); Richard Warren (1784); John Courtenay (1788); Francis Osborne, fifth Duke of Leeds (1792); John Douglas, Bishop of Salisbury, formerly Bishop of Carlisle (1792); and Sir Charles Blagden (1794). Also included are other letters and manuscript material, almost all found in the Boswell Papers, relating to these correspondences: a collection of letters written to and from Langton (among these are twenty letters from Beauclerk);[1] Boswell's *Prologue for the Opening of the Theatre Royal* in Edinburgh; verses written by Boswell to Barnard; and miscellaneous verses and letters pertaining to Barnard, Beauclerk, Richard Burke, Courtenay, Douglas, Macartney, Lord Ossory, and Steevens.[2]

---

[1] Six letters to Langton that turned up among JB's papers have been omitted because they relate in no way to JB or The Club, and would appear to be of little interest to historians on other grounds. They were written to him by Charles Colyear, second Earl of Portmore (two letters); Sir Charles Middleton; Mrs. George Baillie of Jerviswood (two letters, one to Lady Rothes); and a Th. Hall. Also omitted are a Langton family genealogy and three Langton family

letters of the seventeenth and early eighteenth centuries.

[2] Certain letters and other documents written by members of The Club which came to Yale with JB's papers have not been included in the present edition. Thomas Warton's annotated transcript of the letters he had received from SJ (see *post* To Thomas Warton, 13 Apr. 1786) was printed *in extenso* by JB himself in the *Life of Johnson*. Miscellaneous verses by John Courtenay, though presumably

xix

PREFACE

There are no known letters written between Boswell and twenty-three of the first fifty-one members of The Club (those elected during his lifetime): Dr. Christopher Nugent (original); Anthony Chamier (original); Samuel Dyer (1764); Robert Chambers, later Sir Robert (1768); George Colman (1768); James Caulfeild, first Earl of Charlemont (1773); William Jones, later Sir William (1773); Agmondesham Vesey (1773); Sir Thomas Charles Bunbury, Bt. (1774); Dr. George Fordyce (1774); Edward Gibbon (1774); Richard Brinsley Sheridan (1777); John Dunning, later first Baron Ashburton (1777); Joseph Banks, later Sir Joseph, Bt. (1778); George John Spencer, Viscount Althorp, later second Earl Spencer (1778); Jonathan Shipley, Bishop of St. Asaph (1780); Charles Bingham, first Baron Lucan, later first Earl of Lucan (1782); Sir William Hamilton (1784); Henry Temple, second Viscount Palmerston (1784); George Macartney, first Baron (later first Viscount and first Earl) Macartney (1786); John Hinchliffe, Bishop of Peterborough (1792); Major James Rennell (1795); and Richard Farmer (1795). The letters exchanged with Boswell by four other members of The Club, Samuel Johnson and Edmund Burke (original), David Garrick (1773), and Edmond Malone (1782), have been assigned to other volumes in the series.

This volume prints texts of 268 letters. Of this total, 84 were written by Boswell, and 131 were written by various correspondents to him. Fifty-three more, not by or to Boswell, were written by or to other Club members. Of these, 39 are to Langton (one of them is actually addressed to Beauclerk, but was written to Langton as well); one is from Langton to Burke; and 13 are to or from 11 of Boswell's other correspondents in The Club. Fifty-six additional letters (46 from Boswell, 10 to him), for which no texts are known to be extant, receive notice under the proper dates, with as much information about their contents as could be gathered.

collected and preserved by JB, hardly merit publication anywhere. Three letters from Sir William Scott, written to Malone after JB's death, belong properly to Malone's correspondence, just as two letters from Scott and a letter from Earl Spencer to JB's son James belong to the correspondence of the younger Boswell. (He was Malone's executor and literary heir. After his death in 1822 a considerable mass of his and Malone's papers was removed to Auchinleck.) On the other hand, the letter from Thomas Barnard to Sir William Forbes, 27 Mar. 1796, still among Forbes's papers, has been included as a fitting epilogue to the JB-Barnard correspondence.

INTRODUCTION

ADMISSION to The Club was an honour which James Boswell desired and frankly sought. When he began corresponding with Percy, Goldsmith, and Langton, he had not achieved election, though he knew most of the members. His appeal to Percy, 16 April 1773, "remember me at the Club tonight", documents his own admission that he "assiduously and earnestly recommended [him]self to some of the members, as in a canvass for an election into parliament."[1] Without a doubt, membership bolstered his ego. Only seventeen names had been enrolled before his own: he was admitted before Gibbon, Adam Smith, and the Wartons, the last three considerably his elders. Membership in The Club, however, was always more to him than a *cachet*. He was intensely clubbable, preferring good conversation to anything else in life, and where could he find better? Within his opportunities, he was one of the most faithful of all the members in attendance.[2] And of course the tie of The Club led to frequent meetings with members outside, and to correspondence with them. This volume presents part of that correspondence.

The importance of The Club to Boswell is reflected in these letters in his often-repeated request for information ("How does the Club go on?")[2a] and in the responsibility he in turn assumes for reporting its meetings and the activities of its members to fellow members withdrawn to Lincolnshire or Ireland. The Club was important in his correspondents' lives too, as it ought to have been, because of the extraordinary eminence of its members and the range of their talents. In view of the large role that The Club

---

[1] *Life* v. 76 n. 2.

[2] Attendance at The Club was not recorded before 7 Apr. 1775. From that date to the time of his death, JB attended 79 out of 320 meetings, this in spite of the fact that he was not in London at all in 1777, 1780, and 1782, and that in the other years down to 1785 his stay in London could not exceed ten weeks and was generally shorter. After The Club in 1776 gave up weekly suppers for fortnightly dinners during the session of

Parliament (*post* pp. 68 n. 1, 80 n. 5; *Life* i. 478–79), it averaged about fifteen meetings a year. Between 1785 and 1791 only Reynolds, Windham, and Malone had a better record of attendance than Boswell; after Reynolds's death, only Malone and Windham attended more frequently (statistics kindly furnished by Dr. James M. Osborn).

[2a] Quotations for which no sources are cited are from letters in the present volume.

played in the intellectual life of London, reports of its activities were not likely to be mere gossip, or at least not mere trivial gossip. By corresponding with several members when he was exiled in Scotland, Boswell could keep abreast of the literary, social, and political life of the capital.

A considerable number of the letters here printed are themselves interesting as writing. Though Thomas Barnard cannot be classed with great letter-writers like Gray, Walpole, and Cowper, his letters are incisive and witty and furnish a splendid contrast to the shrewd naïveté of Boswell. But undoubtedly the collection is not so much literature as it is matter for biography and history, including the history of literature.

In the first place, for biography of the Johnsonian circle. Some of the correspondences, to be sure, are scanty and biographically un-revealing; unrevealing because Boswell never established real inti-macy with the correspondents in question. (That this lack was not always his choice is shown by the suppressed note in his corre-spondence with the Duke of Leeds.) Others are thin for exactly the opposite reason. Courtenay was an intimate friend, but from the time he and Boswell first met, they were constantly in each other's company, and their correspondence (apart from the formal notes that Courtenay wrote as Boswell's second in the affair of honour with Lord Macdonald) was limited to invitations and regrets. Windham was a similar case. But, as a whole, the collection in a gratifying way widens and deepens our knowledge of several of the figures we associate with Johnson. The *Life*, of course, draws background sketches of various members of The Club, but at all times these sketches remain subordinate to—even contributory to —the portrait of Johnson. George Birkbeck Hill, believing that members of The Club other than Johnson and Boswell deserved to be better known, attempted in *Dr. Johnson, His Friends and His Critics* (1878), to summarize the known biographical material for Langton and Beauclerk. But since he drew the greater part of his information from the *Life*, his portraits are scarcely more detailed than Boswell's; they fail to suppress the Johnsonian presence enough to enable these less vivid figures to emerge clearly. The letters in the present volume, on the contrary, present the members of The Club on their own, brought out from under the shadow of Johnson, that "magnificent Tree", as Boswell described him, "under the shade of which I have long been used to be sheltered".

INTRODUCTION

Langton, who in the *Life* is particularly shaded by Johnson, is allowed to emerge in his own words. Beauclerk—not in his brief correspondence with Boswell but in letters to Langton that somehow came into Boswell's collection—emerges as more complex and humane than he has hitherto been shown to be. Goldsmith wrote Boswell only one letter of any length, but that one is delightfully characteristic. Reynolds, the true founder of the club that is so often called Johnson's, reveals the qualities which caused Boswell (who was surprisingly formal in these matters) to sign himself "Affectionately yours". Percy's letters add something to our reading of the character of the Bishop of Dromore; they refer interestingly to a once famous quarrel of his, not mentioned in the *Life*, over the authenticity of *Fingal*; and they give body to his relationship with Boswell. But it is another bishop for whom this volume does most: Barnard, who in the group portrait of The Club has remained but a shadowy figure. The Bishop of Killaloe is infrequently mentioned in the *Life*, and not nearly so often in the journal as Boswell's epithet of "much-valued friend" would lead us to expect. The letters which Barnard wrote to Boswell present many aspects of the character of a fascinating man; in particular, they make us understand why that man was important to Boswell.

And the letters are valuable for Boswellian biography. First of all, they testify to his personal charm, the abiding attractiveness of his personality. In them almost every other facet of Boswell's character is presented too: hero-worshipper, pamphleteer, Scots lawyer ambitious for an English practice, paterfamilias, eminent biographer, frustrated politician, Steward of the Humane Society, Secretary for Foreign Correspondence to the Royal Academy. They reflect his major interests from 1769 to 1794. During Johnson's lifetime, Johnson the man was naturally the subject most likely to occupy his thoughts while he was writing to other friends of Johnson's. After Johnson's death the writing of the *Tour* takes over briefly, to be followed by the much longer struggle with the *Life* and concurrent ambitious schemes for political advancement. In the letters of the late 1780's one can follow Boswell's public life from its modestly auspicious beginning as counsel to the mayor of Carlisle to his advancement to the recordership of that city. But there it stops, and the rest is frustration and humiliation. The frustration and humiliation are only hinted at in the letters, but hints are enough to convey the pain he felt at the collapse of his towering

xxiii

political hopes. In the last years of his life Boswell seems to have accepted his lot. Although it was far from being what he wanted ("I tried to soothe myself with the consideration of my fame as a Writer"),[3] he made the best of his situation, and his later letters are filled with meetings of the Royal Academy Club and social gatherings with literary and political figures—compensatory pastimes of the Great Biographer.

Boswell had two main ambitions: to become a great man in politics and to win fame as an author. He failed dismally in the first,[4] but he succeeded in the second to a degree probably in excess of his own generous aspirations. These letters in a small way show how central the literary impulse was in him. Having literary ambitions, Boswell was ambitious not only to know literary men, but also to make literary men out of friends who were not literary or had only dabbled in writing. "Why do you not become an Authour . . . as many of your friends have done?" he writes to Langton. "The great advantage of putting one's thoughts in print is that the same effort of mind, which in private intercourse does good only to a few, is made of equal service to multitudes." He is equally determined that Barnard shall publish his essay on the origin of the Scots, even volunteering to get it printed in Scotland. No doubt he felt that Langton and Barnard could make real contributions to learning and literature, but just as surely he thought publication might make them more eminent; and he liked his friends to be eminent, for his sake as well as their own. Both motivations show the respect for and delight in casual publication which marked his own career.

Since most of the letters in this volume were written while Boswell was at work on either the *Tour* or the *Life*, they are concerned with the problems he encountered in gathering, organizing, and polishing his materials. In the *Tour*, the problem was largely a matter of editing a document already at hand. His letters to Barnard, who had begged to see the sheets as they went through the press, show a surprising indecisiveness on his part and a touching confidence in Malone's sense of propriety. Malone "not only winnows [the manuscript journal] from the chaff which in the hurry of immediate collection could not but be in it, but suggests little elegant variations which though they do not alter the sense,

[3] Journ. 13 Feb. 1794. [4] See Frank Brady, *Boswell's Political Career*, 1965.

add much grace to the expression." In addition to the "little elegant variations", of course, Malone also contributed a restraining influence in the selection of material. All of Boswell's deletions and cancels were not the result of his conscience: many were urged by Malone.[5]

The problem of constructing the *Life*, however, was much more difficult. One does not have to read very far into that work to realize the persistence with which Boswell turned to others for information. Although he had an extensive basis in his journals and the accumulation of Johnsonian materials which, as he wrote to Barnard in 1785, he had been gleaning from Johnson and those who knew Johnson "for upwards of twenty years", he felt that they were not sufficient for his purpose. Therefore, he applied again and again to his friends for more facts, more anecdotes, more sayings. The letters in this volume are in great part requests for Johnsoniana and the Johnsoniana requested. And he was well served: some of his friends' letters were incorporated into the printer's copy of the *Life* almost verbatim. It is no exaggeration to say that many of these letters are the *Life* itself, first drafts painstakingly collected, from which Boswell fashioned his completed volumes. They also frequently suggest at least a few of the reasons for Boswell's excellence as a biographer: ambition to excel, devotion to literature and literary men, dogged persistence. It cannot be said that the *Life* occupied any one period of his life. It was the work of almost thirty years, and in the end it was the one solidly successful achievement of a man who started with an ambition for multiple glories. It is principally the *Life* and the preparation for the *Life* which can be said to form the motif of these letters. Boswell and the *Life* are inseparable.

[5] See *Tour*, pp. xiv–xxi and the series of letters that passed between JB and Malone, 5 Oct.–11 Nov. 1785.

JAMES BOSWELL—CURRICULUM VITAE TO 1769

1740 29 October: Born.

1753 Autumn: Entered University of Edinburgh.

1759 Autumn: Matriculated at University of Glasgow.

1760 Spring: Ran away to London with intention of becoming a Roman Catholic.

Published *A View of the Edinburgh Theatre . . . Summer Season 1759.*

Published *Observations . . . on . . . "The Minor".*

1761 Published *An Elegy on the Death of an amiable young Lady.*

Published *An Ode to Tragedy.*

1762 Published poems in *A Collection of original Poems by Scotch Gentlemen.*

7 March: Signed a deed in which he consented to be put under trustees of his father's choosing in case he succeeded to Auchinleck.

Published *The Cub at Newmarket.*

30 July: Passed his trials in Civil Law and received permission to go to London to try to obtain a commission in the Foot Guards.

15 November: Left for London.

1763 Published *Critical Strictures on the new Tragedy of "Elvira".*

Published *Letters Between the Honourable Andrew Erskine and James Boswell, Esq.*

16 May: Introduced to Samuel Johnson.

August: Travelled to Utrecht for further study of law.

1764 June: Left Utrecht for tour through Germany, Switzerland, Italy, Corsica, and France.

1766 11 January: His mother died, he in Paris.

12 February: Returned to London from the Continent.

11 July: Passed examination in Scots Law.

26 July: Passed advocate, printed thesis *De supellectile legata.*

1767 Volunteer in the Douglas Cause, about which he published a number of works: *The Douglas Cause, Dorando, The Essence of the Douglas Cause, Letters of Lady Jane Douglas.*

Published *Prologue for the Opening of the Theatre Royal.*

1768 Published *Account of Corsica, the Journal of a Tour to that Island; and Memoirs of Pascal Paoli.*

1769 Autumn: Published *Verses in the Character of a Corsican.*

25 November: Married his cousin Margaret Montgomerie.

BIOGRAPHIES OF THE CORRESPONDENTS

A BRIEF sketch has been deemed sufficient for most of the correspondents, but Barnard, Beauclerk, Langton, and Percy receive more attention either because not much biographical information has been readily available or because significant new material has recently come to light. It should be noted that it was only after this volume was set in type that a considerable amount of Langton material—family letters and Peregrine Langton-Massingberd's letter-book—came into my hands.

General acknowledgement is made to Sir Lewis Namier and John Brooke, *The House of Commons, 1754–1790*, 3 vols., 1964, no fewer than twelve of the correspondents having been Members of Parliament.

ALEMBERT, JEAN LE ROND D' (1717–83). Mathematician and scientist, d'Alembert was Diderot's principal associate in the *Encyclopédie*, to which he contributed the mathematical articles and the *Discours préliminaire* on the progress and relations of the sciences. He became secretary of the Academy in 1772 and was considered the leader of its philosophic party after the death of Voltaire. The Club had no foreign members, but he is admitted to this collection because of a letter to Topham Beauclerk.

BARNARD, THOMAS (1726–1806). Surprisingly little is known about Thomas Barnard. The *Dictionary of National Biography* lists merely his parentage, his education, the positions he filled in the Church, his marriages, and his associations with the Royal Society and the Johnsonian circle. Almost all accounts of him are inaccurate; all omit certain members of his family. Boswell had very little to say about him in the *Life*, and he was not often mentioned in letters and diaries of his day. With the publication of some of his letters to his niece Isabella,[1] the personality hinted at by Boswell was confirmed; but the hitherto known letters written by the Bishop, both published and unpublished, all cover a period later than that of his friendship with Boswell, and consequently deal

[1] In *Barnard Letters*. Other letters from Barnard to his niece, not published by Powell, are at present in the possession of Miss Joanna Barnard, of Goudhurst, Kent.

only with Barnard's last years. The letters in this edition do much to fill in some of the gaps.

The connexion of this branch of the Barnard family with Ireland was of no long standing. Dr. William Barnard (1697–1768), his father, who came from Surrey and was educated at Westminster School and Trinity College, Cambridge, had made the acquaintance of the Duke of Newcastle while holding the rectory of Esher, Surrey, and had soon afterwards (1728) been appointed the Duke's chaplain. He introduced to the Duke his wife's brother, Andrew Stone, and Stone established himself behind the scenes as a politician with great and continuing influence on the Pelhams. George Stone, Andrew's brother, moved up in seven years from the Bishopric of Ferns, through Kildare and Derry, to the Archbishopric of Armagh, that is, to the primacy of the Church of Ireland. William Barnard, after being made in succession vicar of St. Bride's (Fleet Street, London), prebendary of Westminster, and Dean of Rochester, was appointed Bishop of Raphoe in 1744, and was translated to Derry in 1747 when George Stone moved up to Armagh. Thomas Barnard was born in Surrey in 1726[2] and attended Westminster School, like his father, but then instead of going on to Cambridge, proceeded B.A. (1748) at Trinity College, Dublin. Presumably it was thought that an Irish education would assist him in the career in the Church of Ireland which the interest of his father and uncle and the continuing favour of Newcastle encouraged him to pursue. In 1749 through Newcastle's influence, he obtained the M.A. from Cambridge.[3] In the summer of 1748, during the Congress of Aix-la-Chapelle, he travelled to Hanover with expectation of serving as assistant in some minor capacity to Andrew Stone, either at Hanover or at Aix-la-Chapelle.[4] "I have entreated Mr. Stone," William Barnard wrote to Newcastle on

[2] Most published authorities, following the DNB, give the date as 1728, but he seems to have been born in Nov. or Dec. 1726. He was admitted to Westminster, aged 11, in Jan. 1738 and to Trinity College, Dublin, aged 17, on 24 Oct. 1744 (G. F. R. Barker and A. H. Stenning, *Record of Old Westminsters*, 1928; *Alum. Cant.*; *Alum. Dublin.*). *Gent. Mag.* (1806) lxxvi. 588 gives 1726 as the year of his birth.

[3] *Alum. Cant.*; From William Barnard

to the Duke of Newcastle (1693–1768), 3 July 1750, BM Add. MSS. 32721, f. 210.

[4] Andrew Stone (1703–73), William Barnard's brother-in-law, former private secretary to the Duke, Under Secretary of State, and later tutor to George III. He accompanied George II in his visit to Hanover in May 1748, acting as his private secretary until the arrival of the Duke. He was a man of high Tory principles who had great influence on George III.

14 July 1748, the Duke being then with the King in Hanover,[5] "to present my Son to Your Grace, whom I have committed to his Care, and who will think himself happily honoured by Your Graces Notice and Protection. He had so fine an Opportunity of seeing the World to great Advantage that I could not refuse to consent to it; and withall the hopes that my B[rothe]r might find him capable of being serviceable to Him, was another strong Inducement. He went hence with Lord Pultney."[6]

The date of Thomas Barnard's ordination is not known, but in 1751 he became vicar of Maghera, in his father's diocese.[7] He was married, probably in 1753 or 1754, to Anne Browne, daughter of William Browne, Esq., of Browne's Hill, County Carlow.[8] Burke's *Landed Gentry of Ireland*, 1912 (s.v. Browne-Clayton), says that the marriage occurred on 20 July 1758, but the year can hardly be right, for Barnard is known to have had at least two children before that date. Thomas Barnard, whom he styles his eldest son, was seventeen years old when he matriculated at University College, Oxford, on 7 December 1771 (*post* From Barnard 10 February 1785 and n. 1). And the baptismal register of St. Peter's Church, Dublin, records the christening of William, son of the Rev. Thomas and Anne Barnard, of Digges Street, on 20 July 1757.[9] Neither of these sons is mentioned in any account of the Barnard family hitherto printed, Andrew Barnard (1762–1807) being generally listed as his father's only child, as he no doubt was at the time of his father's death.

In 1761 Thomas Barnard was collated to the Archdeaconry of Derry on his father's presentation and received the degree of D.D. from Trinity College, Dublin. The Bishop's right to present his son was contested in 1762 by one of the Londonderry companies, but nothing came of the action.[10]

Barnard's father, who was extremely ambitious for him, con-

[5] *Gent. Mag.* (1748) xviii. 234, 235, 238, 281.

[6] BM Add. MSS. 32715, f. 359. "Lord Pultney" was William Pulteney (?1731–63), son and heir of William Pulteney (1684–1764), Earl of Bath. John Douglas, one of the other correspondents in the present volume, was Pulteney's travelling tutor.

[7] *Fasti Hib.* i. 390. See also *ibid.* i. 472; iii (1849). 334, 338; J. B. Leslie, *Derry Clergy and Parishes*, 1937, pp. 38–39.

[8] *Gent. Mag.* (1806) lxxvi. 588; *Barnard Letters*, p. 6. The date given for the marriage in *Landed Gentry of Ireland* may be misprinted, 1758 for 1753.

[9] Parish Record Soc. of Dublin, *Register of the Parish of S. Peter and S. Kevin, Dublin, 1699–1761*, 1911, p. 299.

[10] From William Barnard to the Duke of Newcastle, 29 June 1762 (BM Add. MSS. 32940, f. 144).

tinued to address himself to the Duke of Newcastle. In 1761 he solicited "Your Graces Protection for my Family, and if I may presume to point out the Service most desirable to me it woud be that of recommending my Son to the next Lord Lieutenant as a Person under your Graces Protection, whose Advancement woud be agreeable to Your Grace—Give me leave at the same time to assure You that if I did not know his Character to be unexceptionable, I woud not presume to ask this favour."[11] William Barnard was clearly not one of those bishops who caused Newcastle in his later years to remark, "Even fathers in God sometimes forget their maker." But by 1761 Newcastle had fallen from power and his recommendation was of dubious value. Archbishop Stone's formerly dictatorial power had also been curbed, and he died in 1764. In 1765 Thomas Barnard himself requested Newcastle to recommend him to the Earl of Hertford (1718–94), who was appointed Lord Lieutenant in that year.[12] The recommendation, if made, was fruitless, and William Barnard died early in 1768. Thomas Barnard, however, somehow obtained the effective and continuing patronage of Lord Mansfield, and was made Dean of Derry in 1769.[13]

In Derry Cathedral on 13 September 1772, Thomas Barnard preached a sermon before the judges of assize which was later published as a quarto pamphlet of twenty-two pages. Finally, he received the vice-regal favour he had so long sought, being appointed chaplain to the Earl of Buckinghamshire (1723–93), who served as Lord Lieutenant from 1777 to 1780. He was consecrated Bishop of Killaloe and Kilfenora on 20 February 1780.[14] On 12 September 1794 (something like six months after the last letter

[11] 19 Feb. 1761 (BM Add. MSS. 32919, f. 120).

[12] From William Barnard to the Duke of Newcastle, 20 Aug. 1765 (BM Add. MSS. 32969, f. 115).

[13] See ante n. 7 and n. 14 following. There is evidence (*Barnard Letters*, p. 144) that Barnard was on friendly terms with Viscount Townshend (1724–1807), Lord Lieutenant in 1769, but as the compiler of the valuable list cited in n. 14 obviously intended to record all the significant patronage each of the bishops had received, I conclude that Townshend took no active part in Barnard's advancement to Dean.—Lord Mansfield had been a member of two governments headed by Newcastle. Like the Barnards and the Stones, he was an Old Westminster; in fact, had been in both school and college (Christ Church, Oxford) with Andrew and George Stone.

[14] "Dr. Thomas Barnard. Killaloe and Kilfenora—£2,300—Second Chaplain to Lord Buckingham—much patronized by Lord Mansfield" (G. O. Sayles, ed., "Contemporary Sketches of the Members of the Irish Parliament in 1782," *Proceedings* of the Royal Irish Academy, vol. 56, Sec. C [1953–54] p. 284). These

of his to Boswell of which we have any knowledge) he was translated to the united sees of Limerick, Ardfert, and Aghadoe. He entered into a second marriage in 1803 and died on 7 June 1806.

Exactly when Barnard first became acquainted with Johnson and his friends is not known. He and his wife had sat to Sir Joshua for their portraits perhaps as early as 1767, certainly before 1774 when Sir Joshua recorded the final payment. Otherwise the first datable reference to him as an acquaintance by a member of the group occurs in Goldsmith's *Retaliation*, which is generally assumed to have been written in February 1774 and cannot have been written much later, for Goldsmith died on 4 April of that year. He expressly says that he had known Barnard only six weeks.[15] Barnard's being assigned an epitaph in *Retaliation* indicates at least the same degree of acquaintance with Burke, Douglas, Garrick, and Reynolds as with Goldsmith. Beauclerk (who was not a member of the group which figures in *Retaliation*) wrote to the Earl of Charlemont on 18 July 1774:

> The dean of Derry is quite a new acquaintance; he says he is a scholar and I believed him to be so. He seemed a good natured man, and a man of parts, and one proof I am sure he gave of his understanding, by expressing a strong desire to be acquainted with you. . . . His wife, I never saw but once, and that was at the play, and then the dean and I seemed to be both of a mind in trying to avoid her company and conversation as much as possible.[16]

"Sketches" cover the entire personnel of both houses of the Irish Parliament, the object being to indicate in each case how the Member is likely to vote. Lord Buckinghamshire is represented as having "recommended" the appointment of two bishops (one of them another chaplain of his), "translated" two, and "made" two. I interpret the entry concerning Barnard as saying that Buckinghamshire co-operated in Barnard's promotion but that the real pressure came from Mansfield. I have not found the date of Barnard's appointment as chaplain, but there are in the John Rylands Library letters written by him to Sir James Caldwell in 1777 and 1778 from Dublin Castle, the palace of the Lord Lieutenant. See also *ante* n. 7.

[15] Here lies the good Dean, reunited to earth,
Who mixed reason with pleasure, and wisdom with mirth:
If he had any faults, he has left us in doubt,
At least, in six weeks I could not find 'em out;
Yet some have declared, and it can't be denied 'em,
That sly-boots was cursedly cunning to hide 'em.

[16] *The Manuscripts and Correspondence of James, First Earl of Charlemont* (Historical Manuscripts Commission, Twelfth Report, Appendix, Part X, 1891, p. 321).

Barnard was again in London in 1775, and was elected to The Club in February of that year. He was back in town in December, when Percy recorded in his diary that he entertained him twice at dinner in the course of that month. He dined at Reynolds's in the same month, when he wrote his famous verses on Johnson's "politeness",[17] and, as Club records show, spent that winter in London.

The first mention of Barnard in Boswell's journal occurs in a record of the Royal Academy dinner on 23 April 1776, when he told Boswell that "he had a very great respect for Johnson":

> I love him said he; but he does not love me. & he complained of his rough harsh manners saying that when he smiled he shewed the teeth at the corner of his mouth like a dog who is going to bite. He said Johnson is right ninety nine times in a hundred. I think with him but—you do not feel with him said I "No, said the Dean. In short he is not a Gentleman."[17a]

Boswell saw Barnard fairly frequently that spring; when, at one of their meetings, he began drinking wine again, he attributed his backsliding to the example or counsel of Barnard and Reynolds.[18] There is no indication, however, that they became very well acquainted. And there is no mention of Barnard in Boswell's journals again until the spring of 1781, when Barnard apparently returned to London for the first time since 1776. The two men saw much of each other during that spring, and it is clear that they became close friends.[19] Boswell had a serious conversation on religion with Barnard on 29 May, and on the next day, apparently just before the Bishop returned to Ireland, asked for and received his blessing.[20]

One needs only to read Barnard's letters to Boswell to understand why the younger man deliberately cultivated him. Successful, witty, urbane, yet religious, Barnard represented an ideal which

[17] *Life* iv. 431–33, expanded and corrected in F. W. Hilles, *A Copy of Pleasant Verses* (privately printed for The Johnsonians, 1970).

[17a] Quoted from JB's later expansion of his journal note, *Boswell's Note Book 1776–1777*, ed. R. W. Chapman, 1925, p. 18[a].

[18] Journ. 12 May 1776.

[19] The exchange of notes in 1781 (first two letters of correspondence) shows that the two were on fairly intimate terms. On 18 May, the Bishop dined with JB and General Paoli. "Nobody but ourselves. We were quiet and happy. I walked with his Lordship to his door" (Journ.).

[20] Journ.

Boswell could never hope to attain, but from which he could draw inspiration and assistance. Barnard was his Father Confessor. When Johnson died, he seems to have taken his place, at least in part. Like Johnson, he was a high-church Tory. Although much younger than Johnson, he was enough Boswell's elder to be able to give him advice which the younger man could accept and respect. And like Johnson, Barnard seems to have been genuinely fond of Boswell. Although they saw each other for only a few months in London during four of the years after their correspondence began,[21] Barnard faithfully kept up that correspondence for eleven years, sometimes more faithfully than Boswell.

Barnard, of course, played Johnson with a difference. Far less strict in matters of behaviour, far more gentle in his reprimands, he undoubtedly made Boswell feel not quite so much a sinner. When Boswell was in the Bishop's company, the gathering was "jovial and happy".[21a] He felt at ease, and so did Barnard. In 1786, before Boswell had finally determined to make the move to London and the English bar, he breakfasted with Barnard, who "was for a fair trial being made. He went with me to Westminster Hall, and walked about with me in my *Bar dress*. He said we had had a comfortable morning."[22] Barnard was the first person Boswell entertained in his London house.[23] A few days later, the two of them dined at Dilly's with several others. "We had an excellent day," Boswell reported. "But I drank rather too much wine. The Bishop walked home with me to my house and left me to go to bed, it being between ten and eleven."[24] Barnard was more than Boswell's "much valued freind" and "Spiritual Father"; he was "an instructive and pleasing Companion", adviser, and confidant. Their friendship flourished until Boswell's death.

The letters between Boswell and Barnard range over a wider variety of subjects than do the other correspondences in this edition. Mineral waters, dogs, religion, politics, literature, law, and antiquities all find a place. Such a catholic display seems to indicate the diversified nature of Barnard's interests and to show why he was an instructive and pleasing companion. His primary concern is politics. He clearly took his duties as Lord Spiritual seriously and firmly believed that his duties lay also in temporal

[21] Barnard was in London in 1783, 1786, 1789, and 1791.
[21a] Journ. 17 May 1783.
[22] Journ. 7 June.
[23] Journ. 10 June.
[24] Journ. 17 June. JB did not go to bed.

fields. A number of letters written in later years to his niece were dated from the Irish House of Lords. As we know, the years covered by the letters of this edition were years of crisis, not only in Ireland, but also in England. Of all the letters, only these give the reader a sense of the events going on outside the narrow world of letters and English politics. France was in a turbulent state, and the Government, both in England and in Ireland, feared the effects of the Revolution on their dissident people. Barnard clearly felt the threat, and this awareness is revealed in his correspondence. And yet there is never in his comments any indication of fear or hesitation. He is firmly convinced of the rightness of the cause he has espoused. A totally unreconstructed Tory, he intends to defend the *status quo*, without compromise. Only once does he lose the calm detachment which was so much a part of his character: "The Motley Herd that threaten it [the Constitution], composed of Dissenters of all Kinds, atheists and Libertines Included, with that Dog Paine at the Bottom of the Conspiracy." But then, like all true aristocrats of the eighteenth century, he distrusted the mob. And he is quick to point out that he believes the Catholics want no more than what he thinks they should be given.

Barnard's Tory beliefs, of course, found favour with Boswell. That they agreed on many topics was a major reason for their friendship. Boswell was probably also pleased with Barnard's sanguine expectations for the advancement of his career, although Boswell seems to have been the more realistic in his estimate of what he could expect from Lord Lonsdale. Barnard, like Langton and Percy, encouraged Boswell to move to England. One suspects that he could hardly have expected the move to be successful; there is too much evidence in these letters of his penetrating knowledge of Boswell's character. He could only assume, whether rightly or wrongly, that Boswell would be unhappier and, therefore, worse off, if he never made the attempt than if he tried and failed. Boswell placed all his friends in a quandary when he sought their advice on the English bar, and one can hardly blame them for taking the easier way out.

Until these letters were recovered, it was not known that Boswell had gone to the trouble of sending Barnard the sheets of the *Tour* in instalments as they came from the press, nor that he had attempted through Barnard to get the Irish printer of the book to adopt certain changes that he was making in his own second edition. But what makes these letters of 1785 peculiarly pleasant is that they show real affection on the Bishop's part and not a mere willingness to return a favour. His criticism of Boswell's *Letter to the People of Scotland* (1785), which he received when the first instalment of the *Tour* arrived, shows more than almost any other statement how well he understood Boswell: "Your Reasons upon the Matter are Strong and Powerfull, your arguments ad Hominem, and ad Verecundiam, are well and Smartly applied, your Digressions are enlivening, and even your Egotisms, (which are not Infrequent) contrary to the usual Effect of that Figure, amuse the Reader without provoking him." When Boswell tactlessly requests him not to show the sheets of the *Tour* to others, Barnard is only "a little angry", and easily forgives him for mistrusting either his integrity or his understanding. One wonders what Percy's reaction would have been.

It is to be feared that Barnard was somewhat too good a hater. Dissenters got no pity from him; Ireland to him was a land of bulls and potatoes; the Irish, "the Real posterity of the Irish Snakes, Turn'd into men by the Fury Erinyes."[25] The riots at Birmingham merely rejoiced his Tory soul, and though he was a Fellow of the Royal Society, he considered a brick from Priestley's meeting-house a proper trophy. His anger was high-spirited and never mean, but it was nonetheless whole-hearted and persistent. "You may Tell your Sister Sarah . . ."—he is sending a message to a niece who had opposed his marriage at the age of seventy-seven to a young woman of twenty-two, now dying of consumption—"that if I lose my Present wife (as I expect to do) I shall certainly look out for *a Third*, as soon as propriety will permit."[26] (She recovered and outlived him.) One thinks of Swift, but the anger of the Bishop of Limerick is never really of a kind with the *saeva indignatio* that the Dean of St. Patrick's confessed to on his tombstone. It is only a shade in a disposition naturally urbane and sunny.

Having come late into the Johnsonian circle and having spent so little time with Johnson, Barnard could hardly have supplied Boswell with much information for the *Life*. Nevertheless, the few items he could furnish, Boswell used. And if he could not participate extensively in the making of the work, Barnard could and did encourage Boswell in the writing of it. Early in 1785, he writes to Boswell, "You have Collected Materials to do it; You have

[25] *Barnard Letters*, p. 135.   [26] *Ibid.* p. 157.

formerly Declar'd it to be your Intention: The Publick, Expects it from you: and I (as one of them) call upon you to perform your Promise." "You forget that the Publick Curiosity will not wait your Leisure," he reminds him in 1788. And in 1790, he asks him, "When do's your much desired, and Long Expected Work come out? . . . If it do's not soon appear we shall grow as outrageous as the galleries at Drury Lane."

These letters, then, show Barnard to have been a man of varied interests, and a man who was active in the pursuit of these interests. A member of the Royal Society and the Royal Irish Academy, Chaplain to the Royal Academy of Arts, a Protestant bishop of Ireland, and a member of the Irish House of Lords, he found time to participate in almost all their activities. Although away from London most of the time, he led as intellectually stimulating a life as probably could be led in Ireland. Like many of his episcopal brethren, he found time to make researches into the antique past and publish what he found. He served the cause of poor authors by attempting to establish a copyright law in Ireland. That he performed well his duties as bishop cannot be seen in these letters, but in later years, when many Irish bishops were leaving the country because of the danger of a French invasion, Barnard remained, and as a result endeared himself to the Irish.

But the real importance of these letters, I think, is in what they reveal of the relationship between Boswell and Barnard. It was not as a worldly though pious bishop that Boswell particularly valued Barnard, but as a companion and spiritual father. When Boswell first tells Barnard that he has mentioned him in his will, it is with great restraint, as if he were doubtful of the Bishop's response. But when Barnard, undoubtedly touched by "so affecting an Instance of . . . Freindship", requests Boswell not to erase the testimony of his regard even if he should die first, Boswell can express his true feelings: "the clause . . . never will be erased. My heart glowed while I wrote it." And some of this glow comes through in the letters. In Barnard, Boswell found a man who understood him and liked him, and to whom he could unburden himself. And although the Bishop could never replace Johnson, he was an able and satisfying substitute.

BEAUCLERK, TOPHAM (1739–80). Langton's (and later Boswell's) friend, Topham Beauclerk, one of the original members of The Club, is best known, particularly to the readers of Boswell's

Life of Johnson,[1] as a maliciously witty gentleman of fashion who moved in the highest social circles and who was named co-respondent in one of the most notorious divorce cases of the eighteenth century. A great-grandson of Charles II and Nell Gwyn and grandson to the first Duke of St. Albans, Beauclerk matriculated in 1757 at Trinity College, Oxford, where he met Bennet Langton and, through him, Johnson. In his travels with Langton on the Continent, he became involved with Mlle. DuBois, an actress, and the Comtesse de Boufflers-Rouverel.[2] In 1766, his name was linked by gossip with that of Lady Diana Spencer (1734–1808), Viscountess Bolingbroke, the elder daughter of Charles, third Duke of Marlborough. She left her husband, who was notoriously unfaithful, and in September 1767 gave birth to Topham Beauclerk's son. Lord Bolingbroke divorced her; and immediately after the divorce was granted, on 12 March 1768, Topham Beauclerk and Lady Diana were married in St. George's, Hanover Square.

Boswell did not meet Beauclerk until 6 May 1772, and then only briefly, and probably through Reynolds. It was not until the following spring that the friendship between the two men really began. On 7 April 1773, Boswell

> called on the Hon. Topham Beauclerk, who has . . . a house on the terrace of the Adelphi. I was shewn into a very elegant Parlour. I liked his large gilded Lyon, a cast from the Antique, supporting his sideboard. He received me politely; but not with so much ardour as I wish to find. However the truth is, I never was in company with Beauclerk but twice—once dining at Sir Joshuah Reynolds's [6 May 1772], and once supping at Garrick's when I was last in town. He then invited me to see him, when I should return; and Langton told me that my open downright manners had pleased him, and he had said, "I do love Boswell monstrously." Beauclerk's highbred behaviour may have been construed by me as distant coldness. His great veneration for Mr. Johnson, and Johnson's love for him, are enough to make me value him; and from what I have seen of him he appears to be a man of wit, literature, and fashion in a distinguished degree.[3]

Little more need be said of the reasons for Boswell's cultivating

---

[1] See *Life* i. 248–50; ii. 246–47.
[2] *The Diaries of Sylvester Douglas (Lord Glenbervie)*, ed. Francis Bickley, 1928, ii. 292; *Life* ii. 405–06
[3] Journ.

Beauclerk. He states them explicitly. Beauclerk venerated Johnson and was loved in return; he was a man of wit, literature, and fashion. He lived as Boswell no doubt would have liked to live, with a gilded lion supporting his sideboard in an elegant parlour. And by no means least important, Beauclerk announced a liking for Boswell. When Johnson proposed Boswell for The Club, "Beauclerk was very zealous for me."[4] There is no reason to doubt the genuineness of Beauclerk's regard. Boswell was a likable person, and had many qualities that Beauclerk would have found entertaining. Beauclerk jested about him, but his jesting was of the sort that is permitted between friends.[5]

Boswell, however, seemed never to be quite able to drop his guard in Beauclerk's company. Beauclerk was through and through an aristocrat; his tone and bearing were unaffectedly imperious, and he said sharp things perhaps not so much with intention to hurt as without caring whether they hurt or not. He was absolutely fearless, the only man in The Club who unhesitatingly stood up to Johnson's roughness (JOHNSON: "Mr. Beauclerk, how came you to talk so petulantly to me? . . ." BEAUCLERK: "Because *you* began by being uncivil—which you always are").[6] He gave Boswell a cold shiver (Boswell's own expression) by his careless and vivacious scepticism.[7] In 1778 Boswell got really angry with him. It was entirely Boswell's fault: he had burst in, about midnight and uninvited, on a private party of Beauclerk's noble friends, and had not had sense enough to go away promptly. Beauclerk's understandable lack of cordiality stung him. Thick-skinned to most discourtesies, Boswell was very sensitive to anything which he regarded as depreciatory of either his social or his professional status, and he felt that Beauclerk meant to disparage both. In spite of overtures at reconciliation from Beauclerk, he may have left London without forgiving him.[8] But when they met next year, the

---

[4] *Life* ii. 235.
[5] On 20 Nov. 1773, Beauclerk urged the Earl of Charlemont to come to England. "If you do not come here, I will bring all the club over to Ireland, to live with you, and that will drive you here in your own defence. Johnson shall spoil your books, Goldsmith pull your flowers, and Boswell talk to you: stay then if you can" (Francis Hardy, *Memoirs of the Political and Private Life of James Caulfeild,*

Earl of Charlemont, 2nd ed., 1812, i. 347).
[6] *Life* iii. 384–85.
[7] Journ. 23 Mar. 1775.
[8] Journ. 9, 13 Apr. 1778. JB and SJ dined with Beauclerk on 16 May 1778 (*Life*), three days before JB left London, but the journal for that day has not been recovered. *Boswelliana,* ed. Charles Rogers, 1874, pp. 289–90, contains an unpleasant anecdote concerning Beauclerk that JB recorded in 1778.

ice dissolved. Beauclerk was more complaisant than usual and even showed some religious sentiment. Boswell felt (and told him) that he was not only clever but good.[9] Beauclerk died, aged forty, the next spring.

Bad health plagued Beauclerk most of his life. One of his illnesses was the occasion for the single letter to him from Boswell that seems to have survived. It was written on 2 March 1775 and should have been written earlier. Johnson had told Boswell in a letter he had received before the end of January that Beauclerk was so ill that his life was thought to be in danger. Boswell had meant to write a letter showing his concern, but had put off doing so until his own departure for London was imminent. The letter consequently could not but be a little awkward, especially as Boswell could not bring himself merely to say that he would be in London within less than three weeks and would then come around to make inquiries personally. His concern for Beauclerk's health was sincere, but, as in the case of his letter to Goldsmith two years before, he wanted a letter from Beauclerk for his "archives", and was willing to resort to a little duplicity to accomplish his end. So far as we know, his stratagem failed completely. Boswell's journal and the *Life of Johnson* are our principal sources of information concerning the public character of Beauclerk, but for revealing intimate correspondence we have to look to a stray group of letters to Langton.

The Topham Beauclerk most people knew was only part of the man Langton knew and loved. Only the first two of the letters from Beauclerk here printed show the brilliant, witty, fashionable aristocrat whom Boswell described in the *Life*. From these letters, written only about five years after both Beauclerk and Langton left Oxford, it is clear that one of the things that originally brought them together was a common interest in intellectual pursuits. "Why may not we study too? I am become enamoured of the Civil Law, if you know any thing of it come and teach me, else let us study it together." He proved he was no trifler by leaving a library of thirty thousand volumes. To a reader who knows that Beauclerk has only fourteen years to live, there is deep irony in his appetite for learning: "Let others rot, but we will be Immortal," and prophecy in his caution to Langton not to "throw away the poor dregs of life, that we have remaining."

[9] Journ. 15 Apr. 1779.

For the most part, the remaining letters are pathetic requests to Langton to come and see him. He has been ill and confined to the house all day. He knows he will die soon. "You know at all times I preferred your Company to any other, and that preference is not decreased by a very long and painfull Illness, particularly as I have reason to think that it will not be very long before that Illness puts an End to our connection." These are the letters of a man who suffers on his own account and for those to whom he is a burden: Lady Di "has suffered too much already to be deprived of the few Amusements, she can take, and I remain only to be troublesome to my Friends, and to endure excruciating torments myself, without pleasure, Comfort, or hope. The only remaining thing I have is the Conversation of yourself and one or two more Friends."

It is made clear in these letters why many persons believed that Lady Di was fortunate when Beauclerk died. He was not, all agreed, easy to live with. Walpole told Joseph Farington that Beauclerk was "the worst tempered man He ever knew.—Lady Di passed a most miserable life with him. . . . He took Laudanum regularly in vast quantities. . . . Before He died He asked pardon of Lady Di, for his ill usage of her."[10] Lady Pembroke, Lady Di's sister, was somewhat more understanding and seems to have recognized that much of Beauclerk's vile disposition, as these letters so clearly show, was the result of constant pain.[11]

Beauclerk's letters to Langton are valuable for their clear expression of the wretchedness in which Beauclerk ended his days and for the solid evidence which they offer of his friendship for Langton. They are almost the only documents showing Beauclerk's point of view, the only documents which permit a glimpse into his troubled mind. With these letters, Beauclerk assumes a character somewhat different from that which has come down to us in the *Life* and contemporary memoirs and letters. For the first time it is possible to see beneath the surface brilliance of his social mask. And while the view is not pleasant, except as it shows us a lasting

[10] *Farington Diary* i. 66. Cf. *Life* ii. 246 n. 1.

[11] "Mr. Beauclerk dyed last Friday night after ten days illness which was more than sufficient to put an end to the sufferings of his wretched constitution, it is certainly much happier for himself, and he did not act in a manner to be regretted by others" (*Henry, Elizabeth and George*, p. 429). Her husband, Lord Pembroke, wrote to JB, "He was so old in constitution, and suffered so much, both in body, and temper, that his death relieved him, and others from much pain, and trouble" (20 Mar. 1780).

and valuable friendship, it widens our view of the man and, consequently, of those he knew and loved. While Beauclerk undoubtedly enjoyed life in greater splendour, it does not seem extravagant to suggest that he may have been in many ways a more pitiable and unsuccessful person than Boswell, who envied his position and attainments.

BLACKSTONE, SIR WILLIAM (1723–80). Author of the very influential *Commentaries on the Laws of England*, Blackstone was educated at the Charterhouse, London, and Johnson's college at Oxford (Pembroke), was elected Fellow of All Souls, and at about the same time was called to the bar from the Middle Temple. In 1758 he was appointed the first Vinerian Professor of English Law at Oxford, and for several years read the lectures which appeared in print (1765–69) as the *Commentaries*. He held seats in Parliament, 1761–70, and in the latter year was raised to the bench as Judge in the Court of Common Pleas. He was not a member of The Club.

BLAGDEN, SIR CHARLES (1748–1820). Physician, medical officer in the Army, and scientist, Blagden first appears in Boswell's journal in 1790. Two years later he was knighted and on 18 March 1794 was elected to The Club. On the recommendation of his friend, Sir Joseph Banks, he had been elected Secretary of the Royal Society in 1784. Johnson thought him "a delightful fellow". Boswell met him socially several times, but does not appear to have been at all intimate with him. In the correspondence printed in this volume, he turned to Blagden as a scientist for help in deciphering and explaining a technological term in Johnson's difficult manuscript journal of his visit to Paris. Blagden responded with the "copiousness and precision of communication" which had occasioned Johnson's praise,[1] but appears not to have been an unqualified admirer of the book. "Dr. Blagden says justly," wrote Horace Walpole ten days after the *Life* appeared, "that it is a new kind of libel, by which you may abuse anybody, by saying some dead person said so-and-so of somebody alive."[2]

BURKE, EDMUND (1729–97). Irish by birth and education, Burke had settled in London in 1750 to study law, but was never called to the bar, and for nearly a decade appears to have been principally engaged in literary pursuits. He was an original member of The

[1] *Life* iv. 30.
[2] *Life* iv. 30 n. 2; To Mary Berry, 26 May 1791; *Walpole's Correspondence*, Yale Ed. xi. 275.

Club, Johnson from the first holding his powers of conversation to be unparalleled. After a not altogether happy period as private secretary to "Single-speech" Hamilton (see p. li), he moved in 1765 to a much more promising post as private secretary to the then Prime Minister, the Marquess of Rockingham, to whose party he thereafter adhered. Brought into Parliament (he took his seat in January 1766), he immediately established himself as the most admired (though not pragmatically the most successful) orator in the Commons. His speeches on American affairs need only be mentioned. His politics kept him in the Opposition during most of his Parliamentary career: in 1775, when he wrote to Langton, he was allied with Charles James Fox against Lord North's administration. The letter to Langton, the only one from Burke included in the present volume (as noted above, his correspondence with Boswell will appear elsewhere in this series), illustrates that promptness and generosity of assistance of which the best-known recipients were Barry and Crabbe. Though usually in financial difficulties himself, he was always ready to give to others and to use his interest in their behalf.

BURKE, RICHARD (1758–94). The son of Edmund Burke, Richard Burke received his education at Westminster School and Christ Church, Oxford. He was elected to The Club 16 April 1782. Known as The Whelp by The Club, he was "a handsome, earnest, ambitious youth . . . almost too challenging an example of virtue and rectitude. He embarrassed more relaxed individuals. No one would agree with his father, who insisted on thinking him one of the first political geniuses of the age, as well as a moral paragon."[3] It is hard to believe that he would have found Boswell to his taste. Boswell on one occasion thought that he conducted himself "exceedingly well" in a conversation with Johnson, and on another showed impatience with him for keeping Fox from talking at The Club,[4] but in general his references are non-committal.

The letter to Boswell here printed, however, was occasioned not by their frequent meetings at The Club, but by their very exiguous connexions as barristers. Boswell was called to the bar from the Inner Temple on 9 February 1786, and a month later set out on his first circuit, the Northern. Young Burke, who had been called to the bar from the Middle Temple, 24 November 1780, had

[3] T. W. Copeland, *Our Eminent Friend Edmund Burke*, 1949, p. 57.

[4] Journ. 1 May 1783; To Malone, 10 Feb. 1791.

previously been a member of the Northern Circuit, but on 12 March 1786 had written to the Senior a letter from Worcester announcing that he had removed to the Oxford Circuit. As Junior of the Northern Circuit, Boswell was ordered to enter Burke's letter on the records of the Circuit and to answer it. This he did, and his copies of both letters remain today in the Circuit records.[5] Burke at this time was in his twenty-eighth year, Boswell in his forty-sixth.

BURNEY, CHARLES (1726–1814). The elder Charles Burney, father of the novelist Fanny Burney, was one of Boswell's older acquaintances, for on 22 March 1781, "Dr. Burney and I drank to our acquaintance, now *come of age*, as somebody said, it being now exactly 21 years since I first met him at the late Lord Eglintoune's."[6] Burney, who had been a pupil of Thomas Arne, was a success both as a fashionable music teacher and as a man of the world. He was elected to the Royal Society of Musicians in 1749. After a severe illness in 1750, he retired to Lynn Regis for nine years as an organist, but returned to London in 1760. He took the degree of Mus. Doc. at Oxford in June 1769, and in 1773 was elected a Fellow of the Royal Society. The first volume of his successful *History of Music* came out in 1776, the second in 1782, and the third and fourth in 1789. It had a more favourable reception than a similar undertaking of Sir John Hawkins, although many now consider Burney's the inferior work. He was elected to The Club on 17 February 1784. Long a friend of Johnson, he provided a number of letters, anecdotes, and notes for the *Life*. Boswell saw him fairly frequently in London and occasionally visited him at Chelsea College, where he had apartments.

COURTENAY, JOHN (1738–1816), politician, son of a revenue officer in Ireland, began his career by holding in the Army the commissions of ensign and lieutenant. Coming to the attention of Lord Townshend, the Lord Lieutenant, he became Townshend's secretary, and then in 1780 was returned for a seat in the Parliament of Great Britain which Townshend had put at the disposal of Government. A witty and reckless supporter of Government policies, he spoke frequently and effectively. He first appears in

[5] I am deeply indebted to Ian Macaulay, Esq., former Clerk of Assize, Northern Circuit, for making these records available. As authority for details in this sketch not otherwise covered, see G. F. R. Barker and A. H. Stenning, *Record of Old Westminsters*, 1928, i. 143 and James Prior, *Memoir of ... Edmund Burke*, 3rd ed. 1839, p. 219.
[6] Journ.

Boswell's journal in the summer of 1785, apparently having been introduced to him by Malone, also an Irishman, and the two immediately became the closest of friends. Courtenay was elected to The Club on 23 December 1788, his proposer being Sir Joshua Reynolds and his seconder Boswell.

Courtenay actually realized most of Boswell's ambitions. He had been a soldier, he was a Member of Parliament, he was a writer of some reputation, publishing essays, an elegiac epistle (*The Rape of Pomona*, 1773), and a by-no-means contemptible *Poetical Review of the Literary and Moral Character of Dr. Samuel Johnson*, 1786. With Malone he not only cheered Boswell on in his struggle to write the *Life of Johnson*, but also served as audience for and critic of his works.[7] Straitened finances may well also have created a further bond of sympathy between the two, for though Courtenay sat for sixteen years in Parliament, he seems always to have been hard up. "The embarassed state of my affairs overwhelmed my spirits," wrote Boswell in 1791. "Yet here was Courtenay with a wife and seven children, and not a shilling."[8]

Courtenay sympathized with Boswell in his various distresses and often gave him sensible advice. He was one of the few to discourage him from moving to London. At another time Courtenay sensibly reminded Boswell that he had no claim for anything from Pitt "because I had written my pamphlet against Fox's India Bill from principle as against what I thought a bad measure, without regard to party; and that I had no claim from Dundas, because I had afterwards opposed his measure of diminishing the Scotch Judges. All this I was sensible was just."[9] But Boswell would not resign himself to the inexorable logic of it. At still another time, Courtenay made Boswell promise that for three months his "allowance of wine per diem should not exceed four good glasses at dinner, and a pint after it." Before the period was out, however, Courtenay had given Boswell a dispensation.[1]

Although they agreed on many matters, Boswell and Courtenay disagreed in politics and religion. The French Revolution provided a particularly debatable subject for the two of them. "His feelings and notions were so different from mine upon that subject,"

[7] Journ. 15, 20 Apr. 1786; 19 Apr. 1788; 22 Feb., 3 Mar. 1791; To Malone, 31 Mar. 1786; Yale MS. C 842.
[8] Journ. 21 Feb.

[9] Journ. 19 Apr. 1788.

[1] To Malone, 4 Dec. 1790; Journ. 15 Feb. 1791.

Boswell wrote after one of their discussions, "that I should not have argued it with him, for he is a friend to whom I have been much obliged."[2] In addition to having republican tendencies, Courtenay was also an unbeliever. "He said (though I fear a sceptick) that he thought it might be urged in favour of a future state that all men had a hope of it, and yet the belief was not clear, because that would make us do nothing in this life."[3]

In the same conversation in which he indicated his scepticism, Courtenay maintained that "all that was required in an ordinary duel was only to shew that a Man can risk his life. It is not necessary to make a Man who has abused you retract what he has said." Perhaps it was merely to demonstrate this theory of duels that he, in effect, encouraged Boswell to risk a duel with Lord Macdonald. Perhaps; but as Professor Pottle has observed, one feels in him a distinct touch of Sheridan's Sir Lucius O'Trigger. As one reads Boswell's account of that affair, it constantly seems that Courtenay is making matters more difficult and strained than they needed to be—completely without malice, one hastens to add. The correspondence concerning this affair comprises a large portion of the Boswell-Courtenay letters, and in it one can see (and admire) Boswell's firmness and courage in the face of a situation for which he was in great part and somewhat foolishly responsible. The fact that Courtenay was employed in this serio-comic affair so early in his acquaintance with Boswell suggests the strength of the intimacy between the two men.

DOUGLAS, JOHN (1721–1807).[4] Douglas, a graduate of Oxford (Balliol), was appointed in 1744 Chaplain to the 3rd Regiment. Having left the Army, he was ordained priest in 1747 and became travelling tutor to Lord Pulteney, son of the Earl of Bath. In 1758, Lord Bath presented him to the perpetual curacy of Kenley, Shropshire, and in 1762 obtained for him a canonry at Windsor. Under Lord Bath's direction, Douglas wrote a number of political pamphlets. He was also the author of *Milton Vindicated from the Charge of Plagiarism* (1751), which exposed the forgeries of William Lauder, and of an attack on Hume's argument upon miracles, *Criterion* (1752). In addition, he edited the diaries and letters of Lord Clarendon and the journals of Captain Cook. In

[2] Journ. 3 Nov. 1792.
[3] Journ. 31 July 1785.
[4] There is in the British Museum (Add. MSS. Eg. 2181) a brief autobiographical manuscript by Douglas dealing with his life from 1776 to 1796.

1763, he took part with Johnson in the detection of the Cock Lane ghost. Relatively late in life, in 1787, Douglas was made Bishop of Carlisle. After being appointed Dean of Windsor in 1788, he was, in 1791, translated to the Bishopric of Salisbury.

Boswell and Douglas dined together often, and, once at Lonsdale's, Boswell, in a gesture of true respect, "had tea in compliment to the Bishop, and less wine".[5] Boswell further indicated his respect for the older man, who had become somewhat querulous in his old age, by employing considerable restraint in his conversations during a visit he made to Salisbury in 1792:

> But I did not dispute with my worthy friend the Bishop, who was now old, (he having entered at Oxford in 1736,) and from the gout flying through his body had an irritability which occasioned a perpetual fretfulness, which, without any real bad humour, was for ever shewing itself in trifles, particularly towards his son, who however was to blame in *answering*. . . . It is striking to observe how peevishness will lessen the most respectable character till *reflection* brings it up again to it's proper level.[6]

Although Douglas was not elected to The Club until 22 May 1792, Boswell had earlier, on 14 December 1790, proposed him for membership.[7] The correspondence here printed, being primarily social in nature, does not really reflect the strength or warmth of the feelings shared by Boswell and Douglas. The Bishop, nineteen years older than Boswell, seems to have been another of the father-surrogates whom the younger man cultivated.

ELIOT OF ST. GERMANS, EDWARD CRAGGS-ELIOT, first Baron (1727–1804). Eliot travelled on the Continent with the illegitimate son to whom Chesterfield addressed the famous letters; he married Gibbon's first cousin; he was a patron of Reynolds and one of Reynolds's most valued friends. A man of great fortune and political influence, he had seven seats in Parliament at his disposal, his standard price being from two to three thousand pounds. (He seated Gibbon gratis.) Opposed to the American war, he joined the anti-ministerial forces; later he adhered to Pitt. Boswell met him at Reynolds's in 1781, he was elected to The Club on 22 January 1782, and in 1784 he was raised to the peerage.

[5] Journ. 29 Nov. 1787.   [7] *The Club.*
[6] Journ. 19 Aug.

Although he was a man of considerable information and once talked seriously with Boswell about bad spirits (recommending opium when insomnia was in question),[8] the general tenor of their association seems to have been sprightly. On the first evening that Boswell spent with Eliot and his family, Boswell was "too much intoxicated";[9] when Eliot came on Boswell sitting alone at a late breakfast at Reynolds's, Boswell "called out, 'Now we're Whig and Tory.'"[1] To readers of the *Life of Johnson* Eliot is best known as the dispenser of Mahogany ("two parts gin, and one part treacle, well beaten together").[2] Eliot was the kind of man Boswell could without *gêne* invite to dine with him and a new mistress. The brief extant correspondence between him and Boswell suggests that their relation was almost purely a social one.

FORBES OF PITSLIGO, SIR WILLIAM, sixth Bt. (1739–1806). Forbes, who succeeded as a child to a ruined Scots baronetcy, won his way to affluence and nation-wide respect as banker and author (*An Account of the Life and Writings of James Beattie*, 1806). His family had been Jacobite, his religion was Episcopalian, and he became the leader in Edinburgh of the Episcopalians who supported the reigning House. One of Boswell's firmest and most useful friends, he was named by Boswell guardian of his children, one of his literary executors, and the executor of his estate. Boswell paid direct tribute to his public spirit in *The Journal of a Tour to the Hebrides*, 1785, as did Walter Scott in *Marmion*, 1808. Though not a member of The Club, he was on friendly terms with several men who were members, and it was he who served as scribe of the Round Robin, the wary request to Johnson to compose Goldsmith's epitaph in English.

FOX, CHARLES JAMES (1749–1806). Fox was the third and favourite son of Henry Fox, Baron Holland of Foxley. After studying at Wandsworth and Eton, he entered Hertford College, Oxford, in 1764. He left Oxford in 1766, and during the next few years, supported by his father's wealth and indulgence, travelled and gambled through Europe.

In 1768, Lord Holland brought Fox into Parliament for Midhurst, in Sussex. His first speeches in the House were enthusiastically received, and he was considered by many the wittiest speaker

[8] Journ. 1 Mar. 1791.
[9] Journ. 14 Apr. 1781.
[1] Journ. 7 May 1781.
[2] *Life* iv. 78; Journ. 14 Apr. 1781.

of his time. He entered North's administration in 1770 as one of the Lords of Admiralty. Although he had entered Parliament as a Tory, he gradually shifted over to the Whig position between 1772 and 1774. He consistently attacked the King and the war policy, and urged economical reform. Extremely popular with the people, he was elected for Westminster in 1780. On 25 March 1782, he took office as Foreign Secretary in Lord Rockingham's ministry. It was shortly after his appointment that Boswell wrote to him seeking his influence.

Fox was elected to The Club on 4 March 1774, having been proposed by Burke, whom he had known since at least 1766. Though only twenty-five years old, he had been a Member of Parliament for six years, was currently a Lord of Treasury, and was generally thought to be assured of the highest positions in Government. The meeting between him and Boswell at The Club on 24 March 1775 (Boswell's first opportunity to attend since Fox's election) may very well have been their first. The relationship never developed into friendship, and Boswell was perhaps to blame. Coming back to The Club a week later, eager to advance in Fox's esteem, he also came sadly in liquor, and he so showered Fox with vinous compliments that Fox changed places at the table to get away from him. Fox was a man of intense and unyielding dislikes, but even if his personal relations with Boswell had become cordial, Boswell's attempt in 1782 to secure his political interest was foredoomed and indeed inept. He and Fox agreed about the American war, but on all other political matters—especially on the fundamental issue of the power of the Crown—their views were diametrically opposed. Worse than that (for Fox soon after demonstrated a staggering willingness to work in Coalition), Fox probably had seen enough of Boswell to know that he could not be counted on to remain firm in *any* line of action. After 1783, he could not overlook Boswell's considered public attack on the East India Bill which bore his name and was very dear to his heart. Boswell did not seem to understand that although an established politician might attack a man one day and form a coalition with him the next, a man seeking patronage with no political influence and no money had to present a consistent show of loyalty in order to have his requests granted. He never learned, and, as a result, suffered constant disappointment in his futile relations with Pitt, Burke, Fox, Dundas, and Lonsdale. His second letter to Fox illustrates perfectly this inability to understand the ways of politics. However sincere Boswell may have been at the time of writing, Fox, even if he had been able to overlook Boswell's past attacks, could never have been certain that he could be counted on. The needs of party could never be overlooked; but Boswell consistently overlooked them.

GARRICK, DAVID (1717–79). One of Johnson's earliest friends, Garrick had been joint manager at Drury Lane Theatre since 1747. His connexion with that theatre remained unbroken until he retired from the stage in 1776. This greatest actor of his age was elected to The Club 12 March 1773. Since the single letter from him in the present volume is addressed to Langton, discussion of the relations between Boswell and Garrick is reserved for the volume in which their correspondence appears.

GOLDSMITH, OLIVER (c. 1730–74). Goldsmith, one of the most versatile writers of his time, turned to journalism after being rejected for holy orders and after a chequered career as medical student, apothecary's assistant, and school usher. From 1757 on, he produced essays, translations, and various kinds of compilations for booksellers and for such journals as *The Monthly Review, The British Magazine*, and *The Public Ledger*. In addition to his hack work, of course, Goldsmith produced the works for which he is best known: *The Citizen of the World* (1762), *The Vicar of Wakefield* (1766), *The Deserted Village* (1770), and *She Stoops to Conquer* (1773). In 1770, he was appointed Professor of Ancient History to the Royal Academy.

One of the original members of The Club, Goldsmith was a close friend not only of Dr. Johnson but also of Sir Joshua Reynolds and Thomas Percy. Boswell first met him at Tom Davies's on Christmas Day, 1762, and did not particularly take to him: "Mr. Goldsmith, a curious, odd, pedantic fellow with some genius." The pervasive chilliness of his treatment of Goldsmith in the *Life of Johnson*, coupled with certain unflattering remarks that Goldsmith is said to have made about Boswell, has been taken to prove that the two never became true friends. Boswell's journal, however, gives a different impression. No doubt responding in part to Goldsmith's rapid rise to fame and the extremely attractive literary personality displayed in the works that were making him famous, Boswell appears to have grown not only friendly but genuinely cordial, and Goldsmith seems to have responded in kind.

1

The letters here published were exchanged at the height of Goldsmith's success, when the friendship between the two men was at its warmest. Shortly after Goldsmith wrote his letter of 4 April 1773 (*post*), Boswell called on him before he was up. "When he heard that it was I he roared from his bed, 'Boswell.' I ran to him. We had a cordial embrace. . . . He is the most generous-hearted man that exists."[3] The fact that Goldsmith gave Boswell a holograph manuscript of the Song in *She Stoops to Conquer* (C 1379) further suggests that at least in 1773 the relationship was a warm one. Boswell paid graceful public tribute to "my departed Goldsmith" as late as 1785 in his *Letter to the People of Scotland*,[4] but no warmth of personal affection is reflected in the *Life*, which is a pity. His strategy there is to characterize Goldsmith mainly through Johnson's utterances, scrupulously preserving Johnson's emphatic pronouncements that Goldsmith was a very great author and a very great man. But Johnson's utterances in fact consist mainly of vivid and unsparing disparagement of Goldsmith's oddities and foibles; and Boswell refrains from providing the enveloping *personal* appreciation by which he holds in proper scale the unattractive details in his portrait of Johnson. His departure in this case from his general biographical practice puzzled Malone and Reynolds, and has never been satisfactorily explained.

The two men met fairly often in London when Boswell was there, but neither made any attempt to maintain their relationship by correspondence when they were separated. There is no indication that Goldsmith ever wrote to Boswell more than the two letters published here.

HAMILTON, WILLIAM GERARD (1729–96). Not a member of The Club, Hamilton appears in the present collection because of a brief and bad-tempered note to John Courtenay. Known as "Single-speech Hamilton" because of his impressive maiden speech in Commons (almost the only one he ever made there) Hamilton was a friend of Johnson's and was Boswell's second cousin, both of them being great-grandsons of Sir Charles Erskine of Alva, Kt. (d. 1663). He pleased Boswell with the elegance of his "House, table, and manners, and particularly his beautiful language and pronunciation. . . . I flattered myself that I might have one of my sons such a Man as Hamilton."[5] Later he became annoyed when

---

[3] Journ. 7 Apr.
[4] Page 99.
[5] Journ. 15 June 1786.

Hamilton ("That *nervous* mortal") demanded cancellation and revision of certain passages in the *Life of Johnson* which Boswell had taken down from his own dictation, and composed unflattering verses on him.[6]

HAWKINS, SIR JOHN (1719–89). Magistrate, musicologist, and long-time friend of Johnson, Sir John was one of the original and one of the most unpopular members of The Club. He eventually withdrew from the group because of an argument with Edmund Burke.[7] He published in 1760 an edition of Walton's *Compleat Angler*, and then, after many years of preparation, *A General History of Music* in five volumes (1776), a work less enthusiastically received than Burney's *History*, but now generally rated above it. Because they were rival biographers of Johnson, among other reasons, Hawkins and Boswell maintained a fairly cool relationship. Boswell personally resented Hawkins's sole reference to him in the latter's *Life of Johnson* as "Mr. James Boswell, a native of Scotland" (p. 472), but he was by no means alone among Johnson's friends in thinking that the work should be castigated for its "dark uncharitable cast."[8] Hawkins was, on the other hand, on excellent terms with Bennet Langton.

LANGTON, BENNET (1737–1801). Bennet Langton plays a major role in Boswell's *Life of Johnson*, and in both the *Life* and Boswell's journal we learn a great deal about his character. He was a very pious man and too willing to introduce religious topics in mixed company;[1] "as good a Man as lives", "but ridiculous"; "a Man of great knowledge", "but it never lyes straight".[2] He was unable to live within his means. Mrs. Thrale concurs: "Mr. Langton seems to stand in a very odd Light among us.—he is acknowledged Learned, Pious, and elegant of Manners—yet he is always a Person unrespected and commonly ridiculous."[3] In spite of all this, Johnson could say of him, "The earth does not bear a worthier man than Bennet Langton."[4] "I know not who will go to Heaven if Langton does not. Sir, I could almost say, *Sit anima mea cum Langtono*."[5]

---

[6] To Malone, 25 Feb. 1791; Journ. 3 Mar. 1791; Yale MS. M 329.
[7] *Life* i. 479–80; Sir John Hawkins, *Life of Johnson*, 1st ed., 1787, p. 425.
[8] *Life* i. 28; To Temple, 5 Mar. 1789.

[1] Journ. 7 May 1773; 30 Apr. 1783.

[2] Journ. 29 May 1783.
[3] *Thraliana, The Diary of Mrs. Hester Lynch Thrale*, ed. K. C. Balderston, 1942, i. 106.
[4] *Life* iii. 161.
[5] *Life* iv. 280.

Yet the *Life* and other memoirs of the time give us very little from which to construct a *curriculum vitae*. We are told that Langton came from an old Lincolnshire family, that he went to Oxford, that he was somehow involved in the Wey Navigation, that he was a captain and then a major in the North Lincoln Militia, that he went to Chatham as an engineer, and that he lived some years in Rochester. We learn also that he married the widow of a Scots peer and had many children (although authorities have seldom agreed how many), and that he was at times excessively lenient with them. Later studies have not added much in the way of facts. The account of him in *The Dictionary of National Biography* is brief and inaccurate. *Burke's Landed Gentry* misstates his father's name. The notes devoted to him in the Hill-Powell *Life* undoubtedly add to our knowledge, but do not provide many new biographical details. Even Boswell's journal, though it reinforces the great character-sketch of Langton in the *Life*, has not increased our store of facts to any great extent. On the other hand, the letters to and from Langton which were found at Malahide Castle and Fettercairn House have proved of great value in establishing a factual basis for a biography. I have supplemented the information they provide with matter, long since available, from public archives, and with other matter drawn from Langton family papers: a collection of documents in the possession of the present head of the Langton family, J. C. P. Langton, Esq.; the diaries and letter-book of Langton's second son, Peregrine Langton-Massingberd, now deposited in the Lincolnshire Archives; and a collection of letters to and from members of the family recently discovered at Gunby Hall, many of which were transcribed by Peregrine in his letter-book.

Bennet Langton was born in 1737 into a family which traced its descent through the male line from the twelfth century. The Langtons of Langton by Spilsby, Lincolnshire, "lived on and by their land, and kept so fast a hold upon it that parish and advowson have never departed from them."[6] They were apparently content to remain in Lincolnshire, and no member of the family had ever become famous. Bennet Langton's father, Bennet the elder, "so affluent a talker" that "no business [was] done for his declamation",[7] had, according to Mrs. Thrale (perhaps not a completely reliable witness), "no Authority over his Family" and was inept

[6] *The Ancestor*, ed. Oswald Barron, No. vii, Oct. 1903, p. 168.   [7] Journ. 7 May 1773.

in the handling of his finances.[8] He married Diana Turnor, daughter of Edmund Turnor of Stoke Rochford, Lincolnshire. Langton's mother was dissatisfied with country life and constantly teased her husband to take her to London, "never regulating her Family for twenty Years, never buying a Cow, never putting up a Fowl to feed,—never repairing their Furniture or house . . . where they always lived because they were to go to London next Year forsooth and see the Players, who made all the Subject of her Conversation."[9] Bennet Langton the elder's decision to spend most of his time on his estate was perhaps consequent on his having invested in stock of the South Sea Company.[10] According to the Lindsey Sessions Minutes, he was a justice at the sessions of Louth, Spilsby, and Alford at least eighteen times between 1750 and 1767. In 1757, he was Sheriff of Lincolnshire.[11]

Besides Bennet, who was the eldest, his father had at least nine other children, of whom apparently only five lived beyond their third year.[12] Bennet's three surviving sisters, Elizabeth, Diana, and Juliet, are mentioned in the *Life*. There was also a younger brother, George Ferne, who died not long after his matriculation at Trinity College, Oxford, in 1757.[13]

[8] *Thraliana* i. 104–05.

[9] *Ibid.* p. 105. SJ referred to her theatrical "undulation and mobility" (*Letters SJ* ii. 217). There is no evidence of these feather-brain qualities either in the letter Bennet wrote to her in 1764 or in her letter to him of 9 May 1792 (Gunby), apparently the only surviving correspondence between them.

[10] From Bennet Langton the elder to Joseph Banks II, Cavendish Square, London, 8 Dec. 1739, *The Letters and Papers of the Banks Family of Revesby Abbey 1704–1760*, ed. W. F. Hill (The Publications of the Lincoln Record Society, vol. 45), 1952, pp. 183–85. Evidently in the early years of his marriage Langton *did* take his wife to London. He indicates, however, in this letter that he would just as soon not have: "It would be very happy in many respects if the ladies here could be induced to . . . be contented with the amusements that country life affords."

[11] *Lincolnshire Notes and Queries*, Supplement to vol. xxiv (1936), p. 22.

[12] Langton by Spilsby parish register, which records the christenings and burials of four other children who died before completing their third year. Juliet's christening, Diana's marriage, and Elizabeth's burial are also recorded. Bennet and George Ferne Langton do not appear at all in the register, and, with their sisters Diana and Elizabeth, were presumably born elsewhere. Langton's son Peregrine wrote in 1809 that his father was unhappy in the improper marriage of two sisters, one of whom "was burnt to death, as well as a Sister only five years old" (PL-M's diary (1809), p. 72). In his letter-book (p. 100b) he identified Juliet as the elder one who "came to a tragical end; for she died after lingering many months in a dreadful state of suffering from having been burnt". Frances, whose christening is not recorded but who was buried on 12 Nov. 1746, may have been the sister who suffered the same fate at the age of five.

[13] *Alum. Oxon.* II. iii. 818.

The evidence concerning Langton's early education appears to be in conflict, but can be reconciled by assuming that the sources of information complement each other. According to a biographical note sent to me by the late Miss Adela Langton, he was educated "under his paternal roof". Sir William Forbes, however, who knew Langton for nearly thirty years, asserted that he attended the grammar schools of Kensington, Reading, and Beverley before going to Oxford.[14] It is probable that at least some of his education was completed at home, since he did not matriculate at Oxford until he was twenty, which was unusually old for a beginning student. His interest in literature developed fairly early, and was encouraged, as letters printed in the present volume show, by Joseph Spence, author of *Observations*, and by Edward Young, author of *Night Thoughts*. Langton's father was a friend of Spence's, whom he had met through a Lincolnshire neighbour, William Burrell Massingberd (1719–1802);[15] and through Spence the elder Langton may have become acquainted with various literary men whom Spence had known from the early 1750s. Bennet, in short, as a young man in London or Lincolnshire, may have been fairly frequently in the company, not only of Spence and Young, but also of Garrick, Robert Dodsley the poet and publisher, and Joseph Warton. At any rate, he knew Spence and Young well enough to visit them and correspond with them.

When Bennet's brother died, Bennet wrote to Spence concerning his loss. Spence replied in what is actually a sermon on death and on the necessity of reconciling oneself to it; but the letter, a copy of which is in the Osborn Collection at Yale, also indicates that Langton's pious nature was already well developed:

The thoughts which you so well express toward the conclusion, are like yourself; and I hope will in time enable you to bear and conquer your Sorrow, and patiently to acquiesce in the Divine Dispensation. Nay, that I trust you already do: for I know your

---

[14] *Life of Beattie* ii. 264 n. Neither the school at Reading nor that at Beverley has any record of Langton's attendance, but the records up to the nineteenth century are incomplete at both schools. I have found no records at Kensington that suggest that he ever attended school there. The Grammar School was not founded until 1830; no record exists of any other similar school before 1828.

[15] Austin Wright, *Joseph Spence, A Critical Biography*, 1950, pp. 119–20. Professor Wright assumes that Bennet the younger is meant; but he would have been much too young at this period.

good Sense; and what is yet more; how long and how much you have been accustomed to think of the Noblest Principles, in the most Excellent of Religions.

It is apparent from Spence's letter to Bennet in 1756 (*post* Appendix 2) that, no doubt in his capacity as Professor of Modern History at Oxford, he advised the young man on his reading. The letter also seems to confirm the belief that Langton was educated, at least partly, at home. Spence's letter of 1762 indicates clearly that Langton suffered, even as a young man, from the diffusion of interests and lack of direction which were to make his life somewhat futile and, in a scholarly sense, unproductive.

In addition to studying, Langton seems to have tried his hand at writing during the years before going to Oxford; for Edward Young, in 1755 (*post* Appendix 2), advised him to "proceed, Dear Sir, in your litterary Pursuits." If we can judge from the letters Langton wrote, his progress in literary pursuits was not equal to his setting out; but perhaps Young was a flatterer or an incompetent judge. The *New Cambridge Bibliography of English Literature*, 1971 (ii. 1917) lists Langton as co-author, with George Colman, of an essay on modern education in issue No. 22 of *The Connoisseur*, 27 June 1754.[16] If Langton wrote it, at the age of seventeen, it seems likely that it was extensively revised by either Colman or Bonnell Thornton, the other editor of *The Connoisseur*. A satirical piece attacking contemporary education, its style is similar to that of No. 67 of *The Idler*, which Langton is reported to have written while at Oxford.[17] One suspects, however, that Johnson revised that essay before it was printed. Boswell reported that Langton also wrote a number of essays, never published, called "Rusticks", some time during his college career.[18]

Langton matriculated at Trinity College, Oxford, on 7 July 1757, on the same day as his brother. While there he formed a friendship with Topham Beauclerk, also of Trinity, which was to last until Beauclerk's death in 1780. As has been said above in the article on Beauclerk, love of literature and learning (Langton was a fine classical scholar) formed an obvious bond, but otherwise the differences in their characters in later life make the friendship seem

[16] Source of attribution untraced. J. W. Adamson, who edited the section in which it appears in the first edition of the CBEL, has since died.

[17] *Life* i. 330.

[18] *Ibid.* p. 358; see also *Letters SJ* i. 129.

a strange one. Perhaps the differences when they were in college were not as great as they became later;[19] perhaps each found among the other's differences much to admire. Beauclerk's aristocratic and worldly vivacity may have appealed to the sober son of a country squire; the restless and mordant Beauclerk may have felt soothed by Langton's quiet piety. Whatever the reasons, the friendship was enduring and at times touching, as Beauclerk's letters to Langton show. In his last years, Beauclerk seems to have grown even more dependent on the calm strength of Langton's character. His entrusting to Langton the guardianship of his children in case of Lady Diana's death was the final indication of his trust.

Like many young men of good family, Langton travelled on the Continent after leaving Oxford. On 7 August 1762, he and Beauclerk set out from Dover for Calais; they were in Paris by at least the 11th, on which day Langton visited the Louvre and the Tuileries Gardens.[20] Part of their time in that city was spent in seeking out eminent men of learning, as the letter to Beauclerk from the mathematician d'Alembert (*post*) indicates. It is not known whether Langton extended his travels beyond France, although Beauclerk originally had certainly planned to travel in Italy and was reported to have lost £10,000 in Venice;[21] Langton, at any rate, was back in England by March 1763, at which time he seems to have brought back for Johnson a copy of the French Academy's *Dictionnaire*, sent to the Doctor by that body of scholars as an expression of their admiration for his *Dictionary*.[22]

In the years before his marriage, at least from 1763 to 1766, Langton spent most of his time in London, living first in rooms owned by a Mrs. Linant and then at a Mrs. Terry's, and leading an extremely active social life.[23] He attended the theatre and the opera frequently and spent many evenings at Almack's, the Cocoa Tree, the Smyrna Coffee House, and, naturally, at the Turk's Head, with other original members of The Club. Occasional trips to Langton are recorded in his diaries, as are more frequent

---

[19] "Beauclerc very subtily said, 'The belief of Christianity does not influence a man's conduct. I *know*, Langton, it did not keep you from whoring'" (Journ. 23 Mar. 1775).

[20] Langton's diary.

[21] *Life* i. 369, 381 and n. 1.

[22] *Ibid.* p. 298.

[23] Langton's diary does not fix the location of Mrs. Terry's house. One naturally wonders whether it was the house of Thomas Terrie (or Terry), Downing Street, Westminster, where JB had rooms from 26 Nov. 1762 to 7 July 1763.

journeys, generally on Navigation business, down into Surrey. He made a second visit to France, from 27 July to 6 August 1763, travelling to Dunkirk, Lille, Bethune, and St. Omer. There is no indication that Beauclerk accompanied him, although Langton was often in the company of both Topham and his mother, Lady Sidney Beauclerk, at this period.[24] In the autumn of 1764 he wrote to his mother reporting his attendance at the opening of Parliament and expressing his intense disapproval of John Wilkes's recently published *Essay on Woman*.[24a] After 1766 for some years there are few indications of Langton's activities. His father died on 12 June 1769, the estate going to Mrs. Langton, in accordance with the terms of her marriage settlement, until her death, when Bennet would inherit;[25] Langton, in both 1778 and 1779, referred to himself as the "Heir to the Estate of Langton near Spilsby," rather than as its owner.[26]

On 24 May 1770, Langton married Mary, Dowager Countess of Rothes, widow of John Leslie, tenth Earl of Rothes (d. 1767), whom she had married in 1763. Born c. 1743, she was the daughter of Gresham Lloyd and Mary Holt, who later married the seventh Earl of Haddington. Few of Langton's friends approved of the marriage. Johnson said, "He has done a very foolish thing, Sir; he has married a widow, when he might have had a maid."[27] Lady Rothes, who retained her style of peeress in her second marriage, was not popular with her husband's friends. Mrs. Thrale, whose opinions of other women were seldom favourable, maintained that Langton was "tied to a Thing without Beauty, Birth, Money or Talents, widow to an old Scotch Peer who wanted a Son in his Old Age & took a fresh Lawland Lass for that Purpose with more Probability than Success."[28] Langton and Lady Rothes proceeded most effectively to ensure that the estate of Langton stayed in the family. Between March 1772 and October 1787, they had ten children: four sons and six daughters,[29] all of whom lived at least

[24] Langton's diary.
[24a] Gunby. All Langton family letters, unless otherwise noted, are from this collection.
[25] Marriage Settlement of Bennet Langton and Diana Turnor, in the possession of J. C. P. Langton, Esq.
[26] Records at Lindsey County Council, "Militia No. 1. From 1750 to 1822."
[27] *Life* ii. 77.
[28] *Thraliana* i. 106.
[29] George, born 8 Mar. 1772; Mary, 16 July 1773; Diana, 28 Sept. 1774; Jane, 26 June 1776; Elizabeth, 21 Oct. 1777; Peregrine, 29 Jan. 1780; Algernon, 8 Mar. 1781; Isabella, 7 Aug. 1782; Charles, 3 Dec. 1783; and Margaret, 9 Oct. 1787. These birth dates were furnished by the late Miss Adela Langton.

through adolescence, and all of whom, Langton's friends agreed, were "too much about him".[30]

In the autumn of 1772, Langton and his wife paid a visit to Edinburgh, to see relatives of Lady Rothes, arriving on 5 October. Boswell supped with Langton that evening, and the next morning breakfasted with both him and Lady Rothes. The somewhat scanty records of this visit kept by Boswell show that he introduced Langton to a number of the Scottish literati—Drs. Gregory, Blair, Blacklock, and others—and that Langton also met Sir William Forbes, Lord Monboddo, Lord Elibank, and several of Boswell's relatives. Langton and his wife left Edinburgh twice in October, once to visit her mother, the Countess of Haddington. At some time during this stay in Scotland he visited Auchinleck, though Boswell can hardly have accompanied him there. Back in Edinburgh, Langton saw much of Boswell, attended church with him regularly and was entertained at numerous dinners. At Sir Alexander Dick's, Langton and Sir Alexander "talked much of their common friend Spence". Langton left Edinburgh on 17 December; and it was only a few months later that the main body of the correspondence between Langton and Boswell began.[31]

Langton's life during the period covered by the correspondence here printed is fairly well described in his own letters. The letters written to him by others shed some further light. Langton's varied interests in literary, educational, and philanthropic matters are brought out clearly in the letters to him from members of The Club such as Sir Joshua Reynolds, Thomas Warton (his tutor at Trinity College), David Garrick, and Edmund Burke, and in those from others in the Johnsonian circle such as Sir William Forbes and General Oglethorpe. The letter from Robert Orme, historian of the East India Company, whom Langton probably met through Dr. Samuel Parr, a friend of Orme, reveals by implication the wide scope of Langton's reading and his interest in fields other than the classics. Like all country gentlemen at some time, Langton, in the summer of 1775, was called for grand-jury duty. And like many of his colleagues, according to Sir William Blackstone's letter, he failed to appear. Langton apparently did not inherit his father's enthusiasm for public service as magistrate, for his name does not appear once in the records of Lincolnshire justices.

For many years Langton was associated with the Portmore

[30] From SJ, 22 July 1777.   [31] Notes, 5 Oct. to 17 Dec. 1772.

lix

family in the development and management of the Wey Navigation; and there are at Yale two notes to him from the Earl of Portmore (it does not seem necessary to print them) which hint, rather incoherently, at some of the problems that Langton the scholar had to face as a man of business. When he married Lady Rothes, he acquired a new circle of acquaintances, his wife's relatives by her own first and her mother's second marriage. Although the Langtons were already acquainted with the Portmores through their association with them in the Wey Navigation, the marriage of Lady Rothes's stepdaughter to the Earl of Portmore's son undoubtedly brought them together more frequently.

Langton's attendance at Johnson's deathbed has been often described in great detail. After that, aside from the letters in this edition, his life is scantily documented. He edited Johnson's Latin verses for the collected edition of Johnson's works, 1787, and in 1788 succeeded Johnson as Professor of Ancient Literature in the Royal Academy. In 1787, he was involved in the troubled family affairs of John Paradise, whose daughter had eloped with a Venetian count, through the connivance of his wife, who threatened to leave him. Both Langton and Sir John Hawkins were consulted by Paradise, who hoped that legal steps could be taken to prevent his daughter's marriage. He was able to do nothing about his daughter, but Langton and Hawkins were able to bring about a reconciliation between him and his wife.[32] In the summer of 1789 Langton hired a house at Richmond.[32a] In 1790 he took the degree of D.C.L. at Oxford.

Having abandoned, apparently, the task of educating his sons at home, Langton sent them to Dr. Charles Burney's school at Hammersmith. Three of them, Peregrine, Algernon, and Charles, attended at the same time, although Peregrine suffered considerably from an eye ailment, and Langton was forced to withdraw him at least temporarily. The Langtons must have been a trial for any schoolmaster who tried to run his school on any kind of schedule, since their absences seem to have been frequent and their returns from vacations tardy.[33] Between March 1792 and September 1794

[32] Shepperson, pp. 264–73. See also L.-M. Hawkins, *Memoirs, Anecdotes, Facts, and Opinions,* 1824, i. 74.

[32a] PL-M's letter-book, p. 27b.

[33] From Langton to Dr. Charles Burney, Hyde Collection. Another letter from Langton to Burney, excusing the absence of two of the boys because of illness, is in the possession of Mr. Arthur S. T. O'Keefe.

Langton lived much in London, where, according to a number of letters to his daughters, he occupied himself by dining out, attending royal levees, negotiating financial matters, and devising educational projects for his offspring.[33a]

With the death of Boswell, Langton almost disappears from view. Just before Boswell's death, on 24 April 1795, he resigned from the Militia after a military career of twenty-five years.[34] In August of that year, he was at Norwich, whence he wrote to Malone on the third that he had heard from Sir William Forbes that Forbes, Temple, and Malone had been bequeathed by Boswell "the friendly Task of judging which and what parts of his writings left behind him, may be thought of for publication."[35] On the 14th, Boswell's friend William Johnson Temple wrote to him for advice on sending his son to Oxford;[36] and later in the month visited him at Norwich: "Conversation about John's going to Oxford. A fine family. I never saw Mr. L. so entertaining in conversation before."[37] "From Norwich", Peregrine informs us, Langton "again settled in London, hiring a house in Great George Street, Westminster—it was that house which has the *West* end of it over an arch way into a small street leading to the Abbey."[37a] In the autumn of that year, when he visited Euphemia, James, and Elizabeth Boswell in London on the 10th and 11th of October, Temple again saw Langton; but his opinion of Langton's conversational powers was considerably modified: "Mr. L. talks too much and quotes too much and too minutely. I trust too apprehensive about the times we live in: yet full of science and information."[38] It was perhaps his excessive use of quotation, about which even Johnson complained,[39] that gave rise to the story told by the Dean of Winchester of Langton's "coming to town some few years after the death of Dr. Johnson, and finding no house where he was even asked to dinner. . . . Mr. Wilberforce dismissed him with a cold 'Adieu, dear Sir, I hope we shall meet in heaven!' "[40] Whatever

[33a] Gunby: To Mary, 9 Mar. 1792; To Jane, 17–18 Mar. 1792; To Elizabeth, 21 Mar. 1792; To Isabella, 6 Sept. 1794; also From Diana Turnor Langton (mother), 9 May 1792; To John E. Dolben, Nov. 1792.

[34] Musters of North Lincolnshire Militia, Public Record Office, W.O. 13/1295.

[35] Hyde Collection.

[36] *Diaries of William Johnston Temple, 1780–1796*, ed. Lewis Bettany, 1929, p. 135.

[37] *Ibid.* p. 136.

[37a] PL-M's letter-book, p. 63b.

[38] *Temple Diaries*, p. 147.

[39] To Temple, 18 Mar. 1775.

[40] *Autobiography, Letters, and Literary Remains of Mrs. Piozzi* (*Thrale*), ed. A. Hayward, 1861, p. 388. The "Dean of

truth there may be in the Dean's hyperbolic anecdote, Boswell recorded meeting Langton at dinners at Malone's and the Bishop of London's as late as 1794.[41]

Langton's last years are documented primarily by family letters. On 11 April 1796, his daughter Elizabeth wrote to her brother George describing the death of their sister Mary. "My father, thank GOD", she added, "is pretty well, but grown thinner since we left him."[41a] Langton wrote from London to Elizabeth on 8 October congratulating her and her sister Isabella on their studying the Scriptures with the assistance of Dr. Henry Hammond's *Paraphrases and Annotations on the New Testament*. He had spoken recently with Lord Cornwallis; had heard the King's speech at the opening of Parliament; and had met Malone, Blagden, Scott, Burney, and Courtenay at the last meeting of The Club. When his son Peregrine matriculated at Merton College, Oxford, on 4 December 1797, Langton was listed as living at St. Marylebone, Middlesex. On 16 July 1799, he and Malone dined alone at The Club.[42] The day before, he had written to Elizabeth at Langton expressing concern because Lady Rothes had not received a bank post bill which he had sent to her at Skegness, a dreary seaside resort some ten miles from Spilsby, where she was staying because of her health. Algernon, Charles, and Peregrine were apparently with her. Langton also told his daughter that he was writing to Charles to inform him that he had bought for him a copy of the new edition (the third) of Boswell's *Life*, "a very handsome copy in four volumes".[43]

He wrote to Elizabeth again on 5 August expressing concern about Lady Rothes's health and the misbehaviour of Charles, an ensign in the Navy. He reported visits to Miss Reynolds and the novelist Charlotte Lennox (apparently a good friend of the family) and dinner at the Bishop of London's. On 21 September he wrote in another letter to Elizabeth that he had sent by the Spilsby coach "a small Box with the Æther and the Tickells Æther", along with a half-dozen bottles of Calcavella and two volumes of *Christian Theology*. Later in the autumn he had been in bad health, but his condition had improved by the time he wrote to his friend Lt. Col. Pownall from Langton on 30 October describing his journey up

Winchester" was presumably Thomas Rennell, D.D. (1754–1840).
[41] Journ. 20, 23 Mar.
[41a] PL-M's letter-book, p. 66b.

[42] *The Club.*
[43] *Adam Library* iii, facsimile between pp. 149 and 150.

from London and the various visits on the way to friends and relations in Cambridge, Stamford, and Lincoln. He also shared with the Colonel his concern over England's military situation, his interest in the disposal of a church living, and his dismay at a local infestation of sheep rot. "Poor Charles" and his financial problems were also commented on both in this letter and in a briefer one to the Colonel on 3 December. Some time during the winter of 1799, according to Peregrine, the family took a house at Southampton so that Isabella, who suffered from a pulmonary complaint, could benefit from sea air.[43a]

On 10 April 1800, Langton was back in London, whence he wrote to his daughter Jane that he was "very comfortably lodged" at No. 13 Abingdon Street, Westminster. Between May 1795 and July 1799, he had attended thirty-nine meetings of The Club.[44] On Tuesday 13 May 1800, according to a note in his own hand in the Club records, he nominated Dr. Charles Burney (the younger) for membership. The nomination was seconded by Lord Macartney. Burney was not, however, elected until 27 February 1810. Langton attended only two more meetings of The Club, those of 24 June and 8 July 1800.[45] On 15 October of that year he was staying at "a Hotel on our Sea-Coast", where he had been for three weeks, he wrote to a very good friend of the Langtons, Augusta Feilding, a relation of the Earl of Winchelsea. He could not leave until his daughter (possibly Margaret, the youngest), who was very ill, recovered.

Writing from Langton, again to Miss Feilding, on 18 April 1801, Langton commented on the King's late illness (another attack of madness) and on the health of his own daughters, particularly Isabella. Should the doctor recommend a much longer stay at Southampton for her, he wrote, he planned to join "the greater part" of the family there. He apparently joined them shortly thereafter, for letters written by him in May, June, September, October, and November are all dated from Southampton (a letter directed to No. 56 High Street, he informed Miss Feilding, would reach him), although he was considering a move to the Isle of Wight.[45a] He was still at Southampton when he wrote to a Dr. Bland on 18 September, and according to Peregrine, it was during that month

[43a] PL-M's letter-book, p. 111b.
[44] The Club.
[45] The Club.

[45a] From Langton to Miss Feilding, 30 May–5 June 1801.

that he dined with the Duke of Gloucester (with whom he was on fairly intimate terms) at Cowes, Isle of Wight. There he was suddenly seized with a slight fit from which he seemed quickly to recover.[46] No mention of this attack is made in a letter full of fatherly advice he sent to Peregrine on 30 October; but in another, somewhat gloomy, letter to Miss Feilding, which he began on 30 September but did not finish until 6 November, it is clear that the illness influenced his thoughts considerably. After more than a page of apologetic explanation of his tardiness in writing to her, he turned to the subject of his age and the probability of their corresponding further:

> . . . but alas, my dear Madam, what am I talking of? Am I, at near sixty five years old, to be computing for future occurrences by returns of *annual* periods; when, if a few more years should be allotted to me, as in the course of nature might be the case, and the diseases and infirmities attendant on advancing age, be as gradual in their approach to me, as in the more favour'd instances, we may observe it to befal (of which too if I allow'd myself in any sanguine expectations it would be indeed very culpable presumption) yet still, on these better suppositions, memory must be failing, my poor share of intellect more and more clouded, and uneasiness and peevishness too probably augmenting, so as to pervert and distort what offers itself to attention—these are to be sure precious requisites for a correspondent! . . . it is to be hoped, that, if Life should go on with me for a little longer time and the above mentioned effects grow heavily prevalent I may have a chance of detecting them, so as to be in the less danger of persisting to tax your charity to return replies to such an old cross, dull, correspondent, as I should then have compleatly become.

He then recalled to her "some of the lines [271–78] in which my deeply respected Friend Dr. Johnson (in 'The Vanity of Human Wishes') has painted, what I doubt is the most frequent state of Life far advanced—

> Nor Lute nor Lyre his feeble powers attend,
> Nor sweeter musick of a Virtuous Friend,
> But everlasting dictates croud his tongue,
> Perversely grave or positively wrong.

[46] PL-M's diary i (1806–08).

The still repeated Tale and lingering Jest,
Perplex the fawning Niece or pampering Guest,
While growing hopes scarce awe the gathering sneer,
And scarce a legacy can bribe a tear."

From thoughts of his own mortality he turned to the feeble health
of Isabella and Margaret, and to Jane's suffering at the death in
India of her fiancé, Nathaniel Hornby. He then wrote of his disappointment at not being allowed to see the King when His
Majesty was convalescing in Southampton the previous summer,
and called to mind

> the gracious expressions of Notice and Regard with which at
> various times during the last twenty years His Majesty has
> honoured me, and, at such times of recollection I hope it need not
> be deemed too presuming, if, founding the idea on the only
> ground on which it could have any propriety—those gracious
> expressions of Regard—I should have aspired to the wish that
> He should have judged it fit for me to have been on some such
> terms of Access to Him, as might have amounted to my having
> the Honour of being consider'd by Him as an humble Friend. . . .
> But as it now too plainly appears that any such aspiring hope is
> not to be realized I must acquiesce in my Destiny; and thankful
> for the Notice with which His Majesty has thought proper to hon-
> our me, as, with the due Feelings of Attachment towards Him as
> our Great Political Parent; continue to join in the general wish
> and Prayer, that it may be granted to Him "in health and wealth
> long to live", as well as to experience all the other instances of
> Blessings that are so emphatically the subject of Petitions for
> Him, in the Form of Devotion to which I am now referring.

No later letter from Langton seems to exist. Peregrine described
his last days:

> Up to the eleventh of December my father was in his usual state
> of health, and on that Day dined with Dr. Mackie; when finding
> himself indisposed, and that a cough which had lately come on
> troubled him very much, he left the table, and returned home—
> less fear or alarm was entertained as he always desponded, fancy-
> ing himself ill in a 100 ways—Dr. Mackie attended him; he kept
> his bed; his cough was troublesome; but no danger was appre-
> hended; and finding that the cough did not yield to what was

prescribed, Dr. M. gave him leave to take some paragorick elixir, supposing that he would take only occasionally a few drops as the Cough was more or less violent: instead of which he took so large a dose, that when the Dr. attended him on the 17 or 18, he was greatly alarmed, and then, when too late, saw the danger he was in—The intelligence came like a thunderbolt—nobody imagined that anything scarcely ailed him. The state of affliction into which the house was thrown may be supposed—but it is impossible for me to describe it. . . . Neither of his Sons were on the spot when he died, nor had he, till quite the last, any supposition that he himself was dying; so that neither of us could be sent for. He died on the 18 of December, and was buried in St. Michael's Church at Southampton on Goodfriday.[47]

Although Peregrine could not describe the afflicted state of the family, his sister Elizabeth could. She wrote to Augusta Feilding on 31 December:

The source of entertainment, wisdom, and instruction is at end; our pattern and example in every exigence of life is taken away and by the seperation seems to be felt a total destitution of happiness, a sudden abruption of all our prospects, a cessation of all our hopes schemes and desires. If any additional Motives were wanting to prove to us that our loss is *irreparable*, the confirmation of this *sad* truth would be felt in the very remarkable flattering testimonies of regard, approbation and praise paid to the character of him whose departure we now deplore, from a more general and extensive acquaintance than in so finite a station has perhaps been often known, among whom, were the most considerable Men of the Age in which they lived.

Thus died and was mourned the last original member of The Club. The tablet to his memory at St. Michael's Church, Southampton, quotes Johnson's *Sit anima mea cum Langtono*. His death did not go unnoticed, for *The Gentleman's Magazine* for January 1802 printed an "Epistle to Mr. Langton", which was preceded by a letter eulogizing him: "Almost every reader (for there will be few who have not heard something of the excelling goodness of Mr. Langton) will unite in the sorrows of his family for so irreparable a loss! under which they are alone supported by the exertion of that

[47] PL-M's letter-book, pp. 136b–37b.

sublime piety, he also so eminently possessed."[48] Another verse
tribute appeared in the February issue of the same magazine on
"The Friend, the Father, Husband, now no more!"

> Uniting all that polish'd life could please,
> His Johnson's learning join'd with Beauclerk's ease,
> Distinguish'd far above his peers he shone,
> In charms of conversation all his own. . . .
> Unstain'd by vice, pure, pious, calm his mind,
> He died as he had liv'd—to God resign'd.
>
> (lxxii. 157)

Langton first appears in Boswell's company on Tuesday 7 June
1768, when Boswell had collected a company of friends to dine
with Dr. Johnson at the Crown and Anchor Tavern.[49] At this time,
apparently, they were at least acquaintances, if not friends. No
meetings between the two in the next three years are recorded.
Boswell was in London in the autumn of 1769, but Langton's
whereabouts in that year are not known. He was most likely at
Langton. In any case, they did not meet between May 1770 and
15 April 1772, for Boswell reported on the later date that he had
not seen Langton "since his marriage and having a son to keep up
the ancient family which his is."[50] From the spring of 1772,
references to Langton are frequent in Boswell's journals and in the
Life.

Johnson no doubt brought the two men together and their friendship remained rooted in Johnson, but it grew and flourished because each found in the other much to admire and to agree with.
Boswell's first reference to Langton in the existing journal is an
approving comment on the antiquity of Langton's family, "a thing
that becomes very rare amongst either english or Scots Gentlemen."[51] He gave credit to Langton for being a favourite at
Court.[52] He must have been impressed with Langton's friendships

[48] lxxii. 62.

[49] *Life* ii. 63. This is also the first
occasion in which Percy appears in company with JB. The date is fixed by
Percy's diary.

[50] Journ.

[51] Journ. 15 Apr. 1772.

[52] Journ. 2 Mar. 1786. If not a favourite,
he seems to have been well known at

Court, as his remarks to Miss Feilding
(*ante* p. lxv) indicate. Peregrine reported
that "almost upon all occasions" the
King "particularly noticed my father"
and often entered upon "the discussion
of topicks of a literary nature with him,
to know his opinion" (PL-M's letter-
book, p. 27b). Two anecdotes in particular among those Peregrine related to

with Joseph Spence and Edward Young. Always looking for models, he found in Langton the calm piety he wished to emulate.[53] When they were in London, they frequently went together to church; once on Maundy Thursday and once on Good Friday they read the Holy Week *Rambler* together.[54] Boswell was commendably grateful for Langton's quiet attempts to save him from the consequences of his own social barbarities and even to improve his manners. When he arrived drunk at The Club on an evening in 1775 and harassed Fox with fuddled adulation, Langton "very attentively and kindly" put the bottle past him.[55] Langton cautioned him against reporting to people what others said of them,[56] and presented him with a copy of *The Government of the Tongue*. "He gave me the Book," Boswell wrote in it, "and hoped I would read that treatise; but said no more. . . . It was a delicate admonition."[57] But Boswell frequented Langton's company for more than good advice and refreshment of piety. He sought him out for pure fellowship, and wrote in his journal after one of his calls that he was pleased with his conversation, "as usual".[58] Coming from Boswell, that is a compliment indeed. "Amongst the almost innumerable collection of distinguished persons in BOSWELL'S LIFE OF JOHNSON," he wrote in an anonymous newspaper paragraph

illustrate his father's relations with the Royal Family characterize that relationship and suggest the light in which they saw him. When the Langtons were living at Richmond, the King rode by their house. Discovering who lived there, he turned in and began a conversation with Langton, who was in the garden. "The good old King talked to us all in the most gracious manner—Asked my father if he made the elder children teach the younger, as that was a sure criterion by which to know how far those that taught understood what they had learnt" (*ibid.* p. 28b). The second anecdote concerns a conversation by the King, the Prince of Wales, and Lord Lothian about a tutor for the younger royal children. A number were named, and then the Prince of Wales said, "'and why should Your Majesty not propose the Governorship to Mr. Langton. You would then have not only a scholar but a *Gentleman* to superintend my brothers.'

This conversation was repeated to my father by Lord Lothian himself with whom my father was much acquainted. The proposal was never made, nor would it have been accepted—at least I trust not, if proposed. I say I trust not—as it is impossible to imagine any man less fit for such an undertaking than was my father—he had no plan in teaching—he was remarkably indolent, and supine—stood in such supreme awe of rank of any kind, much less [*sic*] of that of Royalty, that nothing would have been learnt from him of any kind" (*ibid.* pp. 29b–30b).

[53] Journ. 24 July 1774.
[54] Journ. 1 Apr. 1779, 13 Apr. 1781.
[55] Journ. 31 Mar. 1775.
[56] Journ. 17 Mar. 1776.
[57] C. B. Tinker, *Young Boswell*, 1922, p. 16 (facsimile). The book is in the Hyde Collection. Langton gave it to JB in 1779 (Journ. 1 Apr.).
[58] Journ. 2 Dec. 1787.

puffing the *Life*, "the character perhaps most highly held forth to the regard of the world, is *Bennet Langton, Esq. of Langton, in Lincolnshire*."[59]

Yet if Langton had been merely a paragon of intelligence and virtue, the relationship would have been much less easy. Boswell undoubtedly drew comfort from the thought that if many people thought him absurd, many people thought Langton absurd too. They maintained that Langton weakly mismanaged his finances: that he chose to live expensively in London when he should stay quietly at home on his estate and save money. They found Langton's humility as ridiculous as Boswell's vanity. Boswell indeed felt himself in some respects so superior to Langton that he could join Johnson in reflections on Langton's lack of family pride and slackness as regards the principle of male succession, his submersion in domesticity, and his bad management.[60] It was far

[59] *Public Advertiser*, 1 June 1791; cutting, Yale P 100:27.

[60] Langton set up a succession to his estate in which his sisters would take precedence of a remote heir male (*Life* ii. 261–62), and told JB that his family had never shown any great men, though it had had ample time to do so (Journ. 24 Oct. 1769); Journ. 1, 11 Apr. 1776; *Life* iii. 128, iv. 146 n. 2; Journ. 18 Mar., 17, 18, 20 Apr., 12 May 1778, 3 June 1784; *Life* iii. 362. The general air of badly managed confusion suggested by those who commented on Langton and his household is vividly supported by the memories of Peregrine: "My father six feet four inches high, thinner than any man I almost ever saw—with a long white flannel dressing gown, which reached to his heels—several papers, and a book or two; with tape to tie his tail; and a comb in his hand, used to make his first appearance seldom before nine oClock, and generally much later—scolding because no body was ready in the parlour to receive him, and wondering at 'the *Girls*' being so late—just as if the other 364 days of the year it had not *always* been invariably the same. After calling and sending messages to 'the Girls', one after the other would drop in dressed very much as if to keep their father in countenance—then the tea was made; *the tail was tied*; during which operation Thomas a Kempis, or some other book of the kind was read out, and breakfast was begun—this would bring us towards eleven oClock—very often the tea was dispatched an hour sooner than otherwise it would have been, that my father might hurry up stairs to doff his long white flannel dressing gown, and put on his Coat and waistcoat; and hurry to Duke Street Chapel . . . or if too late for that place of worship to White hall Chapel—but this also was a custom by no means regular—in which case—if the chapel was neglected—then the breakfast would continue on and on and on till *one*, or probably two oClock; except that sometimes my Mother used to come down stairs, which from very indifferent health she was frequently prevented from doing, and then occasionally I have known the breakfast cloth remain till near three oClock, and immediately relaid for dinner" (PL-M's letter-book, pp. 35a–36a). The lessons Langton conducted after breakfast were equally disorganized: "My father . . . would . . . scrape together a few books, and begin with them before him a desultory conversation that treated of all that was ingenious, and improving, and

from unpleasing to him to see Langton the sudden victim of Johnson's assault: "I so often tost and he laughing—to see his long legs in the air."[61]

Langton no doubt was first glad to make Boswell's acquaintance because Boswell was a highly acclaimed author; like others he became a friend because he was attracted by Boswell's good humour, liveliness, and uncalculating generosity. Once after he and Boswell had seen a regiment of Horse Guards perform their manœuvres in Hyde Park, he complimented Boswell with the remark that it was agreeable to see such a scene with him. "For I was not, like many people, in a state of dull amazement or illhumoured silence, but could talk of what pleased me."[62] Extraordinarily tolerant, he allowed Boswell to print all Johnson's wounding remarks about himself without any remonstrance, though Boswell's occasional suppressions of his name furnished him no real protection. It would seem that, like Boswell, he could tolerate anything Johnson said as soon as he had become convinced that Johnson's love for him was unalterable. Unlike Percy, unlike even Reynolds, Langton was unreservedly co-operative. By such magnanimity, if for nothing else, he deserved his epithet of "worthy".

If Langton and Boswell corresponded before 1772, it cannot have been with any great frequency. The Register of Letters from 1768 to 1771 is not complete, but it is complete enough to have caught a letter here and there if there had been any considerable number

entertaining to the highest degree; but that probably had no reference, after the first five minutes, to the book or books out of which it was intend'd to instruct his children seated around him. A knock of a visitor would be heard at the house door, when instantly the whole party would fly off discomfitted as if attacked by a troop of light horse—the one to one room, the other to another, not being dressed proper to appear before any friend or acquaintance that might call to pay a morning visit—thus all was hurry and confusion, and by the time that it was considered by the parties that their toilette was fit for appearance—then the visitor would be gone—thus the morning lecture generally broke up before it had begun; for although much conversation had been entered into for perhaps two hours or more, it being at least eleven oClock before it began, and towards two or later before anyone usually called; yet some interruption usually took place, so as always to put it off till tomorrow" (*ibid*. pp. 34a–35a). "And yet", Peregrine added ruefully, "this account which is by no means an exaggerated one—is given of a man who of all those with whom I was ever acquainted, had the readiest and keenest taste for Wit, and who would have been the most alive to the ridiculous which it portraits [*sic*] in any other person. What therefore is Sense? I have drawn the picture of a wise, learned, pious, good man" (*ibid*. p. 36a).

[61] Journ. 7 May 1773.
[62] Journ. 15 Apr. 1779.

of them. The first letter to appear in the Register was written by Langton and was received by Boswell on 6 August 1772. It probably announced Langton's intention of visiting Edinburgh. Thereafter they kept up an exchange of letters, with gaps, down to 1794. During the first gap, from the end of 1780 to the middle of 1784, Langton was perhaps completely entangled in his family affairs. The next gap, 1785–89, is satisfactorily explained by the fact that both men were living in London during most of that time. Langton also seems to have been back in London in 1794, which would account for the absence of letters in the last months of Boswell's life.

In spite of interruptions, the correspondence of Langton and Boswell records with some fulness the interests and ideas which bound the two men in friendship. The predominant tenor, as one would expect, is literary. More often than not, the friends they mention are authors; and when they are not, they are often associated with the literary world, if only by being related to Johnson. Johnson is the major unifying element and frequently the principal topic, in the years after his death as well as during his life. The letters resemble the *Life* in showing other members of The Club in relation to Johnson, forming a background for his sayings and doings. Langton's description of the evening gathering at Mrs. Vesey's, with the company crowding four or five deep about Johnson's chair, is typical. Bits of this sort from Langton's letters indeed were incorporated into the *Life* with little editing.

The relations between Johnson and Langton and Johnson and Boswell are naturally more than background material. The first letter recovered on Boswell's side of the correspondence shows him attempting to make up the only serious falling-out between Johnson and Langton that the *Life* records. At Dilly's in London on 7 May 1773, Johnson, who was probably vexed with himself for having called Goldsmith impertinent, reproved Langton angrily for introducing the doctrine of the Trinity as a subject for general conversation. Langton, as Johnson believed and reported to Boswell, went home to Langton "in deep dudgeon" without taking leave.[63] Just before setting out on the Hebridean tour with Johnson, Boswell, in a letter of calculated ingenuousness, attempted to jolly Langton out of his continuing resentment without letting on that he knew anything about it. When Langton failed to reply before Johnson's departure from Scotland, Boswell dropped indirect

[63] *Life* ii. 254, 265.

methods and spoke straight out: "If you have still any discontent, I beg that you may dismiss it, and write to our revered friend at my house in Edinburgh, by the return of the post, that I may have the happiness of thinking that . . . I have contributed to the reconciliation of those who should never have any difference." Langton continued with quiet firmness to think that Johnson's *manner* of checking him had been unkind, but gratefully acceded to Boswell's efforts at reconciliation. Five years later, though the recovered correspondence makes no mention of it, the tables were turned. Boswell got so angry at Johnson's rudeness that he perhaps might have gone back to Scotland without seeing him again if Langton had not arranged for them to meet and talk freely without witnesses.[64]

Even in death Johnson is still with them, in fact, bulks even larger in their correspondence, for Boswell is working on the *Life*, and Langton is one of his chief sources. Johnson had written Langton a good many letters, and Langton had in his memory a larger store of authentic Johnsonian sayings than anyone except Boswell himself. Some passages from Langton's letters to Boswell, as has already been mentioned, were incorporated in the *Life*, and the correspondence contains many requests for material by Boswell and many answers by Langton to specific questions, but relatively little of the matter which Langton furnished will be found here. Though willing, he was exasperatingly dilatory. As early as 1775, Boswell began a persistent campaign to get his Johnsoniana recorded, and finally garnered a gratifying quantity, though mainly by sitting with him, stirring up his memory, and writing the sayings down himself. He compared Langton's mind to "Herculaneum, or some old Roman field". Langton produced only the latter half of his Johnson letters in time for Boswell's first edition, and it was not till after the book was in the press that Boswell got the greater part of the Johnsonian sayings recorded. Langton sent in the other half of his Johnson letters while the second edition was printing, with more Johnsoniana recorded by himself, all this matter too late for chronological insertion.[65]

Neither Boswell nor Langton made a living by literature. Both of them had income from landed property, but both of them

---

[64] *Life* iii. 337–38; *Boswell in Extremes*, p. 329 n. 7.

[65] See Waingrow, index s.v. Langton.

The comparison with Herculaneum occurs both in From Langton, 2 Oct. 1790 and in *Life* iv. 1–2.

throughout considerable portions of the time covered by this correspondence worked at gainful professions to help support their families. From the inception of the correspondence down to 1785, Boswell carried on a busy practice as advocate in Edinburgh through six months of every year. Langton, when he visited Edinburgh in 1772, heard him plead a cause in the Parliament House during a particularly successful period of his practice.[66] Although Boswell does not give anything like a full account of his business in his letters to Langton, he does keep Langton informed as to causes Langton has expressed an interest in, or which he thinks Langton may find interesting: Orangefield's cause, Donaldson's cause, the rather ridiculous cause of Dr. Memis. Langton could appreciate Boswell's satisfaction in receiving more fees than ever before, since he himself knew what it was to lack money. He understood fully why Boswell had to tear himself away from London in order to be on hand at the opening of the General Assembly in Edinburgh. And he could sympathize with Boswell in his severe disappointment at not obtaining the political interest that might have assured him splendid advancement in his profession.

If it has been hard in the past to think of Boswell as a lawyer, it has perhaps been equally hard to think of Langton as a bread-winner. True, we did know that he was an officer of militia, and should probably have asked ourselves how his continuation in this regular and responsible service was to be reconciled with the reputation for general bemusedness and impracticality which the *Life* has established. The letters in this volume show Boswell engaged in the daily round of his profession, and they also show Langton not only as soldier but as engineer and man of business. He served voluntarily for twenty-five years in the North Lincoln Militia, first as captain and then as major, and appears to have enjoyed his military duties and to have performed them commendably. We are now able to see and to approve his serious efforts to recoup the family fortunes by living in Rochester and Chatham and working as a military engineer. These efforts remain no less admirable when we learn that he had to sell a thousand acres after all, surely a sad blow, though he characteristically mutes his distress by referring to the necessary legal transactions as "untoward concerns of business". It is pleasant to discover that at least his moiety of the Wey Navigation proved profitable to him and his family.

[66] Journ. 24 Nov., 12 Dec. 1772.

One important bond between Boswell and Langton was undoubtedly the interest they both took in their families. Langton's paternal fondness is legendary, and Boswell was accused by qualified observers of spoiling his children through too much permissiveness.[67] He did not at all approve of Langton's habit of introducing babes into adult company, nor of making children's doings the subect of conversation at adult gatherings, but he nevertheless spent a great deal of time with his own children, and was tactfully attentive to their needs as persons. Consequently for over twenty years the correspondence alternates a sincere small-beer chronicle of births, illnesses, accidents, and schooling with talk of Johnson, literature, and public events.

What seems to have kept their relationship alive more than any other factor was the need Boswell had for Langton's friendship. His need is shown in his inability to take it for granted. "I am *persuaded* that we esteem and love one another. I am *certain* upon one side. Yet from some unaccountable procrastinating indolence, there shall be sometimes no communication between us for eight or nine months at a time. This may be considered as a proof that we are both so sure from mutual consciousness that our friendship is permanent that we need not repeated assurances of it." But Boswell was not sure, and he required repeated assurances. Unfortunately, Langton was a reserved man; though he may have been in need of Boswell as much as Boswell was in need of him, he could never say so. All the passionate protestations of friendship come from Boswell. Langton showed his feelings in his actions: he answered Boswell's letters; he co-operated fully in the writing of the *Life*; he overlooked what pettier persons would have considered unforgivable invasions of privacy. To whatever degree he may have failed Boswell in their relationship, it was not the result of a lack of good intentions. His sins were those of omission. He was the victim of his own "usual Laziness". "I had been . . . dazzled with the light of confidence in myself—as thinking, that, whosoever Letters I might be in danger of neglecting to answer, no such danger could however happen as to *Yours*; and thus have gone on . . . in a delay." Affection such as this must have worked for good. We ought not to doubt that these two men, both in many ways incorrigible, were happier and to some degree better for their long friendship.

[67] From Elizabeth Boswell, Lady Auchinleck, 16 July, 12 Nov. 1789; From Temple, 13 Feb., 16 Aug., 8 Sept. 1790.

As materials for a biography of Langton, the letters leave one important question still unanswered. They show Langton good, generous, forgiving, learned, and pious, but they do not show him ridiculous, as the *Life* and other trustworthy sources assure us he was. His letters, like his life, are disorganized and undirected; they reflect a mind which diffused itself too widely to be effective. His sentences are too long and too involved; where one word would have sufficed, he uses three.[67a] If he talked like this, it is easy to understand how people who did not know him might have found his conversation boring. But to be a bore is not the same thing as being, to repeat Mrs. Thrale's phrase, "a Person unrespected and commonly ridiculous".

This can hardly be just the case of Goldsmith over again, for we are assured that Langton's manners were highly polished and his conversation always mild. He did not invite ridicule by clumsy efforts to shine. He *looked* ridiculous (he is described as "a very tall, meagre, long-visaged man, much resembling . . . a stork standing on one leg") ;[68] he was always serious, and that may be enough to account for it. In the quick-paced, combative, enormously artful conversation of The Club or Mrs. Thrale's drawing-room, Langton, who was absent-minded, slow in the uptake, rather pedantic, and always desirous of knowing why, must have been a sort of Elephant's Child.

Materials for a life of Langton, however, these letters certainly are. Their most important service, Johnsonian and Boswellian matters apart, is to show that Langton did not weakly acquiesce in his own ruin. But it is surely in connexion with Johnson and Boswell that his life will for the most part continue to be studied. In the present volume Langton's side of his best-known quarrel with Johnson is presented. Though he never won from Boswell the commendation "Bis dat qui cito dat", he did go to extensive trouble to supply him with materials for Johnson's life. Without worthy Langton's complete co-operation, the *Life* would have been a poorer book.

[67a] Commenting on one of his father's letters, Peregrine wrote: "The almost interminable endless long round of nearly unintelligible expressions of thanks, petitions, and excuses, that my excellent father makes in this . . . letter . . . might all of it have been said in three lines" (PL-M's letter-book, pp. 105b–06b).

[68] Henry Beste, *Personal and Literary Memorials*, 1829, p. 62.

LEEDS, FRANCIS GODOLPHIN OSBORNE, fifth Duke of (1751–99). At The Club meeting of 24 April 1792, "The Duke of Leeds [was] proposed by Lord Ossory, who was seconded by Mr. Boswell to be balloted for at the next meeting."[1] On 8 May, he was elected. It is rather difficult to determine, either from the very brief exchange of notes between them or from Boswell's journals, just how well the Duke and Boswell knew each other. Leeds does not appear very often in Boswell's company in the fourteen years of their acquaintance. At the time of their first meeting in 1781, he bore the style of Marquess of Carmarthen. A graduate of Christ Church, Oxford, he had, in 1774, been returned to the House of Commons for the borough of Eye in Suffolk. In 1776, he had been called up to the House of Lords in his father's Barony of Osborne of Kiveton; in 1777, he was a member of the Privy Council, and in 1778, Lord Lieutenant of the East Riding of Yorkshire. In that same year his wife, Baroness Conyers in her own right, eloped with Capt. John Byron; their child was the Hon. Augusta Byron, later Mrs. Leigh. The poet was Captain Byron's only child by a second marriage. Carmarthen served as Secretary of State for Foreign Affairs from 1783 to 1791 and was chosen Knight of the Garter. Although they saw each other seldom, Boswell and this "amiable nobleman of moderate abilities and capricious disposition"[2] seem to have got on well together. The Duke was instrumental in obtaining permission for Boswell to publish the minute of Johnson's conversation with the King; and a certain intimacy is suggested by the fact that after one of the meetings of The Club "The Duke of Leeds and Langton and I sat a long time after the rest were gone."[3] At The Club, only about two months before his death, Boswell got Leeds to witness a deed granting his daughter Veronica £500 of additional fortune because "I was pleased with her infantine attention to my illustrious friend Doctor Samuel Johnson when he was in Scotland",[4] but his main purpose perhaps was to head his list of witnesses with a duke. (The others were Sir William Scott, Viscount Palmerston, and Earl Macartney.)

MACARTNEY, GEORGE, Earl (1737–1806). The glittering array of this handsome Scotch-Irishman's appointments and honours is detailed elsewhere in this volume.[5] He was elected to The Club in

[1] *The Club.*
[2] G. F. R. Barker in DNB.
[3] Journ. 1 Apr. 1794.

[4] *Tour*, pp. 407–08.
[5] *Post* pp. 105 n. 19, 372 n. 8.

May 1786. Boswell held him in admiration and esteem, and Macartney at least thought highly of Boswell's book and was prompt in giving aid whenever Boswell requested it. He tried to find out whether Johnson had ever been translated into Russian;[6] he copied out himself from Lord Bute's papers a letter of Johnson's that Boswell wished to see;[7] and he lent Boswell his own annotations on the first edition of the *Life* for Boswell to use as he saw fit.[8] In 1792 Boswell tried in vain to get an appointment to accompany him to China.[9] One wonders, however, whether Boswell, had he lived to see it, could wholly have relished Macartney's final honour (1796): a barony of Great Britain with the double style Macartney of Parkhurst and of Auchinleck.[10] Baron Boswell of Auchinleck was the title that in a moment of extreme euphoria he had chosen for himself against the day when the King should appoint him Lord Chancellor.[11]

MARLAY, RICHARD (c. 1728–1802). Marlay, an Irishman by birth and education, Dean of Ferns, Bishop of Clonfert, and finally Bishop of Waterford, was described by Sir William Jones as "a man of wit and vivacity" and by Edmond Malone as "a very amiable, benevolent, and ingenious man."[12] He came into Boswell's ken both as admirer of Johnson and friend of Lord Pembroke.[13] Introduced to Marlay in the street in London in 1775, Boswell uncharacteristically forgot Marlay's appearance; when later that spring he met him at Wilton in company with Mrs. Greville, Mrs. Crewe, and the Hon. Miss Monckton, he took him to be "the Parson of the parish and his wife and daughters . . . come on a visit and I would needs from much humanity be very civil and

---

[6] *Post* pp. 280–81.
[7] *Life* i. 380. Macartney's transcript is at Yale: M 146:1.
[8] *Life* i. 13; iv. 12 n. 2.
[9] *Post* p. 372.
[10] *Comp. Peer.* viii. 325. Of course not JB's Auchinleck, an estate of considerable extent in Auchinleck parish, Ayrshire, but a farm of the same name, Auchenleck in Rerrick parish, Kirkcudbrightshire, approximately 5¾ miles east of Kirkcudbright. Macartney's grandfather, who emigrated to Ireland, was a younger son of Macartney of this Auchenleck, and the property remained in the possession of the family till it finally came into

Macartney's hands (P. H. McKerlie, *History of the Lands and their Owners in Galloway*, 1870–79, v. 99–100; *Annual Register . . . for . . . 1806*, 1808, p. 525).
[11] To Temple, 6 July 1784.
[12] *Letters of Sir William Jones*, ed. Garland Cannon, 1970, i. 279; Malone's remarks are quoted by Dr. Powell from the fourth edition of the *Life* in a useful note on Marlay, *Life* iv. 483–84. Marlay is not in DNB. Henry Grattan (1746–1820) was his nephew.
[13] Journ. 24 Dec. 1774; for Marlay's connexion with Pembroke see Journ. 20 Apr. 1779 and below, nn. 14, 1.

encouraging to the good folks."[14] Marlay was admitted to The Club in 1777, but seems never to have become an intimate of Johnson's. Besides meeting Marlay at The Club, Boswell records being guest with him at dinners given by Pembroke, Reynolds, Malone, and Lord Lucan.[15] He apparently thought well of his wit, but recorded only one specimen.[16] When in 1783, after winning an appeal case in the House of Lords, he gave a small dinner "in high tavern style" to Lord Pembroke, Marlay was one of the guests.[1] Boswell seems to have thought of him as an admirable dinner-companion but to have sought no closer intimacy. He never refers to Marlay in his spiritual capacity.

OGLETHORPE, GEN. JAMES EDWARD (1696–1785). General, philanthropist, and colonist of Georgia, Oglethorpe was very active in the social life of London after he left the Army (1745) and politics (1754). For nearly a decade senior general in the British Army, he was well acquainted with several members of The Club; with Boswell since 1768, when he had hunted him up in London and had asked the honour of shaking his hand. ("My name, Sir, is Oglethorpe, and I wish to be acquainted with you.")[2] Boswell for a time entertained a plan of writing his life, and took notes for that purpose.[3] It seems odd that neither Oglethorpe nor Paoli, both so frequently mentioned in the *Life of Johnson*, was ever elected to The Club, but it appears to be a fact that during the first thirty years of its existence The Club admitted no professional military men at all.

ORME, ROBERT (1728–1801). Born in India and educated at Harrow, Orme returned to India in the employ of the East India Company in 1744. While there, he collected materials for his history of the British in India, the first volume of which was published in 1763. He was the possessor of a large library of ancient and modern classics and was elected a Fellow of the Royal Society of Antiquaries in 1770. He was a great admirer of Johnson's conversational powers, but he was not a member of The Club.

[14] Journ. 21 Apr. 1775.
[15] Journ. 27, 28 Mar. 1781, 25 Mar. 1783, 1 May 1787; 13 Apr. 1779, 30 Mar. 1781, 1 Mar. 1791; 14 Mar. 1787; 1 Feb. 1791.
[16] "We talked of Dr. Johnson. I said that he could make himself very agreable to a Lady when he chose it. Sir Joshua agreed. Gibbon contraverted. Dean Marli

said A Lady might be vain when she could turn a Wolf dog into a lap dog" (Journ. 28 Mar. 1781).

[1] Journ. 23 May 1783.
[2] *Life* ii. 350 n. 2.
[3] Journ. 24 Apr. 1779, 9 May 1781; Yale MS. M 208.

BIOGRAPHIES: PERCY

PERCY, THOMAS (1729–1811). Percy, like Johnson, was the son of a tradesman. Born in Bridgnorth, Shropshire, he was educated at Bridgnorth grammar school and Christ Church, Oxford, where he graduated B.A. in 1750 and M.A. in 1753. In the latter year he was presented by his college to the living of Easton Maudit in Northamptonshire, where he remained for twenty-nine years, doing there most of the writing on which his literary reputation rests. Johnson praised him for "extension of mind and . . . minute accuracy of enquiry", and added that his "attention to poetry" had given "grace and splendour to his studies".[1] A devoted and accurate antiquary, Percy had a remarkable talent for antiquarian popularization, discerning aspects of the literature of past eras and of distant lands that would captivate readers of his own and the emerging age. His first publication (1761) was an English version of a seventeenth-century Chinese novel, which he partly edited from a previous unpublished English translation and partly translated from a Portuguese translation. Two years later he published *Five Pieces of Runic Poetry translated from the Islandic Language*. Then in 1765 he produced *The Reliques of Ancient English Poetry*, an ingeniously arranged miscellany of old and relatively modern ballads and other lyrics that proved to be one of the great germinal books of the eighteenth century.

Percy was more patient than Johnson in the cultivation of patrons. *Hau Kiou Choaan*, the Chinese novel, was dedicated to the Countess of Sussex, the chatelaine of Easton Maudit. The *Reliques* were dedicated to the Countess of Northumberland, heiress and representative of the principal Percy line, from a cadet branch of which Percy believed himself to be descended. Lord and Lady Northumberland made him tutor of their second son, the Hon. Algernon Percy, and when that care ended, appointed him domestic chaplain and secretary.[2] In the following year Northumberland was raised to a dukedom. Percy proceeded D.D. from Emmanuel College, Cambridge, in 1769, was made Dean of Carlisle in 1778, and in 1782 became Bishop of Dromore in Ireland. In one of the letters in the present collection (29 Feb. 1788) he says that he is well

[1] From SJ, 23 Apr. 1778 (*Life* iii. 278: Yale MS. M 145 pp. 615–17).

[2] *Percy-Farmer Corresp.* pp. 93–96. See also *The Correspondence of Thomas Percy and Evan Evans*, ed. Aneirin Lewis, 1957, pp. 102–03, and *The Correspondence of Thomas Percy and Thomas Warton*, ed. M. G. Robinson and Leah Dennis, 1951, p. 120 and n. 7. Percy's connexion with Lord and Lady Northumberland appears to have begun sometime in 1764 (Percy's diary).

contented with his situation and has "no desire to exchange it for any other, in or out of this Kingdom".

Percy had been a member of the Johnsonian circle for many years before his correspondence with Boswell began. His friend Dr. James Grainger introduced him to Johnson in 1756[3] and to Goldsmith in 1759. His friendship with Goldsmith was especially close; he collected from Goldsmith and others some very important materials for a memoir which unfortunately was delayed in publication for nearly thirty years after Goldsmith's death. When, early in 1768, it was decided to expand the membership of The Club to twelve, he was one of the three new members elected. It was apparently in this year that he and Boswell first met, both of them, without previous mention of the other, recording a supper to meet Johnson which Boswell had arranged at the Crown and Anchor tavern, 7 June 1768.[4] They had several friends in common: Johnson, Sir David Dalrymple, Lord Hailes (who had been in correspondence with Percy for a number of years on matters concerning Scottish antiquities), Hugh Blair, and William Robertson. To speculate only from the evidence we actually have, either Blair or Robertson (both of whom were at the supper) may have brought Percy as a guest. The formality of Boswell's first note to him in the present correspondence (26 August 1771) suggests that they had not met again since 1768; and when Boswell made his first visit to Percy at Northumberland House on 26 March 1772, it may well have been only the third time of their being in each other's company. "It was agreeable to find Percy in a large room looking into the Strand, and at the same time his room as much a Library,— as crowded and even confused with books and papers,—as any room in a College."[5]

The nature of the relationship between the two men is well indicated by that remark and by a later one of Boswell's that he and Percy "had some lively literary talk".[6] Percy was a literary man: indeed, if one were asked to name the men who gave The Club its secondary designation of "The Literary Club", one might well cite Percy next after Johnson and Goldsmith. For Boswell, Percy would in any case have been interesting as a potential source

[3] *Life* i. 48 n. 2.
[4] For Percy's election see *Life* i. 478 n. 2. For the earliest records showing JB and Percy together see *ibid.* ii. 63;

Percy's diary, 7 June 1768; To Hugh Blair, c. 5 June 1768.
[5] Journ.
[6] Journ. 17 Mar. 1776.

of Johnsoniana. But Boswell also had a keen general interest in literary history, and Percy flowed with literary anecdotes like a mountain brook.[7] Boswell sought him out and saw a great deal of him: in the houses of friends, at The Club, in Percy's study in Northumberland House and his house in Mayfair, in his own house in Edinburgh, in the Deanery at Carlisle. He reported Percy's conversation at length on various occasions.[8] The tone of his remarks in the journal concerning Percy is always friendly and respectful. Not until the printing of the *Life* (a chapter in their relations that calls for special treatment) does any hint of strain appear.

Percy of course had more to offer as a literary man than Boswell did, but there is no reason to suppose that he too did not value the association. He met Boswell when Boswell was in the full blaze of glory following the publication of *An Account of Corsica*; and though Boswell published no other sizable work for many years, he had enough active interest in writing and the problems of authorship to enable him to hold up his end of the dialogue. Percy must have been a clubbable man or he would not have been chosen as one of the first additions to the original membership of The Club. He appears not to have been offended by Boswell's known vices. He no doubt sometimes sighed inwardly as Malone says he sometimes did when Boswell came bouncing into his study, but even when he was busy with urgent tasks he managed matters so that Boswell was not made to feel unwelcome.[9] In 1778, when Johnson tossed and gored Percy in his own house, Boswell earned Percy's warm gratitude by negotiating an apology.[10] When Boswell at the end of 1781 reported his great uneasiness at the state of his wife's health, Percy urged him to take her to Bristol, pausing at Carlisle for an extended visit at the Deanery: "Mrs. Percy is the tenderest and best of Nurses and would be glad to try her Skill on a Lady, who is dear to one we so much value, as yourself." And when after Johnson's death Boswell wrote soliciting material for the *Life*, Percy made a warm and generous reply, subscribing himself "Your affectionate and faithful Servant".[11] It was a style which

[7] Journ. 25 Sept. 1773.

[8] For example, Journ. 26 Mar. 1772, 16 Mar. 1783.

[9] "He was in the constant habit of calling upon me almost daily, and I used to grumble sometimes at his turbulence; but now miss and regret his noise and his hilarity and his perpetual good humour,

which had no bounds" (From Malone to Windham, 21 May 1795, William Windham, *Windham Papers*, 1913, i. 297–98); Journ. 10, 28 Apr. 1778.

[10] *Life* iii. 273–78; Journ. 12, 20, 25, 27 Apr. 1778.

[11] From Percy, 31 Dec. 1781, 23 Apr. 1785.

he very rarely permitted himself in his correspondence, and Boswell ought surely to have noted it and to have responded in kind. Why he did not is hard to explain. He frequently ended his letters to Barnard "Affectionately yours". Perhaps there was something in Percy's personality that made it difficult for Boswell to pass beyond respect and esteem. Percy, if he was not a stiff man, was certainly an ambitious, hard-working, and very systematic man, who by rationing his time managed to accomplish a great deal in the way of his avocation. But on the evidence, if either is to be faulted for failure to express affection, it must be Boswell.

Possibly their correspondence was larger than what now remains, but it is doubtful that it was considerably so. There is no indication in the letters themselves that many are missing, and there are only three unexplained gaps in this correspondence of twenty years. The first is between Boswell's invitation (and reminder) of 16 April 1773 and another invitation written almost three years later. In August of 1773, Percy visited Edinburgh, seeing Boswell on the 9th and 10th.[12] He then went on to Glasgow, returning to Edinburgh on the night of Friday 13 August. He called on Boswell, who had already gone to bed, and since he left for Alnwick at four the next morning, was unable to see him.[13] Boswell did not get to London the following spring; Percy did. Neither mentioned the other in his journal during 1774. They met in London in the spring of 1775, and saw each other fairly frequently while Boswell was in town. The lack of correspondence during this period and the next two years, when they were apart for a long time, suggests that the relationship between them was not particularly close, and that when they had no business to transact or favours to ask, they did not write.

That this is true seems to be borne out by Percy's letter of 20 December 1781, written some months after they had last seen each other in London. "Allow me to request a favour of you," he asks. And a quick survey of the letters will show that not one of them is a spontaneous expression of concern or friendship. They all are written either to request a favour or in answer to a request. And almost always the requests are for literary information or assistance, Boswell returns the list of Johnson's writings which Percy had given him and asks permission to give a copy to Garrick. In giving the permission, Percy requests material for a new book he

---

[12] Percy's diary; Notes, 10 Aug. 1773.
[13] *The Correspondence of Thomas Percy* *and George Paton*, ed. A. F. Falconer, 1961, pp. 67, 69; Notes, 10 Aug. 1773.

is considering, giving Boswell specific instructions for sending packets of information. Boswell, in apologizing for not being able to send anything but "a few pieces" of poetry, thanks Percy for a copy of the Earl of Northumberland's *Houshold Book.*

The letters concerning Percy's part in the Ossian controversy are useful as illustrating his well-known caution about getting into print, but they leave the central issues as puzzling as ever. Why did seasoned scholars like Johnson, Percy, Blair, and Ferguson all tend towards such unqualified positions? Why, when Percy for the second time became convinced that *Fingal* was a fake, did he jump to the conclusion that Blair and Ferguson had imposed on him? John Macpherson could have sung him a Gaelic heroic lay of considerable antiquity, and that lay could have corresponded fairly closely to a passage in *Fingal,* and *Fingal* could still have been a fake. Could both Blair and Ferguson really have forgotten the demonstration to Percy if they had arranged it, and it had taken place just as Percy remembered it? Were they capable (both ministers of the gospel!) of reiterated deliberate falsehood in such a matter? If it be objected that even to formulate such questions implies a knowledge of literary history that nobody could then have had, one can only point to one of Boswell's letters in this volume, which shows that Boswell had quite early come to what we consider the correct verdict: "My opinion was long ago fixed, which is that *some parts* of what is given us as Ossian's Poetry has been repeated in Gaelick *I know not from what æra.*"[14]

Percy's careful concern over details comes out clearly when it is he, rather than Boswell, who is performing the favours. "You must certainly recollect," writes Boswell in a request for Johnsoniana, "a number of anecdotes. Be pleased to write them down, as you so well can do, and send them to me." Although Percy maintains that he can furnish very little and delays sending the anecdotes, the material he finally sends proves of great use to Boswell. He carefully corrects Boswell's errors concerning Francis Barber's schooling; he gives him detailed information on the members of The Club; and, like a true scholar, suggests that Boswell look into the primary source for Club records, the book formerly kept in the Club room at the Turk's Head.

Very little gossip finds its way into the Percy-Boswell letters. The expected references to spouses and children are made

[14] To Percy, 25 Dec. 1781.

lxxxiii

succinctly. Percy encourages Boswell in his hopes of getting into Parliament (as, according to Boswell, he had encouraged him to try his fortune at the English bar), surely not out of conviction but from a pardonable wish to please. A realist and an adept in matters of preferment, well aware through residence in Carlisle of Lonsdale's personality and methods, Percy cannot really have believed that Boswell could subdue his extravagancies and hobble his ego to the extent that Lonsdale's patronage demanded. By and large the letters deal more with public than private affairs: the Cabinet crisis of 1783 in which their friends are concerned, Boswell's pamphlet against the East India Bill, a speech of Burke on the French Revolution. But principally—more than any other correspondence in this volume—the letters are concerned with literary matters. Each partner, believing the other to be interested, writes crisply and directly, forgoing the apparatus of elaborate courtesy.

The correspondence terminates without recrimination, but the friendship collapsed. Percy was always sensitive about controversy and the kind of publication that might seem beneath the dignity of the cloth, and when he became a bishop his caution grew almost morbid. After that he published no new work with his name, even attributing the extensive editorial revision of the fourth edition of the *Reliques* (1794) to his nephew, though he had performed most of it himself. His request to Boswell not to attach his name to the Johnsoniana he had supplied was timid and unreasonable. He had sent these anecdotes freely to Boswell, and had made no request for anonymity. At that time (1787 and 1788) he had clearly not felt that they might expose him to ridicule, but he no doubt took alarm at the newspapers, which ever since the publication of the *Tour to the Hebrides* had been deriding Boswell for his devotion to particulars. Percy's request that the fun about Grainger's rats and mice be suppressed was also unreasonable. He could not deny any of the facts which Boswell presented; the poem had been published and was fair game. His protests about Johnson's aspersions on the moral characters of Grainger and Rolt were however a different matter. There was no doubt that these aspersions were injurious, and they might well have been overstated or mistaken. Boswell made distinctions here, and may sincerely have thought that he was meeting Percy's objections. He kept Grainger's rats, but allowed Percy to defend the poem (and Grainger) in a foot-note. He cancelled Johnson's denigration of

Grainger's morals, and admitted in a foot-note that inquiry in Ireland had failed to substantiate Johnson's charge against Rolt. He went beyond any demand made by Percy in the existing correspondence and cancelled the (completely accurate) statement that Johnson had written the Dedication of the *Reliques* to Lady Northumberland. But he flatly refused to remove Percy's name from the Johnsoniana: "I will do any thing to oblige your Lordship but that very thing. I owe to the authenticity of my Work, to its respectability and to the credit of my illustrious friend, to introduce as many names of eminent persons as I can." And he apparently did not warn Percy in any way that he was including in the book some passages of Johnson's conversation which bore painfully or unpleasantly on Percy himself: Johnson's fleering suggestion that Percy might write the history of the grey ("or Hanover") rat; the report of two occasions on which Johnson had spoken to Percy harshly and rudely. It is not quite enough to say that Boswell's sincerely held theory of biography here brought him into inescapable collision with Percy. He was always reluctant to suppress names, but he nevertheless did do so on many occasions. His treatment of Percy undoubtedly stands in strong contrast to his treatment of Barnard. Johnson's brutality to Barnard on one occasion was notorious, but Boswell mentioned that "smart altercation" only briefly, in the most general terms, out of chronology, and in a foot-note. The fact seems to be that he felt that he had to draw on his Percy conversations as he drew on his Langton conversations to illustrate Johnson's shocking occasional ferocities to his closest friends. As usual when he was dealing with Johnson's unattractive traits, he meant to be perfectly explicit but at the same time to keep the trait subordinate by selecting from his evidence. To present unsparingly Johnson's altercations with *both* Barnard and Percy might overdo matters; and if it came to a choice, the Percy episodes were better, because Boswell had been present at and had recorded those himself, while he had the other only at second hand from Langton and Barnard. And he could not effectively suppress Percy's name in the more important of the clashes because that encounter occurred in Percy's own house and dealt with topics that could not fail to identify him. Moreover, the quarrel had produced a fine letter of apology from Johnson containing praise specific to Percy, and Boswell was determined to print it because it was one of his very best examples of Johnson's magnanimity after assault. Percy had probably not for a moment supposed that Boswell would publish such embarrassingly private matter. It may not be extravagant to suggest that Boswell, though he did not dare ask permission in advance, hoped to mollify Percy *after* publication by suggesting that it did him honour to be included with Langton and Boswell himself in that innermost circle of Johnson's friends—the ones he had caressed after battering them. But he must have known that by not warning Percy he ran the risk of sacrificing a valued friendship.

Joseph Cradock says that Percy had a violent temper.[15] There is no evidence that Percy ever wrote to Boswell after the publication of the *Life*. He did complain to Malone: we do not know all the articles his complaint may have contained, but one of them was a charge of downright duplicity. Malone was able to assure him that the supposed duplicity was merely an oversight. Boswell wrote to Barnard that same summer, "The Bishop of Dromore was it seems much offended, But we made it all up. He was in the wrong I think." We get important additional information from Sir William Forbes, who tried in 1798 to get Malone to censor the *Life*, citing as matter to be excised "the Conversation and Correspondence between Dr. Johnson and the Bishop of Dromore, the publication of which, Mr. Boswell himself owned to me, had hurt the Bishop so much, that it was with difficulty he could be prevailed on ever to speak to him again; or even to come to the Literary Club when Mr. Boswell was present".[16] Boswell cannot have believed for any length of time that Percy had "made it all up". He put back into the second edition of the *Life* matter that he had cancelled in the first edition for fear of offending Percy; and he would hardly have done that unless he had come to feel that the friendship was beyond hope of recovery. That Percy continued implacable is shown by a cautionary note he wrote in 1798 to a clergyman who had proposed to print a private correspondence in which Percy feared some letters of his own might be included: "You were so kind as to furnish me with the 8vo Editn. of Boswell's *Life of Johnson*. You may not perhaps have heard what occasioned his death which soon followd that Publicatn. In consequence of his violating the primary Law of civil Society in publishing in that work Men's unreserved Correspondence and unguarded Conversation, he became so shunned and scouted, that with very agreeable Talents for lively Converse, a fund of anecdotes and a considerable elevation in

[15] *Life* iii. 276 n. 2.   [16] 22 Mav.

Society, he was so studiously excluded from all decent and good Company, as drove him into deplorable habits of drinking, which speedily terminated a Life that seemed radically formed for long duration."[17] It is to be feared that Percy had allowed himself to state as fact what he thought ought to have happened. Boswell's deplorable habits of drinking had been formed long before he published the *Life* and would probably have got worse in any case. Some people undoubtedly shunned him after 1791 (only one specific instance has been reported),[18] but he continued to the end to move in very decent society. During March 1794 (the last full calendar month recorded in his journal) he dined at home eight times (one of those times with invited guests) and twenty-three times abroad, never alone and generally by invitation. His hosts included a former governor general of India, an earl, a marquess, and two bishops—really *three* bishops, for on one occasion he was invited by special request of a bishop, his fellow guest.[19] It is really too bad that one cannot say that one of these bishops was his old friend the Bishop of Dromore.[20]

REYNOLDS, SIR JOSHUA (1723–92). Painter and first president of the Royal Academy, Reynolds was knighted in 1769 and later appointed Principal Painter to the King. He was the author of three numbers (76, 79, 82) of Johnson's *Idler*; and between 1769 and 1791 he published his fifteen *Discourses*, a series of speeches delivered to students of the Royal Academy that touch on almost every major theme of Augustan aesthetic theory.

Reynolds first met Samuel Johnson in 1756, and their acquaintance soon ripened into a close friendship. Together, in 1764, they established The Club. Boswell did not meet Reynolds until 26 September 1769, when he was invited by Goldsmith to dine with

[17] 22 May 1798, to the Rev. Thomas Stedman, Bodleian MS. Percy C 1, ff. 180, 181. A much revised draft.

[18] "From my having indulged myself without reserve in discriminative delineations of a variety of people, I know I am thought by many to be illnatured; nay from the specimens which I have given the World of my uncommon recollection of conversations, many foolish people have been afraid to meet me; vainly apprehending that *their* conversation would be *recorded*" (To Alexander Boswell, 7 Feb. 1794). For the one specific instance see *post*, the letters of JB and Sir William Scott, Before 1 Aug. to 9 Aug. 1791.

[19] Warren Hastings, 22 Mar.; Earl of Inchiquin, 3 Mar.; Marquess Townshend, 25 Mar.; John Douglas, Bishop of Salisbury, 9 and 29 Mar.; Beilby Porteus, Bishop of London, 20 Mar. The bishop who asked his host (John Ross Mackye, 30 Mar.) to invite JB was the Hon. William Stuart, Bishop of St. Davids.

[20] See C. N. Fifer, "Boswell and the Decorous Bishop", JEGP (1962) lxi. 48–56.

him for that purpose. Later, in his *Letter to the People of Scotland* (1785), Boswell spoke of Goldsmith, "who . . . gave me a jewel of the finest water—the acquaintance of Sir *Joshua Reynolds.*"[1] Reynolds was one of that group of older men to whom Boswell looked for advice, affection, and approval; and, for over twenty years, until Reynolds's death, the two men maintained a warm relationship. Reynolds did much to encourage Boswell to finish his *Life of Johnson,* and it was to him that Boswell dedicated his *Magnum Opus.* In his will, Reynolds left Boswell £200 for the purchase of one of his paintings. He had already made Boswell a present of the first portrait he had painted of Johnson, and had forgiven him a debt of £50 for the portrait that Boswell had commissioned in 1785 and never paid for.[2]

Their brief extant correspondence suggests the warmth of their relationship. That they wrote to each other relatively seldom is undoubtedly in great part the result of Sir Joshua's reluctance to write letters.[3] When Boswell was in London, they saw much of each other. When he was in Scotland, they generally communicated through their friends. The number of times Reynolds's name occurs in Boswell's letters is impressive. The fact that Boswell at one time intended to write a life of him further suggests the great respect and affection in which Boswell held him. After Reynolds's death, Boswell frequently felt his loss. After dining with the Earl and Countess of Inchiquin, on 4 September 1793, he "felt painfully the loss of Sir Joshua. They went to the Play, and when I found myself in the street, just warmed with wine and having nobody on whom I could call, I thought the best thing I could do was to steal into bed, which I did a quarter before seven."[4]

SCOTT, SIR WILLIAM (1745–1836). Scott had known Boswell since 14 August 1773, when the two men were introduced by Johnson in Edinburgh.[5] He received in 1764 his B.A. from Christ Church, Oxford, and was elected to a Durham fellowship at University College, where he eventually became senior tutor. He was Camden Reader in Ancient History at Oxford from 1773 to 1785, his lectures (which he never published) being almost as much esteemed as Blackstone's. Inheriting a competency from his

[1] Page 99.
[2] To Alexander Boswell, 25 Feb. 1792; *Life* i. 392; "Friendly Patronage", *Public Advertiser,* 18 June 1791 (by JB): cutting in P 100:32.
[3] From Barnard, 14 Apr. 1785; To Barnard, 1 July 1785.
[4] Journ. The Countess of Inchiquin was Reynolds's niece.
[5] Journ.

father, he resigned his fellowship in 1777, got chambers in the Temple, took the degree of D.C.L. in 1779, was admitted to Doctors' Commons, and was called to the bar, electing to practise in admiralty and ecclesiastical business. He was eminently successful in these special courts, receiving various important appointments from the Crown, the Archbishop of Canterbury, and the Bishop of London, culminating in judgeships in the Consistory Court of London and the High Court of Admiralty. In 1790, at the age of forty-five, he entered Parliament, and from 1801 to 1821 represented Oxford University. He was a consistent opponent to reform. Knighted in 1788, he was raised to the peerage as Baron Stowell in 1821. John Scott, Lord Eldon, was his younger brother.

Scott was elected to The Club on 11 December 1778 and lived to be its senior member. His relationship with Boswell was a fairly close one, and Boswell's journals mention many conversations in which Scott offered him good advice, which he did not take. Although on 10 May 1785 Scott "encouraged" Boswell "to Westminster Hall",[6] he apparently thought better of it later and, taking a more realistic view of him and his chances, "was," Boswell wrote, "for my quietly returning to the Scotch bar."[7] Although Boswell was tempted to accept this advice when it was given, only a few weeks later he "told Scott I *could* not quit the english bar yet, and was now of the Home Circuit. He acquiesced."[8] Like so many of Boswell's friends, Scott apparently was not up to opposing him in his clearly impracticable ambitions. Kind and considerate as he was (and these qualities are shown in his correspondence with Boswell), he was not kind enough to be cruel. It would have taken a friend much closer to Boswell than almost any of the men he knew at that time to deal with his problem realistically. And, perhaps, in the long run, it would have made no difference. Boswell had to learn the hard way.

At times, Scott reminded Boswell too acutely of his failures. There was too great a discrepancy between the careers of the two men, and Boswell was occasionally envious.[9] In addition, Scott, while often encouraging, did not always provide him with adequate sympathy: on 2 November 1792, Boswell "found Sir William Scott at home, and on his assuring me that he was quite at leisure, agreed to stay and eat oysters. I drank here some more port, and

[6] Journ.
[7] Journ. 4 July 1786.
[8] Journ. 30 July 1786.
[9] Journ. 4 July 1786, 30 Oct. 1793.

had excellent Tory Conversation, but could not help feeling very unpleasantly my having no employment; of which I complained to him, but did not perceive much sympathy."[1] This episode, as much as any other, suggests the somewhat over-demanding nature of Boswell. Much as they liked him, much as they sympathized with him, his friends could never be so concerned with his problems as he was. Scott's letters to Boswell about the dinner to which he was not invited reveal the extent of Scott's genuine affection. But it is an affection tempered, as it had to be, with concern for his own and others' well-being and peace of mind. The strength of their friendship is also quite clearly brought out in this exchange, for the nature of the argument was one which could have destroyed a weaker amity. The tolerance shown on both sides is considerable, and the dignity of this particular exchange of views, involving as it does Boswell's damaged pride, reflects credit on both men. Scott plainly understood Boswell; and with that understanding went, along with affection, tolerance. Boswell, on his side, recognized Scott's worth, and thus was willing to accept from him what he might not have accepted from another.

SMITH, ADAM (1723–90). Born at Kirkcaldy, Fife, Smith was educated at Glasgow before obtaining in 1740 a Snell Exhibition to Balliol College, Oxford, where he remained until 1746. After leaving Oxford, he lived in Kirkcaldy and then Edinburgh, where he gave several series of lectures in belles-lettres and jurisprudence. In 1751 he was elected to the chair of logic at the University of Glasgow and, in the following year, was appointed Professor of Moral Philosophy. His lectures in moral philosophy resulted in two influential books, *The Theory of Moral Sentiments* (1759) and the better known *Inquiry into the Nature and Causes of the Wealth of Nations* (1776). Smith was appointed Vice-Rector of the University in 1762 but severed his connexion with it two years later. In 1787 he was elected Lord Rector.

Boswell first met Smith when he attended his lectures at the University of Glasgow in 1759–60. He was particularly impressed by the lectures on rhetoric and belles-lettres, lectures that may very well have influenced his views of literature and even shaped his own prose style. He always spoke highly of Smith as a teacher, "more highly than of any other teacher he had ever had, piling up adjectives like 'beautiful', 'clear', 'accurate', and 'elegant' ".[2] The two

[1] Journ.   [2] *Earlier Years*, p. 42.

men shared a strong interest in minute biographical detail: "I have a pleasure", Boswell wrote, "in hearing every story, tho' never so little, of so distinguished a Man [Pope]. I remember Smith took notice of this pleasure in his lectures upon Rhetoric, and said that he felt it when he read that Milton never wore buckles but strings in his shoes."[3] They also apparently shared a tendency to low spirits, although Smith later denied it.[4]

Elected to The Club shortly before 1 December 1775 (the first meeting he attended), Smith does not seem to have been one of its more popular members. Boswell reported to Langton a little over three months after Smith's election that Johnson had told him "that Adam Smith was a most dissagreable fellow after he had drank some wine, which, he said, 'bubbled in his mouth' ". Langton, in the same conversation, lamenting The Club's "being overwhelmed with unsuitable members", said "that he could perceive Beauclerc had lost his relish for Adam Smith's conversation".[5] And later, Johnson "said Adam Smith was as dull a dog as he had ever met with. I said it was strange to me to find my old Professour in London, a professed Infidel with a bag wig."[6] Even though he defended Smith against a number of such attacks, Boswell seems to have become somewhat disenchanted with his former teacher, in great part because of his liberal and Scottish views. "Since his absurd eulogium on Hume and his ignorant, ungrateful attack on the English University education", Boswell wrote in 1779, "I have had no desire to be much with him. Yet I do not forget that he was very civil to me at Glasgow."[7]

Although Boswell saw Smith a number of times in London, Edinburgh, and even Glasgow, between 1762 and 1788, theirs was not a particularly close relationship. Smith appreciated what he called Boswell's "facility of manners",[8] and the younger man was always grateful for Smith's contributions to his intellectual development, but Smith's rather inelegant manners and the religious views that gave Boswell "reason to fear the deistical influence of scotch professours",[9] plus Smith and Johnson's mutual lack of regard,[9a]

[3] Journ. 18 Oct. 1762.
[4] *Ibid.* 2 Apr. 1775.
[5] *Ibid.* 17 Mar. 1776.
[6] *Ibid.* 13 Apr. 1776.
[7] *Ibid.* 14 Sept.
[8] *Post* From Smith, 1760 or 1761; Journ. 3 Apr. 1775.

[9] Journ. 8 Oct. 1780.
[9a] For an analysis of this relationship, see J. H. Middendorf, "Dr. Johnson and Adam Smith", *Philological Quarterly* (1961) xl. 281–96.

combined to ensure that Smith's influence would remain limited. The three known letters exchanged between them were written before their relationship suffered from Boswell's Anglophil ambitions. There is no evidence that they exchanged other letters during the years of their acquaintance.

SPENCE, JOSEPH (1699–1768). Spence appears in this volume not as a member of The Club, but because of his friendship with the Langton family. Educated at Winchester and New College, Oxford, Spence became a fellow in 1722 and took orders in 1726. His *Essay on Pope's Odyssey* (1726) gained him lifelong friendship with Alexander Pope. Pope's influence assisted Spence's election to the Professorship of Poetry at Oxford, where he gave much admired lectures on the *Iliad* and the *Aeneid*. Besides holding several church livings, Spence ultimately served as prebendary of Durham. In 1742 he received the Regius Professorship of Modern History at Oxford, a lucrative sinecure, which he retained till his death. Between 1730 and 1741 Spence made three extended visits to France and Italy as travelling companion to young aristocrats. These opportunities he turned to account in his *Polymetis* (finally published in 1747). This study of agreement between the writings of Roman poets and the remains of ancient works of art was considered a successful exercise in interdisciplinary investigation. Spence's most important work, a literary record of unique value, was his voluminous notes of conversations with literary and learned men both in England and on the Continent. These notes remained unpublished until 1820, though quarried by many writers on Pope and Dryden: Warburton, Joseph Warton, Dr. Johnson, and Malone. When Boswell came to England in 1768 he carried an introduction to the venerable Mr. Spence from Sir Alexander Dick, but Spence died before Boswell could meet him. Among the Boswell papers are several letters from Sir Alexander reporting Spence's state of health.

STEEVENS, GEORGE (1736–1800). The son of a well-to-do captain in the East India Company, Steevens was educated at Eton before being admitted a fellow-commoner at King's College, Cambridge. He left Cambridge in 1756 without a degree and devoted much of the rest of his life to editing Shakespeare and other writers and contributing anonymous and often scornful critical essays to newspapers and magazines. In 1773 he revised Johnson's edition of Shakespeare (he had edited the quartos in 1766) and later con-

xcii

tributed considerable material for *The Lives of the Poets*. Much as Johnson appreciated Steevens's editorial skills, he had no illusions about his difficult personality and dubious literary ethics: ". . . talking of another very ingenious gentleman [Steevens], who from the warmth of his temper was at variance with many of his acquaintance, and wished to avoid them, [Johnson] said, 'Sir, he leads the life of an outlaw.' "[1] Although he would not agree with Beauclerk that Steevens deserved to be hanged for attacking his friends in the newspapers, he admitted that he was mischievous and might deserve to be kicked.[2]

Johnson, however, thought highly enough of Steevens to nominate him for membership in The Club in February 1774 (he was elected on 4 March). In 1783 Johnson was responsible as well for Steevens's membership in the Essex Head Club. Sir Joseph Banks seems also to have maintained his friendship with Steevens for many years, and Steevens contributed material toward Thomas Percy's edition of Surrey's poems.[2a] Boswell's relationship with Steevens, however, was not a particularly happy one. The two men first met at Johnson's on 27 October 1769,[3] and Boswell records Steevens's presence at The Club on numerous occasions in the years after his election; but they do not seem to have spent much time together elsewhere. Steevens did provide Boswell with anecdotes of Johnson[4] and was responsible for some laudatory paragraphs about Boswell in the *St. James's Chronicle*;[5] but generally the two men seemed to irritate one another. Perhaps they felt themselves in competition. Johnson may have touched on this point in a conversation with Boswell: "Talking of Mr. Steevens, he said he was a great writer in the Newspapers. I thoughtlessly asked, 'What pleasure can he have in that?' 'Nay,' said Mr. Johnson, '*you* can best tell that.' "[6]

It seems likely that it was Steevens who perpetrated a hoax on Boswell at the time of the execution of the Rev. James Hackman whose trial Boswell had attended earlier. Before witnessing the execution Boswell met Steevens at Newgate where he found him "dissagreable [when] unrestrained by Johnson".[7] Quite possibly Steevens found him equally "dissagreable". In any case, although

[1] *Life* ii. 375.
[2] *Life* iii. 231.
[2a] *Percy-Farmer Corresp*. pp. 191–93.
[3] *Life* ii. 107.
[4] Journ. 30 Apr. 1783.
[5] *Ibid*. 26 Feb. 1785.
[6] *Ibid*. 14 Apr. 1775.
[7] *Ibid*. 19 Arp. 1779.

Boswell had simply been admitted to the press yard at Newgate and then ridden in one of the official coaches to Tyburn, where he witnessed the execution, he read that night in *Lloyd's Evening Post* that he had accompanied Hackman to the prison chapel, had ridden in the coach with him to Tyburn, and had even climbed into the cart and prayed with him just before the execution. "In short, his name had been substituted throughout for that of the Rev. Mr. Porter, who really had paid Hackman these mournful attentions."[8] Professor Pottle suggests an explanation for this substitution: "Steevens was an inveterate writer of paragraphs for the newspapers, and the perpetrator of numberless malicious hoaxes on his acquaintances. He had been present at The Club on the night when Boswell had made himself a great man because of his having been at Hackman's trial, and now, seeing Boswell's dislike, may have resolved to give him rather more of Hackman than would be agreeable to him."[9] Against Burke's advice but with Johnson's subsequent approval, Boswell inserted paragraphs in *Lloyd's Evening Post* and the other newspapers printing the account correcting it.[10]

It was Steevens's somewhat underhand behaviour regarding Boswell's *Life of Johnson* that seems to have put an end to their relationship in 1791. Boswell reported on 14 February of that year: "My worthy printer Baldwin endeavoured to cheer me up with hopes that my *Life of Johnson* might be profitable, though Steevens had thrown cold water on my hopes."[11] Later that month Charles Dilly told Boswell "that Stockdale told him it [the *Life*] had been depreciated, and on being pressed, owned that Steevens had talked against it. It vexed me to think that this malicious man had, I feared, access to it at the Printing-House."[12] No further reference to "this malicious man" appears in Boswell's journal, but when he praised Malone for editing Shakespeare without reward except for "*that fame which he has so deservedly obtained*" (*Life* i. 8), Steevens sounded his usual note in *The St. James's Chronicle*, 19 May 1791: "As the Advertisement prefixed to Mr. Boswell's *Life of Dr. Johnson* seems to intimate that Mr. Malone was *singular* in taking no money for the publication of Shakspeare, we are authorized to declare that Mr. Steevens likewise received no pecuniary consideration for his repeated editions of the same authour."[1]

[8] BP xiii. 243.
[9] *Ibid.*
[10] Journ. 20 Apr.; BP xiii. 244.
[11] Journ.

[12] *Ibid.* 20 Feb.

[1] C. J. Horne, "Malone and Steevens", *N&Q*, cxcv (1950). 56.

UPPER OSSORY, JOHN FITZPATRICK, second Earl of (1745–1818). The first reference to Lord Ossory in Boswell's journal occurs on 4 May 1781, but Boswell had almost certainly met him earlier, for Ossory became a member of The Club on 14 March 1777. It is somewhat remarkable, divorce being so rare an event in England in the eighteenth century, that The Club numbered among its members two husbands who had obtained divorces (Sir Thomas Charles Bunbury and the Duke of Leeds) and two co-respondents in divorce actions (Beauclerk and Ossory). Anne Liddell, Ossory's Countess and a favoured recipient of Horace Walpole's letters, had formerly been Duchess of Grafton.

Although infrequent, Boswell's references to Ossory in his journal are cordial ones, and Ossory seems to have been warm in his behaviour to Boswell. On 16 August 1790, Boswell "met Lord Ossory in the forenoon, who had come to town occasionally. I asked him to dine with us [Lord Eliot and his son, Sir Joshua Reynolds, Robert Jephson, and Malone], and he obligingly came. . . . I was struck to observe how Westminster Scholars, however different in age and rank, draw to one another. Lord Ossory and my little James got into close conference, and his Lordship was pleased to say, 'He is the finest boy I ever saw in my life.' It seems he gave James half a guinea, saying, 'I must tip you. I never see a Westminster but I tip him.'"[2] The brief correspondence is pleasing as showing benevolence on Boswell's part and alacrity of assistance on Lord Ossory's.

WARREN, RICHARD (1731–97). Dr. Warren was elected to The Club on 28 December 1784. Boswell appears not to have known him before he met him at The Club on 21 June 1785, and for several years after that he may have met Warren only there. He was much pleased by Warren's cheerfulness, "which though David Hume erroneously calls a *virtue*, is certainly a valuable quality",[3] and suggested to Mrs. Boswell that she employ Warren in place of her usual physician. Mrs. Boswell declined,[4] but by 1790 Warren had become the Boswell family physician, having been especially entrusted with the care of James Boswell the younger.[5] His feeling towards Boswell exactly matched Boswell's towards him. On 27 February 1791, meeting Boswell at an evening party and feeling his hand cold, he reproved him for having omitted his

[2] Journ.
[3] Journ. 12 June 1787.
[4] Journ. 9 Mar. 1788.
[5] Journ. 22, 26 Jan., 17 July 1790.

daily bottle. "He told me that some people had a power of inspiring cheerfulness instantaneously; that when I was myself, I was one of those, and that for some time, he had missed the effect which I used to have upon him." His prescription to drink more wine when in low spirits, which he extended into a general defence of intoxicants, probably indicates a comfortable theory of medicine rather than a belief that Boswell's cause was lost.[6] He attended Boswell in his last illness. The notes between Boswell and him here printed testify to a degree of friendship and regard far in excess of the demands of a physician-patient relationship.

WARTON, JOSEPH (1722–1800). The son of Thomas Warton the elder and brother of Thomas Warton the younger, Joseph Warton published his best known poem, *The Enthusiast*, in 1744. His *Odes on Various Subjects* appeared in 1746; his edition of Virgil, with original critical essays and verse-translations of the *Eclogues* and the *Georgics*, which appeared in 1753, extended his literary reputation. At Johnson's invitation, he contributed some essays (1752–54) to *The Adventurer*. He was appointed usher, or second master, at Winchester College in 1755, and, in 1766, was promoted to the headmastership. He was a notoriously inept disciplinarian, there being three major student mutinies during his tenure. After the third, in 1793, he resigned. Warton is perhaps best known for his critical works and his "pre-Romantic" poems. In his *Essay on the Writings and Genius of Pope*, the first volume of which came out in 1756, the second in 1782, he stressed the importance of invention and imagination in poetry, and degraded Pope to the second rank of poets. Although he quarrelled with Johnson in 1766,[7] they remained friends (albeit irritable ones) to the end of Johnson's life. Warton was elected to The Club in January 1777.[8]

Boswell and Warton met only occasionally. Warton was useful to Boswell as a source of Johnsoniana, but he was not one of the men who played an important part in his life. There is no suggestion that many more letters than are printed here were exchanged between them.

WARTON, THOMAS (1728–90). The historian of English poetry and, from 1785, Poet Laureate, Thomas Warton went to Oxford in 1744 and lived there for the remaining forty-seven years of his

---

[6] Journ. 27 Feb. 1791; 21 June 1785; 19 Dec. 1789.   [7] *Life* i. 270 n. 1; ii. 41 n. 1.   [8] *The Club*.

life. Tutor and Fellow of Trinity College, he considered himself primarily an Oxford don, and passed "with perfect ease and unabated enthusiasm from poetry to criticism, from antiquarian to classical research, from literary history to the editing of his favourite poet."[9] His first published poem appeared without his name in his brother's *Odes on Various Subjects*, in 1746. In 1747, he published his Miltonic *Pleasures of Melancholy*, a juvenile contribution to the Gothic movement. While historically important (Wordsworth and Coleridge found it exciting), it now has little literary appeal. *Observations on the Faerie Queene of Spenser* was published in 1754. In that work, with rich historical illustration, he anticipated his brother's indictment of the insufficiency of contemporary poetic taste. He was for two terms Professor of Poetry at Oxford, as his father had been, but lectured only on classical topics and in Latin. Though indolent and unambitious as teacher and preacher (he asked his pupils each term if they would *wish* to attend lecture, and repeatedly preached the same two sermons, neither of them his own),[1] he was a laborious and learned literary historian and critic.

It was at Oxford, on 20 March 1776, that Boswell, in company with Johnson, met Warton for the first time:

> Then we went to Mr. Thomas Warton of Trinity, whom I had long wished to see. We found him in a very elegant appartment ornamented with good prints, and with wax or spermaceti candles before him. All this surprised me, because I had heard that Tom kept low drunken company, and I expected to see a confused dusty room and a little, fat, laughing fellow. In place of which I found a good, sizeable man, with most decent clothes and darkish periwig, one who might figure as a Canon. He did not say much. . . . There was no vivacity broke forth—no poetick flash. . . . Dr. Johnson said to me afterwards that Warton did not like to be with us. He was not at his ease. He liked only company in which he could reign. "I am sure," said I, "I should have willingly let him reign." "Ay, but he would

[9] Horace Twiss, *The Public and Private Life of Lord Chancellor Eldon*, 1844, iii. 302; Clarissa Rinaker, *Thomas Warton, a Biographical and Critical Study*, 1916, p. 23.

[1] *Ibid.* p. 160, from Alexander Chalmers, ed., *Works of the English Poets*, 1810, xviii. 85 n. Chalmers, who had the sermons, says that one of them was in an old hand and probably his father's; the other was a printed sermon.

not have reigned before us," said he, "for all men who have that love of low company are also timid."[2]

Warton's low tastes would not have disturbed Boswell, but they saw very little of each other after their first meeting. Warton was seldom in London (either before or after his election to The Club on 5 March 1782), and Boswell did not visit him at Oxford, with possibly one exception.[3] Warton's interest for Boswell was twofold: he was a fertile source of Johnsoniana and of material on early Scottish poetry. Their letters are concerned with little else. This is a literary correspondence, like that with Percy, but showing even less intimacy between the writers.

WINDHAM, WILLIAM (1750–1810). Scholar, mathematician, politician, representative of an old Norfolk family, Windham was elected to The Club in December 1778. Educated at Eton, Glasgow, and University College, Oxford, he entered politics rather late with strong reforming opinions, acting steadily for some time with the Opposition to Pitt and as one of the Managers of the impeachment of Warren Hastings. He followed Burke, however, in abhorrence of the French Revolution, ultimately breaking with Fox (whom he had known from his days at Eton), and opposing constitutional change. On 11 July 1794, on Burke's advice and rather against his own desires, he accepted appointment as Secretary at War under Pitt. Boswell, writing on 7 February 1794 to his son Alexander, had predicted that Windham would not take office: "He is a man of high honour, and could not bear being suspected of any interested motive for his supporting government, which he does from sincere patriotism."

Boswell's first recorded meeting with Windham was on 31 March 1783, when they dined at Langton's with Dr. Parr.[4] Shortly thereafter, on 3 April, Boswell "dined at Mr. Wyndham's in Queen Anne's Street, West. It was agreable to be on an easy footing with the Norfolk Wyndham, a Scholar and a Brookes's Man, whose *name* is to me highly classical from Pope. . . . The comfortable house, good Library, and good entertainment, both

[2] Journ.
[3] Warton dined with JB and Malone on 29 Apr. 1786 when they were in Oxford, but there is no indication that

they visited him at his rooms or spent much time in his company (Journ.).
[4] Journ.

xcviii

for the mouth and the mind . . . gave me much satisfaction."[5] This satisfaction seemed to continue throughout their relationship, for Windham was frequently in Boswell's company, even accompanying him on a jaunt of exploration into Wapping, when (as we now know) he really wanted to attend a prize-fight.[6] Windham's assiduous attendance on Johnson in his last illness and Johnson's resulting gratitude must have endeared him to Boswell.

Windham seems to have been, however, strictly a London companion. Although he was much in Boswell's company, with Malone and Courtenay particularly, there is no indication that any attempt was made by either man to correspond during absences from the capital. Their mutual concerns were centred in London. For this reason, their extant correspondence printed here seems particularly appropriate, dealing as it does almost exclusively with London life and interests.

YOUNG, EDWARD (1683–1765). Young was five years older than Pope, and anticipated Pope in the writing of verse satire (*The Universal Passion, or Love of Fame*, 1725–28). Two of his tragedies, written in approximately the era of Pope's Homer, successfully produced at Drury Lane, were rated among the better serious dramatic works of the century. Disappointed in his hopes of great ecclesiastical preferment, he gained his greatest fame at sixty with his sententious *Complaint, or Night Thoughts on Life, Death, and Immortality* (1742–46). Young, whom Boswell never met, was Boswell's favourite poet (*"Night Thoughts* . . . a mass of the grandest and richest poetry that human genius has ever produced").[7] He must have envied Langton, who as a young man had visited Young frequently and, as the letter here printed shows, had submitted some writing of his for the old poet's judgement. Young, who died about a year after The Club was founded, was not a member of it, but comes into the present volume because of this connexion with Langton.

---

[5] Journ.

[6] On 8 Dec. 1787, JB "went to the first night of a new Club, instituted for every saturday Night by Windham. Only he and I there. We had oysters, malt liquor, and punch, and having got upon the extensive and interesting subject of Johnson, did very well" (Journ.). Windham recorded a gathering that took place on 28 Dec. 1790, after The Club had dispersed: "I was tempted to go with Boswell and Langton, after calling on Courtenay, who was gone to bed, to Boswell's lodgings, where, with his daughters and sons and young Langton, I sat disputing with Langton, on the American war, Keppel, etc., with more heat than I liked, till between one and two" (*Windham's Diary*, p. 216).

[7] *Life* iv. 60.

EDITORIAL PROCEDURES

THE TEXTS

Choice and Arrangement of Letters

The copy-text has been the MSS. of letters sent whenever such MSS. were available; failing letters sent, recourse has been had to MS. drafts and file-copies. In a few instances, no original MSS. at all have been forthcoming, and printed texts have been used as copy.

"Not reported" in the head-notes means that though there is evidence that the letter in question was sent, I have no evidence that any kind of MS. of it survived the sender and the recipient. "Not traced", on the other hand, means that a MS. of the letter so referred to was certainly in existence some time after Boswell's death, but that I have been unable to learn where it is now. "Missing" bears the ordinary narrow sense "not in the place where one would expect it to be", as, "the lower half of the second leaf is missing".

Since only three of the correspondences (those with Barnard, Langton, and Percy) are long enough to have much character in themselves, it has seemed best to focus the reader's attention on the changing pattern of Boswell's life by printing in one chronological series all the letters which have some relevance to Boswellian or Johnsonian studies. Letters to Langton from William Blackstone, Robert Orme, Joseph Spence, and Edward Young have been placed in Appendix 2. I have provided alphabetical Tables of Correspondents for readers who wish to follow the separate correspondences.

Transcription

In conformity with the plan of the research edition as a whole, the manuscript documents in this edition have been printed as close to the originals as is feasible in the medium of type. A certain amount of compromise and apparent inconsistency is probably unavoidable, but change has been kept within the limits of stated conventions, and no change that could possibly affect the sense has been made silently. Editorial intervention has been more active in formulary and mechanical elements than elsewhere. The following conventions are imposed without particular notice:

Addresses. Elements appearing on separate lines in the MS. are run together and punctuated according to modern practice. Handwriting is that of the author unless otherwise specified.

Headings. In copies, headings are in the hand of the copier unless otherwise specified.

Datelines. Places and dates are joined at the head of the letter regardless of their position in the MS., and are separated by commas (but see below under *Abbreviations*). Periods following years have been removed.

Salutations. Abbreviations are expanded. Commas and colons after salutations are retained; when the manuscripts show other choices, colons are substituted.

Complimentary closes. Punctuation of complimentary closes has been normalized. Elements appearing on separate lines in the MS. are run together. Complimentary closes separately paragraphed in the MS. are printed as continuations of the last line of text. Abbreviations are expanded.

Signatures. Periods following signatures are omitted.

Postscripts. The punctuation of the symbol P.S. has been normalized, and the postscript is treated as a separate paragraph of the text.

Endorsements. Handwriting is that of the recipient unless otherwise specified.

Punctuation. At the ends of completed sentences periods may replace commas, and are always supplied when omitted. Following a period, sentences always begin with capitals. Punctuation in lists or numerical series has been normalized. Some nonsensical periods have been read as commas, even in hands that ordinarily distinguish the marks clearly.

Interlineations and marginalia. Interlineations and marginalia are inserted in the text at the point indicated by the writer.

Deletions. Insignificant deletions are ignored.

Lacunae. Words and letters missing through a tear or obscured by a blot are supplied within angular brackets. Inadvertent omissions by the writer are supplied within square brackets.

Abbreviations, contractions, and symbols. The following abbreviations, contractions, and symbols, and their variant forms, are expanded both in the text and in the notes: abt (about), acct (account), agst (against), Bp (Bishop), cd (could), compts (compliments), Dr (Dear), Ld (Lord), Lop (Lordship), Ly (Lady), Lyship (Ladyship), recd (received), sd (should), Sr (Sir), wc (which), wd (would), wt (with), yr (your), yt (that), & (and), &c (etc.). All retained abbreviations and contractions are followed by a period. Periods following ordinals have been removed, except in datelines, where they serve as punctuation separating elements of the date. Obscure or misleading abbreviations or contractions are expanded within square brackets.

Superior letters. Superior letters are lowered, except in foreign postmarks.

Titles. Titles of books, periodicals, newspapers, and poems are printed in italics, even when not underlined by the writer.

Quotations. Primary quotation is indicated by double marks of quotation, secondary by single. Omitted quotation marks are silently supplied.

Brackets. Parentheses replace square brackets in the text, brackets being reserved for editorial use.

Devices of emphasis. Underlinings for purposes of emphasis are printed as italics. Words written in particularly large letters or those doubly underlined are printed in small capitals.

Flourishes. Underlinings which seem to be meaningless flourishes are ignored.

The original spelling has been retained, except for obvious inadvertencies, which are corrected in the text and recorded in the notes.

The writers' capitalization has been retained, although in several instances it has been impossible to determine which letters are capitals. This ambiguity is a particular problem in the handwriting of Percy and Barnard, where the C's, M's, N's, and T's, whether capital or small, are frequently identical. In some instances, therefore, my decisions have been arbitrary.

Original paragraphing has been retained.

THE ANNOTATION

Head-notes. Register entries are taken from Boswell's Register of Letters, kept, with gaps, from 7 October 1763 to 20 October

1790. Slight discrepancies between dates of letters and those recorded in the Register have not been annotated. Boswell often recorded the letters from memory and frequently mistook the dates (dates of Boswell's letters in the Register are in any case those on which letters were sent, not the days on which they were written). Postmarks, although partly illegible on some letters, are left unbracketed when not in doubt. Marks on the wrappers other than addresses, postmarks, endorsements, and stamped and written franks are ignored.

Foot-notes. Reference titles in the foot-notes are sufficiently complete for ready identification. When no source is given for the identification of persons in the notes, it can be assumed that the material is available in the DNB or an encyclopedia. No references have been given for information available in the *Encyclopaedia Britannica*, gazetteers, the *British Museum Catalogue of Printed Books*, Robert Watt's *Bibliotheca Britannica*, Joseph Haydn and Horace Ockerby's *Book of Dignities*, and H. B. Wheatley and Peter Cunningham's *London Past and Present*, except where the works have been directly quoted. All dates of members' election to The Club are, unless otherwise noted, taken from the records of The Club.

Reference to all letters which have appeared or which will appear in the Yale research edition is made by correspondent and date when only the text is in question. For context or for annotation, reference may be made to the *Life, Letters of James Boswell, Letters of Samuel Johnson, Private Papers of James Boswell*, etc.

CUE TITLES AND ABBREVIATIONS

This list omits the more familiar abbreviations of standard works of reference and periodicals, such as DNB, OED, and N & Q.

Note: All manuscripts referred to in the foot-notes without mention of a repository are either in the Yale Collection or will be printed in full in other volumes of the present edition. Catalogue numbers are supplied in some instances in order to facilitate identification.

Aberdeen: Beattie Collection, University of Aberdeen.

Adam Library: R. B. Adam, *The R. B. Adam Library Relating to Dr. Samuel Johnson and His Era,* 4 vols., 1929–30.

Alum. Cant. I: John and J. A. Venn, *Alumni Cantabrigienses,* Part I (to 1751), 4 vols., 1922–27.

Alum. Cant. II: J. A. Venn, *Alumni Cantabrigienses,* Part II (1752–1900), 6 vols., 1940–54.

Alum. Dublin.: G. D. Burtchaell and T. U. Sadleir, *Alumni Dublinienses,* 1935.

Alum. Oxon. I: Joseph Foster, *Alumni Oxonienses . . . 1500–1714,* 4 vols., 1891–92.

Alum. Oxon. II: . . . *1715–1886,* 4 vols., 1887–88.

Army List: A List of the Officers of the Army, etc., 1756–.

BM Add. MSS.: *British Museum Catalogue of Additions to the Manuscripts,* 15 vols., 1850–1950.

BP: *Private Papers of James Boswell from Malahide Castle in the Collection of Lt.-Col. R. H. Isham,* ed. Geoffrey Scott and F. A. Pottle, 18 vols., 1928–34. References are to the editorial commentary only. JB's journal is referred to in the present volume as "Journ.", with date. Letters to and from JB are referred to by correspondent and date.

Barnard Letters: Barnard Letters, 1778–1824, ed. Anthony Powell, 1928.

Beattie's Diary: James Beattie's London Diary, 1773, ed. R. S. Walker, 1946.

Book of Company: Records kept by JB from 18 Sept. 1782 to 10 Jan. 1795 of his guests at Auchinleck (Hyde Collection).

Boswell in Extremes: Boswell in Extremes, 1776–1778, ed. Charles McC. Weis and F. A. Pottle, 1970.

Burke's Peerage: Sir Bernard Burke, *A Genealogical and Heraldic Dictionary of the Peerage and Baronetage,* 61st ed., 1899.

Club, The: The Club: the First Half-Century,* ed. James M. Osborn. Forthcoming. This book, based on the official records, supplemented by references in letters, journals, etc., will supplant *Annals of The Club, 1764–1914,* 1914, for the early years.

Comp. Bar.: G. E. C[okayne], *Complete Baronetage,* 5 vols., 1900–06.

Comp. Peer.: G. E. C[okayne], *Complete Peerage,* rev. Hon. Vicary Gibbs, H. A. Doubleday, and others, 13 vols., 1910–59.

Earlier Years: F. A. Pottle, *James Boswell: The Earlier Years, 1740–1769,* 1966.

Farington Diary: Joseph Farington, *The Farington Diary,* ed. James Greig, 8 vols., 1922–28.

Fasti Angl.: John LeNeve and T. D. Hardy, *Fasti Ecclesiae Anglicanae,* 3 vols., 1854.

CUE TITLES AND ABBREVIATIONS

Fasti Hib.: Henry Cotton, *Fasti Ecclesiae Hibernicae*, 5 vols., 1848–60; vol. 1, 2nd ed., 1851.

Fasti Scot.: Hew Scott, *Fasti Ecclesiae Scoticanae*, 7 vols., 1915–28.

Fettercairn Papers: Papers in the collection of Mrs. Peter Somervell, now deposited in the National Library of Scotland.

Gaussen: Alice C. C. Gaussen, *Percy: Prelate and Poet*, 1908.

Gent. Mag.: *The Gentleman's Magazine*, 1731–.

Grand Tour I: *Boswell on the Grand Tour: Germany and Switzerland, 1764*, ed. F. A. Pottle, New York, 1953.

Gunby: Langton family correspondence at Gunby Hall, Lincolnshire.

Henry, Elizabeth and George: Henry Herbert, tenth Earl of Pembroke, *Henry, Elizabeth and George*, ed. Lord Herbert, 1939.

Hyde Collection: Collection of Mr. and Mrs. Donald F. Hyde, Four Oaks Farm, Somerville, N.J.

Johns. Glean.: A. L. Reade, *Johnsonian Gleanings*, 11 vols., 1909–52.

Journ.: JB's journal, Yale. Transcribed conservatively from the MS.

Langton's diary: Eleven small memorandum books for the years 1754–58, 1761–66, containing primarily lists of expenditures; all but the first two vols. in the hand of Bennet Langton. In the possession of J. C. P. Langton, Esq.

Lecky, England: W. E. H. Lecky, *A History of England in the Eighteenth Century*, Cabinet Ed., 7 vols., 1892–93.

Lecky, Ireland: W. E. H. Lecky, *A History of Ireland in the Eighteenth Century*, 5 vols., 1892 and later.

Letters JB: *Letters of James Boswell*, ed. C. B. Tinker, 2 vols., 1924.

Letters Reynolds: *Letters of Sir Joshua Reynolds*, ed. F. W. Hilles, 1929.

Letters SJ: *The Letters of Samuel Johnson, with Mrs. Thrale's Genuine Letters to Him*, ed. R. W. Chapman, 3 vols., 1952.

Life: *Boswell's Life of Johnson, Together with Boswell's Journal of a Tour to the Hebrides and Johnson's Diary of a Journey into North Wales*, ed. G. B. Hill, rev. L. F. Powell, 6 vols., 1934–50; vols. v and vi, 2nd ed., 1964.

Life of Beattie: Sir William Forbes, Bart., *An Account of the Life and Writings of James Beattie, LL.D.*, 2nd ed., 3 vols., Edinburgh, 1807.

Lit. Anec.: John Nichols, *Literary Anecdotes of the Eighteenth Century*, 9 vols., 1812–15.

Lit. Car.: F. A. Pottle, *The Literary Career of James Boswell, Esq.*, 1929; reprinted 1965, 1967.

Lit. Car. Reynolds: F. W. Hilles, *The Literary Career of Sir Joshua Reynolds*, 1936.

Lit. Illust.: John Nichols and John Bowyer Nichols, *Illustrations of the Literary History of the Eighteenth Century*, 8 vols., 1817–58.

Mem.: JB's memoranda, Yale. Transcribed conservatively from the MS.

Namier and Brooke: Sir Lewis Namier and John Brooke, *The House of Commons, 1754–1790*, 3 vols., 1964. See p. xxviii.

NBG: *Nouvelle Biographie générale*, ed. J.-C.-F. Hoefer, 46 vols., 1853–66.

Notes: JB's MS. journal notes, Yale. Transcribed conservatively from the MS.

PL-M's diary: The diary of Peregrine Langton-Massingberd; thirteen leather-bound vols., deposited in the Lincolnshire Archives Office.

PL-M's letter-book: The first (1772–1807) of five vols. containing Peregrine Langton-Massingberd's transcriptions of family letters with his comments, deposited in the Lincolnshire Archives Office. Pagination recommences after p. 104, the first series cited as *a*, the second as *b*.

Percy-Farmer Corresp.: *The Correspondence of Thomas Percy and Richard Farmer*, ed. Cleanth Brooks, 1946.

Percy-Malone Corresp.: *The Correspondence of Thomas Percy and Edmond Malone*, ed. Arthur Tillotson, 1944.

Percy's diary: Thomas Percy's MS. diary, BM Add. MSS. 32336, 32337.

Portraits: *Portraits by Sir Joshua Reynolds*, ed. F. W. Hilles, 1952.

Reg. Let.: JB's register of letters sent and received.

Reiberg: Rufus Reiberg, "The Later Literary Career of Thomas Percy", unpublished dissertation, Yale, 1952.

S.R.O.: Scottish Record Office, Edinburgh.

Scots Mag.: *The Scots Magazine*, 1739–1817.

Scots Peer.: Sir James Balfour Paul, *The Scots Peerage*, 9 vols., 1904–14.

Shepperson: A. B. Shepperson, *John Paradise and Lucy Ludwell of London and Williamsburg*, 1942.

Tour: *Boswell's Journal of a Tour to the Hebrides with Samuel Johnson, LL.D.*, ed. F. A. Pottle and C. H. Bennett, 1961 (New York), 1963 (London).

Waingrow: *The Correspondence and Other Papers of James Boswell Relating to the Making of the Life of Johnson*, ed. Marshall Waingrow, 1969.

Walker: *The Correspondence of James Boswell and John Johnston of Grange*, ed. R. S. Walker, 1966.

Walpole's Correspondence, Yale Ed.: *The Yale Edition of Horace Walpole's Correspondence*, ed. W. S. Lewis and others, 1937–.

Windham's Diary: *The Diary of the Right Hon. William Windham, 1784 to 1810*, ed. Mrs. Henry Baring, 1866.

Works of SJ, Yale Ed.: *The Yale Edition of the Works of Samuel Johnson*, A. T. Hazen and J. H. Middendorf, General Eds., 1958–.

THE CORRESPONDENCE
OF JAMES BOSWELL
WITH CERTAIN MEMBERS OF THE CLUB

From Adam Smith, 1760 or 1761[1]

Not reported. Referred to in To Andrew Erskine, 8 Dec. 1761: "It is a very strange thing that I JAMES BOSWELL Esquire, although possest of 'a happy facility of manners'[2]—to use the very words of Mr. Professor Smith, which upon honour were addrest to the above-mentioned Gentleman—If it was absolutely necessary, I could yet produce the Letter in which they are to be found. . . ." See also Journ. 22 Dec. 1765, 12 Sept. 1773, 3 Apr. 1775.

From Jean le Rond d'Alembert to Topham Beauclerk, 1762 or 1763[1]

MS. Yale (C 29).

ADDRESS: A Monsieur, Monsieur Baucklerc, à l'hotel de Tours, rue du Paon.

POSTMARKS: C, A II [or II V], I^e [?]L^{vee}.

ENDORSEMENT by JB: D'alembert.

[Paris] ce Vendredi à 7 heures

M. D'Alembert est bien fâché de ne pouvoir pas avoir l'honneur de diner aujourdhui vendredi avec Messieurs Bauclerck, et Langhton; un engagement indispensable l'en empêche; il prie ces messieurs de vouloir bien recevoir ses excuses et ses regrets.

[1] It is unlikely that the letter would have been written until after JB had left Smith's class at the University of Glasgow and run away to London on 1 Mar. 1760 (To Hailes, 22 Mar. 1760, National Library of Scotland). From the way in which JB refers to the letter (see its head-note) one would not infer that he had received it recently.

[2] *Letters between the Honourable Andrew Erskine and James Boswell, Esq.*, p. 41, reads "happily possest of a facility of manners". If this was a deliberate change (JB's share of the *Letters* was printed from his retained copies, much revised), it was a change for the worse.

[1] Langton and Beauclerk left England for France on 7 Aug. 1762 and were in Paris by at least the 11th (Langton's diary). On 15 Mar. 1763 SJ wrote to Robert Chambers, "Langton is come home" (*Letters SJ* i. 149). Langton's diary seems to confirm this time of return; for after 16 Aug. 1762 there is no further entry in the volume for that year, and the first entry in the new volume for 1763 is that of 12 Mar., when he was apparently in London.

BEAUCLERK TO LANGTON, MAY 1766

From *Topham Beauclerk* to *Bennet Langton*, *May 1766*[1]

MS. Yale (C 116).

[London]

Negligence, the Bane of all my hopes, has prevented me from answering your letter sooner. Believe me there is nothing, that I lose by it, which I regret more, than that agreable intercourse of letters with you. By what cursed accident does it happen, that we are both of us persecuted by it in so wonderful a manner? Shall we shake it off and become great men? Come to London however, you know the Idiot[2] says, that an Idle man in London must learn something in spight of himself,[3] he is a good Example,—that is he was, for at present he lives in a very clean Room with Books all round it very regularly placed, gets up at nine, and reads Greek for three hours.[4] Why may not we study too? I am become enamoured of the Civil Law, if you know any thing of it come and teach me, else let us study it together. I see such fools rise in this Country, that I should hope we need not despair of Grubbing up some of them. Nothing would make me more eager in any pursuit, than the pleasure of following you in it. As Brickenden[5] said, let others rot, but we will be Immortal. I have made some very agreable literary Acqten. who spend the Summer in Town, and If we find a great desire to see Green Fields, the Duke of Bedford[6] says, that he shall

<hr>

[1] See n. 10 of this letter.

[2] The reference is obviously to SJ. Perhaps it alludes to Hogarth's first meeting with SJ in 1753 when while talking with Richardson he "perceived a person standing at a window in the room, shaking his head, and rolling himself about in a strange ridiculous manner. He concluded that he was an ideot . . ." (*Life* i. 146).

[3] This saying of SJ does not seem to be otherwise recorded.

[4] SJ wrote to Langton on 8 Mar.: "I have risen every morning since New-years day at about eight, when I was up, I have indeed done but little. . . . I wish you were in my new study. . . . I think it looks very pretty about me" (*Letters SJ* i. 185). SJ had moved from Inner Temple

Lane to Johnson's Court, Fleet Street, by at least Sept. 1765 (*Letters SJ* i. 176). For a description of the study, see Sir John Hawkins, *The Life of Samuel Johnson*, 1787, p. 452.

[5] Possibly Francis Brickenden, who matriculated at Trinity College, Oxford, 12 Dec. 1750, received his B.A. in 1754, and his M.A. in 1757, the year Beauclerk and Langton matriculated (*Alum. Oxon.* II. i. 157).

[6] John Russell, fourth Duke of Bedford (1710–71). A prominent politician who headed the "Bedford Whigs"; Ambassador to France (1762–63), he was chief British negotiator of the unpopular Treaty of Paris, and took a leading role in the Grenville Ministry (1763–65). According to contemporaries, he was

4

always have a one horse chair ready to drive you to the Library, which is now removed from Wooburn,[7] while they repair that side of the House. If you like Statesmen in place, better than Statesmen in Disgrace I will carry you to dine with the Secretary Richmond at Holland House,[8] when you please. If you think this is a puff, come and see. The D. of Bedford seriously desired you would spend what part of the summer you pleased at Wooburn. Let us write some work there, and date it at Wooburn by which means we shall torment the future Coopers,[9] as well as the present race. The News here is, that they have discover'd a new Country (where is a secret of State) and that they have seen people the least of whom were eight feet high. This is not an Old Womans Story but is deliver'd into the Admiralty Board and to the King by Capt. Biron,[10] who has been round the World. I want like Formal to spend an Evening with him at the Windmill,[11] he must have seen

honest, obstinate, hasty, passionate, and good-natured. All of them agree that he valued his rank, overestimated his abilities, and was governed by his second wife (see *Comp. Peer.* ii. 83 n. 2). His first wife was Lady Diana Spencer (d. 1735), his second, Gertrude Leveson-Gower (d. 1794). Caroline, daughter by his second wife, married, in 1762, George Spencer, fourth Duke of Marlborough, brother of Lady Diana Beauclerk.

[7] Woburn Abbey in Bedfordshire, chief seat of the Dukes of Bedford. In the Russell family since 1547, the mansion was known for its great collection of art treasures and for its library, "56 feet in length by more than 23 in breadth" (Samuel Lewis, *Topographical Dictionary of England*, 5th ed., 1842, iv. 602). Langton had visited Woburn Abbey with Beauclerk at the end of July 1765, leaving on the 31st, when he gave £5. 5s. to the servants there (Langton's diary). They had apparently been there earlier in the summer, for on 6 July he paid Beauclerk "my Share of the Expenses to Woburn".

[8] Charles Lennox, third Duke of Richmond (1735–1806), was constituted Secretary of State for the South from May to July 1766 in Rockingham's first administration (*Comp. Peer.* x. 840–41). Holland House was the home of Henry Fox, first Lord Holland, the father of

Charles James Fox. Lord Holland had eloped with and married Lady Georgiana Caroline Lennox, sister of the Duke, in 1744.

[9] Cooper not identified. Perhaps a college-mate who envied those who associated with the Great.

[10] John Byron (1723–86) of the Royal Navy, the poet's grandfather, was commander of the *Dolphin*, which had arrived in the Downs on 9 May from a twenty-two-month voyage of discovery in the South Seas. In *A Voyage Round the World, in His Majesty's Ship The Dolphin, and a minute and exact Description of the Streights of Magellan, and of the Gigantic People called Patagonians*, 1767, Byron said of the Patagonians, "Their middle stature seemed to be about eight feet; their extreme nine and upwards; though we did not measure them by any standard, and had reason to believe them rather more than less" (pp. 45–46).

[11] In Jonson's *Every Man in his Humour* (IV. iv) Roger Formall, a magistrate's clerk, desirous of hearing the adventures of Brainworm, a servant disguised as a soldier, offers him a bottle of wine at the Windmill Tavern in Old Jewry: "to hear the manner of your services and your devices in the wars; they say they be very strange. . . ."

strange Serpents.[12] You see my hand writing is not improved, whatever my morals may. The truth is I am writing at a strange house, where the Materials are but bad. Adieu, write me a line by the return of the post to let me know when you come to Town. Believe me to be, Dear Langton, Sincerely yours

T. BEAUCLERK

From Topham Beauclerk to Bennet Langton, Friday 13 June 1766

MS. Yale (C 117).

ADDRESS: To Bennet Langton Esqr. Junr., at Langton near Spilsby, Lincolnshire.

POSTMARKS: 14 IV, J.O.

Charles Street, June 13. 1766

I wrote to you my Dear Langton immediately upon the reciept of your letter, and begged the favour of you to send me a line to inform me, when you intended being in Town, that I might regulate my motions accordingly. Has my letter miscarried, or has your Idleness got the better of you, and prevented you from such an exertion? Qui bene vivendi prorogat horam, you know the rest.[1] Do not let us become examples for children, by throwing away the poor dregs of life, that we have remaining, in so contemptible a manner. Come up to London, go with me to Wooburn, and let us return and study together, if we make nothing of that, at least we shall have the consolation of being sure, that we have lost nothing by the Attempt. Adieu! believe me to be, my Dear Langton, very sincerely yours

T. BEAUCLERK

---

[12] In *Antony and Cleopatra* (II. vii) the drunken Lepidus asks Antony whether there are not "strange serpents" in Egypt and when told that the crocodile is shaped "like itself, and it is as broad as it hath breadth", etc., he remarks "'Tis a strange serpent."

[1] *qui recte vivendi prorogat horam* (Horace, *Epistles* I. ii. 41): "He who puts off the hour of right living." The rest goes on to say that this person "is like the bumpkin waiting for the river to run out: yet on it glides, and on it will glide, rolling its flood forever" (H. R. Fairclough's translation in Loeb ed.).

To Adam Smith,
Tuesday 19 August 1766

Not reported. Sent 19 Aug. (Reg. Let.).

To Adam Smith,
Monday 28 August 1769

MS. Yale (L 1161). A copy in John Johnston's[1] hand.

ENDORSEMENT: Copy Letter James Boswell Esqr. To Adam Smith dated 28th Augt. 1769 Sent off the 30th by post To Kirkaldie.

Edinr. 28⟨th⟩ August 1769

DEAR SIR: As I know your benevolence, I readily take the liberty to Solicite you in behalf of the Widow of Mr. Francis Scot of Johnston, who was a very worthy man, and a Descendant of the Family of Buccleugh.[2]

The Good old woman has a small possession under the Duke,[3] Called knottyholm in the parish of Cannobie, where She is anxious to end her days, She is under Some fears of its being taken from her, I would therefore beg that you may take the trouble to mention this Case to the Duke and prevent an inhumane thing from being done;[4] I am always with much regard, Dear Sir, your obliged humble Servant

(Signed) JAMES BOSWELL

To Adam Smith Esqr. at Kirkaldie

[1] Johnston (?1729–86), for whom JB felt an "enthusiasm of affection" (Journ. 7 Oct. 1764), was a "writer" (solicitor or attorney) in Edinburgh, whom JB had first met in Robert Hunter's Greek class in 1755.

[2] Isabella (Woodhouse) Scott, widow of Francis Scott of Johnston (d. 1761), an Edinburgh solicitor. John Johnston was his cousin and her man of business (Walker, pp. xxxiv and nn. 2–4, 68 n. 8, 121 n. 14, 216 n. 1). Scott's connexion to the Scotts of Buccleuch is untraced.

[3] Henry Scott (1746–1812), third Duke of Buccleuch and later (1810) fifth Duke of Queensberry. Between Feb. 1764 and Oct. 1766 Smith had travelled on the Continent as their tutor with the Duke and his younger brother Hew Campbell Scott. The tour ended abruptly with the murder of Hew in Paris on 18 Oct. 1766. Smith remained on relatively close terms with the Duke for the rest of his life, receiving from him a pension of £300 a year. JB does not seem to have known the Duke, although in 1776 he was convinced that he was simply a tool of the Lord Advocate, Henry Dundas (Journ. 26 Jan., 17 Mar.).

[4] Isabella Scott lived on the pleasant farm of Knottyholm in the parish of Canonbie, Dumfriesshire, a parish completely owned by Buccleuch (Walker, pp. 216–17 and 216 n. 1; Sir John

From Oliver Goldsmith,
c. Friday 22 September 1769[1]

MS. Yale (C 1377).

ADDRESS: To —— Boswell Esqr., Carey Street.

Temple Brick Court No. 2

Mr. Goldsmiths best respects to Mr. Boswell and begs the favour of his company to dinner next tuesday at four oclock to meet Sir J. Reynolds, Mr. Colman, etc.[2]

To Oliver Goldsmith,
Monday 25 September 1769

Not reported. Sent from London 25 Sept. (Mem.: "Note to Goldsmith").[1]

Sinclair, *The Statistical Account of Scotland*, 1795, xiv. 409). On 18 Aug. 1768, Johnston wrote to JB: "I am really anxious about poor Mrs. Scots farm. Nothing can be done at present, as The Duke of Buccleugh leaves Dalkeith on Tuesday next, and it's impossible that a Letter from you Could reach Mr. Smyth before that time, but as I think a Conversation with Mr. Smyth will have a better effect than a letter, we must rest Satisfied till winter when you will have an opportunity of meeting with that Gentleman." Mrs. Scott retained her farm (Walker, pp. 240–41 and 240 n. 2).

---

[1] The dinner occurred on Tuesday 26 Sept. (Journ.). Goldsmith's invitation cannot have been written before Thursday 21 Sept., when JB took lodgings in Carey Street, and hardly after Sunday 24 Sept., the last day on which one would have been likely to refer to the 26th as "next Tuesday". JB no doubt gave Goldsmith his address as Carey Street when they met at Tom Davies's on the 21st (Journ.); he stayed there only two nights (Journ.), but Goldsmith would

not have known that. JB answered the invitation on Monday the 25th (see the next letter), but we have no way of knowing how much it may have been delayed by being sent to the wrong address.

[2] "This day at Goldsmith's I was introduced to Sir Joshua Reynolds" (marginal addition to Mem. 26 Sept. 1769, Yale MS. J 20, 3 Sept.–17 Oct. 1769. This overlaps J 21, Notes, 24 Sept.–3 Oct. 1769). Oddly enough, in his Notes for the day, though he writes "mark company", he does not mention Reynolds, recording only hints for conversation by Colman, Robert Chambers, Baretti, and Goldsmith. George Colman the elder (1732–94), dramatist, along with Garrick and Bonnell Thornton, began *The St. James's Chronicle*, and, with Garrick, wrote *The Clandestine Marriage*. He wrote a number of plays for Garrick, and for himself when he managed the Covent Garden Theatre. He was elected to The Club in 1768.

---

[1] J 20, 3 Sept.–17 Oct. 1769. See n. 2 *ante*.

From Thomas Warton to Bennet Langton, Monday 6 May 1771

MS. Yale (C 3067).

ADDRESS: To Bennet Langton Esq., at Langton, Near Spillsby, Lincoln-shire.

POSTMARKS: OXFORD, 8 MA.

Trin. Coll. Oxon., May 6. 1771

DEAR SIR: I am extremely happy to hear from you. The book you mention is not in the Bodley Catalogue. I am glad my Theocritus[1] has afforded you some Entertainment; as you are one of those who read with taste and Judgement, and with all Due honour for the musty Researches of a Commentator. As to the Story about our Founder,[2] you must observe, that even Wood[3] (malignant as he

[1] *Theocriti Syracusii quae supersunt, cum scholiis Graecis auctioribus emendationibus et animadversionibus in scholia editoris et J. Toupii, glossis . . . indicibus . . . edidit T. Warton*, 2 vols., 1770.

[2] Trinity College was founded in 1555 by Sir Thomas Pope (?1507–1559), a favourite of Henry VIII who was officially involved in the suppression of the monasteries, and, as a result, became one of the richest commoners of the time. Warton was writing Pope's life, published in 1772. A second edition, enlarged, appeared in 1780. There is no mention of Sir Thomas's light fingers in the 1772 edition, but Warton added a section in the later edition in which he dealt with Wood's anecdote, "An anecdote equally ridiculous and scandalous . . . which . . . I shall here examine and disprove" (p. 250). "Although possessed of the proper information and evidence, I had long ago, and for many reasons resolved, never to enter into a particular discussion of this idle calumny. But as, since the appearance of my first edition of this work, it has been circulated both in conversation, and by more biographers than one, as a pleasant anecdote, I could no longer forbear using the means in my power of exposing its falsity and futility" (*ibid.* n. a). In the new section, Warton

describes Henry Cuffe, who originated the anecdote, as a man of a "discontented and arrogant spirit" (p. 251); and he accuses Wood and Dr. Bathurst of misrepresentation and inconsistency (pp. 251–53). He goes on to state that, according to his contemporaries, Wood had "a factious and perverse temper" (p. 254) and (p. 255) was guilty of "turbulence and insolence" (*The Life of Sir Thomas Pope, Founder of Trinity College Oxford*, 1780).

[3] Anthony à Wood (1632–95), antiquary and historian, compiler of *Historia et Antiquitates Univ. Oxon.*, 2 vols., 1674. He was also author of *Athenae Oxonienses* and *Fasti Oxonienses*. The story Warton refers to appears in Andrew Clark, *The Life and Times of Anthony Wood, Antiquary, of Oxford, 1632–1695, Described by Himself*, 1891, i. 424: "[In 1661] Dr. [Ralph] Bathurst told me that one [Henry] Cuffe was of Trinity College and expelled from thence upon this account. The founder Sir Thomas Pope would, wheresoever he went a visiting his freind[s], steel one thing or other that he could lay his hand on, put in his pocket or under his gowne. This was supposed rather an humor then of dishonesty. Now Cuffe upon a time with his fellows being merry said 'A pox! this is a poor beggerly

was, and fond of catching at every opportunity of abuse,) says only, that Sir T.P. on a visit would often pockett a piece of Plate, not out of *dishonesty* but as a *mere Joke*. It is Cuffe[4] who, with equal injustice and ingratitude, gave an unfavourable Turn to this report. Sir Thomas in this matter was guilty of nothing but of a *low piece of humour*, which at the same time we must remember was the fashion and cast of the Age. I beg my best Respects to Lady Rothes, and am, Dear Langton, Yours sincerely

T. WARTON

P.S. The present Greek Professor is Dr. Sharpe[5] of Xt. Church. 40 l. p. Ann.[6]

To Thomas Percy,
Monday 26 August 1771

MS. Hyde Collection.

ADDRESS: To The Reverend Mr. Percy.

[Alnwick] Monday Evening, 26 August 1771

REVEREND SIR: I have been taking a little jaunt in the north of England with my wife for her health[1] and am just arrived at Alnwick, where I am informed you now are. If you are at leisure, I should be very happy to have the pleasure of your company, at the

College indeed: the plate that our founder stole would build such another.' Which comming to the president's ears, was thereupon ejected, though afterwards elected into Merton College."

[4] Henry Cuffe, or Cuff (1563–1601), author and politician. He was elected Professor of Greek at Oxford in 1590. He left the University shortly after Apr. 1594 and later became secretary to the Earl of Essex, to whom he gave bad advice while the Earl was in disfavour with Queen Elizabeth. Cuffe was tried and executed because of his association with Lord Essex.

[5] William Sharp (d. 1782) was Regius Professor of Greek from 1763 until his

death. He was a member of Christ Church, where he matriculated on 14 June 1737, aged 18 (*Alum. Oxon.* II).

[6] The stipend of the Regius Professorship of Greek, which was one of a group of professorships founded by Henry VIII with an annual endowment of £40, was not increased till 1865, when it was made up to £500 (*The Historical Register of the University of Oxford*, 1900, pp. 47, 51).

[1] Before arriving at Alnwick, JB and his wife had visited Newcastle and its environs, and Durham (To Johnston, 27 Aug. 1771).

White Hart.[2] I am with real esteem, Reverend Sir, your most obedient humble servant

JAMES BOSWELL

From David Garrick to Bennet Langton, Saturday 14 March 1772[1]

MS. Yale (C 1344).

ADDRESS: To Bennet Langton Esqr., Langton Hall, near Spilsby, Lincolnshire.

POSTMARK: 14 MR.

London, March 14

DEAR SIR: Let me assure You that I regard Nobody's recommendation more than Yours; but indeed our Theatre at present is so cramm'd with unemploy'd Actors, that we shall be oblig'd at the End of this Season to discharge some, who are a mere Weight upon the property—others, whom we keep because they have been some time with us, have very little to do, and are waiting to be of more Use to us—thus circumstanc'd we cannot open our Doors but to first rate capital performers, and this, I trust from Your knowledge in our affairs, will be receiv'd by You, as a full and equitable Excuse for not Engaging Mrs. Vernsberg.[2] I am greatly

---

[2] Percy recorded meeting JB and Mrs. Boswell, not at the White Hart, but at the Swan, on this date (Percy's diary). According to M. J. Armstrong, *An Actual Survey of the Great Post Roads Between London and Edinburgh*, 1783, p. 28, there were apparently only two inns in Alnwick, the Angel and the Swan. *The Universal British Directory*, ii. 20–21, shows that there were at least two there in 1791: the White Swan and the Black Swan. JB wrote to Johnston of Grange that, on arriving at Alnwick, he "sent for the Rev. Mr. Percy who published the *Reliques of Ancient English Poetry* and he came and sat an hour with us; but was obliged to return to the Castle where the Duke of Cumberland was" (27 Aug. 1771).

[1] Year determined by the publication date of Monnet's book (see n. 6) and by the date of the Garricks' move to the Adelphi (see Margaret Barton, *Garrick*, 1949, p. 251, and *The Early Diary of Frances Burney 1768–1778*, ed. Annie Raine Ellis, 1889, i. 175).

[2] The Burney playbills in the British Museum, C. B. Hogan informs me, indicate that Mrs. Vernsberg and her husband acted at King's Lynn beginning 15 Feb. 1776. They were billed as being from the English Theatre at The Hague. The dates of their births and deaths and their Christian names remain unknown.

11

recover'd from my last attack of the Stone, but not yet so vigorous to take the field against Richmond, or so blood thirsty to make an attempt upon the Life of Duncan;[3] I may yet do both before the Season is finish'd.

Mrs. Garrick is almost kill'd with the fatigue of removing to the Adelphi, where we shall be fix'd in the next week: Mr. Beauclerk is to be our Neighbour[4]—Mrs. Garrick presents her respects with mine to Lady Rothes and Yourself. I am, Dear Sir, Your most Obedient humble Servant

D. GARRICK

I have paid the Subscription to Dr. Hiffernan[5]—you shall repay me when I have the honor of seeing you. Will You give me leave to set your name down for two small french Vols. that will be publish'd next Month by Monnet—call'd the Modern Scarron[6] —price 6 Shillings.

To Thomas Percy, Wednesday 6 May 1772

MS. William Elkins Collection, Rare Book Department, The Free Library of Philadelphia.

ADDRESS: To The Reverend Dr. Percy.

---

[3] Garrick played Richard III on 30 May and 2 June, but did not appear in *Macbeth* during the rest of the season (*Letters of David Garrick*, ed. D. M. Little and G. M. Kahrl, 1963, ii. 792 n. 3).

[4] Topham Beauclerk and his wife remained at the Adelphi until late in 1775 or early in 1776 (see Journ. 17 Mar. 1776).

[5] Paul Hiffernan (1719–77), a miscellaneous writer who had at one time practised medicine and who was in the habit of raising money in odd ways. In 1770, he had dedicated his book, *Dramatic Genius*, to Garrick, and Garrick had raised a subscription for him amounting to over £120. Apparently Garrick had persuaded Langton to subscribe to the second edition, about to be published.

[6] Jean Monnet (1703–85), author and theatre director, *Supplément au Roman comique; ou mémoires de J. Monnet. Ecrits par lui-même*, 2 vols., 1772. *Le Roman comique* of the French burlesque writer Paul Scarron (1610–60), published in 1651, related the experiences of a wandering troop of actors. Garrick lent a helping hand to Monnet in 1749 when Monnet directed a troop of French comedians in London, and the two men remained close friends to the end of Garrick's life (F. A. Hedgcock, *A Cosmopolitan Actor: David Garrick and his French Friends*, 1912, pp. 97–98, 102–07, 371–402).

TO PERCY, 6 MAY 1772

[London] Wednesday[1] 6 May

DEAR SIR: Goldsmith insists that our meeting shall be tomorrow evening at his chambers. Pray come.[2] Your's sincerely

JAMES BOSWELL

To Thomas Percy, Friday 8–Monday 11 May 1772[1]

MS. Hyde Collection.

ADDRESS: To Dr. Percy.

[London]

DEAR SIR: I return you the list of Mr. Johnson's Writings with many thanks. I must tell you however that he allowed Levet[2] to dictate to you several errours, as for instance the Conquest of Goree,[3] and the Preface to Sully.[4] He corrected these errours *himself*

---

[1] MS. "Tuesday". JB saw Goldsmith on Wednesday at Sir Joshua's, and the next evening he supped at Goldsmith's with Reynolds, Langton, "etc." (Notes, 7 May 1772).

[2] JB does not name Percy as being present, but his list does not profess to be exhaustive: see n. 1. Percy's diary contains no entries for May 1772. JB called on Percy on 5 May and on 7 May (Notes).

---

[1] JB made SJ "Angry asking as to works" on 8 May; he left London early 12 May 1772 (Notes). For the "list of Mr. Johnson's writings", see Waingrow, pp. 5–9.

[2] Robert Levet, Levett, or Levit (1705–82), "an obscure practiser in physick amongst the lower people" (*Life* i. 243), who lived with SJ for many years. JB mentioned receiving this joint list from Percy in *Life* iii. 321. Levet introduced Langton to SJ, according to JB (*Life* i. 247).

[3] JB allowed himself to be elliptical, knowing that Percy could not be misled, but his letter got separated from Percy's list and has caused much trouble to bibliographers. See A. T. Hazen, *Samuel Johnson's Prefaces and Dedications*, 1937, pp. 110–13. Percy, as is shown by JB's copy of his list (M 148), did not credit SJ with a *book* (*A Voyage to the Coast of Africa, in 1758; containing a succinct Account of the Expedition to, and the taking of the Island of Goree, by a Squadron commanded by the Hon. Augustus Keppel*, 1759, by John Lindsay, Chaplain of H.M.S. *Fougueux*) but with an "Account" of the book published in *Gent. Mag.* (1759, xxix. 447–51). SJ told JB that "He never heard of Lindsey nor that Gorree was conquered."

[4] *Memoirs of Maximilian de Bethune, Duke of Sully* [1560–1641], *Prime Minister to Henry the Great. Containing the History of the Life and Reign of that Monarch, and his own Administration*

13

to me.[5] Mr. Garrick is very desireous to have a copy of the list; but I must ask your permission before I give it; or I would rather wish you should give it yourself. If you do not forbid me, I will give it.

I hope to hear from you at Edinburgh and am, Dear Sir, your obliged humble servant

JAMES BOSWELL

From Topham Beauclerk to Bennet Langton,
?1772[1]

MS. Yale (C 118).

ADDRESS: B. Langton Eqr.

[London]

If you have nothing better to do I wish you would call here this Evening, but not very late as I am very much out of order with a Cold and Fever.

I wish you would make me acquainted with Mr. Paradise,[2] I

---

under him. Translated from the French [by Charlotte Lennox]. *To which is added, the Trial of Ravaillac for the Murder of Henry the Great,* 3 vols., 1756. The Preface was not by SJ (it is translated from the French original), but the Dedication is much in his manner and has been generally credited to him since Croker. See Miriam R. Small, *Charlotte Ramsay Lennox,* 1935, p. 19; Hazen, pp. 110–13. JB made a note on his copy of Percy's list that Mrs. Williams told him that SJ "wrote Mrs. Lenox's Dedications to translations of Sully and Maintenon", but for some unknown reason he rejected her information. He did assign to SJ a review of the book (*Life* i. 20, 309).

[5] After receiving the list from Percy, JB read it to SJ "article by article, and got him positively to own or refuse; and then, having obtained certainty so far, I

got some other articles confirmed by him directly, and afterwards, from time to time, made additions under his sanction" (*Life* iii. 321–22).

---

[1] No definite date can be assigned. See following notes.

[2] John Paradise (1743–95), son of Peter Paradise, was born at Salonika in Macedonia, where his father was English consul. Educated at Padua, he spent the greater part of his life in London, where he was a good friend of SJ. In 1769 he married Lucy Ludwell (1751–1814), an erratic American who was officially declared insane two years before her death; for the next eighteen years he lived in Charles Street, Cavendish Square. In the same year he was created M.A. of Oxford University; and in 1776 received the D.C.L. degree. A Fellow of the Royal

like him much, but not the prince,[3] I had rather be in the K. Bench prison than in his Company. I am made ill today partly by laughing so immoderately last Night, that is not a common disease with me, I will tell you what at when I see you. One story of Burke I think I can tell you which will amuse you,[4] the rest it is impossible to describe.

Pray send me an Answer when you will come.

From Bennet Langton, c. Sunday 2 August 1772

Not reported. Received 6 Aug. (Reg. Let.). Like JB, Langton during these years visited London only in the spring and early summer; this letter then was presumably written at Langton.

Society, he knew ancient and modern Greek, Latin, Turkish, French, Italian, and English. "The house of Mr. P.," wrote a friend, "has been for a number of years the crouded rendezvous of foreigners of distinction, and on Sunday Evenings open to almost every stranger" (Shepperson, p. 245). Shepperson's biography is corrected importantly by Gleb Struve in "John Paradise, Friend of Dr. Johnson, American Citizen, and Russian 'Agent'", *Virginia Magazine of History and Biography*, 1949, lvii. 355–75. Struve stresses Paradise's associations with continental celebrities and shows that at the end of his life he was in the pay of Russia.

[3] Possibly Prince Stanislaus Poniatowski, nephew of the King of Poland, who came to England in Sept. 1771 to study at Cambridge for a year, "et n'en sortit qu'après y avoir acquis, surtout en fait de sciences exactes, une dose de connaissances peu communes" (S.-A. Poniatowski, *Mémoires*, 1914–24, ii. 215. See Horace Walpole to Lady Mary Coke, 11 Dec. 1771, *Walpole's Correspondence*, Yale Ed. xxxi. 164). On the other hand, the reference might be to Prince Michael Poniatowski, brother to the King of Poland, who visited England in 1772 and was a guest of the Royal Society (Sir Archibald Geikie, *Annals of the Royal Society Club*, 1917, p. 117). "Although not a member of this Club, Paradise was perhaps more frequently invited to dine there than any other outsider. The first of these occasions was on January 25, 1772" (Shepperson, p. 89). JB remarks in the *Life* (iv. 364 n. 2) that Paradise had "a very general acquaintance with well-informed and accomplished persons of almost all nations."

[4] Langton is reported to have thought Burke "rude and violent in dispute" (H. D. Beste, *Personal and Literary Memorials*, 1829, p. 63).

From Thomas Percy,
Monday 24 August 1772

MS. Yale (C 2228). Received 6 Sept. (Reg. Let.).
ADDRESS: To James Boswell Esqr.

> Easton Mauduit, near Castle Ashby,
> Northamptonshire, Aug. 24. 1772

DEAR SIR, I am ashamed to see how long it is since I received the favour of your Letter: in it you expressed a Desire to have leave to communicate the List of Mr. Johnson's Publications to Mr. Garrick: You are intirely at Liberty to gratify any friend of yours with that List, which indeed is as much your own Formation, as mine: and you have certainly all the rights of an Author over it.

I am meditating a New Publication to resemble in form, the former intitled *Reliques of Ancient Poetry*, and to consist like it of 3 Vols. 12mo: but by no means to be a continuation of that Work or any thing like a Second Part, etc. etc. etc. I shall intitle it, *A Collection of Ancient English and Scottish Poems, chiefly of the More popular Cast, together with some few Modern pieces.* 3 Vols. 12mo.[1]

It will take in some very good Songs and Ballads that came too late for the former Work: but then it will not be confined to Pieces of this kind, but will be open to Poems of a more elevated nature; and admit Compositions in all sorts of measures and upon all kinds of Subjects, provided they have poetic Merit.—The principal Aim will be to select such poems, as have either never yet been printed, but lain[2] hid in old MSS. or else such as tho' formerly printed have become scarce and are not commonly read.

I shall accompany the Poems with little Dissertations, Illustrations, Anecdotes, etc. as in the former Work: and to each Volume shall prefix a small Essay. The Subjects which I have thought of at present for Essays are these.

1. On the Origin and Spirit of Chevalry.
2. On the State of Manners on the Borders before the Union of England and Scotland.

---

[1] Percy continued to make plans for this volume for at least two years more, but on 27 Nov. 1778 informed George Paton that he no longer had time for such pursuits (*The Correspondence of Thomas Percy and George Paton*, ed. A. F. Falconer, 1961, pp. 102, 162).

[2] MS. "lian".

3. On the Effect of the ancient English Long-bow.[3]

Pray furnish me with Contributions of Poems towards my Collection: and with Materials for my *Essays*, especially the *Second*. All favours of this kind from you or your friends will be most gratefully acknowledged by, Dear Sir, You[r] much obliged and faithful Servant

THOMAS PERCY

P.S. Any packets may come to me under Cover *to the Earl of Sussex*[4] at this Place: or make a large P on the back of the Outside Cover that is the Distinction of my Letters from his Lordship's.

To Bennet Langton, Monday 12 October 1772

Not reported. Sent from Edinburgh 12 Oct. (Reg. Let.). Langton and his wife, who had arrived in Edinburgh 5 Oct., had temporarily left the city and returned on the 16th (*ante* p. lix n. 31).

From Bennet Langton, c. Monday 21 December 1772

Not reported. Received by JB before the end of Dec. JB failed to record it at the proper point in his Register but inserted it at the end of Dec. as *"Omitted"*. Probably sent from Langton. Langton and Lady Rothes left Edinburgh on 17 Dec. (*ante* p. lix).

To Bennet Langton, Thursday 11 February 1773

Not reported. Sent from Edinburgh 11 Feb. (Reg. Let.).

[3] There is no record of Percy's having written these essays.

[4] Henry Yelverton (1728–99), third Earl of Sussex, was one of Percy's parishioners. His brother, George Augustus, the second Earl, had presented the living of Wilby, Northamptonshire, to Percy in 1756 (*The Correspondence of Thomas Percy and Thomas Warton*, ed. M. G. Robinson and Leah Dennis, 1951, p. 8 n. 25).

17

To Thomas Percy,
Monday 1 March 1773

MS. Hyde Collection. A copy in John Lawrie's[1] hand at Yale (L 1061) shows one substantive difference, clearly an error of transcription.

ADDRESS: To The Reverend Dr. Percy.

Edinburgh, 1 March 1773

DEAR SIR: Your letter which I had the pleasure to receive longer ago than I chuse to mention, began with an apology for your not answering mine sooner. Without intending it, I find myself in the same situation that you then was—*Jam sumus ergo pares.*[2]

Our friend Dr. Blair,[3] and I were at first apprehensive that your intended Plan of other three Volumes of Ancient Poetry would hardly be successful with the Publick. But upon talking of it, with Mr. Langton who passed some time here this winter,[4] we were satisfied that it would do; at least I was quite satisfied. Were I to judge from my own feelings alone, and indeed my own wishes, I should be for your publishing as many volumes of the same kind, as your time will allow; for I defy you to publish more than I shall read with pleasure. I am afraid I shall be able to furnish you with very scanty supplies of Poetry. I shall however give you the offer of a few pieces; and if any of them meet with your approbation, I shall be happy. Your Essay on the state of manners on the Borders before the Union of England and Scotland, will be very pleasing to the Lovers of British Antiquities; especially such as still retain the old feudal spirit, which I own I do, and glory in the consciousness of it. I hope to find some materials for you in the records of the Scottish Privy Council.[5]

[1] John Lawrie, JB's clerk, "a sober diligent attentive lad, very serviceable. . . . He goes to church regularly, which is rare in this loose age, amongst young men of his profession" (Journ. 30 Mar. 1773). See index to Walker.

[2] Martial, *Epigrams* II. xviii. 4: "so now we're quits."

[3] Hugh Blair (1718–1800), Scottish divine and literary man, noted for his excellent sermons. He was Regius Professor of Rhetoric and Belles Lettres in the University of Edinburgh. See *post* From Percy, 20 Dec. 1781 and n. 1.

[4] JB does not record any of this discussion in his journal, but the journal for Oct.–Dec. 1772 is very spare. He and Langton called on Blair at Blair's house on 6 Nov. 1772.

[5] During the late summer and autumn of 1772, JB had been making extracts from the records of the Privy Council of Scotland. He apparently dropped the project until late in 1775, when he "resumed what I had neglected for above two years—reading the records of the Privy Council of Scotland and copying any curious passage. . . . I think that I

TO PERCY, 1 MARCH 1773

TO PERCY, 1 MARCH 1773

My Wife is to lye in this month.[6] If it shall please God to grant her a good recovery, I intend being in London by the first of April, when I shall have the pleasure of meeting you. I am much obliged to you for taking care to send me a copy of the *Northumberland Household Book*.[7] I beg you may return my thanks for it to the Duke most respectfully. I am with sincere regard, Dear Sir, your obliged humble servant

JAMES BOSWELL

From Bennet Langton, c. Friday 5 March 1773

MS. Yale (C 1679). Received 9 Mar. (Reg. Let.).

ADDRESS: To James Boswel Esqr., in James's Court, Edinburgh, Turn at Stilton.[1]

POSTMARK: BOSTON.

Langton, March 1773

MY DEAR SIR, I return You many thanks for Your obliging and friendly Letter—the melancholy Event You wrote me word of I had just had an account of in the Edinburgh Paper—indeed You quite do me Justice in thinking how much Concern it would give me—it is true as You say that, if we were together, we should often, and earnestly, converse about our departed Friend[2]—I see

may make a good publication of these abstracts" (Journ. 24 Nov. 1775). Though he returned to this project in 1779 and 1780, he never completed it. Two folio manuscript volumes of transcripts which may have been his, sold as Lot 514 of the Auchinleck sale, Sotheby, Wilkinson, and Hodge, 23 June 1893, have not since been traced.—Lawrie's copy reads "for you in the Scottish Privy Council".

[6] Veronica was born on 15 Mar. 1773.

[7] *The Regulations and Establishment of the Houshold of Henry Algernon Percy, the fifth Earl of Northumberland*, 1770. For a history and description, see Reiberg, pp. 73–81. JB is one of the persons included in Percy's list of recipients of the book, "Copies of the Household Book given away by his Grace's Order. 1772. Printed about 280 compleat", at the Bodleian (MSS. Percy c. 6, ff. 50–51).

---

[1] Stilton, Huntingdonshire, was where the cross-road from Boston connected to the Great North Road to Edinburgh (Daniel Paterson, *New and Accurate Description of all the . . . Roads in Great Britain*, 3rd ed., 1776, p. 122).

[2] Dr. John Gregory (b. 1724), since 1764 Professor of the Practice of Medicine in the University of Edinburgh, died 10 Feb. 1773. He had practised medicine in London, where he became acquainted with well-known public figures; and, from 1755 to 1764, had been Professor of Medicine at King's College, Aberdeen

19

by the last Paper that the musical Society at Aberdeen have paid a Tribute of Affection to His Memory[3]—Dr. Beattie[4] will feel as much Regret on his Loss, I should imagine, as any of His Friends. As *they* seemed on Terms of the closest Friendship,[5] and Beattie, both by Your and all other accounts of Him, and what appears in his writings, has a high degree of sensibility in his Disposition— it is however a favourable Circumstance to have known Gregory, though for a short time, and for that I have my hearty thanks, Dear Sir, to offer You among the many other Instances in which You contributed to make me pass my Time so agreeably at Edinburgh[6]—I sympathize with You in Your very reasonable Regret at Disappointment in Your hope of bringing Johnson and him whom we are now lamenting to meet; the Satisfaction would I dare say have been reciprocal between Them in consequence of it—His Daughter that was with Mrs. Montague[7] I think he

(*Beattie's Diary*, p. 17). Notice of Gregory's death appeared in *The Edinburgh Advertiser*, 9–12 Feb. 1773, xix. 101. JB attended his funeral on 16 Feb. (Journ.).

[3] *Scots Mag.* for Feb. 1773 (xxxv. 110), after eulogizing Gregory, reported, "The musical society of Aberdeen, the city in which he was born and educated, and had long resided, appointed a funeral concert to his memory; which was held Feb. 19, and conducted with taste and propriety."

[4] James Beattie (1735–1803), poet, essayist, one-time schoolmaster, and Professor of Moral Philosophy in Marischal College, Aberdeen, author of *Original Poems and Translations* (1760). Of greater importance was his *Essay on Truth* (1770), subsidized by his friends Sir William Forbes and Robert Arbuthnot. The *Essay* went through five editions in four years and was translated into French, German, Dutch, and Italian. The first book of Beattie's *The Minstrel*, which repeated the success of the *Essay*, appeared in 1771. Beattie was considered by 1773 the most promising of the younger men of letters in Scotland, a defender of orthodoxy against sophistry and scepticism (*Beattie's Diary*, pp. 22–25).

[5] Gregory, though considerably older than Beattie, was probably his closest friend and was instrumental in introducing him to persons able to advance his career (*Beattie's Diary*, p. 18). Beattie wrote to JB on 1 May 1773, "The air of this town [Edinburgh] is not good for me at present. Every place, and every acquaintance I meet with, puts me too much in mind of the loss, which Society in general, and which his friends, and I in particular, have sustained by the death of one of the most amiable men that ever did honour to our nature.... I dare not trust myself any longer with this subject; otherwise I should become prolix, and depress both your spirits and my own."

[6] See *ante* p. lix.

[7] Mrs. Elizabeth Montagu (1720–1800), leading bluestocking and authoress, had toured Scotland in the summer of 1766 with Dr. Gregory and his elder daughter, Dorothea, to whom she was attracted. In 1772, she adopted the girl as her permanent companion, remaining on excellent terms with her until Dorothea married the Reverend Archibald Allison in 1784. Possibly because she expected her companion to marry her nephew Matthew, Mrs. Montagu became estranged from Dorothea until after

expected home just when we parted—I hope the Family of a Man so much esteemed will be in as agreeable and comfortable a Situation as they can be, deprived of Him[8]—You do not speak particularly of Mrs. Boswel's Health—we hope therefore that She is at least as well as when we left Edinburgh and shall be extreamly happy to hear a favourable account in good time—Lady Rothes desires Sir Her best Respects and Compliments to Yourself and Her and Miss Campbell[9] who is very good in remembering wee George[10] so kindly—Lady Rothes is very much the same as when She was in Scotland; tolerably well when She keeps quiet, but very little able to bear any Fatigue—George with some degree of Illness tho' not very severe, has cut four double teeth since he came to England and seems going on with more but seems to bear up against the uneasiness of it, thank God very happily so far—

I am glad of the Victory You obtained in Your Cause,[11] and to hear that Business has crouded upon You, as You say in Your

Matthew's marriage in 1785 (Reginald Blunt, ed., *Mrs. Montagu "Queen of the Blues"*, 1923, i. 143–270; ii. 131–33).

[8] In addition to Dorothea, Dr. Gregory left another daughter and three sons: James, who succeeded his father at the University of Edinburgh; William; and John.

[9] Jeanie Campbell, stepdaughter of Mrs. Boswell's sister Mary, who was staying with the Boswells (see *Life* iv. 321; Journ. 22 Mar. 1772). Jean Macredie, Jeanie's aunt, had written to Mrs. Boswell the year before to thank her for "the care and affection you show my Dear Nice".

[10] George Langton (8 Mar. 1772–1819), eldest child of Langton and Lady Rothes.

[11] Probably Fullarton (or Fullerton) of Rosemount *v.* Dalrymple of Orangefield and others, a "process of wrongeous imprisonment, oppression and damages". Fullarton (JB's nabob rival in pursuit of Catherine Blair) and Dalrymple were competitors for the post of chancellor of the burgh of Prestwick. In an election-eve brawl, Fullarton struck one John Crawfurd a severe blow, for which he was arrested by Crawfurd's brother, a constable, detained for three hours, and supposedly ill-treated. Fullarton's main complaint was that Dalrymple, as a Justice of the Peace, should have travelled the mile to Prestwick in the middle of the night to extricate him, but he also sued Constable Crawfurd and two other men (John Murray, "Some Civil Causes of James Boswell", *Juridical Review*, 1940, lii. 230–32; "Court of Session Cases"—Lg 21). JB, Alexander Lockhart (Dean of Faculty), Robert Macqueen, and John Maclaurin served as their counsel. All were acquitted, the Lords of Session concluding that "Orangefield had acted, not only without blame, but with the greatest prudence and propriety" (*Edinburgh Advertiser*, 22–25 Dec. 1772, xviii. 404–05, an account probably written by JB himself). JB recorded in his journal for 17 Dec., "Orangefield's cause was won unanimously . . . Mr. Langton went this day." Langton probably left in the morning before the decision was handed down, and would have been interested in the case, having dined with JB on 15 Dec., the day the trial began.

Letter and as You gave me an Intimation that I was very glad to hear, one of the latest times we met—[12]
I am much obliged for the kind Remembrance of my Friends at Edinburgh and will trouble You with my Respects and Compliments to Lord Monboddo[13] and Sir Wm. Forbes, and my other Friends and acquaintance, that You happen to meet—I wonder whether Lord Kamys[14] has seen the 4th Edition of Beattie's *Essay* yet, as it might perhaps reconcile him to it something better by a Note, that, as poor Dr. Gregory said, was added to it, in which there is some apology for a mistake he had made in citing from an earlier Edition of the *Elements of Criticism* what had been corrected in a later one[15]—I should wish to hear how the Study of Greek goes on under Mr. Dalziel (as I think his Name is) the new Professor,[16] and particularly whether the point is settled for the Master of the High School to ground his Pupils in that Language before their being put under the Professor[17] which if it could be properly settled seems a thing so much to be wished for the good of Learning.

I wish my Dear Sir You might have Leisure and Inclination to

[12] JB reported on 12 Dec., "This week had drawn 2 guineas more than any week since I came to the bar—*viz.* 23 guineas. Was rather too much elated, and could not but speak of it. This was wrong" (Journ.).

[13] James Burnett (1714–99), Scottish judge and author.

[14] Henry Home, Lord Kames (1696–1782), Scottish jurist and philosopher.

[15] In a discussion of actual and apparent free will, Beattie wrote, "In the former editions of this Essay, a particular book was here specified and quoted. But I have lately heard, that in a second edition of that book, which, however, I have not yet seen, the author has made some alterations, by which he gets clear of the absurdity exposed in this passage" (*An Essay on the Nature and Immutability of Truth, in Opposition to Sophistry and Scepticism*, 4th ed., 1773, p. 335). The book referred to is not, as Langton states, Lord Kames's *Elements of Criticism* (1762), for which a second edition did not appear until 1774, but his *Essays on the Principles of Morality and Natural Religion* (1751), the second edition of which appeared in 1758. See the second edition of Beattie's *Essay* (1771), p. 366.

[16] Andrew Dalzel (1742–1806) was appointed Joint Professor of Greek at the University of Edinburgh in Dec. 1772. For an extended account of his life, see *Memoir of Professor Dalzel*, by C. Innes (vol. i of *History of the University of Edinburgh from its Foundation*, by Andrew Dalzel, 1862).

[17] Because Robert Hunter (1704–79), Professor of Greek at Edinburgh University, was infirm and inefficient, Alexander Adam began to teach Greek in the High School. Principal Robertson of the University, probably instigated by Hunter, protested to the Town Council on 14 Nov. 1772. The protest was ineffectual, and Hunter retired, selling his chair to Dalzel for £300 and a liferent of the salary. This arrangement was sanctioned by the Town Council and resulted in Dalzel's appointment (Sir Alexander Grant, *The Story of the University of Edinburgh During its First Three Hundred Years*, 1884, ii. 324).

keep adding to Your Grecian Stores; in a Profession so connected with oratory as Yours, and in which You have made such happy advances, it seems a pity that all Demosthenes's Orations and pleadings Should not be familiar to You—I lately read over *that against Midias*, in which there is a striking animation in many parts—among other Passages that pleased me there was one where he says "it may perhaps be objected to me that I have *studied* and *prepared* this Speech;" in his answer to it he says, "No, rather it should be said that *Midias* has written and prepared this Speech of mine as the ill Actions of His Life furnish me the materials of it"—[18]

As to our meeting I do not [know] whether to hope for that Pleasure in London, as I am in doubt whether I shall go there, but I hope You will be so good as to let me know however of the exact time when You go, as I should wish to contrive my Journey there, if I do take it, accordingly—at least I hope in Your Return You can contrive to take this place in Your way—the manner of doing it might easily be settled by Letter.

There is I see just come out a Work that promises to be entertaining, and we have accordingly sent for it at a little Book-Club in our Neighbourhood; it is a kind of History of the English Drama from its very rudest and earliest Beginnings done by an Oxford-Man—Hawkins[19]—who I have heard has taken pains to illustrate his Subject—the poor Man, I find, himself is just dead as his Book is coming out—I have desired them likewise at the same Club to send for the two little Volumes of posthumous Sermons by Farquhar,[20] a great Friend (as he[21] told me) of poor Gregory's, published for his Family's Benefit—I bought them in Scotland and have been much pleased with them—I have brought my Letter to a pretty fair Length and if it was reasonable to say it to You who are so much better employed would wish for as long ones in return—I am, Dear Sir, with great Regard Your affectionate humble Servant

B. Langton

---

[18] *Demosthenes against Meidias*, sections 191–92.

[19] Thomas Hawkins (1729–72), M.A. of Magdalen College, *The Origin of the English Drama, Illustrated in its Various Species*, 3 vols., 1773. Hawkins also edited the 8th edition of Hanmer's Shakespeare, 6 vols., 1770–71. He died

23 Oct. 1772 (*Alum. Oxon.* II. ii. 630).

[20] John Farquhar, A.M. (1732–68), *Sermons on Various Subjects*, 2 vols., 1772. Farquhar was minister of the parish of Nigg, Presbytery of Aberdeen (*Fasti Scot.* vi. 70).

[21] Gregory.

To Bennet Langton,
Friday 19 March 1773

Not reported. Sent from Edinburgh 19 Mar. (Reg. Let.). Referred to *post* From Langton, 20 Apr.: "I thank You very much for Your two Letters and was very glad to hear of the good account the first of them brought of the birth of Your little Daughter."

To Oliver Goldsmith,
Monday 29 March 1773

MS. Hyde Collection.

ADDRESS: To Dr. Goldsmith, No. 2 Brick Court, London.[1]

Edinburgh, 29 March 1773

DEAR SIR, I sincerely wish you joy on the great success of your new Comedy *She stoops to conquer, or the Mistakes of a Night.* The English Nation was just falling into a lethargy. Their blood was thickened and their minds *creamed and mantled like a standing Pool*;[2] and no wonder;—when their Comedies which should enliven them, like sparkling Champagne, were become mere syrup of poppies gentle soporifick draughts. Had there been no interruption to this, our Audiences must have gone to the Theatres with their night caps. In the Opera houses abroad, the Boxes are fitted up for teadrinking. Those at Drury Lane and Covent Garden must have been furnished with settees, and commodiously adjusted for repose. I am happy to hear that you have waked the spirit of mirth which has so long layn dormant, and revived natural humour and hearty laughter.[3] It gives me pleasure that our friend Garrick has written the Prologue for you. It is at least lending you a Postilion since you have not his coach;[4] and I think it is a very

[1] "No. 2 Brick Court" is in an unidentified hand. JB no doubt sent the letter under cover to George Dempster, and the specific direction was added in London. See To Beattie, 20 Apr. 1773. Reg. Let. reports a letter to Dempster on 29 Mar. 1773.

[2] There are a sort of men whose visages
Do cream and mantle like a standing pool.
(*Merchant of Venice* I. i. 88–89)

[3] In these sentences JB echoes what Goldsmith had frequently written about the *comédie larmoyante* in his *Present State of Polite Learning*, his preface to *The Good Natur'd Man*, and very recently in his *Essay on the Theatre; or, a Comparison between Laughing and Sentimental Comedy*, in the first issue of *The Westminster Magazine*, Jan. 1773.

[4] *She Stoops to Conquer* was being acted not at Garrick's Drury Lane but at the rival Covent Garden Theatre.

good one, admirably adapted both to the Subject and to the Authour of the Comedy.

You must know my wife was safely delivered of a daughter, the very evening that *She stoops to conquer* first appeared.[5] I am fond of the coincidence. My little daughter is a fine healthy lively child, and I flatter myself shall be blest with the cheerfullness of your Comick Muse. She has nothing of that wretched whining and crying which we see children so often have; nothing of the *Comedie Larmoyante*. I hope she shall live to be an agreable companion, and to diffuse gayety over the days of her father, which are sometimes a little cloudy.

I intend being in London this spring,[6] and promise myself great satisfaction in sharing your social hours. In the mean time, I beg the favour of hearing from you. I am sure you have not a warmer friend or a steadier admirer. While you are in the full glow of Theatrical Splendour, while all the great and the gay in the British Metropolis are literally hanging upon *your smiles*,[7] let me see that you can *stoop to write* to me. I ever am with great regard, Dear Sir, your affectionate humble servant

JAMES BOSWELL

My Address is James's Court Edinburgh. Pray write directly. Write as if in repartee.

To Bennet Langton, c. Thursday 1 April 1773

Not reported. Sent between Edinburgh and London. See *post* From Langton, 20 Apr.: "I thank You very much for Your . . . second Letter that Mrs. Boswel was doing so well. . . . You was very kind to favour me with a Letter when it could be so little convenient as in Your Journey." JB left Edinburgh Tuesday 30 Mar. and arrived in London 2 Apr.

[5] Veronica had been born on Monday 15 Mar.

[6] JB left for London the very next day, 30 Mar., and had been in London for two days when Goldsmith wrote his reply. For an account of JB's suppressing the date of his departure in order to secure a letter of Goldsmith's for his cabinet at Auchinleck, see BP ix. 107–09.

[7] If this is a quotation, it has not been identified.

From *Oliver Goldsmith*, *Sunday 4 April 1773*

MS. Yale (C 1378).

ADDRESS: To The Honourable James Boswell, James's Court, Edinburgh.

POSTMARK: 5 AP.

London, Temple, April 4th 1773

MY DEAR SIR: I thank you for your kind remembrance of me, for your most agreeable letter, and for your congratulation. I believe I always told you that success upon the stage was great cry and little wool.[1] It has kept me in hot water these three months, and in about five weeks hence I suppose I shall get my three benefits. I promise you my Dear Sir that the stage earning is the dirtiest money that ever a poor poet put in his pocket and if my mind does not very much alter I have done with the stage.

It gives me pleasure to hear that you have encreasd your family, and I make no doubt the little stranger will one day or other, as you hint become a CONQUEROR. When I see you in town, and I shall take care to let Johnson Garrick and Reynolds know of the expected happiness I will then tell you long stories about my struggles and escapes, for as all of you are safely retired from the shock of criticism to enjoy much better comforts in a domestic life, I am still left the only *Poet militant* here, and in truth I am very likely to be *militant* till I die nor have I even the prospect of an hospital to retire to.

I have been three days ago most horridly abused in a news paper, so like a fool as I was I went and thrashed the Editor. I could not help it. He is going to take the law of me.[2] However the press is now so scandalously abusive that I believe he will scarcely get damages. I don't care how it is, come up to town and we shall laugh it off whether it goes for or against me. I am, Dear Sir, your most affectionate humble servant

OLIVER GOLDSMITH

P.S. Present my most humble respects to Mrs. Boswell.

[1] An old saying explained by Erasmus (*Adagia*) as meaning "much labour but small reward". "Great cry and little wool, as the devil said when he sheared the hogs."

[2] For an account of the literary attack on Goldsmith in the *London Packet* (probably by William Kenrick) and of Goldsmith's physical attack on Thomas Evans, publisher of the paper, see R. M.

To Thomas Percy,
Friday 16 April 1773

MS. formerly in collection of Mr. Roger W. Barrett. Printed from a photostat.

ADDRESS: To The Reverend Dr. Percy.

Piccadilly, Friday 16 April

DEAR SIR: I hope you will remember me at the Club tonight.[1] Sir Joshuah, Mr. Johnson and Dr. Goldsmith have obligingly engaged to be for me. They are all to dine at my lodgings on Saturday senight the 24th April.[2] May I beg you will do me the favour to join us. I shall call in upon you tomorrow.[3] But remember not to engage yourself for Saturday se'night. I am, Dear Sir, your obliged friend and humble servant

JAMES BOSWELL

From Bennet Langton,
Tuesday 20 April 1773

MS. Yale (C 1680). Received 22 Apr. (Reg. Let.).

ADDRESS: To James Boswel Esqr.

Stevenage, April 20th 1773

MY DEAR SIR: I thank You very much for Your two Letters and was very glad to hear of the good account the first of them brought of the birth of Your little Daughter and from that and the second Letter that Mrs. Boswel was doing so well, in which Satisfaction Lady Rothes very sincerely partook—You was very

---

Wardle, *Oliver Goldsmith*, 1957, pp. 241–43. Evans allowed Goldsmith to compromise his suit by paying fifty pounds to a Welsh charity. See *Life* ii. 209, 501 for another account.

---

[1] Although Percy was at The Club on the 16th, apparently nothing was done about JB's election (Percy's diary; *The Club*). JB was proposed at the next

meeting of The Club, on 23 Apr., and elected on the 30th.

[2] Percy did not record his attendance at the dinner; the only entry in JB's journal is "Company at dinner. (Fill up.)" He never filled in the names of his guests. SJ was in Oxford (*Letters SJ* i. 320–21), but Reynolds was present, according to his engagement book.

[3] Journal entry for 17 Apr.: "Called Percy."

kind to favour me with a Letter when it could be so little convenient as in Your Journey and though I was much entertained
with the Length of it could not but think it hard that so much of
Your time of Rest should have been taken up by it when both by
what You mention and my own Experience I know the time
allowed for Rest is so short on such occasions—I should have
wrote sooner but have had thoughts some time of a little Excursion
to Town and thought it better to determine first and am now very
happy in the hopes of seeing You very shortly—as I write from a
Place not more than thirty miles from London and hope I shall
be there to morrow about the middle of the day—Lady Rothes
accompanies me and has borne the Journey hitherto very well.
I do not yet know exactly where I am to be in Town as I have
wrote for Lodgings but do not know where they are taken; I shall
be to be heard of at Mr. Charles Thomas's Fruiterer in Bridge
Street Westminster.—I saw the piece You mention, in the
London Chronicle[1] and wish it could be judiciously answered; to
be sure it might be wished that Beattie him self should do it unless
it should be thought not of consequence enough to be worth his
while—however as it may do harm to many that read Newspapers
I wish as You[2] do that somebody would answer it. I shall be glad
to hear some account from You about Lord Monboddo's Book[3]—
but as I find the Post is going out I will not risque losing it; but
defer Chat to our meeting—Adieu and believe me, Dear Sir,
Yours sincerely

BENNET LANGTON

[1] On 23–25 Mar. 1773, in a letter
signed "J. M.," Beattie's *Essay on Truth*,
"which with more propriety, should have
been entitled, *A Proposal to commit David
Hume and his Writings to the Flames*",
was attacked as a work "begun from
personal pique and envy, with a mixture
of vanity". The writer suggested that
Beattie did not understand Hume, and
maintained that Rousseau, whom Beattie
recommended, had "singly done more
harm to Christianity, than all the other
Infidels of the age: his writings are more
dangerous to our religion than Mr.
Hume's, because they are on a level with
common understandings" (xxxiii. 281).
"J. M." concluded by agreeing with
Rousseau "that College and College
Professors serve to propagate falsehood
and folly" (p. 282). The letter was
continued in a later number (17–20 Apr.,
xxxiii. 372) of *The London Chronicle*.

[2] MS. "Yo".

[3] *Of the Origin and Progress of Language*,
vol. i, was advertised as published on 5
Mar. in *The Edinburgh Advertiser*, 2–5
Mar., xix. 149, and on 30 Mar. in *The
London Chronicle*, 27–30 Mar., xxxiii.
303.

From Bennet Langton,
Thursday 17 June 1773

MS. Yale (C 1681). Received 21 June (Reg. Let.).

ADDRESS: To James Boswel Esqr., in James's Court, Edinburgh, Turn at Stilton.

POSTMARK: BOSTON.

Langton (near Spilsby), June 17th. 1773

MY DEAR SIR, I begin to think it a long while that I have not heard of Yourself or Connections—I hope Your Journey down proved tolerably agreeable, and ended in Your finding Mrs. Boswel and Your little stranger quite well—I was sorry that the meeting of Friends We had at Mr. Thrale's the Week of Your Departure wanted the agreeable Circumstance which such a meeting there had last Year of Your being one of the Number[1]— There was a very good set assembled; Murphy was one, who You know is always likely to enliven a meeting of Friends and did so.[2]—Dr. Beattie was asked, but engaged; however for the Time I staid in Town I got a good deal of His Company:[3] it was a very agreeable particular to me that I called at Mr. Burke's with Dr. Beattie and found him at home; as They both seemed to receive as much satisfaction from the Introduction as one should have expected from each of their Characters They would[4]—I had the Pleasure of introducing Him likewise to Sir Joshua Reynolds, with

[1] JB left London on Tuesday 11 May 1773 (*Life* ii. 260). Dinner at the Thrales' was on the following Thursday (see below n. 3). Although JB recorded three gatherings at the Thrales' in Apr. and May 1772 (*Journ.* 22, 28 Apr., 11 May), no mention was made of Langton's presence. 11 May 1772, JB's last day in London that year, is the most likely date.

[2] Arthur Murphy (1727–1805), actor, playwright, journalist, and author of several biographies, among them, *An Essay on the Life and Genius of Samuel Johnson, LL.D.*, 1792; and *The Life of David Garrick*, 1801.

[3] In his diary, Beattie reported on Monday 10 May 1773: "Recd. a note from Mr. & Mrs. Thrale desiring my company to dinner on Thursday, which

I am sorry a prior engagement prevents me from complying with." Beattie and his wife had arrived in London on 7 May, and first saw Langton on the 9th. Beattie recorded in his diary at least four more meetings with Langton between the 9th and the 18th, when Langton left for Lincolnshire (*Beattie's Diary*, pp. 31–35).

[4] Langton introduced Beattie to Edmund Burke on 14 May. "Mr. Burke," Beattie related, "gave me as kind a reception as I ever received from any body, and paid me many complimts. in the genteelest manner. . . . Mr. Burke is one of the most agreable men I have ever seen. Fine accomplishments. Extreme quickness, with humour, and a ready and distinct elocution" (*Beattie's Diary*, p. 33).

whom it appears very fit he should be acquainted from the close Resemblance in justness of thinking and Taste that there is in what each of them have given the publick, and there is the further Reason for wishing them to be acquainted that at Sir J. Reynolds's House he would be likely to meet with so many Persons worthy of his acquaintance[5]—Now I am speaking of Reynolds I do not know whether I have heard You say You had read his speeches deliver'd to the academy,[6] if You have, surely You must have admired them greatly, as they carry Conviction with them I should think even to a Reader that had not particularly applied to Painting, and explain the *Reasons* of *admiring* fine Works in that Art in a manner that seems to hold equally in respect to the other fine Arts, at least very much so as to Poetry, and I should fancy to others[7]—When I saw Dr. Reid at Glasgow I recommended them very particularly to Him and hope he has got them as I should think they would suit him remarkably—You have to be sure looked into his *Enquiry*;[8] when I was in London I thought the Reputation of that work seemed to be high and likely to increase very fast.

I will trouble You with my particular Compliments to Sir Wm. Forbes and to tell Him that I return Him my Hearty Thanks for his obliging Remembrance of me when Dr. Beattie was coming into England to give me the means of his acquaintance;[9] I would have done myself the Pleasure of writing to Him but was apprehensive of giving Him the trouble of answering my Letter which

[5] Beattie was introduced to Sir Joshua probably at a supper given by Langton and Lady Rothes on 17 May (*Beattie's Diary*, p. 35). He found the painter "a man not only of excellent taste in painting and poetry, but of an enlarged understanding and truly philosophical mind . . . it is the truth and simplicity of nature which he is ambitious to imitate" (p. 82). Reynolds and his sister, Frances, entertained the Beatties frequently during their London visit; and on 16 Aug. the poet sat for a portrait, which Reynolds finally presented to him in 1776 (pp. 47–83 and n. 3).

[6] Five of Sir Joshua's *Discourses* had been published at this time: two in 1769; the other three in 1771, 1772, and 1773.

[7] See particularly the second and fifth

Discourses. In his third *Discourse*, Sir Joshua maintained that painting "ranks . . . as a sister to poetry."

[8] Thomas Reid, D.D., F.R.S. (1710–1796), Professor of Moral Philosophy at Glasgow, *An Inquiry into the Human Mind, on the Principles of Common Sense*, 1763. More than five editions of this work were published. JB read the book in Germany in the summer of 1764 and "found it a treasure" because of Reid's "strong reasoning and lively humour" and ability to drive "to pieces the sceptical Cobweb" (Journ. 19 July 1764).

[9] "Dined with Mr. Langton (to whom I gave a letter from Sir W. Forbes) where were Mr. Boswell Dr. Johnson and several others" (*Beattie's Diary*, 9 May 1773).

his Complaisance would perhaps have engaged him in. Lady Rothes desires to join me in Compliments to Him and Lady Forbes to whom will You please to mention that when we were in London Lady Rothes and Her Friend Lady Milsintown[10] met on friendly Terms and all Differences between our Families were agreeably ended—

I have suffered since I had the Pleasure of seeing You with a Cough that increased to a very severe degree, but is now thank God much better, tho' I am still taking Asses Milk for it and ride out twice a Day which seem to have done me the most service of any thing—

You are by this time I imagine enjoying Yourself in recess from Business as I suppose Vacation-Time may be come—You will be so kind as to remember what we talked of in our last Interview; that if any agreeable occurrences in Your affairs fall out that are proper to be trusted to a Letter You will inform me of Them.[11] Pray give my best Respects to all my good Friends—Lord Monboddo, Mr. Hunter, the Hebrew Professor Robertson (I don't know whether Professor Hamilton is one of Your acquaintance or should wish You to remember me kindly to Him)—and all others whom You meet[12]—

Lady Rothes and the little stout Boy are, thank God, very well. She expects to be confined very soon; it was very agreeable to me to find he had not forgot me, he has now cut just as many teeth

[10] Lady Rothes's stepdaughter Mary (1753–99), second daughter of John, tenth Earl of Rothes. She had married, on 5 Nov. 1770, William Charles Colyear (c. 1747–1823), Viscount Milsington, later (1785) third Earl of Portmore (*Comp. Peer.* x. 606, xi. 203–04). The nature of the "differences" between the families is not known. Possibly they took opposite sides in the lawsuit over the estate of Rothes. See *post* From Langton, 12 May 1774, n. 9.

[11] The last interview undoubtedly took place at JB's on 10 May (*post* To Langton, 14 Aug. 1773, n. 2); but the subject of JB's affairs was not recorded as part of their conversation.

[12] James Robertson (1714–95), Professor of Hebrew and Oriental Languages at the University of Edinburgh, 1751–92,

was "the first really qualified Professor who held the chair" (Sir Alexander Grant, *Story of the University of Edinburgh* ii. 289). Langton distinguishes between Dr. James Robertson and Principal William Robertson (1721–93), the famous historian. Robert Hamilton (d. 2 Apr. 1787), Professor of Divinity at Edinburgh, was son of Principal William Hamilton (Grant ii. 283). "Mr. Hunter" was probably Sir William Forbes's partner James Hunter (1741–87), who came from Ayr and had been in Edinburgh College at the same time as JB (Journ. 10 Dec. 1774). In consequence of his marriage to an Ayrshire heiress, he took the name of Blair; he was later an M.P. and made a baronet. Burns held him in high regard.

as he is months old; fifteen—I will only add our best Respects to Mrs. Boswel and Miss Campbell and in hopes to hear from You soon remain, Dear Sir, Your obedient and affectionate humble Servant

BENNET LANGTON

To Bennet Langton, Saturday 14 August 1773

MS. Yale (L 839). A copy in Lawrie's hand (L 840) differs in substance only by the omission of a word, clearly by error. Sent 14 Aug. (Reg. Let.).

ADDRESS: To Bennet Langton Esq., of Langton, near Spilsby, Lincolnshire.

POSTMARK: AU 14.

Edinburgh, 14 August 1773

DEAR SIR: I hope this shall find you in a confirmed state of health, and possessed of two sons to support the ancient race of Langton.[1] I cannot forgive you your *will*.[2] Let Chambers be as bad as others have been in the East Indies,[3] he can do nothing that would shock me more than framing the barbarous deed by which a *Langton* would be set aside to make room for the brood of any fellow who may marry a daughter of the Family. Excuse me dear Sir. I have the masculine feudal principle as firm in my breast, as any old Roman had the *Amor Patriæ*. You must repent. At least you shall not persist without my preaching against you.

I am glad that you introduced Beattie to Mr. Burke and to Sir Joshua Reynolds. You know the high opinion which I have of all of them. I have read Sir Joshua's *Discourses* with great pleasure,

[1] JB's hope was not realized at this time, for Lady Rothes had given birth to a girl, Mary (d. 1796), on 16 July.

[2] On 10 May 1773, JB recorded in his journal: "Langton came to break[fast]. He was going to Chambers to make his will and settle on sisters. I was displeased at him." Langton did not literally settle his estate on his sisters Elizabeth, Diana, and Juliet, but in the table of succession that he drew up he gave them precedence over a remote heir male.

[3] A member of The Club since 1765,

Robert Chambers (1737–1803), later knighted (1777), was Vinerian Professor of Law and Principal of New Inn Hall at Oxford from 1766 until 1773, when he was appointed second judge of the supreme court of judicature in Bengal. He did not leave for India until 1774. JB refers to the increasing graft and corruption in the administration of Bengal by the East India Company from Feb. 1760, when Clive left for England the first time, until Warren Hastings was appointed governor in Dec. 1771.

though I dare say with not quite so high a relish as you who are a Painter.[4] When I was in Italy, I really acquired a considerable degree of taste in pictures.[5] But I find it has decayed from not exercising it. You would rejoice at the honours paid to Beattie at Oxford.[6] I would hope that by this time something substantial is done for him by Government.

I am in very high spirits at present. Mr. Johnson is actually come as far north as Newcastle; and I expect to have him under my roof this night.[7] We shall set out on wednesday next on our wild expedition to the highlands and some of the Hebrides. What an intellectual feast is before me! I shall never murmur though he should at times treat me with more roughness than ever. His roughness is an indication of the vigour of his genius.—You know you and I differ a little upon this head. But I am keen for my own opinion. That however is too ample a subject for a letter. I must only say that I cannot help having a kind of joy in recollecting that you with all your timid caution got a drubbing at Dilly's.[8] The

[4] Langton was, according to his son Peregrine, "in Painting so well able to judge *and* to copy; that when *Sir Joshua Reynolds*, his particular friend, lent him an *excellent* old Battle piece to copy; he returnd for a joke his own as the original [MS. "the original as his own"]: which Sir J. R. said after looking at, he thought it had not been so good, but when his mistake was known to him; said, he was surprized how Mr. L. should be able to paint to deceive him, who had bestow'd so small a portion of his (Mr. Langton) time upon that art" (PL-M's diary, 1806–08, p. 68). In the back of his own diary for 1762, Langton made a list of such art supplies as turpentine, linseed oil, various colours of oil paint, pencils, brushes, a palette-knife, easel, and canvas; and almost every volume of his diary contains pencil and ink sketches, including one of Langton Hall.

[5] JB travelled in Italy from 6 Jan. to 11 Oct. 1765. While there, he took a course in "antiquities" and attended art galleries faithfully. "My present study is Pictures," he wrote to Temple on 22 Apr. 1765. "It is delightfull. I am very fond of it, and I believe I shall form a true taste."

[6] Beattie was awarded the honorary degree of Doctor of Civil Law at Oxford on Friday 9 July 1773, in company with fourteen others. He was pleasantly surprised at the compliments paid to him and remarked, "Of those who received this degree at the same time wt. me, Sir Joshua Reynolds & I were the only persons (so far as I remember) who were thus distinguished by the encomium and applause extraordinary" (*Beattie's Diary*, p. 68).

[7] SJ, who had travelled up with Robert Chambers, left Newcastle on the morning of the 13th (*Letters SJ* i. 341) and arrived in Edinburgh the next evening, when JB "got a card from him about half an hour after 11, that he was at Boyd's. This relieved me" (Journ. 14 Aug.).

[8] At the Messrs. Dillys' (Edward, 1732–79; Charles, 1739–1807), publishers. On 7 May 1773, Langton "ventured to ask Dr. Johnson if there was not a material difference as to toleration of opinions which lead to action, and opinions merely speculative; for instance, would it be wrong in the magistrate to tolerate those who preach against the doctrine of the TRINITY? Johnson was highly offended, and said,

truth is, it was observed when you was here that you assumed a kind of superiority over me, as if you was never touched by that aweful rod, which has so often been applied to my back. It is natural then for me to feel some satisfaction in thinking that you had your share. I shall keep a full and exact Journal of this Johnsonian Tour, which will be very valuable.

My Wife and little daughter and niece are all well. I have had a very successful summer Session.[9] In short in most particulars I am as happy as you could wish me.[9a] All your friends here remember you with regard. Lord Monboddo has a second volume in the Press.[10] My wife joins me in best respects to you and Lady Rothes. I am, Dear Sir, yours sincerely

JAMES BOSWELL

To Bennet Langton, Thursday 4 November 1773

MS. Yale (L 841). A copy. Sent 4 Nov. (Reg. Let.).

Auchinleck, 4 Novr. 1773

DEAR SIR: After one of the most curious tours that can be imagined, which Mr. Johnson and I have made together, the particulars of which are faithfully recorded, we are now reposing ourselves at

'I wonder, Sir, how a gentleman of your piety can introduce this subject in a mixed company.'" Langton, "with submissive deference, said, he had only hinted at the question from a desire to hear Dr. Johnson's opinion upon it. . . . 'It may be considered . . . whether it would not be politick to tolerate in such a case.' JOHNSON. 'Sir, we have been talking of *right*: this is another question. *I* think it is *not* politick to tolerate in such a case'" (*Life* ii. 254). At The Club that night, SJ apologized to Goldsmith for offending him earlier in the day; he did not apologize to Langton (*ibid.* p. 256). See also Journ. 7 May 1773.

[9] He had reason to be gratified. Starting (21–31 May) with five causes before the General Assembly, he had been counsel for the accused in two capital criminal trials. Among his causes before the Court of Session had been Hinton *v.* Donaldson, historically one of the most important he was ever engaged in, for it established in Scotland the principle that an author's copyright did not exist at common law but only as defined by statute. His connexion with "Lord Fife's Politicks . . . a great prize in the lottery of business" which had come his way the previous winter (Journ. 10 Dec. 1772) called for a great deal of "writing", i.e. the preparation of papers for printing (Notes, 7 June–2 July 1773, *passim*). Seventeen printed legal papers from his hand have been reported for this session, a much larger number than for any other period of equal length.

[9a] Lawrie's copy omits "me".

[10] *Of the Origin and Progress of Language*, vol. ii, 1774.

Auchinleck.[1] You are a letter in my debt, but I write this because I understand that Mr. Johnson imagines that the reproof which he gave you at Dilly's has made you angry out of all proportion. It seems you left London without calling for him.[2] I know his sincere regard for you and he well observes that if a friendship of many years is to cease, on account of such a casual speech

> "Who then to frail humanity shall trust
> But limns in water or but writes in dust."[3]

You know I allways was of opinion that you deserved the reproof which you got. But suppose you did not deserve it, are you for so slight a cause to break with one for whom you cannot but have the highest veneration and to whose counsels you have been much obliged? I am uneasy at the thought. Lord Hailes and I have met again on friendly terms on occasion of Mr. Johnson's coming to Scotland.[4] If you have still any discontent, I beg that you may

[1] JB and SJ left Edinburgh on 18 Aug. and arrived at Auchinleck at the end of their tour on 2 Nov. (*Life* v. 51, 375).

[2] SJ had written to JB on 5 July that "[Langton] left the town without taking leave of me, and is gone in deep dudgeon to [Langton]. Is not this very childish? Where is now my legacy [a reference to Langton's will; see *post* From Langton, c. 17 Nov., n. 7]?" (*Letters SJ* i. 334).

[3] The world's a bubble, and the life of man
lesse then a span,
In his conception wretched, from the wombe,
so to the tombe:
Curst from the cradle, and brought up to yeares,
with cares and feares.
Who then to fraile mortality shall trust,
But limmes the water, or but writes in dust.
First stanza of a four-stanza poem, "The World", attributed to Francis Bacon. The text is from Thomas Farnaby, *Florilegium Epigrammatum Graecorum, eorumque Latino versu a variis redditorum*, 1629, pp. 8–10. SJ had quoted to JB the same couplet in the same context at

Aberdeen on 22 Aug. (*Life* v. 89).

[4] Sir David Dalrymple, Lord Hailes (1726–92), Scottish judge and historian, had been offended by JB's behaviour on at least two occasions. He and JB were on opposite sides in the Douglas Cause; when the House of Lords reversed the decision against Archibald Douglas, in Mar. 1769, there were riots in Edinburgh, and sympathizers of Douglas were instructed to light their windows to show their approval. The judges of the Court of Session refused to illuminate regardless of the way they had voted in the cause, and many of them had their windows broken by a mob headed by JB. Lord Hailes, whose windows were broken, suspected JB (From Hailes, 4 Mar. 1769; From Dempster, c. 12 Mar. 1769). In the autumn of 1771, JB, dissatisfied with the way in which General Paoli had been received by Edinburgh officials, wrote, anonymously, two abusive letters to *The London Chronicle* criticizing the Lord Provost, Sir David's younger brother. Dalrymple wrote to JB in December asking if he had written the letters. JB failed to reply, and their relationship became considerably strained (*Lit. Car.* p. 247; From Hailes, early Dec. 1771).

dismiss it, and write to our revered friend at my house in Edinburgh, by the return of the post, that I may have the happiness of thinking that upon the same occasion I have contributed to the reconciliation of those who should never have any difference. I have said nothing to Mr. Johnson of my writing to you. I offer my best respects to Lady Rothes and am with sincere regard, Dear Sir, your affectionate humble servant

From Bennet Langton,
c. Wednesday 17 November 1773[1]

MS. Yale (C 1682). Note at top by JB: This Letter I received in November 1774 [sic] after Mr. Johnson had set out for London.

[Langton]

DEAR SIR, Let me begin with returning You my sincere *Thanks* for Your Letter, (which I received on Saturday last) *which* are certainly demanded of me in the highest Degree by the kind Interest You take in a particular that I esteem of such moment to me, as I do Mr. Johnson's Friendship—Your Letter lies now before me and I will speak to the particulars as they stand in it— in the first place I must mention that there is some Mistake as to my not calling upon Mr. Johnson before my leaving London, which I do distinctly remember to have done; very probably I might not have a Card with me, with my Name, to leave, and *so*, he might not have been told of it—I cannot but be greatly pleased, my Dear Sir, with what You next say, of Your being persuaded of Mr. Johnson's kind Regard for me, as well as of any Regret that he has been so good as to express at any apprehended discontinuance of our Friendship—I do not like to say much on the subject of what I confess has given me pain—You say I deserved the Reproof; to which, as You only say it in general, I cannot attempt speaking particularly, except only, that if the introducing one or two Particulars, in what I said at that time, of too serious a Kind was not well advised, as I am afraid it was not, in the manner at least that I did it; I had no Intention of being any way

---

[1] SJ left Edinburgh on 20 Nov. (*Life* v. 401); the letter probably arrived shortly thereafter. Since letters ordinarily took four days to arrive at Edinburgh from Langton's Lincolnshire home, 17 Nov. seems a likely date.

troublesome to Mr. Johnson, and I hope I did not express myself with any want of Complaisance to Him; I could not therefore but think the manner of his checking me unkind; and as my present Situation, so disagreeable in that Respect, occasions our meetings to be so much less frequent than they have been, to have any unkind or angry Passages happen in those few I can obtain, gives me the more Concern—I will not detain You any further on this head than to repeat my Thanks for this Your kind Endeavour to remove any Misunderstanding there might have been on that occasion we are speaking of.

It gives me sincere Pleasure indeed Dear Sir, to receive Your information of being on Friendly Terms with Lord Hailes; as he appeared to me to be a Man that one should have great Reason to regret being separated from; which I hope, as to You and Him, no untoward Circumstances will ever happen again to effect—I must add to what I was speaking of before, my particular Request that You will use Your best Interest to second the Endeavour I use, in the Letter to Mr. Johnson that accompanies this,[2] to persuade him to give me his Company here as long as convenient on his Return.

Mrs. Boswel and Your little Lady I hope are well; it would be no small satisfaction to Her to see You returned safe from Your Tour—You may imagine how much I long to know the particulars of it—I have constantly consulted my Edinburgh paper with eagerness, to see if there was any Information about You; Yesterday I observed an odd mixture of Articles relating to Your Expedition; one or two of a reasonable and proper kind, and others very pert and silly—it is pretended I see that the account of it is to be printed[3]—though it would be too much to expect that You should be very full in Your accounts, especially with the *Tide of Business* that I hope is coming at large upon You this

[2] Langton's letter to SJ has not been recovered.

[3] Langton probably refers to a series of paragraphs which appeared in *The Edinburgh Advertiser*, 9–12 Nov. 1773, xx. 309. The article announced the arrival of SJ and JB at Edinburgh, and reported, "Dr. Johnson is preparing an account of this tour for the press, in which the learning, prejudices and pedantry of the celebrated Lexicographer will be fully displayed." A brief summary of their itinerary followed. Another paragraph, truly "very pert and silly", facetiously commented, "Dr. Young wrote *The Centaur not Fabulous*. Dr. Johnson will *be* it; for after passing three months in Scotland, and living on oats, the food of horses, he will certainly be half man half horse when he returns to London, so that his friend Sir Joshua Reynolds must give us an *equestrian* portrait of him."

winter, it would be kind if You would now and then, as You have Leisure, put down some of the most remarkable Observations You have made, and send them to me when Your Paper is filled—[4]

I was as You observe a Letter in Your debt, but had deferred my answering Your former Favour till Your Return home as I had no means of directing to You while abroad—in *that* You speak of our valuable Friend Beattie; he informed me, in a Letter, of His Majesty's Kindness to Him;[5] I have been deprived of the Pleasure I had hoped for of seeing Him in his Way to Scotland on account of his being detained in attendance on this Concern; I had however the satisfaction of two Letters from Him[6] in which the amiableness of His Character appears strongly; he speaks of having a Purpose of visiting England next Summer and then encourages me to hope for seeing Him.

Your endeavouring to inspire me with the *feudal Principle* I should wish to pay a proper Regard to, but I cannot say I am quite convinced but rather under some suspence as to my opinion as to the obligation of confining all possessions or Inheritances of Lands to Male-Descendants; I should be very glad to listen to Mr. Johnson on the Subject[7] and hope, as I mentioned above, I shall in no long time have an opportunity of it.

[4] In a letter to Beattie, 2 Dec. (Aberdeen. C. 164), Langton, after mentioning SJ's departure for London, wrote, "I live in hopes that My Friend Mr. Boswel will let me hear some account of Their curious Expedition—He is one of The best Persons that could have been concerned in it—as his memory is very strong; and he is at great care to commit to *writing* things that occur to deserve it—"

[5] Beattie, who had come to London to obtain assistance from the Crown, received notice on 21 Aug. 1773 that the King had been pleased to grant him a pension of two hundred pounds a year; and on 24 Aug. he was given a private audience with the King and Queen at Kew, with only Dr. John James Majendie, instructor to Queen Charlotte and tutor to the Prince of Wales, present. The interview lasted "for upwards of an hour"; and Majendie informed Beattie "that it was a most uncommon thing for a private man and a commoner to be honoured with so long an audience" (*Beattie's Diary*, pp. 85, 88, 124).

[6] Beattie was invited to Langton on 17 May, the day before Langton left London (*Beattie's Diary*, p. 35), and again, in a letter from Langton on 17 June (Aberdeen, C. 114). Beattie recorded in his diary on 2 Sept. (p. 91) that he had written "to Mr. Langton, acquainting him with the reasons that prevent my waiting upon him on my way to the north: he lives thirty miles eastward from Lincoln; to go so far out of our way at this season, might be attended with much inconvenience as well as delay." It is clear from Langton's answer to Beattie on 2 Dec. that the letter recorded in the diary was the second of the two mentioned here. In addition to giving the reasons for the Beatties' not visiting Langton, this letter informed him of the pension and the audience with their Majesties. Langton's invitation was renewed in the Dec. letter.

[7] In the *Life* (ii. 261–62) JB recorded

One Question I should wish to put, as to what You observed in Your Tour, whether the Emigrations from the Northern parts of Scotland are so serious an Evil as the papers represent[8]— which You know they are continually crying out about—

While I recollect it, I have a request to make, which is a Copy of the Prologue You wrote for Mr. Ross at the opening [of] his Theatre, if it is agreeable to You to give it away—

Mr. Johnson I dare say was pleased with Auchinleck; I imagine by the Time of Year that Lord Auchinleck was there as I remember he was so later in the Year when I was there—I imagine You could hardly meet with any thing in Your whole Expedition more romantick than the Fragment of a Castle behind Your House— I imagine You visited the Justice Clerk's curious bridge—[9]

in great detail SJ's opinions on male inheritance and Langton's will: he "maintained the dignity and propriety of male succession, in opposition to the opinion of one of our friends, who had that day employed Mr. Chambers to draw his will, devising his estate to his three sisters, in preference to a remote heir male. . . . 'An ancient estate should always go to males. It is mighty foolish to let a stranger have it because he marries your daughter, and takes your name. As for an estate newly acquired by trade, you may give it, if you will, to the dog *Towser*, and let him keep his *own* name. . . . You, Chambers, made it for him. I trust you have had more conscience than to make him say, "being of sound understanding;" . . . I hope he has left me a legacy. I'd have his will turned into verse, like a ballad.' . . . Johnson could not stop his merriment . . . he appeared to be almost in a convulsion; and, in order to support himself, laid hold of one of the posts at the side of the foot pavement, and sent forth peals so loud, that in the silence of the night his voice seemed to resound from Temple-bar to Fleet-ditch." See also Journ. 10 May, 14 Aug. 1773, for JB's original version of this event.

[8] "A gentleman of very considerable property in the Western isles" wrote to *Scots Mag.* (Sept. 1772) that emigrants since 1768 had carried with them at least £10,000 in specie, but that this loss was less important than the depopulation of the country. He warned that "the continual emigrations from Ireland and Scotland, will soon render our colonies independent on the mother-country" (xxxiv. 515–16). Shortly after Langton wrote this letter, *The Edinburgh Advertiser* stated that a report on the fatal effects of emigration was to be laid before the King and that the problem would probably come under the consideration of Parliament the next year (26–30 Nov. 1773, xx. 348). There was much talk for and against legislation, until the problem was alleviated by the events of 1776. See *Life* v. 205–06.

[9] SJ was to relate of Auchinleck, in *A Journey to the Western Islands*, "I was, however, less delighted with the elegance of the modern mansion, than with the sullen dignity of the old castle. . . . It is, like other castles, built upon a point of rock, and was, I believe, anciently surrounded with a moat. There is another rock near it, to which the drawbridge, when it was let down, is said to have reached" (*Works of SJ*, Yale Ed. ix. 161–62). And JB, in the *Tour* (*Life* v. 379), admitted, "I cannot figure a more romantick scene." See *Life* i. 462; ii. 270; iii. 433, 539; v. 379. The bridge was on the neighbouring estate of Barskimming, belonging to Thomas Miller, the Lord Justice-Clerk, whose son was later to threaten JB with a duel because of an

Lady Rothes desires to join me in best Compliments Sir to Yourself and Mrs. Boswel and Miss Campbell—Her Friend George runs about and tattles very notably—my little Daughter who I think about half equals Yours in age is a fine thriving Child—My best Regards to all my Friends whom You meet— I received a Letter lately from Sir Wm. Forbes[10] which I am going soon to answer—I hope Mr. Johnson and Dr. Blacklock will meet[11]—as I know the high Regard he is held in by the Dr.— Adieu and believe me, Dear Sir, Your obedient and affectionate humble Servant

BENNET LANGTON

To Bennet Langton, Sunday 10 April 1774

MS. BM Add. MSS. 38150, ff. 54–55. A copy in Lawrie's hand at Yale (L 842) omits a word, clearly in error.

Edinburgh, 10 April 1774

DEAR SIR: The death of one friend endears to us still more those who survive. I got the news yesterday that we have lost Goldsmith.[1] It has affected me much; and while I lament his departure,

anonymous letter JB had written in a newspaper against his father (Journ. 6–18 Oct. 1774). The bridge, which still exists, "is a curiosity well worth observation. It is of one entire arch 90 foot high and 81 broad, it is founded in the rock fifteen foot above the surface of the water the banks of which [are] so high that you cannot perceive that there is any river there till you are within [a] few yards of it" (from the journal of John Inglis, H.M. General Register House, Edinburgh [Inglis MSS.], extracts from which were kindly supplied by Sir James Fergusson of Kilkerran, Bart.).

[10] Apparently a letter referred to in the letter from Langton to Beattie, 2 Dec. 1773 (Aberdeen, C. 164): "I had the Pleasure of hearing from Sir William Forbes lately who mentions what I wish may be executed; Your having Thoughts, Sir, of republishing Your Essay with some other pieces that have not yet

appeared; and add his Wishes that the second part of the Essay may soon appear."

[11] SJ and Dr. Thomas Blacklock (1721–91), blind Scottish poet, met at breakfast on 17 Aug. 1773. SJ wrote to Mrs. Thale the same day: "This morning I saw at breakfast Dr. Blacklock the blind poet, who does not remember to have seen light, and is read to by a poor Scholar in Latin, Greek, and French. He was originally a poor scholar himself. I looked on him with reverence" (Letters SJ i. 341). See Life v. 46–48 for a description of the meeting. Some years before, SJ had remarked that Blacklock's descriptions of visible objects "are combinations of what he has remembered of the works of other writers who could see" (Life i. 466).

[1] Goldsmith had died on 4 Apr.

and am warmly impressed with affection and regard to you who are one among the few whom I highly value, it gives me much pain to reflect that I have been so many months indebted to you for an excellent letter without acknowledging it. The same tenderness of disposition which makes me feel my being in the wrong to you, with extraordinary sensibility, makes me at the same time comfort myself with a kind of sympathetick feeling that you will readily forgive me. In that persuasion my worthy Sir, I now sit down, and I trust I shall not be dissappointed.

Mr. Johnson was set out for London before your letter to him arrived. I transmitted it to him by the very first post; and I suppose you would hear from him very soon after. It gave me sincere joy to find that there was no reason for the apprehension that he entertained of your having broke with him. The way in which he expressed that apprehension was a proof of his sincere love for you. I wish your letter had reached him here, that I might have had the immediate pleasure of participating his satisfaction. I had a very friendly letter from him lately.[2] He saw with the eye of a Master of Human Nature, certain unhappy circumstances in my situation of which you and I have talked, and which I am sorry to say still remain as they were.[3] He fortified my mind

[2] *Letters SJ* i. 400–02. JB received the letter on 23 Mar. (Reg. Let.).

[3] The "unhappy circumstances" were no doubt his belief that Lady Auchinleck was ill disposed to him (From Temple, 27 Dec. 1771, 5 Oct. 1772) and Lord Auchinleck's expressed dissatisfaction. In the spring of 1762, in return for a guaranteed allowance of £100 a year, JB had signed a deed empowering his father to vest the estate in trustees of his own choosing if JB should succeed under the terms of his mother's contract of marriage (*Earlier Years*, pp. 80–81, 479). When JB married and settled down, he assumed that his father would voluntarily surrender this deed though continuing (indeed increasing) the allowance, and would make legal provision for Mrs. Boswell in case she should be left a widow. Lord Auchinleck preferred to leave him in uncertainty and under displeasure because he wished JB to join with him in an entail, and JB was violently opposed to the settlement on heirs general that Lord Auchinleck favoured (Journ. 13 Aug. 1769; 21 Mar. 1772). At the end of the Summer Session, 1772, JB asked him outright for the paper of 1762, and Lord Auchinleck refused to give it up. JB, who was "really vexed", thereupon declined to accompany him to Auchinleck (Journ. 9, 11 Aug. 1772; From Pringle, 19 Sept. 1772; 4, 25 Mar. 1773). Langton arrived in Edinburgh at a time when relations were particularly strained. Complaints reported later—of the alleged imprudence and extravagance of JB's marriage, of his jaunts to England, and of his "going over Scotland with a *brute*" (To Temple, 19 June 1775)— may all also have been made by the time the present letter was written. It is not clear that Lord Auchinleck had by this time heard of JB's strong desire to transfer to the English bar (Journ. 22 May 1768; 8 July 1769; 30 Mar. 1772),

with manly resolution, of which he has a noble store. He is certainly to give the World some Account of his Tour to the Highlands and Hebrides. He will not only entertain more richly than an ordinary Traveller; but will furnish much instruction on a variety of subjects. The Emigration of which you hear so much struck him as a very serious Evil; and I am persuaded that he will put it in such a light as to alarm Government.[4] Whether he will be able to point out a method to prevent it, consistently with the British Constitution I much doubt. But he seemed pleased with the idea, when he observed that in France, such a man as Sir Alexander Macdonald would receive a message from his Sovereign.[5]

When I began this letter, I imagined that two pages would contain it; so I wrote upon the opposite page my Prologue which you desired to have. It was published at the time in Newspapers and Magazines. It had a good effect when it was spoken, and calmed a very wild opposition to Ross.[6] Lord Mansfield said to me, It was a very pretty copy of verses; that he liked the judicious

---

but if he had heard, that would probably have been the greatest cause of all for dissatisfaction.

[4] "Many have departed both from the main of Scotland, and from the Islands; and all that go may be considered as subjects lost to the British crown; for a nation scattered in the boundless regions of America resembles rays diverging from a focus. All the rays remain, but the heat is gone. Their power consisted in their concentration: when they are dispersed, they have no effect. . . . Once none went away but the useless and poor; in some parts there is now reason to fear, that none will stay but those who are too poor to remove themselves, and too useless to be removed at the cost of others" (*Works of SJ*, Yale Ed. ix. 131–32).

[5] Both JB and SJ were disgusted with their reception by Sir Alexander and disapproved of his policy of raising his rents, thereby distressing his tenants and causing them to emigrate (*Life* v. 148 n. 1). SJ maintained, "Were an oppressive chieftain a subject of the French king, he would probably be admonished by a *letter* [probably a *lettre de cachet*]"

(*ibid.* p. 206). Sir Alexander (c. 1745–1795), ninth Baronet of Sleat and first Baron MacDonald, later quarrelled with JB over remarks made about him in the *Tour*.

[6] The King, on 22 May 1767, by an act extending the royalty of the city of Edinburgh, was enabled to grant letters patent for establishing an Edinburgh theatre. David Ross and John Lee, former manager of the Edinburgh theatre, both applied for the patent; and it was assigned to Ross. Disgruntled supporters of Lee threatened in the newspapers to boycott the performance, "in case Mr. Ross shall dare to act". Ross promised to resign the patent if the opposition were unsatisfied with his management after two years. The theatre was opened with Henry Jones's tragedy, *The Earl of Essex*, on Wednesday 9 Dec. 1767, with Ross, who spoke the *Prologue*, in the title role (*Scots Mag.* 1767, xxix. 322, 613–14). See *post* Appendix 1 for the copy sent to Langton; and *New CBEL* ii. 1218–19 for a list of newspapers and periodicals in which the *Prologue* appeared.

style of it. It was so conciliating.[7]—Was not this a great deal from a Lord Chief Justice who was Pope's Friend?

Our friend Lord Monboddo's second Volume on the *Origin and Progress of Language*, will, I dare say give you pleasure, though you may not be inclined altogether *jurare in verba*[8] of his Lordship. Lord Kames has published two very dear Volumes of *Sketches of the History of Man*.[9] At least I think them very dear, from what I have read of them. He has a prodigious quantity of Quotation, and there seems to be little of what he gives as his own that is just, or that has not been better said by others. You will have seen *A Father's Legacy to his Daughters* by Dr. Gregory.[10] His amiable mind appears in it. But I could not but agree with a Lady who observed to me, that the publication of it puts his daughters in somewhat an aukward situation, as every body will be comparing their conduct with the model, without making allowance for the difference between speculative and actual propriety. Have you read Warton's first Volume of the *History of Poetry*.[11] He will have a more agreable field as he advances.

---

[7] William Murray, first Baron (1756) and Earl (1776) of Mansfield (1705–93), Lord Chief Justice of the King's Bench and twice Chancellor of the Exchequer, refusing the post of Lord Chancellor, was a friend of Warburton, Hurd, Bolingbroke, and Pope. Pope dedicated to him the *Imitation of the Sixth Epistle of the first Book of Horace*. JB describes him as one of the "bellows" who blew the fire of Garrick's vanity (*Life* ii. 227). He paid the compliment to JB's *Prologue* on 20 May 1768 (Journ.). JB treasured it and quoted it in a memoir of himself he wrote for *The European Magazine* in 1791 (*Lit. Car.* p. xxxvi).

[8] "Swear to every word".

Ac ne forte roges, quo me duce, quo lare tuter:
Nullius addictus jurare in verba magistri.
(Horace, *Epistles* I. i. 13–14)
"Do you ask, perchance, who is my chief, in what home I take shelter? I am not bound over to swear as any master dictates" (H. R. Fairclough's translation in Loeb ed.). The motto of the Royal Society, *Nullius in verba*, was taken from

this passage and indicated the Society's determination to doubt the word of untested authority (Sir Henry Lyons, *The Royal Society, 1660–1940*, 1944, p. 39).

[9] *Sketches of the History of Man*, 2 vols., 1774. Two extracts from it had been published in Mar. in *The Edinburgh Advertiser*, xxi: "On Luxury" (p. 161) and "On the progress of great to small states" (p. 177). The two volumes sold for £2. 2s. bound (*Gent. Mag.* xliv. 229).

[10] London, 1774. The book was a series of paternal essays addressed to his daughters (*ante* From Langton, c. 5 Mar. 1773, n. 7) by Gregory, containing surprisingly liberal advice and opinions on love, friendship, marriage, religion, and feminine behaviour. Extracts from it were published during Apr. in two issues of *The Edinburgh Advertiser* (xxi. 209; 225–26).

[11] The first volume of Thomas Warton's *The History of English Poetry from the Close of the Eleventh to the Commencement of the Eighteenth Century*, containing two dissertations, "On the Origin of

I am not to be in London this spring; but am going through a full[11a] course of Scotch Law, with a brother Advocate.[12] My Wife joins me in respectful compliments to you and Lady Rothes; ⟨and⟩[13] I remain, Dear Sir, your faithful humble servant

JAMES BOSWELL

From Bennet Langton, Thursday 12 May 1774

MS. Yale (C 1683). Received 16 May (Reg. Let.).

Langton, May 12th. 1774

DEAR SIR, The sight of Your Hand in the Direction of Your Letter I assure You was highly acceptable, though You had made me wait so long for that Pleasure, and, with the exceedingly friendly and affecting Contents, I could not but be strongly moved—Poor dear Goldsmith's Loss I deplore feelingly; to hear of it was a Subject both of deep Concern, as well as of great Surprize—one should have thought Him as likely to live at least as any of our Society; I don't know whether You had been a great deal in his Company or not; if You have, I am sure You must often have remarked with high satisfaction those frequent Effusions of a kind and affectionate Spirit towards His Friends which did such Honour to His native sensibility—various Instances of that kind I treasure up in my memory, and shall be likely often to revolve them—

I am happy to find, Dear Sir, that You appear to think favourably of what I expressed in relation to Mr. Johnson and thank You for

Romantic Fiction in Europe" and "On the Introduction of Learning into England", covered the period from c. 1066 through Chaucer. It had only recently been published (*London Chronicle*, 19–22 Mar. 1774).

[11a] Lawrie's copy omits this word.

[12] Charles Hay (1747–1811), a close friend of JB (see *A Series of Original Portraits and Caricature Etchings by the late John Kay*, 1837, i. 169; ii. 392). Later in the summer, JB reported, "Mr. Charles Hay and I this day resumed our study of Erskine's *Institute* where we left

off last vacation. I went to his house then. He agreed to come to mine now" (Journ. 19 Aug. 1774). JB and Hay completed the course of Erskine's *Institute* on Friday 16 Sept. 1774 (Journ.). Hay frequently advised JB in legal matters and aided him in trying to save John Reid, who was hanged for sheepstealing on 21 Sept. of this year, but the friendship did not last. See Journ. 12 July 1777.

[13] Ink faded. Missing word supplied from Lawrie's copy.

Your immediate conveyance of my Letter to Him—I endeavoured in that Letter to avoid any thing that I could apprehend to be disagreeable or an obstruction to being on the most friendly terms with Him, as much as I could; but in what light he received what I wrote, I am unhappily ignorant as I have not heard from Him since; I should be very glad to have Your kind Suppositions verified; that he would be pleased with my Expressions of Respect and Friendship towards Him; but to be sure his Silence makes it the less encouraging to hope so.

I wonder and am concerned at what You mention, relating to particulars in Your own Situation, that what is unpleasant in them is not removed; has the Gentleman who You told me was Your Friend, and, as I understood, was likely to have influence, I mean Sir J. Pringle,[1] used his best endeavours to be of Service? Mr. Johnson is very kind in suggesting those just Thoughts on the occasion he is so admirably qualified to impart—but I earnestly hope there will soon be such an alteration for the better as to leave no Occasion for Your exerting any other Affection of mind than Gratitude and Friendship, and this state of things, that requires Resolution and Patience, prove of short continuance—

The Publication You give Hopes of, of Your Tour by Mr. Johnson will not I hope be long delayed[2]—I cannot but feel it as very disagreeable to continue in such Ignorance of all Your adventures—if You will be so kind as to be a better Correspondent than the last Winter, and let me hear from You soon, do tell me, at least as to one particular, how much was true of what was said in the papers concerning the Laird of Macleod; (I think the Name was) that Mr. Johnson expressed himself in the highest terms of his Abilities, and his improvement of them; as such a Character one naturally wants to know more of[3]—

[1] Sir John (1707–82), Scot, physician, scientist, president of the Royal Society, was Lord Auchinleck's contemporary and warm friend. JB had solicited his intervention in the difficult days of 1762 (*Earlier Years*, pp. 109, 112 n., 489), and again turned to him for help in the autumn of 1772. Pringle did exert himself in the matter, but warned JB that he could not be impartial: "I shall be glad to serve you, but remember in all cases of opposition, I shall be on the minis-

terial side; I mean on that of your father's my oldest and best friend" (From Pringle, 4 Mar. 1773; see also From Pringle, 19 Sept. 1772, 25 Mar. 1773).
[2] *A Journey to the Western Islands of Scotland* was published 15 Jan. 1775 (*Life* ii. 284 n. 2).
[3] "Extract from Notes of Mr. Samuel Johnson's Tour to Scotland and the Western Isles. ... He was a Week at the Seat of the Laird of M'Leod in the Isle of Sky. This young Chieftain is not

It makes me the less regret my not going to London this Spring that You tell me You are not to be there—one Reason, and I imagine the principal one that detains You, is what I have heard that You expect in no long time an addition to Your Family[4]—I wish You had been more express in the mention how Mrs. Boswel and Your little Daughter were in Health—I hope soon to hear a good account of them from You—

Your acquaintance with Lord Hailes I hope goes on in a perfectly agreeable manner since the Reconciliation You told me of—I think I saw lately that there was some Publication in his Name[5]—but my living so much out of the way of getting Books pleasantly or conveniently, makes me often more behind-hand in acquaintance with ingenious new Publications than I should be—accordingly I have not seen Warton's Book yet—from Lord Monboddo's I have seen an Extract, what he says of the Good of being well acquainted with the Classical Greek and Roman Authors[6] seemed to me to be very justly and handsomely expressed—I am sorry to see in the papers the severe occasion of affliction that has befallen him in the Loss of His Son—[7]

It would have been acceptable if You had just mentioned at least how Your Business in Law has gone on; I hope more than answerably to the Improvement of it that You communicated to me before I left Edinburgh—Your side has had a remarkable Victory in Donaldson's Cause—We at a Distance are only left

yet one and twenty, but is an Honour to his Country by his generous Regard for his People: He stops their emigrating to America, by which, while he preserves the Consequence of his own Family, he does an essential Service to the State, by keeping so many brave Men at home for its Defence. Mr. Johnson said, 'he never met with a Man, who, at his Age, had advanced his Understanding so much, who had more Desire to learn, or who had learnt more'" (*St. James's Chronicle*, 29 Jan.–1 Feb. 1774). The "extract" was also published in *The Whitehall Evening-Post*, 19–22 Feb. 1774. It must have been contributed by JB himself, for it combines verbatim two passages from his unpublished journal, 11 and 18 Sept. 1773.

[4] JB's second daughter, Euphemia, was born 20 May 1774.

[5] *Remarks on the History of Scotland*, by Sir David Dalrymple, although published in 1773, was advertised in an Apr. 1774 issue of *The London Chronicle* (xxxv. 375).

[6] Perhaps a reference to a review of Monboddo's book in *The Monthly Review; or, Literary Journal* for Sept. 1773, which quoted an extract on the impossibility of valid philosophical thought without a knowledge and the assistance of the ancients (xlix. 169–70).

[7] Arthur Burnett, Lord Monboddo's only son, aged eleven, died 27 Apr. 1774 at his father's house in St. John's Street, Edinburgh (*London Chronicle*, 7–10 May 1774, xxxv. 446). SJ had been pleased with his Latin (Journ. 21 Aug. 1773).

very imperfectly to guess why Lord Mansfield was silent upon it[8]—I wish much to have heard Your pleadings in the Cause of Lady Rothes, in which I see You was engaged;[9] but sure it was

[8] Langton indirectly refers to two causes, both involving JB's friend, the Scottish bookseller Alexander Donaldson (fl. 1750–94), and the question of literary property. Between 1767 and 1770, Donaldson published, among other books, Stackhouse's History of the Holy Bible, the copyright and publishing rights of which were claimed by John Hinton, a London bookseller. Hinton brought suit against Donaldson and his colleagues, and the hearing began on 20 July 1773 before the Court of Session. JB was one of the counsel for Donaldson. The Lords of Session, among them Auchinleck, Kames, and Hailes, decided in Donaldson's favour, with only Lord Monboddo voting in favour of Hinton (JB's Decision of the Court of Session, upon the Question of Literary Property; in the Cause John Hinton of London, Bookseller, Pursuer; against Alexander Donaldson, 1774). The Scottish court therefore determined that literary copyright existed, not in common law, but by statute, i.e. not in perpetuity but for a limited period of years. Donaldson also had a bookshop in London, for which he printed cheap editions of popular books "in defiance of the supposed common-law right of Literary Property" (Life i. 437). In 1769, the Court of the King's Bench, Lord Mansfield presiding, decided in the cause, Millar v. Taylor, in favour of perpetual copyright at common law. Donaldson challenged this decision by printing The Seasons. Thomas Becket, who had acquired a share of the assumed perpetual copyright, obtained an injunction from the Lord Chancellor in 1772 against Donaldson, who appealed to the House of Lords (A. S. Collins, Authorship in the Days of Johnson, 1927, pp. 95–99). On 22 Feb. 1774, the Lords finally determined the cause in Donaldson's favour and reversed the Lord Chancellor's injunction, thereby confirming the statutory nature of literary property. "Lord

Mansfield was in the House, but did not speak a word on the subject, either as a Judge or a Peer, although he had formerly decided in the court of King's Bench, for the perpetual monopoly, in ... Millar against Taylor. It was much wondered at, (say the London newspapers) that Lord Mansfield did not support that opinion in the H. of Peers, which he had formerly so warmly espoused. . . . This question, which has been litigated for more than thirty years, is now happily determined, both in England and Scotland, and authors are now in a better situation in Great Britain, than in any other country" (Edinburgh Advertiser, 25 Feb.–1 Mar 1774, xxi. 132).

[9] On 2 Mar. 1774, "the Court of Session determined a competition for the estate of Rothes, between Lady Jane Elizabeth Leslie, Countess of Rothes, daughter of the late Earl [and therefore elder stepdaughter of Langton's wife], and the Hon. Andrew Leslie, his Lordship's brother. The question turned upon the import of an entail in 1684, by which the estate is settled upon John Lord Leslie, and his heirs male, or eldest heir female. Mr. Leslie contended, that these words imported, that until the whole heirs male of Lord Leslie were exhausted, no heir female could succeed; and that the word or, here had the same meaning as the usual words whom failing. The Countess maintained, that the clause was only an uncommon method of expressing heirs whatsoever, the explanation of which is plainly heirs male or female; and that the intention of the deed certainly was, that the nearest heir of whatever sex should be preferred ... this not being a male fief, having descended from Countess Margaret, daughter of the Duke of Rothes. The court determined in favour of the Countess. The counsel for the Countess were, the Dean of the Faculty, the Lord Advocate, Mr.

with some repugnance, when in support of the Female Claim; since though I doubt not there were weighty Proofs of the Justice of it—Your feelings could not easily be reconciled to the original appointment from which Her Right is derived, averse as You are to Female Inheritance of Lands and Honours—

I return many thanks for the Prologue, which has given great Entertainment to all I have communicated it to here, and several Copies of it have been requested—it was certainly excellently suited to gain Attention and Favour.

As I have just at present no Franks to Sir Wm. Forbes I trouble You with a Letter inclosed to Him which I beg You to send Him when convenient—He wrote me word of poor Dr. Beattie's accident;[10] I hope poor Man he is well recover'd of it; I see the 2d part of the *Minstrel* is just come out[11]—and must endeavour to get it—

We are all here, thank God, very well—Lady Rothes desires her kindest Compliments Sir to Yourself and Mrs. Boswel—and joins me in hearty wishes that there might be a Chance of the pleasure of seeing You in this part of the world—Adieu, and believe me, Dear Sir, Yours sincerely

BENNET LANGTON

To Bennet Langton, Saturday 31 December 1774[1]

MS. Yale (L 843). A copy in Lawrie's hand (except as noted). Sent 3 Jan. (Reg. Let.).

HEADING in JB's hand: To Mr. Langton.

Edinburgh, 31 Decer. 1774

MY DEAR SIR: Epistolary debtors are like other debtors. As time

---

Andrew Crosbie, Mr. Alexander Murray, and Mr. James Boswell. . . . The estate is said to be worth £2000 per annum" (*Edinburgh Advertiser* xxi. 141). Andrew Leslie appealed to the House of Lords; but the Lords confirmed the decision of the Court of Session on 10 May 1774 (*Scots Peer.* vii. 305, 307).

[10] Beattie fell and broke his arm in the early spring (*Life of Beattie* ii. 25; Margaret Forbes, *Beattie and his Friends*, 1904, p. 104).

[11] Extracts from *The Minstrel; or The Progress of Genius, a Poem*, vol. ii, 1774, were published in *The London Chronicle*, 2–4 Aug. xxxvi. 117, and the book was reviewed in *The Monthly Review* for Sept. (li. 189–93), but I have found no advertisements indicating spring publication.

[1] Apparently only begun on 31 Dec. See last sentence of second paragraph and note. JB recorded a letter sent to

advances, what they owe becomes heavier and heavier; and they sink into a kind of despondency, when by a vigorous exertion they might soon clear themselves. In the unhappy state which I have been describing do I now feel myself, for, indeed, my much esteemed friend, I am seriously distressed with my debt to you. Our common *Banker* Sir William Forbes gives me both joy and uneasiness, by communicating to me, from time to time his letters from you.[2] I rejoice to hear of your wellfare; but I am uneasy to see with how much punctuality you keep up your correspondence, while there are such woefull cessations on my part,—though I cannot tell how.

It would have given me pleasure to have sent you specimens of the curious particulars of Mr. Johnsons Tour to the Hebrides, But, the truth is, I could not select. You will soon have a rich feast by the perusal of Mr. Johnsons Book. I shall be happy when we meet, if the Journal which I kept can afford you any additional satisfaction; and I persuade myself, it will; for I have recorded many of Mr. Johnsons observations which he himself does not remember and I may even presume to say that some of my own descriptions and remarks will entertain you. Sir William Forbes is much pleased with my Journal.[3]

You are now again in London and I hope are in the same cordial intimacy with Mr. Johnson as ever.[4] I intend being up in March,[5]

Langton on 3 Jan. 1775 (Reg. Let.), but none on 31 Dec. 1774. 3 Jan. was a post day from Edinburgh for English mail (*Edinburgh Almanack*, 1775).

[2] In church five months earlier, JB thought of SJ's inevitable death and his "mind was damp'd. I had then a very pretty lively thought that Worthy Langton and others who were touched by that noble loadstone and whose souls would point to heaven like needles to the pole would remain to console me. It is very wrong that I do not write oftener to Langton. Sir W. Forbes shewed me this evening two letters which he had from him" (Journ. 24 July 1774).

[3] JB lent the journal to Forbes on 1 Jan. 1775: "I drank tea by special appointment with worthy Sir William Forbes, to let him read my *Hebrides Journal* to prepare him for Mr. Johnson's Book. He was much entertained and I left him my three

volumes, after reading him a great deal" (Journ.). JB sent him nine more loose sheets of the journal five days later (To Forbes, 6 Jan. 1775, MS. Fettercairn Papers, National Library of Scotland); then lent him the journal a second time on 24 Feb. 1777. Sir William wrote to him on 7 Mar. of that year, praising the MS., a letter JB published in the *Tour* (*Life* v. 413–14) without Forbes's consent or knowledge. For Sir William's strictures on the published *Tour* and his comments on the publication of his letter, see his *Life of Beattie* ii. 378–80.

[4] Langton spent the winter in London. SJ wrote to JB on 21 Jan. 1775, "Langton is here; we are all that ever we were. He is a worthy fellow, without malice, though not without resentment" (*Letters SJ* ii. 4).

[5] JB left Edinburgh for London on Wednesday 15 Mar. 1775 (Journ.).

and please myself with the prospect of enjoying such conversations as delight and exalt me. How does the Club go on? Are the new members an agreeable addition to it?[6] Poor Goldsmith will often be missed.

Why do you not become an Authour as well as many of your friends have done? Your learning and talents in composition should do more than entertain yourself and a smal circle of correspondents. You should in this view think of what Lucan says of Cato *toto genitum se credere mundo*.[7] The great advantage of putting one's thoughts in print is that the same effort of mind, which in private intercourse does good only to a few, is made of equal service to multitudes.[8] There is indeed the risk of censure but that you have no reason to fear. I shall not be satisfied till I have you[9] in my Library in due form. You once I think mentioned to me that you had thoughts of Biography. Mr. Johnson told me that he was for your writing the History of Lincolnshire. That would be an excellent Work for you.

My Wife joins me in best respects [to] you and Lady Rothes; and kind wishes for the prosperity of your young ones.

May I beg that you will put Mr. Beaucler[10] in remembrance of me, and assure him of my grateful attachment. I ever am with real esteem, Dear Sir, your affectionate humble servant

---

[6] Charles James Fox, Sir Charles Bunbury, and Dr. George Fordyce had been elected in Feb. 1774, George Steevens in Mar., and Edward Gibbon some time later that year.

[7] Lucan, *Pharsalia* ii. 383: "[not] to believe himself born [for himself, but] for the whole world".

[8] JB is paraphrasing SJ. Cf. *Life* ii. 15.

[9] The rest of the copy is in JB's hand.

[10] JB's spelling of the name without the *k* indicates that this family name was pronounced in the eighteenth century as it is now: bo-clair.

From Topham Beauclerk to Bennet Langton,
Wednesday, ?February or March 1775[1]

MS. Yale (C 119).

ADDRESS: Bennet Langton Esqr.

Note near seal (probably in Langton's hand): ὁμηρόκεντρα.[2]

Wednesday Morning, Adelphi

DEAR LANGTON, I wish you would dine today with me and Lady
D. alone, she is ill, and I am very much so. If the Greek[3] dines
with you, you may bring him with you, though I much want to
have an hour or two Conversation with you, before we are broke
in upon by other people, which has not happened since you came
to Town.

I have many things which I can talk to you about, that all other
Company interrupt. Our long and uninterrupted friendship makes
this natural. You know at all times I preferred your Company to
any other, and that preference is not decreased by a very long and
painfull Illness, particularly as I have reason to think that it will
not be very long before that Illness puts an End to our con-
ne⟨ction for⟩ Ever. Till then believe me to be with th⟨anks⟩
Sincerely Affectionately yours

T.B.

Pray send an Answer by the Bearer by word of mouth as I
shall not be up when it comes. I write this at two o'clock in the
Morning, though I have dated it Wednesday.

[1] Nicolaida (*post* n. 3) was in London
early in 1775. Langton, who had been in
London since Jan. or earlier, left for
Lincolnshire 26 May (*Letters SJ* ii. 34).
Beauclerk had been very ill since Jan.,
improving in Mar. (*Life* ii. 292; Journ.
21 Mar.).

[2] This word, which has nothing to do
with the contents of the letter, means
poems made up of fragments from
Homer.

[3] Nicolaida, or Nicolaïdes (fl. 1775–
1782), "a learned Greek, nephew of the
Patriarch of Constantinople, who fled
from some massacre of the Greeks"
(John Johnstone's life of Parr, in *The
Works of Samuel Parr*, 1828, i. 84).
Langton, who probably met Nicolaida
through John Paradise (Shepperson, pp.
128–29), invited him to Langton in May
1775 (*Letters SJ* ii. 34).

To Topham Beauclerk,
Thursday 2 March 1775

MS. Yale (L 56). A copy in Lawrie's hand. Sent 2 Mar. (Reg. Let.).
Referred to in Journ.: "St. John's lodge in the evening for a little, having
first written to . . . Beauclerc, a gleam of fine spirits having come."
HEADING: (To Mr.[1] Beau Clerc).

[Edinburgh]

DEAR SIR: Mr. Johnson informed me some weeks ago[2] that you
was very ill. He has not been kind enough to let me know how
you are recovered. Will you excuse me then for perhaps intruding
upon you before you should have the trouble of reading a letter.
I write from a sincere concern for you as I ever retain a most
gratefull sense of your goodness. Will you be so obliging as to
tell me how you are and if you are as well as I would flatter
myself that you may be do me the favour to let me share in the
fruits of your health by imparting a little of your gayity. How is
Mr. Johnsons book[3] liked in the great and fine world? How are
our mutual friends of the Club? I look forward with impatience to
London where I hope to be very happy this spring.

If you are still indisposed please make some of your people
write to me as I am really anxious to know particularly how you
are.

I beg leave to offer my respectfull compliments to Lady Di—
and I have the honour to be, Dear Sir, Your oblidged humble
Servant

From Sir Joshua Reynolds,
Saturday 15 April 1775

Not reported. Sent from London. "I had engaged to go with General
Paoli to Wilton on tuesday. But, there came yesterday a card to me from
Sir Joshua Reynolds, that Mr. Owen Cambridge would be happy to see
me at dinner that day at his house at Twickenham with Sir Joshua and
Dr. Johnson.[1] This was a scene not to be lost, if the invitation was

---

[1] MS. "Th[illegible]" deleted.
[2] 21 Jan. 1775 (*Letters SJ* ii. 4).
[3] *A Journey to the Western Islands of
Scotland.*

[1] JB's great friend Pasquale de Paoli,
General of the Corsicans, had been
living in London since 1769 on a liberal

properly given" (Journ. 16 Apr.). JB breakfasted with Reynolds and, "having found that Mr. Cambridge wished to see me, I resolved to try if I could prevail on the General to wait another day" (ibid.). The General was willing. For a detailed account of the dinner at Cambridge's "beautiful villa on the banks of the Thames" (*Life* iv. 196), see *Life* ii. 361–71 and Notes, 18 Apr. 1775.

From Bennet Langton, Friday 9 June 1775

MS. Yale (C 1684).

Lincoln, June 9th. 1775

DEAR SIR, I hope You had a good Journey home[1] and found Mrs. Boswel, and Your little Ladies well; I reckoned it very unlucky that I could not make use of the kind Intimation You was so good as to send me of Your time of setting out;[2] but I was not able to get away from London till some days after;[3] I should be glad to hear that the Reason You gave Us for Your hasty departure, Your Attendance on the Ecclesiastical Court[4] turned out so as to prove

Crown pension that he owed in some part to JB's *Account of Corsica* (1768). Wilton House, near Salisbury, was the seat of the tenth Earl of Pembroke, who had been moved by JB's book to visit Corsica. Richard Owen Cambridge, poet and essayist, was famous as an entertainer of notables.

[1] JB left London on 22 May (*Letters SJ* ii. 31).
[2] The note, if it was a written message, has not been recovered.
[3] Langton left for Lincolnshire on 26 May (*Life* ii. 379).
[4] The General Assembly of the Church of Scotland, the supreme ecclesiastical court of the kingdom, a body composed of some two hundred ministers and lay commissioners, sat each May in an apartment appropriated to its use in St. Giles's Church, Edinburgh, to hear and decide complaints, references, and appeals which had come up through the synods and presbyteries. Causes were

pleaded by advocates, much as in the Court of Session, judgement being by a majority vote of all the members. In 1775 JB was engaged in two causes. In the first cause, heard on 29 May, Margaret, Lady Forbes, acting for her son, Sir William Forbes of Craigievar, the patron, who was abroad, had presented Mr. John Bonniman to Grange parish, but the Presbytery of Strathbogie had demanded to see her rights and had allowed her till 17 May to produce them. Request for further delay was opposed by Earl Fife, principal heritor, and by Mr. Innes of Edingight, who joined in insisting that no further time should be allowed, and that the Presbytery should claim its right to fill the vacancy, which had then existed six months. The Presbytery gave sentence accordingly and appointed 28 June as the date for considering the settlement, whereupon Lady Forbes appealed. The Assembly instructed the Presbytery to take action on 19 July, "whether any

a good Recompence for Your trouble in hastening down—I found Lady Rothes and my little ones in good Health; but have been forced away from them, as my Date explains, to attend on my Militia Duty at this Place,[5] where I find some degree of Fatigue, as it is the first of the three Years of training the Men[6] and therefore requires an extraordinary Degree of attendance—which the very sultry Weather we have at present makes the more oppressive—I dont know whether I might not have put off the Pleasure of writing till my Return home, where I am going next week, and where I could have had Leisure to have set about it more comfortably—but that I was particularly requested in London by a Gentleman to give him a recommendatory Letter to You, as

farther evidence be produced or not." Boswell and Henry Erskine were counsel for Lord Fife and Mr. Innes. They won their cause, for the Presbytery *jure devoluto* presented Mr. John Duff (whose name suggests a connexion with Lord Fife), and the settlement was sustained by the Court of Session (*Scots Mag.* 1775, xxxvii. 280–81; MS. Minutes of the General Assembly, 1775, S.R.O.; *Fasti Scot.* vi. 315, fuller information in *ibid.* 1870, iii. 204). JB's retainer as counsel for Lord Fife in political causes (a "great prize in the lottery of business": Journ. 10 Dec. 1772) may explain the emphasis in his insistence that he "*must* set off for Edinburgh . . . in time for the General Assembly" (To Temple, 17 May 1775). In the second cause he was less successful. Five elders of the parish of Keith had been deposed by the Presbytery of Strathbogie for suspending the session-clerk on unproven charges of fornication, embezzlement, and mutilation of records. The Synod of Moray had affirmed the sentence of the Presbytery, and the Commission of the General Assembly in 1774 had confirmed both sentences. "Mr. James Boswell, counsel for the elders, protested for liberty to complain of this judgement to the next assembly for redress." He presented a printed petition and complaint, and wrote on 3 June 1775, "Do you know it requires more than ordinary spirit, to do what I am to do this very morning. I am to go

to the General Assembly and arraign a judgement pronounced last year by Dr. Robertson John Home and a good many more of them; and they are to appear on the other side. To speak well when I despise both the cause and the Judges is difficult. But I believe I shall do wonderfully" (To Temple, 3 June 1775). He had no chance to "do" at all, for the Assembly dismissed the petition without a vote (*Scots Mag.* 1774, xxxvi. 330–32; 1775, xxxvii. 284; MS. Minutes of the General Assembly, 1775, S.R.O.).

[5] Langton was commissioned a captain in the Royal North Lincolnshire Militia on 29 Mar. 1770 (War Office, *List of Officers of the Several Regiments and Corps of Militia, Embodied the 26th of March, 1778*, p. 36; bound with *Army List*, 1779). Sir William Forbes reported that he was "an excellent officer. He acquired the esteem and admiration of his brother-officers, not only by his worth and learning, but by his elegant manners, and an inexhaustible fund of entertaining conversation; while he procured the love of the soldiers, by his mildness and humanity" (*Life of Beattie* ii. 266 n.).

[6] Militiamen were recruited for three years' training until the passing of the Militia Act of 1786, when their service was increased to five years (Sir Sibbald David Scott, *The British Army: Its Origin, Progress, and Equipment*, 1881, iii. 144).

he is going a Jaunt into Scotland; upon which I gave Him Your Direction, and engaged to write to You by the time I understood he designd going—I accordingly take the Liberty of doing it, and should be obliged to You, Dear Sir, if You would shew him any Civilities that You might conveniently have Leisure for, when he arrives at Edinburgh—His Name is Paradise; His Father who is living, and is I understand a Man of a handsome Fortune was our Consul at Thessalonica in Greece, where this Gentleman, who is to wait upon You, was born—You will find that he has not compleatly acquired the English Tongue, from having passed so much Time in the Country where he was born—he has been at the University of Oxford to reside some time—and I fancy did not come to England much sooner than the proper time for going to the University—his acquaintance with the ancient Greek Language I take to be pretty considerable—the Gentleman that accompanies Him is named Gosset;[7] I have seen him at Mr. Paradise's, and think he seems a very well-bred amiable kind of Man—His Figure, poor Man, as You will see is very unfortunate—*He* is likewise an Oxford-Man and is in orders—his Father[8] has been long eminent as an Artist in executing Portraits model'd in Wax; some of which You have probably seen—I have just received a Letter from Mr. Beauclerk dated from Muswell Hill;[9] he has been at Bath, but has staid there only two days; finding, he says, that he was in a feverish state he thought it not prudent to drink the waters; and as there was no Company that he was acquainted with there appeared no Inducement to stay; he says Turton[10] has

[7] Isaac Gosset (?1735–1812), bibliographer, book collector, and clergyman. Although his deformity and weakness prevented him from performing much clerical work, he achieved some eminence as a preacher. Interested in literature and theology, he contributed to John Nichols's edition of William Bowyer's *Critical Conjectures and Observations on the New Testament, collected from various Authors* (1782), and was a Fellow of the Royal Society. See *Gent. Mag.* 1812, lxxxii. 596.

[8] Isaac Gosset the elder (1713–99) was a member of the Incorporated Society of Artists, contributing twenty-four portraits to their exhibitions between 1760 and 1778. George II, the Princess Dowa-

ger of Wales, and the Earl of Mansfield were among those who sat to him.

[9] A suburb north-west of London, near Highgate, where Beauclerk had an "elegant villa, and Library worth £6,000". JB and SJ went to see it on 17 May (To Temple, 17 May 1775).

[10] John Turton (1735–1806), physician and Fellow of the Royal Society, was at various times physician to the Queen's household, physician-in-ordinary to the Queen, and physician-in-ordinary to the King and the Prince of Wales. He was also the Langton family physician, and many years later (1795), according to Peregrine, "finding he could be no longer of any service to" Mary Langton, "put her off his hands by sending her to

put him now into a Regimen of taking the Solanum[11] and a Milk Diet—his Case poor Man is I doubt a very serious one. Pray present my best Respects to Sir Wm. Forbes and his Lady when You see them, and please to mention to him, that I design writing him word very shortly what I have been doing in the Concern he last wrote to me upon[12]—You will please likewise, dear Sir, to give my Respects to Lord Hailes and his Family when You see Him—and to any other of My acquaintance You may meet—I have only time to add that I am, Dear Sir, Your affectionate humble Servant

B. LANGTON

To Sir Joshua Reynolds, Saturday 12 August 1775

MS. T. G. M. Snagge.

ADDRESS: To Sir Joshua Reynolds, Liecester Fields, London.

ENDORSEMENT: Boswell.

Edinburgh, 12 August 1775

DEAR SIR: An historical picture of Mary Queen of Scots resigning her crown, painted for me by Mr. Hamilton at Rome is soon to be landed at London from a ship from Italy. I should wish to have the picture in your next Exhibition, if you approve of it.[1] May I beg then that you will receive it into one of your rooms in the mean time; as I do not know where I can place it, in a proper

Clifton:—than which a more unprincipled act I think cannot be imagined". This "abominable" behaviour resulted in "enormous" expenses (PL-M's letter-book, p. 64b).

[11] "Solanum" refers to any of a genus of the nightshade family (*Solanaceae*); although in this case the reference is undoubtedly to the related *Physalis alkekengi*, or winter cherry. "The berries are a singular good Diuretic, and useful against the Gravel and the Stone: Being boil'd in Milk, and sweetened with Sugar, they cure the Heat of Urine, making bloody Water, and Ulcers in the Kidneys and Bladder. They help Jaundice, by opening the obstructions in the Liver and Gall-bladder, and the Dropsy, by carrying off the Water through the Urinary passages" (*A Medicinal Dictionary*, by Dr. Robert James [with a dedication by Samuel Johnson], 1743–1745).

[12] This letter has not been recovered.

[1] The painting, by Gavin Hamilton (1730–97), was exhibited in 1776. For a full account of it see *Earlier Years*, pp. 219–20, 512. Reynolds was not pleased with it, and JB was disappointed when he saw it (Journ. 18 Mar. 1776).

manner, but under your roof. Messrs. Dilly Booksellers in the Poultry are to receive the picture from the ship. Will you be pleased to let them know if it may be sent to you. Or if that is not convenient, will you be so good as give directions where it may be lodged any where else.

The subject of the picture is a very good one. Dr. Robertson has described the scene very well; and Dr. Johnson favoured me with the following inscription for a print from the picture.[2]

Maria Scotorum Regina,	Mary Queen of Scots
hominum seditiosorum	terrified and overpowered
contumeliis lassata,	by the insults, menaces
minis territa, clamoribus victa,	and clamours
Libello per quem regno cedit,	of her rebellious subjects,
Lacrimans trepidansque	sets her hand,
nomen apponit.	with tears and confusion
	to a resignation of the Kingdom.

I will be much obliged to you for your advice and assistance in this matter. I beg you may present my best compliments to Miss Reynolds,[3] and be assured that I ever am with great regard, Dear Sir, your most obedient humble servant

JAMES BOSWELL

From Edmund Burke to Bennet Langton, Monday 18 September 1775[1]

MS. Yale (C 682).

ENDORSEMENT by JB: Edmund Burke To Bennet Langton.

Beaconsfield,[2] Septr. 18. 1775

DEAR SIR, I hope your goodnature will excuse me for troubling

[2] "Mary, when she subscribed these deeds, was bathed in tears; and while she gave away, as it were with her own hands, the sceptre which she had swayed so long, she felt a pang of grief and indignation, one of the severest, perhaps, which can touch the human heart" (William Robertson, *The History of Scotland during the Reigns of Queen Mary and of King James VI*, 2nd ed., 1759 i. 375). An engraving was made by Francis Legat (pub. 2 Jan. 1786), but SJ's inscription does not appear in the one copy so far reported (British Museum).

[3] Frances Reynolds (1729–1807), Sir Joshua's sister.

[1] The second digit of the date has been written over, but it appears to be an 8.

[2] The estate of approximately 600 acres which Burke purchased in 1768. About a mile distant from Beaconsfield, Buckinghamshire, it had formerly been called Gregories.

you with an application. It is for your interest in favour of Mr. Ellis[3] a Clergyman of ingenuity and merit, and who wishes to be made Master of Alford School.[4] I believe, as far as I am capable of judging, that he is extremely well qualified for that employment. He has indeed at present a living in London; but as it is small, and as he has no expectation of further provision in the Church, he is desirous of encreasing his income in order to enable him to provide for a growing family. If you can serve by your Vote and your interest this worthy Gentleman you will lay a particular obligation on me. You will be so good to present Mrs. Burkes and my best Compliments to Lady Rothes, and to believe me with great Truth and Regard, Dear Sir, your most faithful and obedient humble Servant

EDM. BURKE

To Topham Beauclerk,
Saturday 30 September 1775

Not reported. Sent from Edinburgh 30 Sept. "Topham Beauclerc Esq. recommending Sandie Bruce" (Reg. Let.). Alexander Bruce was the son of James Bruce, the overseer at Auchinleck. If he was not already in England, he soon went there, for on 19 May 1776 JB wrote to the Dillys asking them to give him two guineas and to Alexander himself telling him "to improve and come home" (*ibid.*). In the summer of 1776 Alexander wrote to JB, presumably from London, asking if Lord Auchinleck "would have him as Gardener" (*ibid.* "Omitted", entered after 11 July). JB,

[3] William Ellis (1730–1801), Rector of All Hallows, Steyning, 1758–1801, and Master of Aldenham Grammar School, 1757–68. He was appointed Master at Alford, and held the post until his death (*Alum. Cant.* I. ii. 98). In 1782 he published *A Collection of English Exercises, translated from the Writings of Cicero only, for School-Boys to re-translate into Latin; and adapted to the principal Rules in the Compendium of Erasmus's Syntax* (*Gent. Mag.* Jan. 1783, liii. 55–56), a work which had many subsequent editions. His first wife was a daughter of Theophilus Cibber and niece of Thomas Augustine Arne. "He was the personal friend of Sir William Jones, Edmund Burke and other *literati* of his day" (R. F. Scott, *Admissions to the College of St. John the Evangelist in the University of Cambridge* iii, 1903, 573).

[4] The Grammar School at Alford, a town eight miles north-east of Spilsby, was founded in 1565. It was administered by a board of ten managers, six of whom, styled first governors, were inhabitants of Alford and four, "respectable persons *in* or *near* the town . . . called auditors" (*The History of the County of Lincoln,* 1834, ii. 163). A Peter Langton, Esq. contributed to the school in 1658, which could account for Langton's apparent membership on its governing board (*ibid.* ii. 164).

apparently replying in the affirmative, warned him that he could not "expect high wages; but [would] get the same as a homebred Gardener" (*ibid.* 13 July 1776). Alexander proposed £16 in wages plus five shillings a week in board (*ibid.* Aug. 1776), whereupon JB replied to him that his demands were too high and that he might engage himself in England (*ibid.* 13 Aug. 1776). He was JB's gardener at Auchinleck in 1783 (From James Bruce, 5 May).

From Bennet Langton to Edmund Burke, Monday 2 October 1775

MS. Fitzwilliam MSS., Sheffield City Libraries. Printed by permission of Earl Fitzwilliam and his trustees.

ADDRESS: ⟨E⟩dmund Burke Esqr. M.P., at Beaconsfield, Bucks., by London.

POSTMARKS: BOSTON, FREE, 7 OC.

ENDORSEMENTS: [*Probably in hand of Burke's wife, Jane Burke*:] Mr. Langhton, 1775. [Mr. Langhton *later crossed out by an unknown hand, which added above*:] Bennet Langton to E. B. [*and after* 1775:] Octbr. 2nd. [*In the hand of Sir Richard Burke, co-editor of Burke's* Correspondence, *1844, in pencil*:] Not important, R. B.

Langton, Octr. 2d 1775

DEAR SIR, I received the Honour of Your Letter in relation to Mr. Ellis and should have been very glad to have paid the utmost Regard to Your Recommendation; but it was already the Case that the Gentlemen in the ⟨Board⟩ were entirely disposed to elect Him; on my shewing T⟨hem⟩ Your Letter, They agreed that it was a great Satisfaction to receive so weighty an additional Testimony in His Favour; He was elected on Friday last.

I lately received a Letter from Mr. Nicolaides w⟨ritten⟩ in the ancient Greek, which I hope, Sir, to have the ⟨pleasure⟩ of shewing You soon, when we meet in Town; there is the more Reason why I should offer it to Your Perusal; as he expresses in it a very grateful Sense of the Kindness You have shewn him—Lady Rothes desires Sir to join me in best Respects to Yourself and Mrs. Burke. Believe me to be with great Respect and Esteem, Dear Sir, Your affectionate humble Servant

BENNET LANGTON

From Bennet Langton,
Monday 16 October 1775

MS. Yale (C 1685). Received 24 Oct. (Reg. Let.).

Langton, Octr. 16th. 1775

DEAR SIR, Though You will not encourage me in Correspondence by letting me have a Line from You, I cannot help taking up my Pen in consequence of an Article I saw in the last Paper from Edinburgh that Mrs. Boswel was safely delivered of a Son;[1] You and She will please to accept our hearty Congratulations on the Occasion—and I hope will give me a Line to let me know how She and the young Gentleman are going on, as well as the rest of Your Young Family—I hope You received a Letter I troubled You with in the Summer, and am something curious to know whether the Gentlemen I took the Liberty of recommending to You who were coming to visit Scotland, did arrive—

You will have heard of the Excursion to Paris with Mr. and Mrs. Thrale that our venerable Friend has been engaged in; I imagine he may be returned, as Mr. Thrale's duty in Parliament will call him home;[2] it is what I have frequently wished, that Dr. Johnson should visit the Continent—as a Mind like his, amongst other *Food*, should certainly take in that of seeing different Nations; if the conveniency of things had allowed, *You* had the best Claim surely of any one to have escorted him, and profited by his Remarks as they arose, who was the Contriver of that expedition to the Highlands, which it is not easy to imagine would otherwise ever have taken place. I honour Mr. Thrale very much for the undertaking, as it is a very worthy Instance of the Use of his Wealth, and cannot but be surprized to think that among all those of this Land who are in high Stations or opulent Circumstances no one should ever have sollicited Dr. Johnsons Company in visiting such Parts of the World as are worthy of Curiosity.

I hope it will not be long before Lord Hailes's Historical Work comes out; I expect great Entertainment from it, by the Specimen

[1] Alexander Boswell was born on 9 Oct. *The Edinburgh Advertiser* reported, "Yesterday Mrs. Boswell, wife of James Boswell, Esq. younger of Auchinleck, was safely delivered of a son" (6–10 Oct. 1775, xxiv. 229).

[2] SJ set out for Paris with the Thrales on 15 Sept. and returned to England on 11 Nov. (*French Journals of Mrs. Thrale and Dr. Johnson*, ed. Moses Tyson and Henry Guppy, 1932, pp. 69, 165).

You was so kind as to shew me of it in Town[3]—I will trouble You with my best Respects to Him when You see Him—

Poor Mr. Beauclerk, in a Letter I had from him not long ago,[4] speaks of being much better than he was, and seems to attribute it to Tunbridge Waters, though he does not speak distinctly as to what his abatement of ill Health may be owing to; he speaks of intending to go to Bath; it is well however if his Care of himself proves sufficient for a Recovery from so dreadful a Degree of Disease as he laboured under—

We have Thoughts of setting out soon for London, but have one Subject of Regret in relation to that Journey; that our Physician here does not chuse to inoculate any of our little ones as they appear to be all cutting teeth; by which means we must run a risk we intended to have avoided of their catching the small pox—They are all three,[5] thank God, in appearance of being very healthy and strong—

Will there be a Chance of our meeting in London any part of the Winter or Spring? I hope we may have another quiet Walk in *Somerset-Gardens* before They are demolished[6]—for my own part I have little doubt of a Call in no long time to my *Militia* Duty— as it will surely be necessary to have *Them* embodied when so large a Force is sent away as seems to be proposed, and indeed must, if any Effect is expected, in reducing the Americans to Obedience— I think it is agreed that less than 40,000 Men cannot be expected to answer that End—[7]

[3] The work published early in the following year as *Annals of Scotland.* Hailes had sent successive parcels of his manuscript through the post to JB in London the previous spring for SJ's criticism (To Hailes, 1 Apr. 1775; From Hailes, 7 Apr. 1775; To Hailes, 12 Apr. 1775; From Hailes, 15 Apr., 11 May, 7 June 1775).

[4] This letter has not been recovered.

[5] George, Mary, and Diana (b. 28 Sept. 1774).

[6] The gardens of Somerset House, built in the Strand by the Protector Somerset shortly after the death of Henry VIII. The House became the property of the Crown after the execution of Somerset and was usually assigned to the queens. After 1692, it became a nest of apartments for the nobility. When Buckingham House was assigned to Queen Charlotte in 1775, Somerset House was torn down to make way for the present Somerset House, designed by Sir William Chambers. JB and Langton on 12 Apr. had "walked near an hour in Somerset Gardens, where I never had been before. It was very agreable to find quietness and old trees in the very heart of London. My dissipation and hurry of spirits were cured here. We talked of Religion. It was quite such a scene as the *Spectator* [No. 77] pictures. I valued worthy Langton" (Journ.).

[7] *The Edinburgh Advertiser* reported, "It is supposed that this kingdom will find it necessary to keep always in its pay ten thousand foreigners in America

You will be so obliging Dear Sir—as to present our best Compliments to Sir William and Lady Forbes—and to any other of my Friends and acquaintance You may meet—

Did the Alteration of the mistake about the precedency of the two Families in the Highlands, which Dr. Johnson said in his Letter should be inserted in the Papers appear in Donaldsons Paper? If it did I have not happened to meet with it there.

Pray is Your extraordinary Cause decided—as to the Titles of Physician or Doctor in Medicine?[8]

In hopes of hearing from You soon, I remain, Dear Sir, Your affectionate humble Servant

BENNET LANGTON

To Bennet Langton, Tuesday 24 October 1775

MS. Yale (L 844). A copy in Lawrie's hand. Sent 26 Oct. (Reg. Let.).

Edinburgh, 24 October 1775

DEAR SIR: You are much kinder to me than I deserve. Beleive me, I have been resolving day after day to write to you, and have upbraided myself for having so long neglected to acknowledge your favour of last summer. In such a state of mind as these resolutions and upbraidings produce,[1] I had the pleasure of receiving to day your obliging letter of the 16th instant. My wife and I beg that you and Lady Rothes may accept of our very sincere thanks for your congratulations on the birth of our Son. My wife is recovering remarkably well, and young Alexander

to retain that country in due subordination. . . . Together with the foreigners now taken into the service, we shall have 30,000 effective men before the middle of October in America" (1–4 Aug. 1775, xxiv. 75).

[8] Langton refers to the cause of Dr. John Memis (c. 1720–after 1776), who had brought suit against the managers of the Royal Infirmary at Aberdeen for styling him Doctor of Medicine in a translation of a charter which referred to other doctors as physicians. JB was counsel for the managers, and persuaded

SJ to dictate an opinion favouring his clients (Alexander Lyall, "The Case of Dr. Memis", *Medical History*, 1960, iv. 32–48 and *Life* ii. 291, 296–97, 372–73).

[1] Failure to write to Langton was only one of the things which had been troubling JB. "My Father's coldness to me, the unsettled state of our Family affairs, and the poor opinion which I had of the profession of a Lawyer in Scotland, which consumed my life, in the mean time, sunk my spirits woefully, and for some of the last weeks of the Session, I

(named for my father) is a stout little fellow. You know what an acquisition a son is to an old feudal Goth like your humble servant. My earnest study however is to guard myself against being too much attached to what is very uncertain.[2] Indeed it is in vain to think of attaining to such a frame, as to enjoy a good, and not suffer by being deprived of it. Horaces's *Laudo manentem* and careless *resigno quæ dedit*[3] is poetical stoicism and I am persuaded impracticable philosophy. Christianity opens to us a pleasing moderation, which I beleive has been attained.

I sincerely rejoice in the good accounts which you give me of Mr. Beauclerc though they are not determinate. I wish he could certainly know my concern about him. I hope you and he and I shall meet again in London next spring. It is my intention to visit London every spring unless something extraordinary prevents me. I still indulge the scheme of trying my fortune at the English bar.[4] The very curious cause of Dr. Memis is not yet determined.[5] The Lords of Session have granted a proof, that it

was depressed with black melancholy" (Journ., "Review of my Life during the Summer Session 1775"). Then on 9 Oct. his son Alexander was born. JB resolved to "keep a Journal of my life every day from this important æra in my family", but it was not until the 24th, the day he heard from Langton, that he wrote up his journal from the 9th on.

[2] SJ, on hearing of the birth of Alexander, wrote on 16 Nov., "I am glad that the young Laird is born, and an end, as I hope, put to the only difference that you can ever have with Mrs. Boswell" (a reference, JB explained in the *Life*, ii. 387 n. 1, "to my old feudal principle of preferring male to female succession"). JB wrote to Temple on 10 Oct., "You know my dearest friend of what importance this is to me—of what importance it is to the Family of Auchinleck—which you may be well convinced is my supreme object in this World." In his journal for 9 Oct., JB wrote, "When I had seen the little man I said that I should now be so anxious that probably I should never again have an easy hour. ... I was this night most devoutly grateful to God."

[3] laudo manentem; si celeres quatit pinnas, resigno quae dedit et mea virtute me involvo probamque Pauperiem sine dote quaero.
    (Horace, *Odes* III. xxix. 53–56)
"I praise her [Fortune] while she stays; but if she shake her wings for flight, I renounce her gifts, enwrap me in my virtue, and woo honest Poverty, undowered though she be" (translation by C. E. Bennett in Loeb ed.).

[4] The same day in which they walked in Somerset Gardens, JB spent the morning at Langton's "talking of Mr. Johnson and Langton's affairs, and his coming to live in London, which I found he was almost determined to do, and imagined he could live for £800 a year—and of my coming to the english bar, of which he approved" (Journ. 12 Apr. 1775).

[5] The cause was not settled until 30 Nov. 1776. JB did his duty by his employers, though he had come to believe their cause unjust: "Was sorry for poor Dr. Memis when his cause was given against him with costs. I thought him injured" (Journ.). See also To SJ, 14 Feb. 1777 (*Life* iii. 101).

may appear whether there was any *intention* in my clients to *injure* him, by the appelation of *Dr. of Medecine*. For my part I am of opinion that even although an *intention* to make him a little rediculous could be made evident from circumstances such as *altering* the phrase from what it was at first the thing is inconsiderable for judicial cognizance. I take it the intention being proved or not will determine the point of costs which is now become pretty serious—I shall let you know the result.

Mr. Paradise and his Lady and Mr. Gosset came to Scotland last summer, and as I am allways ready to pay attention to any recommendation from you, I shewed them what little civility I could. They were very well directed here, our friend Lord Monboddo was pleased to see a living Greek.

Dr. Johnsons handsome acknowledgement to MacLeod of Rasay was inserted in Donaldsons paper as well as in our other papers.[6] His Journey to Paris is an excellent incident in his Life. I am exceedingly curious to have some account of it from him. A little before he set out he wrote to me very kindly bidding me not be uneasy though he did not write again for sometime as he was going to set out *"on another Journey"* but not a word did he say of a french expedition.[7] This reserve you have remarked to me on lesser occasions.[8]

Lord Hailes has printed above 200 pages in quarto of his *Annals*. I doubt if the book will be published next winter. I send tonight a parcel of the Manuscript to Dr. Johnson for revisal.[9] I shall tell all your friends here of your rememberance of them and they will be glad to hear of it. You promised to me or at least resolved to put down in writing all the sayings of Dr. Johnson

[6] The notice, which was printed in the *Tour* (*Life* v. 412), appeared in *The Edinburgh Advertiser* (Donaldson's paper), 26–30 May 1775, xxiii. 341. The original in SJ's hand is at Yale (C1630).

[7] "I now write to tell you that I shall not very soon write again, for I am to set out to morrow on another journey" (14 Sept. 1775): *Letters SJ* ii. 85–86.

[8] SJ's reticence in revealing details is described in the *Life*: "He himself often resembled Lady Bolingbroke's lively description of Pope: that 'he was *un politique aux choux et aux raves*.' He would say, 'I dine to-day in Grosvenor-square;' this might be with a Duke ... or, 'A gentleman of great eminence called on me yesterday.' He loved thus to keep things floating in conjecture: *Omne ignotum pro magnifico est*. I believe I ventured to dissipate the cloud, to unveil the mystery, more freely and frequently than any of his friends" (iii. 324–25).

[9] *Annals of Scotland, from the Accession of Malcolm II surnamed Canmore, to the Accession of Robert I* was published in 1776. A second volume, *Annals of Scotland, continued to the Accession of the House of Stuart*, was published in 1779.

that you remember. Pray favour me with them, that the crown of his own jewels which I am prepairing may be more briliant. I ever am, My dear Sir, with sincere good wishes for the prosperity of your family Your affectionate humble servant.

Tory as I am I cannot help being doubtfull upon the american controver[s]y or rather inclined to think that our common monarchs subjects in the colonies are hardly treated.[10]

From Topham Beauclerk to Bennet Langton, Monday ? December 1775[1]

MS. Yale (C 120).

ADDRESS: Bennet Langton Esqr.

[London] Monday Morning
DEAR LANGTON, I had entirely forgot when I desired the favour of your Company this day at Dinner, that I had an engagement for this day, but I shall be very much obliged to you if you will dine here on Tuesday, as no person whatever will be here. I left your Book of C. J.[2] which I am afraid was fabricated in this Worthy Town, I will tell you my Reasons when I see you. I likewise left Mad. du Barre's Mem.[3] which I beg the favr. of you to return as

---

[10] In summarizing the events of the summer of 1775, JB wrote in his journal, "The engagements in America roused me somewhat; but notwithstanding Dr. Johnson, I was inclined to the side of the Provincials."

---

[1] Inferred from the dates of publication of the books referred to below in nn. 2 and 3.

[2] Possibly "Cook Journal", and if so, probably *Journal of the Resolution's Voyage, in 1772, 1773, 1774, and 1775. ... Also a Journal of the Adventure's Voyage, in the Years 1772, 1773, and 1774. ...* London, F. Newbery, was published on 25 Nov. 1775 (*London Chronicle*, xxxviii. 511). This anonymous and surreptitious work, which appeared

about eighteen months before Cook's own account, was put in shape from the journal of John Marra, gunner's mate, by some writer in Newbery's employ, who padded it with descriptions taken from the accounts of Cook's first voyage, and other material. See Sir Maurice Holmes, *Capt. James Cook ... a bibliographical Excursion*, 1952, No. 16; also Sydney, Public Library of New South Wales, *Bibliography of Capt. James Cook*, 2nd ed., 1970, No. 1270.

[3] Almost certainly M.-F. Pidansat de Mairobert, *Anecdotes sur Me. la Comtesse Du Barri*, which first appeared, with fictitious London imprint, about Nov. 1775 (*Anecdotes sur la Comtesse Du Barry*, publiées par Octave Uzanne, 1880, pp. xxvi-xxxi).

soon as you have done with it, as two or three people want it. You will read it in an Hour. I forgot to mention that there are some Epigrams etc. made upon the King and Mad. d. B. not fit to be read by the young Lady[4] if she happens to read French; you ⟨had⟩ better therefore not leave it about. You will see that it is a Grub Street performance, but which contains a very curious account of the miserable life of an old Debauchée. All those Anecdotes were publickly known at Paris, therefore you may depend upon the truth of them. The Secrets of the Cabinet are not much to be trusted to. Believe me to be ever yours

T. B.

From Topham Beauclerk to Bennet Langton, ?Winter 1775–1776[1]

MS. Yale (C 121).

[London]

DEAR LANGTON: Ever Since I saw you I have been confined with a Fever, I should otherwise have called upon you. I enquired after your Children from Turton who told me they were perfectly well and that the Smallpox was not likely to come out these three or four days. Lady D. is engaged to go tomorrow to the play, and I can hardly prevail upon her to go as I shall be left alone all day as it is a long day in the H. C.[2] I need not tell you how glad I am always to see you, but if you could dine here to morrow and spend

---

[4] Not Langton's daughter, for his eldest was at this time under three years old. Presumably the unnamed young woman mentioned by JB in his journal for 1 Apr. 1776: "Found [Langton] so domestick in his parlour that . . . I could not bear it, especially as there was a young bleareyed girl some relation of his who lived in the house, and whom he had taught to attend with a keen affectation to what was said, and to put *sensible questions*." *Anecdotes sur Me. la Comtesse Du Barri* does indeed contain a quantity of verse of the sort Beauclerk specifies.

[1] See *ante* From Langton, 16 Oct. 1775, in which Langton expresses his regret that the doctor will not inoculate the children before they go to London because they are cutting teeth.

[2] House of Commons. There were many debates on matters pertaining to American affairs during the autumn and winter of 1775–76 that lasted until 3 or 4 a.m. Such members of The Club as Burke, Fox, and Lord Ossory were frequently very active in these debates. See, for instance, *The London Chronicle* for 26–28 Oct. and 16–18 Nov. 1775 (xxxviii. 415, 488), or for 17–20 and 20–22 Feb. 1776 (xxxix. 176, 184).

the early part of the Evening you would rescue me from some part at least of my Misery. I have been in constant pain night and day for this whole Week, and I am reducd to a feebleness of Body and mind that you cannot imagine. It is no great wonder considering that even my old Friend Laudanum has failed at giving me ease. I have a great Blister just put upon my Back and consequently shall not be able to [raise] my hand to Head to morrow. I know if you can come, you will take pity upon me, for I can neither read, nor think nor hardly bear my Existence, my pain and lowness of Spirits are so intolerable. Believe me to be yours Sincerly

T. B.

L. D. dines early because of going to the play. I have forced her to go, by declaring I would go out if she did not. She has suffered too much already to be deprived of the few Amusements, she can take, and I remain only to be troublesome to my Friends, and to endure excruciating torments myself, without pleasure Comfort, or hope. The only remaining thing I have is the Conversation of yourself and one or two more Friends.

From Topham Beauclerk to Bennet Langton, Saturday ?1776[1]

MS. Yale (C 122).

ADDRESS: Bennet Langton Esqr., Welbeck Street Num. 12, Cavendish Square.

[London] Saturday Morning

DEAR LANGTON: If you have a mind to hear Texier[2] read this

---

[1] Determined, rather doubtfully, by the reference to Le Texier (n. 2) and Beauclerk's health. He was ill apparently most of the year, particularly in the spring, with only intermittent periods of relatively good health (see *Henry, Elizabeth and George*, pp. 75–76).

[2] A.-A. Le Texier, or Le Tessier (c. 1737–1814), was celebrated in France, England, and Holland for his readings of French plays in French at private companies such as is here mentioned. For further information on his career and reputation, see *post* pp. 75–76, text and notes of another undated letter of Beauclerk's which mentions him. He came to England in 1775 and remained there for some years, but most of the references to him in contemporary letters and memoirs are concentrated between 1775 and 1777. Horace Walpole apparently first saw him late in 1775 (*Walpole's*

Evening at Mr. Crawfords,[3] I will carry you there if you will dine here, or be with me at a little past *seven*. I dine at a little past *four* in order to have Time to take my Laudanum before I go to Crawfords, and we must be there at a quarter before eight, for when he has begun reading the Doors are shut and no one allowed to come in, as it interrupts him, and he begins reading at *8* exactly. Pray send an Answer. Shall you be at home today about 2 o'clock? If you are, I will call upon you, if I can, but do not stay at home for me, as it is very uncertain. Believe me to be ever yours

T. B.

From Topham Beauclerk to Bennet Langton, Friday ?5 January 1776[1]

MS. Yale (C 123).

ADDRESS: Bennet Langton Esqr., Turks Head, Gerrard Street, Soho.

[London]

DEAR LANGTON: Perhaps you will like dining with Garrick, if you do I need not tell you that I shall be happy to see you at Dinner tomorrow. There will be nobody but Mr. [and] Mrs. G. and Gibbons. I assure you it is more difficult to get Garrick [to] Dinner than you imagine. I am very ill to day, and Lady D. keeps

Correspondence, Yale Ed. xxxii. 277) and by 1779, thought he had twenty times the genius of Garrick (*ibid*. xxxiii. 87–88). Le Texier stayed with Walpole in June 1776, when Beauclerk and Lady Di, the Garricks, and the Pembrokes were also his guests (To Conway, 30 June 1776). Hannah More reported that she had heard him read at Mrs. Vesey's the same year (William Roberts, *Memoirs of . . . Hannah More*, 1834–35, i. 80). He died "dans un age avancé", in France, some time after 1814 (*Biographie universelle* lxxxiii. 444).

[3] Presumably John "Fish" Craufurd (1742–1814) of Drumsoy and Auchinames, M.P. for Renfrewshire, and admirer of Lady Di Beauclerk (Burke's *Landed Gentry*, 1851, i. 277; *Walpole's Correspondence*, Yale Ed. vi. 79).

[1] The reference to "Club Dinner" limits somewhat the period to which this letter may be assigned. The Club originally met weekly for *suppers*. "After about ten years", the members adopted a new arrangement of dining "once a fortnight during the meeting of Parliament" (*Life* i. 478-79). It is clear, however, that the change from weekly suppers to fortnightly dinners was not accomplished in a single step. There are no Club records showing when dinners were first introduced, but it must have been by 7 Apr. 1775, for JB on that date reports "an institution that there should be a dinner instead of a supper, the first friday of every month" (Journ.; see also To Temple, 4 Apr. 1775). A set of rules and regulations of The Club dated 5 May 1775 states that dinners are to be held on the first *and third* Fridays of the

her Room entirely. Perhaps you will call here after the Club Dinner. Pray tell Gibbons that I was too ill to dine at the Club as I promised, and hope to see him this[2] Evening. Ever Your

T. B.

From Topham Beauclerk to Bennet Langton, after Thursday 22 February 1776[1]

MS. Yale (C 124).

[London]

DEAR LANGTON: Will you come here this Evening as I am still confined at home? If you will come about eight and sup here, you will be very Charitable and will keep me out of harms way. I have staid at home 3 Days entirely alone, and being in low Spirits with my disorder I am afraid I shall not have resolution enough to stay at home any longer, if you do not come. Most people would think this a very good Reason for staying away but I know you think otherwise, and that being able to be usefull to a Friend is as strong a Motive with you to go any where, as a Ball or Lady Derbys[2] dinner to many of my Worldly Friends. Ever Your

T. B.

month, but in fact only one dinner a month was held for some months longer. Members failing to attend a dinner without having sent an excuse paid a forfeit of five shillings. There are three meetings between the institution of dinners and the death of Garrick where the conditions required by this letter obtain—the absence and fining of Beauclerk and the presence of Langton and Gibbon: 5 Jan. 1776, 20 Mar. 1778, and 18 Dec. 1778. Three other meetings, two in 1776 and one in 1777, seem less likely because, although Beauclerk was absent, he was not fined, suggesting that he had not planned to attend. An early date seems more likely than a later one

because of the misspelling of Gibbon's name.

[2] Reading uncertain.

[1] Determined by the date of the Earl of Derby's succession and the report of the Derbys' hospitality in that year (n. 2).

[2] Elizabeth (1753–97), daughter of James Hamilton, sixth Duke of Hamilton, and the wife of Edward Smith-Stanley, Earl of Derby (1752–1834), who succeeded his grandfather on 22 Feb. 1776. At that time "she and her husband were among the most profuse entertainers in London Society" (Comp. Peer. iv. 218 and n. e).

From Topham Beauclerk to Bennet Langton, ?April[1] 1776

MS. Yale (C 125).

ADDRESS: Bennet Langton Esqr.

[London]

DEAR LANGTON, I have sent you your Great Coat which you forgot. I wish you would dine here today and we will read S. Jennings's[2] Book together after dinner or if You cannot dine here if you will come in the Early part of the Evening, but come Early and then you are sure we shall not be interrupted, though I believe no one will come here to night, they are all going to the Opera or play. If you would have My Coach I will send it for you. Ever yours

T. B.

To ?Thomas Percy, Saturday 13 April 1776[1]

MS. Houghton Library, Harvard. Printed by permission of the Harvard College Library. "To the Revd. Dr. Percy afterwards Bishop of Dromore" is pencilled at the foot of the message side in an unknown hand, presumably that of a former owner or of a librarian. The identification of the recipient as Percy is plausible but cannot be regarded as certain.

[London] Saturday 13 April

Dr. Johnson and your humble servant and some more people[2] whom you will be glad to see are to sup this evening at the Crown and Anchor in the Strand. If you return in time, pray be with us. Yours sincerely

JA. BOSWELL

[1] Determined by the date of publication of Soame Jenyns's book.

[2] Soame Jenyns (1704–87), whose View of the Internal Evidence of the Christian Religion was published in Apr. and advertised in The London Chronicle 4–6 Apr. 1776.

[1] On Thursday 11 Apr. 1776, JB called on Sir William Forbes to leave him "a note to engage him to sup with Dr. Johnson at the Crown and Anchor on saturday" (Journ.). In the Life (iii. 41), JB mistakenly described the gathering under 12 Apr.

[2] The others were Sir Joshua Reynolds,

From Bennet Langton,
Saturday 10 August 1776

MS. Yale (C 1686). Received 14 Aug. "Bennet Langton Esq. a kind obliging letter" (Reg. Let.).

London, August 10th. 1776

MY DEAR SIR, Since Your Departure from London[1] I have not had the Pleasure of hearing any account of You till a few Posts ago I was favoured with a Letter from our good Friend Sir Wm. Forbess,[2] who gave me a favourable one of the Health of Yourself and Family—I assure You Dr. Johnson seemed to wonder that he had had no Letter from You since Your leaving Us; though perhaps You may have made up for the forgetting Him in appearance so long by writing, since our Conversation upon it which was some little time ago[3]—I have the Pleasure of informing You, in relation to Him, that when we met last, about a Week ago, he appeared in as good Spirits as I have seen him a great while—He passes his Time a good deal at Streatham[4] but on Saturday next I hope he will give us his Company as that is the Day we have fixed for Christening a little Girl of whom Lady Rothes was lately brought to Bed, to whom he has been so kind as to engage to stand God-father,[5] in which respect my Dear Sir You who know my Venera-tion for Him, will judge how highly I esteem my Child distin-guished. It is not improbable I find that he will make a Visit to

Langton, William Nairne (later Lord Dunsinnan in the Court of Session, and Bt.), and Sir William Forbes (Journ.). Percy did not attend.

[1] JB left London on Friday 17 May 1776 (Journ.).
[2] This letter has not been recovered. Langton's spelling records the usual eighteenth-century Scots pronunciation of the name: Fór-bess, in two syllables. Cf. Sir Walter Scott's tribute to Sir William in *Marmion* (iv. intro.):
Scarce had lamented Forbes paid
The tribute to his Minstrel's shade . . .
The disyllabic pronunciation remains

current in Aberdeenshire, the county of Forbes's origin.
[3] JB wrote to SJ on 25 June and 18 July (*Life* iii. 86, 89). On the 23rd of this month, JB was to write in his journal, "Day after day I have been vexed because I failed to write to him [SJ] and to Mr. and Mrs. Thrale and to Mr. Langton to all of the three last of whom I owe letters; but an inexplicable dilatory disease prevents me."
[4] A quiet country village six miles south-west of London and separated from it by wide commons, where the Thrales had a handsome house (*Life* iii. 452).
[5] Jane Langton, who was born on 26 June 1776.

71

Dr. Taylor this Summer,[6] except that Excursion I hope he will remain in or near London so that one may hope to see Him pretty often—He has greatly increased my Disposition to think favourably of a Book which had before appeared to me to be of great merit from some Extracts I had seen of it—and that is Bryant's 3 Vols. upon ancient History and Mythology[7]—He says he has been reading a great deal of it, and though at first he was not disposed to relish it, as thinking it too fanciful, yet he said as he looked further into it, he found the Author bring together so many particulars in support of his Opinions, that he could not but think it highly remarkable. I find He has met Mr. Bryant at Dinner at Your acquaintance's, Mr. Paradise, where, I understand they seemed to like one another very well.

Since I had writ the Beginning of my Letter Dr. Johnson has given us his Company at the Christening—the *naming* and baptizing the Child had been performed the Day She was born at home but on this occasion the Ceremony of Christening was compleated by attending at the Parish Church, which Dr. Johnson approved of, and mentioned one good Reason why it should always be done; because, from the Fashion that it is to be feared prevails now too much of omitting the Christening at the Church, the *publick* Proof is wanting that the Christening has been performed at all—[8]

By the later meetings I have had with Dr. Johnson I find You have repaired the Neglect of Him which I mentioned in the beginning of my Letter; He says he has heard twice from You of late—On Wednesday last we talked of You a good deal at a Feast where a numerous Company was collected at Mr. Thrale's at Streatham; Count Manucci (if I spell his Name right) was there, and spoke very gratefully of the great degree of Kindness You had

[6] John Taylor (1711–88), one of SJ's last two surviving school friends, held the rectory of Market Bosworth in Leicestershire and a prebendal stall at Westminster. SJ visited Taylor almost every year at Ashbourne; and he and JB had been there on 26 and 27 Mar. (Journ.). Taylor was in London in May, when he consulted SJ on a lawsuit in which he was involved (To Temple, 1 May 1776; Journ. 5, 7 May 1776; *Life* iii. 51–52; *Letters SJ* ii. 125–31, 134–35, 137). On 25 June, SJ wrote, "Whether I shall wander this summer, I hardly know. If I do, tell me when it will be the best time to come to you" (*Letters SJ* ii. 144). There is no record of SJ's having visited Ashbourne again in 1776.

[7] Jacob Bryant (1715–1804), *A New System, or an Analysis of Ancient Mythology: Wherein an Attempt is made to divest Tradition of Fable; and to reduce the Truth to its Original Purity*, 3 vols., 1774–76. See *Life* iv. 272; v. 458.

[8] JB did not include this approval of public christening in the *Life*.

shewn Him at Edinburgh—He seems a very ingenious amiable kind of Man—[9]

I will trouble You to convey the inclosed Letter to Sir William Forbes—and when You can find Leisure shall be very glad to hear how You and Mrs. Boswel and Your Young Family do and hope to have a favourable account—We are all thank God going on very well. Our joint Respects wait Sir on You and Mrs. Boswel— I remain, Dear Sir, with great Regard Your very obedient humble Servant

BENNET LANGTON

We propose continuing in London the whole Summer—where Your Letter will therefore find me if You are so kind as to remember me—

To Bennet Langton, Friday 30 August 1776

MS. Yale (L 845). An extract in Lawrie's hand, to which JB added heading, place, and date. Sent 31 Aug. "Bennet Langton Esq.—of Mr. Hume's death—of Dr. Johnson—thanking him for his kind letter—and apologising for not having supt with him, according to appointment" (Reg. Let.).[1]

HEADING: To Mr. Langton.

Edin., 30 August 1776

David Hume's death[2] will be a topick of conversation in London.

[9] Count Mannucci, a Florentine nobleman and officer of cavalry, had been in Edinburgh during July, when JB, who thought him "a very well-looked man and very knowing and affable", entertained him several times (Journ. 14, 16, 19, 21, 27 July). JB first saw him at the Thrales'; they met him at Rouen in Oct. 1775, while they were travelling with SJ. See *Thraliana* i. 157 and n. 1; *Life* ii. 390, 394.

[1] Probably on the eve of his departure from London, 16 May 1776.

[2] Hume died on 25 Aug. On the 29th, JB wrote, "Grange and I went and saw David Hume's burial. We first looked at his grave in the burying ground on the Caltonhill, and then stood concealed behind a wall till we saw the procession of carriages come down from the Newtown, and thereafter the procession of the corpse carried to the grave. We then went to the Advocates Library, and read some parts of his Essays, of his Epicurean his Stoick, his Sceptick, and on Natural Religion. I was somewhat dejected in mind" (Journ.).

I am sorry to say that I beleive he persisted to the last in his wretched notions, and died in great tranquillity. To speak candidly as our minds are affected in various ways, the firmness of so able a man in infidelity must in some degree shock us.[3] What says Dr. Johnson?[4] May I beg of you to take the trouble of marking down speedily and collecting for me his sayings of which you have now an opportunity of hearing so many. I am obliged to you already for several. Do not wait for striking opinions, acute detections of fallacy or important remarks. Write any vigourous allusion such as the man "talking of making gold as—as a Cook Sir of making a pudding" or any peculiar expression such as "the gloomy malignity of the dog" (Kenrick).[5] By sending me sometimes a little packet of *Johnsoniana*, you will delight me in the meantime, and contribute to the future entertainment of the world.

[3] JB became acquainted with Hume in 1758 through his best friend, Temple (To Temple, 29 July 1758), and maintained the acquaintance to the end of the philosopher's life, even though he despised and feared Hume's ideas on religion. About a month and a half before Hume died, JB, knowing that the older man was dying, called on him. He found him "placid and even cheerful", in spite of his imminent death; and, with true Boswellian tact, brought up the subject of immortality. The conversation was apparently more disturbing to JB than to Hume, for JB "felt a degree of horrour, mixed with a sort of wild strange hurrying recollection of My excellent Mother's pious instructions of Dr. Johnson's noble lessons and of my religious sentiments and affections during the course of my life. . . . I could not but be assailed by momentary doubts. . . . But I maintained my Faith. . . . I left him with impressions which disturbed me for some time" ("An Account of My last Interview with David Hume, Esq.," 7 July 1776).

[4] The next year, when JB and SJ were visiting Taylor at Ashbourne, JB expressed his shock to SJ, who replied that he shouldn't be shocked. "Hume owned he had never read the New Testament with attention. Here then was a man, who had been at no pains to inquire into the truth of religion, and had continually turned his mind the other way. It was not to be expected that the prospect of death would alter his way of thinking, unless GOD should send an angel to set him right" (*Life* iii. 153; Journ. 16 Sept. 1777).

[5] JB did not include either of these dicta in the *Life*, probably because they were in a document he did not review. William Kenrick (?1725–79), miscellaneous writer, attacked SJ's edition of Shakespeare in *A Review of Dr. Johnson's New Edition of Shakespeare; in which the Ignorance, or Inattention of that Editor is Exposed, and the Poet Defended from the Persecution of his Commentators*, 1765. After a later attack, in *An Epistle to J. Boswell, Esq., occasioned by his having transmitted the moral Writings of Samuel Johnson to Pascal Paoli*, 1768, SJ had to restrain JB from replying. Kenrick was, in SJ's opinion, "one of the many who have made themselves *publick*, without making themselves *known*" (*Life* i. 498. recorded in Journ. 9 Apr. 1778).

From Topham Beauclerk to David Garrick, ?Saturday 5 July 1777[1]

MS. Yale (C 126).

ADDRESS: To D. Garrick Esqr.

Hertford Street

DEAR SIR: I have heard from Lord Pembroke,[2] since I came to town, that you are angry with me or Lady D. for something about Teziers[3] Subscription.[4] Now, if it is so, I apprehend somebody must

[1] The date is suggested by the period within which Le Texier was attempting to reconstitute his *Journal étranger* (see n. 4).

[2] Henry Herbert (1734–94), tenth Earl of Pembroke, who was married to Elizabeth, younger sister of Lady Di (*Comp. Peer.* x. 426).

[3] A.-A. Le Texier (c. 1737–1814) (*Walpole's Correspondence*, Yale Ed. xxxix. 273 n. 7) was born in Lyons of a family of sufficient status so that he felt himself barred from a career in acting. At first he became a civil servant, but gave it up in the early 1770s, prompted by his continuing enthusiasm for the theatre (A. D. Wallace, "Le Texier's Early Years in England", *Studies in Honor of John Wilcox*, ed. A. D. Wallace and O. R. Woodburn, 1958, p. 71). As an actor Le Texier's special skill was in taking all the parts in a play "giving the voice, bearing, and suggestion of action suited to each character in turn". He was an immediate and great success in France, and later in England upon his arrival in 1775 (Wallace, pp. 72–73). Because Le Texier's readings were always of French plays in French, his audience was restricted although enthusiastic (W. Roberts, "M. Le Texier: Reader of Plays", *Times Literary Supplement*, 19 Sept. 1936, p. 752). At first Le Texier was Garrick's protégé in England but their friendship apparently deteriorated, especially after Garrick retired from the stage and, early in 1778, started to give readings "à la Texier" (*Walpole's Correspondence*, Yale Ed. xxviii. 347).

Le Texier's name was generally spelled Tessier (Roberts, p. 752).

[4] Le Texier twice collected subscriptions to his *Journal étranger de littérature, des spectacles et de politique*, whose twenty-three issues were published in London from June 1777 to May 1778. At that point, in an advertisement in *The Morning Post* (21 May 1778) he announced his plan to reduce the number of volumes to twelve per year in order to cut the three-guinea subscription in half and broaden the audience. He promised that "'the first volume upon this improved plan will be published at furthest on the 15th of June'". A second advertisement in the same newspaper (29 May 1778) lamented his inability to cut the subscription price, and for this or whatever reasons the *Journal étranger* was never renewed (Wallace, pp. 81–82).

Both Beauclerk and Garrick subscribed to the original *Journal*, the list of subscribers indeed suggesting "a kind of 'social register' for the time" (Wallace, pp. 77–78). When the pages of the present volume were fixed, Beauclerk's letter was doubtfully assigned to 1778 because 1777 seemed early for Garrick to be showing hostility to Le Texier. On review, late June or early July 1777 seems somewhat more likely. The cause of Garrick's anger being at best conjectural, it would seem to be sounder practice to consider chronology and the location of the parties. The first subscription of the *Journal étranger* was advertised in *The Morning Post*, 30 May 1777. Garrick, who attended the celebration of the King's

have told some lie upon this occasion, as I had nothing to do in the Affair good or bad, more than telling Lady D. that you would subscribe to his Book. I wish you would appoint any time when you would call here, as I wish much to have it explained, which cannot be done by Letter. I will tell you honestly all I know about it, and I dare say one quarter of an Hours Conversation will set all right. I would have waited upon you, but I am not well enough to go out. Pray fix what time you will come and I will take care to be ready for you. I dine tomorrow at Mr. Walpoles:[5] any other time I shall be ready to attend you; I wish you could come this Evening, pray send an Answer by the Bearer. Believe [me] to be, notwithstanding[6] Tezier, ever yours

T. Beauclerk

Lady D. had nothing to do in this the fault must be between me and Tezier, and I wish you would call here to see which is in Fault.

From Topham Beauclerk to Bennet Langton, ?Friday 13 February 1778[1]

MS. Yale (C 127).

ADDRESS: To B. Langton Esqr., Turks Head, Gerrard Street, Soho Square.

[London]

DEAR LANGTON, I intended dining at the Club to day, but was siezed with the Gout in my Stomach that I was near dead. I am better, but not well enough to go out.

birthday on 4 June 1777, could have met Pembroke there; Beauclerk, returning to London from Bath at the end of June or early in July, could then first have learned of Garrick's complaint. See *Henry, Elizabeth and George*, pp. 101, 103–04; *General Evening Post*, 5 June 1777; *Letters of David Garrick*, ed. D. M. Little and G. M. Kahrl, 1963, iii. 1156–86; *Letters of Edward Gibbon*, ed. J. E. Norton, 1956, ii. 135, 141; J. H. Jesse, *George Selwyn and His Contemporaries*, 1882, iii. 172; *Walpole's Correspondence*, Yale Ed. xxxii. 365; vi. 458. In any case, Walpole reported Garrick jealous of Le Texier as early as Feb. 1776 (*ibid.* xxviii. 245, 285).

[5] The only specific mention Walpole makes of the Beauclerks' dining with him seems to have been on 6 July 1777 (*Walpole's Correspondence*, Yale Ed. xxxii. 365). This may well be the very dinner here referred to.

[6] MS. "notwithstandind"

[1] This meeting of The Club is the only one held before the last Friday dinner (3 July 1779) at which everyone mentioned in this letter was present and from which Beauclerk was absent (*The Club*). The forfeit placed after his name in the absent list could well mean that he had persisted in an intention to go until it was too late to make an excuse.

Pray ask Jones,[2] Reynolds, Percy, and yourself to dine here on Sunday at 5 o'clock.

I wish you would call here and tell Gibbon, or Jones, or Percy I shall be glad to see them this Evening if they are not engaged. Pray send me an Answer. Ever your

T. B.

Pray tell Jones I have an Oriental Manuscript of Lord Northingtons[3] he cannot find any body Who can tell him what it is. Ask Jones if he will look at it.

To Bennet Langton,
Thursday 26 February 1778

MS. Johnson Memorial House, 17 Gough Square, London. Sent 26 Feb. "Bennet Langton Esq. of my Wife's illness—Begging to have his prayers for her preservation—That I regret not hearing from him etc." (Reg. Let.).

ADDRESS: To Bennet Langton Esq., Welbeck Street, Cavendish Square, London.

POSTMARKS: FE 26, 2 MR.

Edinburgh, 26 Febry. 1778

MY DEAR SIR: There has now been a very long cessation of correspondence between us,[1] which I sincerely regret; and I am

---

[2] William (later Sir William) Jones (1746–94), Orientalist and judge, who was elected to The Club with Garrick in 1773.

[3] Robert Henley, second Earl of Northington (1747–86), an intimate friend of Charles James Fox and later (1783) Lord Lieutenant of Ireland (*Comp. Peer.* ix. 700). The manuscript is unidentified.

---

[1] JB's last letter to Langton was written on 30 Aug. 1776, and as he did not get to London in 1777 he had not seen him for close on to two years. Langton, who now had five small children (the oldest not quite six years old), had subsided into a state of be-

mused domesticity which his friends considered little better than moral paralysis. SJ wrote to JB in Nov. 1776, "Do you ever hear from Mr. Langton? I visit him sometimes, but he does not talk. I do not like his scheme of life; but, as I am not permitted to understand it, I cannot set any thing right that is wrong" (*Letters SJ* ii. 153). He wrote again in Feb. 1777, "Langton lives on as he is used to do" (*ibid.* p. 162). And in July his report was the same: "I have dined lately with poor dear Langton. I do not think he goes on well" (*ibid.* p. 185). For Mrs. Thrale's caustic but brilliant account of the "*Langtonian* Mode of Life" (too long to quote), see *ibid.* p. 193.

pretty sure that I wrote last; so that I may as Merchants say draw upon you for value in your hands. Not that my letter was valuable in any other sense than as expressing that regard which I entertain for you.

The Neglect even though unintentional of so valuable a Friend is harder upon me at present, that I have been all this winter in great anxiety about my Wife, who has for many months been afflicted with a hoarseness and pain in her breast at times, and has upon three different occasions, spit some blood.[2] These are symptoms very alarming to her, because that dismal disease a Consumption has been fatal in her family, her brother and all her sisters having died of it.[3] I flatter myself that her Complaints are occasioned by a severe cold joined with nervous illness; and that when the weather grows mild, she will recover her health. You may figure, My Dear Sir, how dreary a state I should be in were she to die and leave me with three young children.[4] I beg to have your prayers for her preservation.

I have occasion to be in London about the 24th of next Month.[5] I wish to prevail with her to accompany me. But She dislikes travelling; and prefers going to some country place in Scotland, where she can have her children along with her. Perhaps however, she may yield to intreaty.

I hope Lady Rothes and your young ones are well. I had the

[2] JB's journal for the winter of 1777–78 is a record of constant illness on Mrs. Boswell's part and of "dreary and horrible" spirits on his (Journ. 13 Oct. 1777). His bouts of drinking and his nocturnal wanderings caused her no less anxiety than her illness caused him. He reports the spitting of blood on 9 Dec. 1777 and on 5 and 14 Jan. 1778, the second occurrence being largely his own fault.

[3] Mrs. Boswell was the youngest but one of five children. Marion Montgomerie, the youngest, died after 3 Nov. 1764 (Session paper: *Petition of Sir Walter Montgomerie-Cuninghame*, 3 Feb. 1778, p. 2) and before 17 Oct. 1769 (From Margaret Montgomerie); James Montgomerie of Lainshaw died 16 Dec. 1766 (*Gent. Mag.* xxxvi. 600); Elizabeth, who married Capt. Alexander Mont-

gomerie-Cuninghame, and succeeded to Lainshaw, died 3 Jan. 1776; and Mary Montgomerie, who married James Campbell of Treesbank, died 4 Mar. 1777 (Journ. 11 Nov. 1775, 8 Jan. 1776, 6 Mar. 1777).

[4] JB frequently considered the possibility of his wife's death: "The apprehension of losing her, and being left with five young children was frightfully dreary. All my affection for her, and gratitude to her, and the consciousness of not having acted as her husband ought to do, overwhelmed me; and several times I cried bitterly, and one night lay long awake in misery; having wild schemes of desperate conduct floating in my imagination, upon supposition of her death" (Journ. 7 Jan. 1782). Compare Journ. 5 Jan. 1778.

[5] JB arrived in London 17 Mar. (Journ.).

pleasure of seeing Your Mother and sister for a few minutes last Autumn at Ashbourne where I had a cordial meeting with Dr. Johnson.[6] How does the Club go on? And how is Mr. Beauclerc? My Wife joins me in best compliments to you and Lady Rothes, and I ever am, Dear Sir, your most obedient humble servant

JAMES BOSWELL

From Bennet Langton, Saturday 14 March 1778

MS. Yale (C 1687). Received 12 Apr., "Bennet Langton Esq. (returned from Edinburgh)[1] thankful for my remembrance, wishing to see me in London—a little of Dr. Johnson" (Reg. Let.).

ADDRESS: To James Boswel Esqr., in James's Court, Edinburgh.

POSTMARK: 14 MR.

London, March 14th. 1778

MY DEAR SIR, The kind Reproach, in Your Letter with which I was lately favoured, of being a Letter in Your debt is justly founded, and had indeed been so long the Case that I was almost ashamed to renew the Correspondence; however that Negligence enhances greatly my Obligation to You for Your kind Notice of me—When Your Letter arrived I was writing to our Friend Sir William Forbes, and had just been requesting of Him to acquaint You of the state of our respected Friend Johnson's Health, lest You should have observed the disagreeable account of it in the Papers, and not have had any means of knowing that it was erroneous[2]—I hope, Dear Sir, as You observe Yourself, that the

---

[6] JB was in Ashbourne with SJ from 14 to 24 Sept. 1777 (Journ.), and saw Mrs. Langton and Langton's sister Elizabeth on the 23rd.

[1] That is, the letter was forwarded from Edinburgh to London. JB had already left Edinburgh on 13 Mar. and arrived in London on the 17th (Journ.).

[2] On 27 Feb. 1778, *The Morning Post* reported that "the public is likely to suffer an irreparable loss, by the death of the great luminary of the English language, Dr. Johnson . . . he being now attended by Dr. Jebb, without the smallest hopes of ever restoring him to a

tolerable degree of health." The notice was repeated in *The Public Advertiser* for 28 Feb., and *The St. James's Chronicle* for 26–28 Feb. In *The London Chronicle* for 26–28 Feb. (xliii. 208), however, appeared the following: "We have the pleasure to assure our Readers, that the paragraph in one of the morning papers relative to the dangerous illness of the celebrated Dr. Johnson, is without foundation, that gentleman's indisposition being only a slight cold." JB wrote to SJ on 12 Mar.: "The alarm of your late illness distressed me but a few hours; for on the evening of the day that it reached me, I found it contradicted in

improving State of the Season of the Year may greatly contribute to giving Mrs. Boswel Relief in her hoarseness and Cough—as part of Her Complaint You say is nervous, I should suppose a great deal of Air and gentle Exercise would be recommended: by what I understand from Dr. Johnson, in a Letter writ to him since my receipt of Yours,[3] You discourage our having any hopes of seeing Her this Spring when You design giving us *Your* Company; though among other sollicitations a Gentleman, of the Name of Pietri, who is with General Paoli, mentioned, as I understood him, that the General, in a Letter to You,[4] had very much urged her coming—however if She is not to be prevailed upon, I hope at least, Dear Sir, that You will bring us favourable accounts of her advance in Recovery. You will be pleased to assure Her of mine and Lady Rothes's best Respects—The Club, after which You inquire, goes on; it is reduced to *Dinners* only, and those once a fortnight[5]—Our Friend Johnson has been there the two last times, in excellent Spirits, and has displayed his power of Understanding with a Vigour full as considerable as ever—so that increasing Years, and his late Ailments do not appear to operate in any abatement of his Abilities—Among other particulars he talked of two Persons that have exhibited on the publick Theatre remarkably, in their several Walks in the medical Line, which were Dr. Ward and the Chevalier Taylor[6]—He said of them, that,

The London Chronicle, which I could depend upon as authentick concerning you, Mr. Strahan being the printer of it. I did not see the paper in which 'the approaching extinction of a bright luminary' was announced. Sir William Forbes told me of it; and he says, he saw me so uneasy, that he did not give me the report in such strong terms as he had read it. He afterwards sent me a letter from Mr. Langton to him, which relieved me much" (*Life* iii. 221).

[3] It was actually written on the same day as the letter to Langton: 26 Feb. 1778 (*Life* iii. 219).

[4] Paoli's letter has not been recovered, but JB recorded it on 10 Mar.: "General Paoli ... that he has an elegant apartment for me—hopes my Wife will accompany me" (Reg. Let.). JB, who met Pietri on 18 Mar. and then did not learn his Christian name, tells us concerning him only that he was a Corsican and "a young brisk Man" (Journ.). The name is common in Corsica.

[5] The change from weekly suppers to fortnightly dinners was completed in Jan. 1776 (*The Club*). See *ante* From Beauclerk to Langton, ?5 Jan. 1776, n. 1.

[6] Compare Journ. 24 Apr. 1779 (*Life* iii. 389-90), where SJ, probably with some nudging from JB and Langton, gave his judgements on Ward and Taylor in a different and in some respects less interesting version. When he wrote the *Life*, JB should have recalled Langton's letter and quoted it in a foot-note.—Joshua Ward (1685–1761), a quack doctor, supported himself on his "pill and drop" and enjoyed the patronage of the King. Among his medicines was a particularly harmful eyewash. John Taylor (1703–

of the two, Ward he thought was the *foolisher*, and Taylor *the more ignorant*—Ward was, I think he said, a Gentleman by birth, and had been in Parliament, So that he *did* know something of the state of the time he lived in, but Taylor, he said, he believed knew as little of the *present*, as he did of the *future*—Ward he believed might know that *as to an Archbishop and a Duke*, there was some difference as to their situation and Character in Life but Taylor he believed would not have known of any, nor indeed, where discriminations were still much wider—and yet, says Johnson, to these two Men a Nation as enlighten'd and considerable as ours, trusted, to one their Eyes, and to the other their Lives. I have endeavoured to give You a little Sketch of part of what past and wish heartily You had been present to have heard the rest— Garrick sat next him and appeared to *devour* his discourse with very eager Relish—as did Colman likewise who was of our Set that day—Mr. Beauclerk is surprizingly recover'd and generally attends the Club—I told him of Your Enquiry after Him—If You see Sir William Forbes before Your setting out (which will be very near approaching) please to present my Compliments and thanks for his kind Letter which I have just received. Adieu. Yours sincerely

B. LANGTON

To Thomas Percy, Saturday 25 April 1778

MS. Yale (L 1062).

ADDRESS: To The Reverend Dr. Percy, Northumberland House.

Southaudley Street, 25 April

DEAR SIR: I wrote to Dr. Johnson on the subject of the *Pennantian* Controversy; and have received from him an Answer[1] which will

---

1772), an itinerant oculist, made his headquarters in London, but visited almost every court in Europe. Commonly known as the "Chevalier", he was noted for charlatanry in advertising. He was appointed oculist to George II in 1736, and was reported to have gone blind before his death.

[1] For an account of the argument between SJ and Percy over the merits of Thomas Pennant, the traveller and naturalist, see Journ. 12, 20, 25, 27–28 Apr. 1778 and *Life* iii. 271–78, where the letter of SJ which JB here refers to is printed. Percy had complained of SJ's attack to JB, who visited him at Northumberland House on 20 Apr.

delight you. I read it yesterday to Dr. Robertson at the Exhibition;[2] and at dinner to Lord Percy General Oglethorpe etc.[3] who dined with us at General Paoli's who was also a Witness to the high *testimony* to your honour.

General Paoli desires the favour of your company next tuesday to dinner, to meet Dr. Johnson.[4] If I can, I will call on you today.[5] I am with sincere regard Your most obedient humble servant

JAMES BOSWELL

From Topham Beauclerk to Bennet Langton, ?Tuesday 28 April 1778[1]

MS. Yale (C 128).

ADDRESS: B. Langton Esq.

[London]

DEAR LANGTON: I was dressed, and had dined my Chair ready and intended coming to you, but I am so very much out of order, with a violent headach and sickness that it is impossible. I would give ten guine[a]s to have you all here, but I cannot come to you. Pray tell Boswell that notwithstand[ing] the Nonsense of his Anger that I really want to see him, and that he need not doubt it that it is of Consequence to myself. To ballance this, pray tell him that he is the only Man in the World that I ever made an Apology to when I was not in the wrong.[2]

[2] William Robertson, the historian. The Exhibition of the Royal Academy opened on 24 Apr. (advertisement in *Daily Advertiser*, 19 Mar. 1778).

[3] Basil Feilding, sixth Earl of Denbigh, and Lewis Lochee, head of the Royal Military Academy at Little Chelsea, were also there (Journ. 24 Apr.).

[4] Percy did not attend the dinner (*ibid.* 28 Apr.).

[5] JB did call on Percy and copied SJ's letter for him (*ibid.* 25 Apr.). SJ took offence at this, and JB had the painful task of getting the copy back (Journ. 27–28 Apr. 1778; *Life* iii. 276). Percy must have given JB his own letter at the same time.

[1] Langton and JB, with other company including Reynolds and SJ, dined at Paoli's on 28 Apr. (Journ., *Life* iii. 324–31). It seems likely that Beauclerk had been invited and had arranged to eat his invalid's dinner at home and come afterwards; that Langton reported Beauclerk's letter to JB, and that JB "half engaged" to go with Langton to call on him the following evening. (See n. 2.) To assume that the letter was written on the 29th gives a forced meaning to "have you *all* here," and raises the question when JB heard of the letter and made his tentative engagement.

[2] JB's anger was, in great part, the result of his own forwardness and stubbornness. Late in the evening of 9 Apr.,

Contrive sometime that I may spend a few Hours with you before you go to your Regiment as you may be there some time.[3] It is not impossible, considering My state of Health that these may be the last.

From Topham Beauclerk to Bennet Langton, Monday ?June 1778[1]

MS. Yale (C 129).

ADDRESS: Bennet Langton Esqr.

[London]

DEAR LANGTON: It will be great Charity if you will dine with me at Muswell Hill to day, and I will call upon you at 1/2 past two and carry you, and bring you back at eight. If you cannot dine there, I will wait for you 'till after dinner, and call upon you at five o'clock. I hope you will be able to go one or other of these Times, as it is the last time, I shall go. Tomorrow I am engaged. Wednesday I go to Mr. Walpoles for some days and upon my return I go to Brighthelmstone. Ever yours Sincerely

T. B.

after the dinner at Sir Joshua Reynolds's (reported in *Life* iii. 250–60) plus calls on Mrs. Montagu, Lord Mountstuart, and Sir John Pringle, JB appeared uninvited at Beauclerk's, where there was a "Company of Ladies and Gentlemen of their own Class. . . . No sooner had I taken my chair than he [Beauclerk] said, '*When* do you go to Scotland?' I was nettled a little at so abrupt a quest[ion] when I was just come, and answered, 'I won't tell you.' He said He had Bonds there he wanted paid. . . . Supper came up and I slipt away. I know not if I should have had wit enough to do it had I not been nettled. But my stay would have been very unwelcome. Was angry at Beau.'s behaviour. But I should make allowance for his being disconcerted by my interloping." At Langton's on the 13th, Beauclerk spoke to JB again about the bonds and tried to get him to stay after SJ left. "But I was resolute and would not stay and watch late especially at *his* desire." "I had half engaged to go Beauclerc's with Langton," JB recorded

on 29 Apr., "as Beauc. had written to him, desireous to see me and apologising for his behaviour to me. But pride or fear of seeming weak made me resolve not to go. So I was set down at home by Langton who worthily regretted my not going with him." Langton apparently managed to reconcile his two friends later (*post* To Langton, 18 Mar. 1780). See also *ante* pp. xxxix–xl.

[3] SJ reported to JB, on 3 July 1778, that Langton had gone to his regiment (*Letters SJ* ii. 250); the camp broke up on 11 Nov. of that year ("Plans of Encampments", BM Add. MSS. 15533, f. 10).

———

[1] Determined by Beauclerk's presence at Muswell Hill and the impending trip to Brighton. There is no record of a visit to Horace Walpole in 1778, unless one makes it by rather forced interpretation of Mme. du Deffand's "Ce doit vous être une privation l'éloignement des Beauclerk" (To Walpole, 27 Sept. 1778,

From Topham Beauclerk, c. Monday 29 June 1778

Not reported. Received 4 July. "Topham Beauclerk Esq. desireous to know about his York-building Company Bonds—of Langton etc." (Reg. Let.). If the preceding letter is dated correctly, Beauclerk was in London during the last days of June, when this letter was probably written. For the York Buildings Company bonds, see *post* To Langton, 17 Nov. 1780, n. 1.

From Topham Beauclerk to Bennet Langton, ?after Friday 3 July 1778[1]

MS. Yale (C 130).

ADDRESS: To Bennet Langton Eqr.

[?Muswell Hill]

DEAR LANGTON: When we parted, I did not take leave of you as that is a melancholy Ceremony at any time, and I was not all in good spirits, but I assure you I felt it as much, as if, I had expressed it ever so strongly.

A long Absence at any time is very disagreable, but much worse to any Body in my Situation, because the Chances of not meeting again are so much increased. However that may be, you may be assured that whenever I die you will lose a very sincere Friend, and one [who] is perfectly sensible of your Value. I am better than I was and go tomorrow to Brighton. Dr. Fordyce[2] who went to

Walpole's Correspondence, Yale Ed. vii. 73), but the Beauclerks were certainly at Brighton by 24 July 1778 (*ibid.* xxviii. 421; *Letters of Edward Gibbon*, ed. J. E. Norton, 1956, ii. 192, 196). They were at Brighton again in the autumn of 1779, but Lady Pembroke reported in Nov. of that year that the Beauclerks "never go to Muswell Hill now" (*Henry, Elizabeth and George*, pp. 301, 334).

---

[1] This letter would seem to have been written after Beauclerk had been at Walpole's and before he left for Brighton.

Langton had left for Warley Camp by 3 July 1778 (*ante* From Beauclerk to Langton, ?28 Apr. 1778, n. 3).

[2] Possibly Dr. William Fordyce (1724–92), knighted in 1782, who as a young man had served three campaigns as surgeon to the Guards and long retained his connexion with the Army, but more probably his nephew, Dr. George Fordyce (1736–1802), member of The Club, chemist (he instructed Beauclerk in chemistry: *Life* i. 250 n. 1), and in 1791 author of a *Treatise on the Digestion of Food.*—Camps had been established at Warley Common (Essex) and Coxheath

your Camp and Cox Heath in order to poison the Troops with Bread, told Me he saw you in a hard shower of Rain.

If I come to Town I hope to meet you here. Believe me to be very Sincerely and Affectionately Yours

T. BEAUCLERK

To Topham Beauclerk, Monday 6 July 1778

Not reported. Sent from Edinburgh 6 July. "Topham Beauclerk Esq. with an Account of his Bonds. etc. etc. (Copy)" (Reg. Let.).

From Topham Beauclerk, c. Saturday 25 July 1778

Not reported. Received 30 July. "Topham Beauclerc Esq. from Brightelmston, anxious that I will see that justice is done him about his York-building Company's Bonds" (Reg. Let.).

(Kent) in June 1778. Each soldier at Coxheath was allowed "a loaf of wheaten bread, of six pounds weight", which was to serve him for four days, he paying fivepence to the contractor and Government paying the remainder; "he is also allowed three pounds of wood every day for dressing his victuals" (*London Chronicle*, 18–21 July 1778). There was much complaint about bad bread: "several waggon-loads . . . too bad for the men to eat, many being ill on that account" (*Morning Post*, 11 June 1778); "very black, and bad indeed" (*ibid.* 18 June); "the militia [at Warley Camp] in general were disposed to make a considerable disturbance, on account of the bread, which was as displeasing to the sight as to the taste, a dirty black" (*ibid.* 23 June); a subaltern named Joliffe interfered on behalf of the soldiers because of the badness of the bread (*ibid.* 29 June, also *London Chronicle*, 23–25 July; see also *ibid.* 21–23 July; *St. James's Chronicle*, 30 July–1 Aug.; *Public Advertiser*, 6 July; 10, 25 Sept. 1778).—Beauclerk's "poison" perhaps connects this military disturbance of 1778 with a continuing indictment of the use of adulterants in bread, most memorably represented in Smollett's *Humphry Clinker*, 1771 (letter of M. Bramble, London, June 8), though apparently initiated as far back as 1757 by an anonymous furious pamphlet entitled *Poison Detected: or Frightful Truths; and Alarming to the British Metropolis. In a Treatise on Bread.* But at this time bread seems to have been under indictment as being unwholesome even when made of certified ingredients. JB and Charlotte Ann Burney, at a dinner at Hoole's, 7 Apr. 1781, both heard SJ declare that a doctor whose name neither caught had told SJ that he could extract a strong poison from bread (Yale MS. M 39; BM Egerton MSS. 3700B). Miss Burney records that one of the other guests at the dinner, Charles William Boughton-Rouse, thereupon remarked that Dr. William Cadogan (author of a famous treatise on the gout) had said that bread was the most unwholesome food in the world, perhaps because he knew about this poison.

To Sir Joshua Reynolds, Monday 10 August 1778

Not reported. Sent from Edinburgh 10 Aug. "Ommitted 10 Sir Joshua Reynolds recommending Walter Weir a young painter, as a student in the Royal Academy" (Reg. Let.). Walter Weir was probably the son of the painter Alexander Weir (d. 1797), at whose house, "head of Toderick's wynd" (Williamson's *Edinburgh Directory 1774–75*), JB's brother John had been confined (Journ. 9, 11–12 Dec. 1774). Williamson's *Directory 1784–85* lists "Alex. Weir & Son, curious in paintings, St. James Square." In 1809 a W. Weir, "Edinburgh and 98, Mount Street, London," exhibited two paintings at the Royal Academy. "Walter Weir, painter, Toddrick's yard" appears in *The General Post Office Directory*, Edinburgh, 1816–17. There is no record in the Royal Academy of Weir's being admitted a student. Compare *post* To Reynolds, 20 Nov. 1779.

From Topham Beauclerk to Bennet Langton, ?1778 or ?1779[1]

MS. Yale (C 131).

ADDRESS: B. Langton Esqr.

[London]

DEAR LANGTON: Ever since I wrote to you I have been taken up partly by being for a Few Days in the Country, and the rest of the Time by a Law Suit and severe Rheumatism. The Law Suit is compromised, but the Rheumatism remains in full perfection. If you have no other Engagement, I shall be much obliged to you if you will come here this Evening, as I cannot stir Hand or any other Limb. If you come pray send the Servt. on to Mr. Paradise with the Note he has got for him. If you cannot come order him

---

[1] I have been unable to find any record of a lawsuit involving Beauclerk after 1744. His illnesses are never specifically referred to as rheumatism. Evidence for Langton's whereabouts during these two years is lacking for the most part. However, the letter seems to have been written after Beauclerk and Paradise had become fairly well acquainted. The only reference to Paradise's having been entertained by Beauclerk is in *Life* iii. 386: he, Langton, SJ, JB, Reynolds, Jones, and Steevens attended a dinner at Beauclerk's on 24 Apr. 1779. Probably the letter was written late in Beauclerk's life.

to bring the Note back again that is for Mr. Paradise. I am, dear Sir, ever yours

T. B.

From Topham Beauclerk to Bennet Langton, ?1778 or ?1779[1]

MS. Yale (C 132).

ADDRESS: Bennet Langton Esq.

[London]

DEAR LANGTON: I had intended calling upon you this Evening, but I have so very bad a cold, that I cannot go out. I have sent the Coach and if you are not engaged you will be very charitable if you will come in it. I have not been able to stir out since I saw you, and I have a thousand Things to say to you, besides the pleasure I always have in your Company. I hope you will not make a Scruple about my Coach going out for it really has not been out since I saw you, Lady D. and myself both being ill, and ther[e] is not too much work for four Horses.

Mr. Paradise called upon me the other Morning, and has made me a present of a Manuscript.[2] I wish you could prevail upon him to come and sup here with you. But that part as you please yourself. I am, dear Sir, Sincerely and Affectionately Yours

T. BEAUCLERK

To Bennet Langton, Thursday 25 February 1779

MS. Yale (L 846). A copy in Lawrie's hand (except for heading). Sent 25 Feb. "Bennet Langton Esq. A freindly letter (Copy) enclosing one to Mr. Beauclerc" (Reg. Let.); "Wrote lettr. to Langtn. etc. easily" (Notes, 15 Feb. to 9 Mar. 1779).

HEADING: To Bennet Langton Esq.

1 The seal on this letter is identical with that on the letter dated "?after 3 July 1778". There is no seal on the letter which I have placed between these two. Because the references to Paradise and the similarity between the seals are not particularly strong evidence, the dating of this letter must be considered highly conjectural.

2 Unidentified.

Edr., 25 Feb. 1779

MY DEAR SIR: Your indolence and my own in writing letters are very similar. For I beleive we write perhaps as many letters as most people do, and yet though our mutual friendship is very sincere, we delay and delay to write to each other till it becomes an aukward thing to begin a letter. I felt consolation under my indolence when our excellent friend Sir Wm. Forbes told me that you had put off writing to him, I know not how long though it was to receive money which as times go is pretty eagerly seised.

Lady Rothes did us the honour of a visit one forenoon.[1] But we regretted that we could have so little of her Ladyships company and were not a little dissappointed that you did not come to Scotland.

However the time is now I hope near at hand when I shall have the pleasure of meeting you again in London,[2] and if these few lines shall have the good effect to quicken the course of your animal spirits I may flatter myself that the first post after you receive it will have a letter to me in charge from you.

Garricks death affected me much. But I have had such strong health and spirits all this Session that I have been less liable to depression than usual.[3] I regretted my not being in London to make one in the Funeral procession which did so much honour to his memory. I was pleased to see as one of the Divisions *Gentlemen of the Literary Club.* I beleive it had not a name before except the Alehouse designation as Beauclerc says,—of the Turkshead Club.[4] You have encreased your number much since I was in London.[5]

---

[1] On Tuesday 6 Oct. 1778, "Before two, Lady Rothes and her three eldest children paid us a visit with Miss Wauchope of Niddery, her Ladyship being on a visit to that family" (Journ.). See James Paterson, *History of the Family of Wauchope of Niddrie-Merschell*, 1858, pp. 81–83.

[2] JB left Edinburgh on Wednesday 10 Mar., and arrived in London on the 15th.

[3] Garrick died on 20 Jan. JB reported in his notes on the 26th that "Garrick's death dwelt on [my] mind."

[4] The funeral ceremonies, which were held on 1 Feb., began with a procession of thirty-three mourning coaches, in addition to thirty-four others, from Garrick's house on the Royal Terrace in the Adelphi to Westminster Abbey. Among the mourning coaches were five, eighteenth to twenty-second in the procession, carrying the "Gentlemen of the Literary Club" (*London Chronicle*, 2–4 Feb. xlv. 115). JB remarks in the *Life* (i. 477) that the designation "The Literary Club" was first used on the occasion of Garrick's funeral. It was used occasionally by some members after that.

[5] Four new members were elected in 1778: Sir Joseph Banks, William Windham, Sir William Scott, and Lord Althorp.

I trouble you with a letter to Mr. Beauclerc which I am sure you will willingly take care of, as you mediated between us in so very friendly a manner.[6] I have done all that can be done in the present state of matters, about his *Bonds*.

It is long since I have heard from Dr. Johnson, which makes me uneasy. I wish he had more of a kindly tenderness for weaker minds than his own.

My wife joins me in best respects to yourself and Lady Rothes. She and my children are I thank GOD very well. I ever am, my dear Langton, Yours with real regard.

To Topham Beauclerk, Thursday 25 February 1779

Not reported. Sent from Edinburgh 25 Feb. "Topham Beauclerc Esq. giving him all the information I could get as to his York building Bonds etc. (Copy)" (Reg. Let.). Enclosed in preceding letter.

From Thomas Warton, Saturday 27 February 1779

MS. Yale (C 3068). Received 7 Mar.: "Ommitted 7 Mr. Thos. Warton that he will send me if I please two historical Ballads concerning Scotland" (Reg. Let.).

ADDRESS: To James Boswell Esq., of the Court of Advocates, at Edingburgh, Scotland.

POSTMARKS: OXFORD, 1 MR.

ENDORSEMENT: 9d.[1] Received 7 March 1779, Mr. Tho. Warton, offering me two Ballads on Scottish History.

Trin. Coll., Oxon., Feb. 27. 1779

SIR, You once favoured me with a Commission to enquire about a Ballad (as I remember) of the Battle of Halidon-Hill. I have a manuscript (transcribed from the Cotton Library in the British

---

[6] For JB's activities in behalf of Beauclerk and his bonds, and the quarrel between them, see *ante* From Beauclerk to Langton, ?28 Apr. 1778; *post* To Langton, 17 Nov. 1780.

[1] The postage paid for the letter.

Museum) on this subject, written by one Laurence Minot, an obscure Rhymer who lived in the reign of Edward the third. If this is the Poem you mean, I will send it. I have also by the same Author, a Poem on the Battle of *Banocburn*.[2] This also is at your service. I am, Sir, with great Esteem, Your most obedient Servant

T. WARTON

From Topham Beauclerk to Bennet Langton, ?1779[1]

MS. Yale (C 133).

ADDRESS: B. Langton Esqr.

[London]

DEAR LANGTON, I have enquired amongst the Booksellers and find when they have a Copy perfectly clean and well bound of the large paper Cæsar[2] they sell it for 20 Gs. This Copy of Mrs. H.[3] is

[2] Warton probably refers to an incident recorded by JB in his journal on his first meeting with Warton at Oxford on 20 Mar. 1776: "He did not say much; but as Dr. Johnson had some time ago, given him a memorandum from me to inquire about an ancient Ballad for Lord Hailes, he very obligingly told me that he should send me it and asked to have my address." JB was collecting materials for Lord Hailes, editor of *Ancient Scottish Poems. Published from the MS. of G. Bannatyne*, 1770. No mention of these poems is made in the surviving correspondence between JB and Lord Hailes. It was Warton who attributed them to Minot (?1300–?52), who was probably a soldierly minstrel favoured by the Court (see *A Catalogue of the Manuscripts in the Cottonian Library Deposited in the British Museum*, 1802, p. 364). Although Warton printed "The Battle of Banocburn" (Galba E. ix. 49b) on p. 107 of the third volume (1781) of his *History of English Poetry, from the Close of the Eleventh to the Commencement of the Eighteenth Century*, 1774–81, he did not publish "Halidon Hill" (Galba E. ix. 49). Minot's poems

were first printed in their entirety by Joseph Ritson in 1795.

[1] Date determined, rather arbitrarily, by Horace Walpole's comment, on 14 Nov. 1779, "Mr. Beauclerc has built a library in Great Russell Street that reaches halfway to Highgate. Everybody goes to see it; it has put the Museum's nose quite out of joint" (*Walpole's Correspondence*, Yale Ed. xxxiii. 136).

[2] *C. Julii Caesaris quae extant, Accuratissime cum libris editis et MSS. optimis collata, recognita & correcta*, Acceserunt annotationes Samuelis Clarke, Sumptibus & typis Jacobi Tonson, 1712. Clarke (1675–1729) was Rector of St. James's, Westminster. His Caesar was "said to be especially correct in the punctuation, and one of the most beautiful books ever published in England" (DNB). A copy of this folio edition printed by Tonson is listed in *Bibliotheca Beauclerkiana, A Catalogue of the Large and Valuable Library of the late Honourable Topham Beauclerk, F.R.S.*, 1781, p. 70.

[3] Unidentified. JB reported in his notes, 20 Apr. 1781, that he had been told by

90

dirty and must be cleaned, and new bound which will cost 3 Gs. at least. If she chuses to part with it, I [3a] will give her 17 Gs. for it, which is a couple of Gs. More than a Bookseller will give as it must be new bound, and will then only sell for 20 Gs., and they must have some profit in such a Book as this. If I was not sure that 17 Gs. was the very full value I would not offer it. I gave 12 for that I had from White [4] which is new bound and the cleanest Copy that ever was seen. The small paper generally sells for 10 Gs. in good Condition. As this is one of our finest English printed Books I am willing to give the full price for it as I think it a pity not to have one in such a Library as mine. Pray send me an Answer as soon as you can, because if I buy this I must return mine to White and make the best Bargain I can for it, and as I have had it some time, it will not be fair to keep it long, and th⟨en⟩ return it. I am, dear Langton, Sincerely ⟨yours⟩

T. Beauclerk

From Topham Beauclerk to Bennet Langton, Spring 1779

MS. Yale (C 134).

ADDRESS: Bennet Langton Esqr.

[London]

DEAR LANGTON: I have had a very Severe Fever all Night but am now just in that state, the Fever being gone, that I am unable to do any thing but should be glad of some Company in the Evening. If you are not engaged I shall be much obliged to you if you will come here at 8 this Evening, and if you can find Mr. Paradise,

Edward Chamberlayne, "a very communicative literary Man", "that a poor Woman brought Clarkes Cæsar to Beauclerk and asked five guineas. That tho this appeared [a] high price, gave it to her. [He] then went to Elmsley [a bookseller] who told him [it was a] great rarity; would give fifteen guineas for it—Beauc[lerk] sent her the other 10. This Book sold at his Auction for 43 guineas." A marked copy of the sale catalogue in the possession of F. W. Hilles indicates that the volume was sold for £44.

[3a] MS. "I I"

[4] Benjamin White (c. 1725–94), bookseller of Horace's Head, Fleet Street (H. R. Plomer and others, *Dictionary of the Printers and Booksellers*, 1932, p. 261).

I shall be very glad of his Company likewise, besides that I want much to see him before he goes to Paris.[1]

He is civil enough I know to execute a Commission for me that I very much want done there. I am, Dear Sir, ever yours

T. B.

Pray send an Answer. By coming you will not only do me much good but keep me out of harms way for to tell the truth I deserve this Fever, as much as any can do.

To Bennet Langton, Monday 13 September 1779

Not reported. Sent from Edinburgh 13 Sept. "Bennet Langton Esq. to the same effect. (Copy)" (Reg. Let.). "To the same effect", that is, as the preceding Register entry: "General Paoli recommending W. Dick (Copy)." William Dick (1762–96), later Sir William, was the son of Sir Alexander Dick of Prestonfield, Bt. (1703–85), and adjutant in the First Foot Guards (*Comp. Bar.* iv. 446). Before leaving on a jaunt with Col. James Stuart, JB called on the Dicks at Prestonfield "and surprised them with my sudden London Journey, and asked their commands for Willy, whom I promised to see" (Journ. 25 Sept. 1779).

To Sir Joshua Reynolds, Saturday 20 November 1779

Not reported. Sent from Edinburgh 20 Nov. "Sir Joshua Reynolds by Walter Weir again recommending him" (Reg. Let.). Compare *ante* To Reynolds, 10 Aug. 1778.

To Thomas Warton, late November 1779

Not reported. Sent from Edinburgh. Referred to in the following letter.

---

[1] Though France and Great Britain were at war, Paradise was able to make a trip to Paris in this year (arriving 20 May 1779) to solicit the assistance of Benjamin Franklin in preserving Mrs. Paradise's Virginian estate, which was in danger of being confiscated. William Jones accompanied him as legal adviser. Paradise became an American citizen in Oct. 1780 (Shepperson, pp. 132–38, 150–51; *Letters of Sir William Jones*, ed. Garland Cannon, 1970, i. 288–90).

From Thomas Warton,
Tuesday 7 December 1779

MS. Yale (C 3069). Received 13 Dec. "Mr. Tho. Warton asking if he shall send me two Ballads (temp Ed 3)" (Reg. Let.).

ADDRESS: To James Boswell Esq., at Edingburgh.

POSTMARKS: 8 DE, OXFORD.

ENDORSEMENT: 9d. Received 13 Decr. 1779. Tho. Warton asking if two Ballads (Temp. Ed. 3) should be sent to me.

Trin. Coll. Oxon., Dec. 7. 1779

SIR: The favour of your Letter is but just come to hand, being sent after me to Winchester from Oxford. I have almost forgott the Ballads I mentioned to you.[1] If on the Battles of Banocburn and Halidoun Hill, etc. (Temp. Edu. 3.) I have them, and at your's, or Sir David Dalrymple's service. I am, with great Respect, Sir, Your most obedient Servant

T. WARTON

To Bennet Langton,
Thursday 23 December 1779

MS. Yale (L 847). A copy in Lawrie's hand. Sent 23 Dec. "Bennet Langton Esq. Cordial. Begging to have Anecdotes of Dr. Johnson (Copy)" (Reg. Let.).

HEADING: (To Bennet Langton Esq.).

Edinburgh, 23 Decer. 1779

MY DEAR SIR: I cannot let this year come to an end without writing to you. Do you remember how when we were driving down Curzon street in a most cordial frame a short while before I left London last May,[1] we talked how strange and yet how probable it was that we should perhaps not hear from each other

---

[1] Warton mentioned these ballads in his letter of 27 Feb. 1779 (*ante*).

[1] There is no record of this ride. JB left London early on the 4th of May 1779

(*Life* iii. 393; To Temple, 3 May 1779; Notes, 4 May 1779), having heard of his father's illness. There are no entries in his journal between 26 Apr. and 4 May.

during our next separation. I am *persuaded* that we esteem and love one another. I am *certain* upon one side. Yet from some unaccountable procrastinating indolence, there shall be sometimes no communication between us for eight or nine months at a time. This may be considered as a proof that we are both so sure from mutual consciousness that our friendship is permanent that we need not repeated assurances of it. But are we not both losers by such intervals? And should we not rouse ourselves to procure a satisfaction which we both value not a little. I am happy at being the first who writes this time.

You will probably have heard that I had an unexpected jaunt to London last Autumn. I was *Volontaire attaché* to my friend Colonel Wortley Stuart's Regiment;[2] So that Dr. Johnsons joke of *Arma virumque cano* might have been applied to me, though I did not afford so meritorious an occasion for it as you did.[3] I regretted much that you was not in Town when I was there, and that I could not get down to see you at Coxheath Camp[4] which I really intended.

I was a fortnight at *Headquarters* at Chester, where I declare I past my time more happily than I ever did in any place. I know not if I should even except London for the same portion of time. The general hospitality of the people, the curiosity of the town itself and the beauty of its environs and the animation of a Military society gave me the most cheerfull spirits. And your celestial

[2] James Archibald Stuart Wortley-Mackenzie (1747–1818), second son of John, third Earl of Bute, and Mary, only daughter of Edward Wortley Montagu and Lady Mary Wortley Montagu, raised the 92nd Highland Regiment, and was officially appointed its Lieutenant-Colonel Commandant on 27 Dec. 1779. While in Edinburgh in Sept., the Colonel asked JB to go with him to Leeds to see the regiment and then to London to bid farewell to Lord Mountstuart, the Colonel's elder brother, before he left for his embassy at Turin (*Scots Peer*. ii. 301–03; Journ. 21 Sept.). The jaunt began on 27 Sept. with both Mrs. Boswell's and Lord Auchinleck's approval (they felt that the Colonel and his brother might use their influence in JB's behalf), and took JB to Leeds, London, Lichfield, Chester, Liverpool, Warring-ton (where he and the Colonel parted), Carlisle, and back to Edinburgh on 9 Nov. (Journ. 21–23, 26 Sept. 1779; *Life* iii. 399, 411–13, 415–16; Notes 9 Nov. 1799). The journal JB kept on this trip ("truly a log-book of felicity," he wrote to SJ) has been lost; but see *Life* iii. 399–416.

[3] SJ's Virgilian joke on Langton appears to be otherwise unrecorded.

[4] In 1779, according to the Order Book of the 3rd Battalion, the Lincoln-shire Militia was sent into camp at Cox-heath, near Maidstone, Kent, on 16 June, for its training (W. V. R. Fane, *Annals of the 3rd Battalion Lincolnshire Regiment, formerly the Royal North Lincoln Militia, 1759–1901*, 1901, p. 11). The encampment, which began on 7 June, broke up on 29 Nov. ("Plans of Encampments", BM Add. MSS. 15533, f. 7v).

friend the Bishop[5] was pleased to treat me with so much kindness and allow me so much of his conversation, that I felt myself sensibly bettered. I was delighted with his preaching.

I had the pleasure to hear from worthy Sir William Forbes that you and Lady Rothes and the Young ones were well lately.[6] I trust that now you are comfortably settled in the Metropolis, I shall be favoured with hearing from you. How does our Club go on? Do you see Dr. Johnson often. It will be doing me a kindness for which I shall be very gratefull, if you will write down and send me all the anecdotes concerning him, and all his sayings which you recollect. Pray do I beg it of you. My wife joins me in compliments to yourself and Lady Rothes; and I ever am with most sincere regard, My Dear Sir, Your affectionate friend etc.

Pray present my Compliments to Mr. Beauclerc and let me know particularly how he is.

From Topham Beauclerk to Bennet Langton, n.d.[1]

MS. Yale (C 135).

ADDRESS: B. Langton Esqr.

[London] Sunday 3 o'clock

DEAR LANGTON: I am still very ill, I have taken James's powder[2]

[5] Beilby Porteus (1731–1808), Bishop of Chester, later of London. JB wrote to SJ from Chester, 22 Oct. 1779, "The Bishop, to whom I had the honour to be known several years ago, shews me much attention; and I am edified by his conversation. ... The study of the place itself, by the assistance of books, and of the Bishop, is sufficient occupation" (*Life* iii. 413). The Bishop was later (Nov. 1780) blackballed by The Club (*Life* iii. 311 n. 2; iv. 75 n. 3). Peregrine Langton-Massingberd wrote that from Porteus "my father uniformly received much notice. He was my GOD-father; and once gave me two half crowns—which is all that I have to thank him for" (PL-M's letterbook, p. 24b).

[6] Probably by word of mouth. Forbes wrote to JB on 21 Dec. 1779, but with no mention of Langton. The letter mainly concerns JB's Ashbourne journal, which JB had lent him, but shows that the two men had met recently.

---

[1] There is no evidence, either internal or external, on which to base a conjectural date for this letter.

[2] Robert James, M.D. (1705–76), a friend of SJ, patented a powder chiefly made up of calcium phosphate and oxide of antimony, which had a strong diaphoretic action, and was frequently prescribed in cases of raised temperature and inflammatory pain. His flamboyant methods of advertising somewhat

which of Course confines me, if I was well otherwise. I wish you would call here any time this Evening, besides the pleasure of seeing you I have really something to say to you of great Consequence, (that is to myself). I mention this, because it has happened to me that people have appointed a Time to see me having something of Great Consequence to say, I have been very uneasy 'till I saw them, and when I did, I found that it was only of Consequence to themselves. If they had communicated that Secret to me before, I should have been perfectly easy 'till I saw them. Pray come how ever if you can. I am heartily vexed, and that is not good for the Bile. If you can do me no good by your Advice, you will at least relieve me from myself and that is one very good thing. Ever yours

T. B.

Send word at what time you will come that I may not let any one else in.

From Topham Beauclerk to Bennet Langton, n.d.[1]

MS. Yale (C 136). A torn fragment.

[London]

DEAR LANGTON: I wish you would dine here today or call after Dinner early you will find nobody here.[2] I likewise want to ask you a Question, and I do not find it very probable that I shall ever see you again. Believe me to be

damaged James's reputation as a physician; and it was thought by many that the powder was in part responsible for Goldsmith's death. This accusation has since been considerably modified. See *Life* i. 26 n. 1; 81; 159; iii. 500–01; and N & Q, 1925, cxlviii. 351, 390, 412, 425; cxlix. 11–12; 1941, clxxx. 48–49, 68–69.

[1] If one assumes that Beauclerk's

premonitions were accurate, the letter was, of course, written in the last months of his life and could be dated late 1779 or early 1780. But the previous letters show that he might have expressed such fears at any time after 1775.

[2] The sense is probably ". . . after Dinner. Early you will find . . .", but it could be ". . . after Dinner—early, [or] you will find . . .".

To Thomas Warton,
Saturday 1 January 1780

Not reported. Sent from Edinburgh 1 Jan. "Mr. Thomas Warton that the two Ballads (temp. Ed. 3) which he obligingly offers will be very acceptable to Lord Hailes and me. This enclosed to Dr. Johnson" (Reg. Let.). See *Life* iii. 418 and n. †.

From Thomas Warton,
Saturday 19 February 1780

MS. Yale (C 3070). A copy of JB's reply, *post* 2 May, is on fourth page.

ADDRESS: To James Boswell Esq., Edingburgh.

POSTMARKS: OXFORD, 28 FE, [illegible].

ENDORSEMENT: 9d. Received 3 March 1780, Mr. Thomas Warton—that the old Ballads which Lord Hailes and I wish to see are to be in his third volume of the History of English Poetry—But if they are wanted immediately he will send them.

Trin. Coll. Oxon., Feb. 19. 1780

DEAR SIR: I have but just received yours, which has long expected me at Winchester while I was at Oxford. The old Poems I mentioned I will transcribe and send immediately if any great Expedition is necessary: but they will appear soon in print in my third volume of the *History of English Poetry*. I am greatly obliged to Sir D. Dalrymple for the Honour he intended me, but I never received the Book.[1] You will please to inform me if the old Poems are wanted immediately. I am with great Respect, Dear Sir, Your most obedient Servant

T. WARTON

To Bennet Langton,
Saturday 18 March 1780

MS. Yale (L 848). A copy in Lawrie's hand. Sent 18 Mar. "Bennet Langton Esq. that I have seen Mr. Beauclerc's death in the Newspapers. Begging to know about it. etc. etc. (Copy)" (Reg. Let.).

HEADING: (To Bennet Langton Esq.).

[1] No doubt a presentation copy of Sir David's *Annals of Scotland*, 2 vols., 1776–79.

Edr. 18 March 1780

MY DEAR SIR: I wrote to you some months ago but have not been favoured with hearing from you since. I hope you are well notwithstanding the general sickness of this severe season. The *Publick Advertiser*[1] which I received yesterday mentions the death of Mr. Beauclerc on Saturday the 11th and the *London Chronicle*[2] which came today mentions the same sad intelligence. One can never be quite sure that such an article in a Newspaper is true.[3] But I am afraid this is too certain. Pray inform me My Dear Sir; and if we have lost him, be so obliging as communicate to me what particulars you know. Might I hope that your most friendly mild religious suggestions have had some insinuating influence upon him.[4] The death of a Companion so manly so knowing, so brilliant and so high in fashion as Topham Beauclerc damps ones views of life exceedingly. Surely Dr. Johnson will be affected with it.[5] Beleive me, I now with cordial regard remember your benevolent reconciliation of Beauclerc and me.[6]

I shall not be in London this Spring. I have no appeal in the House of Lords nor any case in the House of Commons; and my finances at present will not admit of a jaunt of pleasure to the Metropolis,[7] though indeed I consider it as my great school of instruction. You are to have Lord Monboddo amongst you. He set out a few days ago: You will hear of him at the British Coffee-

---

[1] Monday 13 Mar. 1780, p. 3.

[2] 11–14 Mar. 1780, xlvii. 250.

[3] See *ante* From Langton, 14 Mar. 1778, n. 2, for mention of a false report of SJ's dangerous illness.

[4] On 23 Mar. 1775, JB had been witness to an argument on religion between Langton and Beauclerk in which "Langton quoted passages from Books" and "Beauclerk threw out immediate sparkles from his own mind. I tried to aid Langton a little. . . . It made me somewhat melancholy to find that even Langton who has studied Religion so much, was like myself unable to convince another" (Journ.).

[5] SJ wrote to JB on 8 Apr., "Poor dear Beauclerk—*nec, ut soles, dabis joca.* His wit and his folly, his acuteness and maliciousness, his merriment and reasoning, are now over. Such another will not

often be found among mankind" (*Letters SJ* ii. 336).

[6] See *ante* From Beauclerk to Langton, ?28 Apr. 1778.

[7] Part of JB's financial difficulties was the result of the advances he had made to his wife's nephews, the Cuninghames, until they should receive their patrimonies (Journ. 1, 7 Jan. 1780). In addition, his fees were less than they formerly had been, possibly, he suspected, because his father had been prevented by illness from attending the Court (*ibid.* 11 Mar.). "I never," he wrote in his journal, "before this winter felt real uneasiness from embarrassed circumstances. For I knew not how to raise £200" (*ibid.* 20 Jan.). Charles Dilly, in Jan., agreed to lend JB the £200 for two years (*ibid.* 24 Jan.).

house.[8] Though he has an absurd prejudice against Dr. Johnson, I hope they shall meet.[9] Pray tell me something of the Dr. It is long since I heard from him.

I have from time to time very agreeable conversations with our worthy friend Sir William Forbes. We remember you with joint esteem.

My wife joins me in best respects to yourself and Lady Rothes And I remain, My Dear Sir, Your affectionate humble servant

From Lady Diana Beauclerk to Bennet Langton, Thursday c. April 1780[1]

MS. Yale (C 110).

ADDRESS: To Bennet Langton Esqre., Welbeck Street.

Thursday night, Hertford Street

Lady Di Beauclerk presents her Compliments to Mr. Langton and takes the liberty of sending him Mr. Garricks and Docr. Johnsons Pictures.[2] She flatters her self he will accept of them—she is certain Mr. B. would have wished them so disposed of.

Lady Di is going out of Town tomorrow, hopes to see Mr. L. when she returns.

[8] A place on Cockspur Street much frequented by Scots. A club of Scots, called The Beeswing, met there.

[9] Lord Monboddo, apparently envious of SJ's attainments, could never hear good spoken of him, and, in his *Origin and Progress of Language* (v. 274), belittled SJ and his *Dictionary*. See *Life* ii. 74 nn. 1, 2; iv. 273 n. 1; and v. 74–82. Monboddo had once written to JB (28 May 1777) that SJ was not a fit subject for biography ("no Life of Dr. Johnston —No more Memoirs of Parish Clerks at least none written by you") and that JB should apply himself to the study of Homer. SJ and Monboddo met at Allan Ramsay the painter's on 30 Apr. (*Letters SJ* ii. 348, 351).

[1] Lady Di moved on 14 Mar. 1780 to the house in Hertford Street, where she and Beauclerk had lived before the move to Great Russell Street, having spent the two days after Beauclerk's death with her brother, Lord Robert Spencer (*Henry, Elizabeth and George*, p. 429). Her sister, Lady Pembroke, wrote to Lord Herbert (Elizabeth Beauclerk's future husband) in Apr., "Sister Di has just taken a house [Devonshire Cottage] at Richmond" (*ibid.* p. 464). This note was written probably the day before she left for Richmond.

[2] See *post* From Langton, c. 18 Apr.–18 May 1780 and n. 8, for a description of the portraits.

To Thomas Warton,
Tuesday 2 May 1780

MS. Yale (L 1272). A copy, written on page 4 of *ante* From Thomas Warton, 19 Feb. Sent 2 May. "Mr. Tho. Warton that he need not send the Ballads as they are to be in his third volume" (Reg. Let.).

Edin., 2 May 1780

DEAR SIR: There is no great hurry in our seeing the Ballads. Sir David Dalrymple and I will be happy to find them in your third Volume of the *History of English Poetry*. The sooner *that* comes, the Publick as well as we will be the happier. Enclosed is an order for *The Annals of Scotland*.[1] If you want any thing from this country you may freely command me; or if you would come and see Scotland which is really worth your trouble when you have leisure, you will find me ready to contribute to your entertainment. I am with much regard, Dear Sir, Your obliged humble servant

From Bennet Langton,
c. Tuesday 18 April–c. Thursday 18 May 1780[1]

MS. Yale (C 1688).

ADDRESS (in Lord Lothian's hand): James Boswel Esqr., James's Court, Edinburgh.

FRANK: Lothian.[1a]

POSTMARKS: [3 illegible, one or more of them probably FREE].

HEADING in JB's hand: No date. I received it by post on Monday 22 May 1780.

ENDORSEMENT: Received 22 May 1780 Bennet Langton Esq. An excellent Letter on various topicks. Particularly great respect paid to Dr. Johnson.

---

[1] Probably an order on John Murray (1745–93), the English bookseller for whom Hailes's volumes were printed.

[1] As appears from change of quill and from internal dating, the conclusion of this letter, from "We have had our meeting", was written c. 18 May (JB received it on 22 May). The portion preceding this, probably from "It is so long since I began this Letter", was written on 8 May (see n. 23). The rest shows no certain signs of serial writing, and was perhaps all written c. 18 Apr. (see nn. 3 and 13).

[1a] William John Kerr, Marquess of Lothian (1737–1815), K.T., Colonel of the First Horse Guards, ultimately General in the Army, was a Scots Representative Peer.

[London][2]

My dear Sir, In regard to the former of the two Letters You favoured me with, my usual Laziness, I believe I must confess, prevailed so far, that having let too much time elapse without replying to it, I had begun to look to the expected time of your making us a Visit here in London, to make my excuses vivâ Voce, and then received the disagreeable Intelligence by Your last Letter, that You had not an Intention of coming this Spring— instead of dwelling upon excuses for dilatoriness as to my *writing*, *which* ought to be of much more Value than it is to deserve any length of apologies for delaying it, I will proceed, to acquaint You, that as soon as I had received Your last Letter, I went to an Engagement I had for an Evening Conversation party at Mr. Ramsay's,[3] and imparted to Him and some more of Your Friends who were there, the word I had received from You that You were not coming to Us this Spring—and they expressed their sympathizing with me in Regret upon it—Sir Joshua Reynolds very particularly;—Mrs. Boscawen[4] (as I had taken the Liberty of mentioning that You had frankly said that the Journey was just at present too expensive) wished that some fictitious Charge could be brought against You of a State-Offence that might occasion Your being brought up to Town at the publick Expence, and, when it proved to be a mistake, then, You know, in Equity, the publick must likewise bear Your Expences back again;— which Idea I hope will appear to You, as it did to me, to be a

[2] Langton was in London on 25 Apr. (*Letters SJ* ii. 348) and apparently remained there until he went to Chatham. SJ reported to Mrs. Thrale on 6 June that Langton "is gone to be an engineer at Chatham" (*ibid.* p. 365); and since he had written to Mrs. Thrale six times between 25 Apr. and 6 June, it seems probable that, had Langton left much before the first of June, SJ would have mentioned it earlier.

[3] Allan Ramsay (1713–84), portrait-painter to the King and friend of David Hume and Adam Smith. A man of considerable culture and a good scholar, he frequently entertained SJ and other members of The Club. The only party at Ramsay's at this time recorded by Reynolds in his engagement book was

held on 30 Apr.; SJ was also there (*Letters SJ* ii. 351). But a date so late as 30 Apr. does not square with Langton's statement that he went to Ramsay's as soon as he had received JB's letter of 18 Mar. 26 Mar., the last Sunday in Mar., instead of 30 Apr., the last Sunday in Apr., would be a much more probable date. Reynolds's engagement book is not complete and not always accurate in the recorded entries.

[4] Frances Glanville (d. 1805), wife of Admiral Edward Boscawen, of whom JB wrote, "her manners are the most agreeable, and her conversation the best, of any lady with whom I ever had the happiness to be acquainted" (*Life* iii. 331). Her husband had died in 1761.

handsome Compliment, and which was therefore my inducement for mentioning it—and the more readily as, if Mrs. Boscawen is an acquaintance of Yours, I believe You will agree with me that the Sense and Discernment She possesses give a great degree of Value to Her Praise.

You will have known, as this Letter has lingered too long, by the time it reaches You, that[5] the melancholy Information You had received of Mr. Beauclerk's Death is true. When I received the account of it it startled me very much, for though I had known of his being exceedingly ill, he had appeared to have struggled so far through the Disorder, that I had persuaded myself he would get over it;—What You do me the Honour to intimate as to any good Effects from Suggestions of mine, I am afraid I must not flatter myself with any sanguine hope of—he has conferred a Mark of His Esteem upon me which I cannot but very much prize, which is, jointly with a Gentleman of Cheshire[6] who is a Relation of his, the Guardianship of His Son, on the Contingency of our surviving Lady Die Beauclerk—He has left Her the Use and full Disposal of every thing he died possessed of that he had any power over, in a short Will which he executed in his last Illness; the first direction it contained was, that his Corps was to be carried down into Lancashire and deposited by the side of His Mother in the burying place of Her Family—What he has left will, with proper Care taken of it, prove not an unhandsome Provision both for his Son and his Daughters[7]—Lady Die has made me a Present which I believe You will think of no small Value, a Portrait by Sir Joshua Reynolds of Dr. Johnson, agreed by all who have seen it to be one of the most striking likenesses that ever was taken, and another of Mr. Garrick, likewise a speaking likeness[8]—thus, Sir, I have put together a few particulars

[5] JB excerpted what follows in this sentence to introduce a long quotation from the present letter in the *Life*. See *post* n. 10.

[6] George Leycester, or Leicester (c. 1733–1809), of Toft, Cheshire, Beauclerk's cousin. See *Letters SJ* ii. 336, and *The New Rambler*, July 1948, p. 15.

[7] Beauclerk's mother was Mary, daughter of Thomas Norris, Esq., of Speke, in Lancashire. He left one son and two daughters: Charles-George (d.

1846); Mary, who was married to Francis, Count Jenison Walworth; and Elizabeth, who married her cousin George, Earl of Pembroke, and died in 1793 (Burke, *Peerage*, s.v. St. Albans; *Comp. Peer.* x. 428).

[8] Beauclerk had caused an apt but unsparing quotation from Horace, *Satires* I. iii, to be inscribed on a tablet which formed part of the frame of the portrait of SJ; Langton removed the inscription. SJ said to Langton, "It was kind of you

relating to this poor Man, who has gone to the "undiscovered Country from whose Bourn no Traveller returns",[9] as You seemed to have an anxious degree of Curiosity respecting him— I do not wonder that one of Your Sensibility feels the satisfaction You express at having agreed to Reconciliation with him, which surely ought to be a prevailing mode of Sensation in relation to Those who are departed!—Had his Talents been[10] directed in any sufficient degree as they ought, I have always been strongly of opinion that they were calculated to make an illustrious Figure, and that opinion, as it had been in part formed upon Dr. Johnson's Judgement, receives more and more confirmation by hearing what,[11] since his Death, Dr. Johnson has said concerning them— A few Evenings ago, I[12] was at Mr. Vesey's,[13] where Lord Althorpe,[14] who was one of a numerous Company there,

to take it off," but after a short pause added, "and not unkind of him to put it on" (*Life* iv. 180–81, 451–52). Beauclerk also caused eleven lines from Shakespeare's *Love's Labour's Lost* to be inscribed on the portrait of Garrick (*ibid.* pp. 96–97). Both portraits were replicas, commissioned in 1778 or 1779 from pictures painted for the Thrales (*ibid.* pp. 451–52); James Northcote, *The Life of Sir Joshua Reynolds*, 2nd ed., 1819, ii. 36 n.). The portrait of SJ is now in the possession of Mrs. A. J. L. Murray, Cadlington House, Horndean, Hants. I have been unable to trace the present ownership of the portrait of Garrick.

[9] *Hamlet*, III. i. 79–80.

[10] Sign-posts on the letter and a direction to the printer in the manuscript of the *Life* show that from this point to the end of the paragraph the letter served directly as printer's copy (*Life* iii. 424–26).

[11] The printer misread this word as "that", making nonsense of the passage, and JB failed to detect the error in the proof. It was corrected in the second edition of the *Life* (1793) and listed in *The Principal Corrections and Additions to the First Edition of Mr. Boswell's Life of Dr. Johnson*, 1793.

[12] The *Life* reads "he", though "I" remains unchanged in the copy. If this was a change made by JB in the proof

and not a printer's error, it was careless of JB not to make the further change of "Dr. Johnson" to "him" farther on in the sentence.

[13] Agmondesham Vesey (d. 1785), Accountant-General of Ireland and second husband of Mrs. Elizabeth Vesey, one of the Blue Stockings. He was elected to The Club in 1773. Mrs. Vesey seems regularly to have entertained the members of The Club, with other guests, after the Club meetings (*Life* iii. 424 n. 3), but that this party was not held on a Club night is almost certainly proved by a letter of SJ to Mrs. Thrale, Tuesday 11 Apr. 1780: "On Sunday evening [9 Apr.] I was at Mrs. Vesey's. . . . There was Dr. Barnard of Eaton, and we made a noise all the evening, and there was Pepys, and Wraxal till I drove him away" (*Letters SJ* ii. 339). Sir Joshua Reynolds was also there (Engagement Book).

[14] George John Spencer (1758–1834), styled Viscount Althorp, later second Earl Spencer (1783), Fellow of the Royal Society (1780), M.P. for Northampton (1780–82), Lord Privy Seal (1794), and Knight of the Garter (1799). He collected one of the finest private libraries in Britain. William Jones, formerly his private tutor, proposed him for membership in The Club on 30 Nov. 1778, shortly after his graduation from Trinity

addressed Dr. Johnson on the Subject of Mr. Beauclerk's Death, saying, "Our Club has had a great Loss since we met last" [14a]—He replied, "a Loss, that perhaps the whole Nation could not repair!" The Dr. then went on to speak of his Endowments, and particularly extolled the wonderful *Ease* with which he uttered what was highly excellent—he said that no Man ever was so free, when he was going to say a good thing, from a *Look* that expressed that it was coming; or, when he had said it, from a Look that expressed that it *had* come—At Mr. Thrale's some days before, when we were talking on the same Subject—He said, referring to the same Idea of his wonderful Facility, that Beauclerk's Talents were those which he had felt himself more disposed to envy than those of any Man[15] whom he had known.—At the Evening I have spoken of above at Mr. Vesey's, You would have been highly entertained,[16] as it exhibited an Instance of the high importance in which Dr. Johnson's Character is held, I think even beyond any I ever before was witness to—The Company consisted chiefly of Ladies—among whom were the Dutchess Dowr. of Portland, the Dutchess of Beaufort, whom I suppose from Her Rank I must name before Her Mother Mrs. Boscawen, and Her elder Sister Mrs. Lewson who were[17] likewise there; Lady Lucan Lady Clermont, and others of Note both for their station and understandings[18]—Among the Gentlemen were, Lord Althorpe whom I have before named; Lord Maccartney, Sir Joshua Reynolds,

College, Cambridge; and in writing to inform him of this, ran through the entire list, giving each member a characterizing phrase or sentence, e.g. "Boswell of Corsica, a good-natured odd fellow" (*Letters of Sir William Jones*, ed. Garland Cannon, 1970, ii. 280). In 1781 he married Lavinia, eldest daughter of the first Earl of Lucan (*Comp. Peer.* xii. 154–55).

[14a] "Since you and I met", not "Since the last meeting of The Club". The Club met on 14 Mar., 4, 18 Apr., 2, 9 May, but SJ did not attend any of those meetings. Althorp was present on 18 Apr. and 9 May (*The Club*).

[15] The *Life* omits "Man", almost certainly through a printer's error.

[16] "Highly entertained" changed in JB's hand to "much gratified". This is the only substantive change made by JB in the copy.

[17] The *Life* reads "was", either by printer's error or by change in the proof—again a very careless change if made by JB. In Langton's sentence the first "were" covers the two duchesses, Lady Lucan, Lady Clermont, and "others of note", while the second "were" covers Mrs. Boscawen and Mrs. Lewson. The sentence as printed in the *Life* ("who was likewise there") leaves Mrs. Boscawen out of the company.

[18] Dowager Duchess of Portland: Margaret Cavendish (1714/15–85), only daughter of Edward Harley, second Earl of Oxford, was the widow of William Bentinck, second Duke and seventh Earl of Portland (1708/09–62). (*Comp. Peer.* x. 592–93).—Duchess of Beaufort:

Lord Lucan, Mr. Wraxal, whose Book You have probably seen, *The Tour to the Northern Parts of Europe*, a very agreeable ingenious Man, Dr. Warren; Mr. Pepys the Master in Chancery, whom I believe You know, and Dr. Barnard the Provost of Eaton[19]—As soon as Dr. Johnson was come in and had taken a Chair, the Company began to collect round him till they became not less than four, if not five deep; those behind standing, and listening over the heads of those that were sitting near him. The Conversation for some time was chiefly between Dr. Johnson and the Provost of Eaton while the others contributed occasionally their Remarks. Without attempting to detail the particulars of the Conversation, which perhaps if I did, I should spin my account

Elizabeth (1747–1828), younger daughter of Mrs. Boscawen, was the wife of Henry Somerset, Duke of Beaufort (1744–1803) and Lord-Lieutenant of County Monmouth (*Comp. Peer.* ii. 55). —"Mrs. Lewson": Frances (b. 1746) was married in 1773 to John Leveson-Gower, second son of the first Earl Gower and a captain in the Navy. He was later (1787) appointed Rear-Admiral.— Lady Lucan: Margaret Smith (d. 1814), wife of Charles Bingham, the grandson of Agmondesham Vesey through his elder daughter by his first wife, Charlotte Sarsfield. Bingham (1735–99) was created Baron Lucan of Castlebar in 1776, and later (1795), Earl of Lucan (*Comp. Peer.* viii. 237–38).—Lady Clermont: Frances Cairnes (c. 1734–1820), first daughter of Col. John Murray and Mary, Dowager Baroness Blayney, married William Henry Fortescue (1722–1806) in 1752. He was created Baron Clermont in 1770, Viscount and Baron, 1776, and Earl of Clermont in 1777 (*Comp. Peer.* iii. 276–77).

[19] George Macartney (1737–1806), Lord Macartney, Baron of Lissanoure, later Viscount (1792) and Earl Macartney (1794, all in the peerage of Ireland); Envoy to Russia, 1764–67; Secretary to the Lord Lieutenant of Ireland, 1769–72; Governor of Grenada, 1775–79, of Madras, 1781–85; Ambassador to China, 1792–94; on secret mission to Louis XVIII, 1795–96; Governor of the Cape of Good Hope, 1796–98. He married (1768) Jane, second daughter of the third Earl of Bute (*Comp. Peer.* viii. 323–25). He was elected to The Club in 1786. —Nathaniel William Wraxall (1751–1831), traveller, intriguer, and writer of historical memoirs, had been in the service of the East India Company (1769–72), and was employed in an attempt to restore Caroline Matilda, the sister of George III, to the Danish throne. In 1775, he published *Cursory Remarks made in a Tour through some of the Northern Parts of Europe, particularly Copenhagen, Stockholm, and Petersburgh.* He was also the author of the lively *Historical Memoirs of my own Time* (1815) and *Posthumous Memoirs* (1836). He was created a baronet in 1813 upon the express nomination of the Prince Regent.—Richard Warren, physician.— William Weller Pepys (1740–1825), the brother of Sir Lucas Pepys, was the father of Charles Christopher, first Earl of Cottenham, and Henry, Bishop of Worcester. His wife was noted for her successful bluestocking parties (Alice C. C. Gaussen, ed., *A Later Pepys: The Correspondence of Sir William Weller Pepys*, 1904, i. 6–18). He was created a baronet in 1801 (*Comp. Peer.* iii. 459).— Edward Barnard (1717–81), formerly (1754–65) Provost of Eton, of whom SJ said, "He was the only man . . . that did justice to my good breeding" (*Life* iii. 54 n. 1).

out to a tedious length, I thought, my Dear Sir, this general account of the Respect with which our valued Friend was attended to might be acceptable.

It is so long since I began this Letter that I have some doubts, out of shame at my own Sloth, whether to send it, however the hope that it may [be][19a] of some amusement to You must preponderate—I have thought myself very fortunate in seeing a good deal of Lord Monboddo since he came to Town. He has done me the Favour of supping with me, where he was to have met General Oglethorpe, but we had a disappointment, as the General was obliged to go away early, and Lord Monboddo had imagined that our Hour of meeting was later, than I had intended—however since that I mentioned to Mr. Paradise who was of our Party that Evening, my Wish that a Meeting should take place between the Genl. and Lord Monboddo. He accordingly was so kind as to ask the Genl. to a Dinner where Lord M. was asked at his House, and Yesterday They met and gave me great Cause of Satisfaction at the Endeavour I had used to effect it, as they were very well pleased with each other—both in many other respects and in particular, as You will very readily conceive, from the General's imparting to Lord M. an account of a Gentleman who is come from the East Indies (of the Name of Perry)[20] furnished by what I can understand, with a larger store of Knowledge in oriental Learning, particularly as to the various Languages and Dialects of those Regions, than has perhaps yet been attained by an European—Lord M. is going immediately to endeavour at seeing Him and I hope will be successful in accomplishing it—

To morrow we have a meeting extraordinary called at our Club for considering of filling up the Vacancies, now become two, and of increasing the Number of the Club. The two proposed are Mr. Malone,[21] and the Political Wit Mr. Tickell,[22] who, I should

[19a] Omitted by Langton, inserted above the line by JB.

[20] George Perry, referred to by JB as "the Orientalist" or "Oriental Perry", but identified no further. On 15 May 1781, Perry breakfasted with JB and sickened him with his verbiage (Journ.); on 4 June of the same year, he wrote to JB from Portsmouth, thanking him for the *Account of Corsica*. The letter, signed "George Perry", is endorsed by JB:

"Mr. Perry the Traveller into the East, when about to sail in 1781. Q? Did he ever return?" Garland Cannon reports that he died in a suburb of Calcutta, 12 Mar. 1786 (*Letters of Sir William Jones*, 1970, ii. 790, 814; personal communication).

[21] Edmond Malone (1741–1812).

[22] Richard Tickell (1751–93), pamphleteer and dramatist, grandson of Addison's friend, married in this year

think would be a very good Accession—We have had our meeting and though it was carried for increasing the Club to ⟨the⟩ Number of thirty five, yet the two abovementioned Gentlemen as well as two others that were proposed, in the ballot had one or more black Balls—[23]

One of the occurrences that passed there was that the eleven of Us who were present, subscribed our Names to a Note writ to Davies the Book seller[24] for eleven Sets of his newly-published *Life of Garrick* which were accordingly sent by Him to us at the Tavern; I think it was a good natured Idea. Sir J. Reynolds started it—But I shall make it too late to go to Night if I do not conclude— Accept Lady Rothes and my Best Regards to Yourself and ⟨Mrs.⟩ Boswel—Adieu and believe me to be, Dear Sir, With much Regard Your affectionate humble Servant

BENNET LANGTON

From Lady Diana Beauclerk to Bennet Langton, Tuesday 10 October 1780[1]

MS. Yale (C 111).

ADDRESS: To Bennet Langton Esqre.,[2] at Mr. Adamsons[3] in The Dock Yard, Chatham, Kent.

POSTMARKS: WR, 11 OC.

Mary Linley, sister-in-law of Sheridan. The author of a successful satirical forecast of the proceedings at the opening of Parliament in 1778 ("Anticipation"), he wrote numerous pamphlets supporting the ministry of Lord North, and later supported Fox. After representing himself to Warren Hastings as in deep distress and receiving a loan, he took his own life.

[23] The meeting was held on 9 May, with William Jones presiding. "The number of The Club was increased to thirty-five, but was not to exceed forty. Many members signed a resolve to blackball any candidate when there were actually forty members" (*The Club*). The "two others" proposed are not recorded in the Club minutes. Malone was elected in 1782, but Tickell never became a member.

[24] Thomas Davies (?1712–85), actor

and bookseller, who, on 16 May 1763, introduced JB to SJ (*Life* i. 391–95). With the encouragement of SJ, who supplied the first paragraph and information concerning Garrick's early years, Davies published the *Life of David Garrick, Esq.*, 2 vols., 1780. The biography passed through four editions, and brought Davies both money and reputation.

---

[1] *Post* To Langton, 17 Nov. 1780, concerning the York Buildings bonds, is obviously an answer to the letter Langton wrote in compliance with this request from Lady Di.

[2] The rest of the address is written in another hand.

[3] John Adamson was porter of Chatham Yard (*Royal Kalendar for 1781*, p. 137).

Hertford Street, Oct. 10th.

Sɪʀ: I should be much obliged to you if when you write to Mr. Boswell you would ask him from me about some Scotch Bonds of Lady Sidney's[4]—Clarke[5] it is who tells me he fancy's Mr. Boswell can give me information concerning them. I have no guess at what he means, his manner of explaining not being *very clear* as you may imagine; and therefore should take it as a great favor if Mr. Boswell would throw some light upon all this—I would not have troubled you had I known where to find Mr. B.,[6] but as he may be in Lapland or at the Cape of Good Hope I apply to you. I hope Lady Rothes and all your children are well; Charles[7] is not quite so at present, and I have brought him to Town to see Turton. I hope it is only a Cold—I like his school at Richmond[8] very well, and he is quite unhappy when he leaves it. I beg my Compliments to Lady Rothes, and am, Sir, Your most Obedient humble servant

D. Beauclerk

From Bennet Langton,
between Tuesday 10 October and Wednesday
15 November 1780

Not reported. Sent between 10 Oct. and 15 Nov. See n. 1 to preceding letter. JB's answer, 17 Nov. 1780, indicates that Langton wrote from Chatham.

To Bennet Langton,
Friday 17 November 1780

MS. Yale (L 849). A copy in Lawrie's hand (except as noted) on a folio leaf which appears to have been discarded from a legal paper of

[4] Lady Sidney Beauclerk (d. 1766), Beauclerk's mother.
[5] Thomas Clarke, Beauclerk's *valet de chambre* (Mrs. Steuart Erskine, *Lady Diana Beauclerk, her Life and Work*, 1903, p. 184).
[6] Lady Di's uncertainty was justified by the fact that in Oct. of the previous year JB had appeared unexpectedly in London on a jaunt with Colonel Stuart.

See *ante* To Langton, 23 Dec. 1779.
[7] Charles-George Beauclerk, 1774–1846 (*Burke's Peerage*, 1953).
[8] Since Charles Beauclerk was not yet seven years old, this was probably a day school of which no record remains. The endowed school in Richmond was a charity for poor children (Daniel Lysons, *The Environs of London*, 1792–96, i. 467).

JB's. Mentioned in JB's journal (17 Nov.): "I . . . wrote to worthy Langton."

Edr., 17 Novr. 1780

MY DEAR SIR: Your long letter filled me with gratitude. But your last makes me overflow. Let us not renew the uneasy feeling of our inexp[l]icable indolence but direct our attention to objects more interesting or pleasing.

You are wonderfully jealous of my writing to Lady Di Beauclerc and indeed you well may be so as she is so very fine a woman. But I have not written to her, and you shall be the bearer of all the information I can give about the York Building Bonds.[1] You may perhaps remember how they were the occasion of that difference between Mr. Beauclerc and me, which your kindly worth got accomodated.[2] I exerted myself in having all done by his attorney in Scotland that could be done in the present situation of the York building Estates which are loaded with a multiplicity of debts. It will yet take sometime before the various competitions amongst the Cred[ito]rs are settled, and the estates yet unsold are turned into Cash. But I am happy to hear that there is now a great probability that all the fair debts will be fully paid, and that being

[1] The York Buildings Company was chartered by Charles II on 7 May 1675 to "erect a water work and water house near the River of Thames, upon part of the grounds of York House or York House garden, and to dig and lay ponds, pipes, and cisterns for the purpose of supplying the inhabitants of St. James' Fields and Piccadilly with water at reasonable rents" (David Murray, *The York Buildings Company: a Chapter in Scotch History*, 1883, pp. 3–4). After the Jacobite insurrection of 1715, the estates of the participating nobles and gentry were forfeited to the Crown; and in 1719 and 1720, a change in proprietors having taken place, the York Buildings Company, now a joint stock company, purchased a number of the forfeited estates. The breaking of the South Sea Bubble and the failure of similar ventures in 1720 affected the Company, which was forced to raise money through three rather unsuccessful lotteries and other question-able financial manœuvres. Its troubles were complicated by failure to gain profit from its Scottish estates. By 1739, after futile efforts to gain profits from timber, iron, coal, salt, glass, lead, and copper, the company was insolvent, and its operations shifted to the Court of Chancery. Over a period of years, the price of land having risen, the estates were sold at a profit, and by 1802 most of the claims against the company were settled. In 1829, the company was finally dissolved.

[2] See *ante* From Beauclerk to Langton, ?28 Apr. 1778 n. 2 and Journ. 13 Apr. 1778. JB was piqued because "Beauclerk had not only treated him as a lawyer on a social occasion, but had treated him as though he were a 'writer' or solicitor. Beauclerk would hardly have sought advice about bonds from an English barrister" (*Boswell in Extremes*, p. 278 n. 9).

the case Mr. Beauclerc's Bonds[3] will be more valuable than I imagined they would be. It would therefore be imprudent to sell them at an under value, and I would advise Lady Di to wait patiently till the York B. concerns are fully cleared up which after a very long delay will I hope soon be done. Whenever it becomes necessary that any receipt or deed of conveyance should be granted in England Lady Di will be informed.

Your account of the honours paid to our respected friend Dr. Johnson in the circle of eminent persons at Mrs. Vesey's gave me great pleasure. Let me my Dear Sir repeat my request to you to put down for me in writing at your leisure whatever sayings of his you remember; and I beleive you remember many. Some you have already done me the favour to dictate while I wrote;[4] and they are in sure preservat[io]n. I join with you in admiration of his *Prefaces to the Poets* which we have seen and in longing for those that are to come.[5] I am very well pleased that the Irish have the *Prefaces* printed separately.[6] But this is quite unconnected with the decision upon Literary Property to which I contributed my aid as Counsel.[7] The claim of perpetuity was set aside. But the Statutory

[3] MS. "Bond"

[4] "I had engaged to dine with Langton. I had no great mind to it; but I valued him for his learning and worth, and thought I should get some anecdotes of Johnson from him. ... I got him to talk of Johnson and he told me some particulars which are to be found in the little book which I keep solely for Dr. Johnson's Life" (Journ. 15 Apr. 1776). See *Boswell's Note-book, 1776–1777*, ed. R. W. Chapman, 1925, pp. 18, 24. "I walked to Langton's house with him; and he obligingly gave me some sayings of Dr. Johnson which I wrote down in his presence" (Journ. 15 Apr. 1779). JB distributed the sayings of this latter group throughout the *Life*, and though some portions of the manuscript may survive, it is impossible to identify them with certainty.

[5] The original plan of the London publishers was for the works of each of their poets to be prefaced by that poet's life, which would be written by SJ (*Life* iii. 110–11). But in 1779 a rival edition forced the publishers to bring out the poetry separately in fifty-six small volumes. At the same time and in the same format, they published four volumes of SJ's *Prefaces, Biographical and Critical, to the Works of the English Poets*, containing twenty-two of the fifty-two prefaces that had been commissioned (R. W. Chapman and A. T. Hazen, "Johnsonian Bibliography", *Proceedings of the Oxford Bibliographical Society*, 1938, pp. 155–58). The remaining prefaces appeared in six volumes in 1781.

[6] In 1779 the Dublin booksellers, unauthorized, published in one volume the contents of the first four volumes of SJ's *Prefaces*, but since these were no longer being prefaced to the poetry, the Irish devised, again without authority, a new title, *The Lives of the English Poets; and a Criticism on their Works*. Not until 1781 did the London booksellers follow suit with *The Lives of the most eminent English Poets; with Critical Observations on their Works*.

[7] See *ante* From Langton, 12 May 1774, n. 8.

security of an Authors exclusive right for 14 yrs. or 28 if he shall survive the first term remains firm as before and Irish Editions cannot be had in Britain but as smuggled goods.

Lord Monboddo was I understand very well received in many Companys in London. He returned to us very fond of the Metropolis but preserving his absurd prejudice against Dr. Johnson. There is I fear no cure for him. He has lately had an accident in his family which would have disconcerted the philosophy of most men. His oldest dau[ghte]r has married his clerk. But he does not seem to mind it.[8]

Our excellent friend Sir Wm. Forbes made the Tour of allmost all Wales with his Lady in Autumn last. The letters which he wrote giving an account of what he saw are I really think the best performance of the kind that I ever read.[9]

I have assurance enough to ask the favour of you to write me oftener. You will excuse me for taking the liberty to object to a formal "Sir" which you sometimes interject and I beg you may be assured that I am with the most sincere regard, My dear Sir, your affectionate friend.

My Wife joins me in best compliments to yourself and Lady Rothes. She and the children are all I thank GOD very well. How are you at Chatham so late in the year?[10] I hope to meet you in London in March.[11]

---

[8] Helen Burnett, Monboddo's elder daughter, married Kirkpatrick Williamson, afterwards keeper of the Outer House rolls (Robert Chambers, *A Biographical Dictionary of Eminent Scotsmen*, 1835, i. 427). After calling on Monboddo on 10 Dec., JB reported, "His firm philosophy struck me" (Journ.).

[9] The trip was apparently taken some time in Oct., for Beattie received a letter from Forbes describing it "a few days" before 6 Nov. 1780 (*Life of Beattie* ii. 256–57).

[10] Langton had gone to Chatham, as an engineer, some time before 6 June (*ante* From Langton, c. 18 Apr.–c. 18 May 1780, n. 2), probably to assist in repairing and augmenting the fortifications around the naval magazine and shipbuilding yards there. Fear of a French invasion from 1758 on had resulted in extensive fortification of the area (*The History and Antiquities of Rochester*, 2nd ed., 1817, pp. 331–32). Langton spent much time at Chatham throughout 1784. In *Musters of North Lincolnshire Militia* (W.O. 13/1295, Public Record Office, London), he is listed on Commander-in-Chief's leave assisting the Engineer at Chatham from 25 Dec. 1780 to 24 June 1781, and "on Public Employ" from 25 June to 24 Dec. Because of gaps in the Monthly Returns and Musters, no further record of his activities has been found; nor do the Records of the Ordnance Office preserved in the Public Record Office, or documents in the County Offices of Kent, reveal the nature of his duties. He took a house at Rochester, to which he moved his family in the spring

From Lady Diana Beauclerk to Bennet Langton, ?1780 or ?1781[1]

MS. Yale (C 112).

ADDRESS: To Bennet Langton Esqre.

Little Chelsea[2]

SIR: I shall be very much obliged to you if you could find out from Sir Joshua what he would sell Mary's Picture for, without telling him that I made this inquiry.[3] The case is, that if I find it not beyond what I can afford I should be very happy to buy it. But dare not mention it 'till I know, as it may be a great sum.

Excuse my giving y[o]u this trouble. I am, Sir, your most obedient humble servant

D. BEAUCLERK

To Sir Joshua Reynolds, Tuesday 27 February 1781

MS. Yale (L 1098). Sent 27 Feb. (Reg. Let.). A copy in Lawrie's hand.

Heading by JB: To Sir Joshua Reynolds.

Edinburgh, 27 Febry. 1781

DEAR SIR: During the long intervals of my absence from London,

of 1781. Beattie visited him at that time and wrote to Forbes on 1 June, "He is allowed to be a most excellent engineer" (Aberdeen). SJ visited the family there from 10 to 22 July 1783, although he was apprehensive about sharing a small house with eight children (*Letters SJ* iii. 46, 48, 50–52; *Life* iv. 8 n. 3; 22). Langton's venture at military engineering was undoubtedly an attempt to improve his financial state, which had been getting steadily worse. See *Life* iii. 222, 315, 317, 348.

[11] Last paragraph in JB's hand, standing on a side by itself. This side is numbered "10", and bears the following deleted passage in JB's hand: "The principle of *Family* is indeed of great

consequence in the country. The present Representative [illegible word] has probably". See the head-note above.

[1] Lady Di perhaps asked about the picture within a year of the exhibition mentioned in n. 3.

[2] Apparently erased.

[3] Reynolds's portrait of Mary Beauclerk had been exhibited at the Royal Academy in 1780 as *Una and the Lion*. It must have been too expensive for Lady Di, for it was in Sir Joshua's studio when he died, and was sold in 1796 to a dealer. It is frequently listed as a portrait of Elizabeth Beauclerk, although Walpole, in a note in his copy of the exhibition catalogue, described it as a

I have often wished to have the pleasure of hearing from you; and when we last shook hands at parting[1] you said "Write to me, and I'll answer you"—yet by some strange imbecility or distraction of mind though I have many a time sat down to begin a letter to you this (if I shall make it out) will be the first that I have ended. The truth is that in this dull northern town, I am not the same Man that you see in the Metropolis. I have not that jocund complacency that eager gayety which you have frequently cherished.[2] Allow me Dear Sir to begin our correspondence with returning you my most sincere thanks for your goodness to me, which has increased every year since I was fortunate enough to be introduced to your acquaintance. To make this gratefull acknowledgement is a real satisfaction.

I long much for more of our wonderfull (mirabilis) Friend Dr. Johnsons *Prefaces to the Poets*. The Criticism and Biography of these I have read delight me more and more.[3] What a pity it is that he loathes so much to write[4] and since that is the case what a pity it is that there [is] not constantly with him such a recorder of his conversation as I am. I hope next month to be again in London

portrait of Mary (Algernon Graves and W. V. Cronin, *A History of the Works of Sir Joshua Reynolds, P.R.A.*, 1899–1901, i. 68–69; iv. 1639; Algernon Graves, *The Royal Academy of Arts: A Complete Dictionary of Contributors and their work from its foundation in 1769 to 1904*, 1906, i. ix; vi. 273–74).

[1] JB had last left London on Tuesday 4 May 1779 (Journ.), and no doubt took leave of Sir Joshua on one of his last days there. No record has been recovered for 27 Apr.–3 May.

[2] He had been "sunk into dreadful Melancholy" during a visit to Bothwell Castle in early January by reading necessitarian arguments in Lord Monboddo's *Ancient Metaphysics* and Lord Kames's *Sketches of the History of Man*: "I saw a dreary nature of things an unconscious uncontroulable power, by which all things are driven on and I could not get rid of the irresistible influence of motives." He was in good spirits at the time he wrote this letter, but obviously feared a relapse: "Was

busy with the Ayrshire election business. ... The agitation kept off all melancholy" (Journ.).

[3] Although the first four of the ten volumes had not been published till 1779, JB had read (in proof) the life of Denham as early as 17 Mar. 1778. "It was a Feast to me; and my powers of Admiration in every view were excited. His knowledge, his judgement, his expression filled me with wonder and delight" (Journ.). Two days later, the Dillys had shown him a portion of SJ's life of Cowley. "It was still greater than his Denham. I really *worshiped* him, not *idolatrously* but with profound reverence, in the ancient ... Jewish sense of the word."

[4] "I love to see my friends, to hear from them, to talk to them, and to talk of them; but it is not without a considerable effort of resolution that I prevail upon myself to write," SJ had written JB on 8 Dec. 1763 (*Letters SJ* i. 164). For an account of SJ's indolence and how it interfered with his writing and the completion of literary projects, see *Life* i. 86–87.

and resume that office.[5] But you must write to me by way of a cheering welcome. You must not delay. You must "answer me" as you said you would do. We have lost Beauclerc and Chamier[6] since I was with you. These are sad losses. The first never can be repaired, though his acidity sometimes made me smart.

I saw at Chester a Miss Cunliff whom I liked exceedingly.[7] She was very amiable and painted surprisingly well. She told me she had been obliged to you for allowing her to copy some of your pictures. But she would not be called by me a Scholar of Sir Joshuas. I thought you would be very well pleased to be her Master—"And teach my lovely scholar all I know."[8]

I hope when we meet I shall receive from you some valuable additions to my Boswelliana. I am with great regard, Dear Sir, your obliged and affectionate humble Servant

From Sir Joshua Reynolds, Thursday 12 April 1781 [1]

MS. Yale (C 2351).

ADDRESS: Mr. Boswell.

[London] April 12

DEAR SIR: When I came home last night I found a Card to remind me of my engagement to dine with Mrs. Garrick next Munday to meet Dr. Johnson.[2] This engagement was made at the Bishop of St. Asaphs on Tuesday,[3] but neglecting to put it down in my

---

[5] JB arrived in London on Monday 19 Mar. (Journ.).

[6] Anthony Chamier (b. 1725) died 12 Oct. 1780.

[7] One of the daughters of Sir Ellis Cunliffe, Bt., M.P. Mary was the elder; Margaret Elizabeth the younger. In writing to JB in 1780, his friend Margaret Stuart mentioned the "sense, spirit, and vivacity" of the elder Miss Cunliffe, and then referred later to "your Miss Cunliffe", as if JB's were the other one, the younger (From Margaret Stuart Wortley-Mackenzie, 27 Feb. 1780). Which one painted is not known.

[8] What joy to wind along the cool retreat,
To stop, and gaze on Delia as I go!
To mingle sweet discourse with kisses sweet,
And teach my lovely scholar all I know!
(James Hammond's *Elegy XIII*)

[1] Reynolds's engagement book and JB's journal.

[2] Reynolds's engagement book for 16 Apr. 1781: "4 Mrs. Garrick."

[3] *Ibid.* 10 Apr. 1781: "5 Bishop of St. Asaph." The Bishop was Jonathan

book I thought myself unengaged and gladly accepted the invitation of General Paoli.[4] I must beg therefore you would make my apology to him. Yours sincerely

J. REYNOLDS

From Thomas Barnard, Tuesday 8 May 1781[1]

MS. Yale (C 80).

ADDRESS: James Boswell Esqr., South audley Street.

[London] Tuesday night

MY DEAR BOSWELL: I expected to have seen you at the Club; and it was a shabby thing in you to Desert us for a Catchpenny Printer in the Poultry,[2] but no more of that. Will you eat a piece of Roast Mutton with me and your Freind Sir Joshua on Thursday?[3] If you come I will get a Bottle of the Finest Bristol Water for your drinking at Dinner, and a Flask of Geronsterre or Pouhon[4] for Convivial Society when the Cloth is taken away. I durst not

Shipley (1714–88). JB had accompanied Reynolds and SJ to the Bishop's door before going home for dinner (Journ. 10 Apr.).

[4] There is no record in JB's journal of Paoli's invitation. See *Portraits*, p. 166, for a description of how JB later secured the following invitation from Mrs. Garrick:

> Adelphi, thursday 19 April [1781]
> Mrs. Garrick presents her compliments to Mr. Boswell and if he is not engaged to morrow shall be glad of the favour of his company to dinner at four o clock to meet Dr. Johnson.—If he is engaged to dinner hopes for the pleasure of seeing him to Tea.—An answer is desired.

(MS. Fettercairn Papers, National Library of Scotland.)

---

[1] See next letter, which is clearly an answer to this one.

[2] Charles Dilly.

[3] JB's journal entry for Thursday 10

May shows that he dined with the Bishop that day.

[4] Géronstère and Pouhon are both mineral waters from Spa, Pouhon being the main spring in the town and Géronstère a spring in the environs at a distance of nearly two miles. Barnard could certainly have provided JB with Pouhon (see the advertisement of W. Owen, near Temple Bar, *London Chronicle*, 11–13 July 1776, xl. 47), but Géronstère appears not to have been exported. Barnard had no doubt visited Spa in 1748 (*ante* p. xxix; John Macky, *A Journey through the Austrian Netherlands*, 1725, pp. 74–75; J. P. de Limbourg, *New Amusements of the German Spa*, 2 vols., 1764, *passim*, especially Chs. 3, 8; Philip Thicknesse, *A Year's Journey through the Pais Bas*, 2nd ed., 1786, pp. 114–25; John Murray, *A Handbook for Travellers in Holland and Belgium*, 19th ed., 1876, pp. 188–89). On 6 May JB had apparently been lectured by Paoli for hard drinking and had promised

ask that Great and Excellent man with whom you reside[5] to my Paltry Lodging where I cannot entertain him in a manner Suitable to his Rank and the Sincere Respect I bear him—but as to yourself I shall make you no apology. Being very Truly and affectionately Yours

THOS. KILLALOE

An answer is requested.

To Thomas Barnard, Wednesday 9 May 1781[1]

MS. Yale (L 35). A draft or copy.

S[outh Audley] Street, We. 9 May

MY DEAR LORD, I sincer[ely] thank you for your kind invit[atio]n and shall cert[ainly] be with you. The dinner scene yest[er]d[ay] of Dr. J[ohnson] and Mr. W[ilkes][2] was fixed a month before and we had not calcul[ate]d the eclipse in Ger[rard] St.[3] The liquors you promise are curious. But I am sure of the Champ[agne] of Helic[on] in your comp[an]y. That is the cur[iosa] felic[itas].[4] Beleive me I am a good deal bett[er] in a moral sense, and hope to be more so[5] i.e. "more better," which Ben Jons[on] says is good eng[lish]—nay a beauty.[6] May I be deserv[ing] of your Lordships freind[ship] if that be eng[lish] or whether it be so or not. I have

restraint (Journ.). Barnard must have learned this from JB in some meeting on 6, 7, or 8 May that is not recorded in the existing journal.

[5] General Paoli.

---

[1] Dated by Journ., 8 and 10 May 1781.
[2] JB described the dinner, the second SJ and Wilkes had shared, in *Life* iv. 101–07.
[3] Professor Pottle explains the reference to "the eclipse in Ger[rard] St[reet]" as "an apology by Boswell for keeping Johnson away from The Club to dine with Wilkes at Dilly's. He and Johnson, he says, had not deliberately absented themselves, but the date for the dinner had been fixed a long time in advance, and at the time they agreed upon it, they had forgotten that The Club would meet on 8 May" (BP xiv. 254).

[4] Petronius Arbiter, *Satyricon* cxviii: *Horatii curiosa felicitas*: "the studied felicity of Horace" (Michael Heseltine's translation in Loeb ed.).
[5] JB was uneasy about his "wild life" (Journ. 7 May), and had no doubt confessed his uneasiness to Barnard. See the preceding letter, n. 4, end.
[6] Jonson maintained that "*more*, and *most* . . . are added to the comparative, and superlative degrees themselves", and quoted as an example Sir Thomas More: "Forasmuch as she saw the Cardinall *more* readier to depart." This practice, Jonson asserted, "is a certaine kind of English atticisme, or eloquent phrase of speech, imitating the manner of the most ancientest, and finest Grecians . . ." (*The English Grammar Made by Ben Jonson*, ed. Strickland Gibson, 1928, II. iv. 63).

the hon[our] in the mean time to be, My Dear Lord, Your faithful and affectionate humble servant

From Thomas Percy, Thursday 20 December 1781

MS. Yale (C 2229).

ADDRESS: To The Honourable James Boswell, Advocate, Edinburgh.

POSTMARK: CARLISLE.

Minute of JB's reply (the letter following this) written in the blank spaces of the address side: 25 Decr. 1781. Enclosed the Magazine— The Controversy concerning Ossian is too generally the *Opprobrium Scotorum*. It is indeed amazing with what zeal McPherson has been supported. I have a very bad opinion of Shaw. But Clark of whom I know nothing is from the extracts of his Pamphlet which I have read, a very hardy Bigot. My Opinion was long ago fixed, which is that *some parts* of what is given us as Ossian's Poetry has been repeated in Gaelick *I know not from what æra*. But *how much* is genuine we shall never be able to ascertain.

Carlisle, Decr. 20. 1781

DEAR SIR, Allow me to request a favour of you. I have unluckily been hooked into the Controversy concerning Ossian, and find myself obliged to relate and describe at large a Recitation made to me at Edinburgh which Dr. Ferguson and Dr. Blair (who were present) have utterly forgot. I have reason to believe there has or will be something published concerning *me with respect to this subject*, in a weekly Magazine circulated from Edinburgh: will you have the goodness to forward to me any number or numbers of the said Weekly Magazine, in which my name is or shall be so mentioned. What I particularly want to see is a passage respecting *Clarke's Answer to Shaw* in which he is to qualify by a Note in the said Weekly Magazine, a very hardy Assertion made in his Pamphlet, that he has been authorized by Drs. Blair and Ferguson, to affirm that every circumstance of the Recitation made to me is *altogether False*.[1] Any qualification of this kind that has or may be

[1] Percy had begun by being deeply sceptical of the authenticity of James Macpherson's *Fingal* (1762) and *Temora* (1763), but in 1765 had felt obliged to admit that they were indeed translations of ancient Gaelic poems. According to his own account, Hugh Blair in the autumn of that year, in Edinburgh,

published in the said Weekly Mag[azin]e I beg the favour of you to forward to me under a Cover directed To The Lord Bishop of Carlisle,[2] at Rose Castle near Carlisle, with a D in a Corner of the Superscription for distinction. This I shall esteem a very kind act of Friendship shown to Dear Sir Your very faithful and obliged Servant

THO. PERCY

introduced him to Adam Ferguson, Professor of Philosophy in the University of Edinburgh, a Highlander with knowledge of Gaelic, and Ferguson called in one of his own students (John Macpherson, son of the minister of Sleat in Skye, later Sir John and Governor General of India), who recited and translated bits of Gaelic, which, as translated, bore a convincing resemblance to a passage in *Fingal*. Percy announced himself satisfied by this evidence in a note which he inserted in the second edition of his own *Reliques of Ancient English Poetry*, 1767. He dropped the note, however, in his third edition, 1775, having in the meantime reconsidered the matter and especially having been assured by Macpherson's intimate friend Sir John Elliott, M.D. (1736–86) that Macpherson had repeatedly admitted to him that *Fingal* and *Temora* were almost entirely his own compositions. Percy, who habitually shunned controversy, intended to make no express public statement of the change in his views. But John Smith (1747–1807), minister of Kilbrandon, Argyll, in his *Galic Antiquities*, 1780, cited Percy's 1767 note as supporting his own conviction of the genuineness of *Fingal* and *Temora*; whereupon William Shaw (1749–1831), Gaelic scholar and later biographer of SJ, to whom Percy had talked freely without intending to authorize any publication, replied sharply to Smith in *Enquiry into the Authenticity of the Poems attributed to Ossian*, 1781, pointing out that Percy knew no Gaelic and bluntly asserting that Percy on reflection had come to suspect that he had been the victim of an imposture. Ferguson retorted with an advertisement dated 21 July 1781 which appeared in *The Public Advertiser, The Morning*

Chronicle, and *The St. James's Chronicle* (7 Aug. 1781), declaring that Shaw's statement, so far as it related to him, was altogether false: "I never was present at the repetition of verses to Dr. Percy by a young student from the Highlands." Shaw replied with an advertisement dated 31 Aug., granting that he had his facts at second hand and accepting Ferguson's disclaimer, but insisting that an attempt to deceive Percy had really been made. John Clark (d. 1807), Gaelic scholar and land agent, then replied to Shaw in an abusive pamphlet, *An Answer to William Shaw on the Authenticity of the Poems of Ossian*, 1781, in which he said, "I have personally applied to these two learned and elegant writers; and they have authorised me to assure the public, that the whole is, in every particular, a *falsehood*." Percy, who now felt that he must make some public defence, entered into correspondence with Blair and Ferguson, and found to his consternation that though Blair was willing to disclaim having given Clark authority to speak for him, both he and Ferguson were determined not to remember the recital. Percy thereupon, in a letter dated 10 Nov. 1781, sent his own version of the incident to be published in the same papers that had printed Ferguson's advertisements (Percy to Evan Evans, 24 Dec. 1765, in *Correspondence of Thomas Percy and Evan Evans*, ed. Aneirin Lewis, 1957, p. 117; *Gent. Mag.* Dec. 1781, li. 567–68, Jan. 1782, lii. 11–13, 83–85; *Lit. Illust.* vi. 567–69; John Small, "Biographical Sketch of Adam Ferguson", in *Transactions* of the Royal Society of Edinburgh, 1864, xxiii. 631–40; Reiberg, pp. 232–54).

[2] Edmund Law (1703–87).

P.S. Mrs. Percy desires to join with me in respects to yourself and your Lady, whom we should be very happy to see at the Deanry.

To Thomas Percy, Tuesday 25 December 1781

MS. Yale (*L 1063). Sent 25 Dec. (Reg. Let.).

ADDRESS: To The Revd. Dr. Percy, Dean of Carlisle.

Edinburgh, 25 Decr. 1781

DEAR SIR: Enclosed is the Number of the Weekly Magazine published here, which you desire to have. In it you will find Clark's *qualification* as you well express it, of his assertion concerning the Recitation made to you.[1] The controversy concerning Ossian is too generally the *Opprobrium Scotorum*.[2] It is indeed amazing with what zeal MacPherson has been supported. I have a very bad opinion of Shaw. But Clark of whom I know nothing is from the extracts of his Pamphlet which I have read, a very hardy Bigot. I shall be glad to see what you write upon the subject. My opinion was long ago fixed, which is that *some parts* of what is given us as Ossian's Poetry has been repeated in Gaelick *I know not from what æra*. But *how much* is genuine we shall never be able to ascertain.

I am in great uneasiness about my Wife who has for some weeks

[1] *The Edinburgh Magazine, or Literary Amusement* had begun a review of Clark's pamphlet in the number for 1 Nov. 1781. In the third instalment (15 Nov. 1781. liv pt. 1. 189) it quoted the passage from Clark as given *ante* (n. 1 of the letter preceding this), with the following foot-note: "Lest the general expressions which the author has employed should be misconstrued, he thinks it proper to give the following more particular and accurate account of this matter.—Professor Fergusson, in a printed advertisement, has declared, that he never was present at a repetition of verses to Dr. Percy, by a young student from the Highlands; and that therefore the assertion in Mr. Shaw's pamphlet, so far as it relates to him, is altogether false. [That is, Ferguson has not authorized Clark to say anything, and adheres to what he said in his advertisement.]— What Dr. Blair has authorised the author to publish, is, that his having any concern in introducing to Dr. Percy a Highland student, who was previously taught his part, and was employed as an instrument of imposing on Dr. Percy, is altogether false; but whether any recitation of poetry was at any time made to Dr. Percy by a Highland student, in his presence, is a fact of which, at the distance of sixteen years, he has no recollection, and cannot say whether it happened or not."

[2] "The disgrace of the Scots."

119

TO PERCY, 25 DECEMBER 1781

been ill with a cough, pain in her breast, and other alarming symptoms.[3] I hope she is a little better. She joins me in compliments to you and Mrs. Percy, and I remain, Dear Sir, Your faithful humble servant

JAMES BOSWELL

From Thomas Percy, Monday 31 December 1781

MS. Yale (C 2230). Received 3 Jan. 1782 (Reg. Let.).

ADDRESS: To James Boswell Esqr., Advocate, Edinburgh.

POSTMARK: CARLISLE.

ENDORSEMENT: 8d. Received 3 Janry. 1782. Dr. Percy Dean of Carlisle enclosing his Advertisement on the controversy concerning Ossian. Regretting my Wife's illness, and inviting us to his Deanery.

Carlisle, Decr. 31. 1781

DEAR SIR, Accept my best thanks for your kind and ready compliance with my Request: Should any thing further appear in the same vehicle (your Weekly Mag[azin]e) relating to my share in the Controversy concerning Ossian, etc. I will again beg you to transmit it to me: In return I here inclose my only Copy of the 3 Advertisements, the last of which, I presume, you may by this time have seen in some of the common Newspapers:[1] I am sorry

---

[3] Mrs. Boswell had a miscarriage on 5 Oct. (Journ.), and JB's journal entries for the following weeks reveal her constant bad health. Consumption, of course, was feared.

[1] In a letter dated 24 Nov. 1781 to John Nichols, editor of *Gent. Mag.*, Percy requested that Nichols insert in the next (i.e. the Nov.) number of the magazine the advertisements of Ferguson (21 July 1781) and Shaw (31 Aug. 1781) mentioned *ante* (From Percy, 20 Dec. 1781, n. 1), with his own reply, dated 10 Nov. 1781; also that after the type had been set, Nichols send copies of the three advertisements to seven London newspapers. "The three first [*Public

Advertiser, Morning Chronicle, St. James's Chronicle] I would pay any sum to have my narrative inserted in, as Mr. Ferguson's advertisement appeared in them" (*Lit. Illust.* vi. 567). Percy's advertisement appeared in *The St. James's Chronicle* on 15 Dec. 1781, and all three advertisements appeared in *Gent. Mag.* Dec. 1781, li. 567–68. The enclosure which Percy sent JB, a pre-publication off-print (blank verso) from the type of *Gent. Mag.*, is at Yale. Ferguson then published in *The Morning Chronicle*, 10 Jan. 1782, *The St. James's Chronicle*, 12–15 Jan. 1782, and probably in other papers, a very long undated rebuttal, embedding in it a letter which he had written to Blair on 18 Aug. 1781, and

I have no Frank to send it in—I am extremely concernd to hear the account you give of Mrs. Boswell's complaint, who has our best Wishes of its speedy and effectual Removal: I wish you would try the Soft influence of Bristol Water, and then Carlisle lies in your way, where change of Air and a Visit at the Deanry may be tried before she and you proceed further: Mrs. Percy is the tenderest and best of Nurses and would be glad to try her Skill on a Lady, who is dear to one we so much value, as yourself. We join in best wishes and compliments of the Season to you both. I am, Dear Sir, Your much obliged and very faithful Servant

THO. PERCY

To Thomas Percy, January 1782 to February 1783

Not reported. Sent between Jan. 1782 and Feb. 1783 from Edinburgh. Referred to *post* From Percy, 3 Mar. 1783: "I received some time ago, your very obliging favour."

continuing, "I must now add, that although the facts stated by Dr. Percy might be admitted on less authority than his, yet as they are entirely contrary to any feeling or recollection I have of the matter, and have been employed to convey a very injurious imputation against me, he must excuse me if I do not admit them" (*The Correspondence of Thomas Percy and Evan Evans*, ed. Aneirin Lewis, 1957, p. 117 n. 6; *Gent. Mag.* Jan. 1782, lii. 13). Percy later found, but did not publish, two letters from Blair to himself in which Blair had mentioned the recital of Gaelic poetry. Horace Walpole thought they completely vindicated him (To William Mason, 22 Apr. 1782, *Walpole's Correspondence*, Yale Ed. xxix. 239–40), but JB felt that Percy pushed his evidence (*post* To Percy, 12 Mar. 1783, n. 1). The letters (10 Feb. 1766 and 10 Jan. 1767) are not known to exist, but Blair reported the crucial passages in a letter to Alexander Carlyle, 22 Apr. 1782 (MS. Laing II. 243, Univ. of Edinburgh). They prove that John Macpherson did recite and translate Gaelic poetry to Blair and Percy, but they do not clearly make Ferguson present or place the recital at his house. In 1792 Percy appeared fearful lest JB should publish any of their communications concerning the controversy (*Percy-Malone Corresp.* p. 57). In 1805, at the instigation of Robert Anderson, he allowed Malcolm Laing, in the preface of his *Poems of Ossian*, to divulge on his authority what Sir John Elliott had told him about the authenticity of *Fingal* and *Temora* (*ante* From Percy, 20 Dec. 1781, n. 1). A cryptic remark of Laing's about Percy's moderation and charity towards Sir John Macpherson probably means that Percy, in his communication to Anderson, had named Sir John as the "lad" who had recited Gaelic to him so many years before, but had requested that his name be withheld. Elliott (whom Percy had declined to name in 1781) had died in 1786 (Small's "Sketch of Ferguson", as cited *ante* From Percy, 20 Dec. 1781, n. 1; *Lit. Illust.* vii. 120, 146–47, 150, 153–54; viii. 382, 418–19; R. M. Schmitz, *Hugh Blair*, 1948, pp. 88–89).

To Charles James Fox,
Friday 19 April 1782

Not reported. Sent from Edinburgh 19 Apr. "Hon. C. J. Fox Ditto (Copy)" (Reg. Let.). "Ditto" refers to "asking his interest for the office of Judge Advocate in Scotland." Similar letters were written to Burke, the Earl of Pembroke, and George Dempster[1] on the 18th (Reg. Let.; Journ.). The office had become vacant on the death of Sir James Dunbar, and JB understood that "it must be filled up by one of our Faculty of Advocates, of which Society I was the single man who at any of our meetings openly avowed a detestation of the measures of the late Ministry against our Bretheren in America" (To Burke, 18 Apr. 1782, Fitzwilliam Collection, Sheffield Public Library). Burke wrote a strongly recommendatory letter to General Conway regarding JB, and Pembroke spoke to him in the matter; but neither one was able to give JB a definite answer (C 685, 686). Dempster was also non-committal, and on 4 May JB learned that Mark Pringle had been appointed (Journ. 26 Apr., 4 May). So far as is known, JB never received any answer from Fox.

To Sir Joshua Reynolds,
Monday 19 August 1782

Not reported. Sent from Edinburgh 19 Aug. "Sir Joshua Reynolds, miscellany (copy)" (Reg. Let.).

From Sir William Forbes to Bennet Langton,
Monday 9 September 1782

MS. Yale (C 1270).

Edinb. 9 Septr. 1782

DEAR SIR: I have received the pleasure of your very obliging letter covering two Receits for Lady Rothes's annuity, the one to be exchanged against the receit which I gave to Mr. Tait[1] for the

---

[1] George Dempster (1732–1818), Scots advocate, agriculturist, and M.P. (1761–90), who had abandoned law for politics. He had been a scribbling companion of JB's at least from 1761.

[1] Very likely John Tait (d. 1802), Writer to the Signet, whose wife was a relation of the Boswells. His only son, Craufurd (1765–1832), married a daugh-

former half year: the other for that which is now due; and which I shall endeavor to get from him as quickly as I can, but Mr. Tait is just now in the Country, during the Vacation.

You say nothing of Lady Rothes's health nor the Children's. I hope her Ladyship and they are all perfectly well. Lady F. was delivered safely of a son,[2] a few weeks ago, and is quite recovered. We have now 4 sons and 3 daughters,[3] and all, thank Heaven! as thriving as we can wish them. Our eldest Boy has just finished his third Year at the Grammar-School,[4] and is a very good Scholar for his standing. Of a form of four-score boys he had but one above him, and at a public examination received a very handsome Quarto Greek testament as a premium. I make no apology to you, Dear Sir, for such a trifling detail as this; because I know the important business of education employs no inconsiderable part of *your* thoughts as well as mine.

Dr. Beattie spent some weeks with us lately, and left with me completely finished for the press the Volume of Essays he is about to publish;[5] they will make their appearance in the Course of next Winter. And I am persuaded will give you much pleasure in the perusal.

I am glad you like the periodical paper, *the Mirror*,[6] because

ter of Ilay Campbell, afterwards Lord President of the Court of Session, and their son Archibald Campbell Tait (1811–82) became Archbishop of Canterbury in 1869. Craufurd Tait's daughter Susan (1797–1880) married Sir George Sitwell of Renishaw, great-grandfather of Dame Edith, Sir Osbert, and Sir Sacheverell Sitwell (R. C. Cole, *Genealogists' Magazine*, 1967, xv. 402–06).

[2] Daniel, who died young (Louisa L. Forbes, *Genealogical Table of the Forbes Family of Monymusk and Pitsligo*, 1880).

[3] Mrs. Forbes's *Table* identifies the four sons and two of the daughters: William (b. 1771), John Hay (b. 1776), James (b. 1778), Rebecca (b. 1779), Elizabeth (b. 1781), and Daniel (b. 1782). James (see From Forbes, 18 Dec. 1787) and Daniel died young, and so presumably did the unidentified daughter mentioned as living in 1782. Forbes had at least seven more children born after 1782, of whom one son and two daughters died in

infancy or childhood (*ibid.*; see also Alistair and Henrietta Tayler, *The House of Forbes*, 1937, p. 305). For more information on the sons and daughters who survived childhood, see *Burke's Peerage*, 1956, s.v. Stuart-Forbes; *Burke's Landed Gentry*, 1846, s.v. Macdonnell of Glengarry; *ibid.* 1862, s.v. Skene of Rubislaw.

[4] The High School of Edinburgh. Three years later young William was Dux of the Rector's Class—top boy in the school (William Steven, *History of the High School of Edinburgh*, 1849, Appendix, p. 131).

[5] Beattie was in Edinburgh from the end of July until the middle of August, when he left the manuscript of his *Dissertations* with Forbes to be forwarded to Strahan, the publisher (Margaret Forbes, *Beattie and his Friends*, 1904, p. 184). *Dissertations Moral and Critical* were published in London in 1783.

[6] One hundred and ten issues of *The*

I think, for my own part, that it has much merit.—Some of the papers were written by Lord Hailes, a few by Mr. Baron Gordon, by Dr. Beattie, and by Professor Richardson of Glasgow:—but the laboring oar lay on Mr. McKenzie, author of the *Man of feeling*,[7] by whom the bulk of the Essays were composed, and who had the direction of the publication. It ought not to be forgotten that the profits of the work were bestowed on a public Charity here.[8]— I thank you for mentioning the work of Mr. de Luc[9] which I have heard highly spoken of: but I have not yet had the good luck to meet with it.

You have probably heard by this time that Mr. Boswell has lately lost his Father:[10] whose death could not be considered as a matter of regret; as his faculties were much impaired, and he might be said in some measure to have survived himself.—A melancholy thing! Mr. Boswell now succeeds to a very good family estate; but, with great propriety, does not mean to abandon his profession, in which he has a very fair prospect of arriving at a seat on the Bench, in due time. He speaks of making a short excursion to London about ten days hence, to see you and his

Mirror appeared between 23 Jan. 1779 and 27 May 1780, when they were collected in a volume. Forbes, in his life of Beattie, describes the circumstances of the writing of the publication "by a set of friends, chiefly of the Scottish bar, whose attachment to literary pursuits was congenial" (*Life of Beattie* iii. 289).

[7] Cosmo Gordon (c. 1736–1800), admitted advocate in 1758; M.P. for Nairnshire, 1774-77; Baron of Exchequer since 1777; Rector of Marischal College 1782–83 and 1786–87. JB recorded dislike of him earlier in this year (Journ. 27 Mar. 1782), but clearly respected his opinion in literary matters (Journ. 27 Jan. 1783, 21 Feb. 1785).— William Richardson (1743–1814), Professor of Humanity (Latin) at Glasgow since 1772. He was the author of numerous essays, plays, and poems, including one (*A Poetical Address in Favour of the Corsicans*, 1769) that has mistakenly been attributed to JB (*Lit. Car.* p. 296).— Henry Mackenzie (1745–1831), attorney for the Crown in the Court of Exchequer,

author of the extremely popular novels *The Man of Feeling* (1771), *The Man of the World* (1773), and *Julia de Roubigné* (1777); later friend and encourager of Burns and Scott. He wrote forty-two of the 110 papers comprising *The Mirror*.

[8] "From the sale of the copyright the writers presented a donation of £100 to the Orphan Hospital and bought a hogshead of claret for the use of the [Mirror] Club" (Henry Mackenzie, *Letters to Elizabeth Rose of Kilravock*, ed. H. W. Drescher, 1967, p. xii). For the Orphan Hospital, see Hugo Arnot, *History of Edinburgh*, 1788, p. 561.

[9] Jean-André de Luc the elder (1727–1817), Swiss physician and geologist. He was the author of *Lettres physiques et morales sur les montagnes, et sur l'histoire de la terre, et de l'homme*, etc., 1778–80; and of *Recherches sur les modifications de l'atmosphère*, 1772. He had come to England in 1770 and in 1773 was named reader to the Queen. He later lived in Berlin, but died at Windsor.

[10] Lord Auchinleck died 30 Aug.

other freinds.[11] I cannot help envying him that pleasure very much; or to make use of a better expression, I should feel great happiness in being able to enjoy that satisfaction along with him: but it is a happiness of which I have not at present the most distant prospect.

I shall be much obliged to you, however, to remember me with sincere regard to Sir Joshua Reynolds and Dr. Johnson, or any other literary freind to whom I have the honor to be known, that you may meet with.—Lady F. joins me in respectful Compliments to Lady Rothes and I am with much regard and esteem, Dear Sir, Your most obedient humble Servant

WILLIAM FORBES

I need not say that it will make [me] happy to hear from you, when you find it convenient.

From Sir Joshua Reynolds to Bennet Langton, Thursday 12 September 1782

MS. Yale (C 2353).

Leicesterfields, Sep. 12 1782

DEAR SIR, Tho I am but a tardy correspondent I would not neglect thanking you for your kind invitation, but it is too late in the season to think of any excursion into the country.

I have seen little of Dr. Johnson this year, he is totally absorbed by Mrs. Thrale. I hear however that he is tolerably well and gone to Brightelmstone with Mrs. Thrale,[1] the papers says that they are going afterwards to Italy but of this I have heard nothing from authority, if they go I suppose Miss Burney will be one of the Party as she lives in a manner entirely in that set. I hope you like her last Novel *Cecilia*, Mr. Burke is in raptures and has writ her a complimentary letter,[2] Mr. Fox Says it is a wonderfull performance.

---

[11] JB left Edinburgh for Auchinleck on 17 Sept. (Journ.), and then left for London on the 24th; but he was called back because his wife, who had been in bad health, suffered a pulmonary haemorrhage (Journ. 25 Sept.). JB wrote to Forbes on 20 Oct. to tell him of his being prevented from going to London.

[1] SJ did not go to Brighton with Mrs. Thrale until 7 Oct.

[2] Fanny Burney (1752–1840) had met

The Mirror which you mention I never saw but I have heard a good character of it and that some of the first Scotch Geniuses were engaged in it, some of the Papers are said to [be] written by Wedderburn.[3]

I had a letter from Boswell about a fortnight ago, tho' I think it was more, for it was before his fathers death,[4] he writes in good spirits and expresses his longings after London. Mr. Burke often talks of him and appears to have great affection towards him, he says he is by much the most agreable man he ever saw in all his life.

I hope we shall see you in Town early in the season and [that you will] be a regular attender at the Club. I find Adam Smith intends publishing this winter an Essay on the reason why Imitation pleases.[5] The last day he was there the conversation turned upo[n] that subject. I found it was a subject he had considerd with attention, when I saw him afterwards I told him that my Notions perfectly agreed with his that I had wrote a great deal on detach'd bitts of Paper,[6] which I would put together and beg him to look over it, he Said he could not for the reason above mentiond that [he] was about finishing an Essay on that Subject.

I beg my most respectfull compliments to Lady Rothes. My Niece would join with me but she is in the West,[7] and my sister is at my house at Richmond[8] so that I am quite a batchelor. I am with the greatest respect, Yours

J. REYNOLDS

Burke for the first time three months earlier at Sir Joshua's and had fallen "quite desperately and outrageously in love" (undated letter of hers, quoted by Joyce Hemlow, *History of Fanny Burney*, 1958, p. 151). Her second novel, *Cecilia*, had been published 12 June 1782. For Burke's letter in praise of it see *Diary and Letters of Mme. d'Arblay*, ed. Austin Dobson, ii. 92–94, or *Correspondence of Edmund Burke*, ed. T. W. Copeland, v. 25–26.

[3] Alexander Wedderburn (1733–1805), Baron Loughborough (1780), Lord Chancellor (1793–1801), and Earl of Rosslyn (1801), as early as 1756 had projected and edited a short-lived periodical called *The Edinburgh Review*,

but he was not a contributor to *The Mirror*.

[4] Obviously JB's letter of 19 Aug.

[5] Smith did not live to publish the essay to which Reynolds is referring: "Of the Nature of that Imitation which takes Place in what are called the Imitative Arts". It was included in *Essays on Philosophical Subjects*, published by his executors in 1795.

[6] For examples of such notes see *Portraits*, pp. 175–77.

[7] Mary Palmer (d. 1820) had left her uncle, Sir Joshua, to visit her family in Devonshire on 14 Aug.

[8] The small house at Richmond, built in 1771, was used as a base for a day's outing, generally on Sundays (*Portraits*, p. 175 n. 6).

From Sir Joshua Reynolds, Tuesday 1 October 1782

MS. Yale (C 2354). Received 17 Oct. (Reg. Let.).[1]

ADDRESS in Lord Eliot's hand: To James Boswell Esqre., Edinburgh [*changed in Lawrie's hand to*] of Auchinleck, By Kilmarnock.

FRANK: Ed. Free Eliot.

POSTMARKS: 2 OC, 3 OC, 8 OC, FREE.

ENDORSEMENT: Received 17 Octr. 1782. Sir Joshua Reynolds. An agreable letter of freindship.

London, Oct. 1 1782[2]

DEAR BOSWELL: I take it very kindly that you are so good as to write to me tho I have been so backward in answering your Letters; if I felt the same reluctance in taking a Pencil in my hand as I do a pen I should be as bad a Painter as I am a correspondent. Everybody has their tast. I love the correspondence of viva voce over a bottle with a great deal of noise and a great deal of nonsense. Mr. Burke dined with me yesterday. He talked much of you and with great affection. He says you are the pleasantest man he ever saw and sincerely wishes you would come and live amongst us. All your friends here I believe will subscribe to that wish. Suppose we send you a round Robin, such as we sent to Dr. Johnson,[3] to invite you, will that be an inducement. I think I have many in my Eye that would be eager to subscribe—What dye think of Lord Keppell and the Franker of this letter.[4]

---

[1] In his journal for Friday 18 Oct. 1782, JB, who had fallen behind in his record, wrote, "One of these days had a letter from Sir Joshua Reynolds which agitated me a little, by renewing my eagerness for London. But I felt myself so comfortable and of such consequence at Auchinleck that I doubted if London could upon the whole make me enjoy life more."

[2] Written, like the last paragraph, in a different pen from the rest, and considerably later.

[3] To request that he rewrite Goldsmith's epitaph in English. See *post* From Barnard, 15 Oct. 1785, n. 4.

[4] JB had met both men at Sir Joshua's table in the spring of 1781, Eliot on 30 Mar. and Keppel on 5 May. The latter occasion had been so jovial as to be referred to by JB on the day following as a "Riot" (Journ.). Keppel, the admiral who had been court-martialled and acquitted in 1779 for his conduct in the naval battle off Ushant in July 1778, was a great popular hero because of his anti-Ministerial stance and the oppressive tactics of the Admiralty against him. On the fall of Lord North's Ministry in Mar. 1782, he had been appointed First Lord of the Admiralty and raised to the peerage. Eliot, who became a member of The Club at the beginning of 1782, is characterized

My dear sir I had wrote thus far above a week since but having never spent an evening at home neglected finishing it. I find by the Papers that you have lost your Father[5] for which I sincerely condole with you but I hope this accident will not remove at a further distance the hope of seeing you in London. I am Dear sir, Yours most affectionately

J. REYNOLDS

To Thomas Barnard, Friday 14 February 1783

MS. Yale (L 36). A copy in the hand of John Johnston of Grange.[1] Sent 14 Feb. "Lord Bishop of Kilaloe to begin a long intended correspondence with his Lordship (Copy)" (Reg. Let.). Referred to in JB's journal, 13 Feb.: "In the evening I felt all at once a flow of good spirits, and with great ease wrote several letters for next nights post, one of which was to the Bishop of Kilaloe a correspondence which I had delayed to begin for almost two years, after we had cordially settled it in London. I *must* beleive that Man is in many respects subject to influence quite unknown to him. I have day after day resolved to write to the Bishop yet it has been deferred, though I was vexed at the delay, and loss of real pleasure from his correspondence. On a sudden I have written to him, and now cannot imagine *how* it was put off or *where* was the difficulty. Father of Spirits! I implore thy benignant influence!"

ENDORSEMENT (by Johnston): Copy Letter To The Bishop of Kilaloe 14th. February 1783.

Edinr., 14. February 1783

MY DEAR LORD: I should hardly have believed it possible that after obtaining your Lordship's cordial permission to write to you with an assurance of an answer, I should be almost two years in Scotland without availing myself of so valuable a privilege, But Indolence and procrastination even where our inclinations are warm and eager do sometimes prevail in a marvelous and miser-

ante p. xlvii. Both men were patrons of Sir Joshua, who could hardly have suggested any subscribers to his proposed Round Robin whose names would have delighted JB more.

[5] There is a notice of his death in *The St. James's Chronicle* for 5-7 Sept.

[1] Johnston dined on 14 Feb. with JB (Journ.), who evidently put him to work copying this letter.

able manner. I never experienced the truth of this sad reflection with more regrete than in this instance; The lightness of heart which one feels when the spell is broke by some sudden benignant impulse, is very agreeable, and such is the feeling which I enjoy to night.

The publick revolutions since we parted[2] have been so great, and so various that I shall not say one word of them as I could not avoid being more tedious than one ought to be in a letter, were I to enter upon them at all. But, as a private friend I am very very sorry that Burke was for so short a while in that Hem'sphere which he can so splendidly illuminate.[3] I was not in London last year, But while he was in power he made a very kind exertion to obtain an office for me.[4] He sent me a Copy of his application in my favour which Contained a Character of me which I preferr to the office which I did not get. I still languish for a residence in London. By my Fathers death I succeeded last Autumn to our Family Estate. But I received it under such burdens that unless I can obtain a few hundreds a year from Government I have it not in my power to establish my Family in London. I am an ancient baron,

[2] Lord Cornwallis had surrendered to the Americans on 19 Oct. 1781. North resigned as Prime Minister on 20 Mar. 1782 and was succeeded by the Marquess of Rockingham, a Whig, whose party was determined to end the war. Rockingham died in the summer of 1782, and was succeeded by the Earl of Shelburne, under whose ministry the war was concluded. The provisional articles of peace between England and the United States, signed on 30 Nov. 1782, and the preliminary articles with France and Spain, signed on 20 Jan. 1783, were generally unpopular in England; and Lord Shelburne's cabinet, which had made the peace, gradually split. Several of his cabinet members resigned, ostensibly because of the Government's abandonment of the American loyalists. At the same time, a coalition was formed between the Tory, Lord North, and the liberal Whig, Charles James Fox, formerly bitter enemies. Finally, on 24 Feb. 1783, after a resolution censuring the terms of peace was passed, Shelburne resigned. From that date to 2 Apr., there

was no fixed government, for the King was loath to call Fox, "the Man of the People". Before submitting to Fox, he approached Pitt, Lord Gower, North (without Fox), and Lord Temple; but none was willing to form a government. Finally, on 2 Apr., the King accepted the Duke of Portland as First Lord of the Treasury, Fox and North as joint Secretaries of State, and Lord John Cavendish as Chancellor of the Exchequer.

[3] Burke had been Paymaster General in the ministry of Rockingham, but when Shelburne became Prime Minister on 1 July 1782, Burke and Fox, among others, resigned because they distrusted him.

[4] *Ante* To Fox, 19 Apr. 1782, headnote; Journ. 11 Sept. 1783. The copy of Burke's letter, which was sent to JB on 23 Apr. 1782, is at Yale. To General Conway Burke wrote, "He [JB] is a Lawyer of Ability and of general Erudition, and the pleasantest and best tempered Man in the World. . . . You will have no cause to repent of having attached to you so agreeable a Man as Mr. Boswell."

and I would by no means estrange myself from Auchinleck the romantick seat of my Ancestors, But I am very desirous that when I am absent from it I should be in London rather than in Edinburgh, and I flatter myself with hopes that at length I shall have my desire gratified. Auchinleck is in Airshire not distant from Ireland. I hope your Lordship will do me the honour to come and see me there, perhaps I may prevail on Dr. Johnson to come to it again now that I am Master of it, how happy should I be, how Consecrated should I ever esteem my Groves could I see him and your Lordship there together. I did not fail after your Lordship left London in 1780, to deliver your Message to Dr. Johnson.[5] He was pleased with it, and said, "It would have hung heavy on my heart had I not seen the Bishop before he went." His Calling twice to visit you was an extraordinary Compliment. I had a letter from him a few days ago, in which he rigorously Councels me to drink only water.[6] I have doubtless given him reason to be offended with me for my excess in wine, a sin for which your Lordship has been my Father Confessor. But my moderation for sometime past, makes me bold enough to resist his authority upon this Article. He who has such a superiority over other men may live in any way, But an ordinary mortal who drinks only water will appear but poorly in society. This is my present Creed.

I found at your Booksellers in St. Pauls Churchyard, the only remaining Copy of your pamphlet Concerning the ancient Irish and Scots,[7] which I have read with much pleasure and to my full

[5] 1781 rather than 1780; JB did not go to London in 1780. Barnard probably left London on 31 May ("Bish[op] blessing", Notes, 30 May 1781). JB nowhere records the message which Barnard sent to SJ; in the *Life* he does report the two calls SJ made on Barnard.

[6] "In the evening I received a letter from Dr. Johnson so rigourous against my drinking wine at all, and so discouraging as to my settling in London, that I was a good deal hurt" (Journ. 8 Feb. 1783). In the *Life* (iv. 163) he prints only a brief undated extract from SJ's letter, including none of the matter that had pained him.

[7] Very probably *An Examination of the Arguments contained in a late Introduction to the History of the antient Irish and Scots*, J. Johnson, London, 1772. There is a copy of this work in the library of Trinity College, Dublin (photocopy of the same in the Boswell Office at Yale). It is noticed in *The Monthly Review* (1772) xlvi. 460, and at much greater length and with generous excerpts, in *The Critical Review* (1772) xxxiii. 234–238. *The Monthly Review* reports the price as 2s., *The Critical Review* as 2s. 6d. Gilbert Stuart (B. C. Nangle, *The Monthly Review, First Series*, 1934, p. 238) attributes it to Dr. Thomas Leland (1722–85), probably because Leland's forthcoming *History of Ireland* is advertised on the otherwise blank verso of the last leaf. This attribution is most improbable. If Leland in 1772 had joined in the controversy over the origin of the

satisfaction. I long to see a work of greater length by your Lordship. What it is to be I do not guess; but you said something to us of it the day that we dined with you so agreeably in St. James's street on occasion of my verses on your Lordship's promotion to be Bishop of Kilaloe, of which I inclose a Copy which I should have sent long e're now.[8]

I am to be in London next month[9] and I indulge the Chearing prospect that your Lordship will be there. I am delighted with the Institution of the order of St. Patrick.[10] How happy are the Irish now! Poor Scotland![11] Will your Lordship be kind enough to write to me soon. I have the honour to be with respect and affection your Lordship's faithfull humble servant

—Sign'd—JAMES BOSWELL

Scots which James Macpherson initiated with his *Introduction to the History of Great Britain and Ireland*, one would expect to find some reflection of the arguments in Leland's *History of Ireland*, 1773, but Leland there mentions the Scots of North Britain only casually and incidentally. Barnard certainly crossed swords with Macpherson, as is shown in the letter following this.

[8] JB "Made out Verses on Bishop of Killaloe" at Richmond on 26 Apr. 1781; read them to a company at the Duke of Montrose's 29 Apr. and to Mary Palmer and Edward Eliot at Sir Joshua's on 7 May. But the reference here is probably to the dinner given by Barnard 10 May (Journ.). For the verses as recovered from JB's drafts see Appendix 1.

[9] JB arrived in London on Thursday 20 Mar., after visiting Percy at Carlisle (Journ. 14–17 Mar.).

[10] In order to conciliate the more powerful peers of Ireland, the King, on 5 Feb. 1783, issued a Royal Warrant "for creating a Society or Brotherhood, to be called Knights of the Most Illustrious Order of Saint Patrick" (Sir Nicholas H. Nicolas, *History of the Orders of*

Knighthood of the British Empire, 1842, iv. 3–4). The order was to consist of the Sovereign, a Grand Master (the current Lord Lieutenant of Ireland), fifteen knights, and six officers (*ibid.* pp. 4–5). The institution of the Order was announced in *The London Chronicle* on 11 Feb. (liii. 137).

[11] For the "happy" Irish, see *post* To Percy, 8 Mar. 1784, n. 3. JB felt that Scotland would have been better off had it been allowed to keep its own parliament as Ireland had. In reply to the Bishop of Derry (Lord Bristol), after Bristol had asked his opinion on union with Ireland, he wrote in 1779, "Let us, my Lord, be satisfied to live on good and equal terms with our Sovereign's people of Ireland, as we might have done with our Sovereign's people of America, had they been allowed to enjoy *their* Parliaments or Assemblies as Ireland enjoys *hers*, and instead of calling the Irish 'a deluded people,' and attempting to grasp them in our paws, let us admire their spirit. A Scotsman might preach an Union to them, as the fox who had lost his tail" (*Gent. Mag.* 1785, lv. 742).

From Thomas Barnard,
Sunday 2 March 1783

MS. Yale (C 81). Received 10 Mar. "Lord Bishop of Killaloe Various" (Reg. Let.).

ADDRESS (in hand of the franker): James Boswell Esqr., Aughinleck, Edinburgh, by Donaghadee.

FRANK: ?S. Hamilton.[1]

POSTMARKS: MR 4, FREE.

ENDORSEMENT: Received 10 March 1783. Lord Bishop of Killaloe.

St. Wolstans, March 2d. 1783

MY DEAR SIR: A Letter from You was indeed a most agreeable Surprise, not less acceptable than unexpected. Your Kind Remembrance of an old acquaintance at this distance of Time and Place is perhaps a more flattering Instance of Regard, than if a Letter had follow'd me in a few days after we had been conversing on our future Correspondence, while the Impression both of the Subject and the Person was fresh upon your Memory. At least you must give me leave to Interpret it so, and to return you my Thanks accordingly.

I must now offer you my Congratulations on your accession to the Throne of your ancestors, no longer to be Stiled Esqr. but a Baron; no longer James Boswell; but Aughinleck Himself. Happy should I be if Circumstances would permit me to visit you at your antient Castle, and pay you my Homage. There should I see my Freind at the Head of his Vassals, The Men of Kyle, on "a Milk White Steed most like a Baron Bold,"[2] perhaps meditating an Inroad on the Mtgomeries, or sending out the Burnt Stick[3]

---

[1] Probably Sackville Hamilton, M.P. for the Irish borough of St. Johnstown and Under Secretary to the Lord Lieutenant of Ireland.

[2] Kyle, in which Barnard correctly places Auchinleck, is the middle district of Ayrshire. Barnard quotes a line from "Chevy Chase": "Earl Douglas on his milk-white steed, most like a baron bold".

[3] An allusion of great interest because it antedates by nearly three decades Sir Walter Scott's *Lady of the Lake* (1810),

the third canto of which, with its long accompanying note, is the source of nearly all the popular knowledge of the subject. Barnard's source was probably the same as Scott's—Thomas Pennant's *Tour in Scotland, 1769*, first published in 1771: "In every clan there is a known place of rendezvous, styled *Carn a whin*, to which they must resort on this signal. A person is sent out full speed with a pole burnt at one end and bloody at the other, and with a cross at the top, which is called

to denounce Vengeance against the Cunninghames. Were I still an Inhabitant of Ulster,[4] I should not only hope to see all this, but to partake of the Prey at your hospitable Board. But Providence has Cast my Lot in the South, on the Banks of the Shannon, From whence, even a journey to London will not bring me much nearer to Scotland than I am. Let London therefore be our next rendezvous where I am not without some expectations of meeting you the Ensuing Spring: Even before you have Established your Family at that market of Beef and Pudding which you pretend to prefer to Edinburg, Musarum Sedes, Scientiarum Nutrix.[5]

Your Letter reminds me of the frequent Revolutions in the Publick Affairs since our last parting. You have now another, to add to the list, which again brings some of our Personal Freinds to the Top of the Wheel,[6] the Benefit of whose Influence I trust you will shortly feel. As a Private Man I sincerely rejoice at this Event; But as a Member of the Constitution, I tremble. Two Circumstances however give me a Dawn of Hope that they will not proceed so far, as they Threatned in the Hour of their Hostile Confederacy against the Power of the Crown. One is that the new ministry is likely to be form'd on a Bottom something Broader than either of the last, and composed of more Heterogeneous Principles, which will necessarily produce a certain degree of Moderation in the Cabinet. The second is, that the Expulsion of the Shelburnites has divided the Popular Party against itself,[7]

Crosh-tairie, the cross of shame, or the fiery cross" (pp. 164–65). Remarkably enough, however, Barnard passed over Pennant's arresting phrase "fiery cross" to fix on one in a Latin passage which Pennant in his fourth edition (1776, p. 211) quoted as a parallel. Olaus Magnus, Archbishop of Uppsala in the sixteenth century, says that the northern Scandinavian peoples are summoned to arms by a young man running with a short stick (baculus tripalmaris) burnt at one end and bound with a cord at the other (fustem, seu baculum uno fine combustum, altero fune ligatum), the burning and the cord denouncing fire and the gallows on all who disobey (Historia de Gentibus Septentrionalibus, Bk. 7, Ch. 4, p. 223 of ed. of 1555). The phrase usto baculo (precisely Barnard's "burnt stick") occurs farther on in the passage, and was quoted by Pennant.—The Montgomeries and Cuninghames were prominent families of Cuninghame, the district of Ayrshire north of Kyle.

[4] As rector of Maghera and Archdeacon and Dean of Derry (Londonderry), Barnard had lived in the north of Ireland from 1751 to 1780.

[5] "Seat of the Muses, nursing mother of sciences." I have found no source for this. The scarcity of plural forms for scientia in classical Latin suggests that it is modern, perhaps Barnard's own.

[6] The coalition of Fox and North and the resignation of Shelburne on 24 Feb., which resulted eventually (2 Apr.) in the ministry of Fox and North.

[7] The Rockingham-Shelburne ministry which came to office in Mar. 1782, and which devolved on Shelburne alone after Rockingham's death in July, supported

which was Irresistible when United. Perhaps, now that the Spirit of Faction has totally Destroyd the Imperial Crown of Great Britain, and reduced it only to a Regal one, It may think that it has done Enough; and that 100 millions Expence, with the Loss of America and Ireland[8] is a Sufficient Sacrifice to the Goddess of Liberty, without Attacking the antient Constitution of the Island, under which it has so gloriously flourishd for ages Past, Which Corrupt as it may be and sorely diseased, may still be restored to health and preserved entire without amputation, if Healing Measures be applied. If our new Ministers pursue this System, it is my Sincere and Cordial wish that they may be permanent; for many of them I esteem and some of them I love. In short to use an Expression of our Excellent Freind the Doctor, I wish them as well as an Honest man Can.[9]

On this Side the Water we are at present in a State of Tranquillity in which however we expect soon to be disturbed by a general Election the Source of all discord and Confusion. Our Lord Lieutenant[10] has hitherto made himself very Popular, by the most diligint and uncorrupt attention to the Business of his high Station; joind to a Princely Munificence on every Call of Liberality or Splendour; Tho Nature has denied him the ordinary Talents of pleasing by affability and Courtly address. We shall probably soon loose him (as he belongs to Lord Shelburne) and shall regret his Loss. On the 17th we are to be amused with a grand Installation of the Knights of St. Patrick,[11] in his own Cathedral. Your

economic and parliamentary reform and threatened "the Power of the Crown". Fox, Rockingham's successor, refused to serve with Shelburne; his alliance with North divided "the Popular Party" and marked the end of the reform movement (J. S. Watson, *The Reign of George III*, 1960, pp. 228–34, 240–52).

[8] Barnard blames the loss of the American Colonies on the Opposition to North, composed of the Rockingham and Shelburne factions. Shelburne's fall as Prime Minister was determined by the concessions made to America in the Treaty of Versailles (Watson, pp. 252–59). Barnard also refers to the concessions granted Ireland between 1778 and 1782 (*post* To Percy, 8 Mar. 1784, n. 3).

[9] Mrs. Piozzi says that SJ made this

remark to Burke himself at Beaconsfield at the time of the General Election, autumn 1774 (*Johnsonian Miscellanies*, ed. G. B. Hill, 1897, i. 309–10; *Life* ii. 285 n. 3).

[10] George Grenville, Earl Temple (1753–1813), later (1784) Marquess of Buckingham, was Lord Lieutenant of Ireland from 15 Sept. 1782 to 3 June 1783. When Shelburne resigned, Temple intended to follow his example; but because of the delay in appointing his successor, he was not able to leave Ireland until June (*Comp. Peer.* ii. 406–408).

[11] The Grand Master (Earl Temple) and fourteen Knights-elect were installed at this time. For the official description of the ceremonies, see Nicolas,

written Copy of Verses upon your humble Servant Demand my best Thanks, for however Conscious the Party may be of his own Insignificance, it is flattering Laudari a Te Laudato Viro.[12] But I must a Second time intreat you to Suppress them if you Love me; for tho' between you and me I honest[l]y acknowledge that I am guilty of the atrocious charge of being both a Christian and a Tory, (anglice a Freind to the Constitution in Church and State from Principle) yet I am afraid the first of these Characters you Know must Ruin me with all the men of Sense in England, the second with all the men in Power. Reserve therefore this morsel, if you please, to appear with your Posthumous Works; and (as the Fashion of this World passeth away) Perhaps Religion and Loyalty may again come into Vogue. If not, we shall both be out of the Reach of Censure or applause. I am extremely happy that my Little Tract on McPhersons antient History has given you any Satisfaction: for I find you are one of those *Sturdy* Moralists that Prefer Truth to Scotland, as our Freind Johnson expresses it.[13] The Larger Work which you enquire of will probably never see the Light, as it Concerns a Subject which has ceased to Excite the Curiosity of the Publick. It was a Continuation of the Same Enquiry Concerning the original of the Scottish *Kingdom,* not the Population of that Part of Britain, which I take to be the Posterity of the Antient Caledonians, as Mr. McPherson asserts. But of the Scottish Dynasty which I hold to have Come from Ireland, of which I have as Indisputable Proofs as Exist for the Norman Dynasty having Come from France. Antiquarians generally have Confounded the Ideas of the origin of the People with that of their Princes, which are in Truth very Distinct. We have unquestionable Irish authority, for the Emigration of the Scots Princes and their Knights to Lorn Morven Lochaber Cantyr and Galloway[14] in the second Century with the Names of their cheiftains, like that of

History of the Orders of Knighthood, iv. 25–28.

[12] Cicero, *Quaestiones Tusculanae* IV. xxxi. 67, quoting a lost play by Naevius: "to be praised by you, a man who has received praise".

[13] "A Scotchman must be a very sturdy moralist, who does not love *Scotland* better than truth" (*Journey to the Western Islands,* ed. R. W. Chapman, 1924, p. 108). JB mentioned the state-

ment in both the *Tour* (*Life* v. 190 n. 6) and *Life* ii. 311.

[14] Lochaber, Morvern, or Morven, Lorn, and Kintyre (less commonly Cantyre) are districts, mainly coastal, in the north and north-west of Scotland extending from south Inverness-shire to south Argyll. Kintyre was the seat of the Dalriadan Scottish kingdom. Galloway comprised the counties of Kirkcudbright and Wigtown in south-western Scotland.

the Normans in Domesday Book. These Men founded the Small Kingdom of the Scots in the Western Highlands, as Fordun, Major, Boetius, and Buchanan[15] agree with us in admitting. While all the Respectable Parts of the Country were still possesd by the antient Natives the Picts and Mæatæ.[16] The Scots by degrees Extended their Territories and at last got all the Country into their Hands in the Time of Kenneth the 2d[17] from whom at last the Country took its Name, as England from the Angles; and these Scots are the Lineal Ancestors of the Royal Family and Certain other Septs, such as Dough Glass, Cath, Campbell, Moil, Mcdonald and most of the Mac's etc. But the People at Large Remain still the offspring of the True Caledonians as I verily Esteem the English to be of the Britons, Tho' mixd with the Romans Saxons, Danes and Normans, as the People of Scotland are with their Irish Invaders. Such is my System; in which I have asserted nothing without authority to Enforce it, as well as Probability. Enough of this Subject; of which we will talk more when we meet. You are of Saxon Extraction as well as myself, and therefore not Interested in the Question.

Adieu my Dear Boswell. Write to me again Soon, and Tell me your opinion Candidly and Freely, of Men and things, which at

[15] John Fordun (d. ?1384), Scottish historian, made use of Irish materials in his *Chronica Gentis Scotorum*. Barnard's "Fordun" would have been the *Scotichronicon*, i.e. Fordun continued by Walter Bower. There were editions by Thomas Hearne, 1722, and Walter Goodall, 1759.—John Major, or Mair (1469–1550), historian and scholastic divine, is best known for his *Historia Majoris Britanniae, tam Angliae quam Scotiae*, 1521.—Hector Boece, or Boethius (?1465–1536), wrote a history of Scotland from the earliest times to the accession of James III: *Scotorum Historiae a prima Gentis Origine*, 1526.—George Buchanan (1506–82), poet and scholar, in 1582 published a history of Scotland (*Rerum Scoticarum Historia*) which for a long time was the chief source of information for foreigners.

[16] One of the two confederacies of the native tribes in North Britain at the end of the second century, living, as is now believed, between the Antonine Wall and the Mounth, the name given to the mountains running eastward from Ben Alder to Aboyne (F. T. Wainright, ed., *The Problem of the Picts*, 1955, p. 52; I. A. Richmond, ed., *Roman and Native in North Britain*, 1958, pp. 74–75). The other great confederacy of that time, of tribes living north of the Maeatae, was however styled the Caledonii. The name Pict does not appear till a century later (W. C. Dickinson, *Scotland from the earliest Times to 1603*, 1961, p. 33).

[17] Barnard mistook the numeral or was using a different enumeration from that now accepted. It was Kenneth I (Kenneth MacAlpin), who in or about 841 succeeded to the throne of the Scots and went on to win that of the Picts, apparently by a claim of descent backed by force. After the union of the kingdoms the name of Pict fell at once into disuse (Agnes M. Mackenzie, *The Foundations of Scotland*, 1938, pp. 76, 83).

present is a very Interesting Subject, and be assured that your Thoughts may Safely be Committed to the Breast of your Faithful and Affectionate humble Servant

THOS. KILLALOE

Direct to me at St. Wolstans Ireland. A Packet of any reasonable Size will reach me Free. When you write to Dr. Johnson I beg you to assure him of my Constant Respect, and Most Cordial Esteem. There are two Questions I want to ask him, as I believe He (if any one Can resolve them) first, what is the Meaning of, "That two handed Engine at the Door," in Miltons *Lycidas?* Second. What is "Lukes Iron Crown"; in Goldsmiths *Traveller?*[18] I suppose Thereby Hangs a Tale.[19] But my Reading Cannot Explain it.

From Thomas Percy, Monday 3 March 1783

MS. Yale (C 2231). Received 5 Mar. "Lord Bishop of Dromore desireous to see me at Carlisle in my way to London, and begging to know when?" (Reg. Let.).

ADDRESS (in hand of franker): The Honble. James Boswell, Advocate, Edinburgh.

FRANK: free. G. Rose.[1]

POSTMARK: CARLISLE.

ENDORSEMENT: Received 5 March 1783 Lord Bishop of Dromore.[2]

Carlisle, March 3d. 1783

DEAR SIR, I received some time ago, your very obliging favour,

---

[18] For JB's response to these questions about *Lycidas*, l. 130, and *The Traveller*, l. 436, see *post* To Barnard, 28 Mar. 1783 and 8 Mar. 1784.

[19] *The Merry Wives of Windsor*, I. iv. 159; *As You Like It*, II. vii. 28; *The Taming of the Shrew*, IV. i. 60; *Othello*, III. i. 8. Also found in Cervantes and Rabelais.

---

[1] George Rose (1744–1818), joint

Secretary to the Treasury in Shelburne's Ministry, and again in Pitt's, was an intimate friend of Lord Percy, the Duke of Northumberland's son. He was returned to Parliament in 1784 through the influence of the Duke.

[2] Percy had been consecrated Bishop of Dromore on 20 Apr. 1782, but continued to live in the Deanery at Carlisle for more than a year after that date, his Palace at Dromore being newly built and damp (Gaussen, pp. 194–98).

and in consequence of the information you gave me, sent to London to get an early Copy of Mr. Clarke's Reply to Shaw's last Pamphlet;[3] but as it has never been sent, I fear you were not truly informed on that subject—Indeed, if Clarke knew that the Inquiry was made for me, or on my account, I have no Doubt, but wrong Intelligence would be purposely given.—As March is now arrived, I hope we may indulge Expectations of seeing you soon: which I look forward to, with much pleasure; Only let me beg one Line, if possible, previous to your coming, lest we may be absent from home on a Visit, which we have been solicited to make to a family a few miles from Carlisle.

I had intelligence last night from London; that they are trying to form a Ministry without taking in *the Man of the People*:[4] and this arrangement has been talked of,

Lord Gower, first Lord of the Treasury.
Wm. Pitt and Lord Advocate, Secretaries.
Jenkinson Chancr. of Excheqr.
Macdonald Solicr. General:[5]

[3] Shaw, assisted by SJ, included a *Reply to Mr. Clarke's Answer* in a second edition of his *Enquiry into the Poems ascribed to Ossian*, published in London early in 1782 (reviewed in *Gent. Mag.* Apr. 1782, lii. 184–86). Apparently (his letter is unrecovered and unminuted; see *ante* p. 121) JB gave Percy to understand that a second reply by Clark might soon be expected.

[4] Charles James Fox.

[5] Granville Leveson-Gower, Earl Gower (1721–1803), K.G., Lord President of the Council from 1767 to 1779, was offered the post of Prime Minister but declined it. On Pitt's accession to power he again became President of the Council and served in that capacity from Dec. 1783 to Nov. 1784, when he was made Lord Privy Seal. He was created Marquess of Stafford in 1786.—William Pitt (1759–1806) was first returned to Parliament in 1781, and appointed Chancellor of the Exchequer by Shelburne on 6 July 1782. On the fall of the Fox-North Coalition, after the defeat of Fox's East India Bill, the King appointed Pitt First Lord of the Treasury and Chancellor of the Exchequer, 19 Dec. 1783, making him Prime Minister before he was 25.— Henry Dundas (1742–1811), JB's classmate in the University of Edinburgh and his particular *bête noire* ("a coarse, unlettered, unfanciful dog": To Temple, 22 May 1775), was made Solicitor-General for Scotland at the age of twenty-four and Lord Advocate at thirty-three. Retaining the latter office through the Rockingham and Shelburne ministries (1775–83), he was also appointed by Shelburne Treasurer of the Navy, Member of the Privy Council, Keeper of the Signet for Scotland, and given the patronage of all places in Scotland. During the Coalition Ministry he was replaced as Lord Advocate and Treasurer of the Navy. On Pitt's accession to power, however, he again became Treasurer of the Navy, and was later President of the Board of Control for India, Home Secretary, and Secretary for War. In 1802 he was created Viscount Melville. "For nearly thirty years he was the most powerful man in Scotland" (DNB). For a full account of JB's dealings with him, see Frank Brady, *Boswell's*

In the Mean time Lord North and Cha. Fox are waiting, till they shall be sent for.—I presume the above arrangemt. is that of the Chancr.⁶ Adieu. I am, Dear Sir, Your very faithful Servant

THO. DROMORE

To Thomas Percy, Wednesday 12 March 1783

Not reported. Sent from Edinburgh 12 Mar. "Lord Bishop of Dromore that I hope to find his Lordship at Carlisle on Saturday night¹—that Clarkes Reply to Shaw is not yet published but is in London.² That I wish to be in London in the midst of this political 'Whirlwind.' Would there were an angel to direct the Storm!"³ (Reg. Let.).

Political Career, 1965.—Charles Jenkinson (1729–1808), later (1786) first Baron Hawkesbury and (1796) first Earl of Liverpool, had been Secretary at War from Dec. 1778 to 1782. In 1786, he was made President of the Board of Trade.— Archibald Macdonald (1747–1826), knighted 1788, baronet 1813, was violently opposed to the Coalition, and in Nov. of 1783 opposed the second reading of Fox's East India Bill. He was later (1784–88) Solicitor-General, (1788–93) Attorney General, and (1793) Lord Chief Baron of the Court of Exchequer. He was a younger brother of Lord Macdonald, who gave JB and SJ such unsatisfactory entertainment on the Hebridean tour.

⁶ Edward Thurlow, Baron Thurlow (1731–1806), Lord Chancellor since 1778, and much in the King's confidence. The Coalition Ministry insisted on his resignation, but he resumed the Great Seal when Pitt became Prime Minister.

¹ JB, on his way to London, arrived in Carlisle on 16 Mar. "Was sorry to hear from him, that his only son who had gone to Italy for the recovery of his health from an Asthmatick complaint was given over. But as I perceived that the Bishop could be social notwithstanding, I did not affect to dwell long upon the melancholy subject" (Journ.). On the following day, "the Bishop shewed me the correspondence between him and Drs. Blair and Fergusson concerning Ossian, in which I thought my Countrymen made but a shabby figure; though I also thought the Bishop insisted too much upon the evidence of Minutes kept by him, which he shewed me, and I saw were very curt, and did not mention having heard Earse poetry repeated at Dr. Fergusson's, but only fixed the date of his drinking tea there. The Bishop was very keen and violent upon the subject" (*ibid.*). JB left Carlisle late that day.

² It was published, accompanying a new edition of Clark's *Answer*, some time in 1783, with the title *An Answer to Mr. Shaw's Reply*. Shaw concluded the series with *A Rejoinder to an Answer from Mr. Clark*, 1784 (G. F. Black, *Macpherson's Ossian and the Ossianic Controversy*, 1926, pp. 28, 38; BM Cat.).

³ See Joseph Addison, *The Campaign* (*Miscellaneous Works*, ed. A. C. Guthkelch, 1941), l. 292.

To Thomas Barnard,
Friday 28 March 1783

MS. Yale (L 37). A copy. Sent 29 Mar. "Lord Bishop of Killaloe. Various (Copy)" (Reg. Let.).

HEADING: To the Lord Bishop of Kilaloe.

London, 28 March 1783

MY DEAR LORD: Never was a Correspondent more liberally encouraged than I by Your Lordship. Your letter which I had the honour to receive at Edinburgh has made me your debtor to such an extent that I shall find it very difficult to repay you. But you shall have what I can give you.

It is a week today since I arrived in this Capital, where I expected to get a clear and distinct view of the state of our Government which appeared so dark and mysterious at a distance. But I find the cloud thicker upon approaching it. You know I live with Men of all parties; and I declare that I beleive not one of them can guess what will be the result of the present deliberations of the Cabinet, which I look upon as a great dicebox shaken by a faction. This similitude is not amiss, considering what a share so notorious a Gamester as Charles Fox has in the Storm. To borrow an expression from Churchills *Prophecy of Famine*, "Things are GOD knows how."[1] For my own part I am very seriously concerned to see such a general disregard of all good principles of Government; And I lament that our freind Burke has let himself be drawn so far out of what I am fully persuaded is his natural sphere.[2] I love him most sincerely.

Dr. Johnson was very ill when I came to London. But I am happy to inform your Lordship is now much better. He has charged me with compliments to you as have Sir Joshua Reynolds with whom I past a pleasant evening after the Club last tuesday, and Genl. Paoli under whose roof I live in the same agreable manner you have seen me and I hope shall soon see me again.

I have consulted Dr. Johnson on your Lordships two Queries. "That two handed engine at the door" in Milton's *Lycidas* means

[1] Charles Churchill (1731–64), *The Prophecy of Famine. A Scots Pastoral*, Inscribed to John Wilkes, Esq., 1763, l. 146.

[2] Burke was a member of the Fox-North Coalition, although a man of essentially conservative opinions.

TO BARNARD, 28 MARCH 1783

an Ax or a Sword for the execution of the Prelates of whom there is a gloomy abuse in the Context. The epithet two handed signifies that it is an engine of such weight that it requires two hands to weild or use it. Thus a two handed sword is a common expression for the *Glaymore*.[3] "Luke's iron crown" in Goldsmiths *Traveller* is an allusion to a story which it seems is well known upon the continent of an Hungarian Regicide of the name of Luke[4] whose punishment was having a red hot iron crown put upon his head. Dr. Johnson is not quite sure if Hungary was the country; but thinks it was. The same torture was inflicted on Menteith one of the Murderers of James I or II of Scotland if I recollect right.[5] I am sure it is to be found in the Scottish History.[6] The Dr. observed well that an allusion to any story little known should be explained in a note.

Your Lordship has excited my curiosity much, by the hints which you are pleased to give me of Your History of the Settlement of the Irish Dynasty in Scotland. I hope you will not withhold it

[3] The two-edged broadsword (from the Gaelic *claidheamh mōr* meaning "great sword"), with cross hilt, used by the Highlanders of Scotland.

[4] For a correction of this explanation, see *post* To Barnard, 8 Mar. 1784 and n. 9.

[5] JB's uncertainty as to whether it was James I or James II who was assassinated is a fair indication of the extent of his knowledge of his country's history. James I (1394–1437) was surprised and murdered in the cloister of the Black Friars at Perth on the night of 20 Feb. 1437 by a group of eight or more men led by Sir Robert Graham. Malise Graham, Earl of Menteith, Sir Robert's nephew, was not involved in the conspiracy. The person who according to tradition underwent the torture of the hot iron crown was the King's uncle, Walter Stewart, Earl of Atholl, the prime instigator of the plot, though not one of the actual murderers. As that torture is not mentioned by the one completely trustworthy contemporary source, Walter Bower's continuation of Fordun, modern historians conclude that Atholl, "who had aimed at the crown of Scotland, was

exposed to the public gaze, with a crown of iron fastened to his head and a paper, on which the word 'traitor' was inscribed, before he was led to execution" (E. W. M. Balfour-Melville, *James I, King of Scots*, 1936, pp. 114, 124–25, 149–50, 243, 246–48; *Scots Peer.* i. 436–38; vi. 142–43, 214–15). JB as usual verified his recollection before putting it in the *Life* (ii. 7), where we find "Earl of Athol" and "James I".

[6] JB no doubt means "in any general history of Scotland". Barnard could indeed have found an account of Atholl's hot iron crown in Major, Boece, and Buchanan—that is, in all the historians he himself had named except "Fordun". He could have found it too in a work of the eighteenth century: "Some part of three days was spent in the execution of Athol. . . . On the second day he was placed on a pillar in the view of the people, and a crown of hot iron set on his head, with this inscription, 'Here stands the king of traitors'" (William Guthrie, *A General History of Scotland, from the earliest Accounts to the present Time*, 1767, iii. 351–52).

from the Publick. To do this Age justice it is not deficient in attention to the study of Antiquities; And where authentick proofs can be brought a work upon that subject is particularly valuable— to say nothing of the talents of the writer. I flatter myself with hopes of talking fully of this and other things with your Lordship in this place very soon. I shall be here till the middle of May.[7] I have the honour to be with respect and affection your Lordships most obedient humble servant. May I beg to hear from your Lordship at Genl. Paolis South audley Street. *Attamen ipse veni.*[8]

To Lord Ossory, Thursday 10 July 1783

MS. Yale (L 1255). A copy in Lawrie's hand. Sent 10 July. "Earl of Upper Ossory soliciting his interest with his brother the Secretary at War, in favour of Serjeant John Boswell (Copy)" (Reg. Let.).

HEADING: To The Earl of Upper Ossory.

Edr., 10 July 1783

MY LORD: I have no particular claim to take the liberty of intruding upon your Lordship, except that of having the honour to be a member along with your Lordship of the *Literary Club*, at the Turks head.[1]

But I think I may venture to solicit your Lordships recommendation of Serjeant John Boswell to the Secretary at War,[2] for his Majestys letter as an outpensioner of Chelsea College[3] at a

---

[7] JB did not leave London until 30 May, on which date he departed with Temple (BP xv. 239; *Diaries of William Johnston Temple*, ed. Lewis Bettany, 1929, p. 42).

[8] Ovid, *Heroides* i. 2: "But come yourself."

---

[1] Lord Ossory was elected to The Club on 14 Mar. 1777.

[2] Richard Fitzpatrick (1747–1813), officer and politician, the second son of John, first Earl of Upper Ossory. He was an intimate friend of Fox and had entered the Coalition Ministry of Fox and Lord North in Apr. 1783.

[3] A hospital for invalid pensioned soldiers founded by Charles II; it was built by Sir Christopher Wren.

shilling a day, because he is a branch of my family, who having behaved not so well as he should have done, at an early period of his life, was adjudged to be a Soldier,[4] after which, his conduct was such as to merit approbation, of which a Certificate by the

[4] John Boswell, second son of David Boswell of Craigston, married his distant cousin Margaret Fergusson, heiress of Knockroon, c. 1740 and had one son, John Boswell of Knockroon, and five daughters. JB sometimes called him "Old Knockroon", but the property belonged successively to his mother-in-law, his wife, and his son. He was no doubt "adjudged to be a Soldier" under the Act 29 Geo. II C. 4, which directed Justices of the Peace and others to press into military service all able-bodied men who were unemployed and without means of support. On 22 July 1756 the kirk session of Auchinleck summoned him for examination, "There being a *fama clamosa* in the Country that Mr. John Boswel in Knockroon hath been guilty of repeated Acts of Dishonesty and Injustice of Drunkenness Lying Cursing and Swearing and also that he has been Guilty of Adultery or at least a Behaviour tending thereto with Marion Jamieson who lived lately in Knockroon now in the Parish of Sorn" (MS. Session Minutes of Auchinleck Parish Church, 1745–1819, p. 24). John Boswell appeared before the Session on 24 Aug. and admitted to occasional drunkenness, "which he is sorry for but believes that he has been in a great Measure led to it by being obliged by the disagreeable Situation in his Family and want of the necessary Subsistence at home, to go from home into Company when otherwise he would not have chosen to do so" (*ibid.* p. 25). He could not remember any acts of injustice, and said he had no habit of lying, cursing, or swearing, though on a particular occasion he might lie "to save a greater Mischief" (*ibid.*), and "upon Provocation or in a Passion . . . has unguardedly let slip some words . . . which he is sorry for" (*ibid.*). He absolutely denied the charge of adultery, as did Marion Jamieson, who was examined on 19 Dec. The session however appointed John Dun, the minister, to apply to the Presbytery for authority to examine witnesses. On 13 Mar. 1757 Mr. Dun entered a minute: "John Boswel is gone to the Army so the Process against him is stopt" (*ibid.* p. 34). Five years later (13 June 1762) the minutes of the session for some unexplained reason make this more explicit: "It is necessary to observe that the Reason of the Process being dropt agt. Mr. John Boswel in Knockroon was his being pressed into the Army" (*ibid.* p. 57).—In 1757 notour (notorious) adultery was defined by statute in Scotland as a capital offence, and though sentences imposed by the courts were no longer capital, they might be very severe. As late as 1766 a minister convicted of notour adultery was transported to the plantations and banished for life (John Maclaurin, *Arguments and Decisions in remarkable Cases before the High Court of Judiciary*, 1774, p. 732). When John Boswell "was broke in Dublin" and came home in May 1763 (From James Bruce, 19 May 1763), the kirk session gave him no further trouble, but he clearly did not return to live with his wife, and his mother-in-law as clearly did not provide for him. In 1766 JB had been instrumental in getting him appointed usher to the Lord High Commissioner of the General Assembly of the Church of Scotland, the Earl of Glasgow, who held that office from 1764 to 1772 inclusive (From T. D. Boswell, 4 Apr., 30 May 1766; From John Boswell, 3 Mar. 1769; *Scots Peer.* iv. 215). By 1780 he had been reconciled with his wife and was living with her and her daughters (*Journ.* 2 Sept. 1780).

Earl of Dumfries[5] under whom he served, is lodged with Captain Grant[6] at Chelsea College.

I should hope that a *Gentleman* who has retrieved his character, in the army, may appear to the House of *Fitz-Patrick* a very fit object of his majestys bounty, especially at an advanced age and therefore I presume to address myself to Lord Ossory.

If your Lordship shall be generous enough to patronize Serjeant Boswell upon my application, I shall esteem myself much favoured. I have the honour to be, My Lord, Your Lordships most obedient humble servant

From Sir John Hawkins to Bennet Langton, Tuesday 15 July 1783

MS. Yale (C 1510). Written in the hand of an amanuensis.

ADDRESS: Capt. Langton, Rochester.

POSTMARK: [Illegible].

[London] 15th July 1783

DEAR SIR, From the conversations which I have lately had with Mrs. Williams[1] and Dr. Johnson I guess that by this time you

[5] Patrick Macdowall, later Macdowall Crichton (1726–1803), succeeded his uncle as fifth Earl of Dumfries in 1768. He held a commission as captain in the Army, 5 Mar. 1755, and as captain in the Thirty-first Regiment of Foot, 25 Aug. 1756. He was promoted lieutenant-colonel, 17 Oct. 1761, and appears for six months to have been commanding officer (the first) of the 108th Regiment of Foot. He was commissioned captain in the 3rd Regiment of Foot Guards, 12 Apr. 1762, and held those ranks and that appointment to 1773, disappearing from the *Army List* 1775 (*Army Lists*, especially "Succession of Colonels", *Army List* 1763, p. 238). Since John Boswell was discharged in Ireland (see *ante* n. 4), he could not have been serving under Dumfries when he was "broke", but he may have served in the 108th Foot, which was certainly disbanded after the Peace in 1763. I do not find notice of the disbanding of the 108th, but several other regiments were disbanded or reduced in Ireland at just this time: 121st Foot at Limerick, week of 17 Apr.; 120th Foot at Galway, same date; 105th Foot at Dublin, same date; 123rd Foot at Kinsale, 23 Apr.; 18th Foot same place and date; 16th Foot at Cork, 25 Apr.; 20th Light Dragoons at Limerick, week of 24 Apr. (*London Chronicle* xiii. 412, 436, 454).

[6] Lewis Grant, "son of the Minister of Auchinleck in my Grandfather's time, who is Adjutant to the College" (Journ. 29 May 1783, the anniversary of the Restoration of Charles II). Beginning in 1783, JB regularly attended the anniversary feast at the College. He was on terms of affectionate intimacy with Grant, and according to John Boswell had put him "under the strongest obligation" through his interest with Burke (From John Boswell, 16 July 1785).

[1] Anna Williams (1706–83), "daugh-

have the latter for your guest:[2] a greater act of friendship you could not at this time exercise than by taking him under your hospitable roof, for I am given to understand that, in the opinion of his physicians and those about him, although it has pleased God at present to spare him, his continuance much longer with us, is very precarious.

I visited him twice in his illness, and had some long and very serious conversations with him, that discovered a mind wonderfully at ease, such a faith in the promises contained in scripture as every good christian would wish to entertain, and a perfect complacency and good will towards the world and all around him.[3]

In the last of my visits I took occasion to mention that, at a very advanced period of life, he enjoyed the felicity of seeing his reputation at it's zenith; and, speaking from my own experience and observation, that persons of all ranks, professions, and persuasions concurred in an high opinion of his integrity, worth, and abilities; and that many had signified to me a strong desire that he would give to the public such a collection of his writings, pure and genuine from his own hand, as would perpetuate and prevent injury to his memory.

Besides this motive I was actuated by another, namely the raising, by a subscription for a volume or two of this kind, a sum that might add to his yearly income, and enable him to keep from penury and distress a person very near him, and who, under the calamity of the loss of a sense, in a great measure relies on him for her support.

An undertaking of this kind was formerly recommended to a friend of mine, Dr. Foster[4] the late dissenting minister, and it succeeded to a degree beyond his hopes.

---

ter of a very ingenious Welsh physician, and a woman of more than ordinary talents and literature", who had come to London, hoping to be cured of cataracts in both eyes. An operation, performed in SJ's house, resulting in total blindness, she remained to her death a member of SJ's household so long as he had a home of his own (*Life* i. 232 *et passim*).

[2] SJ was at Rochester visiting Langton from 10 to 22 July 1783 (*Letters SJ* iii. 52; *Life* iv. 233).

[3] Some time during the early morning hours of 17 June, SJ had been seized by a paralytic stroke, which deprived him of his powers of speech. He recovered in time to make the visit, long planned, to Rochester (*Life* iv. 227–33). Hawkins reported the two conversations mentioned in this and the paragraph below in his *Life of Johnson*, 1st ed. (pp. 544–46), but represents the second one as having taken place some months before SJ's illness; the first, some time during the illness.

[4] James Foster, D.D. (1697–1753), *Sermons*, 4 vols., 1744. It was Foster who administered the sacrament to Lord

I obtained from our friend a promise that he would ponder my advice; but do earnestly wish that, in some vacant hour, some favorable opportunity which his presence with you may afford, you would strengthen it with your own; as knowing that coming from you it will meet with the attention it deserves.

The approaching winter will afford the doctor leisure and opportunities for a search and re-collection of papers, occasional compositions, and other materials; beyond which I would wish it not to be postponed. I beg my most respectful compliments to lady Rothes as also that[5] those of my wife may be understood to accompany this letter, together with my best wishes for the health and prosperity of you and your whole family, and am Your sincere friend and humble servant

JOHN HAWKINS[6]

From Lord Ossory, Sunday 27 July 1783

MS. Yale (C 3021). Received 1 Aug. "Earl of Upper Ossory a most obliging letter with one from his brother the Secretary at War, favourable to Serjt. Jo. Boswell" (Reg. Let.).

ADDRESS: James Boswell Esqr., at Edinburgh.

FRANK: Free, Upr. Ossory.

POSTMARKS: 28 ⟨IY⟩, FREE, AMPTHILL.

ENDORSEMENT: Received 1 August 1783. Earl of Upper Ossory. A most obliging Letter with one from his brother the Secretary at War favourable to Serjt. Jo. Boswell.

Ampthill Park, July 27th 1783

SIR, I communicated your request to my brother by letter, not having been in town or seen him since I received it, and I now enclose you his answer.[1]

Kilmarnock at his execution in 1746. Although known for the excellence of his sermons, he would have died destitute but for the subscription referred to by Hawkins, who was his good friend for many years (Sir John Hawkins, *A General History of the Science and Practice of Music*, 1776, v. 325–26).

[5] "that" in Hawkins's hand, above the line.

[6] Signature in Hawkins's hand.

---

[1] The letter is at Yale (C 1266):

War Office, July 26th 1783

DEAR BROTHER, I should be very happy to serve the person recommended by Mr.

I trust Mr. Boswell will be satisfied that, at least, there is no inclination wanting in *the House of Fitz Patrick* to oblige him.

I have the honor to be, Sir, Your most obedient humble Servant

UPR. OSSORY

To John Douglas, Tuesday 12 August 1783

Not reported. Sent from Edinburgh 12 Aug. "Rev. Dr. John Douglas to the same purpose" (Reg. Let.), i.e. "begging his patronage of the Subscription for Mr. Robert Walker's Sermons". Walker (1716–83), who held the first charge in the New (or High) Church, Edinburgh, had died on 6 Apr. 1783. There are around fifty references in JB's journal, 1774–83, to his hearing him preach at the New Church. His *Sermons on Practical Subjects*, first published in 1764–65, went through many editions, one as late as 1851, including one of three volumes in 1783–84, to which JB probably refers. Walker's sermons were well thought of in the Boswell family. JB's journal does not mention his efforts to secure subscribers for the sermons.

To Lord Ossory, Sunday 19 October 1783

MS. Yale (L 1256). A copy. Sent 19 Oct. "Earl of Upper Ossory very grateful for his Lordships obliging attention. Begging his brother may be reminded of Serjt. Boswell, Capt. Grant being to transmit the requisite papers" (Reg. Let.).

HEADING: To the Earl of Upper Ossory.

Boswell, whom I have not the pleasure of knowing otherwise than by reputation. Mr. Boswell may perhaps not be apprized of all the qualifications necessary to enable a Man to receive the bounty of the King's Letter. He must have served as a Serjeant and upon his discharge being recommended to Chelsea he must be in the actual receipt of the out pension. In addition to this he must produce some certificate of good behaviour from some of the Officers under whom he has served. Should Mr. Boswell's friend have all these requisites it may even then be some time before it may be in my power to place him on the List. The Candidates are so very numerous and many of their cases, from wounds and long service, so strong that it may be long before an opportunity offers itself. If you can procure however the particulars already mentioned from Mr. Boswell his name will be entered in the List of applications now in the office, and as soon as he can, consistently with justice, be provided for, he shall. I am Dear Brother, Yours most sincerely,

R. FITZPATRICK

Auchinleck, 19 October 1783

MY LORD: I return your Lordship my most sincere thanks for the very obliging manner in which you have been pleased to attend to my application in favour of Serjeant John Boswell; and I shall be ever desireous of an opportunity to give any proof of my gratitude. I am now at a romantick Seat of my Ancestors in Ayrshire opposite to the coast of Ireland. If your Lordship would take the short passage to that Kingdom by Portpatrick,[1] and honour this Place with a visit in your way, I should be very proud.

It gives me pleasure to understand that Serjeant Boswell has the requisites mentioned in the Secretary at War's letter and I have directed Captain Grant Adjutant of Chelsea College to transmit the discharge with the Earl of Dumfries's Certificate to Colonel Fitzpatrick, who I beg may be reminded of the matter, if that is not too much trouble to Your Lordship.[2] I have the honour to be with much respect, My Lord, Your Lordships most obedient and faithful humble servant

To Sir Joshua Reynolds, Friday 6 February 1784

MS. T. G. M. Snagge. A copy at Yale (L 1099) in John Johnston's hand, endorsed by him: "Copy-Letter To Sir Joshua Reynolds, 6 febry. 1784." Sent 6 Feb. "Sir Joshua Reynolds to have his account of Dr. Johnson's health and etc. etc. (Copy)" (Reg. Let.).

ADDRESS: To Sir Joshua Reynolds, London.

POSTMARKS: FE 7, 11 FE.

ENDORSEMENT: Mr. Boswell.

Edinburgh, 6 February 1784

MY DEAR SIR: I long exceedingly to hear from you. Sir William Forbes brought me good accounts of you, and Mr. Temple sent

[1] Portpatrick, in west Wigtownshire, commands the shortest line of communication between Britain and Ireland. It was for some two hundred years the great thoroughfare to and from the north of Ireland.

[2] John Boswell seems not to have received the appointment. It has been impossible to consult his service record, for his regiment remains unknown, but his name does not appear in the Chelsea Pension Register (W.O. 120/18), 1763–1795.

me very pleasing intelligence concerning the fair Palmeria.[1] But a line or two from yourself is the next thing to seeing you.

My anxiety about Dr. Johnson is truly great. I had a letter from him within these six weeks,[2] written with his usual acuteness and vigour of mind. But he complained sadly of the state of his health; and I have been informed since, that he is worse. I intend to be in London next month, chiefly to attend upon him with respectful affection. But in the mean time, it will be a great favour done me, if you who know him so well, will be kind enough to let me know particularly how he is.

I hope Mr. Dilly conveyed to you my Letter on the State of the Nation *from the Authour*.[3] I know your political principles, and indeed your settled system of thinking upon civil society and subordination, to be according to my own heart. And therefore I doubt not you will approve of my honest zeal. But what monstrous

[1] On 15 Dec. 1783 Temple had written: "I have also met several times, and entertained here your charming Miss Palmer, who has passed great part of the Summer about two miles from me at her sisters Mrs. Gwatkin, who is married to a very agreeable neighbour of mine. I like Miss Palmer extremely; there is some thing peculiarly pleasing and amiable in her manner, her understanding seems good, and she plays, sings and draws with great taste and judgement. As you may naturally suppose, our conversation turned greatly upon you; so much so, that when we met, Miss Gwatkin (Mr. Gwatkins sister, a charming girl) used to say, 'Well now, I do insist upon it that you do not talk about Boswell.' 'Yes, but we will,' replied Miss Palmer, 'and you will talk about him too when you know him, which you shall as soon as he comes to town.' She now has left us and went last wednesday to your friend *Mahoganys*, Mr. Eliots of Port Eliot, for some weeks and then to London. She begged her kind compliments to you." The journal indicates that JB had seen much of Sir William Forbes during the past two months.

[2] SJ had written to JB, 24 Dec. 1783: "I am now a little better. But sickness and solitude press me very heavily. I

could bear sickness better, if I were relieved from solitude" (*Letters SJ* iii. 117).

[3] On 17 Dec. 1783 Fox's East India Bill, which was an attempt to reform the East India Company by substituting a board of seven persons nominated by Parliament for the board then in charge and thereby eliminate bribery and corruption, was defeated in the House of Lords. Previously passed by Commons, it was opposed by the King, who wrote a letter circulated among the Lords in which he maintained that he would regard as an enemy anyone who voted for the bill. Fox was accused of trying to gather patronage to himself, and the bill was considered an attack on property as well as on Hastings. The defeat of the bill rejoiced JB's Tory soul; he "went down to the [Advocates'] Library and drew up an Address to his Majesty from the Dean and Faculty of Advocates to congratulate him on it", which his colleagues refused to send (Journ. 20 Dec.). Undaunted, he began six days later a pamphlet designed "to rouse a spirit for *property* and the *Constitution* in opposition to the East India Bill". It was published the last day of the year with the title *A Letter to the People of Scotland on the Present State of the Nation*.

effects of Party do we now see![3a] I am really vexed at the conduct of some of our freinds.[4]

Amidst the conflict, our freind of Port Elliot is with much propriety created a Peer. But why[5] o why did he not obtain the title of *Baron Mahogony*.[6] Genealogists and Heralds would have had curious work of it, to explain and illustrate that title. I ever am with sincere regard, My Dear Sir, your affectionate humble servant

JAMES BOSWELL

From Sir Joshua Reynolds, Monday 16 February 1784

MS. Fettercairn Papers, National Library of Scotland. Received at Edinburgh 20 Feb. "Sir Joshua Reynolds, account of Dr. Johnson's health etc. etc." (Reg. Let.).

ADDRESS: James Boswell Esq., Edinburgh.

POSTMARK: 16 FE.

London, Feb. 16[1] 1784

MY DEAR SIR: I am glad to hear we shall have the pleasure of seeing you soon amongst us. We find you wanting at our club. The business of the house of Commons has prevented our having had much of their Company this year;[2] we have elected two new

[3a] Copy, "do we see?"

[4] Burke and Fox chiefly. See *post* To Barnard, 8 Mar. 1784.

[5] Copy, "But only why"

[6] Eliot was created Baron Eliot of St. Germans on 13 Jan. 1784. "Mr. Eliot mentioned a curious liquor peculiar to his country, which the Cornish fishermen drink. They call it *Mahogany*; and it is made of two parts gin, and one part treacle, well beaten together. I begged to have some of it made, which was done with proper skill by Mr. Eliot. I thought it very good liquor" (*Life* iv. 78; cf. Journ. 8 Sept. 1792). It was at Sir Joshua's that Eliot had compounded the drink.

[1] MS. "18"

[2] Of the thirty-four members of The Club living on 16 Feb. 1784, eight (Sir Charles Bunbury, Burke, Fox, Gibbon, Lord Lucan, Lord Palmerston, Sheridan, and Lord Ossory) were Members of Parliament. Lord Althorp and Edward Eliot had been M.P.s but had been recently removed to the Upper House: Althorp on 31 Oct. 1783, when his father's death made him Earl Spencer; Eliot on 13 Jan. 1784 when he was created Baron Eliot. The Session had demanded regular attendance and long hours because of the fierce struggle for power going on between the Coalition of North and Fox on the one hand and the followers of Pitt on the other. See the letter preceding this, n. 3. All the members of The Club's delegation except

members, good men and true Lord Palmerston and Sir Willm. Hamilton.[3]

In regard to Dr. Johnson he has not been out of door for some months, I fear grows worse and worse. The Doctors however do not despair. He seldom sees any of his friends, he sleeps half the day in consequence of the quantity of Opium which he [is] continually taking. The answer today to my enquiry was that he was but poorly, his legs are much swelled which I fear is but a bad simptom. We still hope that he will weather it. The loss would be terrible. We have been acquainted for thirty years, if it was possible to supply the place of such a man I am too Old to begin new affections.

I thank you for your book,[4] we are of the same general opinion concerning subordination, but I am not politician enough to know how or to what degree they are applicable to the subject of your pamphlet.

I beg my most respectfull compliments to Sir Wm. Forbes. I thought it very unlucky that Miss Palmer was not in Town to have paid her respects to Lady Forbes. I wishd very much to have had an oportunity of seeing more than I did of that very amiable Lady. I am with the greatest respect, Yours sincerely

J. Reynolds

Eliot and Gibbon supported Fox and his Bill, and Gibbon, who had attached himself to North and since 1778 had voted regularly with Administration, might have voted for Fox's Bill too if he had been on hand. He had left the country in the previous autumn. Fox and his adherents were now engaged in a parliamentary struggle to drive Pitt from office without a dissolution of Parliament. They failed.

[3] Proposed by Reynolds on 9 Dec. 1783, the two men were elected on 10 Feb. 1784. Palmerston had been proposed and blackballed in the previous July (*The Club*; *Life* iv. 232). Henry Temple, 2nd V. Palmerston in the peerage of Ireland (1739–1802), was a Member of the House of Commons of Great Britain continuously from 1762 to 1802. A steady supporter of Lord North, he was appointed to a seat at the Board of Trade, and was made a Lord of the Admiralty and of the Treasury, but obtained greater distinction from his social gifts than as a politician. The great nineteenth-century statesman Palmerston was his son and successor. Sir William Hamilton (1730–1803), grandson of the 3rd D. of Hamilton, envoy extraordinary and plenipotentiary since 1764 at the Court of Naples, collector of antiquities and writer on volcanoes, returned to England in 1784 after an absence of twelve years. His wife had died in 1782. It was in 1784 that he met the beautiful young woman known as Emma Hart, whom he took as his mistress in 1786 and later married—the famous Lady Hamilton. Boswell had met Hamilton and his first wife at Naples in 1765 (Notes 3, 5 Mar.).

[4] *A Letter to the People of Scotland.* 1783.

To Thomas Barnard,
Monday 8 March 1784

MS. Yale (L 38). A draft and copy, the first three sides of which (draft) are written by JB, the fourth (copy), by John Lawrie.

HEADING: To the Bishop of Kilaloe.

Edinburgh, 8 March 1784

MY DEAR LORD: I regret much that there has been no correspondence between us, since I had the honour of a highly valued serious conversation with your Lordship at your lodgings in London last May.[1] Beleive me the good impressions of that conversation are not effaced from my mind,[2] but remain with consolatory effect.

The distractions in the Nation have far exceeded what either your Lordship or I could then have apprehended; and at this moment it seems very doubtful what may be the result. For my own part I have been uniformly steady to my Monarchical principles, and I beg Your Lordships acceptance of a Pamphlet which I have published on the subject,[3] and which I am truly happy to find has had considerable influence. Mr. Pitt has been pleased to write to me upon it in very handsome terms.[4] Dr. Johnson has sent me solid praise.[5] Let *Mitred Kilaloe* give his nod of approbation.[5a]

I rejoice that the Irish appear to be so loyal. But is it not painful My Lord to think that our freind Burke should be so warped in with a desperate faction. I wish he may have philosophy enough or liberality enough to forgive me for my honest opposition to his Party of which I had at first favourable hopes. But the cloven foot appeared in Fox's India Bill.

I intend to be in London about the end of this month, chiefly to attend upon Dr. Johnson with respectful affection. He has been

---

[1] This meeting is not reported in JB's existing journal for May 1783, but that journal shows many gaps.

[2] "and I trust never shall fade" deleted.

[3] *A Letter to the People of Scotland*, 1783.

[4] Paraphrase and direct quotation of Pitt's letter deleted. It ran, "I am extremely obliged to you for the Sentiments you do me the Honor to express, and have observed with great Pleasure the zealous and able Support given to the Cause of the Public in the Work you were so good to transmit to me."

[5] MS. orig. "Nay Dr. Johnson writes— 'Your Paper contains very considerable knowledge of history and of the constitution very properly produced and applied.'" See From SJ, 27 Feb. 1784 (*Life* iv. 261–62).

[5a] Pope, *Epistle to Dr. Arbuthnot* l. 140, adapted.

very ill for some time with dropsical and asthmatick complaints which at his age are very alarming. I should have gone to him immediately upon the rising of the Court of Session on the 11 current. But I stay to support an Address to his Majesty from our County at a Meeting to be held on the 17th.[6] Will your Lordship write to me at Auchinleck near Ayr By Portpatrick?

Why does not your Lordship publish your Account of the Irish Dynasties established in Scotland? I really wish you would do it without delay.[7] This is an age in which the study of Antiquaties is much cultivated, and I have no doubt your Lordships curious labours would receive the applause which they deserve, if I have any title to judge. Might I presume to suggest an advice. I would have you to publish your former Essay[7a] which is out of print, and this in one Volume with your Lordships name.

The explanation which your Lordship gave me in the course of our last conversation, of the holy sacrament of the Lords Supper settled my mind upon a question of solemn difficulty. If your Lordship would be so very kind as to let me have it in writing I should reckon it an infinite obligation; for, the note which I made of it from memory is very imperfect. I earnestly beg of you as a Bishop of Souls to grant my request.

I last year informed your Lordship from Dr. Johnson in answer to your question concerning the meaning of "Lukes iron Crown" that Luke was an Hungarian Rebell. But I can now inform your Lordship better, from the *Respublica Hungariæ*[8] in which we are told of a sedition in that Country in 1514 when *Georgius Zeck* was made King by the rebells and when seized was horribly punished and a red hot iron Crown put on his head. He had a brother called *Luke,* and Goldsmith whose knowledge was wonderfully superficial and inaccurate has put him into his poem instead of George. The passage should be "Zeck's iron Crown" etc.[9] I ever am with

[6] JB attended the meeting and was the author of the loyal address to the King which was adopted after debate. "I was quite happy upon my success," he wrote, "but by no means insolent" (Journ. 17 Mar.). He sent extended accounts to the newspapers: see *The Edinburgh Evening Courant,* 20 Mar. 1784; *The Edinburgh Advertiser,* 19–23 Mar. 1784; *The London Chronicle,* 23–25 Mar. 1784. Yale has a MS. copy of the account in *The*

Edinburgh Advertiser made by Robert Boswell's clerk, Robert Rankin (M 11).
[7] The rest of the letter is in Lawrie's hand.
[7a] See *ante* p. 130 and n. 7.
[8] *Respublica et Status Regni Hungariae. Ex Officina Elzeviriana* (1st ed., 1626). See *Life* ii. 7 n. 2; iii. 52 n. 3.
[9] This explanation of Goldsmith's allusion, which JB later included in *Life* ii. 6–7, itself needs some correction. A

most sincere respect, My Dear Lord, Your Lordships faithful and affectionate humble servant

To Thomas Percy, Monday 8 March 1784

MS. Yale (L 1064). A copy in Lawrie's hand which differs substantively in only four words from the text printed from the original in *Lit. Illust.* vii. 302–03. The manuscript of the original has not been traced.

HEADING (in JB's hand): To The Bishop of Dromore.

Edinburgh, 8 March 1784

MY DEAR LORD: The heavy loss which your Lordship suffered by the death of your Son,[1] soon after my being entertained by your Lordship with very kind hospitality at Carlisle made it so difficult for me to write to you, that I hope you will be good enough to forgive my long delay of expressing my sincere thanks, and I beg your Lordship may at the same time be assured that none of your friends sympathised more with you in your distress. The consolations with which your Lordships mind is stored, have I trust had their benignant effect, so that we may again hope for the benefit of your literary labours.

The state of the Nation has for some time been such, that in my opinion every good subject is called upon to defend the constitution by supporting the Crown. I enclose a pamphlet[2] which I

---

large number of peasants, who had been assembled for a crusade against the Turks, rebelled because of the wretched condition of their country. Their leader was György Dózsa (or Dósa), a Szekler squire and soldier of fortune appointed to direct the holy war against the Muslims. The name Zeck, used as his surname by contemporaries, is apparently a modification of the term Szekler denoting his ethnic origin. The Szeklers are Hungarians who inhabit the upper valleys of the rivers Mures and Olt in Eastern Transylvania. The hot iron crown, reported in several contemporary accounts of György Dózsa's execution, is accepted as historical by modern scholarship. Dózsa's brother, called Luke (Lukács) in the sources used by Goldsmith and Boswell, was really named Gregory (Gergely) (Sándor Márki, *Dósa György és forradalma*, i.e. "György Dósa and his Revolution", 1883, 1886, pp. 2–4, 183–189; see also Sándor Márki, *Dósa György*, 1913). For Goldsmith's source, see *Collected Works of Oliver Goldsmith*, ed. Arthur Friedman, 1966, iv. 269 n. 2.

---

[1] Henry (b. 1763), who died on 2 Apr. 1783 at Marseilles.

[2] *A Letter to the People of Scotland*, 1783.

have published on the subject and which I am truely happy to find has had considerable influence. I rejoice that the Irish appear to be so loyal.[3] If your Lordship thinks that my pamphlet will promote the laudible spirit, and any of the Dublin Publishers chuse to run the risk of reprinting it, I shall be glad to hear of its success.[4]

Be so obliging my Dear Lord, as to let me hear from you, and tell me particularly how your Lady and daughters like the new situation in which you are placed.[5] If you write soon please direct for[6] me at Auchinleck near Ayr By Portpatrick. I intend to be in London about the end of this month,[7] chiefly to attend upon Dr. Johnson with respectfull affection. He has for sometime been very ill with dropsical and asthmatick[7a] complaints which at his age are very alarming. I wish to publish as a regale to him a neat little volume, "The Praises of Dr. Samuel Johnson by Cotemporary writers."[8] It will be about the Size of Selden's *Table Talk* of which your Lordship made me a present, with an inscription on the blank leaf in front, which does me honour.[9] It is placed in the Library at Auchinleck. Will your Lordship take the trouble to send me a note of the writers you recollect have praised our much

---

[3] Between 1778 and 1782, England had modified, to Ireland's advantage, the Commercial Code between the two countries; had relieved Irish dissenters from the sacramental test; had created an Irish volunteer militia; had limited the Mutiny Act; and had eliminated the power of the Privy Council to nullify acts of the Irish Parliament. These reforms, in many cases, gave to the Irish privileges not yet possessed by the English. Because of these concessions, Irish feelings towards England were temporarily less resentful and antagonistic.

[4] The pamphlet was never published in Ireland.

[5] See *ante* From Percy, 3 Mar. 1783, n. 2. Percy wrote to Edmond Malone from Dromore on 5 Aug. (*Percy-Malone Corresp.* p. 2).

[6] *Lit. Illust.* "please to direct to." The second "to" may be right, but the first is almost certainly wrong. Both Malone and Wilkes complained later than this of JB's "please" without "to" as "not English" (From Malone, 5 Nov. 1785; From Wilkes, 1 Oct. 1785).

[7] JB left Edinburgh for London on 22 Mar., but he did not arrive there until 5 May (Journ., *Life* iv. 271). See *post* To Barnard, 14 May 1784.

[7a] *Lit. Illust.* "asthmatical", almost certainly an editorial refinement by J. B. Nichols or his printer. See the preceding letter, where the same sentence is used.

[8] On 8 Jan. 1784 JB had sent Charles Dilly a letter proposing that he or John Nichols go halves on this book. Dilly's letter declining was received 28 Jan. (Reg. Let.). The project was abandoned.

[9] John Selden (1584–1654), *Table Talk: being the Discourses of John Selden, Esq. or his Sense of various Matters of Weight and high Consequence; relating especially to Religion and State*, 3rd ed., 1716. This volume was sold at Hodgson's on 14 Jan. 1932 (Lot 373), where it was described as containing the inscription, "To James Boswell, esq., who is a most happy preserver of the apothegms of his friends . . . presented by his faithful servant Th. Percy."

respected Friend. My address when in London is at General Paoli's, Portman Square.

An edition of my Pamphlet has been published in London, and the first line of the Advertisement was "Reprinted[10] for the PEOPLE of ENGLAND."

This should be adopted in Dublin *mutato nomine.* I ever am, My Dear Lord, Your Lordships faithful humble Servant

From Thomas Barnard, Wednesday 17 March 1784

MS. Yale (C 82).

ADDRESS: James Boswell Esqr., Auchinleck near Ayr, North Britain, by Portpatrick and Donaghadee.

POSTMARK: MR 17.

Dublin, March 17th. 1784

MY DEAR SIR: I cannot suffer a Single post to Depart from Ireland without acknowledging the receipt of your Letter and Pamphlet, with hearty thanks for your Flattering remembrance of an old Freind who Sincerely Loves and Esteems both your Person and Principles. I have not had time to peruse your Letter to your Countrymen, but if it Corresponds with your Quotation prefixed,[1]

---

[10] Reading as in *Lit. Illust.* Lawrie has "Republished", which is almost certainly wrong. I have been unable to find any advertisements, but actually the imprint (which JB probably meant in any case) reads, "Edinburgh, Printed: London Re-printed, for Charles Dilly, in the Poultry. 1784." A unique copy of what appears to be a third edition was found among the Malahide Papers. Entitled *A Letter to the People on the Present State of the Nation* ("London printed, 1784"), it is a cut-down version of the second edition with certain major changes: all specific references to Scotland are omitted; it is addressed generally to the "people"; and JB's expressions of Tory sentiment are softened. (See Frank Brady, *Boswell's Political Career*, 1965, p. 104 n. 2.)

[1] Calm is my soul, nor apt to rise in arms,
Except when fast approaching danger warms:
But when contending Chiefs blockade the Throne,
Contracting regal power to stretch their own;
When I behold a factious band agree
To call it freedom when themselves are free;
The wealth of climes where savage nations roam,
Pillag'd from slaves, to purchase slaves at home;
Fear, pity, justice, indignation start,
Tear off reserve, and bare my swelling heart;

it exactly chimes in unison with my own Sentiments on the present State of Publick affairs. This morning your packet Reachd my hands while I was dressing to attend the House of Lords at a very Early hour to hear the opinions of our Twelve Judges Deliverd Seriatim, on the Subject of the great Cause of Ely and Rochfort,[2] which has already appeared before the British House of Lords in another Shape, and will finally determine the Possession of 16000 pr. annum. The Question is whether the Caption of a warrant of attorney by a Vouchee in a Common Recovery taken out of Court, be Conclusive Evidence of the Sanity of the Party. The answrs. will Determine whether the Cause be sent to a Jury or not. Much Learning has already been Shewn by Three of them; but they are as Tedious as an Emperor, as Dog berry sais in *Much Ado about Nothing*.[3] Hitherto they are all in the Negative to the Question. I only mention this to you as a bit of Law Intelligence in your own Way.

We are all extremely Loyal in this Country, but a little Riotous in favour of a Parliamentary reform. Flood introduced the Motion a few days ago,[4] and it is to be debated on the Second Reading tomorrow; but I believe it will have the Same fate, as it has met with in England, *Pro hac Vice*.[4a] This day being St. Patricks, the Duke of Rutland[5] reviewed the Volunteers of Dublin in the Phoenix Park, and returned them thanks. Then a Dinner for the Knights of St. Patrick in their Collars; and to night a grand Ball

Till half a patriot, half a coward grown,
I fly from petty tyrants to the Throne.

(Goldsmith, *The Traveller*, ll. 379–84, 387–92)

[2] *Post* From Barnard, 14 Apr. and c. 17 July 1785.

[3] " . . . but truly, for mine own part, if I were as tedious as a *king*, I could find in my heart to bestow it all of your worship" (III. v. 22–25).

[4] Henry Flood (1732–91), Irish statesman and orator identified with all great measures of Irish reform, had presented a similar bill from the Volunteer Convention on 29 Nov. 1783 which had been refused. On 18 Mar. 1784, he brought in a bill "to amend the defects of Representation of the People in Parliament" (*London Chronicle*, 25–27 Mar. 1784, lv. 302). The bill was received by the House,

since this time it did not come "commissioned from a body of armed men" (*ibid*. p. 297), but it was defeated. The Volunteers, who were under the command of the Earl of Charlemont, had been organized in 1778 when there was fear of a French invasion. The organization soon became a political force and was vociferous in its demands for reform. Charlemont was not involved in its more radical activities.

[4a] This time around.

[5] Charles Manners (1754–87), fourth Duke of Rutland, who had been sworn in as Lord Lieutenant of Ireland on 24 Feb. and invested as Grand Master of the Knights of St. Patrick on the same day. He was noted primarily for his conviviality and magnificent entertainments (Sir Nicholas H. Nicolas, *History of the Orders of Knighthood*, 1842, iv. 28).

in Fancy Dresses. His administration is Popular, and will be well Supported.

I cannot consent to your Proposal of republishing my Essay in answer to Macpherson, or the other Tract, that I read to you, with my Name annexed, as they are not Subjects which belong to my character and present Station, and may perhaps Draw on answers to which I must Reply. Non Eadem est Aetas, non Mens.[6] But as to your Request of my Explanation of the Sacrament being sent you in writing, I will most readily Comply with it as soon as I have Leisure; and send it to you while you are in London.

I am Sincerly Sorry for the discouraging account you send me of Dr. Johnsons Health. I beg when you see that Excellent Man, you would assure him of my Constant, and Cordial Respect and Esteem. I have not half answerd the Contents of your Letter but you are to look on this only as a Conveyance of my thanks which I wishd to Send to you in time to reach your hands before you left Scotland. Believe me to be, my Dear Sir, Your Faithfull and affectionate humble Servant

THOS. KILLALOE

To Thomas Barnard, Friday 14 May 1784

MS. Yale (L 39). A draft.

London, 14 May 1784

MY DEAR LORD: Your Lordship's truly kind letter of the 17th of March was not received by me till the 8th of May.[1] I had set out for London just before it reached Ayrshire. It was sent after me under cover to my freind Dempster.[2] I stopped at York to be present at the loyal *Comitia* which delighted my Monarchical Soul. The dissolution of Parliament made me return to Scotland for the Election,[3] and as the time of my stay was uncertain,

---

[6] Horace, *Epistles* I. i. 4: "My years, my mind, are not the same" (H. R. Fairclough's translation in Loeb ed.).

[1] Replacing "day before yesterday".
[2] See *ante* To Fox, 19 Apr. 1782, n. 1.
[3] See *ante* To Percy, 8 Mar. 1784, n. 7. JB learned at Newcastle that dissolution

of Parliament was imminent, and paused at York, 24–26 Mar., attending on the 25th a meeting of freeholders of the County assembled to address the King. "Got good place. Was full of english feelings" (Journ.). When news of dissolution arrived, he returned (27 Mar.) to Scotland to present himself as a candi-

Dempster kept my letters till I should come up. He very pleasantly said "Some of them must be of so old a date that I should not be able to read the handwriting." Your Lordship's Epistle does not require Antiquity to give it additional value.

The great cause of Ely and Rochfort appears from your Lordship's short state of it to be very interesting not only from its immense value, but from the question in law and expediency which it involves. I regret I cannot hear the Opinions of your Judges upon it. Whatever is printed concerning it would be a very acceptable present to me. I really love disquisitions of that nature. My practice at the bar in Scotland has habituated my mind to them. I cannot but still be disatisfied that my talents are exerted in a narrow sphere; and I think I am now almost resolved to remove to London, for my Town Residence where I may possibly feed my Ambition, and am sure of gratifying my taste. The Sage Johnson discourages me by two objections. One that I cannot afford the expence of keeping a family here. The other that I shall be estranged from my ancient territory of Auchinleck.[4] To the first I answer, that a Man may live here upon any scale he chuses; and neither I nor my Wife are eager for "vain shew,"[4a] though I acknowledge it would please me, had I a superfluity of wealth. To the second I answer that London is now the Capital of the whole Island of Britain; that the difference of going and coming between London and Auchinleck and between Edinburgh and Auchinleck is just six days in a year, and that I shall be of more consequence at home, and be of more service to my freinds and Neighbours by establishing myself on a good footing here. I have reasonable hopes to distinguish myself in Westminster Hall; and I have not a faint prospect of getting into Parliament.[5] Let me sum up all with the striking thought that I have but one life in this World, and that after years of suspense, I feel that I cannot be

date for Ayrshire if Colonel Hugh Montgomerie should not stand. Montgomerie did stand, and JB went west to give him his support, remaining there till Montgomerie was elected. On 27 Apr. he set out again for London by way of Carlisle and Lichfield (Journ.; Reg. Let.; To James Bruce, 27 Apr. 1784; travel notes in Yale MS. C 2100).

[4] See *Life* iii. 176–79, and iv. 351, 508, for SJ's opinions on JB's projected move.

[4a] Psalms 39. 6.

[5] He means, "My prospect of getting into Parliament is not a faint one." He had received a personal letter of thanks from the Prime Minister, and he believed (mistakenly) that Henry Dundas had promised his interest at a later date under certain contingencies. See Journ. 19 Apr. 1788; To Henry Dundas, 16 and n.d. Nov. 1790; and generally, Frank Brady, *Boswell's Political Career*, 1965.

content until I have tried my fortune upon this great scene of Action. My old freind Sir John Pringle said to me "I know not if you will be at rest there. But you never will be at rest till you are in London." *Nous verrons.* Your Lordship will pardon this long display of my present sentiments concerning myself. I trust You are one of my very best Freinds.

Your Lordship has satisfied me that you have good reasons for not complying with my suggestion to publish your two Archeological performances with your name. But may not that on the irish Dynasties be communicated to the curious world, as the other was? I shall receive your Lordship's explanation of the Holy Sacrament with grateful reverence. Packets addressed to George Dempster Esq. M.P. London come to me in the best manner.

I have the pleasure to inform your Lordship that Dr. Johnson has had a wonderful recovery; and is now really better than we saw him last year. He is clearer a good deal. But he says he feels like a Man who is tired. I wish to get him into the Country; and I beleive I shall about the end of this month accompany him to Lichfield his *Natale Solum*[6] stay with him there some time and then return to London to keep Trinity term in the Inner Temple.[7] I can be called to the english bar about a year hence.

I rejoice that the Duke of Rutland's Administration is popular. But what is this alarming Bill about the liberty of the Press?[8]

Things are excellently well at present on this side of the water,

[6] Nescioqua natale solum dulcedine
cunctos
Ducit et inmemores non sinit esse sui
(Ovid, *Epistulae ex Ponto* I. iii. 35–36). "By what sweet charm I know not the native land draws all men nor allows them to forget her" (A. L. Wheeler's translation in Loeb ed.).

[7] JB wrote to Anna Seward, on 11 June 1784, from Oxford, where he was staying with SJ, "I return to London next week to keep Trinity term in the Inner Temple, having at last resolved to transplant myself from the scottish to the english bar." He left London at the end of June, intending to return for the Michaelmas Term in Nov. (To John Lee, 24 June 1784), but, because his wife and a number of friends and relations opposed his move to the English bar,

remained in Scotland through the winter. See *post* From Forbes to Langton, 21 Jan. 1785, n. 9. He was not admitted to the bar until Feb. 1786.

[8] In this year, the Irish Parliament had failed to impose duties to protect Irish manufactures. As a result, there were numerous disturbances in Dublin, and a seditious press soon appeared. *The Volunteer's Journal* scarcely disguised its advocacy of assassination. The bill, which had been introduced on 8 Apr. (*London Chronicle*, 13–15 Apr. 1784, lv. 364), required that the name of the real printer and proprietor of every newspaper be entered upon oath at the stamp-office and that the printer enter into a cognizance of £500 to answer all civil suits that might be instituted against him for publication.

according to your Lordship's principles and mine. But I am a little affraid of the extensive strength and wealth of the Opposition. Could but the noble spirit of Yorkshire be diffused and preserved we should have a Government quite to my warmest wish.

I am as usual under the roof of my illustrious Freind Paoli who remembers the Bishop of Kilaloe with much regard. I have the honour to be, My Dear Lord, Your much obliged and faithful humble servant

From Thomas Barnard, c. Saturday 15 May 1784

MS. Yale C 82.1 (wrapper only); Fettercairn Papers, National Library of Scotland, a copy in Sir William Forbes's hand (text). Original MS. of text not reported.

ADDRESS: James Boswell Esqr., General Paoli's, South Audley Street, London. [*Redirected in an unidentified hand*:] Upper Seymore Street No. 1.

POSTMARKS: WILLIAMS, [two others undeciphered].[1]

ENDORSEMENT (on text): Copy of a Letter from the Bishop of Killaloe to Mr. Boswell on the Eucharist of which his Lordship was pleased to allow me to take a Copy for my own use, under the same injunctions with which it was originally written to Mr. Boswell. Copied 1st March 1792.

DEAR SIR: You have so often solicited me to give you my opinion concerning the nature and design of the Holy Sacrament of the Lord's Supper; and your last letter was accompanied with so solemn a requisition (I might almost say adjuration) of immediate Compliance, that I will no longer hesitate, or delay communicating

[1] Since this letter was sent under cover to George Dempster (*ante* To Barnard, 14 May 1784), the postmarks must all have been imposed in London. Someone in Dempster's employ redirected it (Paoli had moved in the previous February), and presumably dropped it in the penny post. One of the undeciphered postmarks is circular, the other (overlapping it) is triangular. See *post* From Forbes to Langton, 21 Jan. 1785, n. 1. The letter must have been written before

Barnard had received JB's of 14 May 1784, for it refers to JB's letter of 8 Mar. 1784 (which was the one containing his "solemn requisition") as his "last", but it cannot have been written much before 14 May 1784 or JB would have received it and would not have renewed his request. The last possible day of receipt would be 30 June, when JB parted with SJ (*Life* iv. 337–39; *post* To Barnard, 8 July 1784).

to you my real thoughts on this arduous and very delicate Subject. Conscious however, that *Incedo per Ignes Suppositos cineri doloso*,[2] and that I put my reputation as a Divine to the hazard; yet with the light of God's word in one hand, and the Articles and Catechisms of the Church of Ireland on the other, I trust I shall be able not only to stear the Course of my enquiry clear of Heterodoxy or Superstition, but also to give some Satisfaction to my friend, which he will not find in any of the Controversial Writers on either Side of the Question.

The Christian Sacraments are to be considered in a two-fold light. First,—as certain fœderal Rites,[3] appointed by God, as signs and pledges on his part; by virtue of which (if duly performed on our part) we lay claim to certain benefits, promised and engaged to us in the Covenant of Redemption. Secondly,— As Means of Grace, Viz. the *ordinary* Methods and Channels, (tho' perhaps not the only ones) by which God has promised to convey it to us by Conferring an efficacy and virtue on such visible Signs and Ceremonies as he has instituted for that purpose, wholly foreign to their own nature, and entirely dependent on his original will and pleasure.

A Sacrament is defined in our Church Catechism, *"An Outward* and visible Sign of an *inward* and Spiritual Grace given unto us, as a *means* whereby we receive the same, and a *Pledge* to assure us thereof."* In every Sacrament therefore there are two parts: Viz. *The outward visible Sign*, or ceremonial part; and the inward part, or *thing signified thereby*. But in the Sacrament of the Lord's Supper, even the Outward, visible Sign has a double Signification; one, in the *Exhibition*; the other, in the *Reception* of the Elements: Viz. The Body of Christ broken, and the effusion of his Blood as an atonement for Sin, *exhibited* in the presence of God, under the figure of Bread broken, and wine poured out.—And also, the Strengthening and refreshing of our Souls by the Subsequent *Reception* of that Precious Body and blood; under the type of Bread and Wine, which are the principal Support and refreshment of the animal life and strength of Man.—By the first act of this holy Ceremony, we expect pardon of our Sins, thro' the real atonement thus typified. By the Second, We believe, that We

---

[2] Horace, *Odes* II. i. 7–8: "I tread over fires hidden under a treacherous crust of ashes."

[3] "Constituting or expressing a covenant entered into by an individual with God" (OED, Federal, 1b).

actually receive that Supernatural Support of Our Souls, which Christ has promised to Such as receive his Body and Blood by Faith.

The general idea of the intention and use of this Sacrament being thus laid down; Our farther inquiry into its Nature must be guided by the Words of our Saviour, at its first Institution;— "Take, eat, This is My Body, which is given for you. This do, in remembrance of me." And again, "Drink ye all of this; for this is my Blood of the New testament etc."[4] By the words, *This is my Body*, I do not hesitate to assert My Beleif, that Our Lord meant his natural Body, then just ready to be offered for the Sins of the World. But this does by no means exclude a Spiritual Sense couch'd also under the same Words, expressive of the divine energy, which was to be the Support of those that partook of this typical Body and Blood in Faith.

The first and primary Sense of the Words, *This is my Body*, I hold to be *natural*, but *typical*. That is, Christ did not assert the Bread which he broke, to be really his *Natural* Body: but the Figure thereof.

The Second Sense, in which the Words are to be farther understood, I take to be *Spiritual*, but *Real*. Viz. that a *Supernatural* and *Real*, tho' *Spiritual* presence of Christ in the Soul of the devout Recipient, was therein promised.—And, in order to form a right and Orthodox Judgement concerning this Sacred Mystery; free from Heretical Irreverence on the one hand, and absurd Superstition on the other, it is necessary to keep this distinction of the two Senses still in our minds: the first as relative to the Outward exhibition of the Signs, according to our Saviour's institution; as an Eucharistical Commemoration of his Death: What the Roman Catholicks call the unbloody Sacrifice of the Christian Altar (tho the Protestants do not allow the expression). The Second Sense of the words refers wholly to the *Participation* of those Outward Signs:—In which the Churches of England and Ireland hold that Christ is not only *virtually*, but Truly and Really (tho' not corporally or materially) Present.

Our Lord having declared to his Disciples the nature and import of those Types; proceeds to instruct them in their Use and future Application: *This do, in remembrance of me.*—The English words do by no means come up to the full Sense of the original Τουτο

---

[4] Barnard quotes from the Book of Common Prayer.

ποιειτε εἰς την εμην αναμνησιν.[5] The Greek word αναμνσις implies that kind of Remembrance which we call a *Memorial*: a Term, which expresses with more precision the end of that Sacred Rite, to which it is here applied. For, a Memorial, (in the Scripture-Sense of the word) comprehends something more than a mere Calling to mind a past transaction; as it also imports a Sacred Appeal to God by some Outward Sign appointed by himself, to be exhibited before Him, as a pledge and assurance of some Promise, and a Condition of our laying hold on the Benefits thereof. Such Memorials are, on the Part of Man, so many instruments of Appeal to God's Covenant: Such were the Sacrifices, and many other Rites under the Mosaic Law; which are frequently styled *Memorials*, not, surely, to refresh the memories of those who perform'd them; but as Memorials before Him that instituted them, as Seals of his Promises, and Assurances that they were inviolable, to those who exhibited those testimonies of their Faith and obedience. "This" says Moses (Numb. X.)[6] "Shall be unto you as a Memorial, that Ye may be remembered before the Lord your God."

The word αναμνσις is used by the Author of the Epistle to the Hebrews (and also rendered incorrectly by the English Word Remembrance) when Speaking of the Jewish Sacrifices, as only types of the great Sacrifice to come, the Writer says, that in these "there is a *Remembrance* again made of Sins every Year".— εν αυταις αναμνσις αμαρτιων κατ᾽ ενιαυτον.[7] How far this expression is from reaching the Scope of the Apostle's argument may be left to the English Reader to determine. But if we Substitute the word *Memorial* in its place, and understand it in the Sense already explained, the force of his reasoning will be clear, and Shew that Such Sacrifices could have no efficient Virtue in themselves to take away Sin, because they were only memorials of the Great Sacrifice of Christ, the only *real* atonement; through Faith in which they were accepted as the Sacrament of the Eucharist is at this day.

For these Reasons (and some more which I have neither time nor room to enumerate) I hold that the Exhibition of these Outward Signs of Bread and Wine for a Memorial of Christ, is much more than a Common Act of Calling to mind His Death

---

[5] Luke 22. 19 and 1 Corinthians 11. 24.   [7] Hebrews 10. 3.
[6] Numbers 10. 10.

and Sufferings for us. But that it is rather to be esteemed a Valid Instrument of Claim to the Divine Remembrance; that God would be pleased to Remember his Holy Covenant, and Accept these Memorials for the Sake of Him that ordained them, as they Shew forth the Lord's Death until his Coming again.—Not that we are to infer from hence, that God stands in need of being reminded.—He can no more forget the Death of Christ, than he can change his nature, or falsify his Word.—But our Saviour has given us to understand, that our thus Shewing forth his Death in the presence of his Father, shall be a motive to him to remember it on our account: as the Sprinkling of the Blood of the Lamb on the door-posts of the Israelites in Egypt was a memorial to the destroying Angel to spare that Family where this Ordinance was duly observed; So Shall this Sacred Rite be a Pledge of God's Covenant to pardon our Sins by the Death of Christ, to enable us, thro' his assistance, to perform our Duty here, and to admit us into an inheritance with him hereafter. But if on the contrary we neglect or refuse to make this Memorial of Christs death, according to his institution, we provoke God, not only to withhold from us the spiritual advantages thereof, but to remember Our iniquities, and to Suffer us to perish in them: a just reward for our obstinacy and Presumption.

I have dwelt the longer upon this Point, as many Sincere Christians look upon this Holy Ceremony as a simple Commemoration of the Death of Christ: placing the whole Virtue of the Institution in a mere obedience to a positive Command. The followers of Calvin, Zuinglius,[8] and Hoadley,[9] esteeming this most solemn Rite of the Christian Religion as Calculated only to preserve Communion among Christians, and as a Call to renew our engagements to Repentance, Faith, and New Obedience: but neither expect nor believe that any divine Grace can be convey'd to us thereby. Whereas, if the foregoing exposition be a just one,

---

[8] Huldreich Zwingli (1484–1531), Swiss reformer, greatly responsible for the spread of the Reformation over Switzerland. He first made public his views on the Lord's Supper in 1524, maintaining that it was commemorative and symbolical.

[9] Benjamin Hoadly, D.D. (1676–1761), English divine. One of the principal controversial writers of the eighteenth century, he explained the Lord's Supper as a merely commemorative rite (*A plain Account of the Nature and End of the Sacrament of the Lord's Supper*, 1735). He was answered by (among others) Daniel Waterland (1683–1740) in *A Review of the Doctrine of the Eucharist, as laid down in Scripture and Antiquity*, 1737.

both parts of this Sacrament are equally necessary and important parts of the Christian Worship, as much as the Sacrifice of the Altar was to the Jews under the Mosaic dispensation. For by the first Act, Viz. the breaking of Bread etc. We exhibit in the divine Presence the type of that Real Sacrifice for Sin, through which we demand remission of our own from God's covenanted Mercy: And by the Second, viz. the Reception of those Consecrated Elements in faith, we expect to receive the Actual Strengthening and refreshing of our Souls by the Body and Blood of Christ.

In the *Ceremonial* part of this Holy Rite, we deny the Corporal change of the Elements, at or after the Consecration of them; for then, they would cease to be a *Memorial* of that Sacrifice which they are instituted to represent. They would rather become an actual reiteration of that atonement for Sin, which being once made can never be repeated. But in the Subsequent *Reception* of the Sacrament, the Benefits are no longer typical but Real; as we then believe that we are truly tho spiritually Partakers of the Body and Blood of Christ. By Spiritually, I do not mean Mystically or Figuratively; but only use the Word in opposition to Corporally or Materially. The Soul is Spiritually united to the Body, but not less *really* so. The Deity is Spiritually Present in all places; but that Presence is not surely figurative and ideal.

This Explanation of the real, though Spiritual Presence of Christ in the Sacrament of the Eucharist, is not only consistent with the words of our Lord, at its original institution; but also farther illustrated and confirmed by other declarations and expressions of His, on a different occasion (John VI.)[10] which cannot be understood, if this Sense of the words be not admitted.— "My Father giveth you the true bread from Heaven etc." "If any man eat of this Bread, he shall live for ever; and the Bread which I will give him is my flesh etc." (vide the whole chapter). And when the Jews, taking the words in a literal Sense, are Scandalized, saying, "How can this Man give us his flesh to eat?" Our Lord explains them, by saying, "It is the Spirit that giveth Life; the Flesh profiteth nothing. The words that I speak unto you are Spirit and life." The only Method [by which] the first expressions are intelligible, consistent with the first explanation, is to understand both the Bread of Life, and the Flesh and Blood of Christ, as expressive of that operation of the divine Essence, which is to

[10] Verses 32, 51–52, 63.

166

feed and Support Our Souls both here and hereafter. Not as if we were to eat the Natural Body of Christ Substantially present under the Accidents of Bread and Wine: but yet as if some Supernatural and essential Support was promised to us on that Occasion necessary for the Supply of our Spiritual Strength and Life.—In this Sense the Antient Fathers understood that Petition of our Lords Prayer, *Give us this day our daily Bread* (τον αρτον ημων τον επιουσιον δος ημιν σημερον[11]). Whether such an interpretation comes up to our Lord's Primary Sense of the Words, I will not presume to determine: but Sure I am that it is very Consistent with the general tenor of that perfect form of Prayer; and not unworthy of its divine Author.

This Qualified admission of the Real Presence of Christ in the Sacrament of the Altar, is not more hostile to the doctrine of the Calvinists and Sacramentarians,[12] than to that of the *Modern* Romanists and Lutherans, whether it be of a Material change of the Elements into the Body and Blood of Christ, or their Actual incorporation therewith. For the Human Body of Christ was not that Bread that came down from Heaven (which according to the aforementioned Words of Our Saviour, If a man eat of, he shall live for ever) being entirely composed of the same earthly Materials, as the other Sons of Adam. And therefore, even Supposing that We could, in the literal Sense, eat and drink His Body and Blood, they would be ineffectual to the end appointed, viz. the strengthening and refreshing of our Souls.—

It is true that the Bread and Wine are the types of his *Natural* Body and Blood, the true and proper Sacrifice for Sin: but no change of the type into the reality can from thence be inferred. For it is admitted by all, that the Paschal Lamb was a type of the Same; and yet no one ever supposed that to have been changed into the natural Body of Christ; But in the Participation of this Memorial in Faith (not in the Outward exhibition) we look for the divine Presence to accompany it; even Christ himself dwelling in our Souls, for our Spiritual Support and Sanctification. So that

---

[11] Matthew 6. 11. The words of the Vulgate corresponding to ἄρτον (panem) and ἐπιούσιον (supersubstantialem) appear above the line.

[12] "A name given by Luther to those Protestant theologians . . . who maintained that it is merely in a 'sacramental' or metaphorical sense . . . that the bread and wine of the Eucharist are called the body and blood of Christ. Hence used in the 16th c. (by opponents) as a general name for all deniers of the doctrine of the Real Presence" (OED, Sacramentarian, B1).

altho we reject the Notion of Transubstantiation, as a thing impossible, we may with confidence assert in the words of our own Church Catechism, "That the Body and Blood of Christ are verily and indeed taken and received by the Faithful in the Lord's Supper."

Such are my Opinions on this interesting, but abstruse and delicate Subject.—They are, indeed, crudely expressed, but not hastily Conceiv'd. If any thing appear to you obscure in my Arguments, or unintelligible in my distinctions, I shall be happy to be able to give you farther Satisfaction.—I do not wish that my Opinions Should be publish'd to the World: not that I am afraid to Support them; but that I detest the thought of being obliged to enter the lists of Controversy; which must probably be the Consequence of dogmatising on any very interesting or important Subject.—I therefore trust myself in Your hands, and my papers to your discretion; only requesting that if you Should Communicate them at all, it may be only to Our *Christian* freinds. If Johnson should smite me friendly and reprove me, I will take his Correction in good part. Nay I will even allow that the worthy Genl. Paoli should pity me for not being a good Catholic (though I believe I have the Church of Rome on my side for the first eleven Centuries). But do not permit them to get into the Press if you have any regard to the request of, Dear Sir, Your sincere and affectionate Servant

T. K.

On reading these papers a second time, I find them full of incorrectness, and bad language: but have not time to amend them. I beseech you Not to let them go out of your hands, in[13] their present State on any account.—

To Bennet Langton,
Monday 17 May 1784

Not reported. Sent from London 17 May. "Mr. Langton *short* account of ditto" (Reg. Let.). "Ditto" refers to the previous Register entry: "Rev. Mr. Temple. *Full* account of My *resolution* to establish myself at the english bar."

[13] MS. "on"

To Bennet Langton,
Friday 28 May 1784

Not reported. Sent from London 28 May. "Bennet Langton Esq. that I am to be with him on the 31" (Reg. Let.). A scrap of paper containing a brief itinerary for 11 May to 6 June (J 93) shows that JB was in Rochester on Monday 31 May, and in Chatham on 1 June, obviously visiting Langton before leaving with SJ for Oxford on 3 June (*Life* iv. 283).

To Thomas Percy,
Thursday 8 July 1784

MS. Yale (*L 1065. Collection of F. W. Hilles). Sent 8 July. "Bishop of Dromore—did he receive my last with a political Pamphlet. I hope Dr. Johnson will go to Italy. I have *resolved* with his approbation to try my fortune at the english bar—to which your Lordship animated me here (Carlisle)" (Reg. Let.).

ADDRESS: To The Lord Bishop of Dromore.

Notation by Percy at head: answd. July 29.

Carlisle, 8 July 1784

MY DEAR LORD: Having met with Mr. Buckby[1] a Clergyman of your Lordship's Diocese as a fellow traveller, I take the opportunity of his going to Ireland to write a few lines begging to know if your Lordship received in spring last a letter from me with a political pamphlet?

I have left Dr. Johnson wonderfully recovered, but by no means well. I hope he will go to Italy before Winter.[2] I have at length *resolved* with his approbation, to try my fortune at the english bar,[3] a scheme of which your Lordship talked [to] me in an

[1] Possibly John Buckby, who was collated as prebendary of Kilteskill, Clonfert, on 3 Apr. 1800, and as Treasurer of Kilmacduagh on 12 Apr. of that year (*Fasti Hib.* iv. 195). A Mr. Buckby is mentioned in Percy's diary for Tuesday 17 Nov. 1795.

[2] For an account of the efforts of JB and SJ's other friends, particularly Sir Joshua Reynolds, to obtain money for an Italian trip from the King through the influence of Chancellor Thurlow, see *Life* iv. 326–50; *Letters JB* ii. 323–24; *Portraits*, pp. 168–70; and *post* To Reynolds, 3 Aug. 1784.

[3] SJ's approbation was not without qualifications, for he wrote to JB on 11 July 1784, "The condition upon which

animating strain, when I was hospitably entertained by you at this place.

May I hope to hear from your Lordship *at Edinburgh?* I beg to have my best compliments presented to Mrs. Percy and the young Ladies; and I ever am, My Dear Lord, your Lordships faithful humble servant

JAMES BOSWELL

To Thomas Barnard, Thursday 8 July 1784

MS. Yale (L 40). A copy. Sent 8 July. "Bishop of Kilaloe (Copy) acknowledging receipt of his thoughts on the Lord's supper" (Reg. Let.).

HEADING: To the Bishop of Kilaloe.

Carlisle, 8 July 1784

MY DEAR LORD: Thus far in my way home, I take the opportunity of Mr. Buckby a Clergyman of the Diocese of Dromore to acknowledge with most sincere gratitude the rece[i]pt of your Lordships very kind communication of your thoughts upon the Lords supper. Be assured that I shall obey your Lordships commands not to let them go out of my pos[s]ession. General Paoli was much pleased with them. So was Dr. Johnson. Both of them expressed particular approbation of the learned and just interpretation of αναμνησις. Dr. Johnson was glad to find your Lordship so pious. I had been happy enough for a long time before to be perfectly satisfied of this; and ever since, my regard for your Lordship has been more cordial. Dr. Johnson like myself had doubted whether a man of so much vivacity and *usage du Monde* as Dr. Barnard was sufficiently serious in Religion.[1] *We* who have gay and social dispositions must have some attention to counteract such a suspicion. Dr. Johnson is still by no means well. He did not go to Lichfield. But I was a week with him at Oxford.[2] I hope he will pass next winter

you have my consent to settle in London is, that your expence never exceeds your annual income" (*Letters SJ* iii. 179).

[1] See *Life* iv. 75–76 for SJ's high standards for episcopal behaviour.

[2] JB accompanied SJ to Oxford on 3 June, but returned to London immediately. He was back in Oxford on the 9th and stayed until the 19th, when he and SJ returned to London (*Life* iv. 283–311).

in Italy. I shall write to your Lordship from Scotland concerning the aweful subject of your last letter, and I hope to receive at Auchinleck Ayrshire an Answer to mine from London. I have the honour to remain with great respect and affection, My Dear Lord, your much obliged and faithful humble servant

From Thomas Percy,
Thursday 29 July 1784

Not reported. Probably from Dromore. Referred to in notation at head of To Percy, 8 July: "answd. July 29."

To Sir Joshua Reynolds,
Tuesday 3 August 1784

MS. Yale (L 1100). A copy. Sent 3 Aug. "Sir Joshua Reynolds begging he may be earnest with the Lord Chancellor to get the Royal Bounty extended to enable Dr. Johnson to go to Italy" (Reg. Let.).

HEADING: To Sir Joshua Reynolds.

Edinburgh, 3 August 1784

My Dear Sir, You may beleive I am very anxious concerning the success of my "pious negociation"[1] in favour of Dr. Johnson; and as you kindly undertook to be my Successor in the business, after I left London, and the Lord Chancellor wrote to me that he was to confer with you, I trust you will soon be able to give me good accounts. I have had a letter from Dr. Johnson dated at Ashbourne,[2] in which he informs me that you had written to the Chancellor but had not received an Answer before the Dr. went into the country. I cannot allow myself to think it possible either

[1] JB refers to the efforts he had made to obtain from the King an addition to SJ's pension that would enable him to travel to Italy for his health. He is quoting himself here (To Lord Thurlow, 24 June 1784 and *Life* iv. 328, 348).

[2] Referring to JB's having had to leave London before matters were settled regarding the "pious negociation", SJ wrote on 26 July: "I wish your affairs could have permitted a longer and continued exertion of your zeal and kindness. They that have your kindness may want your ardour. In the mean time I am very feeble, and very dejected" (*Letters SJ* iii. 187). This letter to Reynolds was quite clearly JB's response to SJ's hint that Reynolds's ardour needed strengthening.

that Lord Thurlow would neglect so interesting an affair, after writing me the strong letter of which you have a copy;—or that a still higher Personage[3] would be wanting in liberality after the many professions which he has made to yourself. Dr. Johnson complains chiefly of the Asthma in his last letter; so that a warm climate during next winter would I suppose be of most essential service to him. He is feeble and dejected; and I am in great concern about him. Let me then intreat you my Dear Sir to persevere in exerting yourself to obtain for him that Royal Bounty of which he has been flattered with such hopes, that it would be mortifying should he be disappointed. I am truly astonished that there has been such a delay. Does it not hurt your generous mind?

Pray let me have the pleasure to hear from you soon; and I beg to have my best compliments presented with all sincerity to Miss Palmer, for whose distress I feel the more, that by a letter from my freind Temple I understand her sister cannot recover.[4] Your delightful temper makes you view human life with all its evils as much more agreable than I do—especially when in the provincial dullness of Edinburgh after the felicity of London. I am with great regard, My Dear Sir Joshua, your affectionate humble servant

From Sir Joshua Reynolds, Thursday 2 September 1784

MS. Yale (C 2355).[1]

ADDRESS: James Boswell Esq., Edinburgh.

POSTMARK: 3 SE.

London, Sep. 2d 1784

DEAR SIR: I had no news to write you relating to our friend Dr. Johnson till today when the Lord Chancellor called on me to acquaint me with the consequence of his *pious* negociation. He express'd himself much mortified that it was receivd not with the

---

[3] The King.

[4] On 8 July, Temple had written to JB that Miss Palmer's sister Elizabeth, wife of William Salkeld, "cannot possibly recover, being in the last stage of a

consumption". She died of tuberculosis a few months later.

---

[1] JB refers to this letter in *Life* iv. 348.

warmth he expected. He says he did his utmost but he fears he has not the art of begging successfully—he would take another opportunity "But you know," says he "we must not teize people. However I would by no means have this journey put off if necessary to the establishment of his health on account of the expence. It would be scandalous and shamefull that the paltry consideration of mony should stand in the way to prevent any thing from being done that may any way contribute to the health or amusement of such a man, a man who is an honour to the country." He desired me to inform him that in the meantime he should mortgage his Pension to him (the Lord Chancellor) and should draw on him to the amount of five or six hundred Pounds. The Chancellor explained the Idea of the mortgage to be only this, that he wished this business to be conducted in such a manner as that Dr. Johnson should appear to be under the least possible obligation. I would not neglect acquainting you with this negociation which can hardly be called a successfull one tho I have just wrote a long letter to Dr. Johnson, and have company with me.

Poor Ramsay[2] is dead and your humble servant succeeds him as Kings Principal Painter—if I had known what a shabby miserable place it is, I would not have asked for it; besides as things have turned out I think a certain person is not worth speaking to, nor speaking of so I shall conclude.[3] Yours sincerely,

J. REYNOLDS

From Bennet Langton, Monday 13 December 1784

Untraced. First printed in Croker's 1st ed. of the *Life*, 1831, v. 344.[1] Also in Croker's 2nd ed., 1835, x. 138–39, and in his 3rd, 1848, p. 807 n. 3; the MS. said in 1848 to be in his possession. It is not among the

[2] Allan Ramsay died at Dover on the way home from Italy, 10 Aug. 1784.

[3] Reynolds wrote to the Duke of Rutland on 24 Sept.: "The place which I have the honour of holding, of the King's principal painter, is a place of not so much profit, and of near equal dignity with His Majesty's rat catcher. The salary is £38 per annum, and for every whole length I am to be paid £50, instead of £200 which I have from

everybody else. Your Grace sees that this new honour is not likely to elate me very much. I need not make any resolution to behave with the same familiarity as I used to with my old acquaintance" (*Letters Reynolds*, p. 112).

[1] "The following letter, written with an agitated hand, from the very chamber of death, by the amiable Mr. Langton, and obviously interrupted by his feelings,

Croker papers in the William L. Clements Library, University of Michigan, Ann Arbor.

[London]

MY DEAR SIR, After many conflicting hopes and fears respecting the event of this heavy return of illness which has assailed our honoured friend, Dr. Johnson, since his arrival from Lichfield, about four days ago the appearances grew more and more awful, and this afternoon at eight o'clock, when I arrived at his house to see how he should be going on, I was acquainted at the door, that about three quarters of an hour before, he had[2] breathed his last. I am now writing in the room where his venerable remains exhibit a spectacle, the interesting solemnity of which, difficult as it would be in any sort to find terms to express, so to you, my dear sir, whose own sensations will paint it so strongly, it would be of all men the most superfluous to attempt to—.

To Sir Joshua Reynolds, Thursday 23 December 1784

MS. Fettercairn Papers, National Library of Scotland. A copy in the hand of JB's wife, with corrections by JB. Sent 23 Dec. "Sir Joshua Reynolds for particulars concerning Dr. Johnson (Copy)" (Reg. Let.).

HEADING (in JB's hand): To Sir Joshua Reynolds.

Edinr., 23d Decr. 1784

MY DEAR SIR: On friday night I receivd from Dr. Brocklesby the sad information of Dr. Johnsons death.[1] I can only say that at first it stunned me and that the effect has been ever since more dreary. I have lost a Man whom I not only revered but loved, a

will not unaptly close the story of so long a friendship. The letter is not addressed, but Mr. Langton's family believe it was intended for Mr. Boswell" (Croker's note). It is possible that the reason for Langton's not finishing the letter was his discovery of the wounds SJ had inflicted upon himself in an attempt to draw off the dropsical water. Hawkins reported that Langton apparently thought at first that SJ had committed suicide (*Life* iv.

418 n. 1). JB certainly did not receive from Langton any notification of SJ's death. Both his journal and his Register of Letters were fully posted during Dec. 1784, and both record notifications only from Dr. Brocklesby and Charles Dilly.

[2] Croker 1848 omits this word, probably in error.

[1] See *post* From Forbes to Langton, 21 Jan. 1785, n. 5.

Man whose able and conscientious Counsel was ever ready to direct me in all difficultys. This is a loss which you well know to be a severe affliction for you share it with me.

You may believe I am exceedingly desirous to know every thing that can be told concerning our departed friend, and I therefore earnestly beg you may be so kind as indulge me with a Communication of interesting particulars. It is said in the newes papers and I have no doubt is true that you are one of his executors.[2] I trust to your honour that if my letters to him exist they will be given back to me as they were written in full Confidence as to a Confessor. Probably he has Burnt them as I understand he destroyed in that Manner a little before his death a number of papers. Pray let me know what Manuscripts are saved. I shall be vexed if he has either intentionally or as the newes papers say inadvertently deprived the World of two Quarto Volumes of Memoirs of his life[3] a considerable part of which I have read. They indeed contained a Variety of things which it would have been improper to expose to the *profanum Vulgus*[3a] but his confidential friends might have made a most valuable Selection for I never saw so minute a diary as was kept of the thoughts and actions of that wonderfull Philosopher during certain periods for it was not continued long without interruptions. I owned to him my having read in those Volumes and asked him if he thought I could have resisted the temptation when I found them lying open? He said with one of his complacent Smiles, "I believe you could not." I told him that for once I was tempted to be a thief—to

[2] Reynolds was an executor, along with Sir John Hawkins and Sir William Scott.

[3] "It is with Regret we inform the Publick, from Authority unquestioned, that amongst other MSS. which Dr. Johnson destroyed, some Days before his Death, he unhappily burnt certain material Transactions of his own Life, which, it is said, he had compiled from a Hint given him by a Friend, in Imitation of the *Memoires de sa Vie*, written by the celebrated Mons. Huet, Bishop of Avranches.—Biographers are very busy in preparing Materials for the Life of Dr. Samuel Johnson. Many, we are told, are the Candidates, but the principal which are mentioned are Sir John Haw-kins, and James Boswell, Esq. his itinerant Companion through the Highlands of Scotland" (*St. James's Chronicle*, 14–16 Dec. 1784). *The London Chronicle* for 16–18 Dec. 1784 printed a wordier version of the first paragraph, which concluded, "Finding his health decline, and apprehensive of a sudden dissolution, he was determined, no ill-judging friend, or avaricious bookseller, should have a power of publishing the sweepings of his study, under the title of *his remains*, burnt a great number of unfinished Essays, and undesignedly, as well as unfortunately, burnt the papers containing his Memoirs amongst them."

[3a] "The uninitiated crowd" (Horace, *Odes* I. i. 1).

have carried them off and never seen him more and I asked how this would have affected him. He said "It would have made me mad." I almost regret I did not commit a *splendidum peccatum*[4] which all of us would now have forgiven on account of the Rich stores of Mind which it would have preserved. I have amongst my Johnsonian Collection a transcript of a few passages of his diary.[5] My large stock of Materials for writing his life I mean to arrange and publish. But I shall be in no hurry. I wish first to see many other lives of him that I may both recieve additional information and correct Mistakes and Misrepresentations. I shall be much obliged to you My Dear Sir for your assistance. I have a peculiar treasure which my assiduity has secured—A great number of his Conversations taken down exactly—scenes Which were highly delightfull at the time and will forever afford instruction and entertainment. How dismal a Blank dos his departure make! I stretch after him with enthusiastick eagerness. I cannot doubt that he is exalted to immortal felicity. I should think that the Coldness in a certain quarter of which you inform'd me would now be felt with regret.[6] What a dignified satisfaction must Lord Thurlow enjoy! Pray was the letter in the Newespapers to him from Dr. Johnson genuine? If it was how came it to be made publick.[7] I left with him a half bound Volume of printed Essays which he undertook to revise.[8] Mrs. Desmoulins[9] knew

[4] Cf. "splendide mendax" in Horace's *Odes* III. xi. 35.

[5] These volumes were indeed burned by SJ. See *Life* iv. 405–06 for JB's account of this episode, and Donald and Mary Hyde's "Dr. Johnson's Second Wife" in F. W. Hilles, ed., *New Light on Dr. Johnson*, 1959, p. 133 and the facsimile opposite. JB read the diary on 5 May 1776; his "transcript of a few passages" is now in the Hyde Collection.

[6] A discreet reference to the King. See the second sentence in Sir Joshua's letter to JB of 2 Sept.

[7] The letter, in which SJ thanked Thurlow for the offer of a loan, was genuine, but the original has not yet been traced. For texts from drafts by SJ see *Life* iv. 349–50 and *Letters SJ* iii. 220–21. The circumstances of its publication in newspapers and magazines are

recorded by JB, *Life* iv. 349 n. 2 (see also *Life* iv. 542) and in *Gent. Mag.* Dec. 1784, liv. 892 n.†. The earliest printing I have found is in *The St. James's Chronicle*, Tuesday 16–Thursday 18 Nov. 1784; the letter appears also in *The Gazetteer*, Friday 19 Nov. 1784 (with a comment casting doubt on its genuineness), and in *The General Evening Post*, Thursday 18 Nov.–Saturday 20 Nov. 1784. In its number for Saturday 20 Nov.–Tuesday 23 Nov. 1784, *The St. James's Chronicle* defended the authenticity of its text at great length.

[8] "I read some of my *Hypochondriacks* to Dr. Johnson. And he said 'Sir these are very fine things: the language is excellent the reasoning good—and there is great application of learning. I may say to you what my Wife said to me after I had published four or five of my *Ramblers*. "I thought very well of you before. But I did

of it. I beg you May take Care of it for me. I am soon to publish my Journal of a Tour to The Hebrides in Company with him. I hope you will like it. Upon this very interesting occasion I hope you will pardon my giving you so Much trouble and you may be assured I shall gratefully remember the kindness of your Communications. Let us who remain be still more attached by mutual friendship. I ever am, My Dear Sir, your obliged and faithfull Humble servant

To Bennet Langton,
Saturday 25 December 1784

Not reported. Sent from Edinburgh 25 Dec. "Bennet Langton Esq. for information concerning Dr. Johnson and introducing my brother T. D. (Copy)" (Reg. Let.). Enclosed in a letter to Thomas David Boswell sent the same day.

From Sir William Forbes to Bennet Langton,
Friday 21 January 1785

MS. Yale (C 1274).

ADDRESS: Bennet Langton Esqr., Queens Square, Westminster.

POSTMARKS: WILLIAMS; triangular postmark one side of which reads PENN[Y]; circular postmark J [i.e. one o'clock] W.[1]

Edinbr., 21st. Jan. 1785

DEAR SIR: On my return from a very long expedition thro' the northern parts of Scotland, which detained us till lately, I found

not expect any thing equal to this." I would have you publish them in a volume and put your name to them.' . . . He is to revise them, and then I shall bring them forth in two or perhaps three elegant volumes" (To Temple, 6, 8 July 1784). There are at Yale three collections of *Hypochondriack* papers put together by JB: P 63, 64, and 65. P 63, numbers 1–40, stitched in paper (not "half-bound"), is probably the set here referred to.

⁹ MS. "Desmeuline". Elizabeth Desmoulins (b. 1716), daughter of SJ's

godfather, Dr. Samuel Swynfen, and one of the inmates of SJ's house.

---

[1] Though not made with identical stamps, these are the same marks as appear on the wrapper of From Barnard, c. 15 May 1784. They were imposed by the Penny Post in London, the triangular stamp showing the day the letter was brought to a principal office and the round stamp the hour at which it was given out to a carrier (*Royal Kalendar* . . .

waiting me Your very obliging letter; which gave me the pleasure of knowing that Lady Rothes and Your young family were all well. I hope Your next letter, which in the ordinary course of business I Ought to flatter myself with receiving soon, will give me a continuance of the same good accounts. You are very Kind in enquiring about my son; he goes on very well, still at the Grammar School; which, however, by the ordinary course he quits about six months hence: he ought then, according to the general routine of education to be enter'd of the University here; but as I think it a very great misfortune for a Boy of fifteen years old only to be placed in a situation where by associating with lads much older than himself, he is led to consider himself as a man, I mean to delay his going to the University for at least another Year, and to employ him constantly at Latin and Greek with a private teacher in town of great reputation. Your son is fortunate, indeed! in having such a preceptor as yourself; and I can have no doubt of his progress under such excellent tuition.[2]

I saw Dr. Beattie frequently after his return from England,[3] and left him at Aberdeen in very good health; besides his genius for Music which you say was new to you, he possesses another talent which perhaps you are yet a stranger to; I mean that of drawing: and he is, I think, the only instance I ever knew of the union of the three Sister Arts of poetry painting and music, in practice as well as theory in the same person.[4] I condole with you

---

for the Year 1778, p. 132). A W. Williams is listed among the sorters at the General Post-Office in 1785 and a John Williams appears that same year among the inspectors of carriers, coachmen, and watermen (*ibid.* 1785, pp. 190, 191).

[2] JB reported that SJ "said Langt taught son to save money. Would send him to Parr for nothing" (Journ. 3 June 1784).

[3] Beattie left for England on 6 June 1784 and returned to Scotland in Sept. (Margaret Forbes, *Beattie and his Friends*, 1904, pp. 203–06; see *James Beattie's Day-Book, 1773–1798*, ed. R. S. Walker, 1948, pp. 136–38).

[4] "To a very correct and refined taste in judging of poetry, painting, and music, he added the rare accomplishment

of some actual practice in each. . . . He not only understood the theory of music, but he occasionally amused himself by composing basses and second parts to some of his favourite airs. He was delighted with the organ, on which he often played simple harmonies; and he performed with taste and expression on the violoncello. . . . In the other sister art of painting, he excelled in drawing grotesque figures, and caricatures of striking resemblance; although in this last talent, he very sparingly indulged himself, and at an early period of life laid it entirely aside. . . . Dr. Beattie is the sole instance, of my own acquaintance at least, of a person who possessed the happy talent of being able to practise, with some success, in all three" (*Life of Beattie* iii. 184–85).

very much on the loss of your valuable friend Dr. Johnson, for whose talents and virtues I had a very high respect. Mr. Boswell has favor'd me with the perusal of two letters from Dr. Brocklesby giving a very minute account of his last few days:[5] those Latin pieces which he has left with you,[6] I make no doubt will be a valuable present to the learned World: but it is to be lamented that he should, as Dr. Brocklesby says, have destroy'd many excellent writings, particularly the curious manuscript account of his life:[7] yet I perceive that Sir John Hawkins in his advertisement says he is possessed of a M.S. of the life of Dr. Johnson written by himself.[8] I shall have a curiosity to know, if this be the same with that of which the Dr. destroyed a Copy, or what it is. Our friend, Boswell proposes to write the Dr's. life, for which he is possessed of a variety of curious and important Materials: and he is speedily to publish his own account of their tour to the Hebrides, upon a plan totally different from that printed by Dr. Johnson, as it relates less to descriptions of the Country than to accounts of conversations in which the Dr. bore always a considerable share. Mr. Boswell favored me with a perusal of the Manuscript on their return from that expedition; and it afforded me a very high degree of entertainment.

[5] Richard Brocklesby (1722–97) attended SJ on his deathbed (*Life* iv. 399). On 17 Dec. 1784, JB reported that Brocklesby had "favoured me with a very full letter dated on Monday the 13 the night of his death. ... I had company engaged to sup with us ... and said nothing of the dismal news, but to worthy Sir William Forbes, just as he was going away" (Journ. 17 Dec.). In Reg. Let. under 13 Jan. 1785, JB lists another letter from Brocklesby, c. 27 Dec. 1784: "Omitted Dr. Brocklesby with more particulars of Dr. Johnson's illness and death."

[6] "During his [SJ's] sleepless nights he amused himself by translating into Latin verse, from the Greek, many of the epigrams in the *Anthologia*. These translations, with some other poems by him in Latin, he gave to his friend Mr. Langton, who, having added a few notes, sold them to the booksellers for a small sum, to be given to some of Johnson's relations, which was accordingly done; and they are printed in the collection of his works" (*Life* iv. 384).

[7] See *Life* i. 25, 35 n. 1; iv. 405 and n. 1; *ante* To Reynolds, 23 Dec. 1784.

[8] *The London Chronicle*, 4–6 Jan. 1785 (lvii. 20), contained an advertisement which included the following: "*In the Press, and with all possible Expedition will be published*, In large Octavo, elegantly printed on a fine Paper, A COMPLETE EDITION of THE WORKS of SAMUEL JOHNSON, LL.D. With Notes and Illustrations, and a Life of the Author, collected from a Diary kept by himself, and other documents. By Sir JOHN HAWKINS, one of his Executors." The advertisement went on to mention that a number of unpublished pieces by SJ would be included and to request "additional communications" for the work. For what Hawkins had of SJ's diary see *Works of SJ*, Yale Ed. i. xv–xvi, xxi.

Lady F. joins me in offering respectful Compliments to Lady Rothes: We trouble you likewise to remember us both most kindly to Sir Joshua Reynolds. Mr. and Mrs. Boswell are both in very good health; She, however, always in hazard of attacks of her former complaint. I sincerely rejoice that he has been prevailed on to lay aside thoughts of establishing himself in London,[9] because I was clear from the beginning, it must have been productive to him of ruin ⟨in⟩ the extreme.

I shall be happy to have the pleasure of hearing from you soon, and I beg you will believe me to be most truly, Dear Sir, Your most obedient and faithful humble Servant

WILLIAM FORBES

From Thomas Barnard, Thursday 10 February 1785

MS. Yale (C 83). Received Mar. "Omitted Lord Bishop of Kilaloe of his eldest son's death—of Dr. Johnson etc. etc. An excellent letter" (Reg. Let.).

ADDRESS: James Boswell Esqr., Honble. General Paoli's, South Audley Street, London.

POSTMARKS: IRELAND, 18 FE, FE 1⟨?1⟩.

[9] During his late London jaunt, JB had come to a decision to be called to the English bar and to remove his family to London. The decision had figured prominently in his correspondence (From Temple, 27 May, 3 June 1784; From Mrs. Boswell, 8 June 1784; To Robert Boswell, 10 June 1784; From SJ, 11 June 1784, *Life* iv. 351; From Sir A. Dick, 17 June 1784; To Lawrie, 19 June 1784; To Pembroke, 24 June 1784; From Mrs. Boswell, 3 July 1784), reaching its most elated expression in an enormous letter to Temple written from Doncaster and Carlisle, 6, 8 July 1784: "Let us see if my *resolution* (which after years of wavering came at once upon me with wonderful power,) will make me an eminent Barrister. I am *sure* from what I have allready done upon many publick occasions, that in all Jury trials where popular declamation is of consequence I shall be distinguished. ... May I not indulge the ambitious hope of being a *Baron* indeed—of being created by my Sovereign *Baron Boswell of Auchinleck in the County of Ayr.*" As soon as he reached Edinburgh, general discouragement (To Paoli, 17 July 1784; From Mrs. Stuart to Mrs. Boswell, 19 July 1784) and his own reason convinced him of the imprudence of the scheme. The collapse, like the towering ascent, is best expressed in a letter to Temple: "All is sadly changed. ... I have been harrassed by the arguments of Relations and Freinds. ... I have lost all heart for it. My happiness when last in London seems a delirium. ... I am *satisfied* that my airy scheme will not do" (20 July 1784; see also From Paoli, 27 July 1784; From Temple, 2 Aug. 1784). He may well have announced the scheme to Forbes during his period of elation.

Henrietta Street, Dublin, Feby. 10th. 1785

MY DEAR SIR: It is Pity that, where Mutual Regard and esteem continue unabated the Intercourse of Absent Freinds by Letter should Totally Subside. But without any Such Intention on either Side whether from Real Obstructions that prevent Immediate answers, or the Spirit of Procrastination; (too Common at a Certain Time of Life) Nothing more frequently happens. And, tho' perhaps both Parties Regret it, Neither has the Courage to recommence a long Intermitted Correspondence. Such however, I am Resolved shall not be the Case between you and me.

The Affectionate Letter I receivd from you last Summer was speedily follow'd by the heaviest of all Domestick Misfortunes that could have befall'n me; which totally prevented my attention to every other Call. It was the Death of my Eldest Son,[1] and Bosom Freind; by a contagious Disorder at the Assizes of Cork in the Excercise of his Profession; which he was just beginning to reap the advantages of both in Purse and Character. The Hand which Inflicted the Stroke, has however, effectually Supported me under the Pressure of it: and I am as much myself again, as a Man who, after having lost a Limb, Remains yet in good Health and Vigor of Body, and perhaps retains his Usual Cheerfulness, tho' every moment reminds him of his Loss.

You also, my good Freind, have a Severe Loss to Lament, on which I most Sincerely Condole with you. I am Vex'd and ashamed to read the Paltry accounts of the Life and Conversation of that excellent Man with which the Papers have been Stuffed since his Decease. It is Reserved for you to Vindicate his Fame: You have Collected Materials to do it; You have formerly Declar'd it to be your Intention: The Publick, Expects it from you: and I (as one of them) call upon you to perform your Promise, and give to the World the Memorables of the Modern Socrates for his Honour as well as your own. Give my Sincere and Cordial Respects to the good general Paoli, and entreat him to Join with me in this Request.

Not Knowing whether North or South Britain has the Honour

---

[1] Thomas Barnard, who matriculated at University College, Oxford, on 7 Dec. 1771, aged 17. He was admitted to Lincoln's Inn on 2 Feb. 1775 and called to the Irish bar in Trinity Term 1781 (letter from Thomas U. Sadleir, formerly Deputy Ulster King at Arms, 24 Feb. 1954).

of Possessing you at Present,[2] I venture to direct this to S. Audley Street, as being your Most Probable Residence at this Season.

We are at this moment engaged in the most arduous and critical Business that ever Employd the Deliberations of a Kingdom. Viz. the Final adjustment of our Commercial Intercourse with Great Britain, which was submitted to both houses this Week by Mr. Orde, in the Form of nine Resolutions, on the Promise of Similar ones being adopted in England.[3] Except the 9th which engages on our Part to appropriate a Considerable portion of the Irish Hereditary Revenue, towards the Support of the Naval Force of the Empire, but Subject however to the Direction of the Irish Parliament. Tomorrow they are to be debated. Congress is adjournd without being able to agree on any Specifick Mode of Reform to offer to Parliament.[4] But Parliament seem well agreed to accept nothing that Comes from so exceptionable an assembly. I think this Matter of Reform is the only Political Subject in which you and I differ. I am Inclined to think that whether it be a good or a Bad Measure it is not likely to Succeed in either Country upon the present attempt. However this Matter may be disposed of, I have the Satisfaction to find that the Freinds of Peace and the Protestant Religion are by much the Strongest and most Respectable Party in this Kingdom, and

---

[2] JB was in Edinburgh from 13 Jan. to the middle of Mar. (Journ.); he then left for Auchinleck (*ibid.* 16 Mar.).

[3] Anxious to initiate a commercial union with Ireland, Pitt set up a plan which was submitted to the Irish Parliament on 7 Feb. 1785 by Thomas Orde (1746–1807), chief secretary to the Duke of Rutland. The bill provided for free trade between England and Ireland, equal duties, and preference over foreign importations. It was submitted in the form of ten resolutions, to which Parliament added an eleventh pertaining to Irish contributions to the English Navy. Although the resolutions were violently opposed by Flood and a few others, they were passed; Parliament then imposed additional taxes, enabling Ireland to fulfil her part in the transaction. For a list of the eleven resolutions, see *Gent.*

Mag. (1785) lv. 145–46. For subsequent developments, see *post* From Barnard, c. 17 July, n. 13.

[4] A party of Protestant reformers had arisen in Dublin to fight for the reform of Parliament. A permanent committee was created, and in June 1784 it invited the sheriffs of the different counties to call meetings for the election of delegates, who were to meet as a congress in Dublin the following Oct. The movement was similar to that of the Volunteer Convention, but was not associated with any armed force. Meetings were held both in Oct. and in Jan. 1785, but little was accomplished. The members quickly divided over the Catholic question; and the congress adjourned, having issued only a few declamatory addresses in favour of parliamentary reform which had little effect upon public opinion.

that the Publick Tranquillity is likely to be restor'd here upon a Permanent Basis, in Spite of French Politicks and Popular Madness.

May I trouble you with my hearty Respects and Compliments to Sir Joshua and E. Burke when you see them; (I believe I shall soon write to the Former.) Let me Hear from you when you have no thing better to do, and assure yourself that I am, My dear Sir, with Sincere Esteem and Regard, Your Faithfull humble Servant

THOS. KILLALOE

To Thomas Barnard, Sunday 20 March 1785

MS. Yale (L 41). A copy in the hand of Alexander Millar.[1] Sent 20 Mar. "Lord Bishop of Kilaloe of ditto[2] and of the death of his son (Copy)" (Reg. Let.).

ENDORSEMENT: Copy Letter To The Bishop of Kilaloe 20th March 1785.

Auchinleck, 20th March 1785

MY DEAR LORD: Your Lordship's long silence gave me some concern though I should not presume to flatter myself with a very punctual correspondence on your part whose important Occupations are so various—But the cause of it which your Lordship has now announced to me is truely distressful—As I knew Mr. Barnard and have several times had the pleasure to see your Lordship and him together I can fully conceive what affliction it is to be deprived of such a Son. I indeed never saw a Father and Son so easy with so much propriety. Your Lordships own account of this severe stroke with its effects is just beautiful and consolatory. You may apply to Mr. Bernard but not to yourself Quintilian's pathetick exclamation on the death of his son—"Te omnium spe Atticæ eloquentiæ candidatum Parens superstes ta[n]tum ad

---

[1] "Mr. Millar, my Chaplain" (Journ. 9 Apr. 1787), who, in addition to assisting the minister of Auchinleck by preaching, tutored Sandie, gave JB lessons in arithmetic, and wrote in JB's journal the entries from 29 Oct. to 8 Nov. 1782. The "wee Miller" of Burns's *Holy Fair*, he later became minister of Kilmaurs.

[2] "concerning the Life of Dr. Johnson" (Reg. Let.).

pœnas amisi"[3]—The Bishop of Kilaloe is more divinely instructed than to sorrow as those who have no hope—[4]

The loss of Dr. Johnson is very heavy upon me. It is an extinction of one of the great lights in my intellectual Firmament. It is the fall of a magnificent Tree under the shade of which I have long been used to be sheltered. But he has passed into a better state of Being; and it is my daily prayer that I may be enabled to be a Follower of Him who I trust is through Faith and Patience now inheriting the promises—[5]

Your Lordship encourages me much when you call upon me as one who is able in your opinion to do justice to the memory of that great and good Man. I own it is my Ambition. I have long had it in View: And our illustrious departed Friend was well informed of my design. I am soon to publish my *Journal of a Tour to the Hebrides* in company with him which he read and liked, and which will exhibit a specimen of that Wonderful conversation in which Wisdom and Wit were equally conspicuous. It will be a Prelude to my large Work, *The Life of Samuel Johnson LL.D.* for which I have been making collections for upwards of twenty years, and which I really hope will be a valuable treasure of Literary Anecdotes, and of the genuine emanations of his energy of mind. It will be some time before it is ready for publication; and as I am anxious to make it as perfect as I possibly can, I will be much obliged to your Lords[h]ip if you will send me any particulars concerning him which you may recollect; And pray let me have his character drawn by your Lordships pen. I shall not fail to do justice to your Lordship in the course of my Work. You won Dr. Johnsons heart and his serious esteem; and it is truely pleasing to me to think that I was a benevolent negotiator between you and helped to remove a little misunderstanding.[6]

[3] *Institutio oratoria*, vi. Proem. 13: "Have I lost you who everyone hoped would revive the eloquence of Athens, I, your father, who survive only to suffer?" The passage is corrupt in all the manuscripts and is differently emended in modern editions, but except for one slight change in word-order, JB follows the text usual in the eighteenth century.

[4] 1 Thessalonians 4. 13. This text is quoted in the Collect of the Order for the Burial of the Dead, in the Book of Common Prayer.

[5] Hebrews 6. 12.

[6] This was an episode concerning which JB was strangely reticent in the *Life*, his only reference to it (a brief and general one) occurring out of chronological order and in a foot-note: "There had been once a pretty smart altercation between Dr. Barnard and [SJ], upon a question, whether a man could improve himself after the age of forty-five; when Johnson in a hasty humour, expressed himself in a manner not quite civil. Dr. Barnard made it the subject of a copy of

TO BARNARD, 20 MARCH 1785

Your Lordship's last letter was sent to me to Edinburgh, where I remained last Winter, on account of circumstances which I shall explain to you.[7] I am now at the romantick seat of my Ancestors where I hope to have the happiness of seeing your Lordship one day. It is not very distant from Ireland. I set out tomorrow morning for London, where Packets under cover to Sir Charles Preston Bart M.P.[8] will come safe to me. Or Your Lordship may address directly at General Paoli's upper Seymour Street Portman square. We are now elegantly lodged and can receive your Lordship more *comme il faut*. As often as you have leisure I beg to hear from you and whatever commands you give me shall be accurately obeyd. I have the honour to be with high respect and Warm affection Your Lordships faithful obliged humble Servant

Sic Subscribitur JAMES BOSWELL

To Thomas Percy, Sunday 20 March 1785

Untraced. Printed *Lit. Illust.* vii. 303–04. Sent 20 Mar. "Lord Bishop of Dromore concerning my Life of Dr. Johnson (Copy)" (Reg. Let.).

Auchinleck, 20 March, 1785

MY DEAR LORD, Instead of apologising for not thanking your Lordship sooner, for your last kind letter, which was valued by

---

pleasant verses" (*Life* iv. 115 n. 4). For differing versions of the incident and of the verses, see *ibid*. pp. 431–33; *Boswell's Note Book 1776–1777*, ed. R. W. Chapman, 1925, p. 18 and notes; and especially *A Copy of pleasant Verses*, privately printed for the Johnsonians, 1970, by F. W. Hilles. The altercation took place near the end of 1775, probably on 23 Dec., JB not being present (Hilles, p. 6). On JB's first recorded meeting with Barnard, 23 Apr. 1776, he found Barnard still hurt: Barnard was sure SJ did not love him and thought SJ "not a Gentleman". JB at once reported Barnard's complaint to SJ, who assured him that Barnard was mistaken: he loved him very well, though he disapproved of his living

among wits and frequenting a midnight Club—"that was ours. . . . I was happy in thinking that I could contribute to the reconciliation of two Christians" (*Note Book*, p. 18). By 1781 all hard feelings between the two had evaporated (*Life* iv. 115).

[7] *Ante* To Barnard, 14 May 1784 and n. 7; From Forbes to Langton, 21 Jan. 1785, n. 9.

[8] Preston (c. 1735–1800), of Valleyfield, was M.P. for the Dysart Burghs from 1784 to 1790, and later a commissioner of customs. As a major in the Army, he had defended Fort St. John against the Americans in 1775 (*Comp. Bar.* ii. 426–27). He was first cousin to JB's mother.

me as it ought to be, I shall follow the maxim *ad eventum festina*,[1] and proceed directly to a subject which affects us mutually—the death of our illustrious friend Dr. Johnson. I certainly need not enlarge on the shock it gave my mind. I do not expect to recover from it. I mean I do not expect that I can ever in this world have so mighty a loss supplied. I gaze after him with an eager eye; and I hope again to be with him.

It is a great consolation to me now, that I was so assiduous in collecting the wisdom and wit of that wonderful man. It is long since I resolved to write his life—I may say his life and conversation. He was well informed of my intention, and communicated to me a thousand particulars from his earliest years upwards to that dignified intellectual state in which we have beheld him with awe and admiration.

I am first to publish the Journal of a Tour to the Hebrides, in company with him, which will exhibit a specimen of that wonderful conversation in which wisdom and wit were equally conspicuous. My talent for recording conversation is handsomely acknowledged by your Lordship upon the blank leaf of Selden's *Table Talk*, with which you was so good as present me. The Life will be a large work enriched with letters and other original pieces of Dr. Johnson's composition; and, as I wish to have the most ample collection I can make, it will be some time before it is ready for publication.

I am indebted to your Lordship for a copy of "Pope's Note"[2] concerning him, and for a list of some of his works which was indeed written down in his presence uncontradicted; but he corrected it for me when I pressed him. If your Lordship will favour me with any thing else of or concerning him I shall be much

---

[1] Horace, *Ars Poetica* l. 148: "hasten to the issue". JB has changed the verb to the imperative.

[2] JB copied the note (*Life* i. 143) and Percy's comments on it at Northumberland House on 9 May 1776 (Journ.). Percy had written: "This Billet was written by Mr. Pope when Mr. Johnson published his Imitation of Juvenal entitled 'London'. The merit of that Poem struck Pope and he inquired of Richardson the Painter if he knew the Author, who told him 'it was one Johnson'. Upon which Pope said 'I never heard of him before, but he will be *déterré*.' Afterwards Pope picked up further particulars about him which he wrote down on this Billet. Mr. Richardson gave it to Sir Joshua Reynolds, who gave it to me. Jany. 20 1773. Percy."

To his copy of Percy's remarks JB added: "I copied this Note with Dr. Percy's remark from the Originals, at Northumberland House London, 9 May 1776. James Boswell." JB's copies of Pope's and Percy's notes are at Yale.

obliged to you. You must certainly recollect a number of anecdotes. Be pleased to write them down, as you so well can do,
and send them to me.

I am now, as your Lordship once observed to me, your *neighbour*.
For, while here, at the romantic seat of my ancestors, I am at no
great distance from Ireland. I hope we shall yet visit as neighbours.
At present, however, I am on the wing for London, where letters
addressed to me at General Paoli's, Upper Seymour Street,
Portman Square, will find me. I beg to have my best compliments
presented to Mrs. Percy and the young ladies, and I have the
honour to remain, your Lordship's faithful humble servant

JAMES BOSWELL

From Thomas Barnard, Thursday 14 April 1785

MS. Yale (C 84).

ADDRESS: James Boswell Esqr., Honble. General Paoli's, upper Seymour
Street, Portman Square, London.

POSTMARKS: IRELAND, 19 AP, AP [?15].

Henrietta Street, Dublin, April 14th 1785

MY DEAR SIR: It gives me the most sincere Satisfaction to hear
from yourself that you have actually undertaken a work for which
you are so peculiarly well Qualified, as the Life of Samuel Johnson:
I pray God that I may Live to see it Completed, as I am assured
that it will be equally worthy of the High and Established Reputa-
tions, of the Illustrious Dead and his Biographer. In the mean
time I entirely applaud your design to stay the Stomach of the
Publick by a Taste of Itinerary conversations which I am impatient
to See. And, as a Mark of your Freindship, I request that you will
be so good as to send me your work as it Comes from the Press,
enclosed under Cover to John Lees Esqr.[1] Post office Dublin,
which, I Faithfully promise you, shall not go into the Piratical
Hands of the Irish Booksellers, with whom I am at present rather
in a state of Hostility: having given notice last week in the
House of Lords that I mean to bring in a Bill here for the

---

[1] For Lees see *post* From Barnard, c. 17 July 1785, n. 1.

Protection of Copy Right nearly Similar to that in England.[2] I have been already attack'd by them in all the Dublin News Papers,[3] but I intend to proceed Resolutely in a good Cause; conscious that I deserve the Thanks of the Literary world, and that I shall meet the Support of the Honest and Judicious Freinds of Commerce, as well as those of Learning.

It is some time since you earnestly requested me[4] to republish a Trifling anonymous piece of Criticism, together with a Short tract on the Migration of the antient Scots which I shewd you in

[2] On 4 Apr. 1785, "the Bishop of *Killala* [sic] after pointing out the injuries that authors and booksellers must sustain from a piracy of their works . . . moved, That the House do resolve itself into a Committee, on Tuesday se'nnight, to take into consideration, the best means of securing literary property in this kingdom." The Lord Chancellor asked the Bishop to confine his motion "to a mere notice, that he would throw this matter out to the consideration of the House on Tuesday next, which was moved and agreed to accordingly" (*London Chronicle*, 12–14 Apr. 1785, lvii. 357). The *Journals of the House of Lords of Ireland* record the presentation at this time of no bill dealing with copyright. Barnard probably shelved his bill because he had learned that Administration in Great Britain planned to include something on copyright in the Irish Propositions then before the British Parliament (*post* From Barnard, c. 17 July 1785, n. 13). At any rate, on 12 May 1785, Pitt presented, as No. 17 of his amended propositions, "That it is expedient, that such privileges of printing and vending books, as are or may be legally possessed within Great Britain, under the grant of the Crown or otherwise, and the copyrights of the authors and booksellers of Great Britain, should continue to be protected in the manner they are at present by the laws of Great Britain; and that it is just that measures should be taken, by the parliament of Ireland, for giving the like protection to the copyrights of the authors and booksellers of that kingdom" (*Parliamentary History of England*, 1815, xxv. 575–87, 713). Barnard seems to have intended much more, namely, to protect British copyrights in Ireland.

[3] Barnard exaggerates. *The Dublin Evening Post* (12 Apr. 1785) was personal and flippant: "A Rev. Bishop in our Upper House is 'tremblingly alive all o'er' [Pope, *Essay on Man* i. 197] lest the booksellers of London should sell a dozen or two less copies of each impression of books in Ireland, than they do at present, and is actually about bringing in a bill to protect (what!)—the London booksellers!" *The Dublin Journal* was opposed, but did not mention Barnard. *The Public Register, or Freeman's Journal* (7 Apr. 1785) was highly laudatory: "The Bill, brought into the House of Lords, by the Bishop of Killaloe, for securing literary property in this kingdom, seems to meet the hearty approbation of all, except some few booksellers, who have made a practice for many years to deprive authors of their natural right to the productions of their own brains. It is expected that this bill will pass unanimously through both Houses of Parliament, and will undoubtedly be attended with the noble consequence of calling forth the genius and learning of the kingdom, and ultimately redound to the credit of the national character. Should this bill, therefore be carried into a law, of which there cannot be the least doubt, the learned Bishop of Killaloe will be justly entitled to receive from the writers of this country, the richest wreath of honourable panegyric."

[4] MS. "me me"

Manuscript. Since which, I have revised them Both: and, when you return to Edinburgh, (if you still think them worthy of the Publick attention) I will send them to you to dispose of as you think proper, only requesting that my name may not be affixed to them, and that they may be Printed Rather at Edinburgh than London, where the controversy on those subjects is now gone to Sleep.

On monday next the Inextinguishable Ely Cause is again to be heard before the House of Lords, on a Writ of Error from the Kings bench, as before; and nearly upon the same grounds. The Lords having, last year decreed that the Record of the Recovery was not conclusive evidence of the Sanity of the Party, and orderd a new Issue accordingly; The Court on the Second Trial Still refused the Plaintiff permission to go into Parole Evidence on the Fact. But ass⟨erted⟩ that the Fine and warrant of attorney were Con⟨clusive⟩ Evidence, admitting the Record of the Recovery no⟨t to⟩ be Conclusive, as the Lords had decreed. To us Plain Illiterate men, this seems a Distinction without a Difference; With you Learned Professors it may Differ Toto Cælo:[5] as we shall soon hear Explaind to our Cost in Tedious attention and Exhausted Spirits for Some days.

Pray send me some news (I don't mean Politicks) but about our Common Freinds and acquaintance of whom I have heard nothing for a long time Past, and to whom I beg to be Respectfully remembered. I wrote some time ago to Sir Jos. but can't say that I expected a speedy[6] answer, as, I Know, That species of Painting which *"gives Colour and a Body to the Thoughts"*[7] is not his Favourite Branch of the Business, though no man Executes it Better, when he pleases.

You bid me direct to you Under Cover to an MP. forgetting that the Privilige of Franking between the two Kingdoms is at

[5] "Diametrically."

[6] MS. "speedy speedy"

[7] Phrase untraced. What Barnard means, as JB understood (*post* To Barnard, 1 July 1785, n. 7), was that although Sir Joshua could write well, as his *Discourses* proved, he wrote with reluctance. In *Pleasures of Imagination* (I, lines 46–48 of the earlier version, 1744) Akenside declares that the poet's task is

To paint the finest features of the mind
And to most subtile and mysterious things
Give colour, strength, and motion.
And in lines 118–20 of Book IV (incomplete, 1772) he speaks of the poet whose prevailing hand
Gives, to corporeal essence life and sense
And every stately function of the soul.

an end.[8] I therefore direct as usual, begging you to assure the worthy general Paoli of my Constant Respect and Esteem. I am, My dear Sir, Faithfully and affectionately yours

THOS. KILLALOE

From Thomas Percy, Saturday 23 April 1785

MS. Yale (C 2232).

ADDRESS: To James Boswell Esqr., of Auchenlech, at Edenburgh.[1]

POSTMARKS: IRELAND, AP 23, AP 28.

Dublin, April 23. 1785

MY DEAR SIR: Be assured, it will always give me the highest pleasure to hear from you and to obey any commands or gratify any wishes of yours: Besides the common Tyes of Friendship, our bond of Union in our regard and reverence for our great and good departed Friend Dr. Johnston, will always have a still stronger hold on me, and make me more and more desirous of cultivating an Intimacy with Mr. Boswell.—I am truly glad that you continue the Intention of giving your Johnsoniana to the World.—I will try to rub up my Memory and will transmit to you every thing

[8] A "Bill for establishing certain Regulations concerning the Portage and Conveyance of Letters and Packets by the Post between Great Britain and Ireland" was ordered in the House of Commons, 27 Nov. 1783 (*Journals of the House of Commons*). On 8 Dec. John Ord reported from a committee of the whole House a resolution "that so much of the act of the 4th of his Majesty as relates to the free postage of letters and packets, etc. from Great Britain to Ireland, and from Ireland to Great Britain, be repealed", and this resolution having been passed, the House ordered the Members appointed to prepare and bring in the bill to "make Provision in the said Bill, pursuant to the said Resolution" (*ibid.*; *Gent. Mag.* 1783, liii. 1060). The bill passed the Commons 24 Dec. 1783, was agreed to by the Lords 26 Jan. 1784, and received the Royal Assent 11 Mar. 1784 (*Journals of the House of Commons*). Certain officials of the Lord Lieutenant's office, however, retained the privilege of sending and receiving letters and parcels without payment of postage, and the new Act added to these certain officials in the newly established General Post Office of Ireland. (For the full lists, see 4 Geo. III. Cap. 24 and 24 Geo. III. Sess. 2. Cap. 8.) It is clear from the present letter (n. 1) and letters printed later in this volume that these officials were as ready to accommodate their friends as M.P.s had formerly been.

[1] See *post* To Percy, 1 July, for the result of Percy's failure to address this letter to London as directed by JB.

worth notice, that I can recollect of this extraordinary Man.—I unfortunately neglected to commit to Paper his *Dicta* as they occur'd to me, so that I fear I shall [not] preserve many of these worth your notice.—But I recollect a few facts that I have heard of his early years which are peculiar and characteristic; and as I do not see them retailed in any of the periodical Publications, they may possibly be new to *you also*: These I shall commit to Paper and whatever else I think will answer your purpose and do all I can to *scrattle*[2] for you.—I have a few Letters of his, but they were meer short Billets and not of consequence to merit Publication.

Let me now request a particular favour from *you*. Some Noblemen and Gentlemen in this Kingdom are desirous of Establishing a Society, which shall have for its object the Improvement and Cultivation of *Natural History*, *Antiquities* and *Belles Lettres*:[3] And they wish to collect the Rules and Plan of the several literary Societies in Europe, out of which to form a Code of Laws for their own Observance. We have already applied for those of the Royal and Antiqu[aria]n Societies in London; as also for some of those on the Continent: May I (thro' the medium of your friendship) succeed in procuring those of the Antiquarian Society in Edinburgh?[4] In granting this favour you will oblige not only myself, but others of your Friends particularly Lord Charlemont[5] and the Bishop of Killaloe, who are both favourers of this Scheme and indeed the whole Society, to whom I promised I would write to you. I am, ever, Dear Sir, Your affectionate and faithful Servant

THOS. DROMORE

[2] A dialect verb (intransitive): "To keep on scratching" (OED, Scrattle, 1).

[3] The Royal Irish Academy, Dublin, founded in the spring of this year.

[4] The Society had been founded on 18 Dec. 1780, and had already issued a handsome quarto volume by William Smellie (*Account of the Institution and Progress of the Society of the Antiquaries of Scotland*, 1782, price three shillings) which included the Statutes and By-Laws (pp. 126–33). Percy was an honorary member (29 Jan. 1781; p. 34), but probably had received few communications. JB had been invited to assist in the establishment of the Society, but had declined because he thought its founder, Lord Buchan, "a silly affected being" (*ibid.* p. 3; Journ. 18 Nov. 1780).

[5] James Caulfeild, first Earl of Charlemont (1728–99), was elected first President of the Academy on 2 May 1785 (*List of the Papers Published in the Transactions of the Royal Irish Academy*, 1887, p. 75). In addition to Charlemont, Barnard, and Percy, Malone was also one of the original members of the Academy. Lord Charlemont had been elected to The Club in Mar. 1773.

To Lord Ossory,
Friday 29 April 1785

MS. Yale (L 1257). A copy.

Portman Square, 29 April

Mr. Boswell presents his most respectful compliments to Lord Ossory. Just returned from Richmond Lodge[1] finds his Lordship's card.

On Monday 2 May the Laird of Auchinleck will certainly have the honour to sit down at the table of Fitzpatrick.[2]

From General James Edward Oglethorpe
to Bennet Langton,
Thursday 12 May 1785

MS. Yale (C 2125).

ADDRESS: To ——[1] Langton Esq., Queen Square Westminster.

ENDORSEMENT: Genl. Oglethorpe.

Lower Grosvenor Street, Thursday

DEAR SIR: I thinck we are two Buckets, one goes up when the other goes down.[2]

Mr. Leonardy[3] Has given me two tikets for the House in the

---

[1] The residence of Colonel James Stuart Wortley-Mackenzie, which JB visited frequently. He recorded for Thursday 28 Apr.: "To Richmond Lodge. Miss Monckton there. Comfortable day" (Journ.).

[2] "Dined Lord Ossory's (first time) Lord Palmerston Sir Joshua Col. James Erskine, Andrew Stuart. . . . Lady Ossory was truly Courteous; spoke much of her expectations of my Account of Dr. Johnson. Said her daughter Lady Anne was asked to dine at her Grandmother's [Lady Ravensworth's]. Excused herself because Mr. Boswell was to dine. Her Grandmother sent back word. If she had known Mr. Bos[well was to be] there, would not have asked her. 'There' said

Sir Josh[ua]. 'There's something to write down.' Was brilliant" (Journ. 2 May).

---

[1] What is here interpreted as a dash (cf. *ante* From Goldsmith, c. 22 Sept. 1769) may be a deleted "La". Oglethorpe's hand is very erratic.

[2] Oglethorpe means that he and Langton divide their time between the country and London, but seem never to be "up" at the same time. The old man, who was in his eighty-ninth year, died seven weeks after writing this letter.

[3] Vincenzo Lunardi (1759–1806), secretary to the Neapolitan ambassador, was the first man to ascend in a balloon in England. On 15 Sept. 1784 he had ascended from the Artillery Company's

192

artilery ground which is very convenient to see all the Prossess of filling etc.

I Shall go at 9. of the Clock to Morrow Morning to be there time egnof to see all the Operation. If you have any curiosity and will be here by that tim which is 9 of the Clock I will carry you in my Coach and will take you into the Place I have. Being two tikets I Cary You and My Self which Makes 2. Your most Obedient Humble Servant

J. OGLETHORPE

To Charles James Fox, Wednesday 25 May 1785

MS. Yale (L 555). A copy, in the hand of one of Dilly's clerks, probably John Nornaville.

HEADING in JB's hand: Right Hon. Charles Fox.

General Paolis, Upper Seymour Street,
Portman square, 25 May 1785

SIR: Can you really be liberal enough to read without prejudice, a Pamphlet written by a Man who with honest Zeal opposed your

Ground at Moorfields, sailed over London, and landed at Standon, near Ware. His second attempt, on 13 May 1785, to which reference is here made, was much less successful. "The Public had been induced to believe that a Balloon of sufficient Power to carry three Persons . . . would be launched into the Air. . . . Mrs. Sage and Mr. Biggin . . . were to return from an aerial Tour to the Continent. . . . When the Company, to the Amount of four or five Thousand in the Ground, and eighty or a hundred Thousand in its Neighbourhood, were assembled; Rumours of ill Usage and Dissention were propagated; it was seen by the Preparations that the Power of the Balloon had been falsely estimated; and Lunardi getting into his Car a little after one, in order to be led over the Ground as the Advertisement had taught the Company to expect; the Rope was cut; and he ascended, partly to fulfil his

Promise, partly to escape embarrassing Interrogations. The Wind being at South East he was carried directly over London. It was said when he had reached Holbourn, the Balloon showed a strong Inclination to descend; but that by disposing of his remaining Ballast he with some Difficulty proceeded to the Ground at the End of Tottenham Court Road, from whence he and his Balloon were conducted to the Pantheon" (*St. James's Chronicle*, 12–14 May 1785). Lunardi blamed the failure on a "chemist", no doubt the technician who was to fill his balloon with hydrogen: "La mia seconda salita mi ruinò, facendomi perdere il credito, e ciò per essermi fidato ad un chimico" (G. Morazzoni, *Un Pioniere dell'aereonautica, Vincenzo Lunardi*, 1931, p. 74). JB, however, who witnessed the ascent from Bethlehem Hospital, "was shocked and pleased" (Journ.).

193

Grand Indian Project[1] as much as he could. I do believe you can; and therefore I take the liberty to send you *A Letter to the People of Scotland*[2] against what I think a profligate measure, and if I am able to convince Mr. Fox that it is so, there will be no doubt of its being frustrated. I have the honour to be, Sir, your most Obedient humble servant

JAMES BOSWELL

To Sir Joshua Reynolds, Tuesday 7 June 1785

MS. Yale (L 1101). A duplicate of this, retained by Sir Joshua, is in the possession of T. G. M. Snagge.

ENDORSEMENT: Agreement with Sir Joshua Reynolds, 1785.

London, 7 June 1785[1]

MY DEAR SIR: The debts which I contracted in my Father's lifetime will not be cleared off by me for some years. I therefore think it unconscientious to indulge myself in any expensive article of elegant luxury. But in the mean time, you may die, or I may die, and I should regret much[2] that there should not be at Auchinleck my Portrait painted by Sir Joshua Reynolds, with whom I have the felicity of living in social intimacy.

I have a proposal to make to you. I am for certain to be called to the english bar next february. Will you now do my picture, and the price shall be paid out of the first fees which I receive as a Barrister in Westminster Hall. Or if that fund should fail, it shall be paid at any rate five years hence, by myself or my representatives.[3]

[1] See *ante* To Reynolds, 6 Feb. 1784, n. 3, for an account of JB's opposition.

[2] *A Letter to the People of Scotland, on the Alarming Attempt to Infringe the Articles of the Union, and Introduce a Most Pernicious Innovation, by Diminishing the Number of the Lords of Session*, by James Boswell, Esq., London, 1785. After attacking Dundas for advocating the diminishing of the number of the Lords of Session, JB listed in the *Letter* public men who would oppose the bill, among whom was William Pitt, the Prime Minister, who, JB maintained,

would "send for *the Minister for Scotland*, and tell him, in a determined tone, '*Dundas! Dundas* for shame! Here is a rock upon which we might have split, as *Fox* did upon his *India bill*. I'll hear no more of this Court of Session job! It is a monstrous measure! Let it be quashed!'" (*Letter*, 1785, pp. 78–79).

[1] On this day JB dined at Sir Joshua's.

[2] Sir Joshua's copy, "very much"

[3] It was never paid. "Sir JOSHUA REYNOLDS, with a munificence truly princely, has not only presented Mr. BOSWELL with

If you are pleased to approve of this Proposal, your signifying your concurrence underneath, upon two duplicates one of which shall be kept by each of us will be a sufficient voucher of the Obligation. I ever am with very sincere regard, My Dear Sir, Your faithful and affectionate humble servant

JAMES BOSWELL

I agree to the above conditions
J. Reynolds

London, Sep. 10th 1785

To Thomas Barnard, Friday 1 July 1785

MS. Yale (L 42). A copy.

HEADING: Bishop of Kilaloe.

London, 1 July 1785

MY DEAR LORD: Your Lordship may be perfectly assured that there is no man alive who respects and loves you more than I do, which it might perhaps be presumptuous in me to profess to your Lordship had not you been pleased to give me so many proofs that you think me worthy of your regard. Your last letter does me great honour indeed.

I now send your Lordship *A Letter to the People of Scotland* which I lately published from an honest Zeal to prevent what I seriously think "a monstrous measure"—diminishing the number of our Lords of Session. It has been very successful, and I flatter myself has averted the blow. Your Lordship will be glad to see in it that we no longer differ as to the only point upon which we have formerly disputed—A Reform in Parliament. I have been fairly converted by observing that Reformers can agree upon no one Plan, and that all of them have an inordinate spirit of resistance to

the large portrait of Dr. JOHNSON, from which the capital engraving by HEATH, prefixed to THE LIFE is taken, but also with his friend's own portrait, which appeared in the exhibition of the Royal Academy in 1786: it is allowed to be one of Sir Joshua's very best pictures, both for likeness, character, and colouring" ("Friendly Patronage", *Public Advertiser*, 18 June 1791, by JB, as shown by marked cutting in Yale P 100). The portrait was begun 5 July and finished 10 Sept. (Journ.). It is now in the National Portrait Gallery. Note that Reynolds dated his agreement the day the portrait was finished.

their Superiors coupled with a desire of power over their inferiors, who they hope will be increased by the operation of that speculative novelty which for the time is the object of their *ambitious,* or to speak more properly—*unruly* exertion.

I also send your Lordship the first eight sheets of my *Journal of a Tour to the Hebrides with Samuel Johnson LL.D.* If it in any degree contributes to soothe and sweeten the life of my highly-valued Barnard, I shall think I have laboured to good purpose. Your Lordship shall have the rest of the Book sent to you *by divisions,* to use the military style. I am kept close in London, attending upon the press. The printing goes on more slowly than I supposed it would, for a reason that both I and my Readers will certainly not regret—My *Journal* is revised by Mr. Malone, who I really think is the best critick of our age; and he not only winnows it from the chaff which in the hurry of immediate collection could not but be in it, but suggests little elegant variations which though they do not alter the sense, add much grace to the expression.[1]

I believe the Dublin Booksellers have entered into a resolution not to give any consideration whatever for the first copy of any Book published in England;[2] otherwise I should have troubled your Lordship to negociate for me[3] with some of them. I am happy that your Lordship has stood forth as the Patron of Literature in your House of Lords, and I hope you will prevail.[4]

I should be much obliged to your Lordship for a set of the printed Cases in the great Ely Cause,[5] when you can find a private hand to bring them to Dilly's my Bookseller.

[1] See BP vi. 165–71 and *Tour*, pp. xiv-xxi, for a discussion of Malone's part in JB's *Tour*.

[2] Although there was no statute protecting British copyrights in Ireland, English authors had occasionally secured some profit from the Irish printing of their works by bargaining with a particular Irish publisher to furnish proofs or sheets in advance of English publication, and so give that publisher an advantage.

[3] MS. "to negociate for me to negociate for me"

[4] As stated *ante* (From Barnard, 14 Apr. 1785, n. 2) Barnard's bill was never brought in. Ireland had no law protecting copyright until its union with Great Britain in 1801.

[5] The respective cases of the appellant and the respondent forming the subject matter of an appeal to the Irish House of Lords (as to the House of Lords of Great Britain) were printed and bound in a considerable number of copies at the expense of the appellant and lodged with the House in advance of the trial. The King's Inns Library, Dublin, has copies of the cases in the Ely cause; photocopies are available in the Boswell Office at Yale. See *ante* From Barnard, 14 Apr. 1785 and *post* From Barnard, c. 17 July 1785.

As I have now taken my *resolution* to try my fortune in Westminster Hall, I shall be little at Edinburgh. But as I shall pass my autumns at Auchinleck, I can with all convenience and accuracy publish an edition of the two Works which your Lordship means obligingly to entrust to my care. I wish that your Lordship would permit your name to be affixed. If you are determined against that, I hope you will not object to my mentioning in an Advertisement subscribed by myself that "they are written by a learned Prelate my much respected Friend." In short My Dear Lord, Literary Performances like the Hypochrites have so long had trumpets sounded before them,[6] that the World will not attend to simple merit, and it is not doing a Work justice to send it forth without a trumpet of one kind or other.

Sir Joshua is very well. But he indeed "loaths much to write."[7] He is not sure but he may pay a visit to Ireland this year. The excellent General Paoli remembers the Bishop of Kilaloe with great regard. Pray write to me at his house Portman Square. If your Lordship recollects any *Memorabilia* of Dr. Johnson, pray send me them. I ever am, My Dear Lord, Your Lordship's most affectionate faithful humble servant.

P.S. I cannot refrain from telling your Lordship that I lately made my Will in which I leave your Lordship a small token of remembrance with grateful acknowledgements.[8]

---

[6] Matthew 6. 2: "Therefore when thou doest thine alms, do not sound a trumpet before thee, as the hypocrites do in the synagogues and in the streets, that they may have glory of men."

[7] JB quotes Barnard's sentiment rather than his words (*ante* From Barnard, 14 Apr. 1785, n. 7). Reynolds "would rather run three miles to deliver his message by word of mouth than venture to write a note" (*Letters Reynolds*, pp. xi–xii). At the time JB was writing, Reynolds was preparing to travel to Brussels to see a collection of paintings taken from religious houses which had been suppressed by the Emperor (*ibid.* pp. 129, 133).

[8] A codicil to JB's will, dated 30 May 1785, reads: "And as it frequently happens that there are strange and unaccountable Omissions in Wills so it has happened in mine. . . . I bequeath a gold mourning ring to the Right Reverend Dr. Thomas Barnard Bishop of Kilaloe to whom I am under great obligations as a Spiritual Father, and as an instructive and pleasing Companion in which capacity his Lordship has condescended to live with me, and I trust I have never presumed to be irreverently familiar with him." JB went on to request the prayers of all his "pious friends for my departed soul considering how reasonable it is to suppose that it may be detained some time in a middle state. Their prayers may be conditional and I cannot think will be unlawful" (first of two codicils to JB's will, Register House, Edinburgh).

There was a Dr. Madan[9] of Ireland with whom Dr. Johnson was very intimate. Perhaps some Letters and other materials for the LIFE may be recovered from his heirs.

To Thomas Percy, Friday 1 July 1785

MS. Yale (L 1066). A copy. On verso JB began a copy of his letter to Joseph Cooper Walker,[1] 1 July 1785.

HEADING: Bishop of Dromore.

London, 1 July 1785

MY DEAR LORD: This though in plain prose, might be in verse, for it is "A Complaint"[2] and upon my word a very sincere one. Since I left Scotland[3] I understand that there came to my house at Edinburgh a Letter from Ireland[4] which I am confident was from your Lordship; but by some inexplicable cause it cannot be found; so I have not received it.

After waiting long, in hopes of its appearing, I now despair; and all I can do is to inform your Lordship of the misfortune and earnestly beg that you may be so very kind as to repair it, by writing to me again at General Paoli's, Portman Square, which I shall consider as a very great favour.

I beg to have my best compliments presented to Mrs. Percy and the young Ladies; and I have the honour to remain, My Dear Lord, Your much obliged humble servant

To Sir Joshua Reynolds, Tuesday 5 July 1785

Not reported. Referred to in JB's journal: "Had sent Apology to Sir Joshua for not returning to sit this forenoon as I promised." Reynolds had begun JB's portrait earlier that morning.

[9] Samuel Madden, D.D. (1686–1765), miscellaneous writer and philanthropist. SJ assisted him in preparing for publication *Boulter's Monument, a Panegyrical Poem, sacred to the Memory of Dr. Hugh Boulter, late Lord Archbishop of Ardmagh*, 1745. See *Life* i. 318, 545; ii. 321.

[1] Walker (1761–1810), Irish antiquary, was one of the original members of the Royal Irish Academy.

[2] An allusion to Percy's *Reliques*, which included "Titus Andronicus's Complaint" and "The Complaint of Conscience".

[3] On Monday 21 Mar. 1785 (Journ.).

[4] The preceding letter from Percy (23 Apr.). See *post* To Percy, 12 July 1786.

To Sir Joshua Reynolds,
Tuesday 5 July 1785

Not reported. Referred to in JB's journal: Dining with Reynolds at The Club, "I had told him I was going to the execution next morning, Shaw once Burkes servant being to suffer. Sir Joshua was drawn to it, and said he'd go. I undertook to arrange it all for him. . . . Then I went to Mr. Hearne's and sent a note to Sir Joshua to be at his house at 1/2 past five at latest."

From Sir Joshua Reynolds,
Thursday 7 July 1785[1]

Untraced. Printed in C. R. Leslie and Tom Taylor, *Life and Times of Sir Joshua Reynolds*, 1865, ii. 588–89, where the original is described as an "imperfect draft."

[London]

I am obliged to you for carrying me yesterday to see the execution at Newgate of the five malefactors.[2] I am convinced it is a vulgar error, the opinion that it is so terrible a spectacle, or that it any way implies a hardness of heart or cruelty of disposition, any more than such a disposition is implied in seeking delight from the representation of a tragedy. Such an execution as we saw, where there was no torture of the body or expression of agony of the mind, but where the criminals, on the contrary, appeared perfectly composed, without the least trembling, ready to speak and answer with civility and attention any question that was proposed, neither in a state of torpidity or insensibility, but grave and composed. . . . I am convinced from what we saw, and

[1] Journ.

[2] According to *Gent. Mag.*, on 6 July "the following malefactors were executed before Newgate, viz. John Ivemay and John Honey, for robbing Edward Gray, Esq. on Ealing-Common, of a watch and two seals; Peter Shaw, for stealing in the dwelling-house of Edwin Francis Stanhope, Esq. in Curzon-Street, May-Fair, two gold boxes, six watches, a quantity of medals, &c. and Joseph Brown, for breaking into the dwelling house of Mrs. Goddin, at Hampstead, and stealing a quantity of wearing apparel, &c.; and Robert jackson [*sic*], for forging a letter of attorney from Benj. Bell, late a seaman on board the *Carysford*, with intent to defraud Samuel Danton, and Isaac Clementson. They were all young men, in the prime of life. What pity!" (1785, lv. 566–67).

from the report of Mr. Akerman,[3] that it is a state of suspense that is the most irksome and intolerable to the human mind, and that certainty, though of the worst, is a more eligible state; that the mind soon reconciles itself even to the worst, when that worst is fixed as fate. Thus bankrupts . . . I consider it is natural to desire to see such sights, and, if I may venture, to take delight in them, in order to stir and interest the mind, to give it some emotion, as moderate exercise is necessary for the body. This execution is not more, though I expected it to be too much. If the criminals had expressed great agony of mind, the spectators must infallibly sympathise; but so far was the fact from it, that you regard with admiration the serenity of their countenances and whole deportment.[4]

From Thomas Barnard, c. Sunday 17 July 1785

MS. Yale (C 85).

ADDRESS: James Boswell Esqr., Honble. Genl. Paoli's, Portman Square, London.

POSTMARKS: IRELAND, JY 17, 22 JY.

[Dublin]

MY DEAR SIR: It is full Time to return you my thanks for the Valuable and very acceptable Pacquet You were so good as to

[3] Richard Akerman (c. 1722–92), Keeper of Newgate, JB's "esteemed friend . . . who long discharged a very important trust with an uniform intrepid firmness, and at the same time a tenderness and a liberal charity, which entitled him to be recorded with distinguished honour" (*Life* iii. 431).

[4] *The Public Advertiser*, on 7 July, commented, "The first person who appeared upon the scaffold was Mr. Boswell. *That* was nothing extraordinary but it was surprising when he was followed by Sir Joshua Reynolds. 'Evil communications corrupt good manners'— it is strange how that hard Scot should have prevailed on the amiable painter to attend so shocking a spectacle" (quoted in *Letters Reynolds*, p. 127 n. 2). Strangely enough, that account, like many others in the newspapers reflecting on JB, was almost certainly his own composition. "Up early," he recorded in his journal for 6 July. "Sir Joshua was before me at Mr. Hearne's with his Coach which drove us to Newgate. Convicts were in Chapel. We heard singing. Then we saw irons knocked off—and Man beckon them to a room where they were pinioned. Shaw said (at first when kept waiting) with a sigh 'I wish they were come.' I have given a particular Account in the 'Publick Advertiser.' Sir Joshua and I saw the Machinery perfectly."

send me through the Medium of my Freind Mr. Lees.[1] I attack'd
the Contents with a Voracious appetite; and, tho' the Food was
sufficiently Substantial; it was so highly Season'd as to increase,
rather than Satiate my wishes to prolong the feast. Judge therefore
of my Dissappointment, when, instead of eight Sheets of your
Tour to the Hebrides, I discover'd that there was only Seven.
(Viz. to page 112, ending with the Word Northern).[2] This I
only mention lest you might Conclude that eight sheets had been
sent, as you mention'd in your Letter, and by that means the
eighth Sheet might be omitted in your next, and my book be
incomplete. You may continue to enclose to Mr. Lees, who is an
honest Scotsman in a very Lucrative office here, and very ready to
oblige me in all things. You need not divide the work into pacquets
as his Privilege reaches to any weight.

Your *Letter to the People of Scotland* has made me acquainted
with a Branch of your Constitution, which I did not well understand before; and (having not yet Seen the arguments on the other
Side) I am at present entirely of your mind, as to the Injurious
Consequences of the Intended measure, to diminish the number of
the Lords of the Session. I think you have said enough to animate
both the People of Scotland, and the Faculty, to oppose such an
Innovation totis Viribus, but how efficient those Vires[3] may prove,
in a Country where Influence is so powerfull as it is said to be in
yours, is a matter of Doubt with me. I honour you, for not being
afraid or asham'd to Profess yourself a Tory, anglicé a Freind to
the British Constitution as it is *Still* Establish'd. Tell me in your
next, whether *an Enterprise of great moment* mention'd Page 105,
alludes to any Particular Measure Expected to be brought forward;
or is it only a Possible Case Supposed?[4] Your Reasons upon the

[1] John Lees (d. 1811), created a
baronet in 1804, was secretary to the
Post-Office in Ireland. See *ante* From
Barnard, 14 Apr. 1785, n. 8. A Scot from
Cumnock, he had gone to Ireland as
private secretary to Lord Townshend
when Townshend was Lord Lieutenant.

[2] That is, to Wednesday 25 Aug.,
when JB and SJ were at Strichen. The
seventh sheet ended in the middle of the
following sentence: "Dr. Johnson was
curious to see one of those structures
which northern antiquarians call a
Druid's temple" (*Life* v. 107).

[3] Over this word is a cross made by a
different pen. Perhaps JB considered
quoting what follows in one of his
anonymous newspaper paragraphs.

[4] In the last pages of the *Letter*, JB
explained how, when he had fixed his
opinion upon an important question, he
maintained it as a point of conscience and
honour; "and the SOVEREIGN himself
would find me *tenacem propositi*. . . . Much
would I yield, rather than shake the
reverence due to Majesty by opposition:
But there may come an enterprise of
great moment, as to which it would be

Matter are Strong and Powerfull, your arguments ad Hominem, and ad Verecundiam, are well and Smartly applied, your Digressions are enlivening, and even your Egotisms, (which are not Infrequent) contrary to the usual Effect of that Figure, amuse the Reader without provoking him. The Reading of your Pamphlet, makes me doubly happy to find that we antireformists have got you over to our Side; as I trust that the Pen which might have done us so much mischeif, will now be employd in Defence of the old Constitution.

Though I am much delighted with the Specimen I have reciev'd of the *Tour*, I shall reserve my particular observations for a future Letter after I have read the whole; The receipt of which I shall continue to expect. The Booksellers here have agreed not to purchase any work first printed elsewhere: But I shall take care that none of them shall ever get a Sight of what you entrust to me; so that your English Edition shall receive no disadvantage by their getting the work an hour sooner into their hands than they might otherwise do.

The Printed Cases of the Ely Cause are too large to be sent you in a Letter, but I will take care to convey them to you by the first opportunity of a Safe Hand going to England. In the mean time, as you seem Curious to Know the motives and principles on which we decided that Important Question, I shall make no apology for sending you a Short Sketch of the Matter, which I extract from the Notes I took on the Trials, both of 1784, and 1785.

Mr. G. Hume Remainder Man to the Estate of the late Sir Gustavus Hume brought a Writ of Error into the Kings bench to reverse a Common Recovery, Suffer'd by Nicholas late Earl of Ely, Tenant in Tail, averring that a Warrant of attorney, which made part of the Record and was executed by Nicholas, and accepted by Lord cheif Justice Clayton of the Common Pleas *out of Court* was executed by a Person of Unsound mind, the Tenant in Tail having been an Ideot a Nativitate.[5] Plaintiff and

---

deeply culpable to conceal my sentiments —as to which I may think myself obliged to be a faithful, an intrepid, an inflexible monitor" (*Letter*, 1785, pp. 104–05). In Barnard's terms, this was probably a mere "Possible Case Supposed".

[5] A detailed report of the two trials in the Irish House of Lords, 24 Mar. 1784 and 10 May 1785, will be found in William Ridgeway, *Reports of Cases upon Appeals and Writs of Error in the High Court of Parliament in Ireland*, 1795, pp. 16–121, 204–80; see also pp. 515–75, and,

Defendant Join'd Issue on the Fact of Sanity, and the Cause being Tried in the Kings Bench before The late Lord Annaly,[6] in the year 1782 the Court were of opinion that the warrant of atty. upon the Face of the Record was sufficient Evidence of Sanity, and would admit no Evidence on the part of the Plaintf. in Error to Contradict it. The Plaintiff took a Bill of Exceptions and (upon a writ of Error to the Lords) the Lords reversed the Judgement of the Kings bench and orderd a new Trial according to Law.

Upon this Question before the Lords in 1784. The Judges differ'd in opinion, whether a Common Recovery was alone Conclusive Evidence of the Sanity of the Vouchée, and the Question was decided by the House in the negative by a majority of only one.

The Cause came on to be Tried again before Lord Earlsfort,[7] on a Trial at Bar in the K[ing's] B[ench] Mich[aelma]s Term 1784. Mr. Humes Counsel opend his Cause, and offer'd to maintain the Issue of non Compos by Parol Evidence. But the Defendant in Errors counsel insisted that they had *Conclusive* Evidence of Lord Elys Sanity, and then produced an Inquisition, Commission, and Return, in Jany. 1767, by which Lord Elys Sanity had been found, by Twelve of the most Respectable Persons of the City of Dublin on oath. Which the Court held to be *not* Conclusive

---

for highly important background, the reports of Rochfort v. Earl of Ely, 29 Feb. 1768, and Hume v. Earl of Ely, 2 May 1775, in Josiah Brown, *Reports of Cases upon Appeals and Writs of Error in the High Court of Parliament . . . 1701– 79,* 1784, vi. 329–31; vii. 319–44. A common recovery was a process, based upon an intricate legal fiction, by which a person holding an estate under an entail was able to break the entail and dispose of it as he saw fit. Nicholas Hume-Loftus (1738–69), second Earl of Ely, was the son of Nicholas Hume-Loftus (d. 1766), second Viscount and first Earl of Ely, by Mary, eldest daughter of Sir Gustavus Hume, Bt. (c. 1670–1731), of Castle Hume. Sir Gustavus devised his lands on Mary, later Lady Ely, remainder to her first and other sons in tail male, remainder to her daughters and the heirs of their bodies; and, in default of such issue, remainder to his second daughter Alice, later Mrs.

Rochfort, remainder to her first and other sons in tail male, etc. Each daughter bore as issue a single son, and when the second Earl of Ely died unmarried in 1769, the Hume lands would have passed under the entail to his cousin Gustavus Rochfort, who took the name of Hume. But meantime a common recovery of the lands had been suffered, and under this recovery and the will of the second Earl of Ely, all that Earl's property passed to his uncle and heir, Henry Loftus, Viscount Loftus, two years later created Earl of Ely. Richard Clayton (d. 1770) was Lord Chief Justice of the Court of Common Pleas, Ireland, 1765–70.

[6] John Gore (1718–84), Baron Annaly, Chief Justice of the King's Bench, Ireland, from 1764 to 1784 (*Comp. Peer.* i. 163–64).

[7] John Scott (1739–98), Baron Earlsfort, Chief Justice of the King's Bench, Ireland, 1784–98 (*Comp. Peer.* iii. 331).

Evidence. They next produced a Fine acknowledged before cheif Justice Clayton, on the 8th of July 1767, making a Tenant to the Præcipe in the Recovery, and acknowledged at the Same time that the Warrant (which was Impeach'd) was taken before the *Same* cheif Justice and for the Same Purpose. And it appear'd upon the Record that the Fine, Warrant, and Recovery were different parts of the Same Transaction, at the Same moment and one Conveyance.

The Court held the Fine Produced, and the Warrant appearing on Record in Consequence of the Fine, to be *Conclusive* Evidence of Sanity on the 8th of July 1767 which was the day on which Issue was Join'd; and directed a Verdict for the Defendant, refusing to permit the Plaintiff to go into parol Evidence to Encounter it. The jury then found for Defendant. Plaintiff appeald again to the House of Lords against this Decision of the Kings Bench which was Heard the 18th of april, and de die in Diem, for several days. The Question now was, whether, (admitting the Recovery alone not to be Conclusive Evidence etc. of the Sanity of the Vouchee according to the Late Decision of the Lords in 1784) the Record of the *Fine, Præcipe* and *Concord*, taken on the *Same* day when the Warrant of the Recovery was acknowledged, and Before the *Same* Cheif Justice, was altogether Conclusive Evidence, or not.

This Point was very Learnedly and Elaborately argued on Both Sides; and the Question being again Put to the Judges, they again Differ'd in opinion, tho' not exactly the Same Persons as before; for one of those who had been in the negative as to the Recovery being Conclusive etc. was in the affirmative as to the Fine join'd with the Recovery. However this Difference among the judges obliged the Lords to take a Part in the Decision, contrary to the wishes of most of them, and even to the General Rule of Conduct they have laid down to themselves in all Cases where the opinion of the Judges and Law Lords is decisive. The Majority (of whom I was one) voted for affirming the Judgement of the Kings Bench. I was principally decided in My Judgement by the Following cases, to which I refer you, to see whether you think I was right. Mansfields Case. 12th Coke. Mary Portingtons Case. 10th Coke. Needler and Bishop Winchester. Hobt. 224. Massy and Bean and Whitehead. Burrows Reports.[8] Besides the weight of these

---

[8] "Coke" is Sir Edward Coke (1552–1634) and "Hobt." is Sir Henry Hobart (d. 1625), reporters of cases tried in the King's Bench, 1572–1625. Barnard's references to these collections are reasonably accurate, and were perhaps copied

authorities; I thought in all Doubtfull Cases two Principles ought to govern: one of them being, the Presumption, that in all appeals, the Judgement of a Former Court is more probably right than Wrong. The other being, the High Expediency of supporting, as far as is consistent with Justice; the Common assurances of the Land. So much for the Ely Cause: which has occasiond you an Extraordinary Expence of Postage,[9] and would still farther inhance the Price, if I was to go into it as far as I ought, to give you full Satisfaction.

I most Cordially and Sincerely wish you Success in Westminster Hall: your two cheif Justices are Caledonians already, and I see no reason why you should not be cheif Baron, and send Skinner to Ireland, where we begin to want a New Chancellor; and where an Englishman of *Approved Reputation* will not be Unwelcome.[10] At least if I was you I would always look Forward to one of the Great Prizes; and then, who Knows what may[10a] Happen. I had a Letter last week from the Incomparable Lord Mansfield; in which he sais that he finds himself *growing* old: But his writing Shews no token of it.[11]

Your Hint concerning Publications I will take ad referendum; and say no more on that Subject at present.[12]

from the printed cases. "Massy and Bean and Whitehead", however, are not listed in the Table of Cases of "Burrows Reports" (Sir James Burrow, 1701–82). Barnard perhaps made his notes here from oral pleadings. "Massy" is presumably Massey *v.* Rice, a case of common recovery frequently mentioned in Ridgeway's report (*ante* n. 5) and reported by Henry Cowper (1758 - 1840). "Bean" and "Whitehead" are not mentioned by name in Ridgeway, but may be concealed among his citations, the majority of which are merely to reporters (e.g. Cowp. 346).

[9] The letter filled nine sides of two and a half sheets and cost JB eighteenpence.

[10] William Murray, Lord Mansfield (1705–93) and Alexander Wedderburn, Lord Loughborough (1733–1805), both Scots, were respectively Chief Justice of the Court of King's Bench and Chief Justice of the Court of Common Pleas; Sir John Skynner (1724–1805) was Chief

Baron of the Court of Exchequer. James Hewitt, Viscount Lifford (1709–89), had held the Great Seal of Ireland since 1768 and continued in the office till his death, a longer period than any of his predecessors since the time of Edward I.

[10a] MS. "may may"

[11] Lord Mansfield is said to have been Barnard's patron. See *ante* p. xxxi.

[12] This is the last reference in the correspondence as preserved to Barnard's two investigations of the origin of the Scots (*ante* To Barnard, 14 Feb. 1783; From Barnard, 2 Mar. 1783; To Barnard, 28 Mar. 1783; To Barnard, 8 Mar. 1784; From Barnard, 17 Mar. 1784; To Barnard, 14 May 1784; From Barnard, 14 Apr. 1785; To Barnard, 1 July 1785). So far as is known, JB published neither, if indeed Barnard ever sent him the revised copy. The longer work (*ante* From Barnard, 2 Mar. 1783) seems never to have been published as such, but Barnard read a brief statement of his views before

If I did not return you my warmest acknowledgements for what you tell me of remembering me in your will I should Ill deserve so affecting an Instance of your Freindship; which I esteem a very great Honour, I sincerely assure you. But as I am a much older man than yourself, I have only to request that in case I die first as will most probably happen; that Tes⟨ti⟩mony of your Regard may not be Erased. Adieu my Dear Sir, and be assured that I am with the warmest Sentiments of Regard and Esteem your Faithfull and affectionate Servant

THOS. KILLALOE

My Best respects attend the Great and good Genl. Paoli. When we have disposed of the 20 propositions[13] in our Parliament for which we still wait in Dublin; I will send you some Irish News.

To Thomas Barnard, Wednesday 3 August 1785

MS. Yale (L 43). A copy.

HEADING: To the Bishop of Kilaloe.

London, 3 August 1785

MY DEAR LORD: I ask your Lordship's pardon for my inaccuracy in mentioning that I had sent *eight* sheets of my *Journal of a Tour to the Hebrides,* when in fact there were but *seven.* It gives me very great pleasure to know that your Lordship has been entertained with what I have sent. I now send *eleven* sheets more.

the newly formed Royal Irish Academy (*ante* From Percy, 23 Apr. 1785) on 20 Mar. 1786. This paper, "An Enquiry concerning the Original of the Scots in Britain", was printed in the *Transactions* of the Academy, 1787, Section of Antiquities, pp. 25–41.

[13] The Duke of Rutland, Lord Lieutenant of Ireland, and Thomas Orde, his chief secretary, endeavoured to form a commercial union between England and Ireland which would ensure to each an equal participation in the advantages of trade. Eleven resolutions proposed by Orde and passed by the Irish Parliament were submitted by Pitt to the English Parliament on 22 Feb. 1785. They met with formidable opposition from manufacturers. Nearly twelve weeks were spent in hearing evidence against the propositions, and numerous petitions from manufacturing centres were sent to Parliament requesting their rejection. Pitt again brought forward the scheme in May 1785, in the form of twenty resolutions, some of which were greatly to the detriment of Ireland. In spite of opposition, the resolutions passed; they were then returned to the Irish Parliament.

Your Lordship's *Report* of the Ely Cause is so able, that it makes me jealous as a Lawyer. I shall look at the authorities you mention, and shall venture to give my opinion, be what it may, when formed upon due consideration. I however take it for granted that this cause, like our great Douglas Cause,[1] is now irreversibly settled.

For my own credit, as well as the kindly indulgence of my best feelings, your Lordship may be assured that the clause in my Will in which your Lordship, [with grateful acknowledgements, is remembered] never will be erased.[2] My heart glowed while I wrote it.

Sir Joshua Reynolds is gone to the Continent accompanied by Mr. Metcalf, to be present at a great sale of pictures.[3] When he returns I am confident you will hear from him.

May I beg to be informed that the Parcel I now send has come safe. I am impatient now to have the Book compleated. But I am unwilling to hurry the publication so as in any degree to lessen its accuracy.

General Paoli returns your Lordship his best compliments. I have the honour to remain with the greatest regard, My Dear Lord, Your Lordships very faithful and affectionate humble servant.

The note on p. 215 of my *Tour* refers to a confidential

---

[1] On the death of the Duke of Douglas in 1761, Archibald James Edward Douglas (originally Stewart), son of the Duke's sister, Lady Jane Stewart, was served heir to the estate. The Duke of Hamilton (heir male of the Duke of Douglas) disputed Douglas's claim, alleging that he was a spurious child, that he and his twin brother (deceased) were really stolen children. The case occupied the Scottish courts for five years; on 15 July 1767, the Court of Session decided for Hamilton. Douglas appealed to the House of Lords, which reversed the decision in Feb. 1769 and declared him rightful heir to the Douglas estate. JB was active in the cause of Douglas as a volunteer: in addition to writing *Dorando, a Spanish Tale*, 1767, an *ex parte* allegory of the events of Lady Jane's life, and *The Essence of the Douglas Cause*, 1767, he was one of the editors of *The Letters of Lady Jane Douglas*, 1767, which probably had a great effect on public opinion. In July 1769, JB became one of the regular counsel for Douglas (Journ. 7 July).

[2] "Lordship," ends a line in the manuscript. The restoration assumes that JB in copying omitted an entire line.

[3] Philip Metcalfe (1733–1818), a friend of SJ in his later years and one of Reynolds's executors, annoyed JB with his "boisterous puppyism" (Journ. 8 Nov. 1792). JB is reported to have prevented his election to The Club (*Life* iv. 159 n. 2; 505). Reynolds set out for Brussels on 20 July and was back in England the next month. Disappointed by the paintings from the religious houses, he bought none of them at auction. He did, however, purchase a few from private collections (*Lit. Car. Reynolds*, pp. 73–74; and Journ. 19 July and 10 Aug. 1785).

conversation with his Majesty whom I humbly consulted by a Letter upon the delicate question. The King's behaviour did him the highest honour.[4] I shall be exceedingly happy to communicate the particulars to your Lordship when we meet.

From Thomas Barnard, Sunday 14 August 1785

MS. Yale (C 86).

ADDRESS: James Boswell Esqr., General Paolis, Portman Square, London.

FRANK: Free Thos. Killaloe [*erased*].

POSTMARKS: IRELAND, AU 14, 20 AU, [illegible].

Dublin, Augst. 14th.

DEAR SIR: I sit down with pleasure to acknowledge the receipt of Eleven sheets more of your *Journal*, ending at Page 288, which I have read with equal pleasure as the first seven. I confess I feel sorry that the Travellers are brought so far as Dunvegan already,[1] because I dread that the next importation will bring with it the Conclusion of their Journey.

Your Idea of forming a Set of Professors in every Branch of Literature out of the Club of 1773[2] is pleasantly Imagined, and the Parts of every member are as well cast, as could be, Vesey Excepted, who Knew as much of Irish Antiquities as Johnson himself; and as much of Celtick as Japonese. Architecture was really his Fort, which he understood better than any thing else, and had really a very good Taste in it, as well as some Knowledge, and in that Branch there was a Vacancy for him to fill, as the club had then no other adept to rival him.[3] I am glad however that you have

---

[4] JB wrote to the King on 6 June 1785, asking permission to refer in the *Tour* to "that person who in 1745–6 attempted to recover the throne upon which his Ancestors sat" as Prince Charles rather than as the Pretender. On the 15th of that month, at a royal levee, the King indicated a preference for "the Grandson of King James the Second" (Journ.). See *Life* v. 185 n. 4; 531–32; iii. 499–500.

[1] JB and SJ were at Dunvegan from 13 to 21 Sept. 1773. At this point, Barnard had received a little over half the book.

[2] 25 Aug., *Life* v. 108–09.

[3] JB printed this correction in a footnote to his second edition, identifying the author of it merely as "one of the club". R. W. Chapman in his combined edition of SJ's *Journey* and JB's *Tour*, 1924, p. 468, suggested that the informant was Malone, and this identification was

discretely avoided appreciating the respective Talents of the Present Club in the Same Manner. You have wisely taken the sure method to content us all, by Estimating our merit in the Aggregate.

I much Doubt whether poor Mr. Kenneth McAulay will be quite content with the account you give of his Conversation and the Doctors opinion of his Principles and abilities.[4] If you had served me as you did your Fellow Traveller upon the Road to Glenelg, I should have calld after you as Loudly as he did: and thought your Excuse of going on to prepare for his reception a mere Pretext. You confess that you were better mounted than he; and he might naturally enough conclude that you were willing to take advantage of it and get to your Inn as fast as you Could, regardless of the Perilous Situation in which you left him.[5]

Is not Sir Al. Mcdonald the Present Lord Mcdonald? Whoever he be, or however he may deserve the Contrast you have drawn between him and his Deceased Brother, I am afraid he will not give you a better reception at Slate upon your next Visit than you met with at your first.[6] The first Time you go that Circuit when you are Judge you may make the Experiment.

I am greatly pleased with Johnsons Alcaic Latin ode; not quite so much with his Sapphick,[7] for the Versification is rather hard and inharmonious. The Style however of both is truly classical. But there is one Capital Error which I did not think he was capable of Committing. The 2d Syllable of recedunt in the last

---

adopted by subsequent editors until 1961. Barnard's letter, which was among the papers recovered at Malahide in 1940, did not become available to scholars till 1949.

[4] Kenneth Macaulay (1723–79), Lord Macaulay's great-uncle, had been minister of Harris and of Ardnamurchan and in 1773 was minister of Cawdor (*Fasti Scot.* vi. 439; *Life* v. 505). In the published *Tour*, SJ called him "a bigot to laxness", spoke slightingly of his library and his conversation, and expressed doubts as to his really being author of *The History of St. Kilda*, which he had published in 1764 (*Life* v. 118–23). JB probably thought he had justified his frankness by suppressing SJ's other characterization of Macaulay as "crassus homo" and "the

most ignorant booby and the grossest bastard" (Journ. 27 Aug., 23 Sept. 1773).

[5] Barnard thought that JB rode away from SJ while they were still only part way down the difficult western descent of Mam Rattachan. Actually, as the text makes clear, JB did not venture to leave SJ till they had reached level ground (*Life* v. 144–45).

[6] Sir Alexander Macdonald of Sleat (?1745–95) was created Baron Macdonald of Sleat in the Irish peerage on 25 July 1776 (*Comp. Peer.* viii. 339). See *ante* To Langton, 10 Apr. 1774, n. 5, for an account of the visit.

[7] The Alcaic Ode ("upon the *Isle of Sky*") is printed in *Life* v. 155; the Sapphic ("addressed to Mrs. Thrale"), *ibid.* p. 158.

Line which he has made short, is Long Provehimur Ponto, Terræ-que urbesq. recēdunt. Virg. Lib. 3.[8] A false Quantity is what he would not have Pardon'd in another. If I go on with my observations, I shall not leave room on my Paper for other matters. So adieu *Journal* for the present.

Yesterday Our House of Commons divided on the Bill brought in by Mr. Orde to establish the Commercial Settlement with Great B[ritai]n on the Principles of the 20 Propositions; when notwithstanding the moderation with which it was expressed; yet as the Substance of the 4th Proposition obliging us to adopt from time to time the Laws establishd by the British Parliament for the regulation of the Colonial Trade; it was moved to give a Total Negative to the admission of such a Bill, notwithstanding the Commercial advantages it convey'd. The Debate Continued 17 hours; and the Div. was 127 to admit the Bill, 108 to reject it. The Principal La⟨nded⟩ Interest of the Kingdom being in the Minority. Such a Victory ⟨is there⟩fore look'd upon as a Defeat; for the Matter is yet to be dis⟨cussed⟩ on the Merits. What administration will now do is not Kno⟨wn.⟩ But it is thought they must give it up.[9] Thus have We been Duped by the artifices of opposition in England, to make us reject an advantageous Bargain, that they were afraid we should accept. However something must Speedily be adjusted that shall be admissible here; or this Island will not long be connected with Britain. Woodfall attended this Debate, so you will have it quite Correct.[10] I had the Pleasure of meeting Sir William Forbes the other day, who has been the

---

[8] *Aeneid* iii. 72, "Ponto" for "portu".

[9] Barnard is reporting, not the debate and the division on the bill, but merely the debate and division on the prior motion (12 Aug.) for leave to bring it in. The twenty propositions, as passed by the Parliament of Great Britain, were presented to the Irish House of Commons by Secretary Orde on 15 Aug., and met such violent opposition that they were withdrawn, Orde pledging himself that Government "never would, neither in the present session, nor in any future period, agitate the bill, or present it again to the House, unless it was moved for by the Parliament and people of Ireland" (*Journals of the House of Commons of the Kingdom of Ireland*, xxii. 586–87; *Gent. Mag.* lv. 656–57; *London Chronicle*, 18–20 Aug. 1785, lviii. 169, 176). For the text of the fourth proposition, see *Annual Register 1784–1785*, xxvii. 359, or *Parliamentary History of England*, 1815, xxv 708.

[10] William Woodfall (1746–1803), a parliamentary reporter and drama critic noted for his uncommonly retentive memory, was able to write sixteen columns of parliamentary proceedings without having taken a note. He had been invited to Ireland to report the debates on the Commercial Propositions (*Lit. Anec.* i. 303–04).

Tour of Ireland; He was so good as to call on me with Mr. Lees of the Post office, at [whose] house I am to meet him to day at Dinner; He shall bring over to you the Printed Cases of the Ely Cause.[11] I am come from Dinner, to close my Letter. Lord Hillsborough[12] din'd with us and sais that the Bill will be brought into the House of Lords, or at least a Debate upon it, in order to shew that the most respectable branch of the great Landed Interest of Ireland are not against it. All the Party of to Day dine with me on Thursday. I wish you could make one. I am Faithfully and affectionately yours

THOS. KILLALOE

If this finds you in London, assure the good general Paoli of my Constant Esteem and Respect.

To Thomas Barnard, Wednesday 24 August 1785

MS. Yale (L 44). A copy.

HEADING: To The Lord Bishop of Kilaloe.

London, 24 August 1785

MY DEAR LORD: This is only to express the pleasure it gives me to know that my last packets have been so agreable to you, and to beg that your Lordship may not communicate my *Tour* to many people lest the appetite for it should be blunted before publication; and pray do not let it get into the hands of any printer or publisher till you have the whole which I think will make about thirty sheets. There are some leaves to be cancelled, of which your Lordship shall be informed; and others to replace them shall be sent. I am exceedingly fortunate in having my Book revised by

---

[11] Forbes wrote to JB on 16 Sept. telling him of the visit to Barnard, at which time he had made a copy of the original Round Robin (*post* From Barnard, 15 Oct. 1785 and n. 4). This he offered for JB's use; he also told JB that he would hold the Ely Cause papers until he heard that they were wanted.

[12] Wills Hill (1718–93), first Earl of Hillsborough and first Marquess of Downshire, from 1779 to 1782 Secretary of State for the Northern Department. He took an active part in Irish politics, and was considered a good landlord because of the improvements he made on his estate.

Mr. Malone, who has "discreetly blotted"[1] a great deal. I have the honour to remain with great regard, My Dear Lord, Your Lordships faithful and affectionate humble servant

To Thomas Barnard, Friday 23 September 1785

MS. Yale (L 45). A copy.

HEADING: To the Lord Bishop of Kilaloe.

London, 23 Septr. 1785

MY DEAR LORD: Your Lordship will now be pleased to receive the remainder of my *Tour to the Hebrides,* with five leaves to supply those which your Lordship will observe are to be cancelled.[1] I beg that your Lordship may be so good as to cut out those leaves, and let me know that you have burnt them. I happened by chance to meet Lord Macdonald one night at the Haymarket Theatre; my heart relented, and I softened my account of him.[2]

I set out early tomorrow morning northwards, and shall be very happy to have the honour of hearing from your Lordship at Auchinleck Kilmarnock by Portpatrick. I ever am your Lordships truly faithful and affectionate humble servant.

[1] Poets lose half the praise they should
have got,
  Could it be known what they discreetly blot.
(Edmund Waller, "Upon the Earl of Roscommon's Translation of Horace . . . and of the Use of Poetry", ll. 41–42) JB, in *The Hypochondriack,* No. 28, wrongly attributed the quotation to Pope.

[1] The following leaves were cancelled in the first edition of the *Tour:* C_2 (pp. 19–20), C_7 (pp. 29–30), E_3 and E_4 (pp. 53–56), and M_4 (pp. 167–68). The reason for the first two is not clear; Mr. Pottle has suggested that some accident to sheet C at the printer's rendered these pages unusable, thus enabling Malone and JB to polish. E_3 and E_4 were can-

celled because JB realized that he had taken more liberties with his text than he had originally intended to do. M_4 contained part of the record of the stay with Sir Alexander Macdonald (*Lit. Car.* pp. 114–15, corrected by *Tour,* pp. 408, 411–13; A. T. Hazen, "Boswell's Cancels in the 'Tour to the Hebrides'", *Bibliographical Notes & Queries,* 1938, ii. 7).

[2] On 8 Aug., JB "sat in the first row of a stagebox in my scarlet coat. . . . Wondered to feel myself perfectly easy and fashionable. Lord Macdonald was in the box. I felt remorse for having printed so much severity against him; resolved to cancel a leaf and spare him" (Journ.). He had felt some compunction earlier, but had done nothing about it (*ibid.* 13 July).

The false quantity dec*e*dunt for decidunt was owing to my defect in prosody. It is corrected in the Errata.[3]

From Thomas Barnard to Sir William Forbes, Saturday 15 October 1785

MS. Fettercairn Papers, National Library of Scotland. A large portion of the letter has been eaten by rats.

ADDRESS: Sir William Forbes Ba⟨rt⟩., Edinburgh, North Britain, By Donaghadee Packet, Single Sheet.

POSTMARKS: LIM⟨ERICK⟩ IRELAND, OC 21, OC 26.

[Killaloe]

DEAR SIR: It is now about ⟨three weeks since⟩ I was Honour'd with your very ⟨prompt and most⟩ obliging Letter on your Return to ⟨North Britain,⟩ Thanks for which would have been ⟨Conveyed to⟩ you by the next Post, if our Patriots ha⟨d not⟩ of late so Embarrass'd the Epistolary Intercourse between the two Kingdoms as to amount almost to a Prohibition in all Cases where the Writer was Conscious that the Freight was not worth the Charges.[1] On this motive I was weak Enough to Trust a Letter to you into the hands of a gentleman who told me that he was just setting out for Edinburgh and would deliver it to yourself. But to my Surprise and Confusion He ⟨finally sent it ba⟩ck to me (after Keeping it ⟨for two weeks) at⟩ Dublin, acquainting me at ⟨the same time that he⟩ was prevented from putting ⟨his plan into exec⟩ution. If I have not suffer'd in ⟨your regard from⟩ so apparent a neglect, I can for⟨give him this but⟩ not otherwise.

---

[3] The printer's copy for the *Ode* (Yale, M 133 p. 76), a transcript by JB from SJ's autograph, indeed shows an unambiguous *recedunt*. JB's "defect in prosody" was a national shortcoming, Scots boys not being required to compose Latin verses. For a comparable lapse sanctioned by Sir Walter Scott, see J. G. Lockhart's *Scott*, 1839, vii. 274–81. In this case Malone cannot be entirely cleared of blame, for it was he who wrote on JB's transcript (immediately below *recedunt*) the foot-note of variant readings which accompanied the *Ode* in the *Tour*. JB's *decedunt* in the present instance was careless but implies no lack of understanding of SJ's Latin. *Recedunt, recidunt, decedunt, decidunt* (recede, fall back, subside, fall) would all make sense in the context. The Errata to the *Tour* have correctly "For *Recedunt* r. *Recidunt*."

---

[1] Forbes had to pay the postage. See *ante* From Barnard, 14 Apr. 1785, n. 8.

⟨Mrs. Bar⟩nard and I were happy to hear that ⟨you an⟩d Lady Forbes had got home in Health ⟨and⟩ safety after the Perils of so long a Journey, which nothing could have Render'd a Tour of Pleasure, but your own Willingness to be pleased, with every thing you met with. Your Freinds indeed may Call it so with respect to themselves, as it gave us the unexpected Enjoyment of your Company for a few days; Just long enough to make us regret the Loss of it.[2] We look forward however to the flattering hope of renewing our acquaintance in London at a future Time. Perhaps not very Distant.

The Duke of Rutland is ⟨now visiting the corporation⟩ at Limerick, on his Road ⟨to Killarney, being entertained⟩ there these two Days past ⟨with great splendour. I have⟩ not been to pay my Resp⟨ects, but am happy to learn⟩ from the Reports of the Country ⟨Artillery and gleam of⟩ Feux de Joye (Distinctly audible ⟨and visible) that⟩ the City is in an Uproar on the occ⟨asion.[3] At Killaloe,⟩ however, I have the satisfaction to find my⟨self in poli⟩tical Tranquillity; not a Volunteer to be see⟨n anywhere,⟩ no more Talk of the 20 Propositions than if ⟨they⟩ had never been the subject of Debate.

I had a Letter from Mr. Boswell a few days since,[4] with the Remaining sheets of his *Tour to the Hebrides*, and am highly entertain'd with the perusal. I shall sit down to write him my thanks to his Castle of auchinleck by this Post. Adieu My Dear Sir (Mais jusqu'a Revoir) and be assured that I am with Perfect Esteem and Regard your Faithfull and very obedient Servant

THOS. KILLALOE

[2] Writing to JB on 16 Sept., Forbes reported that "Not the least agreeable part of . . . [the trip to Ireland] was our having the Opportunity of being a good deal with our worthy friend the Bishop of Killaloe, whom we had the good fortune to find in Dublin, and who, with Mrs. Barnard, loaded us with every possible degree of kindness and attention. . . . I know not the time when I have spent so many hours so happily as in the worthy Bishop's Company."

[3] "*Extract of a Letter from Limerick, Oct. 16.* Early last Friday the 14th, his Grace the Lord Lieutenant, and the Duchess of Rutland, arrived in this city, when they were waited on by the Mayor,

Sheriffs, and Common Council. . . . At four o'clock his Grace, attended by the Lord Bishop, went to the cathedral church. . . . Yesterday at three o'clock their Graces rode to the King's Island, and were received by the acclamations of thousands of the citizens; the field re-sounded with 'Long live the Duke and Duchess of Rutland,' returned by twelve rounds from the corps of Artillery. . . . Last night there was a brilliant and crowded assembly" (*London Chronicle*, 22–25 Oct. 1785). From Limerick they proceeded to Killarney and Cork. Killaloe is 17 miles north-east of Limerick.

[4] *Ante* To Barnard, 23 Sept.

Mrs. Barnard and Miss Cooper[5] join me in Compliments to you and Lady Forbes and Miss Hay.[6] If Lord Abercorn[7] be still in Scotland I beg you to assure his Lordship of our Constant and unalterd respects, with thanks for his Remembrance.

From Thomas Barnard, Saturday 15 October 1785

MS. Yale (C 87).

ADDRESS: To James Boswell Esqr., Aughinleck, Kilmarnock, North Britain, By way of Portpatrick. Single Sheet.

POSTMARKS: IRELAND, LIMERICK, OC 21.

Killaloe, Octr. 15th. 1785

MY DEAR SIR: Last Saturdays post brought to my hands your Letter of the 23d of September, and the Remaining Sheets of your *Tour to the Hebrides*, which I have read with equal Pleasure and Satisfaction as I did the foregoing part of the Work; It is a high Treat to the Literary Part of the Publick, for which they are much beholden to you and I trust they will repay you both with Fame and Profit. The Subject itself, is as yet by no means a Stale one; and if it had, The agreeable manner in which you have revived it, the new Light in which you have placed it, and the many additional anecdotes and Sallies of Wit and Wisdom, with which you have Embellishd, and Enriched it, have not only render'd *your* Work a Valuable acquisition to the World; but much Enhanced the Worth of the Original Tour: as, I dare say the Proprietors[1] will find to their Benefit.

I cannot punctually comply with your Requisition, by writing you word that I have actually Burn't the offensive Sheets, to which you have sent me the Succedanea, Because the Remainder of your

---

[5] Unidentified. Probably a relative.

[6] Lady Forbes's sister (?Grace), whom JB had entertained several times (*Journ.* 6 Mar. 1778, 25 June 1779).

[7] James Hamilton (1712–89), eighth Earl of Abercorn. Chosen a Scottish Representative Peer in 1761, 1768, 1774, 1780, and 1784, he voted against the repeal of the Stamp Act in 1766 and against Fox's India Bill in 1783 (*Comp. Peer.* i. 6–7). He possessed a large estate in Ireland.

[1] SJ's *Journey to the Western Islands*, published in 1775 by Thomas Cadell the elder (1742–1802) and SJ's friend William Strahan (1715–85), was reprinted in Oct. 1785.

Work, is now Lock'd up in my Desk at Dublin. But I here faithfully promise you that I will immediately obey your orders as soon as I return thither, and that they shall never be seen by mortal Eye except my own. I think you have acted perfectly right in the Alterations you have made, and cannot perceive that the Vigour of that Part of your Narration, will be in any Degree impair'd by this Castration.

I am a little angry with you for a Short note you sent me some time ago, cautioning me not to trust your Work into the Hands of Booksellers. Did you mistrust my Understanding, or my Integrity? For I must have been a Rogue, or a Fool, to have been Capable of realizing your apprehensions. But I forgive you; and at the same time tell you, that I have been So carefull to prevent any ill consequences from the Confidence you reposed in me, that Though I have read your sheets to many, I have never Suffer'd them to go out of my hands except to Lord Charlemont and Mr. Tighe;[2] and then for so Short a Time as to make Transcription Impracticable. I have been beating my Brains to no purpose to find anecdotes or aphorisms to enrich your Life of Johnson, and can think of none but such as I am sure you are in Possession. Except an Expression of his in Praise of the Irish Nation, deliverd to myself in a Conversation above ten years ago soon after the Publication of his Tour to Scotland. When Speaking of his Taking another Tour to Ireland as a thing not impossible; I said that I did not Know whether we ought to wish for his Company; as from the Severity of his observations on the Scots, we had reason to dread a Similar, or perhaps a still less Favourable representation of our Manners and character. *"Sir"* Sais he *"you have no reason to be afraid of me. The Irish are not in a Conspiracy to cheat the World by false Representations of the merits of their Countrymen: No Sir; the Irish are a Fair People. I never heard them Speak well of one another."*[3] These were as nearly his words as I can recollect. But how pleasing it may be to either Nation to publish them, I leave to your Judgement.

The Round Robin we sent to him from Sir J. Reynolds's to persuade him to alter Goldsmiths Epitaph;[4] might be an anecdote

---

[2] Possibly William Tighe, Esq. of Woodstock, M.P. for Wicklow. He died in 1819 (John Burke, *Commoners of Great Britain and Ireland* iii. 1836, 514). Mary Tighe, the poetess (*Psyche*), was his niece and daughter-in-law.

[3] Printed in *Life* ii. 307.

[4] For JB's account of the Round Robin

so far worthy of notice, as it serves to shew how much he was fear'd by his most Intimate Freinds; who, tho' they agreed in their gaieté de Coeur to pen a Remonstrance against his Composition, yet no one of the Company had the Courage to present it, or even to appear as a Ring leader in the Transaction. Sir William Forbes took the Copy of the original Round Robin when he was in Dublin at my house; and will give you all the particulars of the Business, (being then one ⟨of⟩ the Subscribing parties) if you think it worthy of I⟨nclusion.⟩ We have lately made a very Curious Discovery in the neighbourhood, in the Line of antiquities, which will soon Engage the attention of the Celtick antiquarians. The Ogham or antient Irish Character antecedent to St. Patrick, tho' Spoken of in Books, has by late writers been treated as problematical, and its advocates challenged to produce any undoubted inscription of that Kind.[5] The challenge has been unanswer'd for near a Century past. But this Summer a Young man of the West of the County of Clare said that he had seen a Stone with such sort of writing on it on the Banks of a Lake in that neighbourhood among the mountains far from any road, and almost cover'd with heath. He was desired to go again to the Spot and take a Gentleman who resided in the Neighbourhood and was a man of Letters, with him which he did, and they discoverd

see *Life* iii. 82–85. In the first edition of the *Life* (vol. ii, facing p. 92) he included an engraved facsimile of the document, taken from Barnard's original; a photographic reproduction of this facsimile faces p. 83 in *Life* iii. The original, now in the possession of the Earl of Crawford and Balcarres, was reproduced by photography for Hill's edition of the *Life* (1887, iii. 82). A copy in Forbes's hand is at Yale.

[5] Ogham writing was an alphabet or cipher used in inscribing the ancient Irish language on stone monuments from perhaps the middle of the fifth century to the early part of the seventh century A.D. In its simplest form it consists of four sets of straight strokes or scratches with five characters (each character consisting of one, two, three, four, or five strokes respectively) in each set, incised on an extended straight stem-line which may either be drawn down the middle of the stone or be one of its edges. One, two, three, four, or five strokes perpendicular to the stem-line and below it (or to the right of it) form respectively the letters b, l, v, s, n; the same strokes above (or to the left) the letters h, d, t, c, q; the same crossing the base-line perpendicularly, the letters a, o, u, e, i, and the same crossing the stem-line slashwise, the letters m, g, ng, z, r. See R. A. S. Macalister, *The Archaeology of Ireland*, 2nd ed., 1949, pp. 328–30; Kenneth Jackson, "Notes on the Ogam Inscriptions of Southern Britain", in Sir Cyril Fox and Bruce Dickins, ed., *The Early Cultures of North-west Europe*, 1950, pp. 199–213. As Barnard says, the key to the Ogham alphabet had never been lost, but in 1785 no authoritative corpus of ancient inscriptions existed. The present inscription was in fact the first Ogham inscription on stone to be published.

the Stone as described.[6] It is about eleven feet in Length and Three in Breadth. The Inscription was contain'd in a Long pannel cut out in the Center Thus[7] [consisting of a Long Line cut perpendicularly with shorter ones of various Lengths] which is the Ogham Character as given by Ware[8] and others, together with the Key of it, so that the reading was quite easy as to the Letters, which in the English Character are as follow. F: A N L I D A F I C A C O N A F C O L G A C C O S [O] B M D A *Fan Li da fica Conaf colgac cosobmda*, in English, "Beneath this Stone is Laid Conaf the Fierce, the Swift footed." This might have satisfied an Incurious Reader; But on Reading the same letters Backwards from Right to Left the following words appeard. Adm̃, bo socc, ag Loc, F̤a̤n o̤ca, cifa Dil naf, which in English signifies, "Let him rest at Ease, by the Brink of the Lake under this Oca dear to the Sacred." This double reading verifies in a peculiar the Tradition of the character of this ogham; that it was confined to the Secret and mysterious writings of the Druids. And what makes the Inscription more curious is that the Party, Conaf, was one of the antient Heroes of the Third Century, Cotemporary with Oscar the grandson of Fingal murder'd as Tradition, and antient Manuscripts relate, and afterwards Buried by the Druids. My Paper will not furnish Room for more Particulars; but next winter the publick will be in possession of them.[9] The Stone is un-

---

[6] The young man was Theophilus O'Flanagan, a student of Trinity College, Dublin; the stone was found on Mount Callan, about five miles from Milltownmalbay, Co. Clare; and the gentleman residing in the neighbourhood was Edward William Burton, Esq., of Clifden (*The Transactions of the Royal Irish Academy*, 1787, "Antiquities", pp. 3–16). See n. 9.

[7] Barnard's sketch does not reproduce the actual strokes of the inscription but seems only to have been intended to give a general notion of what it looked like. See the plates, *ibid.*, following p. 16; *Archaeologia*, 1785, vii. 281; also, R. R. Brash, *The Ogam inscribed Monuments of the Gaedhil*, 1879, pp. 297–98; and Brian O'Looney in Sir Samuel Ferguson,

"On the Ogham-inscribed Stone on Callan Mountain, Co. Clare", in *Proceedings of the Royal Irish Academy*, (Antiquities), 1879, 2nd ser. i. 170.

[8] Sir James Ware (1594–1666), Irish antiquary and historian, who was largely responsible for the establishment of Irish history and literature as subjects of study in modern times. For his discussion of Ogham, see *The Whole Works of Sir James Ware Concerning Ireland*, 1764, ii. 19–22.

[9] Barnard refers to "An Account of an Antient Inscription in Ogam Character . . . discovered by Theophilus O'Flanagan. . . . Communicated by the Rev. William Hamilton", which was read before the Royal Irish Academy on 19 Dec. 1785 and collected in 1787 (see

doubtedly genuine and is in my Neighbourhood.[10] Adieu my Dear Sir, give me the Satisfaction of hearing from you when you have Leisure, and believe me to be Faithfully and affectionately Yours

THOS. KILLALOE

n. 6). He seems not to have known that an earlier account communicated by O'Flanagan to Col. Charles Vallency in a letter dated 20 Apr. 1784 had been read by Vallency before the Society of Antiquaries of London on 24 June 1784 and published in *Archaeologia*, 1785, vii. 276–85 (this volume reviewed in *Gent. Mag.* June 1785, lv. 465–67). Both these articles differ from Barnard in giving the name as "Conan", not "Conaf". (Properly "Conav", for present-day Oghamists transliterate as V the character which mediaeval copies of the alphabet render as F. See R. A. S. Macalister, *Corpus inscriptionum insularum Celticarum*, 1945, i. v.) "Conan" was important to O'Flanagan's account, for he says he was moved to hunt for this particular stone because he had read in an ancient Irish poem, *The Battle of Gabhra*, that there was on Mount Callan a sepulchral monument of the Fenian hero Conan, inscribed in Ogham characters. Vallency's plate, presumably based on some kind of sketch sent by O'Flanagan, does in fact show the Ogham characters for "Conan", but the plate accompanying the Irish Academy article, which was engraved from a sketch made by Mr. Burton (a skilled draughtsman), though transliterated "Conan", really reads "Conaf"; and as "Conaf" the name has since been read by a series of responsible archaeologists (Brash, as in n. 7; Brian O'Looney, for Sir Samuel Ferguson, as in n. 7; T. J. Westropp, "Notes on Certain Primitive Remains ... in ... Co. Clare", in *Journal of the Royal Society of Antiquaries of Ireland*, 1917, xlvi. 106). Barnard's "Conaf" can hardly be independent, and surely means that he is following an early version of O'Flanagan's paper. By the time the article was read (or at least by the time it was printed), O'Flanagan had discovered three additional ways of reading the inscription. Of his five readings, four depended on a licence of "commuting the letters F and N, wherever they occur, as the sense shall direct", and one required that the inscription be turned upside down.

[10] The genuineness of the stone was contested from the first, and it has been maintained that the verses which it appeared to corroborate are a modern interpolation. For a summary of the controversy, with full references, see T. J. Westropp, as in n. 9 *ante*, pp. 105–07. R. A. S. Macalister does not admit the inscription to his *Corpus inscriptionum insularum Celticarum*. He says (i. 56), "No notice need be taken here of this inscription, except as a tribute to its notoriety. It professes to be the tomb of the warrior Conan, said in an Irish 'poem' of no very great antiquity to have been slain on Mount Callan, at an assembly convened for sun-worship, and there buried under a stone inscribed in Ogham. Beyond all question it is an eighteenth century forgery." It is theoretically possible to read Ogham backwards and forwards and either side up, as O'Flanagan did, but the poetic, not to say Macphersonese, content of the Callan Mountain inscription is highly suspicious. If it were genuine, it would be *sui generis* among over five hundred ancient Ogham inscriptions now recorded in the British Isles. In general, these consist merely of a personal name or of a name with some kind of pedigree, the commonest type being a name in the genitive case followed by a patronymic: *Doveti maqqi Cattini*, "of Dovetos, son of Cattinos" (No. 157). Furthermore, the "Irish" of O'Flanagan's readings is extraordinary in accidence, syntax, and vocabulary (R. A. S. Macalister, *Studies in Irish Epigraphy*, 1897, i. 12; ii. 95–96).

From Thomas Warton,
Saturday 5 November 1785

MS. Yale (C 3071).

ADDRESS: To James Boswell Esq., at Mr. Dilly's Bookseller,[1] in the Poultry, London.

POSTMARKS: 57 OXFORD, 7 NO.

Trin. Coll. Oxon., Nov. 5, 1785

DEAR SIR, As I am informed[2] that you mean to print a Collection of Dr. Johnson's Letters by way of Appendix to his *Life*, I take the liberty to acquaint you, that I have about twenty of Dr. Johnson's Letters written to me in the years 1755, 1756. If you wish to print them, I will transcribe and send them to you. They are short, but I think they should not be witheld from the Public; and they illustrate a part of his Life when he conversed but little with the world. I am, Dear Sir, Your most obedient humble servant

THOS. WARTON

To Thomas Barnard,
Tuesday 8 November 1785

MS. Yale (L 46). A copy.

HEADING: To the Bishop of Kilaloe.

Edinburgh, 8 Novr. 1785

MY DEAR LORD: Being here but for a day or two to arrange my books and papers before removing to London, I have only time to thank your Lordship for your last very obliging letter (containing more of your much-valued compliments on my *Tour*, and a very curious discovery in irish antiquities) and to give your

[1] Charles Dilly. His brother Edward had died in 1779.

[2] Possibly from the first edition of JB's *Journal of a Tour to the Hebrides*, in which, in an advertisement following p. 524, he discussed the materials for SJ's life: "With these will be interwoven . . . a great number of letters from him at different periods." In the second edition (1785), Warton is one of those thanked in the expanded advertisement for "valuable communications" (following p. 534).

Lordship the trouble of ordering a correction to be made in the irish edition of my Book, in case it be not printed off before this reaches Dublin.

I have had much uneasiness on account of young Mr. Tytler[1] who is mentioned on p. 485–6, in a manner which it seems hurts him much. I solemnly declare he told me last winter he had no objection to my inserting the passage. But unluckily he has totally forgotten this; and I have with some difficulty satisfied him that I did not intend to injure or affront him.

The correction I am to make is etc.[2]

Your Lordship will have the goodness to forgive me for taking so much liberty with you, as to beg that you may send some person to find out who it is that is reprinting my Book in Dublin,[3] so that if it be not too late the correction may be made.

[1] Alexander Fraser Tytler (1747–1813), later raised to the bench as Lord Woodhouselee, expressed a belief that *Fingal* was genuine because he had heard a great part of it repeated in the original, and was forced by SJ to admit that he had no Gaelic. "Did you observe," said SJ afterwards to JB, "the wonderful confidence with which young Tytler advanced, with his front ready *brased?*" (*Life* v. 388 n. 2). JB, after agreeing to alterations proposed by Tytler, had tried unsuccessfully through the mediation of Professor Dugald Stewart to get Tytler to apologize for expressions in his first angry letter of complaint. After arriving in London, JB consulted Edmond Malone and John Courtenay, who told him that a written apology was absolutely necessary. Several more letters passed before the affair was settled to the satisfaction of both parties. See Journ. 18, 30 Nov. 1785, and correspondence (twelve letters) between Stewart, Tytler, and JB, 14 Oct.–1 Dec. 1785; also Claire Lamont, "James Boswell and Alexander Fraser Tytler", *The Bibliotheck* (1971), vi. 1–16.

[2] See *Life* v. 388 and n. 2 for the text both as originally printed and as amended. J. C. Walker, writing to JB from Dublin on 13 Nov. 1785, reported that the Irish edition of the *Tour* had gone on sale the previous day. On 31 Dec. 1785

he wrote, "White [see the note following this], by direction of a learned friend of yours, has softened the Anecdote of young Tytler in the remaining Copies. I am happy to possess it in its pristine state." The "softening" could have been accomplished only by a cancel leaf (I i ₃, pp. 485–86). The Yale copy of the book, like Walker's, shows the "pristine state".

[3] The Irish edition was published in Dublin by Messrs. White, Byrne, and Cash. They were also among the eight Dublin booksellers for whom the Irish edition of Mason's translation of du Fresnoy's *Art of Painting* (1783) was printed. Luke White (1740–1824), starting life as the servant of an auctioneer of books, "is said to have realised the largest fortune ever made by trade in Ireland" (*Annual Register*, 1854, p. 330). He bought and sold libraries, imported books from the Continent, and was one of the booksellers authorized by Government to sell tickets in the Irish State Lottery. He published an annual catalogue from at least 1780, and in 1786 brought out *The Complete Dublin Catalogue of Books ... printed in Ireland*, listing several thousand titles of which he offered to sell all that were in print. He published SJ's *Lives of the Poets* in 1779. In 1803 he offered through the

I do not enclose this to Mr. Lees, being uncertain if he be yet returned to Dublin.[4] I shall have the honour of writing to your Lordship fully from London, and I ever am with great respect and affection, My Dear Lord, Your Lordships very faithful humble servant.

P.S. If the Book should be all printed off, I beg that the obnoxious passage may be cancelled, and the leaf reprinted at my expence.

To Thomas Warton, Friday 18 November 1785

MS. Yale (L 1273). A copy.

HEADING: To The Rev. Mr. Tho. Warton.

London, 18 Novr. 1785

REVEREND SIR: I arrived here yesterday, and this day found at Mr. Dilly's your letter which was lying for me.

I am very much obliged to you for your kind offer of Dr. Johnson's letters to you, which I thankfully accept, and shall be glad to have them as soon as you can conveniently let me have them, as my plan is to carry on his Life chronologically, with letters interweaved. I am with great regard, Dear Sir, Your much obliged humble servant

Lord Lieutenant to lend Government £500,000 at five per cent., half paid down, half in two months. He was High Sheriff of Co. Dublin, 1804, and of Co. Longford, 1806; M.P. for Leitrim, 1812–24. He purchased the estate of Luttrelstown from the Earl of Carhampton, in whose family it had been since the time of Henry VI. His son Henry (1789–1873) was created Baron Annaly in the peerage of the United Kingdom, 1863 (*Burke's Peerage*, 1953, s.v. Annaly; *Comp. Peer.* s.v. Annaly; A. J. C. Hare, *The Story of two Noble Lives*, 1893, i. 13–15; information gathered from Dublin newspapers by Professor R. C. Cole).—Patrick Byrne, bookseller and stationer in College Green, also a buyer and seller of libraries, joined White in 1785 in publishing SJ's *Poems*.—John Cash, bookseller with a shop in Capel Street, was also authorized to sell lottery tickets. His name appears in the newspapers more frequently than for the publishing or selling of books (R. C. Cole, as above in this note).

[4] See *ante* From Barnard, 14 Apr. 1785.

From Thomas Warton,
Saturday 19 November 1785

MS. Yale (C 3072).

ADDRESS: To James Boswell Esq., at Mr. Dilly's, Bookseller in the Poultry, London.[1]

POSTMARKS: 57 OXFORD, 22 NO.

Trin. Coll. Oxon., Nov. 19th, 1785

DEAR SIR: You shall receive Dr. Johnson's Letters to me, before the sixteenth day of next Month. I hope I do not mention too late a day; and am with true regard, Dear Sir, Your most obedient humble servant

THOS. WARTON

To John Courtenay,
Thursday 8 December 1785

MS. Yale (L 385). A copy kept by JB (L 386) shows only one substantive difference.

ADDRESS: To John Courtenay Esq.

Portman Square, 8 Decr. 1785

MY DEAR SIR: I now send you the whole series of the correspondence concerning the disagreable affair between Lord Macdonald and me,[1] in which I am conscious of no intentional wrong, though there may have been inadvertency; and therefore having done all I possibly could as a Gentleman to conciliate, I

[1] A signed message of six lines, written on the back of the letter while it was still unopened, has been carefully covered by JB with deleting scrawls. It reads, "Mr. Dilly wishes to see Mr. Boswell when he has occasion to come to Mr. Baldwin's office and will be at home in the afternoon and thro the Evening— Weds. 23d Nov." Calling at Dilly's on the 24th, JB was introduced to Richard Cumberland (Journ.).

[1] For a complete account of this "disagreable affair", see BP xvi. 139–45, 221–59 (where all the related letters and documents are printed), and Lit. Car.

pp. 117–18. Because of a number of unflattering passages printed in the Tour dealing with his penuriousness and his inadequacies as a person and as a landlord (see, for instance, Life v. 148 n. 1, 149, 150 n. 3, 157 n. 2, 161, 279, 315–16, and 415 n. 4), Lord Macdonald (Sir Alexander Macdonald at the time of SJ's and JB's tour) on 26 Nov. wrote to JB an "abusive" letter. After consulting with Courtenay, General Paoli, Malone, and William Bosville, JB decided to ignore the letter; but he "wrote a letter to Mr. Bosville (not at all referring to it) begging of him as a common friend to tell Lord Macdonald that I had some weeks

beg² you may at once bring the business to a crisis for I am resolved it shall not hang on. With every sentiment of esteem and gratitude I am, My Dear Sir, Your much obliged and faithful humble servant

JAMES BOSWELL

From Lord Macdonald through John Courtenay, Friday 9 December 1785

MS. Yale (C 1832).

ENDORSEMENT in Courtenay's hand: No. 7.¹ Lord Macdonald's Answer— 9th Decembr. 1785.

[London] Decembr. 9th. 1785

"Lord Macdonald does not choose to publish Mr. Boswell's Letter to Mr. Bosville,² not being at liberty to put to the press abstract Correspondence."

Copy'd from Lord Macdonald's *hand writing*.

J. COURTENAY

before entirely of my own accord left out some passages which might be disagreable to him". Bosville complied with JB's request and reported that "there would be no more of it" (Journ. 28 Nov. 1785). On 6 Dec., however, Courtenay informed JB that he thought it possible that Lord Macdonald might show, or even publish, his letter to JB; therefore he and Malone advised JB to make sure, before he left for Scotland, that such a procedure was forestalled. JB wrote a note to this purpose, and the next day Courtenay took it to Lord Macdonald, who wanted time to consider it. On the 8th, Courtenay returned to Lord Macdonald who dictated to him a long but unsatisfactory message. Courtenay and Malone advised JB to write another paper, which Courtenay was to take to Macdonald the next day. The letter printed here is, then, in a sense, JB's formal appointment of Courtenay as his second. The documents he encloses are Macdonald's original letter to JB, JB's note to Macdonald in which he indicates

that this letter should not be shown or published, the long message dictated to Courtenay by Lord Macdonald, JB's second paper (written on the 8th), and a copy of JB's letter to William Bosville.

² L 386 (mistakenly), "have done all I possibly could as a Gentleman to conciliate. I beg"

¹ The documents pertaining to this affair were all numbered either by JB, Courtenay, or Malone. JB enclosed all the papers in a wrapper, endorsed "Papers Between Lord Macdonald and Mr. Boswell", and gave them to Malone, who numbered the unnumbered ones, added "No. 1 to No. 15 inclusive" to JB's wrapper and folded them in a second wrapper endorsed, "Papers between Lord Macdonald and Mr. Boswell delivered to me by Mr. Boswell. Edmond Malone. No. 1 to No. 15 inclusive." See BP xvi. 257. It is not known how the packet came back into JB's archives.

² In his letter to Macdonald, written on 8 Dec. and delivered on the 9th, JB

To John Courtenay,
Saturday 10 December 1785

MS. Yale (L 387).

ADDRESS: To John Courtenay Esq.

ENDORSEMENT: No answer having been sent by Lord Macdonald on friday, Mr. Boswell waited till eleven o'clock on saturday forenoon and then wrote to Mr. Courtenay as follows. No. 9 Letter Mr. Boswell to Mr. Courtenay.

[London] 10 Decr. 1785

DEAR SIR: I sent a note to Lord Macdonald yesterday requesting an explicit answer at five o'clock,[1] but have received none at eleven this morning.

I beg therefore that you will be pleased to wait on his Lordship with the enclosed papers.[2] I am, Dear Sir, your faithful humble servant

JAMES BOSWELL

enclosed "a copy of the letter written by him to Mr. Bosville dated Novr. 28 which Lord Macdonald may communicate in any manner his Lordship pleases, provided that no use publick or private is to be made of the unsigned letter sent by Lord Macdonald to Mr. Boswell." The letter to Bosville "contained an admission that he had overstepped the bounds of propriety in printing certain of the reflections on Macdonald, that he had deleted those passages in the second edition, and that he was sorry they had ever appeared" (BP xvi. 244).

[1] Not understanding Lord Macdonald's reference to "abstract Correspondence" in the message sent to him by Courtenay (previous letter), JB had written to Macdonald, on 9 Dec., at 4 p.m., "to know . . . whether his *sole* objection to his proposition is, that the letter is addressed to Mr. Bosville, and not to Lord Macdonald himself. . . . He hopes and expects

that Lord Macdonald will favour him with an immediate and explicit Answer, which his Lordship will be pleased to send to Berners Street No. 7 where Mr. Boswell will send for it at five o'clock."

[2] A challenge to a duel (facsimile in BP xvi. 248) which Courtenay was to present to Macdonald if he failed to comply with JB's request, and a letter dated 10 Dec. "eleven o'clock forenoon" which stated JB's position and concluded as follows: "Such being the state of the case between Lord Macdonald and Mr. Boswell, it is for his Lordship to consider that if he refuses to comply with the reasonable condition of making no use publick or private of his letter to Mr. Boswell, Mr. Boswell must understand that his Lordship means to asperse him by shewing it; and therefore Lord Macdonald lays him under the absolute necessity of asserting his honour in the only way which his Lordship has left him."

To John Courtenay,
Monday 12 December 1785

MS. Yale (L 388).

ENDORSEMENT by Edmond Malone: No. 13.

[London] Monday Morning, Decr. 12, 11 o'clock

DEAR SIR: I must request the favour of you once more to wait on Lord Macdonald, and desire an explicit answer to my requisition of the 10th instant; that his Lordship should "make no use publick or private of his letter to me of the 26th November."

The letter of the 11th instant addressed by his Lordship to you, which you were so obliging as to communicate to me last night, contains in my apprehension no answer whatever to that requisition.

His Lordship was pleased to say in a paper delivered by him to you on saturday last,[1] that he should "deliberate upon my paper of that day and take advice upon it from his confidential friends." I observe that in his letter to you, his Lordship mentions that "he has consulted a friend"; and after an attentive examination of every part of his letter to you, the only paragraph that I can find relative to the subject of my note of Saturday the 10th instant is that in which his Lordship declares his willingness to obliterate and consign to oblivion certain passages of his letter of the 26th of November.[2]

If any passages *could* be expunged from a letter written and delivered a forthnight ago, it would cease to be the same letter.

It is not necessary for me to point out the injurious parts of

---

[1] 10 Dec. 1785, From Lord Macdonald through John Courtenay.

[2] JB refers to the first paragraph of Macdonald's letter: "In consequence of the resolution which I had taken yesterday morning to conferr with a friend upon the Subject of the writing delivered me by you from Mr. Boswell; I laid before him the proceedings at large upon the Business, which I had not done before. Having accurately weighed my original Letter—he said he saw no necessity for me to insist upon retaining publishing or exposing some passages which I had inserted relative to my disbelief of the Conversation alledged by Mr. Boswell to have passed between Dr. Johnson and me—Complimenting Mr. Boswell upon his Memory and the delicacy of his feelings and conscience, he said the Passages were too ridiculous in themselves to occasion any warmth or Controversy—I feel no difficulty in expunging them from the Letter in question, although I do not on my conscience recollect any thing of a like nature to have passed upon that occasion."

that letter which have laid me under the necessity of requiring what I have done. His Lordship is certainly at liberty in any letter of *a new date* addressed to me or any other person, or in any other mode that he shall think proper,—to avail himself of any observations in his letter of the 26 of November on me or my Journal, provided they are expressed in terms not personally injurious to the feelings of a man of honour.

But if his Lordship should still decline to comply with my requisition I have once more to request you to communicate to his Lordship the contents of that paper of the 10th instant which yet remains in your hands,[3] substituting only the date of this day for that of the 10th.

I have the honour to be with great regard, Dear Sir, your much obliged and faithful humble servant

JAMES BOSWELL

From John Courtenay,
Tuesday 13 December 1785

MS. Yale (C 835). Written on a blank side of the preceding letter.

Lord Macdonald, means to leave out the *scratched* passages in the Original letter. of the 26 Novembr. to Mr. Boswell which may be deemed as personal; Consequently—the Ostensible letter which will be receiv'd by Mr. Boswell,—will be the *only* record, which his Lordship means (either public or private) to make Use of, in Answer to Mr. Boswells Remarks in his *Tour*—Lord Macdonald has of himself oblitera[te]d some additional passages, which He thought, might be misconstrued.—

[3] The challenge. Courtenay was not required to deliver it, for it was decided that Lord Macdonald's agreement to expunge certain passages to be marked by Courtenay was adequate satisfaction. In his last letter to Courtenay, dated 13 Dec., Lord Macdonald stated that he had "of himself obliterated certain passages which he apprehends might be misconstrued, and from motives of reciprocal Courtesy agrees to leave out in his second Edition [a witty gibe at JB's revisions in the *Tour*] some few passages which came scratched to hand in the original Letter to Mr. Boswell. Consequently the ostensible Letter will be the only surviving record which Lord Md. means at any time to use either publicly or privately in answer to Mr. Boswell's remarks upon him in his first Edition of a tour to the Hebrides. Lord Macdonald now positively closes this business leaving Mr. Boswell to attend the call of his friends in Scotland."

227

From Thomas Warton,
Thursday 22 December 1785

MS. Yale (C 3073).

ADDRESS: To James Boswell Esq., at Mr. Dilly's, Bookseller in the Poultry, London.

POSTMARKS: 57 OXFORD, 23 DE.

Trin. Coll. Oxon. Dec. 22, 1785

DEAR SIR: I shall be in town within a fortnight, when I will bring the Letters with me. But if wanted sooner, I will send them almost immediately.—In the mean time, I am to beg pardon for not sending them before the 16th instant, according to promise. But the hurry of an Election (in which I have succeeded)[1] deranged everything. I hope you will admitt this excuse; and am, Dear Sir, Your most obedient Servant

T. WARTON

P.S. Excuse my awkward direction of this—I know not your address exactly.[2]

To Thomas Warton,
Monday 27 February 1786

Not reported. Sent from London 27 Feb. "Rev. Mr. Tho. Warton begging he may now send me his letters from Dr. Johnson" (Reg. Let.).

From Thomas Warton,
Monday 27 February 1786

MS. Yale (C 3074). Received 3 Mar. "Rev. Mr. Tho. Warton, that

[1] Warton was elected Camden Professor of History at Oxford on 1 Dec., according to the Convocation Register for that date.

[2] JB had apparently not given Warton the address at which he was actually staying (General Paoli's, No. 1 Portman Square) because he was in a state of painful indecision as to fixing in London, and felt less compunction about asking Dilly to take in valuable papers than to put the burden on the General. The Macdonald affair having been settled and the last sheets of the second edition of the *Tour* having been revised, he had left for Scotland on the day that Warton dated his letter, hoping that Mrs. Boswell would help him make up his mind (Journ.).

Dr. Johnson's Letters to him are to be at Mr. Hamiltons (late Printer) Bedford Row on monday or tuesday next" (Reg. Let.).

ADDRESS: To James Boswell Esq., London.

Oxon., Feb. 27th, 1786

DEAR SIR: You will receive the Papers on Monday or Tuesday next, by the hands of Mr. Hamilton[1] (late Printer) of Princes street Bedford Row.

I am exceedingly obliged to you for the Present of your most entertaining *Tour*. I was very unfortunate in not finding you in town.[2] I am with great Regard, Dear Sir, your most faithful and obedient servant

T. WARTON

To Richard Burke the Younger, Saturday 18 March 1786

MS. copy in JB's hand in the records of the Grand Court of the Northern Circuit (The Crown Court, Liverpool), the entire text within quotation marks, which are ignored below. "The Grand Court is holden with a view to the discipline of the Bar, but chiefly in the High Jinks fashion, to bring mock charges against the members" (Lord Campbell, *Lives of the Lord Chancellors and Keepers of the Great Seal of England*, 8th ed., 1880, viii. 381 n. 2). JB's draft, containing some variations and dated 20 Mar., is at Yale (L 336). Only the most interesting variants are reported.

York, 18 March 1786

MY DEAR SIR: Your farewell letter addressed to "John Wilson Esq. Northern Circuit" was read by me to the Grand Court, with an audible, but faultering voice;[1] as indeed from the tenderness

---

[1] Archibald Hamilton the elder (?1719–93), who started *The Critical Review* and printed Smollett's *Compleat History of England*, was a friend of JB. In addition to a villa at Ash in Hampshire, he had a town residence in Bedford Row, where he died in his 74th year (*Lit. Anec.* iii. 398–99).

[2] JB had been in Edinburgh from 28 Dec. 1785 to 27 Jan. 1786. Since 1 Feb., he had been in London (*Journ.*).

[1] Young Burke, who had been a member of the Northern Circuit (of which JB was now the junior member), had just written to the Senior announcing that he had removed to the Oxford Circuit. In JB's hand in the records of the Grand Court of the Northern Circuit appears the following: "The Junior was requested to read it to the Court which he did accordingly, and it was ordered to be entered on

of your own feelings you may conceive how we were affected upon being informed that we had lost you.[2]

Such was the melting musick of your pathetick periods that even the knotty oak Old Lignum[3] himself seemed to weep like one of Phaeton's sisters after they were turned into trees. *Our "Withers"*[4] were *not* "unwrung with grief"; dejection was visible even in the bluff countenance of Sir John Cockell;[5] and a general cloud hung over the whole legal hemisphere.

the records. Follows the tenor thereof.

'To John Wilson Esq. Northern Circuit.

'Dear Wilson

'If I recollect right (and I think my memory is not likely to fail me in this instance) it was in your company that I first went the northern circuit, and for that reason seemed to myself to be introduced to it by you, and under your patronage. I make a much less agreable use of your friendship, in begging you to be the instrument of my farewell. I never shall forget that I once made part of so respectable a body. My fortunes now call me a different way; but wherever they call me, I shall always recollect with a satisfaction mixed with regret, the many agreable hours I passed amongst you: but I shall recollect with an unmixed satisfaction the many valuable and pleasant acquaintances the northern circuit brought within my reach, and I shall always desire to cultivate them. The time is approaching which brings *you* all together in the Grand Northern Court. I might once have said *us*; and indeed if I am rightly instructed, allegiance is indelible by any change of place and circumstance. I am sure that of true affection is so, and by *that* I am still bound to the northern circuit. May I beg therefore that though I have no longer a strict right, and cannot avail myself of my privileges, and am utlegatus [*properly* utlagatus, *outlaw*] homo, may I beg that from old regard I may be permitted to be considered as virtually present, and thus to renew my oath of fealty [and] homage. I have only to add my request to be remembered to all the gentlemen of the circuit, individually and generally, and according to the old mode to return many thanks for all favours.

'We have hitherto had a pretty good circuit. Nothing however has happened which it would be much entertainment to you to be made acquainted with. Believe me to be Dear Wilson your ever affectionate and obliged humble servant (signed) Richd. Burke

'Worcester, March 12, 1786.'

"The Junior was requested to write an Answer to the aforesaid letter, and the same was ordered to be entered in the records." The Senior, John Wilson (1741–93), had been called to the bar in 1766 and joined the Northern Circuit the next year. Appointed judge to fill a vacancy in the Court of Common Pleas, he was knighted on 15 Nov. 1786.

[2] Draft, "so amiable a brother"

[3] George Wood (1743–1824), later a judge. From 1796 to 1806, he was M.P. for Haslemere, Surrey. In 1807, he was appointed a Baron of the Exchequer and knighted.

[4] William Withers, one of the counsel on the Northern Circuit; he appears to have resided at York (*Browne's General Law List*, ed. John Browne, 1790, pp. 224, 288). He was 25 in 1772 and was called to the Bar of the Society of Lincoln's Inn 26 Nov. 1773 (*Calendar of the Inner Temple Records*, 1926, v. 279, 301).

[5] JB is jocular both here and in the list of counsel ("Sir J. Cockell") he recorded as present at the York Grand Night, Lent Assizes, 18 Mar. 1786. There was at the time no knight or baronet named Cockell. "Sir John Cockell" was undoubtedly William Cockell, whom JB saw admitted serjeant-at-law a year later (Journ. 7 May

But you know, My Dear Sir, (and happy it is that we can with truth say so) that Melancholy cannot last long with *us*; and I am sure your benevolence will be pleased when you are informed that we soon resumed that merriment which is the genius of the northern circuit, and joined heartily in those excellent songs that I doubt not will for ever vibrate in your ears.[6]

As we fear you are too delicate a plant for our northern blasts, we unite in wishing that more gentle breezes may blow propitious to your fortunes. May your fate at Monmouth be very different from that of it's Duke.[7] May you be as successful with the Ladies at Shrewsbury as Captain Plume[8] was. May you be a pretty fel*low* at Abingdon.[9] May your Alma Mater Oxford celebrate the triumphs of your eloquence; and may Stafford, Hereford, Gloucester and Worcester join in the chorus not without libations of ale, cyder and Perry.[10]

I have only to add, that if you should repent, and wish to return to us, it is resolved that you shall be received; but it will be upon condition of your performing the ancient ceremonial for unchaste Dowagers at West Enborne in Berkshire. You must come into the Grand Court riding backward upon a black ram, and say the words following.

> Here I am
> Riding upon a black ram
> Like a deserter as I am.

1787). In 1790 William Cockell was the only serjeant-at-law on the Northern Circuit (Browne, p. 224). He died at Pontefract, 16 Apr. 1811: "William Cockell, esq. the King's antient Serjeant. He was called to the degree of a Serjeant in 1787; and was for many years an eminent leading Counsel on the Northern Circuit" (*Gent. Mag.* lxxxi pt. 1. 497). Sir John Cockle is the miller in "The King and Miller of Mansfield", a ballad published in Percy's *Reliques*. Compare Robert Dodsley's farce, *Sir John Cockle at Court*. Originally JB began this sentence in the draft: "Discontent [altered to "Distress"] for a moment altered the looks of (the jovial) Sir John Cockell."

[6] Draft, "auricular recollection"

[7] The Absalom of Dryden's poem, James Scott (1649–85), a natural son of Charles II, who led an unsuccessful rebellion against James II and was executed.

[8] One of the recruiting officers in George Farquhar's *The Recruiting Officer* (1706), who is successful in love but unsuccessful in recruiting soldiers. The play is set at Shrewsbury.

[9] JB has clearly underlined (also in the draft) the last two letters of "fellow". Conceivably the allusion is to some excellent song that vibrated in the ears of the group.

[10] The places named were all on the Oxford Circuit. Burke had matriculated at Oxford (Christ Church) 22 Dec. 1772 and received his B.A. in 1778. In the draft this paragraph originally ended: "May the delicious John Dories be ever at their best and in the greatest plenty when you are at Exeter and may you

My contrition sincere O Grand Court don't disdain
But good Mr. Junior let me have my place again.[11]

If you should not be able to find a black ram, Mr. Serjeant Walker and Mr. Samuel Heywood[12] have with equal publick spirit and private friendship generously offered that you should have your choice of either, to exhibit in that capacity.

By authority of the Grand Court of the Northern Circuit

(signed) JAMES BOSWELL, JUNIOR

To Thomas Warton,
Thursday 13 April 1786

Not reported. Sent from London 13 Apr. "Rev. Tho. Warton thanking him for his valuable communications concerning Dr. Johnson—putting a few queries—begging to know if I can be of any service to him to make some return. May perhaps be a week at Oxford this vacation" (Reg. Let.) The "communications" were Warton's transcripts (now at Yale) of SJ's letters to him, sent for JB to use in the *Life*. Warton had written a number of notes, but JB found other passages in need of explanation. Warton replied almost at once: see the letter following this. JB was at Oxford from 27 Apr. to 1 May, dining with Warton on 29 Apr.

drink the richest Cyder without being troubled with the Devonshire colick."

[11] JB recalls the ceremony described in *Spectator* 614: "At *East* and *West Enborne*, in the County of *Berks*, if a customary Tenant die, the Widow shall have what the Law calls her *Free Bench* in all his Copy-hold Lands . . . *while she lives single and chaste*; but if she commit Incontinency, she Forfeits her estate: Yet, if she will come into the Court riding backward upon a Black Ram, with his Tail in her Hand, and say the Words following, the Steward is bound by the Custom to re-admit her to her *Free Bench*.

    Here I am,
    Riding upon a Black Ram,
    Like a Whore as I am;
    And, for my *Crincum Crancum*,

    Have lost my *Bincum Bancum*,
    And, for my Tail's Game,
    Have done this worldly Shame;
    Therefore, I pray you Mr.
      Steward, let me have my Land
      again."

On 27 Dec. 1764 JB had heard Voltaire jokingly recite these lines.

[12] Thomas Walker, mentioned in JB's journal 25 Aug. 1778, 16 June 1785, 29 Mar., 2 Apr. 1786, had been created serjeant-at-law in 1772 (Alexander Pulling, *The Order of the Coif*, 1897, p. xxvii). Samuel Heywood (1753–1828), a warm friend of Charles James Fox, had considerable practice on the Northern Circuit and became serjeant-at-law in 1794.

From Thomas Warton, Saturday 15 April 1786

MS. Yale (C 3075). Received 16 Apr. "Rev. Mr. Tho. Warton—Answers to my queries concerning Dr. Johnson"[1] (Reg. Let.).

ADDRESS: To James Boswell Esq., at Mr. Dilly's, Bookseller in the Poultry, London.

POSTMARKS: 57 OXFORD, 15 AP.

Oxon., April 15th, 1786

DEAR SIR: Miss Jones[2] lived at Oxford, and was often of our parties. She was a very ingenious poetess, and published a volume of poems; and on the whole was a most sensible, agreeable, and amiable woman. She was sister of the Rev. Oliver Jones, Chantor of Christ Church Cathedral at Oxford, and Johnson used to call her the *chantress*. I have heard him often address her in this passage from *Il Penseroso*,

> Thee, chantress, oft the woods among
> I woo, etc.—

She died, unmarried, about fifteen years ago.

Of Miss Roberts, if you please, we will say nothing more.[3]

My *Spenserian design* was hindered by taking pupils in this College.[4]

I suppose Johnson means, that my *kind intention* of being the *first* to give him the good news of the Degree being granted, was *frustrated*, because Dr. King brought it before my intelligence arrived.[5]

---

[1] See the head-note of the letter preceding this, and Waingrow, p. 141 n. 1.

[2] Mary Jones (fl. 1740–61). This paragraph, except for the last four words, JB printed as a note to SJ's letter to Warton, 21 June 1757 (*Life* i. 322). JB misread her brother's name as River Jones, an error that has appeared in all printings of the *Life* since (*Life* vi. 1964, 488).

[3] A niece of Bennet Langton the elder (*Life* i. 430), mentioned in SJ's letter of 14 Apr. 1758. I am unable to explain Warton's unwillingness to discuss her

further.

[4] SJ's letter of 28 Nov. 1754 (*Life* i. 275–76) refers to a second book on Spenser that Warton had planned. JB adapted this sentence as a note to the letter.

[5] This note (*Life* i. 280 n. 1) JB copied into Warton's transcript, which was being used as printer's copy. The degree was the M.A. conferred on SJ by Oxford in 1755. Dr. William King was principal of St. Mary Hall, Oxford. He brought SJ the diploma.

I must forever most heartily regret, that I neglected to committ to paper many of his conversations, now totally forgotten; for in his earlier visits at Oxford, he lived with me almost intirely. And in town, I have passed much time with him. I am, Dear Sir, your most faithful humble Servant

T. WARTON

P.S. Excuse my Address, as I do not exactly know when you are in town.[6]

From George Steevens, Sunday 23 April 1786[1]

MS. Yale (C 2543). With this were enclosed anecdotes of SJ: see Waingrow, pp. 148–52. The address and endorsement which Waingrow gives for this letter (p. 146) are properly those of C 2544 (From Steevens, 12 Apr. 1787).

[Hampstead Heath] Sunday Evening April 23. DEAR SIR: In the eleventh book and second chapter of *Tom Jones* (3d. edit. 12o. Vol. 8. p. 179.) you will find the following passage. —"The other, who, like a Ghost, only wanted to be spoke to, readily answered, etc."

As for Tom Tyers, or Tom Tit, I am always happy to assist at what our late friend would have styled the *deplumation* of a thievish bird, who wishes to parade in borrowed feathers, nay receives compliments on their beauty, without once acknowledging whence he had them.[2]

---

[6] JB had been on the Circuit to the assizes at York and Lancaster since 9 Mar.; he was back in London on 10 Apr. (Journ.). His address was Portman Square, where he stayed with General Paoli until he moved to Great Queen Street.

---

[1] Between 1784, the year of SJ's death, and 1791, the year of publication of the *Life*, 23 Apr. fell on a Sunday only in 1786. This year is also indicated by JB's use of information from this letter in the third edition of the *Tour* (see n. 2 below).

[2] Thomas Tyers (1726–87), the son of Jonathan Tyers (founder of Vauxhall Gardens) and author of *A Biographical Sketch of Dr. Samuel Johnson*, was "bred to the law; but having a handsome fortune, vivacity of temper, and eccentricity of mind, he could not confine himself to the regularity of practice. He therefore ran about the world with a pleasant carelessness, amusing every body by his desultory conversation" (*Life* iii. 308). In the *Tour*, JB quotes SJ as saying, "Tom Tyers described me the best. He once said to me, 'Sir, you are like a ghost: you never speak till you are spoken to' " (*Life* v. 73). In the third edition, which was published shortly before 28 Sept. of this year (*Percy-Malone Corresp.* p. 36), JB

I enclose a few anecdotes set down in the first words that offered. You may either burn these papers, or take such hints from them as you judge to be worth notice. I wish you may find a niche for the earliest of the two letters,[3] as[4] it tends to prove that Dr. Johnson was not wholly disgusted by the encrease of the club, to which he himself contributed at the very time when Mrs. P. represents him as having lost all confidence in it, on account of the introduction of "new faces."[5]

I think I shall find other Letters etc. for you, and am always Your very faithful and obedient

G. STEEVENS

From Thomas Warton, Wednesday 3 May 1786

MS. Yale (C 3076). Received 6 May. "Rev. Mr. Tho. Warton sending an authentick copy of Dr. Johnson's letter on receiving his Doctor's Diploma" (Reg. Let.).

ADDRESS: To James Boswell Esq., at Mr. Dilly's, Bookseller in the Poultry, London.

POSTMARKS: 57 OXFORD, 4 MA.

Oxon., May 3d. 1786

DEAR SIR: I have just recovered Dr. Johnson's Letter of Thanks

---

annotated Tyers's statement, using Steevens's information without acknowledgement. Steevens's use of *deplumation*, Dr. Powell suggests (Waingrow, p. 147 n. 2), may very well have been inspired by SJ's *depeditation* of Foote in the *Tour* (*Life* v. 130). SJ's characterization of Tyers as Tom Restless in *Idler* No. 48 supports Steevens's reference to "borrowed feathers".

[3] As Waingrow says (p. 147 n. 3), most likely those of 21 Feb. and 5 Mar. 1774 (*Life* ii. 273–74), now in the Hyde Collection. JB printed only two other letters from SJ to Steevens: 7 Feb. 1774 (*ibid.* p. 273) and 25 Feb. 1777 (*Life* iii. 100).

[4] MS. "at"
[5] The letter of 21 Feb. 1774 notifies Steevens of SJ's desire to nominate him for membership in The Club. Steevens is perhaps being too sensitive, since Mrs. Piozzi places this increase of "new faces" rather indeterminately "in the year 1775 or 1776" (*Anecdotes of the Late Samuel Johnson, L. L. D.*, 1786, reprinted in *Johnsonian Miscellanies*, ed. G. B. Hill, 1897, i. 229–30). SJ, however, did approve of increasing the number of Club members from twenty to thirty in 1777, saying, "we have several in it whom I do not much like to consort with" (*Life* iii. 106).

for his Doctor's Diploma from Oxford,[1] 1775. I have sent it, as I thought you might wish to see it as soon as possible. Very faithfully your most obedient

T. WARTON

From William Windham to Bennet Langton, Friday 16 ? June 1786[1]

MS. Yale (C 3131).

ADDRESS: B. Langton Esqr.

ENDORSEMENTS: [*In Langton's hand*:] Mr. Windham. [*In JB's hand*:] Mr. Windham.

Hill Str., Friday Eveng. 16th.

DEAR SIR: If you should by good fortune, be disengaged tomorrow, and will suffer me to escape the effects, due to my own negligence for not sending to you before, you will meet a party at my House tomorrow, consisting of Dr. Parr, Sir Joshua Reynolds, etc., whom your company will make very happy, as well as, Dear Sir, Your Obedient and faithful Servant

W. WINDHAM

We shall dine at about 5.

To Thomas Percy, Wednesday 12 July 1786

Untraced. Printed in *Lit. Illust.* vii. 304–05. Sent July. "Bishop of Dromore for material for Dr. Johnson's Life" (Reg. Let.).

---

[1] "175" cancelled. The diploma, dated 7 Apr. 1775, is printed in *Life* ii. 332–33.

---

[1] Because of engagements and out-of-town trips recorded by both Windham and Reynolds, there are only three possible dates for this letter: 16 June 1786, 16 Feb. and 16 Mar. 1787. John Johnstone's edition of Parr's *Works*, 1828, does not indicate whether Parr was in London on any of the three dates; William Field's *Memoirs . . . of the Rev. Samuel Parr*, however, suggests (p. 243) that he was not there in Feb. or Mar. 1787. Samuel Parr, schoolmaster, divine, and controversialist, was known as "the Whig Johnson" because of his oddities and his great classical learning. He composed the epitaph for the monument of SJ in St. Paul's Cathedral.

London, July 12th, 1786

My Dear Lord, My friend Malone undertook to convey to your Lordship a copy of my *Journal of a Tour to the Hebrides*, which I hope you have received.

Your Lordship's last letter to me, which had been unaccountably mislaid in some corner of my house at Edinburgh, has at last been found. I am very sorry that it is now too late to obey your Lordship's commands to procure you a copy of our Scottish regulations, of which I understand from the Bishop of Killaloe[1] you have formed, for your Royal Society, the best in the world. But I beg leave to renew my solicitation, and to remind your Lordship of your obliging promise to let me have any materials in your possession that can illustrate the Life of Dr. Johnson, which I am now preparing for the press. I beg that your Lordship may be kind enough to favour me with them as soon as you can, as I now have occasion for all that I can get. Be pleased to direct for me at Mr. Dilly's, bookseller, London. Though the magnitude and lustre of his character make Dr. Johnson an object of the public attention longer than almost any person whom we have known, yet there is some danger that if the publication of his life be delayed too long, curiosity may be fainter. I am, therefore, anxious to bring forth my quarto. Pray, then, send me your kind communications without delay.

I am much pleased with the edition of the *Tatler*,[2] with notes; but I should have been better pleased had the notes been all *by one hand*; your Lordship will understand me.[3] I long to have the *Spectator*, my early favourite, illustrated in the same manner.

What a dreary thing (I cannot help feeling it) is it to have one's friends removed to a distant country! When I recollect the many pleasing hours which I have passed with Dr. Percy in London, and the few at Alnwick, and the few at Edinburgh, and a good many at Carlisle, how much do I wish that he were well established

---

[1] Barnard was in London during the summer of 1786.

[2] *The Tatler, with Illustrations and Notes, Historical, Biographical, and Critical*, 6 vols., 1786. In 1763–65, Percy had undertaken for Tonson an edition of *The Spectator, The Guardian*, and *The Tatler*, in which he had been assisted by John Calder, formerly private secretary of the Duke of Northumberland. When Percy abandoned the project, he turned over his materials to Calder (see *Life* ii. 501–03). A more detailed discussion of his part in the edition is found in Reiberg, pp. 134–142.

[3] Percy annotated this: "The Bishop of Dromore had no hand in this edition. T. D."

in England! I am resolved, however, some time or other, to see Ireland all over; and with what glee shall we talk over old stories at Dromore!

I am now at the English bar, of which I long wished to make a fair trial. How long I shall continue will depend upon circumstances. I beg to have my best compliments presented to Mrs. Percy and the young ladies; and I have the honour to be, my dear Lord, your faithful humble servant

JAMES BOSWELL

From Sir Joshua Reynolds, Wednesday 18 October 1786[1]

MS. in possession of T. G. M. Snagge.

ADDRESS: James Boswell Esq.

Wednesday

This being St. Lukes day, the Company of Painters dines in their Hall[2] in the City, to which I am invited and desired to bring any friend with me.

As you love to see life in all its modes if you have a mind to go I will call on you[3] about two o'clock, the black-guards[4] dine at half an hour after. Yours

J. REYNOLDS

[1] "I dined often at Mr. Malone's, and once at Sir Joshua Reynolds's; and on St. Luke's day he carried me to dine with the Painter Stainers in their Hall. A City feast pleased me, and I think I relished it almost as well as if I had been free of bad spirits" ("View of my Life [from 20 Sept.] till 1 November 1786 when no diary"). *The Morning Chronicle* for 21 Oct. 1786 commented on the dinner and mentioned that the painters were "accompanied by Sir Joshua Reynolds, Mr. Boswell, and several of the Royal Academicians."

[2] In Little Trinity Lane, on the south side of Thames Street. Sir Joshua had been presented with the Freedom of the Company in 1784.

[3] Reynolds struck out "I will call on you" and in a new start wrote what appears to read "I will can you." Possibly, writing in haste, he omitted a syllable, and we should read "I will car[ry] you." Regardless of what he *wrote*, that, or something like it, must be what he *meant*. See the quotation from JB's journal in n. 1.

[4] Because of their ungentlemanly hour of dining. G. B. Hill suggested that Reynolds was showing "vexation at losing two or three hours of his working day" (*Johnsonian Miscellanies* ii. 460 n. 2).

To Thomas Barnard,
Saturday 6 January 1787

MS. Yale (L 47). A draft. Sent 6 Jan. "Bishop of Kilaloe of various particulars. (Copy)" (Reg. Let.).

HEADING: To The Bishop of Kilaloe.

Great Queen Street, Lincolns Inn Fields, 6 Janry. 1787[1]

MY DEAR LORD: As I reckon your Lordship to be one of my most sincere Friends, I am sure you will be glad to hear that after the uneasy state of despondency as to my success as an English Lawyer, concerning which I troubled your Lordship with too many complaints, when you were last here,[2] I have lately had a fortunate opening of encouragement and hope. The Earl of Lonsdale carried me down to an election at Carlisle, as Counsel for the Mayor.[3] The business lasted fourteen days, and I was happy enough to acquit myself much to his Lordships satisfaction, and let me add, to my own. This of itself is quite sufficient to satisfy me for the first year of my ambitious attempt to follow my

[1] MS. "1786"

[2] See especially Journ. 7 June 1786.

[3] JB's relations with Sir James Lowther (1736–1802), Earl of Lonsdale from 1784, are studied at length in Frank Brady, *Boswell's Political Career*, 1965: see especially pp. 131–43. Lonsdale, an immensely wealthy, resolute, and unpopular politician, ordinarily returned nine members to the House of Commons. He had been latterly one of the chief opponents of the American war, had given Pitt his first seat in Parliament, and by continuing adherence to Pitt had won a peerage. JB in 1778 had been struck by his "swarthy turklike stateliness" (Journ. 22 Aug.), and confessed that Lonsdale's introduction as a peer made his mouth water (Notes, 3 June 1784). In his *Letter to the People of Scotland*, 1785, an attack on the power of Henry Dundas, he had made a direct appeal to Lonsdale: "HE whose soul is all great— whose resentment is terrible; but whose liberality is boundless" (p. 28). Lonsdale had invited him to dine on a turtle (Journ. 21, 22 July 1786; JB was engaged), and in the following Nov. made to him the flattering proposal here reported. JB left London on 25 Nov. and returned on 22 Dec. 1786 (Reg. Let.). Lonsdale already controlled one of the seats for Carlisle, but was now engaged in a struggle to take the other away from the Duke of Norfolk. To accomplish his end, he had forced the Corporation to admit huge numbers of non-resident colliers and farmers as honorary freemen. JB's task was to find law for the Mayor when these "mushroom" voters were challenged at the polls. He also found himself unable to resist the opportunity to publish as leaflets or broadsides a signed legal opinion and at least five unsigned political squibs (*New CBEL* ii. 1213–14). Lonsdale's candidate was easily elected but a Select Committee of the House of Commons seated his opponent.

profession in a wider sphere; and I flatter myself it will lead to future employment.

We are all indulging the agreable expectation of having your Lordship among us this winter. I dined at Sir Joshua Reynolds's on Wednesday with your irish Secretary of State and his son,[4] Mr. Courtenay, Mr. Malone, Mr. Windham, Mr. Batt[5] and Mr. Metcalfe. We had an excellent day. I dined with him again yesterday, upon a sudden call, with only the Laureat,[6] and we were hearty and pleasant. On tuesday we are to have an extraordinary meeting of the Literary Club as usual at this season when the two Wartons can attend.[7] This is Life!

Sir John Hawkins's edition of Dr. Johnson's Works with his Life will be published in a few weeks.[8] The Life is a large Octavo volume, of above 600 pages. It has been printed off several months. I have seen no part of it; but Mr. Langton has read it all, and tells me that he must not anticipate particulars; but that upon the whole it is very en[ter]taining. I understand it is full of digressions, in the Knights manner of writing, which somebody[9] very well characterised by *a rigmarole way*. My great Volume will not be finished for some time. I have waited till I should first see Hawkins's compilation. But my friends urge me to dispatch, that the ardour of curiosity may not be allowed to cool.

Parliament will soon put us all in agitation again. The Commercial Treaty with France[10] will occasion violent debates; and to tell you fairly my own opinion, though the theory is beautiful

[4] John Hely-Hutchinson (1724–94), noted for his "unblushing venality and subservience to government" (DNB) and an intimate friend of Edmund Burke and William Gerard Hamilton, was Principal Secretary of State for Ireland from 1777 until his death. He had six sons.

[5] John Thomas Batt (1746–1831), attorney, who was at one time a Commissioner of Bankrupts, at another, a Commissioner for Auditing Public Accounts. He is mentioned frequently in the journal as JB's dinner companion.

[6] Thomas Warton was appointed Poet Laureate on the death of William Whitehead, 14 Apr. 1785.

[7] Of the sixteen meetings of The Club attended by one or both of the Wartons between 1777 (when Joseph was elected) and Dec. 1789, all but one were held in Jan. (*The Club*).

[8] *The London Chronicle* announced on 27 Mar. 1787 that a complete edition of SJ's works, with a life by Hawkins, had been published that day, in eleven volumes. The *Life* was sold separately (24–27 Mar. 1787, lxi. 293).

[9] Probably Malone, who in his notes on the book listed ten digressions under the heading "Rigmarole" (B. H. Davis, *Johnson before Boswell*, 1960, p. 192).

[10] The treaty, concluded on 26 Sept. 1786, established between England and France complete liberty of navigation and of commerce in all articles not specifically excepted. It was opposed by Fox, Burke, Flood, and others.

I am affraid that our Ministry[11] will be found to have gone on with too much precipitation, and the result may be the same with that of the irish propositions. I must communicate to your Lordship an admirable repartee of our Lord Thurlow's. He was last summer at Wedgewood's[12] manufactory; and Wedgewood after shewing it to his Lordship said with an exulting air, "Well My Lord; we got the better of you at last as to the irish propositions. But it was the Irish that did it for us." "True Sir" said the Chancellor; "but had the Irish believed one word of what you swore at the bar of the House of Commons they would not have done it for you."

My Wife and children came up with me in September, and agree very well with London.

Pray come soon and be so good as bring with you the Opinion upon a certain will which a young friend of mine at the bar[13] drew up with great care. He wishes to have it again as a precedent for himself. Your Lordship may order a copy to be taken. I have the honour to be with great respect, My Dear Lord, your Lordships most faithful and affectionate humble servant

---

[11] JB originally wrote "our young Ministers".

[12] Josiah Wedgwood (1730–95), pottery manufacturer, who was instrumental in directing The Great Chamber of the Manufacturers of Great Britain, which opposed the Irish commercial resolutions. He was one of those who spoke against the resolutions during the hearings on the bill (ante From Barnard, c. 17 July 1785, n. 13).

[13] JB himself: see ante To Barnard, 3 Aug. 1785. Hume v. Burton, the appeal to the House of Lords of Ireland which Barnard had taken part in and had reported to JB (ante From Barnard, c. 17 July 1785) did not concern a will, but a will had been one of the principal matters of contention in a previous stage of what was generally styled "the Ely Cause": the appeal to the House of Lords of Great Britain, 27 Apr. 1775, styled Hume v.

Earl of Ely. Nicholas Hume, second Earl of Ely, in a will signed 6 Nov. 1769, had bequeathed his personal estate to the Hon. Henry Loftus, his uncle and successor in the title (House of Lords *Cases* in Hume v. Earl of Ely: see *ante* To Barnard, 1 July 1785, n. 5 and From Barnard, c. 17 July 1785, n. 5). This will would have been of particular interest to JB because in Scots law it would have been totally invalid as having been made on deathbed. Lord Ely had signed it while dangerously ill and had died without remission of his illness five days later. For the will to have been valid in Scots law, Lord Ely would either have had to survive the signing by sixty days or in a lesser time have shown himself unsupported at kirk in the time of divine service, or at market during the time of public market.

From Thomas Barnard, Tuesday 23 January 1787

MS. Yale (C 88).

ADDRESS: To James Boswell Esqr., No. 56 Great Queen Street, Lincolns-inn Fields, London.

POSTMARKS: IRELAND, JA 24, FEBY H 2.

Henrietta Street, Dublin, Jany. 23d. 1787

MY DEAR SIR: I most Cordially and Sincerely Congratulate You upon the Fair Prospect of Success and Reputation that now Seems to open before you, from the consequences of your Carlisle Expedition: If you had been permitted to Chuse out of the British Dominions a Patron the most Capable of conducting you to Honor and Profit you could not have pitch'd upon one more fit your Purpose than Lord Londsdale; He has Wealth, He has Interest, he has Business enough to Keep you Employ'd, and He has other Boroughs left, tho' he looses Carlisle.[1] So Corragio, my Freind; Something will turn up Trumps yet at Westminster Hall, and a Fico for Sweet Edinburgh. I have told your Freind the Bishop of Dromore of your Atcheivements, and he entirely agrees with me in opinion. He had already heard of them with much pleasure from some of his Cumberland Correspondents in the opposite Interest,[2] How with your deluding Tongue you persuaded the Enemy to give up their usual Triumph of Chairing the Successfull Candidate.[3]

---

[1] See ante To Barnard, 6 Jan. 1787, n. 3, and Frank Brady, *Boswell's Political Career*, 1965, pp. 142–43. It was the *second* seat for Carlisle that was presently in question. Lonsdale did "loose" it, through action of a Select Committee of the House of Commons, but he still had his "ninepins": two members each for Cockermouth, Haslemere, and Westmorland; one each for Appleby, Carlisle, and Cumberland (*ibid*. pp. 132–33).

[2] That of the Duke of Norfolk, who was "himself the patron of eleven seats" (*ibid*. pp. 142–43).

[3] It was intimated on 14 Dec. that Stephenson, the Duke of Norfolk's candidate, would be chaired, he having completed his poll with a majority of over

200 if the votes of the "mushrooms" were disregarded. JB thought this "an absurd and insolent scheme", and really feared that Stephenson's life might be in danger from the gang of colliers and sailors whom Lonsdale had lodged in his house "in readiness to quell any riot". A handbill prepared (it was said) by Lonsdale's candidate, Knubley, was circulated, saying that it would "be justly considered as a wanton insult to their *majority*, as declared by the *Poll Clerk*, should Mr. Stephenson be chaired", and "they give notice that it *will not be suffered*" (Yale MS. Lg 43; P 29:3). The Mayor (Sir Joseph Senhouse) read a proclamation prohibiting the chairing, and followed it up with a second handbill

If you can thus Soften the Iron Hearts of the North, English Judges and Middlesex Juries will melt like Wax before you.

I envy you the Happy days that you pass with our Mutual Freinds at London. I hoped to have been amongst You this Spring, But the great and Interesting Business that is now before our Parliament here,[4] calls for my attendance upon my Post, and the Joint Exertions of every Freind of the Establish'd Church to prevent its enemies from seizing upon the Inheritance of the Clergy, or themselves from Surrendring it upon Composition for their own present ease and Convenience. I thank God that the great Landed Interests of this Country see the Matter in its true Light, and I trust we shall be well Supported on Both Sides of the House if we do not desert ourselves. You will see the Speech and addresses in your Papers, on which tho' there were Divisions in both Houses, yet upon those parts of the addresses that related to the Support of the Church, there was but one Sentiment.[5] Notwithstanding this, when the Matter comes to be considerd in detail, there will be many Insidious plans of adjustment and Compensation Proposed, and these are what we must beware of, and take care to deliver the Constitution down to our Successors

(P 29:4). Next day (15 Dec.) a third handbill was circulated: "Opinion of James Boswell, Esq; of the Inner Temple, Barrister at Law. Chairing a person who is declared by the proper officer to be *duly elected*, is a very *ancient custom*, and from *long usage*, which is the foundation of *common law*, may be considered as a part of, or as an appendage to an ENGLISH ELECTION, and therefore may be permitted and protected by the Magistrate. But, *chairing an unsuccessful candidate*, is a defiance to established authority, and an insult to the returning officer. Therefore, a number of persons assembling to chair an unsuccessful candidate, is an *unlawful convocation*, and truly a *Mob*, which the Magistrate may, and ought to disperse" (Yale P 29:5). It must have been this opinion that Percy's correspondents reported. JB's own records fail from this point, but *The Morning Chronicle*, 27 Dec. 1786, reports that Stephenson was nevertheless chaired on 16 Dec., "attended by almost every gentleman of the county, and an in-

numerable concourse of spectators . . . accompanied by banners and musick". Lonsdale's "mushrooms" had undoubtedly made him very unpopular in Carlisle.

[4] At the end of Jan., a very stringent crimes act (the Whiteboy Act) was passed by the Irish Parliament to prevent uprising and effectually to punish riots, illegal combinations, etc. The Whiteboys were illegal groups of peasants, first organized to resist the enclosure of the commons in 1761. Later the movement was directed chiefly against extortionate and sometimes illegal tithes extracted from the peasants. Occasionally landlords and clergymen of the Established Church received threatening letters, and some property was destroyed; but the movement was primarily agrarian, and not sectarian. Whiteboy activities had spread during the later months of 1786, and the Act of 1787 made most of their outrages capital offences.

[5] See *The London Chronicle*, 25–27 Jan. 1787, lxi. 89–91; 27–30 Jan., lxi. 99.

in as good a Condition as we found it; which I trust we shall be able to do if we are true to ourselves. As to the Commercial Treaty meeting the same Fate with the Irish Propositions, I hope you will prove a false Prophet; it certainly is not disliked by the Trading Part of England some very few branches excepted; and the objections seem rather to be the Cavils of Party (which would have equally attended it, if it had been ten times more advantageous than it is) than the Voice of candid and Judic[i]ous disapprobation: and Supposing that to be the Case I trust that the Ministerial majority, tho' perhaps equally Biass'd and Corrupt, will be strong enough to Carry it through Parliament with their usual Success in Both Kingdoms.

The opinion you gave me in a Certain Case,[6] I carried with me to Killaloe upon my Return to Ireland; and my Brother[7] having been at that time apparently at the Point of Death, I was prevented from laying it before him. It is no⟨w⟩ lock'd up in my Desk in the Country; So that I have it not here to send you; but a Freind whom I can trust with the Key will go thither next month, and I shall then take care to have it brought to Town that I may send it to you.

Pray indulge me with a Letter now and then, that I may Know how you live and Thrive: Your Bench threatens many Vacancies to make room for you; at least at the Bar;[8] we have one Vacant here and another will probably be so in less than a Month.[9] Rare times, for young Lawyers! Adieu, my Dear Sir; be assured that I am, and with my Warmest wishes for your Happiness and Success, your Faithfull and affectionate humble Servant.

THOS. KILLALOE

My best respects to Mrs. Boswell. Pray Remember me to My dear Sir Joshua.

[6] The "certain will" referred to in the previous letter.

[7] The Reverend Dr. Henry Barnard (1738–93), rector of Maghera, Co. Londonderry.

[8] Barnard means that the vacancies on the bench made by the death or retirement of the judges will be filled from the bar. If JB does not get a judge's appointment, at least some of his rivals at the bar will be eliminated.

[9] The Chief Justiceship of the Common Pleas, Ireland, was vacant by the death of Marcus Paterson, who had been Chief Justice since 1770; the death predicted was presumably that of Christopher Robinson, who had been Puisne Justice of the King's Bench, Ireland, since 1758. Paterson was succeeded by the Solicitor General, Hugh Carleton (1739–1826), later Baron and Viscount Carleton; Robinson by John Bennett. Both new justices were sworn in on 10 May 1787 (*London Gazette*, 19–22 May 1787).

From Joseph Warton,
Monday 29 January 1787

MS. Yale (C 3063). "Rev. Dr. Joseph Warton with letters to him from Dr. Johnson" (Reg. Let.).[1]

ADDRESS: James Boswell Esqr.

ENDORSEMENT: Rev. Dr. Joseph Warton.

Winchester College, Jan. 29 1787

DEAR SIR, I Here send you the Two Letters which I mentioned of our old Freind Dr. Johnson,[2] of which you [may] make what use you please. I long very much to see your Work; and think with pleasure of those Hours which I spent with you in London. Believe me, Dear Sir, very sincerely your obedient humble Servant

Jos. WARTON

I beg my best Compliments to Mr. Malone when you see Him.

From Thomas Percy,
Tuesday 6 March 1787

MS. Yale (C 2233). Percy's first draft, dated 5 Mar., riddled with deletions and with at one point a paragraph pasted over a deleted one, is among the Boswell papers at Yale (*C 2232.9). With one exception, which is noted, the draft differs from this text only in punctuation, capitalization, the placement of two or three passages, and minor word changes. Received Mar. "Bishop of Dromore with a few Johnsoniana" (Reg. Let.).

ADDRESS: James Boswell Esqr., at Mr. Dilly's, Bookseller in the Poultry, London.

POSTMARKS: MR 6, MARCH 10.

Dublin, March 6th. 1787

DEAR SIR: My delay in answering your obliging Letters, I beg you will ascribe to the true Cause; the not being able to satisfy myself, That any Particulars I could recover concerning our

---

[1] This letter and a letter from the Rev. Daniel Astle, dated 23 Jan. 1787, are entered in the Register at the end of January, after 27 Jan. but without the ditto mark that would indicate that they were definitely received on that date. JB probably made the entries at some distance of time, remembering only that he received the letters late in January.

[2] See *Life* i. 253; ii. 115.

friend Dr. Johnson were worth your Notice, much less would answer the Expectations I had formed to myself, or excited in you, when we regarded the Subject at a Distance. Yet I have often reproached myself for not submitting them to you; and at length have determined to send them such as they are; with the addition of a Greek Epitaph made by Dr. Johnson on poor *Oliver Gold-smith*,[1] which I lately[2] procured from a Gentleman in this Country to whom Johnson gave it himself, (Mr. Archdall[3] who had been educated under Dr. Sumner[4] at Harrow.) I send you Mr. Archdall's own Transcript of it, hoping it will prove a Peace-Offering and restore to me the pleasure of your Correspondence.[4a]

In Conversations of Dr. Johnson and Mrs. Williams, I have heard them mention the following Circumstances of his Childhood: That he was put to learn to read, or improve his reading, to a School-Dame[5] at Litchfield: Who upon Account of the Defect in his Eyesight, usually followed him home lest he should be run over in the Streets: And he was so near sighted, that he was obliged to stoop down on his hands and knees to take a View of the Kennell[6] before he ventur'd to step over it; but if he observed the Old Woman following him, he would turn back in anger and kick her Shins.[7] This Old Dame lived to hear that he was a great Author, and once when he came to Litchfield brought him a Pound of Gingerbread declaring He was the best Scholar she had ever had.[8]

When he was a boy he was immoderately fond of reading Romances of Chivalry, and he retained this fondness thro' Life, so that spending part of the Summer of 1764,[9] at my Parsonage House in the Country, he chose for his regular Reading the Old

[1] Printed both in *Life* ii. 282 and *Letters SJ* i. 411.

[2] Draft, "two days ago"

[3] Richard Archdall, who was at Harrow c. 1766. He later attended Trinity College, Dublin, and was M.P. for Ardfert, Killybegs, Kilkenny, and Dundalk (*The Harrow School Register, 1571–1800*, ed. W. T. J. Gun, 1934, p. 1). He was a member of the Royal Irish Academy (*The Transactions of the Royal Irish Academy*, 1787, p. 164).

[4] Robert Carey Sumner (1729–71), Master of Harrow. He was SJ's friend and the Master of Sir William Jones and

Dr. Parr.

[4a] It is at Yale: *Life* Papers Apart (M 145 p. 513).

[5] Ann Oliver (d. 1731), wife of a Lichfield shoemaker (*Johns. Glean.* xi. 348). See also *ibid.* iii. 77–79; and *Life* i. 525–26.

[6] That is, "canal": "the surface drain of a street; the gutter" (OED, Kennel, *sb.*[2]).

[7] This incident, but as told by SJ to JB, is related in *Life* i. 39.

[8] *Life* i. 43.

[9] MS. "1784". See *Life* i. 486, and the note following.

Spanish Romance of *Felixmarte of Hircania,* in folio, which he read quite through. Yet I have heard him attribute to these extravagant Fictions that unsettled Turn of mind which prevented his ever fixing in any Profession.[10]

After he had gone thro' Dr. Hunter's[11] School in Litchfield, his Father removed him to that at Stourbridge, where he was received as a kind of assistant, who was to have his own Instruction gratis for teaching the Lesser Boys. I have heard him remark, That at one of these he learnt much in the School, but little from the Master: in the other, much from the Master, but little in the School.[12] Not far from Stourbridge is the endowed Grammar School of Tresull in Staffordshire;[13] Of which, I believe, Pope endeavour'd to procure him to be elected Master thro' the Interest of Lord Gower,[14] as is mentioned in the Billet written by Pope to Richardson the Painter, of which you have a Copy.

Dr. Johnson's Father, before he was received at Stourbridge, applied to have him admitted as a Scholar and Assistant to the Revd. Samuel Lea,[15] M.A., Head Master of Newport School in Shropshire (a very diligent good Teacher, at that time in high Reputation; under whom Mr. HOLLIS is said in the Memoirs of his Life[16] to have been also educated.)[17] This application to Mr. Lea was not successful; but Johnson had afterwards the supreme Gratification to hear, that this Old Gentleman, who lived to a very

[10] This paragraph, somewhat modified, is quoted by JB in *Life* i. 49. It is not contained in Percy's first draft.

[11] John Hunter (?1674–1741), Master of Lichfield Grammar School from 1704 until his death, noted for his floggings (*Life* i. 44).

[12] *Life* i. 50. Percy had related the remark earlier (17 Oct. 1786) to Malone, asking him to pass it on to JB, but had written "nothing" in place of "little" (*Percy-Malone Correspond.* p. 43).

[13] To Malone Percy had written, "the School in Staffordshire, for which Pope applied to Lord Gower for his interest to procure for Johnson, I believe was at *Treasle* near *Stourbridge*; if it was not at Stourbridge itself, at each of which Places, I believe there is an endowed School" (*ibid.*).

[14] John Leveson-Gower (1694–1754),

first Earl Gower (*Comp. Peer.* vi. 37–38).

[15] Graduate of Jesus College, Cambridge, Rector of Bucknall, Staffordshire. He died in 1773 (*Alum. Cant.* I. iii. 65; *Johns. Glean. passim,* see Index).

[16] Thomas Hollis (1720–74), considered an atheist and a republican because of his fondness for seventeenth-century republican literature and his habit of decorating the covers of books with daggers and caps of liberty. Francis Blackburne published the *Memoirs of Thomas Hollis* in 1780. See *Life* iv. 97; Journ. 30 Nov. 1764.

[17] Asterisk inserted by Percy, who added a note at the bottom of the page: "As was also your humble Servant many years afterwds." JB repeated Percy's note in the *Life:* "As was likewise the Bishop of Dromore many years afterwards. BOSWELL" (i. 50).

advanced age, mentioned it as one of the most memorable events of his Life that he was VERY NEAR having "that great Man for his Scholar."[18]

S. Johnson was at length admitted of Pembroke College in Oxford, where the pleasure he took in vexing the Tutors and Fellows, has been often mentioned. But I have heard him say, what ought to be recorded to the honour of the present venerable Master of that College, the Reverend WILLIAM ADAMS D.D.[19] who was then very young and one of the junior fellows, That the Mild, but judicious Expostulations of this Worthy Man, whose Virtue awed him, and whose Learning he revered, made him really ashamed of himself, "Tho' I fear," said he, "I was too proud to own it."

I have heard from some of his Cotemporaries That he was generally seen LOUNGING at the College Gate, with a Circle of young Students round him, whom he was entertaining with his Wit and keeping from their Studies; if not spiriting them up to Rebellion against the College Discipline: which in his maturer years he so much extoll'd.[20]

He ascertain'd the Æra of his coming to London, by recollecting that it happen'd within a Day or two of the Catastrophe of Eustace Budgell[21] the Relation and Friend of Addison, who having loaded his pocket with Stones, called for a Boat and in the midst of the Thames leap'd over and was drown'd.—He remember'd also to have once walk'd thro' the New exchange ⟨in⟩ the Strand,[22] among the Milleners' Shops mentiond in the *Spectator*,[22a] before that building was pulled down and converted into private houses.

When in 1756 or 7 I became acquainted with him, he told me [he] had lived 20 years in London but NOT VERY HAPPILY.

The above Particulars are what I chiefly remember to have heard him mention of his Early Life; and you see how little they

---

[18] This paragraph quoted in *Life* i. 50.

[19] (1706–89), Master of Pembroke College, Oxford, and friend of SJ.

[20] Above two paragraphs quoted in *Life* i. 74.

[21] Budgell (b. 1686), a miscellaneous writer and cousin of Addison, became somewhat eccentric after losing £20,000 in the South Sea Bubble. He also was involved in suspicious financial dealings, which ruined his reputation. He committed suicide on 4 May 1737.

[22] A kind of bazaar on the south side of the Strand, so called to distinguish it from the Royal Exchange. The first stone was laid on 10 June 1608, and it was torn down in 1737.

[22a] Nos. 155. 211.

are worth recording. The subsequent Part you know as well as myself.

Having a treacherous Memory and neglecting at the time to commit his *Bon Mots* to writing (which I now regret,) I cannot add much to your Treasures of that sort, of which you have so rich a Store: Yet I will conclude with one, which I heard fall from him, and I hope I have not heard it in vain.[23]—I was in his Company once, when a Person told him of a Friend of his, who had very fine Gardens, but had been obliged to sue to his Neighbour, with whom he was not upon very cordial Terms, for a small piece of adjoining Ground, which he thought necessary to compleat them.—"See," said the Sage, "how inordinate Desires enslave a Man! One can hardly imagine a more innocent Indulgence than to have a fine Walk in a Garden: Yet observe, even the Desire of this slight Gratification, if carried to excess, how it humiliates and Enthralls the proudest Mind: Here is a Man submits to beg a favour from one he does not love, because he has made a Garden-Walk essential to his happiness."[24] I am, Dear Sir, Your most obedient Servant

THOS. DROMORE

P.S. I have heard, with great pleasure of your late Success in the North. I hope it will lead to a lasting Connection with a Nobleman, distinguished for the Zeal and Spirit, with which he serves his Friends; and I already anticipate the happiest consequences to you from that Connection; especially his bringing you into Parliamt. for one of his numerous Boroughs, an Event which I consider as no less certain than splendid to your Fortunes and Establishmt. in England.

N.B. I have not yet received the Copy of your book,[25] but I believe it is now travelling to me. Accept my thanks for it.—I hope to hear ⟨that th⟩is came in time.

---

[23] Percy's first draft of the preceding part of this paragraph is in a confused state. There are two versions. The second version, added to the end of the letter apparently after Percy decided not to send it, is printed in *Lit. Illust.* The meaning of each, although not the expression, is identical.

[24] This anecdote was not published in the *Life*.

[25] The *Tour*.

From Lady Diana Beauclerk to Bennet Langton, shortly before Sunday 8 April 1787

MS. Yale (C 115).

ADDRESS: Bennet Langton Esqre., Westminster.

Notes by Langton on address side: Hops? *from* London. Malt not divided as to Distances. Q. £. 91000. 910

$$\begin{array}{r} 5 \\ 4550 \\ 910 \\ \hline 5460^1 \end{array}$$

[London]

SIR: I am very sorry I could not see you when you call'd, I was really too ill. I trouble you now with this note to beg you will make my excuses to Lady Rothes for not yet having been to wait upon her, which I trust she will be good enough to accept of, when I name them,—bad health,—and marrying my Daughter Elizabeth.[2] I have been lately subject to dreadful Cramps or Gout, in my stomach—The ⟨flurry⟩ and bustle this fortunate ⟨alliance p⟩uts me in, I fear will ⟨prevent me⟩ for some little time lon⟨ger from waiting upon⟩ Lady R. I am ⟨sure that you will⟩ for my sake and Mr. Bs. be glad to hear that Eliz. has been so wonderfully lucky as to please such a man as Lord Herbert; indeed every circumstance joins to make me happy in this event. I am Sir your most Obedient humble servant

D. BEAUCLERK

When the wedding is over I shall wait upon Lady Rothes.

From George Steevens, Thursday 12 April 1787

MS. Yale (C 2544).

ADDRESS: James Boswell Esqr., Great Queen Street, Lincolns Inn Fields.

ENDORSEMENT: From Mr. Steevens.

[1] A calculation perhaps of interest (6 per cent of £91,000) due on a loan. The hops, malt, and interest may all have concerned the Wey Navigation. See *post* From Langton, 1 Mar. 1790, n. 4.

[2] Elizabeth Beauclerk (d. 25 Mar. 1793), younger daughter of Beauclerk and Lady Di, was married to George Augustus Herbert (1759–1827), her cousin, on 8 Apr. 1787. He was styled

Hampstead Heath, April 12th. 1787

DEAR SIR: One of the inclosed letters, and the note, are additional proofs[1] of the attention shown by our late friend to the club. The other letter refers to a sum raised by him toward the relief of a female relation of Dr. Goldsmith.[2] I am, Dear Sir, very faithfully Yours

G. STEEVENS

From Richard Marlay, Monday ?28 May 1787[1]

MS. Yale (C 1973).

ADDRESS: To James Boswell Esqre., Great Queen Street.

POSTMARKS: PENY POST PAYD S TU, ?T [hour illegible].

[London] Monday Night

DEAR SIR: I am extremely concerned I can not have the pleasure of waiting on you next Wednesday. That day I am engaged to dine in the country. Yours very sincerely

R. MARLAY

From George Steevens, Wednesday 13 June 1787

MS. Yale (C 2545).

ADDRESS: James Boswell Esqr., Great Queen Street, Lincolns Inn Fields.

POSTMARKS: PENY POST PAYD T TH, 2 OCLOCK T.

Lord Herbert until 3 Feb. 1794, when he became eleventh Earl of Pembroke (*Comp. Peer.* x. 427–28).

Club because of Mr. Thrale's death (*Life* iv. 84). Steevens endorsed it on the verso: "Note to the Club, on Mr. Thrale's Death" (C 1603).

[1] Proofs in addition to the letter of SJ's which he had already sent to JB (*ante* 23 Apr. 1786).

[2] See *Life* iii. 100, for the letter concerning Goldsmith's relative. The other letter is unidentified, but the note, as Waingrow (p. 212 n. 2) suggests, is probably the one to Sir Joshua Reynolds in which SJ declined "the Call" of The

[1] Determined by Journ. Wednesday 30 May 1787, reporting a dinner at which JB had three Irish guests: Courtenay, Malone, and Gen. Edward Stopford, brother to the Earl of Courtown. JB lived in Great Queen Street from 16 May to about 31 Dec. 1787; Marlay became Bishop of Clonfert 12 Nov. 1787.

[Hampstead Heath], June 13th. 1787

DEAR SIR: I have just now been informed, by a letter out of Sussex,[1] that the Dialogues of Lord Chesterfield and Dr. Johnson, are the Production of Mr. Hayley.[2] Yours very faithfully

G. STEEVENS

From John Courtenay, Friday 15 June 1787

MS. Yale (C 836).

ADDRESS: Jas. Boswell Esqr., Great Queen Street, Lincolns Inn Fields, London.

FRANK: Bath June fifteenth 1787. Free J. Courtenay.

POSTMARKS: JU 16 87, BATH 110, FREE C.

[Bath]

MY DEAR BOSWELL: Excuse[1] the irregularity of recei[vi]ng

---

[1] Steevens's Sussex correspondent is unidentified.

[2] *Two Dialogues; Containing a Comparative View of the Lives, Characters and Writings of Philip, the Late Earl of Chesterfield, and Dr. Samuel Johnson,* 1787. William Hayley (1745–1820), poet and biographer of William Cowper, was the author of many poems, including *The Triumphs of Temper* (1781) and *The Triumph of Music* (1804), both ridiculed by Byron in *English Bards and Scotch Reviewers.* JB had read his verse *Essay on History* (1780) "with pleasure" (Journ. 28 Dec. 1780). A friend of Anna Seward, he had given JB, through her, permission to make use of his "impromptu on the Colossal Critick", a "Liliputian Poem" (Waingrow, p. 96 and n. 1). JB's later quarrel with Miss Seward meant a quarrel with Hayley. See, for instance, JB's contemptuous comments in *Gent. Mag.* for Nov. 1793 (lxiii. 1011) on "the scraps of letters between her and Mr. Hayley [published in the Mar. issue (pp. 197–99)], impotently attempting to undermine the noble pedestal on which the

public opinion has placed Dr. Johnson". Others than JB were curious about the authorship of *Two Dialogues,* and various persons were suggested in the months after its publication. As late as 31 Dec., Elizabeth Robinson Montagu, apparently accused by her sister, Sarah Robinson Scott, of being its author, wrote to her sister to deny it: "You do me unmerited honour in suspecting me of the Dialogue you mention between Johnson and Lord Chesterfield. They are well contrasted, the one endeavoured by pleasing manners to grace Vice, the other by his brutal insolent manner disgraced Virtue, and by his low superstition and bigotry even renderd piety less respected. It would puzzle one to determine whether he who placed the Syrens in the Temple of Vice or he who put the Gorgons head at the entrance of the Temple of Virtue did most mischief. I wish much to see the Dialogue, pray let me know where it is to be got" (Huntington Library MS. MO 6159, quoted by permission of the Library).

---

[1] MS. "Exclusive"

your letters thro' my hands—. They go to my *late* House in Berners Street—and Are sent to me—to forward—[2]

I Am wonderfully well—the Bath Water agrees with me, as well as wine with you. But as to *Society*—none; that Is there Are *Everyday People Enough here*;—but I am grown fastidious— Remember me to Malone, and Sir Joshua—I wish you were all here—Yours faithfully

J.C.

To John Courtenay,
Thursday 28 June 1787

Not reported. Sent from London 28 June. "John Courtenay Esq. Account of some agreable dinners so he sees the truth of Dr. Johnson's remark: London Sir is the place for a man whose pleasures are intellectual; sending him No. 13 of *Olla Podrida*" (Reg. Let.). For the Johnsonian remark, see *Life* iii. 378 ("London is nothing to some people; but to a man whose pleasure is intellectual, London is the place"). As a note to the *Life*, JB wrote (iv. 426 n. 3), "In the *Olla Podrida*, a collection of Essays published [in weekly numbers in 1787–88] at Oxford, there is an admirable paper upon the character of Johnson, written by the Reverend Dr. Horne, the late excellent Bishop of Norwich. The following passage is eminently happy:—'To reject wisdom, because the person of him who communicates it is uncouth, and his manners are inelegant;—what is it, but to throw away a pine-apple, and assign for a reason the roughness of its coat?'" The quotation is from No. 13.

To Joseph Warton,
Friday 3 August 1787

MS. Yale (L 1270). A copy. Sent 3 Aug. "Rev. Dr. Joseph Warton concerning Dr. Johnson's Life (Copy)" (Reg. Let.).

HEADING: To The Revd. Dr. Joseph Warton.

London, 3 August 1787

REVD. SIR: I am certainly very much to blame for not hav[in]g long ago acknowl[edge]d the favour of your oblig[in]g letter

---

[2] Courtenay had apparently left London for Bath on 1 June (Journ.).

with two to you from Dr. Johnson. My only excuse is that I waited from time to time for something to communicate by way of making you a return and now I can only heartily thank you.

The Life of our great Friend in which his letters are to be introduced chronologically is not yet so near to its conclusion as you may suppose. Profes[siona]l and social avocat[io]ns have retarded my progress.[1] But the work will cert[ain]ly be published in the course of the next sess[ion] of Par[liamen]t.

I think Sir you ment[ione]d to me that you might perhaps find among your pap[er]s something concern[ing] Collins. If you do I beg you may favour me with it. Pray was the orig[inal] Life of Collins all written by Johnson or did you furnish a part of it as I have been told?[2]

You were so good as to say that you would give me some partic[ular]s which you recollected of Dr. Js convers[ation] with the King.[3] Will you let me have them now? or will it be better to wait till I have drawn up that article as completely as I can from the materials of which I am allready possessed so that you may see it.

All our common friends who are in town are well and remember you with great regard. Mr. Langton has this moment left me,[4] and joins in best compliments to you and to your brother who I suppose is with you. I am with very great regard, Dear Sir, Your obliged and faithful humble servant.

Any communications for me may be sent under cover of The Hon. Wm. Ward M.P.[5] London.

[1] In July, JB had attended the Assizes at Hertford and Chelmsford; he had also been "jovial" frequently, dining out four times in the five days preceding the writing of this letter.

[2] The poet William Collins (1721–59) and Warton were schoolfellows at Winchester. JB refers to the character of Collins published in 1763 in *The Poetical Calendar*. SJ later included this piece in his *Life of Collins*. Warton presumably disclaimed any part in it, for JB in the *Life* (i. 22, 382) assigned it without qualification to SJ.

[3] SJ's conversation with the King occurred in Feb. 1767 (*Life* ii. 33–41).

Warton is among several whom JB thanks for the details of this conversation (*ibid.* p. 34 n. 1).

[4] JB does not record this visit in his journal, there being no entry for that day. He had dined at Langton's on the first of the month (Journ.).

[5] Ward (1750–1823), later third Viscount Dudley and Ward of Dudley, was the husband of Julia, second daughter of JB's "chief", Godfrey Bosville of Thorpe and Gunthwaite in Yorkshire. From 1780 to 1788, he was M.P. for Worcester (Namier and Brooke iii. 606; *Life* iii. 541). JB saw him occasionally in London (Journ. 6, 8 Aug. 1785).

From William Windham,
Sunday 5 ?August 1787[1]

MS. Yale (C 3132).

ADDRESS: Mr. Boswell.

[London] Sunday. 5th.

MY DEAR SIR: I lament much, that this combination of accident and mismanagement will have deprived me of the pleasure of your company. I know not now, how to arrange a party for an earlier day.—With respect to the other matter, my hands and thoughts are so full at present, with a business in which I have imprudently engaged myself, and with my usual neglect, delayed to the last minute, that I cannot well fix any time for looking out the papers, you mention, (if I have them here) till after Tuesday.—Yours etc.

W. WINDHAM

To John Douglas,
Monday 1 October 1787

MS. Yale (L 438). A draft. The second paragraph was extracted from the original (not traced) by William Macdonald in the memoir prefixed to *Select Works of John Douglas,* 1820, pp. *77–*78.

HEADING: To The Lord Bishop of Carlisle.

Great Queen Street, Lincolns Inn Fields, 1 October 1787

MY DEAR LORD: My Lord Lonsdale who did me the honour to stop with me for an hour at Stamford, where I had the good fortune to meet his Lordship in my return from Scotland,[1] gave

---

[1] The date is questionable, but the papers Windham refers to are quite possibly the three letters SJ had written to him. These Windham sent to Malone in Sept. 1787 (From Malone, 14 Sept. 1787). The only Sunday the fifth in that year was in Aug. Windham had just arrived in London from Norfolk (Windham's *Diary,* p. 123), having missed at least two dinner meetings of the committee for SJ's monument, 31 July and 1 Aug., that JB attended. The two dined together at Malone's on the 7th. JB was out of town (in Croydon on the Home Circuit) on the 8th, 9th, and 10th. Windham dined with JB on the 11th.

[1] There is no mention of the meeting with Lonsdale in the journal. JB and Mrs. Boswell passed through Stamford on Friday 28 Sept. 1787 (Journ.).

me a most cordial satisfaction by informing me authentically of your promotion to the Bishoprick of Carlisle.[2]

I[3] certainly have no pretentions to the gift of prophecy,[4] but I recollect, with some degree of exultation, what passed between your lordship and me at the bishop of Chester's,[5] a few[6] years ago, when we were kept waiting for dinner till he should come from the House of Lords. I said, I hoped to wait for you for the same reason; you answered, "I am obliged to you, but I have no such expectations now; all my friends are dead." I replied, "no Doctor, your best friend is alive, yourself, your own merit."

I rejoice in looking upon Dr. Douglas now as a *Neighbour* and I flatter myself that I shall persuade your Lordship to visit Auchinleck and walk with me in those romantick scenes of my ancestors to which Dr. Johnson has given celebrity.[7] I am with most sincere respect, My Dear Lord, Your Lordship's very faithful humble servant

From John Courtenay, *?shortly after Saturday 19 January or Saturday 19 April* 1788[1]

MS. Yale (C 837).[2]

ADDRESS: J. Boswell Esqr.

[London]

Should you happen to See Dr. Brocklesby—Say nothing of my dining at Malone's On Saturday;—as I put off a *philosophical*

[2] Douglas was appointed to the Bishopric of Carlisle on 18 Oct. 1787 (*Fasti Angl.*). Lonsdale had recommended him for the bishopric and was apparently in great part responsible for his promotion (From Lonsdale to Douglas, 23 June 1791, BM MSS. Eg. 2186, ff. 34–35). He wrote to Douglas on 21 Sept. 1787 informing him of the King's consent to his appointment (*ibid.* MSS. Eg. 2185, f. 121).

[3] This paragraph follows the text printed in *The Select Works of John Douglas* (see head-note).

[4] MS. of draft, orig. "to a prophetick spirit"

[5] JB possibly referred to this occasion when talking with Sir Joshua Reynolds

on 5 June 1784: "I mentioned Dr. Douglas at the Bish[op] of Chesters saying '*One* other glass if your Lordship pleases' with his sly glistening look. Said Sir Josh[ua] 'Squinting—with one eye fixed on the bottle one on the Bishop'" (Journ.).

[6] MS. of draft, orig. "some". Several other similarly minor false starts in this paragraph are not reported.

[7] See *ante* From Langton, c. 17 Nov. 1773, n. 9.

[1] Determined by JB's record of large parties at Malone's. The second one was followed by an all-night jaunt to Hampstead involving both JB and Courtenay.

[2] Courtenay, perhaps by accident,

engagement with him (with an Excuse) to meet that party[3]—
I Can't resist temptation.—Just now very ill, and have been So—
these two days;—and going to take An Emetic.—The Virtue of
Bath Waters is soon exhausted;—I dont much Care—how soon
the Vis Vitae[4] may be so too—Yours in the mean time faithfully
and Affectionately

J.C.

To Thomas Barnard,
Saturday 9 February 1788

Not reported. Sent from London 9 Feb. "Bishop of Kilaloe of my being
elected Recorder of Carlisle—State of my Life of Johnson—Power of
Pitt—Spirit of Fox—Hastings's Trial" (Reg. Let.).

To Thomas Percy,
Saturday 9 February 1788

MS. Berg Collection, The New York Public Library. Sent 9 Feb. "Bishop of
Dromore—two first articles as above.[1] Mrs. Piozzis Letters—Malone's
Shakespeare—can he tell me any particulars of Dr. Johnsons Frank at
Bishop Stortford" (Reg. Let.).

ADDRESS: To The Lord Bishop of Dromore, [Dublin *deleted*; *added in
another hand*:] Dromore.

POSTMARKS: FE 11 88, [two others illegible].

London, Great Queen Street, Lincolns Inn Fields,
9 Febry. 1788

MY DEAR LORD: Procrastination we all know increases in a pro-
portionate ratio the difficulty of doing that which might have once
been done very easily. I am really uneasy to think how long it is

selected for this note a piece of paper
folded in two leaves which already bore
the beginning of an abandoned message
on the verso of the second leaf: "Mr.
Courtenay requests that M". On folding
the note to seal it, he scratched out as
much of the sentence as showed on the
address side.

[3] Brocklesby was a Fellow of the Royal
Society and published papers in the
Philosophical Transactions.

[4] "Force of life."

[1] That is, as entered for a letter to
Barnard of the same date: "my being
elected Recorder of Carlisle—State of my
Life of Johnson" (Reg. Let.). JB was
elected Recorder of Carlisle on 11 Jan.
1788, the announcement appearing in
The London Chronicle, 12–15 Jan. lxiii.
56, and in *The General Evening Post*,
15–17 Jan.

since I was favoured with your Lordships communications concerning Dr. Johnson, which though few are valuable, and will contribute to increase my store. I am ashamed that I have yet seven years to write of his Life.[2] I do it chronologically, giving year by year his publications if there were any, his letters, his conversations, and every thing else that I can collect. It appears to me that mine is the best plan of Biography that can be conceived; for my Readers will as near as may be accompany Johnson in his progress, and as it were see each scene as it happened. I am of opinion that my delay will be for the advantage of the Work, though perhaps not for the advantage of the Authour, both because his fame may suffer from too great expectation, and the Sale may be worse from the subject being comparatively old. But I mean to do my duty as well as I can. Mrs. (Thrale) Piozzi's Collection of his letters will be out soon, and will be a rich addition to the Johnsonian Memorabilia. I saw a sheet at the printing House yesterday and observed Letter CCCXXX, so that we may expect much entertainment.[3] It is wonderful what avidity there still is for every thing relative to Johnson. I dined at Mr. Malone's on Wednesday with Mr. W. G. Hamilton, Mr. Flood, Mr. Wyndham, Mr. Courtenay, etc. and Mr. Hamilton observed very well, what a proof it was of Johnson's merit, that we had been talking of him almost all the afternoon. But your Lordship needs no refreshment upon that subject.

I have two or three letters from him to Francis Barber while that faithful Negro was at school at Easter[3a] Mauduit. Can your Lordship give me any particulars of Johnson's conduct in that benevolent business?

[2] More than three years were to elapse before his book appeared.

[3] *Letters to and from the late Samuel Johnson, LL.D. To which are added some poems never before printed.* Published by H. L. Piozzi, 2 vols., 1788. JB was not exactly entertained when he received a copy of the book from Dilly the day before it was published: "I was disappointed a good deal, both in finding less able and brilliant writing than I expected, and in having a proof of his fawning on a woman whom he did not esteem—because he had luxurious living in her husband's house, and in order that this fawning might not be counteracted, treating me and other friends much more lightly than we had reason to expect. This publication *cooled* my warmth of enthusiasm for 'my illustrious friend' a good deal. I felt myself degraded from the consequence of an ancient Baron to the state of an humble attendant on an Authour, and what vexed me, thought that my collecting so much of his conversation had made the World shun me as a dangerous companion" (Journ. 7 Mar. 1788).

[3a] Correctly, Easton.

Your Lordship would I am sure be pleased to see that I was lately elected Recorder of Carlisle. Lord Lonsdale's recommending me to that office was an honourable proof ⟨of⟩ his Lordship's regard for me; and I may hope that this may lead to future promotion. I have indeed no claim upon his Lordship. But I shall endeavour to deserve his countenance.

Malone flatters himself that his Shakespeare will be published in June. I should rather think that we shall not have it till winter.[4] Come when it may, it will be a very admirable Book.

Our Club goes on as it has done for some time past. Shall we not have the pleasure of seeing your Lordship among us this year? However much I may rejoice at your Lordship's elevation, I cannot but feel a very sincere regret at your absence. I recollect with fondness the happy mornings I have passed in that capital Study in Northumberland House, and elsewhere. Does not your Lordship sometimes wish to be in old England again?

I offer my best compliments to Mrs. Percy and to the young Ladies. How do they like Ireland? I ever am, My Dear Lord, with great regard, your Lordships very faithful humble servant

JAMES BOSWELL

From Thomas Barnard,
c. Thursday 28 February 1788

MS. Yale (C 89). Received 4 Mar. "Bishop of Kilaloe that he has better hopes than I have of my consequential advancement from being made Recorder of Carlisle—In favour of Hastings—That he is to pass either next summer, or next winter in London—Wishing my Life of Johnson to be hastened" (Reg. Let.).

ADDRESS: Jas. Boswell, Esqr., No. 56, Great Queen street, London.

POSTMARKS: FE 28, MR 3 88.

[Dublin]

MY DEAR SIR: Your Letter was a very agreeable Surprise to me as I had almost despaired, of your ever Intending to write to me again, which, however, I was vain enough to ascribe to want of Leisure, or any other Cause rather than forgetfulness of an old Freind. I Sincerely congratulate ⟨yo⟩u, good Mr. Recorder of

---

[4] Malone's *Shakespeare* was not published until late Nov. or early Dec. 1790.

Carlisle upon your new Dignity; and tho' you do not seem very Sanguine in your Expectations of its consequences, I have better hopes; I have always heard that His Lordship is very generous *where he Likes*: And though perhaps he may not be the very first Man one would chuse for a Patron, He is no bad one as Times go.

I am concern'd and disappointed to hear that you have Still Seven years of Johnsons Memorabilia to finish; as I flatter'd myself that your work would have been publishd long since. You forget that the Publick Curiosity will not wait your Leisure. It will have some other Object to engage its attention in a year or two; and in twice that Time, Anecdotes of Johnson will be a Subject for an Antiquarian rather than a Biographer. I have no Doubt that your work will be Immortal let it appear never so late; But I would have it also Popular: and you Know Still better than I do, how much Depends upon Seizing the Critical Moment in order to Ensure Success.

The accounts I hear, and Read of our Freind Burkes Exertions in Westminster Hall,[1] make me sorely regret my absence from so Brillant an Exhibition of those Abilities which I have ever admired and Revered, even when they were out of Fashion. When this matter was in a very Early Stage of ⟨its⟩ Progress, I expressed to him my wishes that Both He and Hastings might come off with Honour, a wish that he then Ridiculed as a Solecism. But I have the Satisfaction to find that it is already Completely gratified on one Part; and am not without hopes that it may be equally So on the other. I should lament most Sincerely if ever the Man to whom these Kingdoms have such obligations should at last fall the Victim of their Stern Justice; which, however merited, Posterity will always ascribe to the Ingratitude of his Country. When you read of the Banishment of Themistocles,[2] ?do you not hate the Athen-

---

[1] Burke, who was active in preparing the charges against Hastings, was head of the managers for the impeachment. On 10 May 1787, before the House of Lords, he accused Hastings of high crimes and misdemeanours; on 15 Feb. 1788, he began his opening speech, which continued during four sessions and, according to *The London Chronicle*, "comprehended one great and magnificent display of unequalled abilities and unrivalled knowledge of history, law, politics, religion, philosophy, ethics, sciences in all their branches and ramifications; together with a complete acquaintance of the propensities of mankind" (16–19 Feb. 1788, lxiii. 169). The speech was reported in *The Dublin Chronicle*, 19–21 Feb. (i. 1018) and 23–26 Feb. 1788 (pp. 1034–35).

[2] Themistocles was banished to Argos around 470 B.C. when he opposed the party which favoured friendship with the Spartans.

ians? or of Cicero[3] ?the Romans?[4] And yet the Conduct of Both these Heroes and Patriots was not defensible by the Laws of their Country, any more than that of the Governour of Bengal. The Execution of Lentulus[5] was Legally a Murder as much as that of Nuncomar,[6] and I have no Doubt that the Prosecution of Cicero, was then as popular at Rome as that of Hastings or Impey[7] can be now at London. Our Government Here goes on Swimmingly, and I believe our Sessions will Conclude by the End of March. Mr. Grattans attack upon the Tythes has occasion'd a Debat⟨e⟩ and Some Conversation. It was Virulent in the Extreme, but quite weak, both in argument, and the Support it met with. His Speech is publish'd at Length in a Pamphlet,[8] and will not do much Honour even to his abilities, or Information. At present we are Engaged on a Bill for the Lowering Interest to Five per Cent, which has past the Com⟨m⟩ons, and is to be debated in the Lords on Saturday, wh⟨en⟩ I hope it will be rejected;[9] For in truth I do not think ⟨w⟩e are as yet Ripe for such a Measure.

I hope to see you in England e'er it be Long. I am as yet

[3] Cicero was banished in 58 B.C. for refusing to accept public office under Pompey, Caesar, and Crassus, when his acceptance of a post would have implied submission to the Triumvirs and ensured his personal safety.

[4] Barnard here follows a style, surely very rare in English, of putting a mark of interrogation at the beginning of a question as well as at the end.

[5] Publius Cornelius Lentulus Sura, former Roman consul, praetor and member of the Catiline conspiracy, was strangled in 48 B.C. with four of his associates on the orders of Cicero, then consul.

[6] Raja Nand Kumar, or Nuncomar, Indian ruler, had at one time preferred charges of corruption against Hastings. Later, he was tried for forging a bond and was sentenced to death by the Supreme Court of Bengal. He was executed on 5 Aug. 1775.

[7] Sir Elijah Impey (1732–1809), Chief Justice of Bengal, presided at the trial of Nuncomar. He was accused of rushing the defendant's execution in order to stifle his charges against Hastings. Actually,

Nuncomar, during Impey's absence, had been denied leave to appeal by Hastings's enemies. Impey was also accused of extending illegally the jurisdiction of his court, and in Dec. 1787, charges were brought against him in the House of Commons. The committee of the whole house debated on 4 Feb. 1788 whether the accusations justified impeaching him. He defended himself, and the impeachment was dropped on 9 May 1788.

[8] On 14 Feb. 1788, Henry Grattan (1746–1820) moved for a committee of the Irish House of Commons to inquire into the state of tithes, recommending that they be commuted in order to relieve the peasants. The House defeated the motion 121–49 (*The Speeches of the Right Honourable Henry Grattan*, 1822, ii. 25, 71). The speech was published as *A Full Report of the Speech of the Right Hon. H. G. in the House of Commons . . . the 14th of February 1788*, 1788. See *The Dublin Chronicle*, 16 Feb. 1788, i. 1004.

[9] The bill was defeated in the Irish House of Lords on Tuesday 4 Mar., by a majority of ten (*London Chronicle*, 13–15 Mar. 1788, lxiii. 260).

undetermin'd whether I shall Come over in Spring, as soon as the Parliament is prorogued and return the latter end of summer, or whether I shall first Go to my Diocese and stay till September, and then pass the next winter in London.[10] This will be decided in a fortnight. In either case I shall bring my Family with me, and a Very pretty Niece[11] to shew Sir Joshua Reynolds, (to whom I beg my very Affectionate Compliments when you see him), and pray write to me when you have an hour of Leisure who am always, Dear Sir, most Sincerely Yours

THOS. KILLALOE

I request you to present my Respects to the good genl. Paoli; and to Sir Wm. Forbes. As I Know you Interest yourself in every thing that gives pleasure to your Freinds, I will tell you that my Son Capt. Barnard,[12] has been in Italy for a year Past, most of which he has spent at Naples, where, by good Fortune the King[13] happend to take a Liking to him, and Invited him to pass a fortnight with him at Caserta, Since which he was consider'd as a Sort of Enfant de Famille, and an Immediate protegé of his Majesty, even to be admitted to Dine with the Queen. These Marks of Royal Favour detain him there nine months, and in consequence of it, he has met with Receptions of the most advantageous Kind at Rome (where he now is) by Royal Recommendation; and writes me Word that he has no occasion for any thing of that nature from England for the Time to Come, as he is already in a much Superior Line of acquaintance to that of any

[10] Barnard apparently decided to spend the winter in London, for JB gave a dinner there in his honour on 26 Jan. 1789 (To Mrs. Boswell, 28 Jan. 1789).

[11] Isabella Barnard, daughter of the Bishop's brother Henry by his first wife. She lived at Barnard's for some time (*Barnard Letters*, p. 12).

[12] Andrew Barnard (d. 1807) first appears in the *Army List*, 1783, p. 97, being then Captain in the 27th (or Inniskilling) Regiment of Foot, with commission dated 4 June 1782. In 1782 this regiment was in America (*Army List*, 1782, p. 97). His company was reduced in 1783, Barnard remaining on half pay until 1795, when his name no longer appears in the *Army Lists*.

[13] Ferdinand IV of Naples, III of Sicily (1751–1825), son of Charles III of Spain, had succeeded to the throne at the age of eight. His queen, Maria Carolina, daughter of the Empress Maria Theresa, whom he had married in 1768, was much more able and ambitious than he was. In 1779, at her instigation, an Englishman, John (later Sir John) Acton (1736–1811), had been made Commander-in-Chief of the Neapolitan navy, and soon gained direction of both the internal administration and the foreign policy of the kingdom. The Queen sought independence of the Spanish connexion and *rapprochement* with England and Austria.

Englishman, not in the same fortunate circumstances with himself: and that this advantage will follow him to every city in Italy as long as he chuses to remain there.

From Thomas Percy, Friday 29 February 1788

MS. Yale (C 2234). Received 6 Mar. (but see postmark). "Bishop of Dromore congratulating me on my Recordership of Carlisle—Of the Literary Club" (Reg. Let.). A "copy much altered", dated 28 Feb., in *Lit. Illust.* vii. 310–12, should be read entire as there printed: it differs so widely from the letter sent as to make piecemeal reporting of variants impracticable. As the date suggests, it was probably not a copy but a draft which Percy systematically condensed in transcribing so as to keep it within the bounds of a folio half-sheet. Even so, every bit of space available for writing was covered.

ADDRESS: James Boswell Esqr., Great Queen's Street, Lincoln's Inn Fields, London.

POSTMARKS: DROMORE, MR 3, MR 7 88.

Dromore House, Feb. 29. 1788

DEAR SIR: I had lately seen in the Papers Mention of your being Elected Recorder of Carlisle and was preparing to congratulate you on that appointment, when I received your truly Acceptable Favour of the 9th Inst.—Be assured I do and ever shall rejoice at every event which gives you pleasure or affords a Tribute to your Merit, as I think this may fairly be consider'd. And it does great honour to my Lord Lonsdale, thus to look out and attract to himself men of distinguished Abilities; as he has done by his Patronage of you and the New Bishop of Carlisle.—Yet I cannot, but regret that the connection of both with that City and Diocese should not have taken place, till mine had wholly ceased there: And cannot but consider it, as an odd Fatality, that your Removal to England, which I so often and strongly urged to you, should have been delay'd till I had migrated from thence.—In other respects I am very well contented with my present situation and have no desire to exchange it for any other, in or out of this Kingdom.

With regard to our departed Friend Johnson, He spent a good

part of the Summer of 1764 at my Vicarage House at Easton Mauduit in Northamptonshire,[1] and was there attended by his black Servant Francis Barber:[2] but he returned with him to London, and never was at School there. He had formerly, I believe been placed by his Master at one of the cheap Schools in Yorkshire: and after 1764 at a School at Bishops Stortford in Hertfordshire;[3] where poor Frank I fear, never got beyond his accidence.[4] But I know nothing of the Particulars.

I found lately a Memorandum of the time of my admission into the Club at the Turks Head in Gerrard Street[5] etc. and shall[6] here collect some other particulars on that subject; concerning which Mention has been made both by Sir John Hawkins and Madm. Piozzi. But both of them have omitted what I have heard Johnson assign as the Reason why the Club was at first begun with so small a Number as 8 or 9; and for many Years was not allowed to Exceed that of TWELVE Members: He said It was intended the Club should consist of SUCH men, as that if only Two of them chanced to meet, they should be able to entertain each other, without wanting the addition of more Company to pass the Evening agreeably.[7]

Whether they answer'd this expectation must be judged from the following List of their Names as it was compleated soon after the beginning of the year 1768 when (in Consequence of Sir John Hawkins's secession)[8] the remaining Members agreed to extend their Number to Twelve, at which it remained fixed for some years; who then more or fewer constantly supped and spent the evening at the Turk's Head every *Monday* in the Winter and

---

[1] *Life* i. 486. SJ was at Percy's vicarage from 25 June to 18 Aug. (*ibid.* pp. 553–54).

[2] Barber (c. 1742–1801), who served SJ from 1752 until SJ's death, later provided JB with some information for the *Life*.

[3] He was there from 1767 to early in 1772 (see *Johns. Glean.* ii. 16–22).

[4] That part of grammar which treats of the inflections of words; thus, by extension, the rudiments or principles of any subject (OED, Accidence[2]), in this case, Latin.

[5] Some time after JB's death, Percy wrote another memorandum, incorporat-

ing the information included here with material on The Club's later history. It is in the possession of The Club, and is printed in *The Club*.

[6] MS. "shall shall"

[7] The same statement is found in the Percy memoir of Goldsmith (*The Miscellaneous Works of Oliver Goldsmith*, 1801, i. 70) and *Life* i. 478 n. 2. See *post* To Percy, 12 Mar. 1790, n. 8, and From Percy, 24 Apr. 1790, n. 1.

[8] Hawkins's account of his secession is found in his *Life of Samuel Johnson* (1st ed., p. 425). For a discussion of the various reasons given for it, see *Life* i. 479–80 and n. 1.

Spring Months. This was afterwds.[9] chang⟨ed⟩ I think to *Friday Evening.*

The List alphabetically was as follows.

1. Topham Beauclerc Esq. 2. Edmund Burke Esq. 3. Mr. Robert Chambers, then Vinerian Professor of Law in Oxford, now Sir Robt. the Judge in India. 4. Anthony Chamier Esqr.[10] sometime Under Secretary[11] at War. 5. Geo. Colman Esq. 6. —— Dyer Esq.[12] (a great Friend of the Burke's,[13] and apparently a very amiable agreeable Man). 7. Dr. Oliver Goldsmith. 8. Dr. Samuel Johnson. 9. Bennet Langton Esqr. 10. Dr. Nugent[14] (Father of Mr. Burke's Wife.) 11. Revd. Thomas Percy. 12. Mr. Reynolds, now Sir Joshua Reynolds.

I was first admitted into the Club on 15th Feb. 1768. And about the same time Mr. Colman and Mr. Chambers were elected New Members also: The rest I believe were original Members. But Mr. Beauclerc had for sometime left the Club, and afterwds. returned to it.[15]—For further Particulars I must refer you to Sir Joshua Reynolds, Mr. Langton and Mr. Burke, who are the only original Members now remaining. It was not I think till after the Deaths, 1st of Mr. Dyer 2dly of Mr. Chamier, that the Number of Members was extended to more than 12.—Nor had it the name of the *Literary Club,* till on the Death of Garrick, it was so called in the Account of his Funeral given in the Papers. I am, Dear Sir, Your very faithful Servant

THOS. DROMORE

N.B. In the old Club Room at the Turk's Head was a book of

[9] Dec. 1772 (*The Club*).
[10] Chamier (1725–80), through the influence of his sister-in-law's husband, Thomas Bradshaw, was in 1772 appointed deputy Secretary at War, and was created in 1775 Under-Secretary of State for the Southern Department. He was in Parliament from 1778 until his death. See *Life* i. 478 n. 1.
[11] Percy inserted "query" above the line at this point. See the preceding note.
[12] Samuel Dyer (1725–72), translator, was a close friend of Burke, an excellent classical scholar, a good mathematician, and master of French, Italian, and Hebrew. By speculating with and losing £8,000 inherited from his brother, he

somewhat damaged his reputation; and when he died shortly thereafter, he was suspected of having committed suicide. See *Life* i. 480 n. 1.
[13] Asterisk inserted by Percy, who has added a note at the bottom of the page: "If desired I believe I could procure and send you the Eloge which Mr. Edmund Burke published in the Papers on Dyer's Death." Burke's character of Dyer appeared in *The Public Advertiser* for 17 Sept. 1772.
[14] Christopher Nugent (d. 1775), physician and Fellow of the Royal Society. Burke married his daughter, Jane Mary, early in 1757. See *Life* i. 477 n. 4.
[15] *Life* i. 478 n. 2.

entries and Forfeitures of absent Members which would show the variable State of the Club for many Years.

To Sir John Hawkins, Wednesday 16 April 1788

MS. Yale (L 634). A copy. Referred to in JB's journal, 19 Apr.

HEADING: To Sir John Hawkins Knight.

Great Queen Street Lincolns Inn Fields, 16 April 1788

SIR: I have received a letter from Mr. Francis Barber residuary legatee of the late Dr. Samuel Johnson, authorising me to demand from you all books or papers of any sort which belonged to him, that may be in your possession.[1]

You will be pleased to appoint a time when I shall wait upon you to receive them. I am Sir your most humble servant

From Sir John Hawkins, Thursday 17 April 1788

MS. Yale (C 1511). Written in the hand of an amanuensis (?Hawkins's eldest son), except for the signature. Referred to in JB's journal, 19 Apr.: "I had received from the Knight a very civil answer."

ADDRESS: James Boswell Esq.

[London] 17th April 1788

SIR, I have no Books that belonged to Dr. Johnson, in my possession; the printed ones are sold, and the value of them accounted for. Those in manuscript, that is to say his Diaries and Notes, have been delivered to Mr. Nichols.[1] Two or three

---

[1] Barber had written to JB on 2 Apr., appending to the letter the authorization JB mentions. The form of the authorization was suggested by JB in a letter to Barber on 20 Mar., in which he instructed him to copy it "over in your own hand, dated, and signed and addressed to me." JB had written to Barber even earlier, on 3 Mar., requesting authorization (Reg. Let.), but Barber had failed to send it.

[1] John Nichols (1745–1826), printer, author, and sole manager of *Gent. Mag.* from 1792 until his death, was an intimate friend of SJ and among many Johnsonian books had printed Hawkins's *Life of Johnson*. He seems to have volunteered to procure for JB the Johnsonian materials Hawkins had acquired, and turned over these materials to JB 20 July 1787 (Journ.; To Francis Barber, 3 Mar. 1788). Perhaps included in what JB

Pamphlets and a few useless Papers are all that remain, and those I wish to be rid of, and shall be ready to deliver to you, on the production of the Order of Mr. Francis Barber, on Saturday next at 6 in the evening.[2] I am, Sir, Your very humble Servant

JOHN HAWKINS

To John Courtenay, Thursday 5 June 1788

Not reported. Sent from Auchinleck 5 June. "John Courtenay Esq. A few lines as to the beauty of Auchinleck etc. and that I will keep an account of penny postages with his servant for letters which I send under cover" (Reg. Let.). Letters to Courtenay were delivered to his house free, but postage had to be prepaid on the enclosures when they were put in the Penny Post.

To John Courtenay, ?September 1788

Not reported. Probably sent from Auchinleck. Referred to in next letter.

From John Courtenay, Monday 29 September 1788

MS. Yale (C 838). Written on first page of From Malone, 29 Sept., which also contains a note to JB from Robert Jephson.

ADDRESS: Jas. Boswell Esqr., Recorder of Carlisle.

FRANK: Cobham Septembr. Twenty ninth 1788. Free J. Courtenay.

POSTMARKS: 21 COBHAM, FREE S, SE 30 88.

received were the 1729–34 diary, another for 1765–84, and that for the French tour of 1775 as well as notes on reading like "Repertorium" (*Works of SJ*, Yale Ed. i. xv–xxi).

[2] On Saturday, 19 Apr.; because JB was engaged for that day at six, Hawkins had changed the time of meeting to eleven in the morning. The business was settled "in perfect good humour. . . . There were but three pamphlets the three diplomas of degrees from Dublin and Oxford, and a few papers for which I gave a receipt

[see *Life* i. 281–82, 489; ii. 332–33]. . . . We sat most serenely opposite to each other in armchairs, and I declare, he talked so well, and with such a courteous formality, that every five minutes I unloosed a knot of the critical cat o'nine tails which I had prepared for him. . . . How much might human violence and enmity be lessened if men who fight with their pens at a distance, would but commune together calmly face to face" (Journ.).

Cobham Park, Sepr. 29, 1788[1]

DEAR BOSWELL: You would be delighted with the *Aristocratic* dignity and Convenience of this Mansion;[2]—especially with the Addition of Malone's Hospitality.—Dont think of quitting the Joys of wine—as you threaten in your last; if you do—Your life of Johnston will resemble—Sir J. Hawkins.—Mr. Jephson[3]—is much pleased—with your Connubial *Ode* to the Signora.[4]—He wishes to see—and hear you—Let him speak for himself.—Best Compliments and wishes to Mrs. Boswell—and Believe me— Yours faithfully and Affectionately

J. COURTENAY

From John Courtenay, Tuesday 30 ?December 1788[1]

MS. Yale (C 839).

ADDRESS: Jas. Boswell Esqr.

[London] Tuesday 30th.

MY DEAR SIR: John Wilkes has promised to dine with me, on *Friday*:—the party will not be Compleat without the two North Britons;—the *literal* and metaphorical *One*. Yours faithfully

J. COURTENAY

To Thomas Warton, Tuesday 10 February 1789

Not reported. Sent from London 10 Feb. "Omitted 10 Rev. Tho. Warton recommending Mr. Dilly as the purchaser of his edition of Milton's Juvenile Poems" (Reg. Let.).

[1] Place and date in Malone's hand.

[2] Since Malone's house in London was being painted, he had taken a house in Surrey for himself, his sisters, and his brother's wife, Lady Sunderlin (From Malone, 17 June, 12 Aug. 1788).

[3] Robert Jephson (1736–1803), dramatist and poet. Malone wrote the epilogue for his tragedy, *The Count of Narbonne*, and the prologue for *Julia, or the Italian Lover*. He was frequently in the company

of JB, Malone, and Courtenay.

[4] *Ode by Dr. Samuel Johnson to Mrs. Thrale, upon their Supposed Approaching Nuptials.* For discussions of this ribald and tasteless poem see *Life* iv. 550–51; *Lit. Car.* pp. xxii–xxiii, 131–34.

[1] Five dates are possible because JB and Courtenay were seeing more than usual of Wilkes at this time, but the date suggested is the most likely.

From Thomas Warton,
Wednesday 11 February 1789

MS. Yale (C 3077). Received 12 Feb. (but see postmark). "Omitted 12 Rev. Tho. Warton that his Juvenile Poems of Milton[1] are engaged" (Reg. Let.).

ADDRESS: To J. B. Garforth Esq. M.P.,[2] at James Boswell's Esq., Num. 38 Queen Anne's Street West, London.

POSTMARKS: 57 OXFORD, FE 13 89.

Oxon., feb. 11th, 1789

DEAR SIR: I was unhappy to be called away so soon from Town; but I was obliged to attend an old Aunt who was supposed to be dying.[3]

On the score of your Recommendation only, I should have been very willing to deal with Mr. Dilly; with whom I should be very glad to be acquainted, on the hopes of the pleasure of meeting you at his table. But before I left London, I had engaged with Robinson in Pater Noster Row and his Partners.[4] I am, Dear sir, very sincerely Your's

T. WARTON

From Bennet Langton,
between Monday 30 March and Monday 13 July 1789

Not reported. Established by entry in Reg. Let. for To Langton, 17 July 1789. Sent between 30 Mar. and 13 July, probably from Langton.

---

[1] *Poems upon Several Occasions* . . . with Notes . . . by T. Warton. Second Edition; with Many Alterations, and Large Additions. (Appendix, Containing Remarks on the Greek Verses of Milton, by C. Burney.) Published in 1791 by G. G. J. and J. Robinson. The first edition, in 1785, had been published by J. Dodsley.

[2] John Baynes Garforth (c. 1722–1808), M.P. for Haslemere, the Earl of Lonsdale's "capital Manager and one of his Members of Parliament with whom I had got acquainted while the Carlisle Election was before the Committee" (Journ. 22 July 1786). He apparently served as a kind of messenger boy for Lonsdale and frequently carried messages and instructions between Lonsdale and JB. For a time, JB had his letters sent to Garforth to save postage (To Mrs. Boswell, 5 Dec. 1788). Warton's oddly mixed address cost him fourpence.

[3] Not further identified.

[4] George Robinson (1737–1801), in 1784, took into partnership his son George (d. 1811) and his brother John (1753–1813), who were his successors.

Langton appears to have been in London at least to 29 Mar. (To Mrs. Boswell, 27 Mar. 1789) and to have been at Langton when this letter was written (see head-note for next letter but one).

From Sir Joshua Reynolds, Monday n.d. [1]

MS. Yale (C 2361).

ADDRESS: James Boswell Esq.

[London] Monday

DEAR SIR: I have promised to call on a person in St. Pauls Church yard this morning at half past three, to see pictures. The Coach therefore will be at your door a quarter before three when I hope you will be ready.

To Bennet Langton, Friday 17 July 1789

Not reported. Sent from Auchinleck 17 July. "Bennet Langton Esq. of my wife's death in answer to his—Comfortable to think he is at Langton —To write down Johnsoniana" (Reg. Let.). Mrs. Boswell died on Thursday 4 June, the day that JB and his sons set out from London to join her. He remained at Auchinleck until 10 Aug. (Book of Company).

To Bennet Langton, between Friday 17 July and December 1789

Not reported. Written in reply to a letter (not reported) from Lady Rothes (see next letter but one). Place of writing uncertain. Except for 10–28 Aug., when JB made a trip to Lowther and Rose Castle, and 21–24

---

[1] This letter could have been written at almost any time after JB settled in London, 1 Feb. 1786, down to 4 June 1789, when Mrs. Boswell's final illness recalled him to Auchinleck. When he returned again to London at the beginning of Oct., Reynolds had suffered total loss of vision in his left eye and was afraid to paint, to read, or to write (Journ.; C. R. Leslie and Tom Taylor, *Life and Times of Sir Joshua Reynolds*, 1865, ii. 539–40; To Temple, 13 Oct. 1789). See *post* From Barnard. 20 Dec. 1790, n. 3.

TO LANGTON, BETWEEN 17 JULY, DECEMBER 1789

Sept., when he was on a trip to Carlisle, he remained at Auchinleck from 7 June on (To Temple, 23 Aug. 1789; Book of Company). He left Auchinleck for London on 1 Oct. (*ibid.*; To Temple, 13 Oct. 1789).

From John Courtenay, Sunday 11 ?October 1789[1]

MS. Yale (C 840). Notes for *No Abolition of Slavery* written on blank spaces of this letter.

ADDRESS: Jas. Boswell Esqr., Queen Anne Street *East*.

[London] Sunday Morng. 11th

DEAR BOSWELL, Send me—a Scotch tongue, and You will Oblige Yours

J.C.

To Lady Rothes, Wednesday 23 December 1789

MS. Mrs. F. Hamilton Lacey, Hove, Sussex. Sent Dec. "Omitted Countess of Rothes to know where Mr. Langton is, and get some information from him about Dr. Johnson" (Reg. Let.). A note on side 4 (in an unidentified hand which appears also on To Langton, 23 Feb. 1790) reads, "This letter was addressed to the Countess of Rothes the wife of

---

[1] James Bruce's Housebook records payment of charges for "two Barrels for Apples and Tongues for London", 2 Dec. 1789, and for carriage for barrels and a box for London by Mauchline, Glasgow, and Carron, 7 Dec. 1789. The actual shipment would have occurred considerably earlier: for example, carriage for the moorfowl which JB and his company (including Courtenay) ate on 19 Nov. 1789 (To Sandy, 23 Nov. 1789) is charged in the Housebook under date of 17 Dec. 1789. JB, who had been away from London since 4 June 1789, arrived back with all his children except Euphemia on 6 Oct. 1789 (From Veronica Boswell to Euphemia Boswell, 12 Oct. 1789), and the tongues must have been waiting for them or have arrived shortly afterwards. 11 Oct., a Sunday, was no doubt the date of Courtenay's letter. JB's address was 38 Queen Anne Street *West*, but the difference between numbers east and numbers west on Queen Anne Street was inconsiderable. The notes for *No Abolition of Slavery* which appear on the blank spaces of this letter were probably not made much before 15 Apr. 1790, when JB sent the Countess of Crawford "Specimens of my *Slavery* and *Love* Poem" (Reg. Let.). This example warns us that it is not always safe to assume that JB had recently received the letters he used as scratch paper.

Bennet Langton of Langton Lincolnshire by James Boswell Esqre. the Biographer of Dr. Johnson." There is also on this side an arithmetical computation, apparently in Langton's hand.

London, 23 Decr. 1789

DEAR MADAM, I hope Mr. Langton received my letter in which I returned thanks for that with which I was honoured by your Ladyship. As I am uncertain where he now is I take the liberty of addressing this to your Ladyship though it refers to particulars which he only can answer. I presume that he is either at Oxford,[1] or that your Ladyship can soon convey a letter to him. We have had various reports concerning him: His absence from London is missed by none more often I think than by Mr. Courtenay and myself. As for me, the want of such a comfortable house as yours was to me at all times is much felt, especially now when I have much need of comfort. I flatter myself that we shall have the pleasure of seeing my worthy friend here soon. He will surely do as much as the Wartons and come to the Club in the Christmas Holidays.

My Life of Dr. Johnson is at last very near being put to the press.[2] I am at a loss for a small circumstance or two.

When Mr. Langton was asked to look at his watch at Oxford and see how much time there was for writing an *Idler* before the post went out was it half an hour? or how long?

What year was Dr. Johnson at Langton?

Who was the General that was very civil to him at Warley Common and what remarks did Johnson make.

What is the *gentlest* account of Sir John Hawkins's putting up a

---

[1] Langton seems to have lived in London from the end of 1784 until the spring of 1789, making occasional visits to Langton during that time (Journ. 12 July 1785 and *passim*). From about 15 Aug. to at least 6 Oct. 1786, he was at Cowes, Isle of Wight, possibly in connexion with his engineering duties (Alice C. C. Gaussen, *A Later Pepys*, 1904, ii. 268; *Johns. Glean.* ii. 65). Some time between 29 Mar. 1789, when Veronica was to dine at the Langtons' in London (To Mrs. Boswell, 27 Mar. 1789), and Oct. of that year, when Lady Rothes and the children were in Holywell St., Oxford (From Langton to his daughter Mary, 28 Oct. 1789, Hyde Collection), the Langtons moved to Oxford in order to be, according to Peregrine, close to their son George at University. Peregrine, who could not remember whether the move was in 1789 or 1790, wrote, "it is impossible that a more ill judged step could have been taken", because of "so moderate an income, and so large a family" (PL-M's letter-book, p. 41b).

[2] Printing of the *Life* began early in 1790 (Journ.).

Manuscript Volume of Johnson's, and what followed? What were Johnson's various remarks?[3]

My eldest son longs much to see George. He is now an Eton Scholar, and though he did not like it at first is now quite content. He is at home for the Holidays.[4]

It will give me most sincere pleasure to hear that all your Ladyships family are well.—I offer the best compliments of the season, and have the honour to be with great regard, Dear Madam, Your most obedient humble servant

JAMES BOSWELL

Please to let my letters come under cover of Richard Penn Esq. M.P.[5] London.

From Sir Joshua Reynolds and Others to John Douglas, c. Tuesday 5 January 1790

MS. Yale (*C 2355.8). Except for the signatures, in the hand of a professional scribe.

ENDORSEMENT: Burke Reynolds Boswell and Malone, Jany. 1790.

[London]

MY LORD: We have the honour to inform your Lordship, that at a meeting of the Friends to the memory of the late Dr. Samuel Johnson, held on the 5th of Janry. pursuant to publick advertisement, it was resolved that a Monument shall be erected to him in Westminster Abbey as speedily as may be[1] after a sufficient number

---

[3] JB refers to a book of SJ's "meditations and reflections" which Hawkins found in SJ's room and which he took with him, ostensibly to keep it from the hands of George Steevens. The "gentlest" account is undoubtedly that of Hawkins himself (*Life of Samuel Johnson*, 2nd ed., 1787, p. 586). For JB's version, see *Life* iv. 406 n. 1.

[4] On 23 Dec. 1789, JB "was now studying Prosody with Sandie, who was quite reconciled to Eton and visibly *imbutus* with its spirit allready" (Journ.).

[5] Penn (1736–1811), grandson of William Penn, had been Deputy-Governor of Pennsylvania from 1771 to 1773. From 1784 to 1790, he was M.P. for Appleby, Westmorland; and was returned for Haslemere, Surrey, in 1790. Since Penn was one of Lord Lonsdale's henchmen, JB saw much of him in the winter and spring of 1789–90, and considered him "a worthy mild consoler" (Journ. 16 Nov. 1789). He once promised to make JB his secretary if he were appointed ambassador to America (*ibid.*).

[1] At a dinner 19 Dec. 1789 at Sir William Scott's, Reynolds, Sir Joseph Banks, Malone, Metcalfe, Dr. Laurence,

of subscriptions shall have been procured for that purpose; and that they have requested us to apply to your Lordship and several other persons as likely to aid and patronize such an Undertaking.[2] We have the honour to be, My Lord, Your most humble and obedient servants

J. REYNOLDS
JAMES BOSWELL
EDM. BURKE
EDMOND MALONE

Lord Bishop of Carlisle

The bearer is authorized to receive the subscriptions of those who may be pleased to contribute to this design.

From Sir Joshua Reynolds, Friday ?8 January 1790[1]

MS. Yale (C 2356).[2] In Mary Palmer's hand.

ADDRESS: Mr. Boswell.

[London] friday Morn.

Sir Jos. Reynolds and Miss Palmer request the favor of Mr. Boswells company this Evening if he is not engaged to play at Whist.

and JB agreed "that there should be a publick meeting advertised of friends to the memory of Dr. Johnson on the 5 of Janry. to sanction a Subscription" (Journ.). For the meeting and subsequent events connected with the subscriptions see *Life* iv. 423–25, 464–69.

[2] It was Malone who suggested sending out this circular letter to about two hundred persons "selected from all the Nobility, Gentry, and Scholars of the Kingdom" (*ibid.* p. 467).

---

[1] "I went by invitation to Sir Joshua Reynolds's, drank tea and played whist. Metcalfe and Malone were there, and we staid to cold meat" (Journ. Friday 8 Jan. 1790). JB also played whist at Sir Joshua's on Friday 23 July 1790, but as

we are not assured that he went that evening by invitation, the earlier date has been preferred.

[2] JB used all the blank spaces of this letter for jotting down Johnsoniana which were somehow to be worked into his draft of the *Life* as he revised it. Of these notes, one may well have derived from the conversation at Sir Joshua's on one or the other of the evenings when he played whist there: "When it was first mentioned at Club that Burke was elected a Memb. of Parlt. and Sir J. Hawk. seemed surprised Johnson said 'Now we who know him know he will be one of the first men in this country.'" Compare *Life* ii. 450, a passage added to the draft, where Reynolds is named as JB's informant.

To Bennet Langton,
Tuesday 23 February 1790

MS. Yale (*L 849.6). A note above and below the first line of the letter (in an unidentified hand which also appears on To Lady Rothes, 23 Dec. 1789) reads "To Bennet Langton Esqre. of Langton from James Boswell the Author of Life of Dr. Johnson".

London, 23 Febry. 1790

MY DEAR SIR, A considerable time ago I wrote to Lady Rothes addressed Oxford,[1] trusting that the contents of my letter would reach you wherever you should happen to be, as to which I was uncertain. I am really uneasy that I have neither heard *from* you nor *off* you, and write this merely to *hail*[2] you intreating that if it comes to your hands you will be so kind as to write to me, and then I will trouble you with a few inquiries concerning Dr. Johnson, my Life of whom is now in the press.[3] My two sons have both been ill of a rash fever,[4] but I thank GOD are now pretty well.

I offer my best respects to Lady Rothes, and love to your children and am with most sincere regard, My Dear Sir, your faithful humble servant

JAMES BOSWELL

Please to write under cover of Richard Penn Esq. M.P., London.

From Bennet Langton,
Monday 1 March 1790

MS. Yale (C 1689).

ADDRESS: To James Boswell Esqr.

ENDORSEMENT: Bennet Langton Esq. 1 March 1790.

---

[1] *Ante* 23 Dec. 1789.

[2] Since JB emphasizes "off", that form can hardly be an inadvertence. Perhaps an untraced quotation. The sentence sounds as though it might have been spoken by a nautical character in a play.

[3] JB had decided on the format of the *Life* by 13 Jan. By 22 Feb., he was going to the "Printing House to quicken" the printing (Journ.).

[4] Alexander ("Sandy") was ill in late Dec. and early Jan.; Jamie, off and on between 11 Jan. and the end of the month (Journ.). Only Jamie's illness was identified by JB in the journal as rash fever.

Oxford, March 1st. 1790

MY DEAR SIR, Let me begin my Letter with assuring You, that, in so great a degree of delinquency as subsists in your not having had notice taken of your Letter, Lady Rothes has no manner of share—She delivered it to me on receiving it;—and, as to me, alas! may I have leave to say, that it seems as if I had been, in this instance, dazzled with the light of confidence in myself—as thinking, that, whosoever Letters I might be in danger of neglecting to answer, no such danger could however happen as to *Yours*; and thus have gone on,—sure that I was going immediately to treat myself with writing to You, in a delay, to which, *both* the lines of the distich, "Truditur dies die, Novæque pergunt interire Lunæ,"[1] as I am ashamed to think, are applicable. But I will not weary You any longer with apologies, unless, in giving You some account of the manner in which I have been of late engaged, as You are so kind as to wish me to do, I should be so fortunate as to have You think that my Engagements have been such as to extenuate a little the blame of my tardiness—I was detained in Lincolnshire from the time of my last writing to You, for a time, by some not comfortable concerns of business,[2] and, afterwards, from severe ill health prevailing in more than one Instance of very near Relations to me,[3] till the midst of December last; when I arrived here, and found Lady Rothes in a state of health a good deal improved from what had been the case, and the rest of my numerous family tolerably well on the whole; Your Letter arrived towards the end of that month, and, very soon after, I had to go into Hampshire on the Concerns of a Canal[4] that I believe You

[1] Horace, *Odes* II. xviii. 15–16: "Day treads upon the heel of day, and new moons haste to wane" (C. E. Bennett's translation in Loeb ed.). Topham Beauclerk once told JB that SJ had repeated this ode "one moonlight evening in London, soon after he got acquainted with him". JB himself memorized it some years later (Journ. 22 Mar. 1776).

[2] This business, to which Langton refers again (*post* 2 Oct., 30 Nov.), was possibly the disposal of the Oxcombe estate (over 1,000 acres), which had been in the family since about 1641. His father, in 1762, was the last Langton to present to Oxcombe Church. One John

Grant presented to the church on 26 Feb. 1798, having apparently purchased the estate from Langton (*Lincolnshire Notes & Queries* vii. 84–87).

[3] Lady Rothes had been ill, and he had reported to his daughter Mary on 28 Oct. 1789 that his sister was not well: "Your Aunt Langton continues a good deal the same" (Hyde Collection). Elizabeth Langton died early in Jan. 1791 (notes in Foster Library, Lincoln, from Parish Register of Langton by Spilsby; *Gent. Mag.* 1791, lxi. 91).

[4] The Basingstoke Canal, which ran from Basingstoke, Hampshire, to the River Wey Navigation, near Weybridge,

have heard me speak of, where I was detained some little time; when I returned here; I had a subject of some anxiety of consideration to attend to; that of fixing on the manner in which I was to place my Son in the University; the result of which has been (not to trouble You with detailing particulars) that he has been entered as a Gentleman-Commoner at Christ-Church[5]—he dines every day in the Hall there, and associates to a due degree with the Society, but sleeps at home, in my habitation—The Dean of Christchurch[6] has been very obliging to me in his friendly communication with me on the occasion—in a manner, that, if I could have the satisfaction of our meeting, I should hope it might be of some entertainment for me to recount but that hope of our meeting, I have no grounds for allowing myself; unless You would be so kind as to give us your Company here for some little time that You could Spare us—as I have it not in view to make any visit to Town, within any time that I can assign—the very kind regret, Dear Sir, that You mention having, with some other of my friends, entertained, among whom you particularize Mr. Courtenay, at my having shifted my situation,[7] demands my best Gratitude and to him and whoever others have honoured me with expressing such kind regard, I will beg You to offer my due acknowledgements—

It is agreeable to find, Sir, by your last Letter that You were relieved from the anxiety You must have been under by the Fever that the two young Gentlemen have been attacked with—I hope

Surrey. The proprietors of the Wey Navigation received one shilling per ton for all boats passing from the canal through the Wey (sometimes called the Wye) Navigation into the Thames. Langton had inherited a moiety of the Wey that had come into the family with his grandmother, Mary Tindall. The second moiety was in the possession of the Portmore family. Although the Basingstoke Canal did not benefit those who invested in it, the undertaking proved profitable to Langton and the Portmores (Owen Manning and William Bray, *The History and Antiquities of the County of Surrey*, iii, 1814, lvii–lviii). See N & Q (1956) cci. 347–49 for my account of Langton's connexion with the Wey Navigation.

[5] George Langton matriculated at Christ Church College on 1 Mar. 1790

(*Alum. Oxon.* II. ii. 818). He was placed, according to his brother Peregrine, "among a most expensive class of young men, without any allowance—without any means of keeping pace with them." He was later moved from Christ Church "for his excessive irregularity, his debauchery, his inattention to all rules . . . and was placed at Corpus Christi, where if possible, his conduct was more improper still" (PL-M's diary, June 1811–May 1813, pp. 406–07).

[6] Cyril Jackson (1746–1819) was Dean of Christ Church from 1783 to 1809. He was later (1799) to refuse the primacy of Ireland and the bishopric of Oxford (*Alum. Oxon.* II. ii. 734; *The Historical Record of the University of Oxford to 1900*, 1900, p. 550). See *Letters SJ* ii. 145.

[7] The move to Oxford.

their Recovery from it is quite compleat—and am glad to understand that the eldest is pleased on the whole with his Situation as
an Eton Scholar—I fancy I had better not keep what I have
written, till I have replied to the queries You send relative to Dr.
Johnson, as I find four or five days have stolen on already since I
began it— and that might make more addition of delay than I could
wish; but I intend resuming the writing and giving my replies
almost immediately after dispatching this—I have only one thing
further at present to say; which is, that You told me, on my
having some apprehension that some of the particulars I had
communicated might not be what I should chuse to have published
that I should have the reading over of all You had received from
me, which I very much wish could have been the case; which to be
sure the distance of situation makes something difficult to accomplish—however at present, as I have said, I will send my paper
away, adding only that I am (with all our best Regards), Dear Sir,
Your faithful humble Servant

BENNET LANGTON

To Thomas Percy,
Friday 12 March 1790

MS. collection of Arthur A. Houghton, Jr. Sent 12 Mar. "Bishop of
Dromore sending him Burke's Speech on french affairs and Lord Stanhope's answer; obliged to him for some information concerning Johnson
—apology for long silence—Death of valuable wife—left with five
children. Am to get additions to Goldsmith's works to communicate to
him" (Reg. Let.).

HEADING (in an unidentified hand): Mr. Boswell.

Queen Anne Street West, 12 March 1790

MY DEAR LORD: I am indeed ashamed of my long silence. But
although I felt very gratefully the kindness of your Lordships last
obliging letter containing some good information for my Life of
Dr. Johnson many things have since my receiving it made me
rather an irregular correspondent. As the great cause of all my
dissipation of mind, I have to mention the loss of a most valuable
wife, who died in June last of a consumption[1] which being an
hereditary complaint had afflicted her for many many years. I have

[1] 4 June.

three daughters the eldest of whom is only sixteen and two sons the eldest of whom is only fourteen.[2] I have therefore a great charge for which I am very unfit; but I must do my best. I was every day wishing to write to your Lordship, for that consolation which your office enables you to give. I thank GOD for having afforded me more than I at first supposed possible.

It gives me great pleasure to hear that your Lordship and family intend a visit to us next summer.[3] I shall by that time be well advanced in my *Magnum Opus* of which a hundred pages are now printed. I hope we shall have many of those happy days which *olim meminisse juvabit*.[4]

I engaged to Sir Joshua Reynolds to send your Lordship Mr. Burkes Speech on the french affairs.[5] It accordingly comes under cover as your Lordship mentioned. I have added to it Lord Stanhope's Answer,[6] which I will venture to call somewhat blackguard.

Sir Joshua has been shamefully used by a junto of the Academicians.[7] I live a great deal with him, and he is much better than you would suppose.

[2] Veronica (b. 1773), Euphemia (b. 1774), Elizabeth (b. 1780), Alexander (b. 1775), James (b. 1778).

[3] JB probably heard of Percy's intention from Reynolds. Percy did not get to London until 1791.

[4] Virgil, *Aeneid* i. 203: "it will some day be a joy to recall" (H. R. Fairclough's translation in Loeb ed.).

[5] Reynolds wrote to Percy, on 13 Mar., "I have put the little business that you intrusted me with into the hands of Mr. Boswell, who, indeed, desired it, as he said he owed your Lordship a letter" (*Letters Reynolds*, p. 201). The pamphlet was *Substance of the Speech of the Right Honourable Edmund Burke, in the Debate on the Army Estimates in the House of Commons, on Tuesday the 9th day of February, 1790. Comprehending a Discussion of the Present Situation of Affairs in France,* 1790. The speech had been made in reply to praise given to the French Revolutionists by Fox. Burke deplored the violence and anarchy, contrasted the events in France with the Glorious Revolution of 1688, and concluded that the French were not ready for liberty.

[6] Charles Stanhope (1753–1816), third Earl Stanhope, *A Letter to the Right Hon. Edmund Burke. Containing a short Answer to his late Speech on the French Revolution,* 1790. Stanhope was president of the Revolution Society, which sent a message of approval to the French Assembly (see also From Barnard, 14 July 1791 or shortly after, n. 3). In 1789, he had introduced a toleration bill into the House of Lords designed to repeal a number of obsolete religious laws. The bill was defeated.

[7] Reynolds's disagreement with the Academy was brought about by his efforts to promote the election of Joseph Bonomi as professor of perspective rather than Edward Edwards, an artist preferred by a number of Academicians. When Sir Joshua ordered the two men to submit drawings, Edwards refused, believing, like most of the Academy, that such a display of samples was unconstitutional. Henry Fuseli being elected, Reynolds resigned his presidency and membership, returning only after the members admitted that his requiring the display of drawings was within his rights. This they did on 13 Mar.; and Reynolds

Pray how does your edition of Goldsmith[8] go on? I am in the way of getting at many additional works of his which I shall communicate to your Lordship.[9] I offer my best compliments to Mrs. Percy and the young Ladies and ever am your Lordships faithful humble servant

JAMES BOSWELL

From Thomson Bonar to Lord Macartney,
Saturday 13 March 1790

MS. Yale (C 170).

ADDRESS: Lord Macartney, Curzon Street.

ENDORSEMENT by JB: As to Russian Translations.[1]

POSTMARKS: PENNY POST PAID G SA, 7 [O]CLOCK.

Broadstreet Buildings, 13 March 1790

MY LORD: There are a great many English Novels translated into the Russian Language. *Tom Jones*, *Joseph Andrews*, and *Amelia* are among the number. Of our Poets, Popes *Essay on Man*, is the

resumed the chair on the 16th (C. R. Leslie and Tom Taylor, *Life and Times of Sir Joshua Reynolds*, 1865, ii. 553–85, *Lit. Car. Reynolds*, pp. 174–76, 249–76); Although JB here seems to side with Reynolds, he told Joseph Farington some years later that he thought Sir Joshua was at fault (*Farington Diary* i. 95).

[8] In 1773 Goldsmith had dictated some memoranda concerning his life to Percy, who planned to become his biographer. These, with other valuable papers he had collected, Percy turned over to SJ in 1776, but SJ died before writing the proposed life. Once more Percy decided to undertake the task, intending to write a memoir that would be prefaced to a new edition of Goldsmith's writings. This edition eventually appeared in 1802 (K. C. Balderston, *The History and Sources of Percy's Memoir of Goldsmith*, 1926, pp. 11–30). See *post* From Percy, 24 Apr. 1790, n. 1.

[9] What these works were, or whether JB ever sent any, is not known.

[1] JB had apparently asked Macartney, who had twice gone to Russia as envoy extraordinary, whether *The Rambler* had been translated into Russian (*Life* iv. 277 and note). Macartney had referred the question to Thomson Bonar (1743–1813), second son of the Edinburgh banker Andrew Bonar. Bonar, mistakenly named Thomas in *The Universal British Directory* of 1791, was a merchant with offices at 7 New Broadstreet Buildings. He had lived in St. Petersburg, where his son, Thomson Jr., was born in 1780. He is listed in the *Royal Kalendar* as an assistant in the Eastland Co. in 1792 and as an assistant in the Russia Co. from 1795 until the end of his life (John Burke, *Landed Gentry*, 1855; *Gent. Mag.* 1813, lxxxiii. pt. 1. 582–83).

only one I recollect. I think they have translated also, Johnson's *Prince of Abyssinia*, but no other of his Works.[2]

If Your Lordship wishes for more certain information, I will write about it to Petersburg.[3] I am very truly, Your Lordships very Humble Servant

T. BONAR

To John Douglas,
Tuesday 16 March 1790

MS. Yale (L 439).

HEADING: Copy. To The Lord Bishop of Carlisle.

[London] Queen Anne Street West, 16 March 1790
MY DEAR LORD: General Paoli having received the most earnest solicitations from his brave countrymen to return to them, is to depart next week.[1] He is to oblige his faithful and attached friend by taking a dinner with him in a hut in Queen Anne Street West on *Monday 22 March* at 5 o'clock.[2] I am engaging a few very select friends pour dire adieu to the Corsican Hero, and I presume to request the honour of *my own Bishop's*[3] company on the occasion.

[2] A telescoped Russian version of *Rasselas* had been published in 1764 and two of SJ's *Rambler* papers in 1766 (J. S. G. Simmons, "Samuel Johnson 'on the banks of the Wolga'" in *Oxford Slavonic Papers*, 1964, xi. 28–37).

[3] Macartney could have handed this letter to JB when attending the dinner JB gave before Paoli's departure (see n. 2 of next letter). JB had attended a meeting of The Club on 16 Mar., but according to the Club records Macartney was absent.

[1] Shortly after the French Revolution broke out, Paoli was recalled from England, where he had been in exile since 1769, to rule again over Corsica. He left London on 29 Mar. 1790 (*Public Advertiser*, 2 Apr. 1790). He ruled until 1794, when the British, with his approval, took over the island.

[2] A card, one of three preserved in the

Boswell Papers from this period, lists the names of the company who attended JB's dinner: General Paoli, "Ministre de Sardagne" [i.e. Count St. Martin de Front, Envoy Extraordinary], Ministre de Portugal [i.e. Cipriano Ribeiro de Freire, at this time Secretary of Legation], Sir John Dick, Mr. [John] Osborn, Sir Joseph Banks, Mr. [Richard] Cosway, "Don Titus" [i.e. T. D. Boswell], and Lord Macartney (Yale, part of J 110).

[3] JB refers to their official associations with Carlisle. "Mr. Boswell had not been long at the English bar when he was elected Recorder of the ancient city of Carlisle, and soon after his learned and respectable countryman Dr. John Douglas was appointed Bishop of the Diocese. These two promotions gave occasion to the following epigram:

'Of old, ere wise Concord united this Isle,
Our neighbours of Scotland were foes at Carlisle;

I ever am with great respect. My Dear Lord, Your most obedient humble servant

JAMES BOSWELL

From Thomas Percy,
Friday 19 March 1790

MS. Yale (C 2235).

ADDRESS (in William Bennet's[1] hand): James Boswell Esqr., Queen Anne Street West, London.

FRANK: Dublin, March the twenty third 1790. Wm. Bennet.

POSTMARKS: MR 25 90, [illegible], FREE.

ENDORSEMENT: Bishop of Dromore 19 March 1790.

Dublin, March 19th. 1790

DEAR SIR, I lose no time in acknowledging your very obliging favour of the 12th—which the last Packet brought over and at same time I had Sir Joshua's kind but short Billet of the 15th which I will beg you to mention with my best Compliments, when you see him. I very sincerely thank you for the 2 Pamphlets, Mr. Burke's Speech and Lord Stanhope's (*illiberal*) answer to it: both highly acceptable to us on this side the Water; Who are often much behind hand with respect to the fugitive Publications. For as they generally are sent by Sea from London to Dublin; the Passage down the Channel and round to the Bay of Dublin requires so many different Winds, that a Voyage to America is frequently performed in less time. But by the favour of Dr. Bennet's Privilege who is Under-Secretary to the Lord Lieut. any small Pamphlets will come free by the Post.—I see advertized a Pamphlet contain-

But now what a change have we here on the border,
When Douglas is Bishop and Boswell Recorder'"
("Memoirs of James Boswell, Esq.," from *The European Magazine*, May, June 1791, quoted in *Lit. Car.* pp. xlii, 235). The "Memoirs" were written by JB, and the epigram is his also (cutting from *Public Advertiser*, 13 May 1788, with JB's mark of authorship, in P 116).

---

[1] The Rev. William Bennet (1746–

1820) had been for many years chief tutor at Emmanuel College, Cambridge, where the Earl of Westmorland was his pupil. When Lord Westmorland was appointed Lord-Lieutenant of Ireland in 1790, he nominated Bennet as his chaplain and under-secretary. The latter appointment gave Bennet the privilege of franking letters to Great Britain. See *post* in this letter and From Barnard, 14 Apr. 1785, n. 9. On 12 June 1790, Bennet was appointed Bishop of Cork and Ross, and in 1794, Bishop of Cloyne.

taining an Account of the Debate on the proposed Repeal of the Test-Act:[2] I should be very glad to have it sent me by same Conveyance; and hope you will allow me to settle, for all similar Disbursemts. with you when I come to England, as I hope to do this summer.

I was truly concerned for your very afflicting Loss: well knowing what I should have felt myself under a similar Affliction. I could only have refer'd you to the Comforts which Religion offers in such Cases of irremediable Distress, and those a friend of Dr. Johnson could not want to have suggested. May you and your young Family always enjoy them in their utmost Extent, in every Exigence of Life.

I am much indebted to your candid acceptance, if you can find any admission for the petty anecdotes I sent you: Which, I am so perfectly sensible are of little value, that I hope you will grant the request, which I now make, viz. that you will not give my *Name* to the public along with them: but mention if at all necessary that they were communicated by a Person, who had heard them in Conversation from Dr. Johnson himself, or from Mrs. Williams, when he was present and admitted the Particulars to be true. In granting this favour you will much oblige me, and if it should be necessary to cancell a Leaf or two, I will thankfully repay the Loss to the Bookseller.—The indulging me in this Petition, will encourage me to add any supplemental Intelligence, that may hereafter occur when we meet on the other side the Water.

Mrs. Percy and my Dau[ghte]rs join with me in best Compliments to you and your young Family: Who am very truly, Dear Sir, Your very faithful humble Servant

THOS. DROMORE

---

[2] An advertisement in *The London Chronicle* (6–9 Mar. 1790, lxvii. 231) announced the publication of *The Debate in the House of Commons March 2, 1790 on the Repeal of the Corporation and Test Acts; containing the Speeches of Mr. Fox, Mr. Pitt, Mr. Burke*, Printed for John Stockdale, opposite Burlington-house, Piccadilly. The advertisement appeared under the heading: "Debate on the Test Act, with a correct List of the Members who voted for and against the Repeal, and a List of the Absentees." Fox introduced the subject in Commons, arguing that it was wrong to assume that men holding certain speculative opinions would necessarily commit actions immoral and harmful to society, and that the acts should be repealed. The cause of the dissenters was hampered by the political alliance (at least in theory) of some of their members with the French Revolution; and Burke and the others who opposed Fox's motion believed that many of the dissenters had no religious motives, but were interested in destroying church and monarchy. The House divided 294–105 against the motion.

P.S. Goldsmith's new Edition has been delay'd by the Dublin Bookseller's having left off business, who first ingaged in it:[3] but it is now resumed by an eminent Printer in London,[4] and I hope will proceed properly: Can you tell what became of his MS. Prospectus for his intended Diction[ar]y of Arts and Sciences? This would be a valuable Acquisition.[5] When will Mr. Malone's Shakespear come forth.

From John Courtenay, ?between Friday 26 and Monday 29 March 1790[1]

MS. Yale (C 841). On verso, notes in JB's hand of a conversation with Archdeacon Pott.

ADDRESS: J. Boswell Esqr.

[London]

DEAR BOSWELL: I perfectly forgot yesterday in the hurry of talking, that I have been engaged—since Tuesday and in a way I cannot get off.—Believe I am extremely sorry for it;—I would have wrote, but concluded you would not wait[2]—Ever faithfully Yours

J. C.

[3] Presumably Henry Whitestone, who died 16 Oct. 1787 (K. C. Balderston, *The History and Sources of Percy's Memoir of Goldsmith*, 1926, p. 25, and *Gent. Mag.* 1787, lvii. 937).

[4] On 2 July 1789 John Nichols agreed to publish the life and works. The agreement, however, was not consummated, although Nichols did print the volumes published in 1802 (Reiberg, pp. 157, 169). See also To Percy, 12 Mar. 1790, n. 8, and From Percy, 24 Apr. 1790, n. 1.

[5] Percy had unsuccessfully asked Malone for this in 1786 (Balderston, p. 27). Nor, as JB's answer to this shows, could JB discover it.

[1] The suggested dating is based on Courtenay's "Tuesday" and the assumption that JB had recently received the letter when he first met Archdeacon Pott. That meeting occurred shortly before

9 Apr. 1790 (To Langton of that date) and probably at the Anniversary Feast of the Humane Society, Tuesday 30 Mar. (date obtained from *General Evening Post*, 30 Mar.–1 Apr. 1790). See n. 2.

[2] JB recorded remarks of Charles Macklin (?1697–1797), the old actor and playwright, dated Sunday 28 Mar. 1790, in the blank spaces of his copy of To J. Warton, Saturday 27 Mar. One can make sense of Courtenay's puzzling "I would have wrote" by assuming that on Saturday he had agreed to go with JB next afternoon or evening to meet Macklin at Macklin's lodgings or at a tavern, and that on Sunday he wrote JB a note that JB would not see till he got home. The note says in effect, "I recollected as soon as we parted yesterday that I was engaged for today, and would have written instantly to let you know, but I felt sure that you would not wait for me."

For Gods sake, keep yourself a little quiet:—for drinking too much every day—will harden your blood.[3]

To Joseph Warton, Saturday 27 March 1790

MS. Yale (L 1271). A copy. On verso, anecdotes of Charles Macklin (M 173).

Queen Anne Street West, 27 March 1790

REVEREND SIR: I take the liberty to beg that you may let me know by return of post which two papers in *The Adventurer* signed T were written by Colman.[1] One of my sheets waits for your answer.[2] I go on steadily, but cannot be out before October. All our common friends are well and remember you with much regard. I ever am, My Dear Sir, your faithful humble servant

JAMES BOSWELL

If you can recollect the origin of Johnson's prejudice against G[r]ay's poetry, pray let me have it.

From Joseph Warton, Tuesday 30 March 1790

MS. Yale (C 3064). Received Apr. "Rev. Dr. Jo. Warton information about Johnson" (Reg. Let.).

ADDRESS: James Boswell Esqr.

ENDORSEMENT: Rev. Dr. Joseph Warton 30 March 1790.

[3] If this postscript stood alone, one would probably assign it to the end of 1790, when we know that JB gave Courtenay his word that he would "drink no more than four glasses and a pint of wine a day" till the first of Mar. 1791 (Journ. 15 Feb., 1 Mar. 1791). The end of Mar. 1790, however, appears also to have been a time when Courtenay would have been alarmed at JB's drinking. The journal lapses from mid-Feb. to the end of Mar., but we know from various scraps (J 110, M 194, 173, 316) that JB was dining out a great deal during that period (from 14 Mar. to 29 Mar. almost daily) and can have no doubt that he was drinking heavily. If, as surmised in n. 2,

Courtenay saw JB on Saturday 27 Mar., he might well have found him in bad shape. JB had supped the previous evening with the Stewards of the Humane Society (date fixed by M 194), and these suppers were remarkably jovial (Journ. 7 Mar. 1791).

[1] For JB's account of SJ and *The Adventurer* see *Life* i. 252–54. It is corrected by L. F. Powell in the introduction to his edition of *The Adventurer* (in *Works of SJ*, Yale Ed. ii. 323–35).

[2] Sheet S. A facsimile of the proof-sheet of p. 135 appears in R. B. Adam's *Reproduction of Some of the Original Proof Sheets of Boswell's Life of Johnson*, 1923.

Winton,[1] March 30 1790

DEAR SIR, I do not delay a moment to answer the letter with which you have favoured me, relating to the authors of the *Adventurer*. It was *Thornton*,[2] not *Colman*, who wrote several papers. And it was always imagined, tho I have not positive proof, that Thornton wrote all the papers, marked *A*. viz[3] Numbers—3. 6. 9. 19. 23. 25. 35. 43. And that *Johnson* wrote ALL marked *T*, except the two from *misargyrus*.[4] That is *all* the papers marked *T*. after n. 45. Just about that time *Thornton* engaged with poor[5] *Colman* in writing the *Connoisseur*.[6] By the two particular friends[7] Johnson certainly meant—*Hawkesworth* and *Bathurst*. I did not then know *Hawkesworth*.

With respect to our friends strange aversion to *Gray's* poetry, I never could find any other cause of it, than that he was particularly fond of that sort of poetry, that deals chiefly, in nervous, pointed, sentimental, didactic Lines.

I know not whether you would like to mention that Johnson once owned to me, knowing how enthusiastically fond I was of the Greek Tragedies, that he never had read a Greek Tragedy in his Life.[8]

[1] That is, Winchester.

[2] Bonnell Thornton (1724–68), miscellaneous writer. See W. C. Brown, "A Belated Augustan: Bonnell Thornton, Esq.", *Philological Quarterly* (1955) xxxiv. 335–48, for an account of his literary career. Warton wrote a Latin inscription for his grave in Westminster Abbey.

[3] MS. "marked. *A.* viz".

[4] In addition to Powell's comments (n. 1 to preceding letter) see V. L. Lams, Jr., "The 'A' Papers in the *Adventurer*: Bonnell Thornton, not Dr. Bathurst, Their Author", *Studies in Philology* (1967) lxiv. 83ff.

[5] In 1789, Colman had had his second paralytic stroke, which affected his brain; consequently in Aug. of that year he was placed permanently in a private asylum at Paddington. He lived in that unfortunate condition for five years before he died (E. R. Page, *George Colman the Elder*, 1935, pp. 296–97).

[6] The first issue of *The Connoisseur* was dated Thursday 31 Jan. 1754; the last one, No. 140, Thursday 30 Sept. 1756.

SJ maintained that the publication "wanted matter", but JB came to its defence: "No doubt it has not the deep thinking of Johnson's writings. But surely it has just views of the surface of life, and a very sprightly manner" (*Life* i. 420). For an account of it, see the "Historical and Biographical Preface" to vol. xxv of the 1823 edition of Alexander Chalmers's *The British Essayists*, pp. xv–xxxix.

[7] As Professor Waingrow points out, JB, after making his copy, must have added to the original of the preceding letter a query as to whom SJ meant by this phrase in a letter to Warton, 8 Mar. 1753 which JB was printing in the *Life*. Dr. John Hawkesworth (?1715–1773), a miscellaneous writer, member of the Ivy Lane Club, biographer and editor of Swift, was an intimate of SJ (see *Life* i. 190 n. 3); Dr. Richard Bathurst (d. 1762) was also a member of the Ivy Lane Club. Francis Barber, SJ's black servant, had been his father's slave.

[8] SJ acknowledged to Cumberland that "his studies had not lain amongst"

I long to see your Work, as I am very sure it must be very entertaining and interesting. I rejoice with you and with every Lover of great Genius, and the Arts, that our dear and amiable friend Sir Joshua, is restored to that Seat, that He alone is fit to fill and adorn.[9] I shall, as I said to you in Town,[10] be sincerely glad if ever you will give me the pleasure of your Company at this Place, and I am, Dear Sir, Your faithful and obedient humble Servant

Jos. Warton

To Thomas Warton, before Wednesday 7 April 1790

Not reported. Sent from London before 7 Apr. "Rev. Mr. Tho. Warton for Johnsonian information" (Reg. Let.).

From Thomas Warton, Wednesday 7 April 1790

MS. Yale (C 3078). Received Apr. "Rev. Mr. Tho. Warton Ditto ["information about Johnson"]" (Reg. Let.).

ADDRESS: James Boswell Esq., Queen Anne's Street West.

Woodstock, Apr. 7th, 1790

DEAR SIR: I have just had the favour of yours at this place, eight Miles from Oxford,[1] and therefore do not answer it so soon as you might expect.

the Greek dramatists (*Johnsonian Miscellanies*, ed. G. B. Hill, 1897, ii. 78); but his writings and other statements do not bear out Warton's categorical assertion: he comments on Greek tragedies in *Life* iv. 16, and discusses the use of allegorical figures in the *Prometheus* of Aeschylus and in the *Alcestis* of Euripides in *Lives of the English Poets*, ed. G. B. Hill, 1905, i. 185. Warton may very well mean that SJ did not read these dramatists in Greek.

[9] Warton refers to Reynolds's quarrel with, and temporary resignation from the presidency of, the Royal Academy.

[10] There is no specific reference to this conversation in JB's journal.

[1] Warton had been curate at Woodstock, Oxfordshire, from 27 Apr. 1755 to 3 Apr. 1774. In Oct. 1771, "he was presented to the small living of Kiddington, near Woodstock, which he retained until his death" (Clarissa Rinaker, *Thomas Warton*, 1916, pp. 159–60). See "Wartoniana" in *The Literary Journal*, 1803, i. 280–81, 601–03, for an account of Warton's connexions with Woodstock.

At Oxford, *Lodgings* is the word elleiptically for the *Master's,* or *President's,* etc., Lodgings. Thus if I had been visiting our President, I should say, I have been *at the Lodgings.* At Cambridge they say, surely very improperly, the *Lodge.*[2] I am, Dear Sir, very sincerely Yours

T. WARTON

To Bennet Langton, Friday 9 April 1790

MS. BM Add. MSS. 36747E, ff. 50–51. Sent Apr. "Bennet Langton Esq. pressing him for answers to Johnsonian Queries etc." (Reg. Let.).

London, 9 April 1790

MY DEAR SIR: You cannot imagine how I was comforted by receiving your kind letter, as my *brooding* mind had begun to form strange groundless apprehensions that you were somehow offended with me. Let us *engage* that no such sad circumstance shall ever take place, without fair warning given, and then we shall be at least *negatively* easy.

As a Steward of the Humane Society[1] I lately got acquainted with the Reverend Mr. Pott, Archdeacon of St. Albans[2] who

---

[2] The OED confirms Warton's distinctions, although it makes no value judgement on the relative correctness of the two terms. JB had obviously questioned the use of *lodgings* in Warton's memorial of SJ's 1754 visit to Oxford, printed in *Life* i. 271–72.

---

[1] The Humane Society (later the Royal Humane Society) was instituted in 1774 by Dr. William Hawes "for the Recovery of Persons apparently dead by Drowning". JB's friend, Dr. John Coakley Lettsom, was Treasurer of the Society and was probably instrumental in getting JB elected Steward. The Society's archives do not record his election, but it probably took place at the Anniversary feast on 24 Mar. 1789 (To Mrs. Boswell, 24, 25 Mar. 1789; Journ. 28 Feb. 1791 indicates that elections were made at the anniversary meetings). He attended a supper meeting of the Stewards on 26

Mar. 1790, the Anniversary feast on 30 Mar. (on both these occasions singing songs of his own composition), and some kind of meeting recorded merely as "Humane Society" on 8 Apr. (M 194; *General Evening Post,* 30 Mar.–1 Apr., 1–3 Apr. 1790; *Edinburgh Advertiser,* 6–9 Apr. 1790; Journ. 8 Apr.). His name appears in the list of Stewards in the Society's annual reports for the years 1791, 1792, and 1793, but there is no mention of his name after that (letter from Col. G. W. M. Grover, Secretary of the Royal Humane Society, 8 Jan. 1959).

[2] Joseph Holden Pott (1759–1847), archdeacon successively of St. Albans and London. In the *Life,* JB praised two of his sermons that had appeared in the spring of 1790 as *Two Sermons for the Festivals and Fasts of the Church of England* (reviewed *Gent. Mag.* Apr. 1790, lx. 348; *Life* ii. 458–59, 536).

preached an admirable sermon for our Charity.[3] He told me he had a living for some time in Lincolnshire, near to Langton from which he regretted that you were absent. I found he knew *your character well*[4] he described Langton as a respectable ancient place, and said he passed it with a sigh.

You may rest assured that you shall see your Johnsoniana before I print them. I shall either send them to you, or (what I really wish much) come to you for a day or two and have *chocolade* for my mind. How can I lodge myself most comfortably.

We are now collecting our cash for Johnson's Monument. Pray give orders to pay your five guineas to Mr. Metcalfe Saville Row who is our cashier.[5]

I have printed twenty sheets of my Magnum Opus. It will be the most entertaining Book that ever appeared. Only think of what an offer I have for it—*A Cool thousand.*[6] But I am advised to retain the property myself.

Now my dear Langton let me request to have your answer to my queries directly; for *one* of the articles will be in the press in a day or two. How *can* you be so indolent? With best respects to Lady Rothes and love to your young race I am ever most affectionately yours

JAMES BOSWELL

Write under cover of Richard Penn Esq. M.P. who calls you his old friend.

---

[3] Pott's *Sermon Preached . . . for . . . The Royal Humane Society* had been preached at St. Dunstan's in the West on Sunday 28 Mar. At the Anniversary Meeting it was ordered "that the Archdeacon be earnestly requested to publish the same". This was done; it was reviewed in *Gent. Mag.* (July 1790), lx. 640. A copy of this rather rare pamphlet is in the Boston Athenaeum. On the verso of the dedication page is a list of Stewards for the year 1790, eighteen men, including JB.

[4] Possibly a reference to Pope's *Essay on Criticism* i. 119: "Know well each Ancient's proper character." Pott had been collated to the prebend of Welton-Brinkhill in Lincoln Cathedral, 17 Mar. 1785.

[5] On 23 Dec. 1788 Langton had signed, along with eight other members of The Club, a resolution agreeing to contribute five guineas towards the expense of the monument (*The Club*).

[6] Almost nine months later, JB was tempted to take up this, or another offer for £1,000, from George Robinson, bookseller, which Malone had reported to him. JB wanted to buy the estate of Knockroon and needed at least the £1,000 for a down payment. Charles Dilly, although he would lose in the transaction, advised him to sell the copyright, "yet Malone had raised my hopes high of the success of my Work, and if it did succeed, the Quarto edition alone would yield me above £1200" (Journ. 20 Feb. 1791).

To Thomas Percy,
Friday 9 April 1790

MS. Berg Collection, The New York Public Library. A copy in James Ross's[1] hand, except for the heading, is at Yale (L 1067); there is one significant difference between the texts.

London, 9 April 1790

MY DEAR LORD: Stockdale has promised a list of the members who voted on both sides on the great question on the Corporation and Test Acts.[1a] But he is so very long about it that I will wait no longer, but send you the Debate as published by him. I most heartily rejoice to find that the Church is so respectably established in the opinion of the Laity.

As to suppressing your Lordship's name when relating the very few anecdotes of Johnson with which you have favoured me, I will do any thing to oblige your Lordship but that very thing. I owe to the authenticity of my Work, to its respectability and to the credit of my illustrious friend,[2] to introduce as many names of eminent persons as I can. It is comparatively a very small portion which is sanctioned by that of your Lordship, and there is nothing even bordering on impropriety. Believe me My Lord you are not the only Bishop in the number of great men with which my pages are graced. I am quite resolute as to this matter.

Pray who is it that has the charge of Goldsmiths Works here? I should like to talk with him. I know not where the Plan of his Encyclopedia is, or if it be preserved.[3]

Our amiable friend Sir Joshua Reynolds has received from the

---

[1] JB's Scots servant. See *post* To Leeds, 19 June 1792, n. 1.

[1a] John Stockdale (?1749–1814), the publisher of the pamphlet in which Percy is interested.

[2] MS. "friends". In Ross's copy the word is also plural, but the *s* has been struck out, presumably by JB, who wrote the heading.

[3] John Bowyer Nichols used the original MS. of the present letter as printer's copy for *Lit. Illust.* vii. 313–14. At this point he inserted an asterisk as sign for a foot-note ("It is not in Mr. Prior's edition of *The Miscellaneous Works*

of Goldsmith"), but must have supplied copy for the note in the proof or written it on a separate piece of paper now missing. See *post* n. 5. In 1773 Goldsmith projected a grandiose Dictionary of the Arts and Sciences which he was to edit, with his distinguished friends (Burke, Reynolds, Garrick, Burney) as contributors. He drew up a prospectus which was perhaps never published; at any rate, no copy of it is now known to exist. The scheme was soon dropped (R. M. Wardle, *Oliver Goldsmith*, 1957, 1969, pp. 262–263; Arthur Friedman, *New CBEL* ii. 1202).

Empress of Russia the present of a very fine gold snuffbox beautifully enamelled with her head on the lid set round with five and thirty capital diamonds.[4] Within it is a slip of paper on which are written in her own hand these words—I think I recollect them exactly.—Pour le Chevalier Reynolds en temoignage du contentement que j'ai ressenti de ses excellens discours sur la Peinture.[5]

I offer my best compliments to Mrs. Percy and the young Ladies, and have the honour to be, My Dear Lord, Your Lordships faithful humble servant

JAMES BOSWELL

From Bennet Langton, Friday 16 April 1790

MS. Yale (C 1690).

ADDRESS: To James Boswell Esqr.

Oxford, April 16, 1790

MY DEAR SIR, I do not by any means wonder that, as You mention, You should have inclined to suppose that I had been in some idle Whim of taking offence, which had prompted my length of Silence; at least I do not see any reason for your calling *yours* a *brooding mind* on that account—when I had blameably given so much occasion—and, *now*, I have slid into my old course, and, till the last day for the post from hence in this week stares me in the face, I have suffered the time to while away without replying to your late favour—

I am afraid I cannot speak satisfactorily to the first of Your Queries—viz. what was the precise time that Dr. Johnson reduced himself to, in writing a Paper of the *Idler*, at my room—

[4] The Empress, Catherine II, had commissioned Reynolds to paint a picture for her, leaving to him the choice of subject. He chose the strangling of the serpents by the infant Hercules, and the painting, shown at the Royal Academy Exhibition in 1788, was sent to her in 1789 together with copies of his *Discourses* in English, French, and Italian (F. W. Hilles, "Sir Joshua and the Empress Catherine", in *Eighteenth-*Century Studies in Honor of Donald F. Hyde, ed. W. H. Bond, 1970, pp. 267–277).

[5] Asterisk inserted here by John Bowyer Nichols (see *ante* n. 3), followed immediately by copy in Nichols's hand for a foot-note for *Lit. Illust.*: "These passages are printed in Prior's *Life of Goldsmith* i. 454." Prior in fact printed all of the present letter but the first and the last paragraphs.

for, unless one could be quite strict in it, it seems not to be of any value to attempt only suppositions or *near* guesses at it—I think it must surely have been more than *half an hour*, the time *You* speak of[1]—but how much more I am afraid it is rather too uncertain to attempt saying—

As to the 2d Query—Dr. Johnson was at Langton in the beginning of the Year 1764—[2]

The General who was so polite to the Dr. was *General Hall*[3]— these answers I apprehend may be sufficient at present—if You will *come*, as You are so kind as to suggest we could then, jointly, pay further regard to such other particulars as I observe in Your Letter—I am charmed on all accounts to be informed of the magnificent offer You have received; on your own, and on that of our deeply honoured and revered Friend, to observe that his fame by the agency of Your powerful offices of affection and respect is thus striking out deeper and wider Roots, in such sort that one may conceive it as probable for Socrates to cease to be remembered and extolled as for our Friend to experience such a fate—

Lady Rothes, Dear Sir, and my Daughters desire with their best Regards that I would urge, if You fulfil Your design of coming to us (and which I think I may now call a debt of honour) that Miss Boswell will give us the favour at the same time of Her Company, as we can manage to offer two apartments—such as Friendship must make up the defects of—in our habitation here— pray give me a Line of information—and, *in our favour*, as soon as you receive this—though it is a great deal more than I deserve— Believe me to be, my Dear Sir, most affectionately Yours

BENNET LANGTON

My best Compliments to Mr. Penn—and all friends—

---

[1] Unable to hold up the press, JB, who had left a blank in his copy, compromised with "about half an hour" (*Life* i. 331). SJ's visit to Langton at Oxford was in July 1759.

[2] See *Life* i. 476–77, for the particulars of this visit supplied to JB by Langton, and *ibid*. n. 1, for an additional episode.

[3] Probably Gen. Thomas Hall (d. 1809), the only General Hall mentioned in the *Army Lists* for that period. He was commissioned a major-general on 29 Aug. 1777, and in 1778, the year of SJ's visit to Langton's camp, was on half pay (*Army List*, 1778, p. iv; *The Royal Kalendar for the Year 1778*, p. 173). A Major-General Hall was one of three generals on the staff of the Essex or Eastern District assigned to Warley Camp that year with the militia ("Plans of Encampments, and Dispositions of the Army in Great Britain from 1778 to 1782", BM Add. MSS. 15533, f. 3).

From Thomas Percy,
Saturday 24 April 1790

MS. Yale (C 2236).

ADDRESS (in William Bennet's hand): James Boswell Esqr., Queen Anne Street West, London.

FRANK: Dublin, April twenty fourth [*corrected from* fourteenth *correction initialed* WB.] 1790. Wm. Bennet.

POSTMARKS: AP 24, AP 28 90, FREE.

ENDORSEMENT: From the Bishop of Dromore.

Dublin, April 24th. 1790

DEAR SIR, I received very safe the *Debates on the Corporation and Test Act,* and return you my best thanks for this fresh Instance of your kind Attention:—I much doubt whether Stockdale will venture to publish a List of the Members, who voted pro and con. that (to us of the established C[hur]ch) very important Question. —In the Part of Ireland, where I live, a great Proportion of the inferior People are descended from Emigrants from Scotland in the Reigns of James I, Cha. I and Cha. II, who fled from the predominant Episcopalians in those anti-Calvinistic (or rather anti-Presbyterian) Reigns, and retain a good deal of the original Prejudice against Episcopacy, etc.—The Fate of the above Question will have a very good effect in our Country, as they had been made to believe that the People of England were not interested in our support or preservation. They were growing very insolent, and this already appears to quiet and compose them.

Be assured, my dear Sir, that I cannot but esteem it an honour to be mentioned in any Work of yours: My only Scruple was about the peculiar matter with which my Name might be connected. As the Anecdotes, I sent you were of the lowest and most trifling kind, I could have wished (and still intreat) that the mention of me expressly by name might be reserved to any Communication which I have sent, or may hereafter send, that may not expose me too much to ridicule from the non-importance of the Particulars. This favour I hope I may obtain from your Friendship that I may be allowed to see before Publication, such Passages as my Name is produced in form to support: as perhaps upon Review I may add something to increase the weight of my Testimony: or the value of my Communication.—If you do not indulge me in this request, I shall really take it ill.—I hope to be in London before Winter, and perhaps that may be soon enough to grant me what I here solicit.

Goldsmith's works are in some degree under my Direction, but the intended Life is in the hands of another Gentleman.[1]—When I am in London I shall be glad to converse with you on the Subject.

I rejoice at every Honour paid to the great Merit of our excellent Friend Sir Joshua Reynolds to whom I beg you will give my best Respects.

Shall I obtain the favour of you to deliver the inclosed Letter to Mr. Wilton (your neighbour)[2] with my Compliments and Request that he will be so obliging as to convey it to his Son-in Law, Sir Robt. Chambers. Believe me most truly, Dear Sir, Your very faithful Servant

THOS. DROMORE

P.S. Pray inform me, when next you write, if my Letter to Sir Robt. Chambers is not too late to be sent this Spring: It is to thank him for an obliging Present of the *Asiatic Researches* published at Calcutta, 4to.,[3] which I have at length received from Londn. having had notice of its being sent upwds. of 3 Months: So slow is the passage of Ships hither from thence.

[1] See *ante* To Percy, 12 Mar. 1790, n. 8. Percy's caution is characteristic: he must have known that the "Gentleman" was no stranger to JB. (See also From Percy, 19 Mar. 1790 and n. 4.) About the time the present letter was written, he entrusted the writing of the memoir to Thomas Campbell, the Irish clergyman whose *Diary of a Visit to England in 1775* (first published in 1854) is well known to Johnsonian scholars. After Campbell's death in 1795 he engaged another Irish man of letters, the Rev. Henry Boyd, to revise and expand Campbell's work. The publishers grew impatient at Percy's delays, and when a quarrel over terms developed, they appointed their own editor, Samuel Rose, who brought out memoir and works in 4 vols. 1802 (dated 1801). Rose made "interpolations" in the memoir which Percy disliked (Balderston, *The History and Sources of Percy's Memoir of Goldsmith*, pp. 30–52).

[2] Joseph Wilton (1722–1803), sculptor, was one of the founding members of the Royal Academy and served as its Keeper from 1790 until his death. Sir Robert Chambers married his daughter, Fanny, on 8 Mar. 1774. Wilton lived on Queen Anne Street East.

[3] *Asiatick Researches: or, Transactions of the Society, Instituted in Bengal, for Inquiring into the History and Antiquities, the Arts, Sciences, and Literature, of Asia,* vol. i, 1788. The Asiatic Society of Bengal (now the Asiatic Society, Calcutta), of which Sir William Jones was President, was founded in 1784. The first volume of its *Researches* contains articles by Jones, Warren Hastings, and others.

To Bennet Langton,
c. Friday 7 May 1790

Not reported. Sent c. 7 May 1790 from London. Referred to *post* From Langton, 10 May: "The Favour of Your Letter reached me Yesterday."

To the Duke of Leeds,
Saturday 8 May 1790

MS. Yale (L 856). A draft.[1]

Queen Anne Street West, 8 May 1790

My Lord: Several years ago I had the honour to be presented to[2] My Lord Carmarthen by Mr. Burke at the Royal Academy Dinner.[3] It is not however upon this circumstance which I do not

---

[1] There is among JB's papers a draft (L 855) for another letter from him to the Duke, presumably written before the present letter but not sent. Since it occurs in the same sheet of paper as JB's notes for his tragedy *Favras*, and since JB referred to that work as being in preparation in a paragraph (P 117) which he sent to *The Public Advertiser*, 24 Mar. 1790, it may be plausibly dated in Mar. or Apr. 1790. (Thomas de Mahy, 1745–90, Marquis de Favras, a French royalist, was martyred in the cause of the French monarchy. Accused of complicity in a plot to kill La Fayette and other leaders, he was hanged on 19 Feb. 1790.) JB's draft runs as follows: "Duke of Leeds. Hear you are one of the most agreable men in the World. Wished much for the honour and pleasure of your acquant. for fear of interested imputation waited till you should be out of administration. But as I see no prospect whatever of that take this mode and to prevent possibility of trouble to your Grace or meaness in me enclose a *promissory* Note which will at least aid me [to] receive one [*illegible*]. I refer your Grace for what I am to Lord Mcarteney or Sir Joshua Reynolds to any body who knows me—but Dundas—All I have to

add is that if this does not hit your Grace's fancy that I have only to request that you will not laugh at me. If you should I shall say like 'downright Shippen' [Pope, *Satires* II. i. 52] when Sir R[obert] W[alpole] knowing him to be a Jacobite smiled when he observed him taking the oaths, 'Bob that is not fair.'—I promise to pay to F. D. of Leeds One thousand pounds lawful money of Great Britain one day after my soliciting him directly or indirectly for any post place or pension whatsoever his Grace's word of honour to be admitted as evidence of the fact in all the Courts of Great Britain."

[2] "the Marq" deleted. A number of other false starts of no importance remain unannotated. Leeds was styled Marquess of Carmarthen before he succeeded to the dukedom.

[3] 28 Apr. 1781: "Burke. 'Allways happy to meet you. My Lord Carmarth[en] allow me to introduce my freind Mr. Bos[well].' Just saw his Lordship. Gen. Paoli said he was hurt his horns were too heavy for his head. 'Or rather I should say that after being too heavy for his head their roots are grown down to his heart'" (Journ.). Lord Carmarthen had divorced, on 31 May 1779, Lady Amelia D'Arcy, daughter of Robert

flatter myself is remembered by your Grace, but trusting to the general courtesy of Literature[4] that I presume to mention that Your Grace may contribute towards the illustration of the life of Dr. Johnson in writing which I am now engaged. Should your Grace be so disposed you will oblige me very much if you will be pleased to appoint a time when I may have permission to wait upon your Grace.[5]

At any rate I beg your Grace may forgive the liberty which I have ventured to take. I have the honour to be with great respect, My Lord, Your Graces most obedient and most humble servant.

From the Duke of Leeds, Sunday 9 May 1790

MS. Yale (C 1714).

ADDRESS: James Boswell Esqr., Queen Anne-Street West.
SUPERSCRIPTION: Leeds.[1]

[London,] May 9. 1790

The Duke of Leeds presents his compliments to Mr. Boswell

D'Arcy, fourth Earl of Holdernesse, because of her elopement with Capt. John ("mad Jack") Byron. The Hon. Augusta Byron (later Leigh) was her daughter by Byron. The poet was Captain Byron's son by a second marriage.

[4] JB had made use of the same phrase in a letter to the Earl of Carlisle, 29 Dec. 1789 (Waingrow, p. 296; cf. *Life* iv. 246).

[5] JB no doubt wished to secure permission to print in the *Life* a letter of the Duke's which had come into his hands. On 1 Mar. 1786 he had "waited on Sir Francis Lumm who had obligingly procured me from Sir John Caldwell a Minute of the conversation between the King and Dr. Johnson [on 10 Feb. 1767; see *Life* ii. 33–40 and F. Taylor, "Boswell's Use of the Caldwell Minute", *Bulletin of the John Rylands Library*, 1952–53, xxxv. 226–47] which was in the late Sir James Caldwell's repositories. . . . He gave me Lord Carmarthen's Letter to him containing his Majesty's permission that the Minute should be delivered to me to make what use of it I should think proper in my Life of Dr. Johnson" (Journ.). In addition, he hoped to get Leeds to persuade F. A. Barnard, the King's Librarian, to permit him to print a letter of professional advice which SJ had written to Barnard. See To Frederick Augusta Barnard, 10 June 1790, in Waingrow, pp. 322–23.

[1] Written in the style of a frank, but the note clearly did not go through the post and was presumably delivered by a servant. There are a dozen or more other examples of the mode among the Boswell papers, the authors of the letters being generally peers or high Government officials.

and shall be happy to see him in Grosr. Square tomorrow at half past one,[2] if that hour is not inconvenient to Mr. Boswell.

James Boswell Esqr.

From Bennet Langton, Monday 10 May 1790

MS. Yale (C 1691).

ADDRESS: To James Boswell Esqr.

Oxford, May 10th. 1790

MY DEAR SIR, The Favour of Your Letter reached me Yesterday— to be sure it would require more confidence than I would wish to possess, if I was to press a charge against You for not replying to mine in earlier time, after my own offences that way—but I am sorry You did not write, and fix a time such as would by this time have given us your Company—as, though I cannot but approve and admire the reason You give for your *present* delay of coming,[1] I am fearful that things may turn out so little pleasantly for me as to make it difficult to judge when, now, I may hope for that satisfaction—to explain myself,—I am at present hesitating whether I may request an excuse, *this* time of meeting, of my attendance in Lincolnshire for the assembling of the Militia, which on several accounts it would be of a good deal of Inconvenience to me to go to, but, if, on considering of it, there appears any kind of necessity for me to be there for some part of the time at least, I cannot judge when exactly I may find my way homewards again— all I can say in the mean time is that I will take care to let you know as soon as, after a little farther considering of it, I have come to a

[2] JB's request to print Leeds's letter was granted, and the letter duly appeared in a foot-note to the *Life* (ii. 34 n. 1). JB also obtained from Leeds a clear opinion that SJ's letter to F. A. Barnard (see the preceding letter, n. 5) did not concern the King's business, and that there could be no objection to its being published. This failed, however, to impress Barnard, who refused on his own account to allow the letter to be made public (To F. A. Bar- nard, 10 June 1790; From F. A. Barnard, 11 June 1790: Waingrow, pp. 322–24).

[1] Besides being engaged on the *Life*, JB was subject to the orders of Lord Lonsdale. Lonsdale insisted that JB go with him to his seat at Laleham, Middle- sex, on 15 May 1790, even though he knew that JB's friend Temple had just arrived for a visit on the 14th (Journ.).

determination, which I must do within this fortnight hence at furthest—

With regard to the particulars of which You wish me to give some account, and that are now occurring to be treated of in the course of Your Work—I have been dwelling upon them since the receipt of Your Letter, and have attentively read over what Sir J. Hawkins says,[2] which appears in the main to be correct enough— I am sorry it is out of my power to send You the paper You speak of; that, of Sir Joshua Reynolds's writing, when he put down the Names of those proposed to be applied to for agreeing to meet as a Club[3]—but it unluckily is somewhere among my papers in London, and which I have not any means of giving a direction for finding— but I do not know of any difference that there would be found *in it* from the list given in the 415th page of Sir John's *Life, 1st Edition*.[4] On that page it is said that "the first movers in this Association were Johnson and Sir Joshua Reynolds"—whereas it would have been more close to what I remember of the fact if it had been said, that Sir Joshua was the mover of it; as Johnson did not with entire Readiness accede to the Scheme.

You say in yours, that the Commencement of the Club comes in, in the Year 1763—I apprehend that to be a mistake; as exactly as I can trace it in recollection, it was, in the beginning of the year 1764 that it was first talked of, and very soon after it was first named it was actually instituted—I see, in the 425th page of Sir J. Hawkins, he says "the Institution of this Society was in the Winter of 1763"[5]—but that should have been said, "in the Spring of 1764"—it was about eight or ten weeks after the Return of Johnson and me from Lincolnshire—which was, in the beginning of February 1764[6]—I do not know of any other particulars as to

[2] About the founding of The Club (pp. 414–16).

[3] List untraced.

[4] "Johnson, Sir Joshua Reynolds, Mr. Edmund Burke, Christ. Nugent, M. D. Oliver Goldsmith, M. B. Mr. Topham Beauclerk, Mr. Bennet Langton, Mr. Anthony Chamier, and Myself [Hawkins]."

[5] "The institution of this society was in the winter of 1763, at which time Mr. Garrick was abroad with his wife, who, for the recovery of her health, was sent to the baths at Padua." Hawkins incorrectly maintained that SJ kept Garrick out of The Club when the actor returned.

[6] The date of the first meeting of The Club seems never to have been positively determined. However, Reynolds recorded a dinner at the Turk's Head for half past three on Monday 16 Apr. 1764, which is almost exactly ten weeks after the beginning of Feb. The engagement book containing notice of the dinner is a full one, which would seem to indicate that no possible earlier meeting of The Club was left unrecorded by him. See N & Q (1956) cci. 302–03.

the first fixing of the Club that You are not as well apprized of at least as I am—any other questions You favour me with I will be as exact in replying to as I can—and with all our kindest Regards I am, Dear Sir, Your affectionate humble Servant

BENNET LANGTON

From Bennet Langton, Monday 31 May 1790

MS. Yale (C 1692).

ADDRESS: To James Boswell Esqr.

Oxford, May 31st. 1790

MY DEAR SIR, I write (according to the Intention I expressed in my last Letter of acquainting You, as soon as I could understand whether I should be obliged to attend at the meeting of the Militia) to say that I have just received the Favour of an excuse from going to Lincoln this time of assembling—I hope then You will find it convenient to fulfil the Intention You were so kind as to signify of giving us Your and Miss Boswell's company—pray let us know as soon as You receive this what hope of seeing You we may be encouraged to form—You will have been, I doubt not, sharply affected by the dismal Event of poor Warton's decease[1]— As Johnson has said, and on an occasion that bears a resemblance to what I am now adverting to, "What are the hopes of Man!"[2] I had formed an Image to myself of the agreeable addition it might be to any satisfaction You might receive at this place, to have had the opportunity of some social Interviews with the poor departed Friend of whom I am speaking—and had accordingly mentioned to him the hope we had of seeing You here, at which he expressed much satisfaction.—But I will not run the risque of hindering my Letter from going by this post by continuing to write more and therefore, with our best Regards as due, will beg You to believe me to be, Dear Sir—affectionately Yours

BENNET LANGTON

[1] Thomas Warton had died 21 May, the day after suffering a stroke in the common-room of his college.

[2] "But what are the hopes of man! I am disappointed by that stroke of death, which has eclipsed the gaiety of nations and impoverished the publick stock of harmless pleasure" (on Garrick's death, from the life of Edmund Smith, *Lives of the English Poets*, ed. G. B. Hill, ii. 21, par. 76). JB quoted it in *Life* i. 81–82.

To Thomas Percy,
Wednesday 16 June 1790

MS. collection of Charles N. Fifer.

ADDRESS: To The Lord Bishop of Dromore, Dublin.

London, 16 June 1790

MY DEAR LORD: I have the pleasure to acquaint your Lordship that both your letters to Sir Robert Chambers[1] were in time to go out this season.

The sudden dissolution of Parliament[2] throws us all into a disagreable hurry. I have the honour to be, My Dear Lord, your Lordships faithful humble servant

JAMES BOSWELL

To Bennet Langton,
Friday 27 August 1790

MS. Yale (*L 849.7). Signature cut away.

London, 27 August 1790

MY DEAR SIR: Since I was favoured with your last kind letter I have been driven about not very pleasingly, having been suddenly hurried away by Lord Lonsdale to do duty as Recorder of Carlisle[1] where I was kept I may say a prisoner in a tedious state of uncertainty, which vexed me the more that the progress of my Life of Johnson was in some degree retarded, though Mr. Malone was

[1] The letter referred to in Percy's letter of 24 Apr. and one, dated 29 Apr. 1790 (Bodleian, MS. Eng. Poet b. 6, f. 56), which Percy had written upon receipt of a ten-page letter (BM Add. MSS. 32329, ff. 124–29) from Chambers. The letters of both men, in addition to dealing with the *Asiatic Researches*, were concerned with a fragmentary manuscript of some Rowley poems which Percy had given Chambers some years earlier.

[2] The session ended on 10 June, and Parliament was dissolved by proclamation on 12 June.

[1] JB had written to Lord Lonsdale on 1 Dec. 1787, soliciting the Recordership of Carlisle. He was informed on the 20th of that month that the position was his (Journ.) and was duly elected 11 Jan. 1788. Lonsdale's patronage, however, proved completely unsatisfactory, and the relations between the two men became steadily worse. The crisis came in June 1790. JB was informed by Lonsdale, on 14 June, that he would have to go to Carlisle for the coming election. JB was reluctant to go, partly because he did not want to leave Temple, who was then

so very kind as to superintend the press in my absence.[2] I have resigned the Recordership having found that the proper discharge of its duties was incompatible with my other engagements. Many people supposed that the great Man who recommended me to that office would have given me a seat in parliament; but it seems he did not chuse that. What I shall do to gratify my ambitious cravings I am at a loss. You my valuable friend know how they disturb my tranquillity, and how unlucky I have hitherto been.

My daughter Euphemia who passed the winter at a boarding-school at Edinburgh, met me at Carlisle and I brought her to town with me, and now that Mrs. Buchanan the Lady in whose house Veronica lived, is gone to Scotland, I have both my eldest daughters in the house with me, and my sons one an Eton and one a Westminster Scholar are at home for the vacation, which is by much too long. Little Betsy is doing very well at a boarding school at Chelsea.[3]

visiting him. The Earl "talked meanly of this being all I had to do for my £20 salary" (Journ.). In the coach on the way to Carlisle on 17 June Lonsdale informed JB that he had never had any intention of putting him in Parliament. In the conversation which followed, JB angered the Earl "so as to raise his passion almost to madness, so that he used shocking words to me, saying 'Take it as you will. I am ready to give you satisfaction. . . . You have kept low company all your life. What are *you*, Sir?' 'A gentleman My Lord, a man of honour, and I hope to shew myself such.' He brutally said 'You will be settled when you have a bullet in your belly.'" A duel was averted (apparently Lonsdale was no more anxious to fight than JB), but JB "was now obliged to submit to what was very disagreable to me without any reward or hope of any good" (*ibid*. 17 June), and he "felt a dead indifference, as to the election, now that all prospect of ambition by means of Lord L. was cut off" (*ibid*. 3 July). JB left for London on 15 July.

[2] Though JB from the first turned to Malone for general advice about the *Life*, he did not submit the text to him for criticism until he had nearly completed

the draft of the entire work (To Temple, 10 Jan. 1789). It was his practice then, with Malone's assistance, to submit the draft to "nice correction" and send it in parcels to the printer. The actual close collaboration on the text began on 13 Oct. 1789 (To Temple, 13–14 Oct. 1789) and continued from that date till 19 or 20 Nov. 1790, when Malone left for a visit to Ireland, the text having by that time been revised nearly three-eighths of the way through vol. 2 (To Malone, 4 Dec. 1790, Hyde Collection; From Malone to John Jordan, franked by Courtenay Friday 19 Nov. 1790, in *Original Letters from Malone . . . to John Jordan*, ed. J. O. Halliwell-Phillips, 1864, p. 48.—On his return from Carlisle on the present occasion JB "had found that by my kind and active friend Malone's aid my Book had gone on in my absence five sheets" (Journ. 19 July 1790).

[3] Euphemia had not been happy at school. On 24 June, JB wrote that "I had yesterday received a letter from my brother David communicating from Lady Auchinleck, Euphemia's uneasiness at staying longer at the Edinburgh Boarding School. I resolved to relieve her" (Journ.).—Veronica had gone the year before to live with Mrs. Buchanan, "the

I have a very great desire to be with you at Oxford, and your most kind invitation to accomodate both me and my daughter in your house warms my heart; for in truth there is very little of such cordiality to be experienced. My difficulty is in leaving London, while my Life of Johnson is in the press. It will be a much larger Work than was calculated. I was very desireous to confine it within one quarto volume, though it should be a very thick one; but I now find that it must be two, and these more than 550 pages each. I have printed as yet only 456; but am next week to put on two compositors, so as to advance in a double ratio.

The Collectanea with which you were pleased to favour me, you may depend upon it shall not be inserted without being revised by you, and ⟨this is one of⟩[4] the reasons which make ⟨me desirous of meetin⟩[4]g with you. Could you without much inconvenience meet me halfway, we might pass a comfortable day together, and go through your Memorabilia and adjust them having no interruption, and my visit to you might be deferred till the conclusion of my *Magnum Opus*. Pray try if you can oblige me so much, and if you can, be pleased to fix day and place. I hope this request will induce you to write without delay, before the *mould* of indolence has had time to gather.[5]

I heartily wish you joy of the degree of L.L.D. so *worthily* conferred.[6] I was at a loss whether to direct to you by that title. Pray let me know.

Though I fear that my visit to your agreable family cannot take place for some time, I should not only be exceedingly happy, but esteem it as of valuable service to my two eldest daughters to have that pleasure, and they would be very happy in such an opportunity. We join in best compliments to yourself and Lady Rothes and all under your roof.

⟨James Boswell⟩[7]

Pray write under cover of J. B. Garforth Esq. M.P.

good Widow Lady with an accomplished daughter" (To Temple, 2 Aug. 1789). Sandy entered Eton on 15 Oct. 1789 (To Temple, 28–30 Nov. 1789); Betsy entered Blacklands House on 12 Nov. 1789 (Journ.); Jamie entered Westminster School 7 June 1790 (Journ. 6 June 1790).

[4] Lacuna caused by signature's being cut away.
[5] Perhaps a Johnsonian phrase (cf. *Life* iv. 352).
[6] Langton had received the D.C.L. degree from Oxford 16 June 1790.
[7] See *ante* n. 4. A complimentary close was probably also cut away.

From Thomas Barnard,
Saturday 11 September 1790

MS. Yale (C 90).

ADDRESS: James Boswell Esqr. Aughinleck, Edinburgh, North Britain, By Donaghadee Packet.

POSTMARKS: LIMERICK, SE 13, SE 17.

Killaloe, Sept. 11th 1790

My Dear Sir, Not Knowing in What Part of the United Kingdom you at present Reside,[1] I am forced to Form my Conclusion from Probabilities, and, Supposing the Long Vacation to be the Natural Season for a Man of Business Propriis Rebus Vacare,[2] I direct this to your own antient Metropolis, In hopes That, if it do's not find you there, it will at least be convey'd safely to your hands.

It is now Upwards of a Year Since I promised to reserve for you a Dog of the Breed of Spaniels, of which you saw a Specimen with me in London: and I fear that by this Time, either my good Faith or my Memory has Suffer'd considerably in your opinion for at Least these Six months' Past. But the true Cause of this long Delay has been a Disappointment in the first Litter of Puppies, which turnd out a Parcel of mere mongrels. The Second however has been more Successfull; they are Thorough Bred on Both Sides and are as Beautifull a Set of Red Spaniels as I have ever Seen. Of These, I have reserv'd for you, one of Each Kind, which are now Six weeks old, and shall be sent to you as soon as I receive your orders to that Purpose, and the Proper Directions, where, and to whose Care I am to Consign them. You will have time to take the Necessary Steps to prepare your Correspondent to receive them, and take Care of them, before they will be fit to take their Voyage, as opportunities may not offer every Day. I think you spoke to me of Sending them to Whitehaven,[3] which I believe will be the easiest method of Conveyance; But Still I must be inform'd of the Name

---

[1] JB was in London from 1 to 11 Sept., when his journal stops temporarily. There are extant letters of his written from London 13, 14, 15, 16, 17, and 22 Sept., and the journal begins again on the 26th. There is no indication that he left

the city during the month.

[2] "To have time for his personal concerns."

[3] A seaport in Cumberland on the Irish Sea, thirty-six miles south-west of Carlisle.

of the Person who is to receive them, and shall wait for your Commands.

This Country furnishes no Intelligence worthy of your attention; We are all in perfect Tranquillity, and good Humour, Notwithstanding the Furious Menaces, and Measures of Whig clubs,[4] and angry Citizens in Dublin; The Sollicitor general[5] dined with me here yesterday, and tells me that even in Dublin they are coming back to their Right Senses, as they find it not possible to get a Sufficient Party on their Side to make themselves Formidable. Our Lord Chancellor[6] is also stealing a fortnight of Leisure to look at his Estate, and is now within seven miles of me, but I have not seen him yet.

When do's your much desired, and Long Expected Work come out? Quousque Jacobe abutere Patientiâ Nostrâ?[7] if it dos not soon appear we shall grow as outrageous as the galleries at Drury Lane. Shall we have it next Season or not? Confess the Truth.

Have you had any Late account from the good General Paoli? I hope his Reception at home has been such as it ought to be, and that the Evening of his Life may be both Honourable, and Serene.[8]

[4] In June 1789, a large number of the principal men in Ireland, including Charlemont and Grattan, formed themselves into a Whig Club for the purpose of maintaining the Constitution of 1782 and "endeavouring by all legal and constitutional means to check the extravagance of Government and its corrupt influence in the Legislature" (Lecky, *Ireland* iii. 4). A Northern Whig Club was later formed in Belfast. A resolution of the Whig Club was published in the papers in July respecting the election of the Lord Mayor of Dublin and accusing the Lord Chancellor and the Privy Council of interfering with the election (*Dublin Chronicle*, 27 July 1790, iv. 300). The Lord Chancellor brought up the resolution in the House of Lords and deplored the issuing of such statements, which excited public discord and were dangerous to the public peace (*London Chronicle*, 29–31 July 1790, lxviii. 111). The text of the resolution is printed in *The Dublin Chronicle*.

[5] John Toler (1745–1831), later (1827) Earl of Norbury, was Solicitor General of Ireland from 1789 to 1798. He was noted chiefly for his jocular disposition and complete lack of qualifications for the positions he filled. He opposed all attempts to give Catholics emancipation in Ireland.

[6] John Fitzgibbon (1749–1802), later (1795) Earl of Clare, was practically the directing head of the Irish government from 1783 until the Union. He was made Lord Chancellor and created Baron Fitzgibbon of Lower Connello in 1789. Although he pressed for law reform, he constantly opposed Catholic emancipation.

[7] Barnard paraphrases the first line of Cicero's *Oratio in Catilinam Prima*: "Quo usque tandem abutere, Catilina, patientia nostra?": "[In heaven's name,] Catiline [James], how long will you abuse our patience?" (Louis E. Lord's translation in Loeb ed.).

[8] See *ante* To Douglas, 16 Mar. 1790. In Apr. 1790, Paoli was received by Louis XVI and appointed military commander of Corsica. The General wrote to JB on 7 and 28 Apr. and 14 June

I felt some Concern I assure you at His putting forth to Sea again, and thought he had much better have staid where he was well, and where he was almost b⟨ecome⟩ an Englishman.

I shall Expect to hear from you as soon as is Conv⟨enient⟩, and if this finds you in Scotland, tell me something congenial to the place of your present Residence, and the People among whom you are; whom I assure you I very much Honour and Esteem. And Believe me to be always, My Dear Sir, very truly and Sincerely yours

THOS. KILLALOE

Mrs. Barnard desires her Compliments.

From Dr. Charles Blagden, Saturday 18 September 1790

MS. Yale (C 154).

ADDRESS: James Boswell Esq.
ENDORSEMENT: From Dr. Blagden.

Percy Street, Sep. 18, 1790

DEAR SIR, Upon further consideration I have no doubt but the term Baretti meant to convey to Dr. Johnson was *"Marc* d'eau forte"* (which is pronounced *Mar*)[1] signifying the residuum found after the distillation of Aqua fortis.[2] Chemically speaking, this,

describing his reception in France and the eagerness with which the Corsicans awaited his return to the island. In Corsica he was elected mayor of Bastia and commander-in-chief of the national guard.

[1] SJ had recorded the term when he was in Paris in the autumn of 1775 with the Thrales and Baretti (*Life* ii. 384–401). JB published in the *Life* (ii. 389–401) the contents of a "small paperbook . . . entitled 'FRANCE II' . . . a diurnal register of [SJ's] life and observations, from the 10th of October to the 4th of November, inclusive, being twenty-six days, [which] shows an extraordinary attention to various minute particulars"

(p. 389). It is this book which JB asked Blagden to inspect. The entry for 23 Oct. describes the process of making looking-glasses. "Those that are to be polished, are laid on a table covered with several thick cloths, hard strained, that the resistance may be equal; they are then rubbed with a hand rubber, held down hard by a contrivance which I did not well understand. The powder which is used last seemed to me to be iron dissolved in aqua fortis: they called it, as Baretti said, *marc de l'eau forte*, which he thought was dregs. They mentioned vitriol and saltpetre" (p. 396). SJ's manuscript actually reads "mar" (*Life* ii. 396); hence Blagden's emphatic *marc* and his comment on the pronunciation.
[2] Nitric acid.

when washed, hardly differs from colcothar[3] prepared expressly by calcining vitriol of iron, though possibly its mechanical properties may not be exactly the same; and as large quantities of aqua fortis are distilled for various manufactures, its residuum may very probably be the principal source of the colcothar used by the glass-grinders. With great esteem I am, dear Sir, Your very faithful humble Servant

C. BLAGDEN

From Dr. Charles Blagden, Friday 1 October 1790

MS. Yale (C 155).

ADDRESS: James Boswell Esq., Queen Anne Street West.

ENDORSEMENT: From Dr. Blagden.

Percy Street, Oct. 1, 1790

DEAR SIR, It gives me some satisfaction that I have been able to make out all your difficult words except one. That of Oct. 23d is unquestionably *dregs*, being the usual translation of *Marc*, though in the present case not strictly applicable.—In the article of Nov. 2d[1] the first word is *Ant-Bear*, with which animal the description agrees; and the second is *Toucan*, a well-known bird, with a most enormous beak. As to the others, the word after "Two" I cannot decypher; it looks to me like Fansans,[2] but there is no such name

---

[3] The brownish-red oxide of iron which remains after the heating of ferrous sulphate. It is used as a polishing agent.

[1] On 2 Nov., SJ's party visited Chantilly. "The cabinet," SJ wrote, "seems well stocked: what I remember was, the jaws of a hippopotamus, and a young hippopotamus preserved, which, however, is so small, that I doubt its reality.—It seems too hairy for an abortion, and too small for a mature birth.—Nothing was in spirits; all was dry.—The dog; the deer; the ant-bear with long snout.—The toucan, long broad beak.—The stables were of very great length.—The kennel had no scents.—There was a mockery of a village.—The Menagerie

had few animals.—Two faussans, or Brasilian weasels, spotted, very wild" (*Life* ii. 400). JB comments, in a note, "The writing is so bad here, that the names of several of the animals could not be decyphered without much more acquaintance with natural history than I possess.—Dr. Blagden, with his usual politeness, most obligingly examined the MS. To that gentleman, and to Dr. [E. W.] Gray, [Keeper of Natural History and Antiquities] of the British Museum, who also very readily assisted me, I beg leave to express my best thanks" (*Life* ii. 400 n. 1). See the note following.

[2] SJ wrote "fausans". JB's note, presumably supplied by Dr. Gray, is: "It is thus written by Johnson, from the

that I can find in any language; the words next to "or" are *Brasilian WeEsels*;[3] the animal properly so called, however, is not spotted. Can the former word be an adjective of place, like Brasilian? but on that supposition I cannot reconcile the letters to the name of any country.

I shall always receive your commands with great pleasure; and am, very respectfully, dear Sir, Your most obedient humble Servant

C. BLAGDEN

From Bennet Langton, Saturday 2 October 1790

MS. Yale (C 1693). Received 9 Oct. "Bennet Langton Esq. a long letter; various" (Reg. Let.).

ADDRESS: To James Boswell Esqr.

Oxford, Octr. 2d. 1790

MY DEAR SIR, It may justly have appeared to you to be the case with me, that I had not attended to your request and Injunction, *not to suffer the mould of Indolence to gather*, as I have, in the way so usual between us, delayed a reply to Your last Letter—but I have something more to alledge, than I have had at most other times of this kind of negligence in excuse, for not having taken notice of your proposal; of our meeting half way, for the looking the papers over—for, in some untoward concerns of business, I am engaged in such unpleasant sort, as to be probably obliged to take a Journey into Lincoln shire, in a very short time,[1] and am under uncertainty what my continuance of stay there must be; for these three or four Weeks past, I have expected every post, to have the time fixed for my setting out; but, not receiving such word from the Sollicitor who manages my business for me, I have written

French pronunciation of *fossane*. It should be observed, that the person who shewed this Menagerie was mistaken in supposing the *fossane* and the Brasilian weasel to be the same, the *fossane* being a different animal, and a native of Madagascar. I find them, however, upon one plate in Pennant's 'Synopsis of Quadrupeds'" (*Life* ii. 400 n. 2).

[3] Blagden's E serves the purpose of a *sic*. Though SJ's own *Dictionary* opts for *weasel*, he did indeed on this occasion spell the word with three *e*'s (BM Add. MSS. 35299 kindly examined by W. H. Kelliher, Assistant Keeper).

[1] *Ante* From Langton, 1 Mar. 1790, n. 2.

307

again in order to have the matter duly fixed—thus you see, dear Sir, this rather strange suspence that I have been and am kept in, has been an obstacle to the plan of meeting; but it has not been the only one; for, a part of the time, it would not have been in my power, on account of a very disagreeable accident that has happened to my Son George;—in returning home to Oxford after having taken a ride, just as he was coming into the Town, his Stirrup and Girth broke as the horse was going with great Speed,[2] and he was thrown violently to the ground; he was taken to a publick house that was near, whither a Surgeon came to him and from thence he was brought home in a Chaise; it was found that there was a wound in his head of about three Inches in length, and that the Skin and flesh were torn up, to the breadth of above an Inch—he had a good deal of blood immediately taken from him—but the Surgeon, after examining carefully, said, he hoped the Skull was not affected by any fracture, which, as the wound has gone on to closing and healing in a favourable way, we hope we may now trust to have been a right judgement of the case—he was kept to as much quiet and to as low a habit of diet as possible, which of course reduced and weakened him a good deal—this, dear Sir, You will conceive has given us a good deal of anxiety—it has been however productive likewise of Sensations of an opposite kind, arising from experiencing very generally among our Friends and acquaintance here, both on Georges account and on that of the rest of the Family, a very kind and good natured degree of Solicitude— This Letter I had begun at Oxford on the day when it is dated, but (as I am afraid I ought to say "ut mihi constem")[3] I am finishing it at a place, not having dispatched it when I ought, at some distance from thence. Mr. James, a near Relation of Lady Rothes's[4]

---

[2] George's brother Peregrine recorded in his diary that George rode like a madman (PL-M's diary, 1809, p. 330). This habit was perhaps at least one cause of the accident.

[3] "To keep myself in character", a paraphrase of Horace, *Ars Poetica* 125–27:

Si quid inexpertum scaenae committis,
  et audes
Personam formare novam; servetur
  ad imum
Qualis ab incepto processerit, et sibi
  constet.

"If it is an untried theme you entrust to the stage, and if you boldly fashion a fresh character, have it kept to the end even as it came forth at the first, and have it self-consistent" (H. R. Fairclough's translation in Loeb ed.).

[4] Walter James James (1759–1829) of Langley Hall and Denford Court, Berkshire, formerly Walter James Head, second son of Sir Thomas Head and Jane Holt, Lady Rothes's aunt. He succeeded his elder brother in 1777 and in 1778 assumed the name of James (as had his brother) by act of Parliament, having in-

whom I believe You have met at our house, has very kindly and pressingly urged our coming to his House in Berkshire, and as my Summons for Lincolnshire was not arrived, I have accompanied Lady Rothes hither, in the mean while;—George and my two eldest Daughters are come with us where we are very obligingly received by Mr. James and Lady Jane, his Lady, who is a Daughter of Lord *Camdens*;[5] it would have been a pleasant addition to other agreeable Circumstances in the Excursion, had it proved a time when *he* had been come to make his Son in Law a visit, which he usually does some time in the Autumn.—Mrs. Montague is a Neighbour, of about seven or eight miles distance from hence; a Message has been exchanged since we came, but I have not seen her yet—

To conclude my narrative that I have been obliged to trouble you with of our situation and engagements, I have the further particular to mention, that a Female first Cousin of mine[6] has been making a Stay with us of some weeks, and while we are upon this visit at Mr. James's, takes the occasion of being with a Friend of hers, with whom She had promised to pass some days, and is to return back for a further abode at our house—so that we cannot at present hope for the pleasure of seeing Miss Boswells—it gives me

herited the estate of his uncle, John James. He seems to have written the anonymous *Defence of Mr. Boswell's Journal of a Tour to the Hebrides*, 1785 (Charles Ryskamp, "Boswell and Walter James" in *Eighteenth-Century Studies in Honor of Donald F. Hyde*, ed. W. H. Bond, 1970, pp. 207–24). He was created baronet on 28 July 1791 (Burke, *Peerage*, pp. 1098–99; *Comp. Bar.* v. 268). He was, apparently, an eccentric, "whose Character", his cousin Peregrine Langton-Massingberd wrote later, "it would take the pen of My Lord Clarendon to describe: so heterogenious an animal is he; and so various, and uncertain at different times" (PL-M's diary, 1806–1808, p. 116). Peregrine then devoted nine pages of the diary to explaining and describing James, and included an illustrative anecdote: "He asked the Butler whether the Cook had had a fall, one day as we were all sitting quietly at dinner; the Man said no. Why. Said Sir Walter,

I am sure this is the mark of her [Peregrine has erased a word] upon the Potatoes" (p. 122).

[5] Lady Jane Pratt (1761–1825), youngest daughter of Charles (1714–1794), first Earl Camden, former Lord Chancellor and Lord President of the Council. She was married to James on 25 Apr. 1780 (Burke, *Peerage*, p. 1098, s.v. Northbourne).

[6] Possibly Miss Roberts, identified in the *Life* (i. 336, 430) as old Mr. Langton's niece. The Langton genealogies are not helpful. A Miss Roberts married one of Bennet Langton's uncles, but unless the uncle assumed his wife's surname, their daughter would have been Miss Langton. On 26 June 1765, Langton had paid £2. 0s. 2d. "To Miss Judy Roberts wch she had pd. for my mother"; and during the week of 16–22 June 1766, he had reminded himself "To write an acct. to Miss Roberts that dividends are due to Her" (Langton's diary).

likewise concern to be sure that this engagement of Business that I have mentioned, hinders our having the meeting we have so long been fruitlessly concerting, for the revisal of the papers—the best that seems now to be said is that as soon as I should find myself released from my Lincolnshire Business and returned to Oxford, I would take care to let You know and then we might betake ourselves to planning again and I hope with better effect—

You do me Justice, my dear Sir, in thinking that I feel with You and for You, on occasion of your disappointments in your views,[7] and, indeed I think, your *claims*, of the ambitious kind— and surely I am not a little confirmed in the propriety of my having used the word, *claims*, by recollecting, that no less a Man than Mr. Burke, said to you when he and his Friends were in office, that it would be right for them to think of shewing You some Mark of Respect and Regard, for their *own* sakes[8]—then I call to mind the very emphatick praise that Lord Thurlow gave to your Work, of the *Tour*[9]—You have I am strongly persuaded a large Harvest of Reputation to look to when Your great Work shall appear, but to be sure the added importance of Character that *that* may be expected to confer, is not of the kind that immediately forwards success in the active or political course of Life—I observe Your mention of the great kindness of Mr. Malone in having superintended the printing in Your absence,[10] which topick, Mr. Courtenay who favoured me with a Call not long ago in going through Oxford, explained upon likewise, and mentioned his having deferred an intended Journey to Ireland that he might be of Service in forwarding the work[11]—I cannot but at times feel a wish, that,

[7] *Ante* To Langton, 27 Aug. 1790.

[8] Oddly enough, JB himself seems to have recorded this fine compliment of Burke's only in the "Memoirs of James Boswell, Esq." which he wrote for *The European Magazine* at the time of the publication of the *Life of Johnson*: "In 1781, when Mr. Burke was in power, that celebrated Gentleman shewed his sense of Mr. Boswell's merit in the warmest manner, observing, 'We must do something for you for our own sakes', and recommended him to General Conway for a vacant place, by a letter in which his character was drawn in glowing colours" (*European Magazine*, 1791, xix. 406; *Lit. Car.* p. xl).

[9] JB sent to Lord Thurlow on 23 Sept. 1785 a copy of the *Tour* which was acknowledged on 11 Oct. On 26 Feb. 1786, JB called on Thurlow: "'Your Lordship did me the honour to read my *Tour*.' C[HANCELLOR]. 'Yes, every word of it; and yet one cannot tell how. Why should one wish to go on and read how Dr. Johnson went from one place to another? Can you give a rule for writing in that manner? Longinus could not'" (Journ.).

[10] See *ante* To Langton, 27 Aug. 1790, n. 2.

[11] It seems likely that Malone would have postponed his trip in any case until he had read final proof of *The Plays and*

instead of merely passing a few hours together, for the reviewing such particulars as have been recovered out of what You have been pleased to style my *Herculaneum*,[12] we might have the means of devoting a quantity of time as much larger as there might prove to be any topicks to interest relating to our revered Friend, for the endeavouring, by consultation and conference, to throw any additional Light that might be on such parts of his Character and opinions as I happened to have means more peculiarly of knowing from having lived so much with him—but what I speak of I am afraid is not practicable, and to be sure, if at all endeavoured at should have been an earlier proceeding than now, when so much of the work is actually printed[13]—But it grows time, with our best Regards as due—to release you—believe me, my dear Sir, to be sincerely and affectionately Yours

B. LANGTON

To Bennet Langton, between Saturday 9 October and Tuesday 30 November 1790

Not reported. Sent between 9 Oct. and 30 Nov. Referred to *post* From Langton, 30 Nov.: "I am very glad to be favoured with your Information that my Letter was acceptable."

To John Douglas, Friday 15 October 1790

Not reported. Sent from London. To his son Sandy JB wrote, 15 Oct., "I . . . have this day written to the Bishop of Carlisle requesting to know at what time I may be sure to find him, and on what days of the week he is most at leisure."

Poems of William Shakespeare. The eleven volumes were not published until at least 29 Nov. 1790. (*The London Chronicle* of 25–27 Nov., lxviii. 517, announced that they would be published on that date, but did not announce actual publication until the issue of 2–4 Dec. [*ibid.* p. 541]. The paper had reported in its issue of 16–18 Nov. that "the last sheet . . . was last week printed off" [*ibid.* p. 483].) Malone left for Ireland on 19 or 20

Nov. JB wrote to him there on 4 Dec.
   [12] JB compared the "good store of *Johnsoniana*" treasured in Langton's mind "to Herculaneum, or some old Roman field, which, when dug, fully rewards the labour employed. The authenticity of every article is unquestionable" (*Life* iv. 1–2).
   [13] On 5 Oct. 1790, JB wrote to his son, Sandy, that fifty-six pages of the second volume had been printed.

From George Steevens, c. mid-October 1790

MS. Yale (C 2546).

[Hampstead Heath]

I have just been told there is in the King's Library the original MS. of Dr. Johnson's *Irene*,[1] containing many unpublished speeches etc. If you have not seen this Curiosity, you may wish to see it. Yours very faithfully

G.S.

From John Douglas, Sunday 17 October 1790

MS. Yale (C 1100).

ADDRESS: To James Boswell Esq., Queen Anne Street-West, Cavendish Square, London.

FRANK: Windsor, October seventeenth 1790. free. J. Carliol.

POSTMARKS: OC 18 90, FREE A.

Windsor Castle, Sunday Octr. 17th. 1790

DEAR SIR: I shall be happy to see you at the Deanry,[1] when you come down, and a Bed will be ready for you. I can answer for my dining at home this Day Sevennight, and, unless I hear to the contrary, shall expect you on Saturday Evening. Till then I remain, Dear Sir, Your's sincerely

J. CARLIOL

Your Son,[2] I hope, will dine with me, the Day you favor me with your Company.

[1] King's MS. 306 (*British Museum Catalogue of Western Manuscripts in the Old Royal and King's Collections*, by Sir George F. Warner and J. P. Gilson, 1921, iii. 56).

[1] Douglas had been appointed Dean of Windsor 21 Mar. 1788. The Deanery, built in 1500, had been "much improved by Dean Keppel in the middle of the eighteenth century" (William March, *The Official Guide to Windsor Castle*, 1926, p. 34).

[2] Sandy, his elder son, a student at Eton.

From John Douglas,
Thursday 21 October 1790

MS. Yale (C 1101).

ADDRESS: To James Boswell Esq., Queen Anne Street West, London.

FRANK: Windsor, October twenty first 1790. free. J. Carliol.

POSTMARKS: OC 22 90, FREE C.

Windsor Castle, Thursday Octr. 21st. 1790

DEAR SIR, I write, only to mention, that we do not dine till four o'Clock on Saturday, and I think you may, without inconvenience be with us, by that hour. After Dinner, you will have time to go to Eton, if you choose, and let your Son know I expect to see him on Sunday at our dining hour.[1] I am, Dear Sir, Your's sincerely

J. CARLIOL

To George Steevens,
Saturday 30 October 1790

MS. Hyde Collection.

ADDRESS: To George Steevens Esq., Hampstead Heath.

POSTMARKS: Two triangular and one circular Penny Post Paid, all illegible.

[London] Saturday 30 Octr.

DEAR SIR: My having been in the country[1] has prevented my acknowledging sooner the favour of your polite note.

The Original *Materials* of *Irene* Mr. Langton had from Johnson, and presented them with a fair copy made by himself to the King;[2] but with his Majestys permission kept a copy for himself, which he obligingly communicated to me, and I have given some extracts from it.[3] I breakfast every day almost at home at ½ past nine. Pray

---

[1] There is no journal for this period, but this was the time when JB talked with Fanny Burney at St. George's Chapel (*Diary and Letters of Madame d'Arblay*, ed. Austin Dobson, iv. 1905, 431–33).

[1] At Eton to visit his son Sandy. See *ante* From Douglas, 17, 21 Oct. 1790.

[2] Langton's fair copy is also at the British Museum (King's MS. 307). See *Life* i. 108 and n. 1.

[3] *Life* i. 108–10.

come and *dejeunez* after your walk.[4] I am your most obedient humble servant

JAMES BOSWELL

I go to Kent today and return Monday or tuesday.[5]

From George Steevens to Edmond Malone, Tuesday 23 November 1790

MS. Yale C 2547 (wrapper only); the Folger Shakespeare Library, Washington, D.C. (text). Text printed by permission of the Folger Library.

ADDRESS: Edmond Malone Esqr., Queen Anne Street East, near Portland Chapel, London. [*Crossed out:*] Novr. 23d. [*Redirected in an unidentified hand:*] at Baronston, Mullingar, Ireland.

POSTMARKS: PENNY [POST] PAYD [illegible]; NO [illegible]; [illegible] OCLOCK W; NOV 25 [9]0; NO 28.

Note in another hand near seal: Dance.

Hempstead Heath, Novr. 23. 1790

Mr. Steevens presents his best compliments and thanks to Mr. Malone, for his very acceptable present of two sets of Shakspeare. Though Mr. S. has no occasion for a third Copy, he begs leave to acknowledge the liberality of Mr. Malone's offer.

Mr. Malone's favour is dated Novr. 17. but the books (unaccountably) did not reach Hampstead till a few minutes ago.[1] Mr. Steevens's thanks would otherwise have been less tardy.

---

[4] Steevens regularly walked into London from Hampstead early in the morning, visiting friends, publishers, and bookshops prior to returning home, still on foot, early in the afternoon (DNB).

[5] JB spent two days with John Cator of Beckenham in order to receive from him some anecdotes of SJ. He returned to London on Monday 1 Nov. (To Charles Jenkinson, 1 Nov. 1790). See Waingrow, p. 341 n. 3, for further information on this visit.

[1] Since the last sheet of Malone's edition of Shakespeare was probably printed off during the second week of Nov., the delay seems neither unaccountable nor excessive. See *ante* From Langton, 2 Oct. 1790, n. 11, for further information on its publication.

314

From Bennet Langton,
Tuesday 30 November 1790

MS. Yale (C 1694). A separate scrap of paper, bearing a note on one side and some verses on the other (both in JB's hand), is sewn to the last page of the letter. From "It was in the Summer of the year 1778" to "I have not a moment more before the post goes out" JB edited the entire document for inclusion in the printer's copy of the *Life* as a "Paper Apart". He ended, however, by admitting much less than he had prepared, apparently effecting the abridgement in the proofs.

Oxford, Novr. 30th. 1790

MY DEAR SIR, I am very glad to be favoured with your Information that my Letter was acceptable—as to the hope of my seeing You, I am still (in consequence of "the Laws delay"[1] that affects some business that I am concerned in) in the same disagreeable uncertainty—I am threaten'd with having very soon a necessity to go a long Journey—into Lincolnshire, but it, at present, seems as if I must, after accomplishing that, find my way to London, on one or two accounts, neither of them any way connected with Inclination, which, however, in their effect will coincide with a third motive of a very agreeable kind—that, of the hope of seeing my Friends there—

But to come to the point of replying to Your Enquiries—The Book, to which I esteem it as a great honour that You should have remembered my referring, is *The natural History of Iceland*, translated from the Danish of *Horrebow*. The Chapter is, the *72d* and its title,—"Concerning *Snakes*" (not Fishes) and the whole words of the Chapter are,—"There are no Snakes to be met with throughout the whole Island"—Though I had forgot having made the Allusion, it occurs easily to see what it pointed to—and I think I feel a little remorse at having been so pert in my remarking, when You say, that the only word or two he *did* utter was, "pretty Dear," to one of the Children—and further, as I owed the means of my having the passage, to make the Allusion, from our Friend himself;—who, as it appeared to me, with an effect of a good deal of Humour, had brought it out in company; when mention was made of Horrebow's Book, he said with an affected gravity "I can repeat an entire Chapter of that Work"; and, when we expected

[1] *Hamlet*, III. i. 72.

315

a pretty copious recitation—he *did* repeat it, as above inserted[2]—
There is another such title and Chapter in the Book—"Concerning
Owls" "There are no Owls of any kind in the Island"[3]—Next, as
to what relates to his visiting the Camp—I believe I had better
write down any particulars I remember, loosely as they may occur,
and You will then make any use of them or put them in any order
that you may judge proper—[4]It was in the Summer of the year
1778—that he complied with my Invitation to come down to the
Camp at Warley—and he staid with me about a Week—The
Scene appeared, notwithstanding a great degree of ill health that
he seemed labouring under, to interest and amuse him—as
agreeing with the disposition that I believe you know he constantly
manifest[ed] towards enquiring into Subjects of the Military kind—
He sat, with a patient degree of Attention, to observe the proceedings of a Regimental Court Martial that happen'd to be called
in the time of his stay with us—and one Night, as late as at eleven
o'Clock, he accompanied the Major of the Regiment, in going,
what are styled, the *Rounds*, where he might observe the forms of
visiting the Guards, for the seeing that they and the Sentries are
ready in their duty on their several posts—He took occasion to
converse at times on military topicks, one in particular, that I see
the mention of, in Your Journal,[5] which lies open before me:
Page 132,[6] as to Gun-powder;—which he spoke of, to the same
effect, in part, that you relate[4]—but as You may perhaps, my
dear Sir chuse that I should tell you pretty fully what I can recollect, I will venture being tedious rather than being too succinct;
and You will make any use, or as little use as You please of any
part of what I write—As to the granulating Powder, he observed,
that, to a certain degree it is necessary, for if, on the contrary, You
reduce it to a state like meal, it will not explode at all; but, what
is in that state, consumes in succession; which is what is called
wild fire—such, I remember, he said, as the School-boys make for
sport—the good, then, of having powder in grains, he said, appears
to be, the *air* that is by that means admitted; which, being in-

---

[2] *Life* iii. 279. JB had recorded the
incident in his journal (13 Apr. 1778),
but had failed to catch the name of the
author and to recall the exact wording of
the famous short chapter.

[3] See *ibid*. n. 2.

[4-4] Included, with minor textual revision, not all of which is here directed by
JB, in *Life* iii. 361.

[5] "of a Tour to the Hebrides" inserted above the line by JB.

[6] Converted by JB to a foot-note: "3
Edit. p. 111."

stantaneously[7] rarified, on firing it, produces the explosion, and the other consequent effects—how *large* the grains ought to be, he said, was the matter of next consideration—it would seem that *that* size of them is to be preferred, that, in the same dimensions, would admit of the most air; and, for an experiment to that effect, he said, he would make use of two measures, of a Bushel exactly each; and fill one with Leaden Bullets, the other with small Shot, such as is used in fowling pieces—then he would weigh them, when so filled—and whichever (as the dimensions of each Measure were to be exactly equal) proved to be the heavier— would evidently have the least Air admitted—if the bullets weighed heavier, and so appeared, by the larger form in which the Lead was cast, to exclude the air the more—*that* would determine him not to have the Powder in *large* grains—if the small shot weighd heavier—and *so*, excluded air the more—it would induce him not to granulate the powder into smaller grains—He said further, on this article of Gun powder, that, in order to judge whether it was good, his expedient would be, as, in the three Ingredients of it, Salt petre, Sulphur, and Charcoal, the much larger part ought to be Salt-petre (upwards of seventy parts in a hundred—the Charcoal about fifteen, the Sulphur about nine) but that as, from the comparative dearness of Salt petre, the temptation is, to put less of that than its due proportion—he would put a quantity exactly weighed of the powder into *Water*, which would dissolve the Salt petre, and then pour the Water off, which would carry the Salt petre with it—and he would then weigh the mass that remained; which would serve to detect the deficiency (if any) and how great, as to the ingredient most essential and most in danger of being deficient—The above mentioned experiments, I am aware, may, to experienced Men of the military and Chemical professions, possibly appear imperfect and slovenly, in comparison of such as they may be apprized of—but, considering that Dr. Johnson had so little means of being well versed in such discoveries and experiencies as belong to professional skill they may perhaps be allowed to be considerable efforts of mind, compared with his means of information—and may lead to the thought, among so many other grounds for the same Idea concerning him—to what his Efforts of Understanding might have attained, if exerted with the same Vigour (in any Profession to

---

[7] MS. "instantanteously".

which he should have applied) on the stores of knowledge that he would have found therein accumulated—Thus far I had written, when it occurred to me, that, as what has been mentioned as said by Dr. Johnson is of some length, which makes it the more desirable that it should have been founded on correctness of knowledge in the Subject, if there should be thoughts of giving it to the Publick—it might be better to enquire a little, of those qualified to judge, as to the correctness of it—which I have accordingly been doing—and from two respectable Gentlemen of the University whom I conferred with—and to confirm what had been said by them—from our principal Physician here Dr. Wall[8] who was for five years our Chemical Professor, I learned that what external air there may be among the particles of the Gun powder is by no means to be reputed the cause of the explosion in firing it—but that it is the confined nitre that by its vast expansion occasions it—there being then this allay, of incorrectness in the Notion—though the expedient proposed by Johnson according to the principle he had supposed is highly ingenious—perhaps you will think it as well not to insert what he said upon it, in any particular manner[9]—and as to the other device, to detect the deficiency of the Salt-petre, Dr. Wall explained upon that head, so as to shew that there would be no certainty in the effect—for that they can adulterate by putting common salt with Salt petre, which has no effect in the explosion, and yet would be equally dissolved by the water that Dr. Johnson proposed to make the trial by—so that if the *remaining* Ingredients, after the water was poured off, weighed no more than they ought in their due proportion still he might be mistaken in thinking that what had been carried off by the water had been only genuine Salt petre—*this* therefore, my dear Sir, in like manner I suppose, you will omit the particular mention of—but I thought

---

[8] Martin Wall (c. 1747–1824), a Fellow of New College, was Clinical Professor from 1785 to his death. He received his D.Med. in 1777 (*Alum. Oxon.* II. iv. 1488).

[9] "See Note" inserted by JB. The note, on a separate scrap of paper sewn to the letter, reads as follows: "Note on Mr. Langton's Letter at the word *manner*: Although there is it seems a defect in point of experimental science in Dr. Johnson's observations they are so ingenious and shew such a vigorous aptitude of research that I should be sorry to omit them." Eventually, as remarked above, JB decided not to include them in the published work. On the reverse side of the scrap of paper bearing this note are eight lines from Addison's *Cato* (I. iv. 64–71) which JB had copied out to complete a quotation on luxury made by General Oglethorpe on 14 Apr. 1778 (*Life* iii. 282).

I would however send you this paper, both to shew you that I have been at work; and apprehending that You would chuse to have the particulars communicated, for your own amusement and the interest You take in what relates to our Friend—should it not be altogether fit for publication—I have further to mention— that [10]on one occasion that the Regiment were going through their exercising, He went quite close to the Men at one of the Extremities of it, and watched all their practices attentively, and when he came away his remark was—"the Men indeed do load their musquets and fire with wonderful Celerity;[10] the Sportsman is twice as long about it—he first puts in his powder and rams it down and then his Shot which must be rammed down likewise—whereas your Men charge with both powder and ball at once"—which You, I suppose are Soldier enough to know;— that what they call the Cartridge, is made up with both the powder and Ball—[11]He was likewise particular in requiring to know what was the weight of the Musquet-Balls in use, and within what distance they might be expected best[12] to take effect when fired off—In walking among the Tents, and observing the difference between those of the Officers and private Men, he said that the superiority of accommodation, of the better conditions of life, to that of the inferior ones, was never exhibited to him in so distinct a view—The Civilities paid to him in the Camp were, from the Gentlemen of the Lincolnshire Regiment—one of the Officers of which accommodated him with the Tent in which he slept—and from General Hall, who very courteously invited him to dine with him; where he appeared to be very well pleased with his entertainment—and the civilities he received on the part of the General —the attentions likewise of the General's Aid de Camp, Captain Smith,[13] seemed to be very welcome to him, as appeared by their engaging in a great deal of discourse together—The Gentlemen of the East York Regiment likewise, on being informed of his coming, sollicited his company at dinner—but by that time, he had fixed his departure, so that he could not comply with the Invitation[11]—the last particular of this tattle that I will offer

---

[10-10] Printed, with slight changes, in *Life* iii. 361.

[11-11] Printed, with slight changes, in *Life* iii. 361.

[12] Omitted in the *Life*, probably by a printer's error.

[13] Possibly Capt. Lieut. Robert Smith of the South Lincolnshire Regiment (*Army List* for 1779, "Militia", p. 37).

you is, that he met one day with Dr. Cadogan,[14] who was our Camp Physician, at my tent—who, with a chearfulness and good humour that is constantly prevalent in his manners, asked him as to his state of health—Dr. Johnson, who was clouded with Illness and Uneasiness, replied in a half peevish manner that he was by no means well—Dr. Cadogan then asked him what *plan* he followed with a view to better health—he answered very impatiently "I pursue no plan!" Dr. Cadogan then said, I thought very pertinently, "If You had said Dr. Johnson that You were in a good health and did not pursue any plan I should have thought you very right, but declaring yourself to be ill, surely it is eligible for you to consider of any Regimen or plan that might give a chance for restor'd health"—[15]

I have not a moment more before the post goes out than to give all our due regards and to say that I am, Dear Sir, Yours faithfully

BENNET LANGTON

From Thomas Barnard,
Saturday 4 December 1790

MS. Yale (C 91).

ADDRESS: James Boswell Esqr., 36. Queen Anne Street West, London.

POSTMARKS: DE 4, DE 9 90.

St. Wolstans, Decr. 4th. 1790

DEAR SIR: It is now upwards of Two months Since I wrote to you from Killaloe to acquaint you that in consequence of your Request, and My Promise, I had reserv'd for you two Spaniel Puppies of the Red Breed the same of which you Saw a Specimen in London, But, if possible more Beautifull than their Dam; and I requested you to direct me how I should dispose of them, whether I should send

---

[14] Dr. William Cadogan (1711–97) was the successful author of two medical books, one on the nursing and management of children, the other on gout, both of which passed through many editions. Shortly after receiving his medical degree from Leyden in 1737, he was appointed a physician to the Army. See *Life* v. 210–11. Having received half pay since 11 Nov. 1762, he was placed on full pay on 27 June 1778, the time of the encampment, and finally retired on half pay on 13 June 1780 (William Johnston, *Roll of Commissioned Officers in the Medical Service of the British Army*, Aberdeen University Studies No. 76, 1917, p. 38).

[15] An X made by JB at this point indicates the end of the portion of the letter to be printed. He finally decided to omit the anecdote concerning Dr. Cadogan.

them to Whitehaven according to your first Instructions, and to whom I should Consign them?

To these Queries I have not been honour'd with an answer; Though I think my Letter, (being directed to Jas. Boswell Aghinleck Esqr. Edinburgh) ought to have Reach'd your hands, even tho' you had not been in North Britain. I should not however have troubled you with a Second, if I had not thought it more Probable that the Post Should be negligent than Mr. Boswell. I shall therefore wait some time Longer for your Commands before I dispose of the Survivor of the Two Dogs; for one of them unfortunately Lost his Life about a month ago by falling into a Boiling Copper, unobserved, till he was taken out completely Dress'd in company with a Round of Beef.

I have just, and But just, Finish'd Burkes inimitable Pamphlet.[1] C'est un chef d'Œuvre s'il y en avoit jamais. It is above all Praise. How Superior is he, not only to all other writers but even to his former Self, now he speaks the genuine Language of his Heart,[1a] instead of that of his Party? Such Information Such argument, enforced by Such a Stile, and Embelish'd with such Luxuriance of Fancy! And Fancy Employ'd, as it ought to be, to adorn Truth and not to disguise it, by substituting it in the Place of Argument. Whether it will make many Proselytes I doubt: for Modern Politicians seldom act from any Principles, except Self Interest or Revenge. A Few honest Englishmen may however be Kept Steady to the good Cause of the Constitution by the Information they may draw from That Source, and even this is something.

I see by the Newspapers that you are not Neuter in these Busy Times, when all Honest Men ought to Lend a hand.[2] Macte tua Virtute.[3] Whatever you are ⟨doing⟩ you have the Sincere and Cordial good wishes of, Dear Sir, Your Faithfull and obedient Servant

THOS. KILLALOE

---

[1] *Reflections on the Revolution in France, and on the Proceedings in certain Societies in London relative to that Event. In a Letter intended to have been sent to a Gentleman in Paris*, 1790.

[1a] "But still I love the language of his Heart" (Pope, speaking of Cowley, *First Epistle of the Second Book of Horace*, l. 78).

[2] On 9 Nov., at the Lord Mayor's Feast, JB sang a ballad of his own com- position, "William Pitt, the Grocer of London", praising Pitt for having forced the Spanish to agree to a convention which guaranteed Great Britain trading privileges on the north-west coast of America (*Lit. Car.* pp. 141–44). The ballad was widely published in the newspapers in mid-Nov. See *New CBEL* ii. 1227, 1231.

[3] "Well done!"

If you honour me with an answer tell me something of our Freinds. Have you heard from the good Paoli? If you Chance to see Mr. Burke, Pray assure him of my unalterable Respect and Regard: To tell him how much I admire his work is needless, for who do's not? Even those who most feel the Severity of his Strictures; must reluctantly confess its Merit. Non illud carpere Livor—Possit opus.[4]

To Thomas Barnard,
Tuesday 7 December 1790

Not reported. Referred to in next letter, and also in To Malone, 7 Dec.: "I shall be indebted to you for half the postage of this; as I enclose a letter to the Bishop of Killaloe to send me the *Round Robin*, and wish to be sure of a *certain* and *speedy* conveyance, and therefore trouble you."

From Thomas Barnard,
Monday 20 December 1790

MS. Yale (C 92).

[St. Wolstans] Decr. 20th

DEAR SIR: In Answer to your very obliging Letter of the 7th, I send you herewith, The True original Round Robin on the Subject of Goldsmiths Epitaph according to your Request. (Disclaiming however all Recollection of any *Promise* to that Effect.) I confess that I was a Principal in that Mutinous act, being Employ'd to draw it up at the Table; And though I might be a Little Pot Valiant, when I wrote it, I am still of the Same opinion. I refer you to Sir Joshua Reynolds for the Particulars of the whole Transaction, as it pass'd at his Table. When you have made what use of it you think Proper, I request you to return it to me, that I may preserve it as an archive.

By the Date of your Letter I Imagine that you had not receiv'd a Second that I wrote you a Few days before, to tell you of the Loss of one of the Dogs by Falling into a Boiling Copper. How-

---

[4] Ovid, *Metamorphoses* vi. 129–30: "nor work" (F. J. Miller's translation in Envy himself could find a flaw in that Loeb ed.).

ever, Since you are at present in London and likely to stay there some time, so that you would not be in the Way to recieve your Dog and take him under your own Protection, And as I Know by Experience the Danger of Trusting any Commission of that Kind to Masters of Coal Ships, especially when they Can Frame a Thousand Excuses (of Death, or Loss by running away, or being Stolen etc.) for not delivering their charge to the person it was consign'd to; I think it much the safest Way to wait till you are return'd to Aughinleck before I part with the Dog from my own Care; and in the mean time I hope to have a second, ready to accompany him, as the Dam is preparing for another Brood.

I am extremely happy to hear from yourself, that your young Family Promises you so much Credit and Comfort; I have no doubt of your Instilling into them *good* Principles, Both Religious and Political. Make them Christians, instead of Philosophers, good Subjects, instead of Virtuous Citizens; and British Patriots, instead of general Philanthropists. Oh! how I hate all that Cant, from a Set of Rascals who in Reality act from *no* Principles at all, and how I honour Burke for Exposing the Ill Tendency of their Plausible Pretenses!

Since I wrote the above I have been Searching for General Paolis note[1] to send it you with the other Paper, but Cannot find it, though I am sure I have not destroy'd it. Whenever I do meet it, I will not fail to Enclose it to you. I cannot suppose that you want it for your present Work, so the delay can be of no Consequence.

I rejoice at the good account you give me of our Freind Sir Joshua, whom I sincerely Love, and ever Shall. Ille habeat Secum Servetque Sepulchro.[2] I do not regret his Leaving off the Excercise of his art:[3] He has Lived enough to the World; and I hope he has

---

[1] Possibly a reference to a note written by Paoli on 10 May 1776. JB had vowed to the General that he would give up wine, but at a dinner at Barnard's on the above date he was "plag[u]ed about waterdrinking . . . I was really poor. Wrote [to General Paoli] for dispensat[ion]; good return" (Notes). See *post* From Barnard, 9 Aug. 1791.

[2] Virgil, *Aeneid* iv. 29: "May he keep it [my love] with him and guard it in the grave" (H. R. Fairclough's translation in Loeb ed.).

[3] On 13 July 1789, the sight of Sir Joshua's left eye "became so much obscured that he was obliged to leave off painting, and within ten weeks the sight of that eye was entirely gone" (C. R. Leslie and Tom Taylor, *Life and Times of Sir Joshua Reynolds*, 1865, ii. 540). No entry of a sitter occurs in his engagement book after July 1789 (ibid. p. 549). Sir Joshua wrote to Richard Brinsley Sheridan on 20 Jan. 1790, "there is now an end of the pursuit; the race is over whether it is won or lost" (*Letters Reynolds*, p. 191).

still some years to Live to *himself*, and have only to Enjoy his well Earn'd Praise, His Fortune, and His Freinds. Apropos to that, Pray how goes on the Club,? and who attends it? I am afraid it is become a Little too *Fine* for the Taste of its old Members.[4] Clonfert has just Left this Neighbourhood for Bath, but goes to London for the Remainder of the winter after the Christmass Holidays.

Well, I Long for your Shrove Tuesday Cock to make his appearance. But However he will have one Disadvantage; He will be a *Dilly*, (I suppose) and in that Case you Know he must have a great Deal of *Lead* in him. Perhaps you dont call them in Scotland by that Name, and so my Pun is Lost upon you.[5] But whether he be Lead or Feathers Dead or alive I must have him before the Irish Printers get hold of him, and I desire you to order your Printer on the day of Publication to send me one by the mail coach, Directed to the Care of Mr. Jackson, Holy head,[6] For the Bishop of Killaloe Dublin, who is, My Dear Sir, Your Faithfull and affectionate humble Servant

THOS. KILLALOE

P.S. I wonder how your Letter of the 7th travell'd to me For it came Free, and had the Irish Postmark of Mullingar upon it. Is Malone come to Ireland, and did he convey it? I can account for this Mystery no otherwise.[7]

---

[4] See *post* From Barnard, 25 Mar. 1794 and n. 3.

[5] JB had written to Malone on 16 Dec., "My utmost wish is to come forth on Shrove Tuesday (8 March). 'Wits are game cocks etc.'" The quotation is from the last lines of Gay's fable, "The Elephant and the Bookseller":

No author ever spar'd a brother,

Wits are game-cocks to one another.

Barnard's strained witticism, as Waingrow (p. 375 n. 4) has noted, depends upon puns on "Dilly" (JB's printer and a nursery name for duck) and "lead" (printer's lead or bird-shot) and perhaps also the custom of shying (throwing) sticks, etc. at cocks on Shrove Tuesday.

[6] Innkeeper of the Eagle and Child in Holyhead (*Universal British Directory* [?1798] iii. 387).

[7] Barnard's accounting for the mystery was correct. Malone had gone to Ireland to visit his brother, Lord Sunderlin, at Baronston, near Mullingar. A letter from Malone to JB, dated 19 Dec. 1790, was written from Baronston.

From Thomas Barnard,
Sunday 2 January 1791

MS. Yale (C 93).

ADDRESS: James Boswell Esqr., Queen Anne Street West, London.

POSTMARKS: LEIXLIP, JA 3, JA 8 91.

Jany. 2d. 1791[1]

DEAR SIR: I have made a Terrible Mistake by enclosing to you (in the Same Pacquet with the Round Robin that you requested) a Letter intended for another Gentleman[2] and substituting your Letter in its Place, which, he has return'd to me by this Days Post, and I now transmit it to you unalter'd, Requesting you, in the *First* Place to Pardon my mistake; owing to a Multiplicity of Letters to be sent off by that Post. *Secondly* relying upon your Candour, to Keep the Mistake to yourself, and not make a *good* Story of it to the Club. *Thirdly*, to send me back my Letter *Immediately*, as the right owner is anxious to recover it, and you see the Contents are Important. I rely on your granting all the above, and am most Sincerely Yours

T. KILLALOE

Direct to me at St. Wolstans, Leixlip, Ireland.

From John Courtenay,
c. Friday 14 January 1791

Not reported. Sent from Bath. Referred to in To Malone, 18 Jan.: "Poor C. has been at Bath for some time. I had a few lines from him a day or two ago. His situation is deplorable. I would fain have the seat in Parliament turned to account, and I found him not averse; but that must be negotiated if at all, by others." Courtenay, a formidable member of the Opposition, had been seated for Tamworth by Lord Townshend in 1780 to support Lord North's Government, and had been returned again by Townshend in 1784, though by that time Townshend had gone over to Pitt while Courtenay supported Fox. Townshend may have acted thus "handsomely" (*Farington Diary* i. 132) in order to continue Courtenay's immunity to arrest for debt. JB wishes that Courtenay would use his seat as a bargaining counter to obtain from Government some

---

[1] MS. "1790"   [2] Unidentified.

employment or office which would relieve his financial embarrassment. No such arrangement seems to have been made. Courtenay had to give up his seat in 1796, but came in for Appleby on Lord Thanet's interest, apparently at Fox's request, and Lord Townshend returned a friend of Government for Tamworth (materials for this note largely furnished by E. L. C. Mullins, Secretary to the Editorial Board of The History of Parliament Trust).

To John Courtenay, Thursday 10 March 1791 [1]

MS. Yale (L 389). A draft.

[London] Thursday 10 March

MY DEAR COURTENAY: I am under the necessity of paying £150 *this day se'night*, being the first installment of £500 for my unhappy Relation in the India Service whom I mentioned.[2] What I am to beg of you is that you may inform me *this week*, whether the small matter can be replaced *certainly* before this day se'night,[3] that if it cannot, I may have three days to exert myself.[4] Yours faithfully

[1] 1791 is the only possible year in which 10 Mar. fell on a Thursday. See also the following notes.

[2] JB wrote to Malone on 18 Jan.: "£500 which I borrowed and lent to a first cousin an unlucky Captain of an Indiaman were due on the 15th to a merchant in the City [Alexander Anderson, Lothbury]. I could not possibly raise that sum, and was apprehensive of being hardly used. He however indulged me with an allowance to make partial payments £150 in two months £150 in eight months, and the remainder with the interests in eighteen months. How I am to manage I am at a loss." JB had borrowed the money ten years before to assist in outfitting Bruce Boswell, son of Dr. John Boswell. Bruce Boswell's voyage, 1781–86, had been an imbroglio of disasters, and he had repaid no part of the loan. When the debt to Anderson fell due, JB was already under great financial pressure being under the urgent neces-sity of raising money to complete the price of the old Boswell property of Knockroon which he had rashly pur-chased. In his harassed state he was tempted to accept an offer of £1,000 for the *Life* which he had heard that Robin-son the bookseller had said he would give. Dilly and Baldwin generously came to his relief, their loans to be repaid from the profits of the *Life* (Journ. 9 Apr., 31 May 1781; 13 Nov. 1786; 20 Feb. 1791; 24 Nov. 1792; "View of my Affairs", 1787–91, 1793, Yale MS. A 52; "A Narrative of the Voyage of the Ship Earl of Chesterfield", Yale MS. C 306; To Malone, 18, 29 Jan., 10, 25 Feb., 8 Mar. 1791).

[3] Courtenay's debt to JB must have been trifling, for it is not listed in JB's "View of my Affairs, 21 February 1791" (Yale MS. A 52).

[4] The following, except for the word *manner*, is deleted at this point: "I am truly vexed that I should have to write in

From Thomas Percy,
Saturday 12 March 1791

MS. Yale (C 2237).

ADDRESS: James Boswell Esqr., Great Portland St., London. Single.

POSTMARKS: IRELAND, ⟨MR⟩ 12, MR 16 91.

Dublin, March 12th. 1791

DEAR SIR, I am happy to find by our Friend Mr. Malone, whom I saw yesterday, that your Life of Dr. Johnson may soon be expected: He tells me however, that he thinks 3 or 4 weeks may pass, before you will be able to come forth. This induces me to request a particular Favour, which, if granted, will exceedingly oblige me.—It is to beg to be indulged with a sight of that sheet of your book, wherein you mention a common Friend of Dr. Johnson's and mine,—Dr. Grainger[1] the Translator of Tibullus:—I have a particular Regard for the memory of poor Dr. Grainger, and as he, thro' his Wife was connected with some very respectable Families, but especially as he left an only Daughter a young Lady of great Beauty and Merit, just now in her bloom, to whom a very considerable Fortune was lately bequeathed by a maternal Uncle,[2] I cannot but feel a particular solicitude for their and her feelings lest they should be wounded and her happiness, nay even the Chances of her establishment in Life affected, by any unguarded Account of her deceased Father, in a book, which She will naturally have on her Shelf.

—Now Dr. Grainger was not only a man of Genius and Learning, but had many excellent Virtues, being one of the most

this wretched manner. But I beg you may not be vexed; for I shall try friends enough."

---

[1] James Grainger (?1721-66), physician and poet, who from 1759 lived on St. Kitts, West Indies. When he died, he bequeathed to Percy his MSS., which were published by Robert Anderson as *The Poetical Works of James Grainger, M. D., with Memoirs of his Life and Writings*, 1836. The ballad, "Bryan and Pareene", in vol. i of Percy's *Reliques* was contributed by Grainger. Mrs. Grainger was the former Miss Daniel

Mathew Burt, daughter of the Chief Justice and Treasurer of St. Kitts (V. L. Oliver, *History of the Island of Antigua*, 1894, i. 88).

[2] Grainger is said to have had two daughters, Louise and Eleanor, but there is no evidence that Louise was living in 1790. Eleanor certainly was, for she was married in 1798 to Thomas Rousell, Esq., of Wandsworth. She was Percy's goddaughter (*Lit. Illust.* vii. 230). Her maternal uncle, William Mathew Burt, was Governor of Leeward Islands and died 27 Jan. 1781 (*London Magazine*, 1781, l. 149).

generous friendly and benevolent Men I ever knew: yet as there was one Story, which Johnson used to tell; I mean the Recital of the passage in his *Sugar-Cane* (where he introduces the Vermin, Rats etc. which destroy the Canes) by Tom Warton;[3] that I take for granted you have inserted;[4] I could wish to prevail on you if not (what I could most wish) to *omit* that Story, yet to accompany it with a proper and just representation of what occasioned such a Peculiarity, in a Poem, which otherwise has great Merit, being the first Collection (I believe) of poetical Flowers, which have ever been gather'd across the Atlantic.[5]—The passage in question was originally not liable to such a Perversion; for the Author having in this Part of his Work occasion to mention the havock made by *Mice, Rats,* etc.—had introduced the subject with a k⟨ind⟩ of Mock-Heroic, and a Parody of Homer's battle of Frogs and Mice, invoking the Muse of the Old Grecian Bard, in manner that was not ungraceful: and in that State I had seen it: But afterwards unknown to me and his other Friends, he had been over-persuaded to alter the passage, (contrary to his own better Judgment) so as to produce the Unlucky effect above alluded to[6]—.

[3] *The Sugar-Cane: A Poem in Four Books,* with Notes, 1764, written by Grainger at St. Kitts, had been sent in manuscript to Percy and others for reading and correction. The "Story" is variously told by JB, Miss Reynolds, and Mrs. Piozzi (*Life* ii. 453–54, 532–34), but the point of all the accounts is that when the poem was read aloud from a manuscript (Percy's identification of the reader as Thomas Warton is new and probably correct), the company burst into laughter at the words, "Now, Muse, let's sing of *rats*!" Alone of the three, JB adds that one of those present who got a sight of the manuscript observed that "The word had been originally mice, and had been altered to rats, as more dignified."

[4] He had: see the note preceding this. As Waingrow (p. 394 n. 6) says, Malone had probably told Percy so, and may even have alerted him to the presence in that same leaf of two pleasantries of SJ directed at Percy himself: "Percy was angry at me for laughing at 'The Sugar Cane;' for he had a mind to make a great thing of Grainger's rats" (*Life* iv. 556); and instead of Percy's "writing the history of the wolf in Great-Britain . . . I should like to see '*The History of the Grey Rat, by Thomas Percy, D.D. Chaplain in Ordinary to His Majesty*' (laughing immoderately)" (*Life* ii. 455).

[5] Percy must have suffered a lapse of memory. Oscar Wegelin, *Early American Poetry,* 2nd ed., 1930, lists over two hundred poems or collections of poems written in America and published by 1764. It was no discredit to Percy to have been unaware of most of them, but he surely knew George Sandys's popular and influential *Ovides Metamorphosis* (1626), and he ought to have known that the latter fifteen books of it were written on the voyage out to America or in Virginia, where Sandys was treasurer of the Colony. By an odd oversight Wegelin overlooked Sandys too.

[6] A manuscript draft of the poem in the library of Trinity College, Dublin (see *Times Literary Supplement,* 13 Aug. 1938, p. 531; 16 Feb. 1951, p. 108) fully confirms Percy's description of the original

Now this is what I Want to have mentiond in a Note by way of extenuation, accompanied with a just Character of the Doctor who was both a very valuable Man and an ingenious Writer: For his Poem on Solitude, in Dodsley's *Misc[ellan]y*[7] contains some of the sublimest Images in Nature. He also wrote a very valuable medical Tract on the Treatment of Negroes and their peculiar Maladies.[8] If you will therefore allow me to see your Account of my Friend, I will submit to you such Illustrations or Annotations, as may perhaps induce you to cancell the Leaf (for which I will gladly pay out of my own pocket) and both add to the general Information ⟨and⟩ Evince your own Candour as well as exceedingly oblige, Dear Sir, Your very faithful Obedient Servant

THOS. DROMORE

N.B. Any thing bulky will come Post-free under Cover to *The Lord Bishop of Cork*[9] *at the Castle in Dublin.*

To Thomas Percy, between Wednesday 16 and Sunday 20 March 1791

Not reported. Sent from London. Referred to in next letter.

text. The passage in question occurs early in Book II:

Where shall the Muse the muster-roll begin?
Where breathless end? Say shall she sing of mice?
Critic forbear the supercilious smile.
Great Homer deignd to sing of little mice:
And do not faithful chroniclers relate
How Famine worst of Heavens relentless foes
Hath ghastly trod their desolating steps?
Nor by the planter are unfelt the woes
The puny whisker'd vermine-race produce.
With these associate shall the numerous claw
Of rats be joind; an unrelenting crew?
Whatever canes these fell marauders gnaw,
Fall prostrate, snapt off by the slightest breeze!

Corresponding to this passage the printed text has only two lines:

Nor with less waste the whisker'd vermin race
A countless clan despoil the lowland cane.

[7] "Solitude, An Ode", in *A Collection of Poems in Four Volumes*, By Several Hands, 1755, iv. 233–43.
[8] *An Essay on the more common West India Diseases; and the Remedies which that Country itself produces. To which are added, some Hints on the Management of Negroes*, 1764. This work was published anonymously.
[9] William Bennet.

From Thomas Percy,
Thursday 24 March 1791

MS. Yale (C 2238).

Dublin, March 24th. 1791

DEAR SIR, I esteem it quite providential, that by casually mentioning the subject to Mr. Malone I was induced to write you about my poor friend Dr. Grainger, and there by prevented you from suffering the Pain you would have felt at doing injustice to his Memory, and perhaps irreparable Injury to his amiable and innocent Daughter.—I am astonished at the severe Censure which you tell me Dr. J. passed upon that worthy Man: for such I will aver him to have been, from the fullest Conviction and long Acquaintance with him. I knew him much better than Dr. J. and do not recollect a single Instance of Misconduct, or any one Action of his Life (that ever came to *my* knowledge) that could abate my esteem of him.—As to the cruel Censure that he was destitute *of any principle*, or *Obligation of Duty*:[1] I know not how we are to judge of Men's principles, but by their operation on their Conduct: and I do declare, that as to the *relative Duties* Dr. Grainger was quite exemplary: His parents died when he was young, but he was one of the most grateful and affectionate Brothers, of the most indulgent husbands, of the most tender Fathers, and, most disinterested Friends I ever knew: as I could support, if needful, by remarkable Instances.—Nor did I ever once hear him throw out any sentiment, even *in sport*, that could justify such a severe Imputation, as that "he was quite destitute of principle I mean any Notion of Obligation to rectitude any principle of Duty." etc. etc.—I am persuaded, that Dr. J. would upon reflection have been very sorry to have had, what was perhaps a hasty escape, been made History and certainly to have recorded such a Censure

---

[1] "He was an agreeable man, and would have done one any service in his power; but was, I think, quite destitute of principle,—I mean quite without any notion of obligation to rectitude,—any principle of duty." SJ continued with a narrative character of Grainger intended to illustrate both his facility in matters of obligation and his haplessness. Since Percy makes no reference to this charac-ter, it is probable that neither Malone nor JB reported it to him. Though JB had considerably softened his record of SJ's remarks as they appeared in his journal (21 Mar. 1776), where the "young woman" Grainger had fallen in love with was a "wench", the character would still have annoyed Percy and would have been painful to Grainger's daughter. See *Life* iv. 556.

(being, as I believe in my *Conscience* it is, unfounded) would have been as injurious to the Memory of the Relater, as to the Sufferer, and have entailed Discredit on any Book that should have recorded it.—Excuse me therefore, my dear Friend, if out of regard to the memory of that revered Character, whose Virtues and Talents you wish [to] preserve from Oblivion: If out of regard to your own future Comfort; and from many other Considerations, which to you I need not urge;—I beg and intreat you before it be too late, to take a retrospect thro' your Book, and cancel any accidental Escapes of the same kind where Dr. J. has thrown out Severe Censures on the personal Characters of Individuals.—You know how liable he was to Prejudice, and what severe things he would sometimes say of his nearest Friends: Such effusions he never did nor could seriously mean, should be recorded and transmitted to Posterity, as giving their decided Characters.—Allow me also to request the favour of you to let me see the proof Leaf, of your amended Characters of my poor Friend Grainger: If I should propose an amended Sentence or Phrase, you are at last at Liberty to adopt or reject it: What I wrote last was a meer hasty application and I believe incorrect: I think I used the word *ungraceful*, instead of *elegant and well-turned* etc.:—I will repay whatever expence it occasions at press and will return it by first Post.[2]—It may come inclosed to me under a Cover To the Lord Bishop of Cork, at the Castle Dublin; and will forever oblige, Dear Sir, Your affectionate and faithful Servant

THOS. DROMORE

[2] Malone, writing to JB on 14 Apr. 1791, said that he had talked recently with Percy about Grainger and was glad that JB had "satisfied him, for he was very earnest about it" (C 1926). It does not appear, however, that Percy actually saw the amended text until the *Life* was published. JB left his account of the unlucky reading of *The Sugar-Cane* and SJ's verdict on the poem pretty much unchanged, but he allowed Percy to defend the poem in a foot-note compiled from Percy's letters of 12 and 24 Mar. 1791. He suppressed SJ's assertion that Grainger totally lacked principle, deleted the greater part of SJ's character of Grainger, and moved the part of it he did retain farther on in the page, presenting it as "the singular history of an ingenious acquaintance" who had settled as a physician in the Leeward Islands. Of SJ's two gibes at Percy, he completely suppressed the first, but let the second stand, tempering it by an added sentence: "Thus could he indulge a luxuriant sportive imagination when talking of a friend whom he loved and esteemed."

From Sir William Scott, Monday 4 or Tuesday 5 April 1791 [1]

MS. Yale (C 2440).

ADDRESS: Mr. Boswell.

[London]

DEAR BOSWELL: I shall be glad if you will take a family Dinner with us on Thursday 1/2 past 4 to meet Miss Bagnall. [2]

W. SCOTT

From Thomas Percy, Wednesday 6 April 1791

MS. Yale (C 2239).

Dublin, April 6. 1791

DEAR SIR, Since I troubled you with my last, Mr. Malone and I have talked over the Anecdote you had heard from Dr. Johnson concerning Mr. Rolt: [1] viz. That coming over to Ireland, he had here printed an Edition of Dr. Akenside's *Pleasures of the Imagination*, as his own Production. [2]—As I wish to prevent every Im-

---

[1] Determined from JB's journal entry and To Temple, 6 Apr. 1791 (see n. 2).

[2] Frances Bagnall (d. 1832), the younger daughter of John Bagnall of Earley Court, Berkshire, and sister to Scott's wife. JB wrote to Temple on 6 Apr., "I am to dine with Sir William Scott the King's Advocate at the Commons, tomorrow, and shall have a serious consultation with him, as he has always encouraged me. It is to be a family party where I am to meet Miss Bagnal (his Lady's sister) who may probably have six or seven hundred a year. She is about seven and twenty, and he tells me lively and gay *a Ranelagh girl*, but of excellent principles, in so much that she reads prayers to the servants in her Father's Family, every sunday evening." In his journal for 7 Apr., JB wrote, "Dined at Sir William Scott's to meet his sister in law Miss Bagnal of whom we had talked in a kind of jest as one to whom I should make love. She proved to be a fine girl enough; but did not please me much. Her father was there." Miss Bagnall later (1793) married the Hon. Thomas Windsor (see *The Victoria History of the County of Berkshire*, 1923, iii. 217).

---

[1] Richard Rolt (?1725–70), miscellaneous writer, who was related to Ambrose Philips. His second wife was related to the Percys of Worcester. After his death, Percy allowed her a pension.

[2] Mark Akenside (1721–70), *The Pleasures of Imagination*, 1744. Akenside gave the title *The Pleasures of the Imagination* to a heavily revised version which he left uncompleted at his death. Modern bibliographical research has failed to establish the existence of any edition of

putation of Misinformat[io]n from being fasten'd on the Memory of our departed Friend; I have been making it my business to inquire into the truth of this Fact and to day I saw one of the best informed Men of Literature in this Country;[3] One, who I verily believe has seen every Edition of any work of Taste, which has pass'd the Irish Press within this Century: and he had never seen or heard of any Impression of the aforementiond Poem, which had ever been printed by, or attributed to Rolt: Nor did he believe the Fact was true.—I cannot help concluding therefore that Dr. Johnson had been imposed on: And I submit to you, whether in that Case, this Anecdote should not be suppressed.

I understand, that it is at present under Consideration with the Members of the Club, whether Dr. Johnson's Monument shall be erected in St. Paul's, or in Westmr. Abbey. If my Suffrage is required, I desire it may be given for St. Paul's; as I beg you will mention, with my Compliments to Sir Joshua Reynolds, who, I am told, inclines to the same Opinion. Excuse this trouble in, Dear Sir, Your very faithful Obedient Servant

THOS. DROMORE

P.S. Rolt has a Widow living, who may possibly take up the Pen in Vindication of the Character of her deceas'd husband, or get some brother Author of his to do it, if his Memory should be branded with an Imputation false and groundless: Which had better be prevented.

Excuse my troubling you with the inclosed, which may be forwarded by the Penny Post, to Mr. Stirling[4] and by the general Post to Mr. Percy.[5]

the *Pleasures* with Rolt's name on the title-page. See To Malone, 25 Feb. 1791, and *Life* i. 547. In the first edition of the *Life* JB let his text stand with a foot-note saying that he had had inquiry as to this story made in Ireland but did not find it recollected there: he was giving it on the authority of SJ and *The Biographical Dictionary*. He expanded the note in the third edition (*Life* i. 359 n. 2).

[3] Probably Joseph Cooper Walker, who was in close touch with Percy at this time. See *Lit. Illust.* vii. 702–47. Walker indeed might be a better candidate than Percy for the authorship of the "excellent memoir" of Rolt in *The European*

Magazine (1803) xliv. 9–11 which J. B. Nichols attributes to Percy (*ibid.* p. 62 n.). The memoir is dated "Dublin, June 18, 1803". But "in the summer of 1803", Percy "was lying in a darkened room, deprived of the sight of one eye and threatened with the loss of the other" (Gaussen, p. 302).

[4] Possibly the Rev. Joseph Stirling, or Sterling, author of *Poems*, 1782, who corresponded with Percy and occasionally forwarded books and pamphlets to him (*Lit. Illust.* viii. 284–85, 302–03). See also Gaussen, pp. 223–26, 273.

[5] The London penny post handled mail only within the confines of London,

From Joseph Warton,
Saturday 9 April 1791

MS. Fettercairn Papers, National Library of Scotland.

ADDRESS: James Boswell Esqr.

Wint[on] Ap. 9 1791

MY DEAR SIR: As I know you love to be accurate, I trouble you with a line to say I have found the passage of *Dryden* which I mentioned to you. It is in his Dedication to Juvenal—the words are these—

"*Donne*—affects the *metaphysics*, not only in his Satires, but in his amorous Verses; where Nature only should reign; and perplexes the minds of the fair sex with nice Speculations of philosophy—In this—Mr *Cowley* has copied Him to a fault"[1]—Here is a plain proof that *Dryden first* spoke of the *metaphysical* poetry, as I said in my *Essay*—

When do we see your *Opus* magnum? Your *monument* will be as long in making its appearance as the marble one? Is the *Latter* to be in St. Pauls or in Westminster abbey? Is Malone returned?[2] Favor me with an answer to these Questions, and believe me, Dear Sir, sincerely and faithfully yours

J. WARTON

To Joseph Warton,
April–May 1791

Not reported. Sent from London. Referred to in the next letter.

where there were from four to eight deliveries daily. The general post carried the mail to the rest of the country. "Mr. Percy" was probably the Bishop's nephew, Thomas Percy (1768–1808), who in 1791 was a student at St. John's College, Oxford.—This was probably the last letter that Percy ever wrote to JB. When the *Life* appeared, he was deeply offended, and not only by matter of offense still remaining in the Grainger cancel. See *post* To Barnard, 16 Aug. 1792 and n. 12 on that letter.

[1] The passage is from Dryden's "Discourse concerning the Original and Progress of Satire: Addressed to the Right Honourable Charles, Earl of Dorset and Middlesex", the dashes indicating omissions (*Essays of John Dryden*, ed. W. H. Ker, 1926, ii. 19); Warton had cited it in his *Essay on the Genius and Writings of Pope*, § 12, n. 64. When he mentioned it to JB is not recorded. Cf. *Life* iv. 38.

[2] Malone was still in Ireland with his brother. He wrote to Percy on 26 Apr., "I mean to sail for England early next week" (*Percy-Malone Corresp.* p. 54).

From Joseph Warton, Sunday 8 May 1791

MS. Yale (C 3065).

ADDRESS: James Boswell Esqr.

ENDORSEMENT: Rev. Dr. Warton.

Winton, May 8 1791

MY DEAR SIR: You make me very happy by saying I shall so soon receive your great Work, for which I am greatly obliged to you, and return you my warmest thanks. I will beg you to direct them— To me—at the College Winchester, by *Collyer's Coach*, which goes from the White Horse, Piccadilly.[1] I am, Dear Sir, very faithfully your obliged friend and servant

Jos. WARTON

My best Compliments to Mr. Courtenay.

From Richard Warren, Wednesday 11 May 1791

MS. Yale (C 3060). Draft of JB's reply on same sheet.

ADDRESS: Mr. Boswell.

ENDORSEMENT: Dr. Warren *Before* Publication.

Sackville Street, May 11. 1791

DEAR SIR: Lady Duncannon[1] sets out for Bath at ten o'clock on Saturday morning, and the advertisement says that your Book will be published on Monday[2]—Lady Duncannon will be four days in

---

[1] "Collyer's coach sets off from the White Hart Inn, in this city every morning at seven o'clock, and arrives at the Bell-Savage, Ludgate-Hill, about seven in the evening. Leaves London about four in the morning, and arrives here about three in the afternoon" (*Universal British Directory*, 1798, iv. 918 s.v. Winchester).

---

[1] Henrietta-Frances Spencer (d. 14 Nov. 1821), second daughter of John, first Earl Spencer, who married, on 27

Nov. 1780, Frederick Ponsonby (1758–1844), Viscount Duncannon. He succeeded his father as third Earl of Bessborough on 11 Mar. 1793 (Burke, *Peerage*, s.v. Bessborough). At this time, Lady Duncannon was extremely ill and under the care of Warren, who was the family doctor not only of the Duncannons, but also of the Spencers (The Earl of Bessborough, *Lady Bessborough and her Family Circle*, 1940, p. 60).

[2] "On 30 April (p. 413) the *London Chronicle* announced 16 May as the day

335

going to Bath and is impatient to see your book—will it not be in the power of your bookseller, at your request to let her have a copy on friday night—I shall be very much obliged to you for indulging her in this favour, and verily believe by granting it that you will greatly lessen the fatigues of her journey and contribute to her cure—I am, my dear Sir, Yours most sincerely

R. WARREN

To Richard Warren,
Wednesday 11 May 1791

MS. Yale (L 1269). A draft on same sheet as preceding letter.

Great Portland Street, Wednesday 11 May
DEAR SIR: I am flattered beyond measure by Lady Duncannon's impatience to see my Book, but at the same time am really frightened. My bookseller Mr. Dilly will have copies of it in readiness by friday morning; and I understand it will that day be in the hands of several other booksellers. I am with most sincere respect, Dear Sir, your obliged and faithful humble servant

From Joseph Warton,
Sunday 15 May 1791

MS. Yale (C 3066).

ADDRESS: James Boswelle Esqr.

ENDORSEMENT: Rev. Dr. Warton.

Wint[on] May 15 1791
MY DEAR SIR: I seize the very first post to acquaint you that I last night received safe your valuable Volumes, for which I return you my sincerest thanks: and from which, even from what I have already eagerly devoured, I promise to myself the highest Entertainment. I am, my Dear Sir, very faithfully and sincerely Yours

JOS. WARTON

of publication, repeating the advertisement of 31 Mar. . . . I find this same advertisement repeated on 7 May (p. 437), after which it disappears" (*Lit. Car.* p. 167).

From John Douglas,
Monday 16 May 1791

MS. Yale (C 1102).

ADDRESS: To James Boswell Esqr., Queen Ann Street, East,[1] London.

FRANK: Windsor, May sixteenth 1791. free. J. Carliol.

POSTMARKS: WINDSOR, FRE MA 17 91.

ENDORSEMENT: Lord Bishop of Carlisle (Dr. Douglas).

Windsor Castle, May 16th. 1791

DEAR SIR, I take the earliest Opportunity of expressing my thankful Acknowlegements, for the very unexpected honour conferred upon me, by so valuable a Present.[2]—I had ordered a Copy to be sent me; but your partiality having already supplied me with One, our Library will receive the other, when it arrives.— I hope soon to have an Opportunity of thanking you personally at the Deanry; and am, Dear Sir, Your much obliged and obedient humble Servant

J. CARLIOL

To John Douglas,
before Tuesday 14 June 1791

Not reported. Sent from London. From Douglas, 15 June, is obviously an answer to a letter written by JB.

From John Douglas,
Wednesday 15 June 1791

MS. Yale (C 1103).

ADDRESS: To James Boswell Esqr., Great Portland Street, London.

FRANK: Windsor, June fifteenth 1791. free. J. Carliol.

POSTMARKS: WINDSOR, FREE JU 16 91.

[1] JB had been living in Great Portland Street since leaving Queen Anne Street, *West,* on 19 Jan. The address is correct in the Bishop's other letters. Edmond Malone lived on Queen Anne Street, East, and Douglas may have confused the two addresses.

[2] The *Life,* published on the day Douglas wrote this letter.

Windsor Castle, June 15th 1791

DEAR SIR, It will be very convenient for me to receive you on Saturday next, and we shall be happy to see you. On that Day, however, I am to dine with the Officers of the Regt.[1] at their Mess; which Engagement I must not neglect; but if you arrive at the Deanry before Four o'Clock, my Wife and Daughter[2] will make you welcome to a family Dinner.—Your Son, I suppose, will learn from yourself the time of your arrival, and you will be so kind as to desire him to dine with us on Sunday.—I am, Dear Sir, Your most obedient humble Servant

J. CARLIOL

To John Douglas, Friday 17 June 1791

MS. BM Add. MSS. Eg. 2182, f. 65. A copy in the hand of James Boswell the younger at Yale (L 440) does not differ significantly from the original.

Great Portland Street, 17 June 1791

MY DEAR LORD: Sir Richard Symons[1] having asked me to a very pleasant dinner party tomorrow, I shall not have the honour of making my bows in Windsor Castle till Sunday morning. My son shall obey your Lordship's summons, and learn from his Father to respect *John Carliol*, as Sir Joseph Banks[2] calls your Lordship, of

[1] The Twenty-ninth (or the Worcestershire) Regiment of Foot, of which Charles Stanhope, Earl of Harrington, was colonel (To Harrington, 22 June 1791; To Harriet Milles, 4 July 1791).

[2] Probably Elizabeth, who died unmarried.

[1] Symons (c. 1744–96), born Richard Peers, took the name of Symons when he inherited the estate of his maternal grandfather, Richard Symons of the Meend, Herefordshire. He was M.P. for Hereford City from 1768 to 1784 and was created baronet in 1774 (*Comp. Bar.* v. 173).

[2] Banks (1743–1820), botanist and President of the Royal Society, was elected to The Club on 11 Dec. 1778, shortly after he was chosen to head the Royal Society (*Life* iii. 365). "John Carliol" was Douglas's correct *signature* but was not a proper style for address or reference. Douglas was sixty-six when he was made a bishop. Banks's usage must have been deliberately humorous and was also no doubt jubilant, as much as to say, "He's made it at last." Douglas was in fact about to be translated to Salisbury and to change his signature to John Sarum.

whom I ever am, with all sincerity, the much obliged and faithful humble servant

JAMES BOSWELL

From *William Windham,*
Sunday 19 June 1791 [1]

MS. Yale (C 3133).

ADDRESS: James Boswell Esqr., Portland street.

[London] Sunday morn. 19th.

DEAR BOSWELL: The absence of a week [2] makes me so keen for the pleasures of London Society, that I cannot prevail upon myself to lose a moment; and wish to assemble, therefore, some gallants to meet here tomorrow.

My Brothers wife [3] is with me, on her way through Town, and with two young Ladies, [4] not very handsome but far from disagreable, will make the basis of a party [5] (the *fond* the Anglo-Gallicans would say) on which I want to engraft some choice fruits,—Yourself, Courtnay, and Malone.—Yours very truly

W. WINDHAM

To Lord Eliot,
Friday 1 July 1791

MS. Yale (L 502). A copy.

HEADING: Copy. To The Right Honourable Lord Eliot.

[1] Determined by references in Windham's *Diary*. See n. 2.

[2] Windham had been on a trip to Bath from 10 to 17 June 1791 (Windham's *Diary*, pp. 229–30).

[3] Catherine Doughty, the wife of George William Lukin (1740–1812), afterwards Dean of Wells, Windham's half-brother. Windham was extremely fond of her: "Where shall I ever find one so amiable, so worthy, of understanding so acute, of integrity so confirmed, of disposition so pure, and attached to me from feelings of such genuine affection?"

(Windham's *Diary*, p. 143). Mrs. Lukin had been at Bath and apparently returned to London on the 18th (*ibid.* pp. 229–30). (See *Alum. Oxon.* II. iii. 881, and *Alum. Cant.* II. iv. 233.)

[4] Probably Mary (d. 1800) and Kitty, the daughters of Mr. and Mrs. Lukin. Mary had certainly been staying with Windham in Bath and London since 12 May (Windham's *Diary*, p. 230).

[5] There are no entries in Windham's *Diary* between 18 and 24 June. JB was presumably at Windsor with Bishop Douglas on the 19th.

TO ELIOT, 1 JULY 1791

[London] Friday 1 July 1791

MY DEAR LORD: The gay little *Parisienne*[1] wishes to know whether tomorrow evening or Sunday evening will be most convenient for your Lordship manger un morceau de poulet avec une bonne salade chez elle. Il faut qu'elle en soit avertie un jour d'avance. As I have the honour to be her negociator, and have an interest besides as the only other person who is to be present at a very agreable petit souper I request that your Lordship may favour me with your answer directed to me No. 47 Great Portland Street. I look forward with pleasure to our meeting tomorrow at Sir Joshua's;[2] and ever am Your Lordships faithful humble servant

LE BARON BOSWELL

From Lord Eliot,
Friday 1 July 1791[1]

MS. Yale (C 1191).

ADDRESS: To James Boswell Esqre.

Spring garden,[2] Friday Night

MY DEAR BARON: Unfortunately I am Engaged both tomorrow and Sunday Evening.

Nothing can be more certain, than that the Party you propose would have been highly entertaining and pleasing to Myself, Yet the Entertainment and Pleasure must have been confined to Self; being fully Sensible that I could have contributed none to so agreeable and lively a Company, *a la Fleur de leur Age.* I have the honor to be—the Baron's very obedient and faithful humble Servant

C. E.

We will have a chat at Sir Joshua's.

[1] Her name was Divry, "a little french Mademoiselle whom I knew some time in London" (Journ. 3 Sept. 1792). JB had arranged for her to write to him while he was visiting Bishop Douglas in June (Yale MS. L 432). By the time he wrote the identification above he had come to regard her as "a mercenary and base creature".

[2] There is no record of this occasion; JB seems to have kept no journal for the period 11 Apr. 1791 to 16 Aug. 1792, nor is there a Reynolds engagement book for 1791.

[1] Dated from the preceding.

[2] No. 16 (*Royal Kalendar* for 1791, page following 21). Spring Gardens, a small and fashionable street just south of Charing Cross, had formerly been part of a garden attached to the King's palace at Whitehall.

340

From Richard Warren, Sunday 3 July 1791

MS. Yale (C 3061).

ADDRESS: The Lord Bishop of Killaloe or Mr. Boswell, 78 St. James's Street.[1]

[London] Sunday July 3. 1791

DEAR SIR: I shall be extremely happy in the Company of the Bishop of Killaloe and yourself at dinner to day—a little before six—Yours most sincerely

R. WARREN

From Thomas Barnard, Thursday 14 July 1791 or shortly after

MS. Yale (C 94). The appearance of the letter suggests that it was wrapped around the brick that accompanied it.

ADDRESS: James Boswell Esqr., 47 Portland Street, Portland Road, London.

[?Birmingham]

SIR: The Eminent Character you Bear for your attachment to our glorious Constitution, and Zeal for its Defence in These troublesome Times, will plead my apology for sending you the Present which accompanies this Letter.

It is a Real and genuine Brick,[1] one Belonging to the Meeting House of the great Doctor Priestly at Birmingham, and torn off by these Hands from its Smoking Remains[2] while scarcely Tangible,

---

[1] Presumably Barnard's lodgings.

---

[1] The brick is missing.

[2] The Constitutional Society of Birmingham held a dinner on 14 July 1791 to commemorate the fall of the Bastille. Joseph Priestley (1733–1804), scientist and dissenting clergyman, was invited but did not attend. Angry crowds, however, assumed that he was the leader of the group and broke into the hotel where the meeting had been held. Not finding members of the Society there (they had left early), they proceeded to the New Meeting, where Priestley usually preached, and burned it down. After burning down another meeting-house, they attacked Priestley's home, a mile away from Birmingham. He and his family escaped without injury, but the house, his books, papers, and apparatus were all destroyed. For a detailed description of the riot, see *The Universal British Directory*, 1791, ii. 204–06; *Dublin Chronicle*, 23 July 1791, v. 286–288.

and totally Untenable for a Moment. I thought it however a Prize well worth the Hazard of Burning my Fingers to acquire it.

It is not Indeed a Stone like the Chevaliere D'Eon's Present from the Bastile;[3] But it is a much more Proper Material for the House of Schism; being of the Same Species with that which composed the Famous Tower in the East, at which the First *Separation* among Mankind originated, The most antient Monument of *Confusion* that ever Existed. I hope Therefore that you will esteem it as a Relique Equally Valuable, and not Less Curious Than the other, From, Sir, Your most humble and obedient Servant

Α.ΔΗΛΟΣ[4]

From Charles Burney, Saturday 16 July 1791

MS. Yale (C 705).

ADDRESS: To James Boswell Esqr., Great Portland Street.

ENDORSEMENT: Dr. Burney.

Chelsea College,[1] July 16th. 1791

DEAR SIR: So much time has elapsed between the publication of our friend's life and my being possessed of leisure sufficient to finish the perusal of it, that I shall seem to have waited till I could join the general Chorus of your praise. The approbation of an individual can now afford you but small gratification:[1a] the effects of praise and abuse are always proportioned to our wants and expectations.

[3] Charles-Geneviève-Louis-Auguste-André-Timothée D'Eon de Beaumont (1728–1810) had come to England in 1762 as an agent for the French and was later *chargé d'affaires* at London. In exchange for secret documents he had in his possession, he eventually received a pension of 12,000 livres from the French government but was required to dress and behave as a woman for the rest of his life. On 14 July 1790 "she" sent to Lord Stanhope, who was presiding at a meeting in London in honour of France's newly acquired freedom, a stone taken from the arch of one of the chief gates of the Bastille (Pierre Pinsseau, *L'Étrange Destinée du Chevalier d'Eon*, 2nd ed., 1945, p. 246).

[4] "Unknown." The letter, however, is in Barnard's undisguised hand. See *post* From Barnard, 25 Feb. 1792, and To Barnard, 16 Aug. 1792.

[1] In 1783, Burke obtained for Burney the post of organist at Chelsea Hospital, commonly called Chelsea College (Roger Lonsdale, *Dr. Charles Burney*, 1965, pp. 295–96). Burney moved into the Chelsea apartment during the summer of 1787 (*ibid.* p. 335).

[1a] MS. "gratificatification"

Johnson had enemies, who of course will try to depreciate your work. The number of these will perhaps be somewhat augmented by your success, as well as by the severity of his private opinions; but to all else, the book is so uncommonly alluring, that I have hitherto met with no unprejudiced readers who have not been sorry when they were arrived at the last page.

Some indeed have thought that too many of the weaknesses, prejudices, and infirmities, of this truly great and virtuous Man have been recorded; but, besides the reputation which you will acquire for the fidelity of your narrative in telling all you knew, it will elevate the Character of our Hero: for what other Man could have had his private life so deeply and minutely probed, without discovering vices, or at least foibles, more hurtful to Society than those which you have disclosed? The most gratifying information which I can give you concerning the effect of your narrative, is, that it has impressed your most hostile readers with a much more favourable opinion of the goodness of our friends heart than they had before conceived, though some of them were never insensible to his merit as a writer.

I believe it may be said with truth, that it is impossible to open either of your two Volumes without finding some sentiment of our venerable Sage worth remembering. His wit and his wisdom are equally original and impressive; and I have no doubt but that both will become proverbial to Englishmen, and long continue to direct their taste as well as morals.[2] For my own part, I think myself infinitely obliged to you for embalming so many of his genuine sentiments which are not to be found in his works. Indeed if all his writings which had been previously printed were lost, or had never appeared, your book would have conveyed to posterity as advantageous an Idea of his character, genius, and worth, as Xenophon has done of those of Socrates.[3] I have often found your own reflexions not only ingenious and lively, but strong; and the latter

[2] A paragraph mark is inserted at this point, and a line is drawn in the margin opposite the sentences beginning "For" and "Indeed". JB was undoubtedly making a collection of complimentary comments on the *Life*. Cf. To Wilkes, 25 June 1791.

[3] Burney was not the only reader of the *Life* to be reminded of Xenophon. Ralph Griffiths, reviewing the work six months later, remarked, "Xenophon's *Memorabilia* of Socrates may, possibly, have first suggested to Mr B. the idea of preserving and giving to us the *Memorabilia* of Johnson" (*Monthly Review*, 1792, n.s. vii. 2; see B. C. Nangle, *The Monthly Review, Second Series*, 1955, p. 92). JB himself had mentioned Xenophon at the end of his *Journal of a Tour to the Hebrides* (*Life* v. 414).

part of your narrative, though I already knew its chief circumstances, has in it so much pathos, that it renovated all my sorrows, and frequently made me weep like a tender-hearted female at a Tragedy.

I am now more and more inclined to recommend to your diligence, zeal, and biographical abilities, the collecting and writing *Memoirs of the deceased members of* our *Club*, in your more lively manner than that of Crescimbeni's *"Notizie istoriche degli Arcadi morti."* [4] *Vous aurez beau jeu* in speaking of such men as Garrick, Goldsmith, Lord Ashburton, Bishop Shipley, Beauclerk, Dyer, Chamier, T. Warton, etc. [5] Indeed you may make even Hawkins[6] entertaining, for the first time. If your own manner of pourtraying Johnson had not been so much approved, you might have borrowed the Pencil of Fontenelle[7] or D'Alembert; but the *Eloges* of the former, though admirably written, are rather too much confined

[4] Giovanni Mario Crescimbeni (1663–1728), an Italian *abate* and poet, was first Custode Generale of an academy of poets, called Arcadia, formed to correct the abuses of poetic taste. The poets, in accordance with their pastoral ideals, gave each other Greek names. The academy gained great prestige both in Italy and in the rest of Europe. The *Notizie*, edited by Crescimbeni, was published in three volumes in 1720–21 (*Biographie universelle ancienne et moderne*). Burney probably did not know that JB was an Arcadian. See F. A. Pottle, "Boswell as Icarus" in *Restoration and Eighteenth-Century Literature*, ed. Carroll Camden, 1963, pp. 389–406.

[5] John Dunning, first Baron Ashburton (1731–83), Solicitor-General, M.P., pro-American, mover of the famous resolution that "the influence of the Crown has increased, is increasing, and ought to be diminished", generally conceded to stand in ability at the head of the English bar, seems to have been elected to The Club by May 1777.—Jonathan Shipley (1714–88), Bishop of St. Asaph, friend of Benjamin Franklin and outspoken opponent of the Ministerial policy towards the American colonies, was elected on 21 Nov. 1780 (*Letters of Sir William Jones*, ed. Garland Cannon, 1970, i. 451).—Samuel Dyer (1725–72), classical

scholar and translator, original member of the Ivy Lane Club, intimate friend of Burke, was the first member elected to The Club (1764) by the nine founding members.—Anthony Chamier (1725–1780), deputy Secretary at War, Under Secretary of State for the Southern Department, M.P., proposed by SJ for the chair of commercial politics in the imaginary college at St. Andrews in which each member of The Club was to teach his specialty (*Life* v. 109), was an original member.

[6] Burney and Hawkins were not on particularly friendly terms. Hawkins's five-volume *General History of the Science and Practice of Music* followed the first volume of Burney's *History* by only four months in 1776, and Burney was not pleased with the competition (Lonsdale, pp. 189–225). For discussions of Burney's antipathy to Hawkins with detailed description and copious quotation, see P. A. Scholes, *The Great Dr. Burney*, 1948, i. 297; and his *Life and Activities of Sir John Hawkins*, 1953, pp. 140–48. See also B. H. Davis, *A Proof of Eminence*, 1973, pp. 145–47, 149–51.

[7] Bernard Le Bovier de Fontenelle (1657–1757), *Éloges des académiciens de l'Académie Royale des Sciences, etc.*, 2 vols., 1731. He was known as "the Nestor of Literature".

to mere panegyric; while *l'Histoire des Membres de l'Academie Françoise*, of the latter, though more miscellaneous and enlivened with anecdotes, has less strength, Originality, and elegance.

It was Johnson's wish that our Club should be composed of the heads of every liberal and literary profession, that we might not talk nonsense on any subject that might be started, but have somebody to refer to in our doubts and discussions, by whose Science we might be enlightened. The Stalls of Divinity, Classics, Civil Law, History, Medicine, Politics, Botany, Chemistry, Criticism, and Painting, were already well filled.[8] *Biography* now claims you as her chairman. Take into consideration how best to fulfill her views in executing the office assigned to you, and believe me to be with true regard, dear Sir, Your faithful and affectionate Servant

CHAS. BURNEY

To Sir William Scott,
before Monday 1 August 1791

Not reported. Sent from London before JB left (presumably 1 Aug.) for the assizes at Chelmsford (To Temple, 22 Aug. 1791; *Gent. Mag.* July 1791, lxi. 677). In it JB seems to have announced his intention of attending a dinner given by Scott, though Scott had not replied to his request to be invited.

From Sir William Scott,
Tuesday 2 August 1791

MS. Yale (C 2441). A draft of JB's answer on p. 3.

ADDRESS: James Boswell Esq., on the Home Circuit.

FRANK: London, August second 1791, Wm. Scott.

POSTMARKS: FREE AU 2 91, AU 2 91.

[London]

DEAR BOSWELL: You *will* force a Passage and I have only to say that *I* am always glad to see You, let me have what Company I

---

[8] Burney's division of The Club into stalls is similar, though from a later per- spective, to SJ's and JB's imaginary college. See n. 5.

may. But excuse me if I state the true Reason that makes [me] sometimes ask other Friends of our Connexion, when I do not take the Liberty of asking You. I have *other* Acquaintance, Men whom I very much value on many Accounts, but Men who are perhaps more shy and delicate than I am, and who, in my Hearing, have often expressed a proper Respect for your Talents but mixed with a good deal of Censure upon the Practice of publishing without Consent what has been thrown out in the freedom of private Conversation.[1] I don't discuss the rectitude of their Opinion upon that Matter, but I know they are sincere in it; and I really have felt a repugnance to asking Gentlemen to meet, whose Company might excite Sentiments of Uneasiness or Apprehension for a Moment to each Other. For believe me, it is not the Gaiety of the present Hour nor the most joyous Display of convivial Talents for the Moment, that are an equivalent with Many Men for the Pain of being brought out, against their Consent or without their Knowledge, into the Glare of public Light, when they supposed themselves to be merely discussing in a private Society. You will understand me, I am not censuring *You*, but am defending *myself*, for doing what you might otherwise deem to be an Act of Unkindness. *I* shall be glad to see You, I repeat it, as *I* always am; but no *Letter Press* upon the Occasion! I wish I could remove from my Friends the Apprehension of a Consequence which renders your Company less acceptable than, I am sure, it would be on *every other* Account. Yours faithfully

W. SCOTT

I dine on Saturday at 5 *precise*.

---

[1] This was not the first time that JB had encountered such censure; the *Tour*, published as far back as 1785, had exemplified to the full his practice of recording and publishing private conversation, often without notice to the persons concerned. Malone wrote to him on 14 Sept. 1787 that his habit of recording was the cause of Burke's coolness, and advised him to give up the practice after he had completed the *Life*. On 7 Mar. 1788 he confessed to a feeling that his collecting so much of SJ's conversation had made people shun him "as a dangerous companion" (Journ.). That the publication of his two Johnsonian books caused him to lose some invitations must be true, but the present letter is the only specific memorial of exclusion among the Boswell papers at Yale.

From Sir William Scott,
c. Thursday 4 August 1791[1]

MS. Yale (C 2442).

ADDRESS: James Boswell Esq., Queen Ann Street East, Cavendish Square.

POSTMARKS: PENNY POST PAID G TH, W 10 O'CLOCK.

[London]

DEAR BOSWELL: I do not know whether You have received from me a Letter upon the Circuit. If you have not, I send this Note to say that I shall be very glad to see you at Dinner on Saturday 5 o clock. My Letter contained my Reasons for not asking You before. Yours

W. S.

To Sir William Scott,
Friday 5 August 1791

MS. Yale (L 1140). A draft, written on p. 3 of From Scott, 2 Aug.

Great Portland Street, Friday 5[1] August 1791

DEAR SIR: After receiving your letter communicating a circumstance of which I had not the least apprehension, I certainly could not *force a passage*. I should be curious to know *who* they are that are conceited and absurd enough to imagine that I could take the trouble to publish *their* conversation,[2] because I have recorded the

---

[1] Date established by the preceding letter and the first (triangular) postmark. The "W" of the second (round) postmark appears to stand for "Westminster", the sorting office.

---

[1] MS. "6"

[2] Those who attended the dinner were Malone, Windham, Thomas Erskine, Sir William Wynne, Sir Joshua Reynolds, and a Mr. De Vyme, son of a French refugee, who had lived for many years in Portugal and had witnessed the earth-quake at Lisbon (Sir James Prior, *Life of Edmond Malone*, 1860, p. 409). The only possible objectors to JB in this group would have been Erskine and Wynne, and Erskine seems ruled out by Scott's reference to the objector's shyness, delicacy, timidity, and natural reserve (From Scott, 2 Aug. and c. 5 Aug. 1791). Sir William Wynne, knighted the same year as Scott, was official principal of the Court of Arches and master of the Prerogative Court of Canterbury (W. A. Shaw, *The Knights of England*, 1906, ii. 300).

wisdom and wit of Johnson. But I own I wonder my dear Friend at *your* saying *No Letterpress upon the occasion.* It is too ridiculous. Yours ever very faithfully

From Sir William Scott, c. Friday 5 August 1791

MS. Yale (C 2443). The draft of JB's answer is on pp. 2–4.

ADDRESS: James Boswell Esq., Queen Ann Street East.

[London]

DEAR BOSWELL: Be so good as to remember that you have published not only the Wit and Wisdom of Johnson, but a little of the Folly of other People mixt with it; amongst the rest, some of your humble Servant's,[1] though I make no grumbling about it. Dont impute to Absurdity and Conceit what is owing to timidity and natural Reserve; You must know that there are Persons who do not choose to face the Light. When I talked of *no Letter Press*, I certainly did it more jocularly than otherwise; and when I talked of *forcing a Passage*, you must suppose that I did it with reference to your own Letter which held out the same Idea; you cannot think me brutal enough to use such an Expression seriously, without supposing that I meant a quarrel, which I should certainly consider as a real Misfortune.

If you dont persist in thinking me *too ridiculous*, pray come. I shall be extremely sorry if you do not, as I go out of Town in a very few Days for the Summer. Yours faithfully

WM. SCOTT

[1] Scott may very well be referring to an anecdote he told about Blackstone's use of wine while at work on his *Commentaries* (*Life* iv. 91). Although he does not grumble here, he later caused JB to amend the anecdote in order to eliminate the impression that Blackstone was a drunkard. In a letter to Malone, written early in 1799 (Yale, C 2449), Scott reported that he "remonstrated sharply" with JB about the anecdote. If this anecdote is the "Folly" mentioned here, the discrepancy in Scott's attitude towards it is not a problem, since it could easily have changed after he had learned of the Blackstone family's reaction. He later apologized to them (*Life* iv. 91 n. 2).

To Sir William Scott, Tuesday 9 August 1791

MS. Hyde Collection, lower right corner of first leaf missing. JB's draft (MS. Yale, L 1141), written on pp. 2–4 of the preceding letter, shows only slight substantive differences, all of which are reported below. The draft supplies with certainty all but one of the words missing from the letter sent.

Maidstone, 9 August 1791

MY DEAR SCOTT, The little *mal entendu* which has happened between us I do not regret, as it has given me the comfort of being satisfied that you value me more than I could fully allow myself to believe: For, *ed anche Io son Pittore*,[1] I—roaring boy[2] as I am—have my *nerves* and my *diffidence* as well as you. My resolving not to come to you was owing to a very little *pique*, and a considerable degree[3] of *propriety*; for I did think that it would not be right for me to throw the least damp upon your company however conscious I was that it must be owing to misapprehension. I therefore resisted your second[4] kind note, and went to Mr. Cator's at Beckenham Place,[5] on Saturday morning, in order to pass two days in the delightful County of Kent, between the Assizes at Chelmsford and at Maidstone.[6] He carried me that day to dine with his neighbour Mr. Jenner[7] the Proctor a good man and true; and there I gave Sir William Scott as my toast and drank a bumper to his health; and by mentioning that I was asked to dine with him had that share of the feast, which to me is something, the

---

[1] *Anch'io son pittore* ("I too am a painter"), supposedly said by the painter Correggio after a close scrutiny of a painting by Raphael.

[2] "*Roarers*, or *roaring boys*, was a cant name for a set of quarrelsome bullying blades, who, when this play [*Philaster*, 1611, V. iv] was written and long after, infested the streets of London: the allusions to them in our early drama are innumerable" (Alexander Dyce, ed., *Works of Beaumont and Fletcher*, 1843, i. 300).

[3] Draft, "My resolution . . . considerable deal"

[4] Draft, "your kind note,"

[5] John Cator (1730–1806), timber merchant and friend of Mr. Thrale. His seat at Beckenham JB considered "one of the finest places at which I ever was a guest" (*Life* iv. 313).

[6] The assizes began at Maidstone on Monday 8 Aug. (*Gent. Mag.* lxi. 677).

[7] Robert Jenner (1743–1810) of Doctors' Commons, proctor, lived at Chislehurst, Kent, about three miles from Beckenham (DNB s.v. Sir Herbert Jenner-Fust).

vanity of being one of his convivial friends. You see then there was no malice or ill will lurking in my breast.

Yesterday I received here your obliging letter, the *principle* of which I readily admit and thank you ⟨hearti⟩ly[8] for setting me quite at ease. But as to the *application*, be so good as to recollect that I have not published any of *your* folly, for a very obvious reason; and what I have published of your share in the Johnsonian Conversations was revised by yourself, upon which occasion I enjoyed one of the pleasantest days I ever passed in my life.[9] *You* therefore, my good Sir William, have no reason even to *grumble*. If others, as well as myself, sometimes appear as shades to the GREAT INTELLECTUAL LIGHT, I beg to be fairly understood, and that you and my other friends will inculcate upon persons of timidity and reserve, that my recording the conversations of so extraordinary a man as Johnson with its concomitant circumstances, was a *peculiar* undertaking, attended with much anxiety and labour, and that the conversations of people in general are by no means of that nature as to bear being registered and that the task of doing it would be exceedingly irksome to me. Ask me then My Dear Sir with none but who are clear of a prejudice which you see may easily be cured. I trust there are enough who have it not.

I can return you the compliment that I should certainly consider a quarrel with you as a real misfortune. I now do not apprehend that there can be even any coldness, but on the contrary that our friendship is strengthened; and I assure you that I am with great respect and affection, My Dear Scott, Your obliged and faithful humble servant

JAMES BOSWELL

Pray let me know *on the Home Circuit* that you have received this letter.

---

[8] Supplied by conjecture. The draft has no adverb: "and thank you for setting"

[9] "I dined with Sir William Scott, by appointment to *sit* upon my Record of the conversation between Johnson and him [10 Apr. 1778]. . . . We revised my Johnsonian leaves, and I staid supper and sat till the venerable St. Paul's had struck one" (Journ. 10 June 1790). See Waingrow, p. 438 n. 3.

From Thomas Barnard,
Tuesday 9 August 1791

MS. Yale (C 95).

ADDRESS (in the hand of R. Hobart[1]): James Boswell Esqr., 47 Great Portland Street, London.

FRANK: Dublin, August ninth 1791. R. Hobart.

POSTMARKS: AU 9, FREE AU 15 91 A.

ENDORSEMENT: Bishop of Killaloe.

St. Wolstans, August 9th 1791

MY DEAR SIR: I promised you that you should hear from me soon after my Arrival in Ireland, and having now got a Frank, and an hours Leisure, I sit down with Pleasure to discharge my Conscience, and my Engagement. But what Interesting Intelligence Can this Land of Bulls and Potatoes furnish for the Entertainment, of such a Mind as yours? Politicks are become a Bore, and Scandal is only amusing to those who Know the Parties, Literature is gone to Sleep till next Winter, and Even the *Life of Johnson* is not yet republish'd here, in Octavo:[2] Eating, and Drinking seems to be the only Occupation of the Kingdom (Since the 14th of July is Past;) and all Parties Concur in promoting it, with an unanimity that must be highly pleasing to every Virtuous Citizen, or Loyal Subject. You Know, my worthy Freind, you were always of Opinion that nothing produced Harmony and mutual affection among Mankind so much as *Hot meat* often taken in each others Company, and I am Convinced you are perfectly right in your Observation.[3] We had a Tolerably pleasant Journey to Ireland, and a Short Passage, and have now been comfortably Settled for above a Fortnight, But Tomorrow must decamp once more and Change our Quarters to the Banks of the Shannon, where I mean to stay about Two months, and make some excursions to the remote parts of my Diocese; But shall reserve Killarney, till next Summer. Mrs.

---

[1] Presumably Robert Hobart, later fourth Earl of Buckinghamshire, who was at this time Chief Secretary to the Lord Lieutenant of Ireland. Cf. *ante* From Percy, 19 Mar. 1790, n. 1.

[2] *The Life of Samuel Johnson, LL.D.*, 3 vols., Dublin, 1792. JB apparently had

no connexion with the Dublin edition and was probably not particularly pleased with it, since it must have harmed the sale of the second edition (*Lit. Car.* p. 167).

[3] JB's "Observation" appears to be otherwise unrecorded.

Barnard will stay behind me at St. Wolstans, as she is too much an Invalid to undertake a Long Journey.

I suppose my Freind Sir Joshua has told you already of the Honour intended me by the Royal Academy,[4] and that, (in Consequence of the Kings declaring, that he should entirely approve of my accepting it, and that it would be agreeable to him that I should,) I have acquiesced in his Majesty's opinion, as the most Decisive authority I could appeal to, and withdrawn the objection I made when it was first proposed to me. If he has not shewn you my Letter to him on that subject, I presume he will, if you ask him: I think I desired him to do it, and to remind you that you were now become a Part of my Charge.[5] I shall be very much

[4] Honorary appointment to the Academy was made on the nomination of the President, subject to the approval of the Council and General Assembly and the confirmation of the Sovereign (W. R. M. Lamb, *The Royal Academy*, 1951, pp. 167–68). Sir Joshua Reynolds, after consultation (perhaps informal) with the Council, had written to ask Barnard if he would accept election as Chaplain. Barnard had replied that he did not wish the machinery of election to be set in motion unless it could previously be ascertained "by private application" that his election would be genuinely agreeable to the King. Reynolds then asked Barnard to write him an ostensible letter to that effect. Barnard complied, and Benjamin West was commissioned to show the ostensible letter to the King and to get his opinion of the appointment (correspondence to this point not recovered; details inferred from the two letters cited below and *Farington Diary* iv. 82–83). Reynolds reported on 19 July (unpublished letter *penes* the Earl of Crawford and Balcarres) that "The King . . . *Very Much* approved of it, and added that it was a great honour to the Academy to have a person of your rank, a litterary character and so agreable a man, for their Chaplain." The letter went on to tell how when West also handed the King a minute of the action of the Council, 25 June 1791 (Minutes of the Council) electing JB Secretary for Foreign Correspondence and subscribing out of the Academy's "*Own*" fund 100 Guineas towards defraying the expences of Dr. Johnson's monument, He (His Majesty I should say) was *Graciously* pleased to draw his pen across, that it might not be supposed, he said, that he gave his approbation to that measure when he signed the Election of Boswell to the Secretaryship, both being on the same paper." Barnard replied on 29 July that he was accepting the office, "chiefly because it will tend to preserve that connexion with *you* which it has ever been my ambition to cultivate and cement, and which I hope will remain in full force as long as we both shall live" (C. R. Leslie and Tom Taylor, *Life and Times of Sir Joshua Reynolds*, 1865, ii. 623). Barnard was elected by the General Assembly on 10 Dec. (*ibid.* p. 622).

[5] On the motion of Benjamin West JB had been unanimously elected Secretary for Foreign Correspondence of the Academy at a meeting of the General Assembly on 2 July 1791. In his letter to Reynolds, Barnard wrote: "Tell my brother Boswell that I expect to receive *his* congratulations on becoming his fellow-servant; and as he will be now under my more immediate care and inspection, I shall give him good advice as often as I hear he has occasion for it, of which you will be so kind as to inform me from time to time whenever you think he wants it" (*ibid.* ii. 623).

obliged to you if you will send me that Little Tract upon the Sacrament of the Lords Supper, which I communicated to you in Confidence some years ago, as I have no Copy of it in my Possession, and I have some thoughts of making a Few additional observations Tending to a Farther Explanation. I have not yet been able to Find Paoli's Letter on Water Drinking, But I am sure I have it safe, and will search for it, when I have Time, Till I find it.

In the mean Time pray let me have the pleasure of hearing from you; I assure [you] I feel very Sincerely Interested in your happiness, and prosperity, and the Success of your Various Plans both for your own advantage and that of the Publick. Tell me also some news of your Party *Since* the Fourteenth of July; Is it now— *Triumphant Tories, and Desponding Whigs?*,[5a] or are the Revolutionists getting head again, Since their Birmingham Defeat? When did you see our Freinds in Duchess Street,[6] and How do they do? When do you Leave Town for Aughinleck? and how long do you stay?[7] To all these Queries I shall expect a Solution; and as [much] more *Spontaneous* Intelligence, as you can Supply me with. If any thing occurs on this side the water worth communicating you shall Certainly have it, But at present I can think of nothing more to add, except to assure you That I am with much Regard, My Dear Sir, Your Faithfull and[8] Obedient humble Servant

THOS. KILLALOE

My Son begs to present his Compliments with mine to you and the young Ladies.

From *William Windham,* Tuesday 9 August 1791[1]

MS. Yale (C 3134).

ADDRESS: James Boswell Esqr.

[London] Tuesday August. 9th.

DEAR BOSWELL: I am afraid there is but little chance of your being

---

[5a] Jonathan Swift, *Description of a City Shower*, l. 41.

[6] Lady Anne Lindsay (1750–1825), later Barnard's daughter-in-law, and her sister, Lady Margaret Fordyce, daughters of the Earl of Balcarres.

[7] JB arrived at Auchinleck on 28 Aug. and left on 18 Oct. (Book of Company).

[8] MS. "and and"

[1] The year is fixed by the next letter and To Scott, 9 Aug. 1791.

in Town to day: but, in case you should return,[2] be it known, that the Gang[3] meets at my house to day, and that we shall complain, if we do not see you.—Yours etc. etc.

W. WINDHAM

From Sir William Scott, Friday 12 August 1791

MS. Yale (C 2444).

ADDRESS: James Boswell Esq., Home Circuit.

FRANK: London, August thirteenth 1791, Wm. Scott.

POSTMARKS: FREE AU 12 91 A, AU 12 91.

[London]

DEAR BOSWELL: I am just stepping into my Chaise for a Month's Ramble, and have barely time to tell you that I am glad to find that you see Things in the Way they were meant. Don't be[1] so *fier* of your Country[2] Maxim, *Nemo me impune*[3] etc. as to smell Provocation where none was intended. Yours very faithfully

W. S.

We had a pleasant Day at Windham's on Tuesday.[4]

From William Gerard Hamilton to John Courtenay, Wednesday ?17 ?1790–93[1]

MS. Yale (C 1491).

ADDRESS: J. Courtnay Esq.

[2] JB was on the circuit at Maidstone, Kent, on 9 Aug. (see *ibid.*) and clearly did not return to London on that day.

[3] Philip Metcalfe's name for Reynolds, Malone, Courtenay, and JB (Journ. 4 Jan. 1790). Windham presumably did not name his other guests (see next letter) because he wanted to get Scott and JB together, and feared that JB would shy off if he knew that Scott was to be of the party.

[1] MS. "Don't me be"
[2] MS. "county"
[3] The motto of Scotland (*Nemo me impune lacesset*): "No one will attack me with impunity."

[4] Present besides Scott were Malone, Sir Joshua, Dr. Laurence, and Sir Harry Englefield. The chief topic of conversation apparently was Mrs. Piozzi (Sir James Prior, *Life of Edmond Malone*, 1860, p. 412).

[1] The only certain evidence for dating this letter is the "Wednesday": the numeral looks like a "7" corrected to a "17", but is by no means certain. JB's relations with Hamilton and Courtenay

[London] ?17 Wednesday

DEAR C.: Nothing can be more mortifying than your Excuse. The General[2] and I will dine alone. At all events come as soon as you can. Yours etc.

W. G. H.

To Thomas Barnard, Sunday 12, Wednesday 15 February 1792

MS. Yale (L 48). A draft.

HEADING: To the Lord Bishop of Killaloe.

London, Great Portland Street, 12 Febry. 1792

MY DEAR LORD: Your Lordship has apparrently great reason to accuse me of culpable negligence in not acknowledging the favour of your letter of last autumn long before this time but you will excuse me when you know the real truth. I went down to Auchinleck[1] to look after the business of my Estate; but I had not been there above a day or two, till the effect of[1a] finding myself in that house where I had been uncommonly happy with a most valuable wife who was to be seen there no more brought back a miserable state of mind to which I have long been subject at intervals and whatever external exertions I have forced since this last return of Melancholy, I have not yet had one day of good spirits.[2] I am

---

were closest in the years 1790–93. If, as has been suggested, he begged and preserved the note as an illustration of Hamilton's cantankerous nature, he probably acquired it not long after his trouble with Hamilton over cancels in the *Life* (To Malone, 25 Feb. 1791; Journ. 3 Mar. 1791) or not long after he demanded payment for them (To W. G. Hamilton, 25 Feb. 1793). Possible dates in those years are 17 Aug. 1791; 17 Apr., 17 July 1793.

[2] Possibly General William Dalrymple (1735–1807), who is almost always mentioned in JB's journals in company with Courtenay and, less frequently, with Hamilton. The second son of George Dalrymple of Dalmahoy, he became colonel in 1777, major-general in 1782. In 1793, he was promoted to general;

and, in the next year, was appointed colonel of the 47th Regiment. From 1784 to 1790, he was M.P. for Wigtown Burghs. His son became seventh Earl of Stair (*Scots Peer.* viii. 150–51).

---

[1] c. 28 Aug. 1791 (Book of Company).

[1a] "solitude (for my eldest son who was there" deleted.

[2] Compare To Temple, 22 Nov. 1791. At this point, several attempts to begin the next sentence have been deleted (the symbol > means "this changed to"): "In such a state there is an avers > In such a state work > In such a state [an] attempt to write > I am just beginning to emerge from the dismal cloud, by what cause I know not; but I avail myself of my first > I am just beginning to be a little easier, and I avail myself of the first".

just beginning to be a little easier, and I seise the first better moment to write to my much valued friend.[3]

Having been interrupted, I now[4] resume my pen; but alas I am to give your Lordship very bad accounts of our excellent President of the Royal Academy. When I came to town in October, I found him in great apprehension of losing the sight of his other eye; on which account he had taken a number of medicines, and lived very low, so that he was relaxed and dejected. He by Dr. Warren's advice made some efforts to rouse his constitution; but he soon sunk again, and by degrees became so ill as to be confined to his room, and for more than a month he has kept his bed. The Physicians were long entirely in the dark as to his case. Dr. Warren said to me that it was a dissolution of his frame occasioned by some disorder which could not be discerned. A few days ago they thought they had discovered it to be a diseased liver, and they are now treating him accordingly but have no hope of his recovery. He does not wish to see his friends, takes laudanum, and dozes in "tranquil despondency" as Burke expressed it. His death will be an irreparable loss to the Academy and to his numerous friends.[5] The thought of it hangs heavy upon my mind. The CLUB yesterday (Sir William Scott Sir Charles Bunbury[6] Windham Malone Courtenay Lord Lucan and myself) joined in sincere concern. I am very sorry that he did not imbibe Christian piety from Johnson. No clergyman attends him; no holy rites console his languishing hours.[7] I heartily wish that your Lordship were here.

A number of the members of the Royal Academy hold a dining club once a forthnight.[8] I like it much, and so I am sure would our Chaplain; but this sad illness of Sir Joshua throws a damp upon us.

Sir William Forbes has been here some time. I read to him your Lordship's letter to me on the Holy Sacrament. He begged of me to present his best compliments to your Lordship and to request as

[3] Catchword, "On", follows, but JB did not begin as he had planned on the second page.

[4] "15 Febry." written above the line.

[5] Sir Joshua died between 8 and 9 o'clock on Thursday evening, 23 Feb. 1792, and was buried at St. Paul's on 3 Mar.

[6] Sir Thomas Charles Bunbury (1740–1821), M.P. for Suffolk and brother of Henry William Bunbury, the caricaturist

(*Comp. Bar.* iv. 118). He was elected to The Club in Feb. 1774.

[7] "languid hours" deleted.

[8] The Royal Academy dining club met every other Friday evening from Nov. to Apr. or May at Free Mason's Tavern. JB regularly attended its meetings, "which I never missed when in town, and was exceedingly unwilling to miss on any consideration whatever" (Journ. 14 Feb. 1794), from 1792 to 1794.

a very great favour that he may have a copy of it for his own private use. I told him that your Lordship intended to revise and enlarge it.

My *Life of Johnson* has had wonderful success, there being now 1500 copies sold; but indeed as John Wilkes said, "it is a wonderful Book." I am preparing a second edition in Octavo.[9]

I have called once in Duchess Street.—not at home and as yet have had no summons. I offer my compliments to Mrs. and Captain Barnard and have the honour to remain your Lordships much obliged and faithful humble servant

From Thomas Barnard,
Saturday 25 February 1792

MS. Yale (C 96).

ADDRESS: James Boswell Esqr., Great Portland Street, London.

POSTMARKS: IRELAND, FE 25, FE 29 92.

Rutland Square [Dublin] Feby. 25th 1792

DEAR SIR: I confess, I have been not a Little Mortified at your Long Silence, and was once very near transcribing one of your own Letters to Johnson on a Similar occasion,[1] (Mutatis Mutandis) and sending it to you, as an Epistola objurgatoria, But you have given me such Solid Reasons for it, As have quite Disarm'd me, and I can only Pity and Condole where I meant to Blame. I will not therefore Retaliate, by Delaying my Thanks for your very obliging and acceptable Letter, but it is on Condition that you make me some amends for what is past, by a very *Speedy* Reply, to this; With such Farther accounts as you can Collect of the State of my Dear Freind Sir Jos. both in Body and Mind. I have very little hopes of seeing him again on This Side of the grave, But it would be some Consolation to think that he had left this World with the Sentiments of a christian, in Faith and Hope; and that, For the Comfort of his Real Freinds; He never should Realise that Dreadfull Scene which [he] has so feelingly Painted.[2] But That "*If*

---

[9] The second edition of the *Life* did not appear until 17 July 1793, although it went to press in the spring of 1792 (see *Lit. Car.* pp. 157–59).

[1] See, for instance, To SJ, 25 June 1774, 24 Apr. 1777, 22 Oct. 1779.

[2] A reference to "The Death of Cardinal Beaufort", from Shakespeare's *2 Henry VI*. "The Cardinal in the last

He Hoped for Heavens High Bliss," He should at Least, "Make Signal of that Hope."[3] I never Observ'd, nor yet Believe, His Sober Thoughts to have been tainted with Infidelity, But his attention to his Profession for 7 days in the Week, with all the morning dedicated to Business and every Evening to Social Dissipation, Left no Room for Religion in his mind; His Spiritual Faculties lay Torpid, for want of Excercise, and it is now, I am afraid, too late to Call them into action again. I shall be most Happy to hear from you that I am Mistaken.

I beg you to give my Compliments and Cordial Respects to Sir Wm. Forbes, and tell him that he is heartily welcome to Copy the little Tract I sent to you; and when that is done, I shall be obliged to you if you will return me the original, as I have Kept no Copy of it myself. Pray is it true that you Rec[e]iv'd last Summer from an unknown Hand a Valuable Relique from the Conflagration of Priestly's Meeting House with a Letter accompanying it? Tell me the Circumstances, and What Reception it met with.

We have been Employ'd here for this fortnightpast on a very Interesting Question in Parliament; viz. How far we shall Repeal or Relax the Popery Laws in this Kingdom. A Bill has passd the Commons yesterday, granting the Roman Catholicks, full Liberty of Educating their children, either in their own Seminaries, or in the University, with ours (Degrees Excepted) Licence to Intermarry with Pr⟨otes⟩tants, and admission to the Bar, (Tho' no⟨t⟩ the Honors of it). On Monday we shall ta⟨ke it⟩ into Consideration in our house; and I believe it will Pass, tho' with much opposition. But this do's not Content them. They want the Elective Franchises, which will not be given them.[4] Rich. Burke, is

---

agony of death; Warwick, Salisbury, and King Henry standing by the bedside; the king with hand and arm uplifted; on a table the Cardinal's hat; above the pillow is a demon's head glaring upon the dying priest, a part of the claw seen, ready to clutch the departing spirit" (*A Catalogue Raisonné of the Engraved Works of Sir Joshua Reynolds, P.R.A. from 1755 to 1822*, by Edward Hamilton, 1884, p. 142). Sir Joshua painted the picture in 1787 for Alderman Boydell. Leslie and Taylor call it "a very poor and flimsy piece of painting" (*Life and Times of Sir Joshua Reynolds*, ii. 503).

[3] Lord Cardinal, if thou think'st on
   heaven's bliss,
Hold up thy hand, make signal of
   thy hope.
      (*2 Henry VI*, III. iii. 27–28)

[4] The Relief Bill of 1792, which had been suggested by the British ministers but extensively revised by the Irish Parliament, was passed. It improved the position of the Catholics in Ireland considerably. They were not, however, granted the elective franchise or the right to bear arms.

their avow'd agent, and I am sorry for it; for he has neither done Them, nor himself any Service by it.[5] E. Burke has written (and Printed here) an Excellent Pamphlet in their Favour;[6] But the Principle of Self Defence is too strong in the Human Breast to yeild to Eloquence, or Even argument: The Protestant Interest here is too deeply concern'd in preserving its own Security, to give up its Present Ascendancy to the pretended Rights of Man, Especially when Their Estates as well as their Religion may hereafter be Involved in the Question.

I thought you had expressed an Intention of Paying us a Visit at this Season. You would have heard some Debates not unworthy of your attention, and met some of your Freinds who would have been very glad to see you among them, none more So, than, Dear Sir, your affectionate and Faithfull Servant

THOS. KILLALOE

My Son left me last Wednesday and I suppose is by this Time at No. 20 Parliament Street. Duchess Street I believe goes on as usual. You Know, I suppose that Lady A. was in France last november.[7] I presume you have seen them by this Time.

I rejoice at the great Success of your Book. Did you not promise us a *Supplement?*[8] I hope your Young Ladies are well and your Son answering all your Expectations at Westminster.

[5] The Catholic Committee in 1790 employed Richard Burke as a legal adviser, and in Sept. 1791 appointed him its agent in England. By July 1792, however, the Committee no longer considered him useful. He was accused by various groups of unduly raising the hopes of the Catholics, of neglecting their cause, of antagonizing the Irish government, and of embarrassing the English government. Distrusted by all sides, he left Ireland in Nov. 1792 (*The Correspondence of Edmund Burke*, vii, 1968, ed. P. J. Marshall and J. A. Woods, pp. xiii–xix).

[6] *A Letter to Sir Hercules Langrishe, Bart., M.P., on the Subject of Roman Catholics of Ireland, and the Propriety of Admitting them into the Elective Franchise,* etc., 1792. An edition was printed in London the same year.

[7] Lady Anne Lindsay had gone to France to be near William Windham, with whom she was in love. Although fascinated by her, Windham never asked her to marry him, and she finally gave him up. Andrew Barnard, although twelve years younger than Lady Anne, who was 38, had asked her to marry him, but she had refused because of the discrepancy in their ages. The Bishop was distinctly opposed to such a marriage, although he had great respect and liking for Lady Anne. She left Paris in Oct. 1791 (Dorothea Fairbridge, *Lady Anne Barnard at the Cape of Good Hope*, 1924, pp. 4–7). See *post* pp. 417–18.

[8] *Post* To Barnard, 16 Aug. 1792, n. 11

From Sir William Forbes to Thomas Barnard, Thursday 19 April 1792

MS. Fettercairn Papers, National Library of Scotland. A draft.

ENDORSEMENT: Bishop of Killaloe, Dublin, 19 Apr. 1792.

[Edinburgh] 19 Apr. 1792

The dissipation and distractions of a town life prevented me while I remained in London, from making a suitable acknowlegement to[1] your Lordship as I fully intended, for your very great goodness in permitting Me to take a copy of your letter to our friend Mr. Boswell, on a very Solemn and interesting Subject.[2]— I now beg leave to make offer of my grateful thanks for this very confidential communication, which I receive as an additional Mark of that kindness and attention with which your Lordship has been pleased so frequently to honor me.—Your Lordship may rely that the paper shall remain entirely with myself.—It is a Subject on which I have thought and read a good deal; and in regard to which I have often felt no inconsiderable degree of uneasiness, lest I may have form'd a wrong judgement on so serious and important a Part of religious duty.—

If I have ever the good fortune to meet with your Lordship again, I will still solicit the favor of some farther explanation of some points[3] in order that I may the more fully apprehend your Lordship's meaning. I am extremely desirous of adopting your Lordship's interpretation; which is that in which I was originally instructed; and it is only of later years that some publications I have read, have made me waver a little in regard to it—a state of all others the most uncomfortable!

I had gone to London with my eldest daughter[4] to place her in a Boarding school, and had much satisfaction in again meeting with some valuable acquaintance after nearly a five years absence;

---

[1] "thanking" deleted. Further reporting of deletions is selective.

[2] "The Nature of the Eucharist" deleted. See *ante* From Barnard, c. 15 May 1784, for the letter. It is fortunate that Forbes made a copy, for no other text is now known.

[3] "than what is contained in your Lordship's very Candid letter to Mr. Boswell" deleted.

[4] Probably Rebecca (1779–1841), married (1802) Alexander Ranaldson Macdonell of Glengarry and Clanranald (Louisa L. Forbes, *Genealogical Table of the Forbes Family of Monymusk and Pitsligo, 1460–1880*, 1880). But see *ante* From Forbes to Langton, 9 Sept. 1782, n. 3.

which was only allayed by the loss of our excellent and valuable friend Sir Joshua Reynold[s] whose death is a deep and a severe misfortune to his friends.[5] It was well observed by Mr. Malone, that Sir Joshua was a point of concentration, as it were, to those who had the happiness to enjoy his society, which it is scarcely to be expected any other can Supply.

I staid a few days after having fix'd the period of my departure that I might have the honor of assisting in paying the last duties to his remains. It was a most solemn and affecting scene, the procession thro' the Cathedral; Such as I never witnessed before, And I believe I may say with great truth that never was any Man attended to his Grave by a more respectable assemblage of friends nor more sincerely attached to him.[6]

Lady F. who has been in a very poor state of health for more than a twelvemonth, so as not to be able to accompany me to London, begs to join me in offering our duty to your Lordship and Mrs. Barnard.—I earnestly Solicit the Continuance of a place in your remembrance.

From John Douglas to Lord Macartney, Wednesday 23 May 1792

MS. Yale (C 1104).

Park Place, May 23d. 1792

My Lord: I consider my Election into the Society, where you presided Yesterday, as an honour conferred upon me; but my Satisfaction is heightened by the very obliging Manner in which Your Lordship has been pleased to communicate the Information.[1]

---

[5] "whose death is a misfortune to his friends which they can scarcely hope to see repaired" deleted.

[6] For an account of Reynolds's funeral, see *Gent. Mag.* (1792) lxii. 273–74, which, after describing the procession in great detail, commented: "It is remarkable that the funeral of this illustrious painter was honoured by the attendance of one knight of the Thistle, two knights of St. Patrick, three knights of the Garter, three dukes, and four lord-lieutenants of Ireland."

[1] "My Lord, I have the honor to acquaint you, that your Lordship was this day elected a Member of the Club: I am particularly happy that it falls to my lot to communicate this Information to your Lordship and am with great respect, My Lord, Your Lordship's most faithful and most humble servant. Macartney, President" (Lord Macartney to Douglas, 22 May 1792, BM Add. MSS. Eg. 2186, f. 61). Douglas had been proposed for membership on 24 Apr. by

—While I express my thanks, I am happy to have an Opportunity of assuring your Lordship, that I am, with great Respect, My Lord, Your Lordship's most faithful and obedient Servant

J. SARUM

Lord Macartney.

To Bennet Langton, late May 1792

Not reported. Sent in late May probably from London (To Barnard, 16 Aug. 1792). Referred to in next letter.

From Bennet Langton, Monday 11 June 1792

MS. Yale (C 1695).

ADDRESS: James Boswell Esqr.

ENDORSEMENT: Bennet Langton Esq.

[Oxford] June 11th. 1792

MY DEAR SIR, I am not in fault for not more readily replying to your Letter, for I did not reach home till Saturday Evening; at least I have only let one Post go by; I should have met you at the Club; but that the Contractor for the Canal[1] was very desirous that I and some of my Associates should take a View of his Works, and He had so much to shew us, that too late an Hour of the day was come on for reaching London in time—and I directed my course to Weybridge, where a worthy man resides, of whom I think you must have heard me speak, if You have not met him when with me, who is our Agent for managing the River Wye, of the name of Granger;[2] he has for some time been in a lamentable

Fox, seconded by Malone. On 14 Dec. 1790, JB, seconded by Sir Joseph Banks, had proposed Douglas for membership, but he was not elected at that time (*The Club*).

---

[1] Unidentified.

[2] One John Granger, Esq. is listed in the Quarter Sessions records for the County of Surrey as an inhabitant of Weybridge from 1780 to 1795, for which years his tax assessments are recorded (letter from C. H. Thompson, County Archivist for Surrey, 23 Sept. 1953). A John Granger also appears on the retainer given to JB by the Earl of Portmore and Langton in Feb. 1787 (see Journ. 30 Mar. 1787). The retainer is at Yale (Lg 46).

state of ill-health; I wished therefore to make him a visit, and found him in appearance wonderfully recovered, so that it may be hoped he may yet do more of that considerable service to me and my Family, which his good conduct of the concern has effected for some length of time past—In returning homewards I thought I might as well, as Windsor was in my road, make a little stop there; and on arriving in the evening on Friday, I was glad to find that my respected Friend Dr. Heberden[3] was arrived there for his Summer residence; I waited on him, and sat with him near two Hours; and, the next morning, at eight, o clock, met him again, at the Royal Chapel; as we stood in the Portico to make our Bows— The King came up to us, and took notice in a very obliging manner of us both, and staid some little time in Chat—as he asked me where I was come from, I of course introduced the mention of the Canal-business where I had been attending—and when some talking had gone on, upon that Subject, and he seemed going away; he came a step back again in order to mention your Book—which furnished discourse for some little time longer—I thought this might be acceptable—as I know You respect the Influence of the Georgium Sidus[4]—After breakfasting with good Dr. Heberden; I went to our Friend, the Bishop of Salisbury,[5] and sat with him I believe near an hour—and by what he told me, it seems that all your Friends, and I ought to add the Community at large, are much indebted to him, in that he hindered you, by a persuading that at last with some difficulty prevailed, from repairing to the Scene of the Riots in Mount Street,[6] where I sincerely think your

---

[3] Dr. William Heberden the elder (1710–1801), "one of the most eminent English physicians of the eighteenth century" (DNB), was the first physician to describe angina pectoris. A classical scholar, he wrote on both medical and philosophical topics. SJ, who called him "ultimus Romanorum" (*Life* iv. 399 n. 4), bequeathed him a book in recognition of his attendance on him (*ibid.* p. 402 n. 2).

[4] "The George star." Sir William Herschel (1738–1822) had so named the planet which he discovered in 1781. The name was disliked outside England and finally gave way to "Uranus", proposed by the German astronomer J. E. Bode (1747–1826).

[5] John Douglas, who had been translated from Carlisle on 28 July 1791 (*Fasti Angl.*). He had also been Dean of Windsor.

[6] On 5 June 1792, a group of about forty servants of both sexes, who had assembled at the Pitt's Head, Little Stanhope Street, Mayfair, "to make merry by a dance" in celebration of the King's birthday, were arrested and taken to the watch-house in Mount Street, Grosvenor Square. On the following day, a mob demanded their release and broke the windows of the watch-house. Most of the servants were released that morning; but the mob assembled again in the evening, breaking into the watch-house and causing considerable damage in the

peril would not have been inconsiderable, which I am led to think from hearing that one whom I am well acquainted with, in consequence of having asked some of the Rabble why they assembled in such a riotous sort, had his head laid open to the Skull by a blow which beat him down and then the Wretches that were nearest fell to trampling upon him, so that he has very narrowly escaped with his life—I am afraid I have continued prating till it is time to send away my letter so that perhaps I had better send off what I have writ and defer any thing there may be to say as to the Johnsoniana till next post, when I propose to dispatch my observations, which however I am afraid will amount to very little; indeed I had thought that you had been aware of all that concerned those few particulars contained in the paper that you have sent me back[7]—the worst of it is that there will be postage to pay for them as our Friend Courtenay will have set out on his grand Tour[8] before the Letter can arrive: and I am afraid that my remarks (as Hamlet says of his th⟨anks⟩⟩ "will be too dear at a Halfpenny"[9]— I have only time to add all our kind regards to Yourself and the Ladies and that I am, my dear Sir, Yours very faithfully

BENNET LANGTON

From Charles Burney, Tuesday 19 June 1792

MS. Yale (C 706).

ADDRESS: To James Boswell Esqr. Great Portland Street, No. 47.

neighbourhood. Foot and horse troops were necessary to restore order (*Annual Register 1792*, Rivington, 1798 pt. 2, pp. 23–24). See also *London Chronicle*, 5–7 June 1792, lxxi. 543–44, for an account of the riots. JB apparently kept no journal from 11 Apr. 1791 to 16 Aug. 1792, and did not mention the incident in any known surviving letter.

[7] Langton contributed greatly to the second edition, sending JB thirteen letters of SJ (printed at end of second volume) and additional anecdotes. Some of these were printed on pp. 274–77 of the third volume (*Life* iv. 27–30), but Langton is

here probably referring to what he sent to JB so late that it was printed in the preliminaries of the first volume, *x– *xiii (*Life* iv. 30–33). On 11 June 1792, the very day Langton wrote this letter, JB wrote to James Abercrombie that his second edition was "now in the press".

[8] That is, they could not be sent to JB through Courtenay, who as an M.P. had franking privileges. Courtenay was back from Paris, where he had attended the debates of the Legislative Assembly, on 9 Oct. 1792, when JB dined with him (To Alexander Boswell, 12 Oct. 1792).

[9] *Hamlet*, II. ii. 282.

Chelsea College, Tuesday Morng. 19th. June 1792
DEAR SIR: I am truly concerned, that it will not be in my power to have the honour of waiting upon you and Miss Boswells to Morrow. But I have been long engaged to dine with Dr. Haydn[1] and all the Musical graduates[2] that are in town, on that day. I hope for the happiness of meeting you at the Club to day. Having had but one dinner there during the present year,[3] I hunger and thirst for another.

Believe me to be with great regard and Affection, dear Sir, Your obliged and faithful Servant

CHAS. BURNEY

From the Duke of Leeds,
Tuesday 19 June 1792

MS. Yale (C 1715).

ADDRESS: James Boswell Esqr., etc. etc. etc.,[1] Parsloes.[2]

ENDORSEMENT: Duke of Leeds.

Gros[veno]r Square, June 19. 1792
DEAR SIR, I am very sorry it will not be in my power to dine at the Club[3] today being engaged to the Duke of York.

[1] Franz Joseph Haydn (1732–1809), the Austrian composer, "from whose productions I have received more pleasure late in life, when tired of most other Music, than I ever received in the most ignorant and rapturous part of my youth, when every thing was new, and the disposition to be pleased was undiminished by criticism, or satiety" (Burney's *History of Music*, 1789, iv. 599). Haydn, with whom Burney had corresponded for many years, had been in England since Jan. 1791 (Roger Lonsdale, *Dr. Charles Burney*, 1965, p. 352). About to return to Vienna, he gave a dinner-party at Parsloe's in St. James's Street on 20 June 1792.

[2] The Musical Graduates' Meeting, established in London on 24 Nov. 1790, was an organization of men who had degrees in music. Each graduate was required to entertain the other members. Haydn had received the D.Mus. from Oxford eleven months earlier (Percy Scholes, *The Great Dr. Burney*, 1948, ii. 119–20).

[3] Burney and JB did meet at The Club on 19 June; the only previous meeting attended by Burney in 1792 was that of 5 June (*The Club*).

[1] JB was President of The Club for this evening (*The Club*). Leeds's etceteras may stand either for the other members of The Club or for possible honours of JB's concerning which Leeds was uninformed but punctilious.

[2] Where The Club met.

[3] The Duke had been elected to The Club on 8 May 1792.

The Duchess and myself will be very happy if you will honour us with your company tomorrow at Dinner, in case you are not better engaged. Beleive me, Dear Sir, your very faithful and Obedient Servant

LEEDS

James Boswell Esqr.

To the Duke of Leeds, Tuesday 19 June 1792

MS. Yale (L 857). A copy in James Ross's[1] hand.

Parsloes, Teusday 19 June 1792

MY DEAR LORD: I do most sincerly thank your Grace for your kind invitation to dinner tomorrow. But unfortunatly I have a few friends who have engaged to eat and drink at my board[2] which humble as it is has an host aspiring enough to ask one day the Duke of Leeds to sit down at it and by his brilliant rays to make its[3] defeciencies be forgotten. I go to Margate for two days at most on thursday.[4] When I return I entreat a renewal of the much valued invitation on any day except Monday and teusday next week.[5] I have the honour to be, my Lord, Your Graces much obliged and faithfull humble servant

(Sign'd) JAMES BOSWELL

To His Grace the Duke of Leeds.

[1] JB's servant, "sober and honest, and can serve very well; but even Sandie now says that he is grown more negligent and impertinent" (To Mrs. Boswell, 9 Feb. 1789).

[2] JB appears to have kept no journal from 11 Apr. 1791 to 16 Aug. 1792, and his known surviving letters do not name his guests on 20 June 1792.

[3] MS. "it"

[4] JB had received from the London Committee for the General Sea-bathing Infirmary notice of his election to the Committee and an invitation to be present at the laying of the foundation-stone of the Infirmary in West-sea-bath Bay near Margate, on 21 June 1792. He at first declined but sent his acceptance on receiving a letter of "earnest solicitation" from the Committee (From the Committee, with nine signatures, 15 June 1792; copies of JB's reply to John Pridden, Secretary, and to the Committee, both 16 June 1792, in Kent Archives Office, Maidstone, Cat. No. MH/T1). For an account of the proceedings and a list of those participating (JB is mentioned), see *Gent. Mag.* (1792) lxii. 571–72. A dated memorandum (J 115.8), apparently scribbled by JB at Margate, shows that he did remain there to 22 June, as he indicated he might.

[5] On the 25th, JB gave a dinner for the composer Haydn (From Earl of Exeter, 26 June; From Sir John Gallini, 22 June). On the 26th, he attended the celebration

From William Windham,
?before Wednesday 20 June 1792[1]

MS. Yale (C 3135). Notes for Boswelliana (M 67) on verso.

ADDRESS: Mr. Boswell.

[London]

DEAR BOSWELL: I would join you at breakfast this morning, but have a person, who is to be here on business at 11.[2] Yours truly
W. W.

From Thomas Barnard,
Wednesday 4 July 1792

MS. Yale (C 97).

ADDRESS: James Boswell Esqr., 47. Great Portland Street, London.

POSTMARKS: LIMERICK, JY 6, JY ?10 92.

Killaloe, July 4th 1792

DEAR SIR, I have been just now reading one of your Dolefull Epistles to Johnson, Complaining, not unjustly, of his Neglect for a Tedious Intermission of his Correspondence: and I had a great mind to have transcribed it, (Mutatis mutandis,) and sent it to you as an objurgatory Epistle from myself;[1] who have Equal Cause of Complaint against Your Worship. How can you Express your own Impatience on that occasion with So much Energy and Pathos, and yet have so little Consideration for the Feelings of

of the anniversary of Alderman Curtis's election to Parliament, singing a song (later published as a broadside: Yale, P 160) which he had composed for the occasion. An account of the celebration appears in *Gent. Mag.* lxii. 572; see also *Diary,* 27 June 1792; *Morning Chronicle,* 5 July 1792; *Public Advertiser,* 4, 5, 6 July 1792. There is no indication that the Duke's invitation was renewed.

1 Determined by one of the notes on the verso of this, which refers to "the King's

birthday [4 June] 1792", and by the fact that Windham was at Felbrigg from 20 June (Windham's *Diary,* pp. 256–60).

2 The only entries in Windham's *Diary* for June 1792 (11, 13, 14, 15, 16, 17, and 20) suggest neither the person nor the business with which he was concerned.

1 Barnard seems to have been taken by this idea of employing JB's letters against their writer. Compare the similar opening *ante* From Barnard, 25 Feb. 1792.

Another, as to Suffer a Letter (that certainly demanded some Answer even tho' Future Correspondence were to Cease) to lie Dormant more than Seven Months without a Reply?

What have you to say for yourself? aye What? Has the Foreign Correspondence of the Royal Academy entirely occupied Your Pen? Do's a Third Volume of the Ἀπομνημονευματα[2] totally Engross your Time and attention? (I wish you may have so good an Excuse to alledge.); or dos your Care of the Constitution, ne quid Detrimenti capiat Respublica,[3] Keep you as Busy as it did last year in preparing ammunition against the 14th Inst.?[4] That or any other Excuse, (*Even Mere Indolence and Dissipation*) you have still Leave to Plead, Provided you no longer Persist in Your Laches,[4a] But make compensation for your Past Silence by a Full account of yourself, and all your Adventures from Christmass Last. When you have Dispatched This; I expect some particular Intelligence of our Club Freinds, and How have they Stuck together Since they have Lost the Common Cement that First United Them?[5] What is the State of Literary Society in the Metropolis at Present? Who are your own Political associates This year? Who are your Convivial? I shall Expect a Full detail of all this Interesting Matter in your next, and as much more as you please to Add. And to Remove every motive for Delay, (Real or pretended) I give you Leave to Keep my Paper *another month*, if You wish to transcribe it, Rather than it should serve you for a Fresh Excuse. Now Therefore,—*Accingito et omnes Pelle Moras.*[6] I shall Calculate the Posts that *ought* to Elapse till I receive your Letter, and the more Postage I pay for it, the more acceptable it will be.

And now my good Freind let me Thank you for the Kind, and Freindly manner in which I hear you have Spoken of me at a Certain House.[7] Accept my Sincere acknowledgements, but do *not*

---

[2] "Memoirs."

[3] "That the Republic shall receive no harm", the injunction given in ancient Rome to the Dictator when he was invested with the supreme authority.

[4] JB had conducted an anonymous newspaper campaign of depreciation and ridicule against the meeting in London on 14 July 1791 by the Celebrators of the Anniversary of the French Revolution. See *New CBEL* ii. 1228, 1234.

[4a] Remissness, negligence.

[5] Sir Joshua Reynolds.

[6] "Gird yourself, overcome all delays!" —Ovid's *Metamorphoses* vii. 47–48 (paraphrased).

[7] Undoubtedly the house in Duchess Street. JB must have volunteered to present the Bishop's point of view on his son's relations with Lady Anne. See From Barnard, 9 Aug. 1791, n. 6, 25 Feb. 1792, n. 7, and the antepenultimate paragraph of To Barnard, 16 Aug. 1792.

mention them again, for tho', I think, nothing is more pleasing than Such Communications as convey the mutual Regard of absent Freinds to each other, and therefore Both Parties ought to be obliged for it, yet some People do not Chuse that *any* part of Confidential Correspondence should be divulged. *Verbum Sapienti*.

Pray how came you to Disappoint your Freinds last Spring of your Intended (and Promised) Visit to Dublin? I had prepared you a good Reception when you Came among us, and you would have met it, I can assure you.

I am now Settled at Killaloe for the Remainder of the Summer, and I thank God, my Health and Spirits continue as well as usual. Better, I think, than when you saw me last. I see with much Satisfaction every appearance of permanent Tranquill⟨ity⟩ in this Country, Notwithstanding the Efforts of Payn⟨e⟩ and Napper Tandy to disturb it.[8] All the Property of the Kingdom, whatever be their Parliamentary conduct or Party seem determin'd to Support the Constitution against those who have nothing to Loose, and Therefore, as Little to Risque, by what they Call a Reform; and therefore I trust that Such Beggarly adventurers, numerous as they are, will succeed as Ill *here* as they are likely to do with You.

And now, *Bad as you are*, I bid you heartily Farewell, and with much Sincerity assure you That I am, Dear Sir, very Faithfully and affectionately yours

THOS. KILLALOE

To John Douglas,
Thursday 9 August 1792

Not reported. Sent from London. Referred to in next letter.

[8] The second part of *The Rights of Man*, by Thomas Paine (1737–1809), appeared in 1792 and was widely distributed in Ireland, where it made many converts. James Napper Tandy (1740–1803) was one of the leaders of the Volunteer Movement, and, with Archibald Hamilton Rowan, was in the process of raising in Dublin two battalions of National Guards, made up principally of Catholics.

From John Douglas,
Sunday 12 August 1792

MS. Yale (C 1105).

ADDRESS: To James Boswell Esq., Great Portland Street, London.

FRANK: Salisbury, August twelfth 1792. free. J. Sarum.

POSTMARKS: SALISBURY, FREE AU ?13 92.

Salisbury, Sunday Augt. 12th. 1792

DEAR SIR, Your's of the 9th could not be answered sooner; for I got back to Salisbury from my Visitation, only in the Evening of yester-day. On tuesday, Wednesday, and Thursday next, the Clergy of four Deanries are to be visited here and my House will be crouded during those three Days, as they must all dine with me. On Friday, I am to have the honor of a Visit from their Majesties,[1] which will put it out of my Power to receive any other Company on that Day; so that I cannot be at Liberty till Saturday next; when Mrs. Douglas and I hope to have the Pleasure of giving you and the Ladies[2] our family Dinner at four o' Clock: and of lodging you that night. I am, with great haste, Dear Sir, Your's sincerely

J. SARUM

P.S. We can give you beds on Saturday and Sunday; but after that, we expect our house will be full.

To Thomas Barnard,
Thursday 16 August 1792

MS. Yale (L 49). A copy, in the hand of James Ross, with a few corrections in JB's hand.

HEADING in JB's hand: To the Lord Bishop of Killaloe.

[1] "On Friday afternoon, at a quarter past five o'clock, their Majesties and the six Princes arrived in perfect health at Gloucester Lodge, Weymouth. They set out from Windsor soon after five, breakfasted at Hartford Bridge, partook of a cold collation at the Bishop of Salisbury's at Salisbury Palace, and dined at Weymouth" (*London Chronicle*, 18–21 Aug. 1792).

[2] JB, Veronica, and Euphemia left London 17 Aug., arriving on the 18th at the Bishop's "in good time to dinner. Our company was the Bishop, his Lady son and daughter, Miss (say Mrs.) Rooke Mrs. Douglas's sister, Mr. Hudson the Bishop's Secretary, and Dr. Ash the Physician and his niece Miss Bishop" (Journ.). JB and his daughters stayed through Sunday 19 Aug.

London, 16 August 1792

My Dear Lord: Your Lordships goodness in favouring me with a second letter has cost me many a pang for my *unaccountable* procrastination. Now that I am fairly *en train* I shall endeavour to make some amends.

The excellent letter accompanying the brick from Preistley's meeting-house at Birmingham came to my hands in due course. I was much pleased with the letter, but suspected a joke till Malone informed me of the truth. Both the letter and curious fragment of Antihierarchical seditious *edification* shall be carefully deposited at Auchinleck. Every thing concerning the loss of our ever to be lamented Sir Joshua Reynolds has long ago reached your Lordship. I heartily wish that in one respect he had been such as *we* are. But we must make allowance and hope the best. Cosway[1] says he will be *retarded* in his spiritual progress. The blank which he makes in the Circle in which I have long moved is sad indeed. Malone is editing his discourses and some other writings concerning his art.[2] The world will have it that I am to be his Biographer. I did begin last winter to collect some particulars of his early life from him. Tomorrow I am to set out on a jaunt[3] into Devonshire and Cornwall and I doubt not shall pick up a variety of materials for his History. But whether I shall attempt what as yet seems not quite well suited to me I know not.[4] Sir Joshua was indeed a man of pleasing and various conversation but he had not those prominent features which can be seised like Johnsons. Our friends of the Royal Academy urge me to the task by telling me that I may make a very good Book of the late Presidents life interwoven with the History of the Arts during his time and they will contribute all their lights.[5] We have a most agreable Royal Academy Club

---

[1] Richard Cosway (1740–1821), painter and member of the Royal Academy. Paoli had been on terms of close friendship with him and his wife, and JB now saw him frequently at Academy functions.

[2] *The Works of Sir Joshua Reynolds, Knt. Late President of the Royal Academy, to which is prefixed an Account of the Life and Writings of the Author*, by Edmond Malone, Esq. one of his executors, 2 vols., 1797.

[3] MS. "juant". With Veronica and Euphemia, to visit Temple at St.

Gluvias, Cornwall, where they arrived on 24 Aug. (Journ.).

[4] To Andrew Erskine, 6 Mar. 1793, JB wrote: "The last year of his Life I began to take notes from him of his early years, and also indeed of other periods . . . and when I was in Devonshire and Cornwall last autumn, I got several anecdotes concerning him. But I doubt much whether I could write a *Life* of him." Only one page of notes has apparently survived. See *Portraits*, pp. 19–26.

[5] They also discussed the possibility

consisting of a select number who dine together once a fortnight during the Winter. Would that our Chaplain were with us. West acquits himself admirably.[6]

The literary Club has flourished this last Winter. We have had numerous meetings, and those excellent ones. We have a choice accession in the Duke of Leeds who likes it extremly and the Bishops of Peterborough and Salisbury[7] with the latter of whom I and my two eldest daughters who accompany me on my Jaunt are to be Saturday and Sunday next at his Palace. Lord Macartney has done his part well among us and we are proud that the Ambassadour to China[8] is of our Number. Will your Lordship believe it? I seriously solicited to go with him but every place was filled up. I am now not sorry that I was not taken at my word for the Voyage would have been distressing to me and the banishment from London dispiriting and I much suspect that he will not be received: or if he is that he will be hoodwinked.

As to political connections I realy cannot say that I have any. I did this ministry essential service in 1784 for which I have never yet been considered though I have Dundas's promise.[9] *Il faut attendre.* I have little to do in my profession. My cheif appearance last winter was endeavouring to defend the tithes of an honest Rector against an Inclosure Bill in a Committee of the House of Lords. The business lasted eight days and I did very well.[10]

My *Life of Johnson* has done wonderfully. Only think of upwards

of JB's writing a history of the Academy (Journ. 21 Dec. 1792).

[6] Benjamin West (1738–1820), American-born painter, elected President of the Academy on Reynolds's death.

[7] John Hinchliffe (1731–94), Bishop of Peterborough, was elected to The Club in Mar. 1792. JB misspelled his name as "Hinchcliffe" when he inserted it in the revised list of members of The Club in the second edition of the *Life* (i. 445; *Life* i. 479). John Douglas was elected on 22 May 1792. JB hoped to get particulars of his life during his projected visit (Journ. 19 Aug. 1792).

[8] George Macartney, Viscount Macartney of Dervock, was appointed Ambassador Extraordinary and Plenipotentiary to the Emperor of China in 1792. The purpose of his mission, which left in September of that year, was commercial

(*London Chronicle*, 8–11 Sept. 1792, lxxii. 242).

[9] JB refers to his *Letter to the People of Scotland*, 1783, and to the two loyal addresses to the King from Ayrshire and Edinburghshire which he managed in 1784 (Journ. 7–18 Mar.). Dundas had promised JB, in Dec. 1784, that he would talk to Pitt "and see whether I could get an office of some hundreds a year", and "promised he would be in earnest to assist me" (Journ. 12 Dec.). JB seems to have expected Dundas to hold to his promise in spite of JB's attack on him in the *Letter to the People of Scotland*, 1785.

[10] On 2 Apr. 1792 a bill carried on by George Finch-Hatton (1747–1823), M.P. for Rochester, 1772–84, father of the tenth Earl of Winchilsea, providing for an enclosure in the parish of Weldon,

of 1660 sets of two Vols. Quarto at two Guineas being sold a considerable time ago. My octavo edition in three Vols. is in great forwardness. It will contain a variety of additions which I shall print in Quarto and give to the purchasers of the first edition.[11] The Bishop of Dromore was it seems much offended, But we made it all up. He was in the wrong I think.[12] But no more of that.

Northamptonshire, was sent to the Lords from the Commons; it was read for the second time on 5 Apr. and referred to Committee. On 17 Apr. the Rector of Weldon, the Rev. William Raye, presented a petition to be heard before the Committee to protest against the commutation of his tithes which would result from the adoption of the bill. JB and Robert Graham (1744–1836), later Baron of the Exchequer and knighted, were counsel for Raye, while Spencer Perceval (1762–1812), later Prime Minister, and Serjeant Simon Le Blanc (d. 1816), later puisne judge of the King's Bench and knighted, appeared for the bill. Hearings, which consisted mainly of examination of witnesses, were held on 25, 30 Apr.; 7, 8, 11, 14, 15, 16 May; on 8 May JB succeeded in getting a witness rejected. On 16 May Perceval summed up for the bill and Graham replied for Raye. The Committee adjourned till 22 May that there might be a conference of the parties. If Raye gained any advantages, it was out of court, for on 30 May the Bishop of St. David's (Samuel Horsley, 1733–1806) reported the bill to the House without amendment; it was passed on 31 May and on 11 June received the royal assent (*Journals of the House of Lords*; Lg 65; *Public Advertiser*, 1, 10, 22 May 1792; *St. James's Chronicle*, 3–5, 8–10, 17–19 May 1792).

[11] A 44-page pamphlet, entitled *The Principal Corrections and Additions to the First Edition of Mr. Boswell's Life of Dr. Johnson*, 1793.

[12] See *ante* From Percy, 12, 24 Mar., 6 Apr. 1791. Percy had been warned (*ante* To Percy, 9 Apr. 1790) that he must expect to find himself named as authority for certain anecdotes of SJ which he had

given JB (*ante* From Percy, 6 Mar. 1787), but in the lack of statement to the contrary, he may have assumed that JB would not report those occasions on which SJ had treated him roughly, or would at least not name him as the butt of SJ's anger or roguishness. When he read the *Life* he must have been deeply hurt; and in at least one matter he felt sure that JB had shown downright duplicity. The index of the *Life* gave a reference to Percy's *Reliques* for a page that contained no mention of Percy, but did say that SJ had written dedications for authors who were unwilling to have the fact mentioned. (SJ had in fact written the dedication of the *Reliques* to the Countess of Northumberland.) Percy complained of this as a "very unfair and unpardonable proceeding", not to JB (an ominous sign), but to Malone, and further tried to find out from Malone whether JB was preparing additional enormities for the second edition. Malone consulted JB, who assured him that the supposed foul play was mere oversight. The page in question was a cancel; the index (which JB did not make himself) was compiled from a pre-cancel sheet; nobody thought to amend it after the cancel was made. "With respect to the other matters", Malone reported, "Mr. B. said that there was no change whatsoever in his new edition, except one sentence, which is added relative to Granger's Poem" (6 June 1792: *Percy-Malone Corresp.* pp. 56–57). This last statement does not square at all with what one finds in the second edition. JB never restored SJ's severe abstract judgement of Grainger's principles, nor SJ's statement that he helped Percy write a flattering review of *The Sugar-Cane* but did it with his tongue in his cheek. He

Sir Wm. Forbes and his Lady have been in England some time. Your Son favoured me with his company one day to meet them as did Sir Wm. Scott. We exulted in the thought that four more zealous Church and King men could not be found. Lady Forbes is much better. Sir Wm. very wisely takes her to Italy to have her health confirmed.[13] She is a most valuable Wife and mother. Duchess Street is as agreable as ever. I pay all attention to your Lordships *Verbum sapienti.*

How horrible is the present state of France.[14] Thank God Great Britain and Ireland are so wise as well as so happy. The Proclamation[15] though it did appear to me a little ticklish has proved to be of very great advantage.

I ever am with the most sincere respect and affection, My Dear Lord, Your Lordships much obliged and faithfull humble Servant.

allowed SJ's character of Grainger to continue to wear the transparent disguise of "an ingenious acquaintance". But otherwise in one way or another he put back in nearly everything that he had taken out of his original text. He could hardly have forgotten what the state of his text was when Malone put Percy's question to him, and he was a truthful man, but it is possible—indeed likely—that the passage was not yet printed off (see *Lit. Car.* pp. 167–68) and that something caused him to make further changes. That something may have been the emergence of ineluctable evidence that Percy had not "made it all up", as JB wanted to think at the time he wrote the present letter. Having been forced to conclude that Percy was hopelessly estranged (see *ante* pp. lxxxv–lxxxvi), he may well have decided to please himself as to the text of his book. It is a pity that he did not confine his comments on *The Sugar-Cane* to what he had heard SJ say, but he unfortunately added some obscure judgements of his own. See *Life* ii. 454 lines 3–8 and the third paragraph of n. 1.

[13] Forbes wrote to JB on 12 Mar. 1793 from Naples, "We have now been here three months, during which time the mild Climate has agreed so well with her, that I flatter myself before we return home next winter, her health will be entirely restored." Sir William and Lady Forbes, because of a banking crisis, left Rome on 8 May 1793 and arrived in Edinburgh on 16 June of that year (Sir William Forbes, *Memoirs of a Banking House*, 1860, pp. 79–80).

[14] The French, who declared war on 20 Apr., had been soundly defeated in their first battle with Austria (War of the First Coalition against France). Louis XVI had broken with his Girondin ministers, but his firmness was too late: on 20 June, his palace was besieged and captured by an armed mob, and he was forced to wear the red cap of Liberty while exposed for hours to the insults of the mob. On 10 Aug., he was dethroned and imprisoned with his family.

[15] Because of the multiplication of small democratic societies corresponding with France, the wide circulation of seditious writings, and particularly the appearance of the second part of Paine's *Rights of Man*, the Government issued a proclamation against such writings and societies. For the text of the proclamation, which produced long debates in both Houses and divided the Opposition, see *The London Chronicle*, 19–22 May 1792, lxxi. 488). Publication of the proclamation also produced strained relations between the Government and France.

When I return to Town a Copy shall be made of the paper which was communicated to Sir Wm. Forbes and shall be sent to your Lordship.[16]

To the Lord Bishop of Killaloe Ireland

From John Courtenay, ?September 1792[1]

MS. Yale (C 843).

ADDRESS: James Boswell Esqr.

[Brussels]

MY DEAR BOSWELL: Here we are, after travelling thro the Austrian Netherlands, the fines[t], richest and best cultivated Country I ever saw; the farmers and peasants seem quite at their ease; their houses and cottages neater—and better furnished than I ever saw in England—. By coming thro Antwerb (thirty miles out of the direct road) we have just come a hundred miles; and till we came to this Court and Capital—we scarce met a beggar.— The Peoples minds are big with expectation thro the Country;— and they certainly (as who does not but Tories) wish well to France and Liberty.—At Ghent—on Tuesday last—several wounded Austrians were brought in.—and five great detatchments of the Armies—were but four leagues from us;—and skirmishes every hour—and we are told here (and from the best authority) that the french behave with great spirit—. Vive la loi—et la

---

[16] Whether this was done or not remains unknown. As indicated *ante* (From Forbes to Barnard, 19 Apr. 1792, n. 2), JB's papers at Yale contain neither original nor copy, but Forbes's copy survives.

---

[1] Courtenay was on the Continent in the autumn of 1792, returning to London by 9 Oct. (To Alexander Boswell, 12 Oct. 1792; *ante* From Langton, 11 June 1792, n. 8). His references to the position of the French armies suggest a Sept. date, for by that month, the German armies were retreating, "and a consequent attack upon Flanders, under the auspices of General Dumouriez, gave a new direction to the revolutionary current of France; from being invaded, [she] became the invader. She not only pushed to the Rhine, but, crossing that river, made various conquests in Germany" (*Annual Register 1792*, Otridge, 1799, p. 109). Ghent finally fell to the French on 12 Nov., Brussels on the 14th (*ibid.* p. 117). Courtenay apparently was travelling south to Paris. Were this letter sent later than Sept., he probably would have written *Vive la loi—et la république*, since France was declared a republic on 21 Sept.

nation; I wish You were here—you should drink it in burgundy Every day.—

I beg my Dear Boswell—that You will call on Faulder the bookseller[2]—he has commenced an Action against me on two notes—and his Attorney has made some progress this term;— One of these notes shall be very soon paid;—as Mr. Sharp[3] has now a bond in his hands—on which I hope we shall soon raise money to Answer—these demands;—but the law expences double the debt—and are intolerable—. If possible, on these assurances (which you can speak to from your own knowlege) prevail on him to stop proceedings—. I'll write to you Again—when there is any thing worth mentioning—. In the mean time—Believe me Ever Most faithfully and Affectionately Yours

J. COURTENAY

To Lord Eliot, before Friday 7 September 1792

Not reported. Sent from St. Gluvias. Referred to in next letter.

From Lord Eliot, Friday 7 September 1792

MS. Yale (C 1192).

ADDRESS: To James Boswell Esqre., St. Gluvias, Penryn, Cornwal.

FRANK: St. Germans, September the Seventh 1792, Craggs Free Eliot.

POSTMARK: ST GERMANS.

Port Eliot, Sept. 7 1792

MY DEAR SIR: I must write in a hurry or I shall lose this post.

Your Letter is just come to my hands—It would have got to London sooner.

I shall be very happy to see you, and your friend Mr. Temple

---

[2] Robert Faulder, who had a place in New Bond Street. He published JB's *No Abolition of Slavery*. Since he did not publish any of Courtenay's writings, his action was undoubtedly to recover loans he had made to Courtenay. I can find no record of the loan or of Faulder's legal action.

[3] Probably Richard ("Conversation") Sharp (1759–1835), whom JB knew fairly well. Like Courtenay, Sharp was a radical Whig.

here on[1] Wednesday next the 12th instant.[2] I have the honor to be, My Dear Sir, your very faithful humble Servant

CRAGGS ELIOT

James Boswell Esqre.

From William Windham, Friday 26 October 1792[1]

MS. Yale (C 3136).

ADDRESS: James Boswell Esqr., Portland street.

[London] Friday Eveng. 26th.

DEAR BOSWELL: There is a scene in life, to which amidst all your researches, I doubt if you have ever been witness, and which merits nevertheless all the attention, that a Philosophick observer can bestow. It will be a sad scandal, if an attender on executions, and an explorer of Wapping[2] should never have been present at a

---

[1] "Tuesday next the Eleventh" deleted.

[2] JB and Temple did not arrive at Port Eliot until Saturday, 15 Sept. JB was "struck" with the appearance of the mansion and pleased with the cordial reception of Lord and Lady Eliot: "Good service—Good dinner of two courses and desert — Madeira — hock — Sherry 27 years old port—Claret—and always after dinner a bottle of Champagne and also Canary. Excellent Cyder and admirable Beer—the Wheat the malt and the brewing all *home*. His Lordship pleasantly and kindly said this was the first time a *Laird of Auchinleck* had been at Port Eliot, and he drank *Auchinleck* as a Cornish Baron drinking to a Scottish Baron. . . . I warmed myself well with wine; but was unreasonably displeased that neither My Lord nor his son were *jolly* as the phrase is; that is encouraged a brisk circulation of the bottle, which in many houses is required as a test of hospitable reception" (Journ.). The two friends were still at Port Eliot on the 16th, when JB consumed considerably more liquor and Temple apparently berated him for his excessive thirst, but JB did

not record the date of their departure. JB and his daughters were at Bickham, near Plymouth, on 21 Sept.

---

[1] Date determined by references in *Life* iv. 201 n. 1, and in Windham's *Diary*, p. 265.

[2] A section of east London on the north bank of the Thames chiefly inhabited by seafaring men and tradesmen. Seamen were hanged at Execution Dock, below Wapping New Stairs, as late as the close of the eighteenth century. SJ had recommended to JB and Windham that they "*explore Wapping*, which we resolved to do. We accordingly carried our scheme into execution, in October, 1792" (*Life* iv. 201 and n. 1). Windham was, as this letter suggests, an unenthusiastic companion: in his diary for 23 Oct. (an error for the 27th, since the fight was held on the latter date), he complained, "I let myself foolishly be drawn by Boswell to explore, as he called it, Wapping, instead of going when everything was prepared, to see the battle between Ward and Stanyard, which turned out a very good one, and which

boxing match. Information has just been brought to me, that a contest of that sort will take place tomorrow, between two heroes, —one of them of great fame in the annals of pugilism,—at about 12 or 14 miles from London.[3] Instead of going to Wapping suppose we go thither. My nephew[4] if He is at liberty will be delighted with the scheme; and we shall be back in London by 4 o'clock. Though I am a great admirer and approver of these things, my ardour is so far abated.—as what does not time take away? That without an eager or an intelligent companion, I shall hardly attend on the occasion. It is sufficient indeed for me in general, that such things take place, whether I have the satisfaction of seeing them or not. I am quite persuaded of their salutary influence on the manners of the Common people; particularly for the purpose of rendering them more *liberal* and *humane*: and keeping at a distance, that rancorous spirit, and thirst for blood, that we see rage with such violence among our neighbours.[5] Depend upon it, that the manly and honourable spirit of our common people, is in a great measure produced by, as it has produced, the practice of such kind of contests. It is only the vulgar and the Short sighted who imagine, that these contests render the people ferocious.—If you have a mind to go, come[6] breakfast here tomorrow at nine or a little after.[7]—Yours truly

W. Windham

would have served as a very good introduction to Boswell" (Windham's *Diary*, p. 265).

[3] "The battle between Stanyard and Ward took place at Langley Broom, on Saturday, upon a stage erected for that purpose, when, after a hard contest of twenty minutes duration, victory declared in favour of Ward. The immediate cause of this was his breaking the jawbone of his antagonist, who, till then, had exhibited much bottom; nor was he deficient in skill and manoeuvre, till he had been put off his guard by the address of Ward's second. Johnson, who backed Stanyard, was the principal loser. The Birmingham men were not less disappointed, having formed the most sanguine expectations upon Stanyard. . . . Nearly all the amateurs attended" (*London Chronicle*, 27–30 Oct. 1792, lxxii. 412). Windham attended numerous prize-fights (see *Diary, passim*).

[4] Robert Lukin (b. c. 1772), third son of the Rev. George William Lukin and Mrs. Lukin, demy of Magdalen College, Oxford. He had been at Felbrigg earlier in the autumn (*Alum. Oxon.* II. iii. 881; Windham's *Diary*, pp. 260, 261, 262, 264).

[5] Windham refers to the September massacres.

[6] Not clear. Possibly "come" written over "eat".

[7] Neither JB nor Windham records this breakfast.

From Thomas Barnard, Sunday 9 December 1792

MS. Yale (C 98).

ADDRESS: James Boswell Esqr., No. 47 Great Portland Street, London.

POSTMARKS: LEIXLIP, DE 10, DE 14 92.

St. Wolstans, Decr. 9th 1792

MY DEAR SIR: I hope you will think this Letter well worth the Postage, when it is to acquaint you that I have fortunately recover'd that Letter of Gen. Paolis to you, *Quem non Fœcundi Calices Fecere Disertum*,[1] which you were so desirous to repossess, and which I had mislaid for several years Past. It now waits your orders. But I will not enclose it in This, lest it should Miscarry, as I am not perfectly Sure of your Present address; and [it] were a Thousand Pities that so Valuable a Document of that, *Mixtum cum gravitate Lepos*[2] which so well became your Departed Freind should be Lost.

I have another motive for Detaining it, Because I am pretty sure it will *extort* from you a Letter; and I want to Know How and about you (as we Irish happily Express it). I shall, therefore, now Expect to receive your Commands in a Few days. And, as you write a very Extensive Hand I request you to take a sheet of Folio Paper, and when it is Fill'd with an account of Your Self, and our Mutual Freinds; and all the Political Intelligence you can send me at this most Interesting Crisis;[3] *Scriptus et in Tergo*[4] Seal and Commit it to the Bellmans Care and it will be most graciously Receiv'd.

In Return you shall have your Precious Letter of Paolis; Enveloped in the History of our Politicks which at this moment are

---

[1] Horace, *Epistles* I. v. 19: "whom have not abundant cups made fluent", here introduced ironically. Paoli's letter on water-drinking has apparently been lost.

[2] "Union of charm and dignity", paraphrasing Cicero's "gravitate mixtus lepos" in *De re publica* II. 1. The solecism in "mixtum" is surprising in Barnard.

[3] France had threatened to invade Holland, which had entered into an alliance with England in 1788. England promised to live up to the treaty should

Holland's neutrality be violated. Although England made attempts to forestall hostilities, it was felt that war with France was inevitable, and military preparations were made. The militia had been called out on 1 Dec., partly to prevent subversion within the country by the numerous democratic societies; and the meeting of Parliament had been moved up to 13 Dec.

[4] Juvenal, *Satires* i. 6: "written even on the back".

not Less Interesting than your own. Three Millions of Irish Catholicks demand the Right of Voting at Elections as well as other Dissenters. A Convention of 2 Delegates from every County are now sitting in Dublin.[5] Five *new* Irish ambassadors are just ready to Sail with their address to the King on that Subject.[6] The Republicans have offer'd to join them to Enforce their Demands; and the Protestant Landed Interest of the whole Kingdom have almost unanimously Declared at their County Meetings their Resolution to oppose them. Government in the mean Time seem to stand Neuter, and profess not to Interfere in so great a National Question; Two Regiments are already raised and Clothed by the Party, and (in Imitation of the French) call'd National Guards. They were to have made their first appearance in arms this Day[7] (if the Weather had permitted), and the Commanding officer of the Garrison had declared his Resolution to attack them if they did, and make them Lay down their arms. But there is a Whisper abroad that they have some private assurances from the Common Soldiers that they will not fire upon them. All Dublin is in a Ferment; at this Period, Some in hope some in Fear, all anxiously waiting for the Result of these Formidable preparations; *Now sits Expectation in the air*.[8] And so must yours do for some time Longer, for I will not Wait for tomorrow to tell it you. For my own Part I feel Bold when I think that the Constitution in Church and State is supported by all the Respectability in the Kingdom. The Motley Herd that threaten it, composed of Dissenters of all Kinds, atheists and Libertines Included, with that Dog Paine at the Bottom of the Conspiracy, puts me in

[5] Earlier in the year, the Catholic Committee sent out a circular letter "inviting the Catholics in every parish in Ireland to choose electors, who, in their turn, were in every county to choose delegates to the Catholic Committee in Dublin in order to assist in procuring 'the elective franchise, and an equal participation in the benefits of trial by jury'" (Lecky, *Ireland* iii. 63–64). The convention was violently opposed by Protestant organizations, partly because of the actual or imagined connexions of the Catholic leaders with the French Revolution. The meetings began on 3 Dec.

[6] The Catholic Convention, having determined to petition the King directly about their grievances, sent five delegates to London, where the King received them graciously. The English Government informed them that England was in favour of a relief bill, but no exact measures were specified.

[7] The leading members (Tandy and Rowan) of the new National Guards invited all Volunteer companies in Dublin to meet on 9 Dec. to celebrate the triumph of liberty in France. The meeting was prevented by a proclamation issued on 8 Dec. forbidding all seditious assemblies and ordering magistrates to subdue them, if necessary, by force.

[8] *Henry the Fifth* II. Prologue. 8.

mind of Virgils Description of Caesars and of Anthonys party at Actium.[9] On one side Augustus,

> Cum Patribus *Populo*que,[10] penatibus et Magnis Dis.
> Hinc ope Barbaricâ Variisque Antonius Armis; etc.
> omnigenumque Deum Monstra, et *Latrator* anubis.
> Contra Neptunem etc.
> gaudens Vadit Discordia Palla
> Quam cum Sanguinio Sequitur Bellona Flagello;

Under which, that they may all Smart, God of his mercy grant if they proceed much Farther. Not the Catholicks, (for I really think they ask No more than we may Safely grant them.) But those Rascally Republicans; who pretend Reform, but mean destruction. Who from the beginning of the american War have join'd with the Enemies of their Country to Blast its Councils, and Counteract its arms, who have Croak'd like Illomen'd Birds over its Successes and rejoiced at its Defeats, and now when it has risen to prosperity in spite of All their efforts to Keep it down, Like Envy in Ovid, *Vix retinent Lachrymas quia Nil Lachrymabile Cernunt.*[11]

And so I think our Freinds Late of Duchess street have escaped out of that genteel Neighbourhood, and have bought our old Dwelling in Berkely Square[12] of which they are to make a good House by adding a great Room and a second Stair Case. But what is to become of their Evening Parties for the Ensuing winter. I have no more Room but to assure you that I am most Faithfully and Sincerely yours

THOS. KILLALOE

[9] *Aeneid* viii. 679–703. Barnard quotes only lines 679, 685, 698–99, 702–03: "With peers and people, and the great gods of the Penates./Here, Antonius with barbaric might and varied arms;/Monstrous gods of every form and barking Anubis/Wield weapons against Neptune and Venus and against Minerva/ ... and in rent robe Discord strides exultant,/While Bellona follows her with bloody scourge" (H. R. Fairclough's translation in Loeb ed.).

[10] Barnard has underlined "*Populo*"

and inserted "Not the Mob" above the line.

[11] "They scarce restrain their tears because they see nothing to weep at", an adaptation of Ovid's description of Envy, *Metamorphoses* ii. 796.

[12] According to Dorothea Fairbridge (*Lady Anne Barnard at the Cape of Good Hope*, 1924, p. 4), Lady Anne bought the house in Berkeley Square "for the reason that it commanded a 'squinting view' of Windham's house, and that she could see him going in and out of his door".

Pray is Lady Inchiquin[13] Breeding? It is rumour'd here that she is! Remember me to our Worthy President, Mr. Secretary. *Direct to Me in Dublin.*

From William Windham, Saturday 18 May 1793

MS. Yale (C 3137).

ADDRESS: James Boswell Esqr., Portland Street.

ENDORSEMENT: May 18. 1793, Right Hon. William Windham a handsome apology for not dining with me.

[London] Saturday morng.

MY DEAR SIR: I am not more ashamed than sorry, at being obliged to make my excuses for not dining with you to day. On your principles[1] it might not be a bad Apology, that I am to dine with a Lord.[2] But my Aristocracy does not go that length.—I should prefer the Commoners dinner,[3] and had counted upon it with great satisfaction: but on examining my engagements I found that there was one for to day, which I had wholly overlooked, and overlooked partly from a cause, which makes it less capable of being set aside, namely, that it is of very long standing. I must submit to fate; and beg you only not to add to my losses, your reproaches for my not discovering this mistake earlier. Yours truly

W. WINDHAM

[13] Mary Palmer, Sir Joshua Reynolds's niece, who was married on 25 July 1792 at the home of her trustee, Edmund Burke, to Murrough O'Brien, Earl of Inchiquin. He was later (1800) Marquess of Thomond and (1801) Baron Thomond of Taplow. She died without issue on 6 Sept. 1820, in her seventieth year (*Comp. Peer.* xii. pt. 1. 714–15).

[1] Windham is probably alluding to JB's avowal in the *Life of Johnson* (i. 442–43): "I said, I considered distinction of rank to be of so much importance in civilised society, that if I were asked on the same day to dine with the first Duke in England, and with the first man in Britain for genius, I should hesitate which to prefer."

[2] There is no entry between 16 and 20 May 1793 in Windham's published diary. He dined with a number of peers at Lord Spencer's on the 16th (Windham's *Diary*, pp. 275–76).

[3] Malone was also invited to JB's dinner. JB comprehended the other members of the party under the general designation "good men and true" (To Malone, 17 May).

To Bennet Langton, Monday 15 July 1793

MS. Yale (*L 849.8).

ADDRESS: To Major Langton of the Lincolnshire Militia, Warley Camp.[1]

POSTMARK: CHELMSFORD.

Note by Langton on side 4 (see *post* n. 8): *Men* for furlough.

Chelmsford, Monday 15 July 1793

MY DEAR SIR: I came here last Wednesday to attend the Circuit. On friday I went to General Sir John Dalling's[2] at Danbury Place about five miles off, and have sojourned there till today, when I am returned to attend the Sessions, which begin tomorrow morning. They will finish on Wednesday; so that either that night, or early on thursday morning, I can pay my respects to you at Warley Camp. Pray write me a line directed at Mr. Stanes's, Bookseller[3] here; to tell me when it will be best to come. I wish to see what is to be seen. If therefore, there be any thing particular at night, I can come on Wednesday take a bed at Brentwood,[4] and be with you again early next morning, and after having fully felt *Castrajuvant*[5] (on a peaceful common) proceed to TOWN in the evening to prepare for my Tour to *Valenciennes*[6] *another*

---

[1] Langton had been commissioned a major on 5 Feb. 1791 (letter from A. S. White, Librarian, The War Office Library, London, 21 Dec. 1953).

[2] Dalling (c. 1731–98), then a lieutenant-general, was created baronet 11 Mar. 1783. From 1777 to 1782, he was Governor of Jamaica; from 7 Dec. 1784 to 11 Apr. 1786, Commander in Chief in Madras. He was promoted to general on 3 May 1796 (*Comp. Bar.* v. 231).

[3] William Stanes was also a bookbinder and agent to the Royal Exchange Assurance Office (*Universal British Directory*, 1791, ii. 516). JB first stayed with him in July 1786, when attending the Chelmsford Assizes (Journ. 26 July). Stanes brought JB a client in July 1787 (Journ. 12 July), and in the fall of 1791 bound two sets of the *Life* for him (From Stanes, 7 Nov. 1791).

[4] A town four miles north of Warley.

[5] Horace, *Odes* I. i. 23: "Multos castra juvant": "Many delight in the camp."

[6] JB had originally planned to go "abroad on a tour to Holland and Flanders and to pass some time with the combined armies" (British and Austrian allies who were besieging Condé and Valenciennes) in June 1793 (To Andrew Gibb, 31 May 1793), but the trip was prevented by an accident. Coming home drunk on the night of 5 June, he was attacked by a footpad, robbed, and knocked down. He received a severe cut on the back of his head and a contusion on both arms. See *London Chronicle*, 8–11 June 1793, lxxiii. 557. By 21 June he was feeling "pretty well", and wrote to Temple that the continental trip was to hold. See *post* To Langton, 24 July 1793.

guess matter.[7] I ever am, My Dear Cavalier, yours most cordially

JAMES BOSWELL

Observe that I write in the *form* of your Tutor Tom Warton.[8]

From Bennet Langton, Tuesday 16 July 1793

MS. Yale (C 1696).

ADDRESS: James Boswell Esqr., at Mr. Stanes's, Bookseller, Chelmsford, Essex.

POSTMARK: BRENTWOOD.

Warley Camp, July 16th. 1793

MY DEAR SIR, I am just favoured with your Letter, and propose to send my Answer to it of course by the return of the Post, but have some apprehensions whether that will answer for the being in time; I observe indeed that *your* date is of yesterday, but have some doubt whether a Letter will get down to Chelmsford quite so quick, as yours has done the opposite way; however it is all I can do; but why would you not write a Line a post or two sooner, from Sir John Dallings; and then all might have been *certainly* effected—either to morrow afternoon, or Thursday morning we shall be happy in seeing you here—As to accommodation, you can, if you have no objection, sleep in Camp—in the Tent of one of our Lieutenants of Grenadiers—who is no other than my Son[1]—He will be much mortified at being absent when you favour us with your Company—but it is the turn of our Regiment

---

[7] That is, quite another affair. See OED, Guess, *sb.* 3.

[8] "The word 'form' seems to refer to the unusual arrangement of the written text. The letter begins on the third page of an ordinary sheet of writing paper, once folded. When this page was filled, Boswell turned the sheet and wrote across the opposite, or left-hand page, so that the writing on one page is perpendicular to that on the other" (C. B. Tinker in *Letters JB* ii. 448 n. 5). *Ante* from T. Warton, 15 Apr. 1786, shows the same arrangement.

[1] George Langton was commissioned a lieutenant in the Royal North Lincoln Militia on 18 Sept. 1792 (letter from A. S. White, Librarian, The War Office, London, 21 Dec. 1953). He was promoted to captain in Apr. 1794 (Lindsey County Council, carton labelled "Militia No. 1. From 1750 to 1833").

to furnish a Detachment for guarding the Powder Magazines at Purfleet—and he is one of the Officers that is gone with it—I have ordered Sheets to be spread out for you in the hot Sun, and hope you may find things convenient—Not a word do you say about the *Life*: the last thing you told me in London, was that you would come to our Camp, and bring it with you—As I was writing the above, the Marquis's[2] Aid de Camp, Captain Gardner,[3] came to my Tent, to let me know that his Lordship was come to see me. I went out to him, and we stood and chatted a little while, chiefly, a vôtre Sujet, on my mentioning our expecting here the satisfaction of your company—But, to resume the *Life*; what can be the meaning of this delay? You must prepare, you see, to give me an account of it, but I do not think you can give a good one—But I must not close, without giving you some Latin, in return for your quoting Horace, as I should be ashamed to be outdone, with reference to that practice, of Scraps of Greek and Latin—therefore, I think I will warn you, that you do not suffer yourself to be seduced by the good Fellowship that is going on here, till you are in the condition of him who is represented as talking to his feet, in the following Distich—

Sta, Pes! sta, mi Pes! sta, Pes! ne labere, mi Pes!
Ni steteris, lapides hi mihi lectus erunt![4]

[2] George, first Marquess Townshend (1724–1807), a general in the Army from 1782, was General on Staff, Eastern District, from 1793 to 1796 (letter from A. S. White, 21 Dec. 1953). He was Lord Lieutenant when JB visited Ireland in 1769. "The congeniality of their dispositions united them in the most pleasant manner" ("Memoirs of James Boswell, Esq.", *European Magazine* xix. 404: *Lit. Car.* p. xxxvii).

[3] Documents in the Public Record Office and in the War Office Library do not list a Captain Gardner as aide-de-camp to Lord Townshend. The adjutant of the North Lincolnshire Militia in 1793, however, was a Richard Gardiner.

[4] Langton's distich is a version of one attributed to the Dutch scholar Daniel Heinsius (1580–1655), who is said to have exclaimed as he reeled up a stone staircase,

Sta pes, sta bone pes; sta pes, ne labere, mî pes;
Sta pes, aut lapides hi mihi lectus erunt.

J. S. Watson, who translates, "Stand, stand, my trusty feet; firm be your tread; Stand firm, or else these stones must be my bed", applies the anecdote and the lines to Richard Porson (1759–1808), the learned but intemperate Regius Professor of Greek at Cambridge (*The Life of Richard Porson, M.A.*, 1861, p. 282). One wonders whether Langton might not earlier have associated the lines with Porson—perhaps even heard Porson apply them to himself. Langton knew Porson well: "Porson frequently spent his evenings with the present venerable Dean of Westminster [William Vincent], with Dr. Wingfield, with the late Bennet Langton, and with another friend. . . . The above individuals being

They are characteristical, you see, of the supposed condition of the Person—Garrick, poor fellow, would have spoken them, with an effect, as I conceive, equal to any of his comick touches—Adieu! believe me, my dear Boswell, to be most affectionately and regardfully Yours

BENNET LANGTON

To Bennet Langton, Wednesday 24 July 1793

MS. Hyde Collection.

ADDRESS: To Major Bennet Langton, of the Royal North Lincolnshire Militia, Warley Camp, Essex.

POSTMARK: JY C24 93.

Note on address side in Langton's hand: Vol. 2 P. 216—sententiarum gravitate quique venerabilem.[1]

London, 24 July 1793

MY DEAR SIR: Tomorrow's (friday's) Chelmsford Coach will bring for you two copies of my second edition of Dr. Johnson's *Life*,[2] which are directed for you to be left at the White Hart Brentwood. I beseech you to correct a strange *erratum* on the last page but one of the Additions prefixed to Vol. I: for *without* much regret read *with* etc.[3]

all of them very regular in their hours, used to give him to understand, that he was not to stay after eleven o'clock, with the exception of Bennet Langton, who suffered him to remain till twelve; corrupted in this instance perhaps, by Dr. Johnson" (William Beloe, *The Sexagenarian*, 1817, i. 228).

[1] Langton here notes two errors in the Latin of SJ's Oxford D.C.L. diploma as printed in the *Life*, 2nd ed., ii. 216–17. Line 5 of the first paragraph has incorrectly *sententiarum gravitatis*, which Langton corrects to *gravitate*. Line 8 of the first paragraph has incorrectly *quique venerabilem Magistrorum Ordinem* for *quique in venerabilem*, etc. (The scribe who engrossed the diploma had omitted *in* and added it in smaller letters above the line.) Langton in this case copied the Latin as it stood, perhaps not being certain of the emendation. The first edition had correctly *gravitate* but also omitted *in*. (The original diploma, and a copy from the Register, found among JB's papers, were presented by Colonel Isham to the Bodleian Library.) This error seems not to have been corrected until the Hill-Powell edition.

[2] *The Life of Samuel Johnson, LL.D.*, by James Boswell, Esq., The Second Edition, Revised and Augmented, 3 vols., 1793.

[3] "I cannot help mentioning without much regret, that by my own negligence I lost an opportunity of having the

I was sorry to leave you sooner than you kindly wished. But it was really necessary for me to be in town; and, as I candidly owned to you, I had enough of a Camp. In my convalescent state, another disturbed night would have hurt me much.

O London! London! there let me be; there let me see my friends; there a fair chance is given for pleasing and being pleased.

I beg you may present my best respects to the Gentlemen of your Regiment, whose civilities to me I never shall forget; and if your son be with you give my kind compliments to him. Above 400 of the new Johnsonian Volumes are already sold. WONDERFUL MAN!

I hesitate as to Valenciennes;[4] though I should only *survey* a camp there. Yet my curiosity is ardent.—In all places I ever am, My Dear Sir, yours most sincerely

JAMES BOSWELL

From Bennet Langton,
c. Tuesday 30 July 1793[1]

MS. Yale (C 1697).

HEADING in JB's hand: Bennet Langton Esq. from Warley Camp 1793.

[Warley Camp]

Accept, my dear Sir, of my best thanks for your welcome present; it is unnecessary to attempt explaining to you *how* welcome it must be, to me to dwell on the Scenes of the Life of a Man, whom I so much honoured by whom I was so kindly regarded, Scenes in which I had so frequent a share, and in the accounts of which the mention of course is introduced of a Set of men eminent for

history of my family from its founder Thomas Boswell, in 1504, recorded and illustrated by Johnson's pen" (*Life*, 2nd ed., i. xxi).

[4] JB was still in doubt on 31 July, when he wrote his sons, "I still hesitate a little about my expedition to the Combined Armies; but I cannot quiet my curiosity; and as I this moment have received the news that Valenciennes has surrendered, I shall see a happy and victorious Body of Troops. I therefore

believe I shall set out next week." But he still wavered; and when on 22 Aug. he heard that his "Chief's" younger son, Col. Thomas Bosville, had been killed in Flanders, he felt his *"military ardour . . . quite extinguished"*, and "resolved not to go to the Continent this year" (Journ.).

─────────

[1] JB sent copies of the second edition of the *Life* on the 25th (see the letter preceding this). The suggested dating

their abilities, with most of whom I was in a state of intimacy, and with some of particular friendship—I have been of course rivetted to the perusal and re-perusal of the Volumes by night and by day since their arrival—a few mornings ago, it happened that the thundering Morning Gun, which you were in such a state of fearful preparation for, surprized me not yet gone to bed, and if I was not at the moment reading your book, it had at least been accessary to my sitting up so late—One thing, my dear Sir, occurs to me as I am writing, as a subject of regret, which is that I have never found an opportunity of requesting you to allow me the perusal of the Letters of thanks and praise of your Work that you have had the satisfaction of receiving, particularly the Letter you received from such a Man as Dr. Parr[2]—it must have been a high delight to me to see feelings and opinions so corresponding with my own so much better expressed, as they would of course be by him, and perhaps by many others of those who have writ to you (than I could presume to suppose my having the power of doing)—

Now that I have given some vent to expressions, of admiration on this reperusal of your Work, and of the delight it has given me—let me take up an opposite task—that of pointing out some mistakes—wherein I am naturally led to one, that is in front of those communications of mine that you have judged proper to make use of, and which communications unluckily stand forward and prominent, as being premised to the mass of the work[3] and therefore should, you will allow me, be more than commonly correct, as well as good in their kind—I do not know whether it may not be the best way of managing what I have to say, to tell you, that, on my being desired to lend the book, which I think need not be objected to in instances where it does not particularly appear that a copy of it would otherwise be purchased, (I speak

assumes that five days would have sufficed for the perusal, seeing that he read the book "by night and by day" and was already familiar with the first edition.

[2] Parr praised the *Life* in two letters to JB: in the first, written 11 Dec. 1791 (collection of F. W. Hilles), he gave "hearty" and "full" applause to JB's work; in the second, [25] Dec., he wrote, "As to the composition of the book I upon the whole think it very good, and so good as to justify you in making it better for a future edition."

[3] Langton's contributions referred to here are on pp. *x–*xiii of vol. i of the second edition, and are introduced by the following heading: "From Mr. Langton I have the following additional Particulars." As a result of this letter JB printed an extra page (*xxxviii) headed "Additional Corrections", not found in copies already distributed (*Lit. Car.* pp. 158–59).

of the unfairness it would be in me to lend a book that you had presented me with, unless the circumstances were as I have said that there seemed not to be an intention of purchasing it—and *then* I think it may contribute in no small degree, by diffusing its reputation to increase the chance of its being purchased, if occasions are taken of *so* lending it)—on lending the book, I drew up a corrected form of two passages, which I laid between the leaves,[4] as not chusing that my poor contributions should go out with their imperfections on their heads—and this paper which I put into the book I will transcribe, and shall be glad to receive word of what occurs to you on the matter—the following is the Copy of it—

"The Communication from Mr. Langton in Page Xth of the Additions to Dr. Johnson's *Life* premised to the first Volume, by some accident is very much mis-stated—it should have been to the following effect:

"On occasion of Dr. Johnson's publishing his Pamphlet of *The False Alarm*[5] there came out a very angry answer (by many supposed to be by Mr. Wilkes). Dr. Johnson determined on not answering it, but, in conversation with Mr. Langton mentioned a particular or two, that, if he *had* replied to it, he might perhaps have inserted—In the Answerer's Pamphlet, it had been said with solemnity 'Do you consider, Sir, that a House of Commons is to the People as a Creature is to its Creator?' 'To this Question,' said Dr. Johnson, 'I could have replied, that, in the first place, the idea of a Creator,[6] and so on, as it is in the printed book, down to

[4] This very sheet, or a duplicate of it in Langton's hand, measuring $6\frac{1}{16}$ by $7\frac{3}{16}$ inches, folded in half parallel to the longer side and written on the first three pages thus formed, is in the collection of F. W. Hilles. It is endorsed on the fourth page in an unidentified hand, "from the Revd. J. W. Morgan of Colchester." John W. Morgan, rector of St. Giles's, Colchester, from 1818 until his death in 1857, was son of John Morgan of Chelmsford with whom Jamie Boswell stayed for two weeks in Aug. 1792 (*Alum. Oxon.* II. iii. 981; From Jamie, 21 Aug. 1792; From J. Morgan, 3 Sept. 1792). The copy with the inserted leaf was presumably lent at some time or other to John Morgan, who failed at least to return the corrections. His son (if one may continue the speculation) was later persuaded to turn the leaf over to a collector of autographs.

[5] It was published in 1770.

[6] JB's original text reads merely: "'Talking reverently of the SUPREME BEING, he uttered these sentences:

'Do you consider, Sir?

'In the first place—the idea of a CREATOR must be such as that he has power to unmake or annihilate his creature.

'Then it cannot be conceived that a creature can make laws for its CREATOR.'" Langton's correction was printed in JB's "Additional Corrections" (*ante* n. 3).

the figure, '3,' that refers to the Note[7] in all which latter part the statement given by Mr. Boswell is correct—

"The Remark then, was not a general one, which it surely would have been unnecessary for Johnson to make, as containing only such very evident truth; but its excellence was in its particular application to what his Opponent had said.

"In Page XIII of the Additions, there is a confusion in the statement of the Remark on the Shield of Achilles[8] which will be disentangled if we read it as follows, and as it should have been given—

"'He may hold up that Shield against all his enemies,' was an observation on Homer, in reference to his description of the Shield of Achilles, made by Mrs. Fitzherbert, Wife to Mr. Fitzherbert of Derbyshire[9] and respected by Dr. Johnson as a very fine one—'He had in general' etc. as in the book."

I trust then, my dear Sir, that you will see the necessity there is for explaining and correcting the Passages I have been noticing —a few more mistakes I have marked—which I will enumerate— "Bender," Vol. 2d. P. 37,[10] should I have no doubt be, "Belgrade"—Oglethorpe served against the Turks under Prince Eugene—and I am almost certain that He never besieged Bender— Apothegm,[11] surely should be spelt Apophthegm—The Greek word Vol. 3d. P. 360—is wrong printed—ευσροποι—which should be ευστροφοι[12]—In Vol. 3d. P. 582, It is said that Mr. Burke

[7] The note reads as follows: "His profound adoration of the GREAT FIRST CAUSE was such as to set him above that 'Philosophy and vain deceit,' with which men of narrower conceptions have been infected. I have heard him strongly maintain that 'what is right is not so from any natural fitness, but because GOD wills it to be right;' and it is certainly so, because he has predisposed the relations of things so as that which he wills must be right. BOSWELL."

[8] "'He may hold up that SHIELD against all his enemies;'—was an observation by him on Homer, when referring to the description of the shield of Achilles, made by Mrs. Fitzherbert, wife to his friend Mr. Fitzherbert of Derbyshire, and respected by Dr. Johnson as a very fine one. He had in general a very high opinion of that lady's understanding." JB printed Langton's correction in his "Additional Corrections".

[9] William Fitzherbert of Tissington, Derbyshire (1712–72), was a Fellow of the Royal Society and Vice-President of the Society of Antiquaries. His wife, the former Judith Alleyne, died 12 Mar. 1753 in childbed at the age of 31, "in the flower of her age, distinguished for her piety and fine accomplishments" (Gent. Mag. 1753, xxiii. 148). Fitzherbert hanged himself in 1772 (Johns. Glean. vi. 169). See Life iii. 148–49; iv. 33.

[10] "Dr. Johnson said, 'Pray, General, give us an account of the siege of Bender.'" Cf. Life ii. 181 and n. 1. Corrected in "Additional Corrections".

[11] ii. 221. It was changed in the third and later editions (cf. Life ii. 348).

[12] Imperfectly corrected in "Additional Corrections", the tau being omitted. Cf. Life iv. 105 n. 4.

stood forth in defence of his Friend, which perhaps might be the case, but the Person that I heard Johnson speak of as his defender on that occasion was Mr. Fox, as I particularly well remember; perhaps Mr. Burke might also have come forwards[13]—*Vol. 1st.* *525*—You say Mr. Gibbon was chosen Professor of ancient Literature in the Academy—having previously said that *that* was *my* Professorship,—Mr. Gibbon's is—of ancient *History.*[14] Vol. 3d. P. 269—The errour continues—of saying "it is well known that the Trial of Lord Charles Hay[15] never came on"—The Trial did come on, and was carried through—and, at the Time of Lord Charles's death—the Sentence was probably according to the usual forms before the King for his consideration. In Vol. 2d. P. 274 The expression as you give it from Johnson's Journal "little more than half as much for"[16] (In this erased part I had not at first taken the import right, but, on a re-attention, my difficulty disappears)—Vol. 2d. P. 284—"*Frenon,*" the Journalist, I am pretty sure should be *Freron*[17]—These I think are all the

[13] The passage referred to relates how Burke defended in Parliament the granting of SJ's pension in recognition of his literary merit. JB let it stand, but Langton was correct (*Life* iv. 318 n. 3).

[14] Corrected in "Additional Corrections" (*Life* ii. 67 n. 1).

[15] After a distinguished army career, Lord Charles Hay (d. 1760), a major-general, was sent to Halifax in Nova Scotia under General Hopson to join the expedition under the Earl of Loudoun preparing to attack the French. Loudoun's inaction caused Hay to say, it was charged, that "the general was keeping the courage of his majesty's troops at bay, and expending the nation's wealth in making sham sieges and planting cabbages when he ought to have been fighting." Hay was arrested, sent back to England, and tried before a court martial 12 Feb. to 4 Mar. 1760. At Hay's request, Langton introduced SJ to him. Decision on the case was not made public, it being referred to the King, and Hay died (1 May) before the King could make up his mind. JB had originally written: "It is well known that his Lordship died before the trial came on." In JB's MS. of Johnsoniana dictated by Langton, 17 Dec. 1790, the last five words are underlined and queried—not by JB (Waingrow, p. 373 n.). Langton's "The errour continues" suggests that he is the one who had queried the phrase before it appeared in the first edition. But Langton overlooked JB's correction, the substitution of "sentence was made known" for "trial came on", which appears in the second edition under "Corrections" on p. *xxxv.

[16] Langton has crossed out this partial sentence. All but one word of the phrase he quoted appears on p. 273 and not p. 274. Taken from SJ's French journal, it reads: "We then went to Sans-terre, a brewer. He brews with about as much malt as Mr. Thrale, and sells his beer at the same price, though he pays no duty for malt, and little more than half as much for beer."

[17] In the copies of the second edition I have examined, the name *is* Frenon, although in "Additional Corrections" the reader is directed to change *Frenon* to *Freron*. If Langton is correct, the misprint was probably corrected while the sheet was printing. Élie-Catherine Fréron (1719–76), journalist and literary critic, published *L'Année litteraire* and

Errata I have observed—and have only remaining time to insert my Compliments and my Sons to the Young Ladies and Gentlemen—and those of all the Gentlemen of our Corps to yourself and am, Dear Sir, Your faithful humble servant

B. LANGTON

From Sir William Scott, Saturday 2 November 1793

MS. Yale (C 2445).

ADDRESS: James Boswell Esq., Portland Street, Queen Ann Street.

POSTMARK: PENY POST PAID G TH.

ENDORSEMENT: Sir William Scott (without date but) 2 Novr. 1793.

[London]

DEAR SIR: I am much obliged to you for the Present of your Additions[1]—but it was unnecessary, because I had bought your 8vo Edition;[2] as I cannot do without having the Book in a portable convenient form, fit for a Post-Chaise—*jucundus* comes in *vehiculo*[3]—I hope Malone did not take amiss my deserting Him;[4] there are few Men whom I should be less willing to disoblige. Yours etc. etc.

WM. SCOTT

engaged in numerous quarrels with Voltaire (*La Grande Encyclopédie*, 1886–1902, xviii. 149–50).

[1] *The Principal Corrections and Additions to the First Edition of Mr. Boswell's Life of Johnson*, 1793.

[2] The second edition of the *Life*.

[3] Scott paraphrases a saying of the Roman mime writer, Publilius Syrus (fl. 43 B.C.): "Comes facundus in via pro vehiculo est": "A talkative companion on a journey is as good as a coach." *Jucundus*

means "pleasant" or "agreeable". A version with *jucundus* must have been widely current in the eighteenth century, for JB gives the *sententia* in that form in inscribing to Wilkes a copy of the *Letter to the People of Scotland*, 1785 (BM).

[4] On 30 Oct., JB "Called on Malone. Called also on Sir William Scott, who was to have dined with us, but sent an excuse. I was dejected by contrasting my idle dejected state, with his occupation and prosperity. Only Courtenay and I dined at Malone's" (Journ.).

From Charles Burney,
Wednesday 29 January 1794

MS. Yale (C 707).

ADDRESS: To James Boswell Esqr.

ENDORSEMENT: Dr. Burney 29 Janry. 1794.

Chelsea College, 29 Jany. 1794

Dr. Burney presents his best compliments and thanks to Mr. Boswell for the honour of his enquiries as well as present.[1] Dr. B. has been confined by indisposition, and crippled hand and foot, for near 3 Months; but is now so far recovered that he is able to hold a pen and put on a shoe.[2] Notwithstanding sickness and indifference about most other things, roused by the advertisement of Mr. Boswell's additions to his admirable life of their great friend Johnson,[3] he procured, and greedily perused it, the day it came; and found that it procured him more ease, or at least, diverted attention from self, more than any medicine he had taken. He will however gratefully preserve the gift as a flattering testimony of Mr. Boswell's kind remembrance, and hopes soon to be able not only to thank him *vivâ voce*, but to meet him at *the* Club, at which he is always mortified when not able to attend.

From William Windham,
Friday 31 January 1794

MS. Yale (C 3138).

ADDRESS: James Boswell Esqr., Portland street.

ENDORSEMENT: Right Hon. W. Windham, 31 Janry. 1794.

[1] *The Principal Corrections.*

[2] In the summer of 1793, Burney suffered from "a species of evil which for some time had been hovering over him, and which was as new as it was inimical to his health ... namely, a slow, unfixed, and nervous feverishness, which had infested his whole system. ... This disstressing state lasted, without relief or remittance, till it was suddenly and rudely superseded by a violent assault of acute rheumatism; which drove away all minor or subservient maladies, by the predominance of a torturing pain that nearly nullified everything but itself" (Mme. D'Arblay, *Memoirs of Dr. Burney*, 1832, iii. 175–76).

[3] In *The London Chronicle* for 11 July 1793 (lxxiv. 39) appeared this advertisement: "On Wednesday, July 17, will be published ... The Life of Samuel Johnson, LL. D. ... The Second Edition ... While no pains have been spared to improve this very popular work, the CORRECTIONS and ADDITIONS are printed separately in quarto, for the accommodation of the purchasers of the First Edition" (quoted in *Lit. Car.* p. 168).

[London] Friday 31st.

MY DEAR BOSWELL: Will you dine here on Sunday next to meet Malone, and I hope Sir Willm. Scott etc.?—I am sorry to have sent so late; though I hope not too late.[1] Yours etc.

W. WINDHAM

We will dine as soon as we can.

To Thomas Barnard, Wednesday 19 February 1794

MS. Yale (L 50). A copy.

HEADING: To The Lord Bishop of Killaloe.

London, Great Portland Street, 19 Febry. 1794

MY DEAR LORD: Better late than never.—A common Proverb I trust will serve to procure a favourable reception to my congratulating so long after the time, your Lordship on your son's marriage[1] according to your Lordship's wish, a wish to which with the circumstances concerning it I had the honour of being made a confidant by your Lordship a considerable time ago; and I can say with great truth that a secret could not be better kept. Captain Barnard and Lady Anne were set out for Ireland before I had time to pay my respects to them in person. May I request of your Lordship to act as my proxy in wishing them all happiness. I dined last saturday in company with Mrs. Abington,[2] who gave me the latest intelligence of your Lordship, between whom and her I

[1] The dinner did not take place. On 1 Feb., "Windham called on me, and he and I went to Malone's, Windham having asked us to dine with him next day, and having recollected a prior engagement which made him put it off. . . . I parted with Windham at his own door, feeling my inferiority, when I thought of him as an active Statesman" (Journ.). JB dined at home on Sunday and "was quiet all the evening".

[1] Andrew Barnard married Lady Anne Lindsay at St. George's, Hanover Square, 31 Oct. 1793. Although the Bishop had been astonished at the

engagement, he took over his son's debts and raised his income to £800 (Dorothea Fairbridge, Lady Anne Barnard at the Cape of Good Hope, 1924, p. 10).

[2] Frances Abington (1737–1815), the actress, who last appeared on the stage on 12 Apr. 1799. She was noted for her elegant taste in dress. JB reported, "Mrs. Abington's fame, and elegance and vivacity pleased me much, notwithstanding that she was now past fifty and grown very fat' (Journ. 15 Feb. 1794). In the course of the conversation, she suggested that JB should write the life of Richard Steele.

know there is no love lost.[2a] She retains her elegance of dress and manners, and *gayeté de cœur* wonderfully.

Your Lordship would see in the Newspapers that our Royal Academy resolved on a celebration of its twenty fifth year.[3] We had very long and tedious debates on the subject, for two evenings. The President proposed a splendid plan of an Exhibition of the choicest works of members of the Academy during that quarter of a century. But it was thought both extremely difficult, if not impracticable, and that it might occasion violent animosities, and even be seriously injurious to living artists. At length we agreed (subject to the approbation of his Majesty our Founder and Patron) that we should dine together at our own Apartments at Somerset House;—that a loyal and dutiful Address to the King should be signed by all the members present, and afterwards presented to His Majesty;—That a medal with his Majesty's head on one side and a suitable device on the reverse, with proper inscriptions, should be struck on the occasion, four in gold for the King, Queen, Prince of Wales and Princess Royal; and one in silver for each member of the Academy—the expence of the whole to be defrayed out of the funds of the Academy.[4] His Majesty most graciously approved. We had a most admirable dinner of two courses and a desert, and variety of excellent wines,[5] on 31 Decr. at which were no guests but Cramer, Borghi, Shield etc. who favoured us with Musicks Charms;[6] and the choice spirits staid and partook of a very pretty supper.[7] The Address was signed before dinner. But I must observe that we maintained a becoming decorum, and were joyous without excess. Our medal will be

[2a] "I know there is mutual affection." Down to the nineteenth century the phrase was ambiguous, being capable both of this sense and that now current. See OED, Love, *sb*. 8d.

[3] See *Farington Diary* i. 27–32 for an account of the preparations for the celebration.

[4] JB attended meetings on 3 and 17 Dec. At the last meeting, the Academy decided to hold the commemoration, but rejected West's idea in favour of Joseph Farington's, which JB here describes (Journ.).

[5] "Madeira sherry port and claret, and a glass of Champagne", according to JB's journal (31 Dec. 1793).

[6] Wilhelm Cramer (?1745–99), violinist; Luigi Borghi, violinist; and William Shield (1748–1829), composer, violinist, and conductor. JB, however, was not charmed: "We were in the best convivial frame, and should have enjoyed ourselves to the utmost, had not Mr. West, with good meaning, but injudiciously engaged Cramer, Borghi Shield, in short a number of Musicians both vocal and instrumental, whose performances interrupted the flow of our festivity, and irritated many members" (Journ.).

[7] JB was naturally one of the "choice spirits" who stayed late and saw the New Year in.

finely executed. Your Lordship I am sure will value yours. We regretted much that our Right Reverend Chaplain was not with us. There is now a vacancy of the Professorship in Ancient History, by the death of Mr. Gibbon.[8] Great caution must be used in filling it up respectably. Many of the Academicians, I know will consult with me. I really do not at present think of a proper person. Can your Lordship assist me? Gibbon has left a very curious account of his own life, in which he traces minutely the progress of his mind and studies, and short political history, and intersperses many touches of character. Mr. Malone has read and heard read a good deal of it. Lord Sheffield, who is his Executor, is to publish it.[9] The Bishop of Peterborough and Mr. Gibbon have made two vacancies in the LITERARY CLUB.[10] How they are to be supplied I know not. I doubt not we shall have some *black-balling*.[11]

I need not say a word to your Lordship of publick affairs, except that we really *do* expect an invasion by those detestable desperadoes of France. It is right we should expect it, and be well prepared for it. *Good men and true* talk of it freely, and say *Who's afraid?*[12]

Will your Lordship give me leave to beg the favour of your giving me or procuring for me a letter to Lord Hobart[13] recommending to his Lordships notice a first cousin of mine Mr. George Webster, who has resided several years at Madras, in the employment of the East India Company. He is a son of the late Dr. Alexander Webster[14] a very respectable Clergyman of the

---

[8] Gibbon died on 26 Jan. 1794.

[9] *Miscellaneous Works: with Memoirs of his Life and Writings, composed by himself. Illustrated from his Letters; with occasional Notes and Narrative*, By John Lord Sheffield, 2 vols., 1796.

[10] John Hinchliffe, Bishop of Peterborough, had died on 11 Jan. 1794.

[11] Since only one vacancy was filled within the year, that of Sir Charles Blagden, Secretary of the Royal Society, in Mar., it is probable that other candidates were blackballed. The Club minutes furnish no evidence.

[12] "Good men and true" are presumably Tories. See *ante* From Windham, 18 May 1793, n. 3.

[13] Robert Hobart, styled Lord Hobart, later fourth Earl of Buckinghamshire

(1760–1816), Chief Secretary to the Lord Lieutenant of Ireland, 1789–93, Governor of Madras, 1793–97. He was nephew of Barnard's patron, the Lord Lieutenant 1777–80. See *ante* p. xxxi and *post* p. 414 and n. 1.

[14] Dr. Alexander Webster (1707–84), clergyman and pioneer in actuarial statistics, leader of the "high-flying" or conservative party in the Church of Scotland, was JB's uncle by marriage, his wife, Mary Erskine, being sister to JB's mother (John Ramsay, *Scotland and Scotsmen in the Eighteenth Century*, 1888, i. 262). He was a devoted supporter of the Hanoverian succession, had been chaplain both to the King and to the Prince of Wales, and had served as Moderator of the General Assembly.

Church of Scotland (I should say *Kirk*, I believe,) at Edinburgh. I will be truly obliged if I can obtain it, and I should suppose your Lordship may yourself do me that kindness. I ever am with the warmest regard Your Lordship's faithful humble servant

From *William Windham, Thursday ?13 March 1794*

MS. Yale (C 3139).

ADDRESS: James Boswell Esqr., Portland Street.

ENDORSEMENT: Right Hon. W. Windham 11 March 1794.[1] N. B. The Meeting did not hold. We were all engaged.

Hill st. [London] Thursday Mrng.

DEAR BOSWELL: Though you rejected the Eumelian yesterday,[2] you will perhaps consent to eat your mutton here to day, to meet Malone, and Sir Charles Blagden, (if they are to be had) and any other that I may be able to pick up.—What say you? Do the Gods oppose? or will Curtis and Dilly yield you for one day to our wishes?[3] Yours etc.

W. W.

From *William Windham, Friday 14 March 1794*

MS. Yale (C 3140).

ADDRESS: James Boswell Esqr., Portland street.

ENDORSEMENT: Right Hon. W. Windham 14 March 1794. N. B. I went

[1] Windham's "Thursday" is somewhat more likely to be right than JB's "11 March 1794" (a Tuesday). JB did dine with Dilly on Wednesday 12 Mar. 1794 (Journ.), and in the spring of 1788, at least, the Eumelian Club met on a Wednesday (Journ. 30 Apr.).

[2] "A Club in London, founded by the learned and ingenious physician, Dr. Ash, in honour of whose name it was called *Eumelian*, from the Greek 'Εὐμέλιας; though it was warmly contended, and even put to a vote, that it should have the more obvious appellation of *Fraxinean*, from the Latin. BOSWELL" (*Life* iv. 394 n. 4).

[3] William Curtis (1752–1829, created a baronet in 1802), banker and speculator, alderman of London (Lord Mayor, 1795–96), an extremely prominent man, was M.P. for London for twenty-eight years. JB had composed and sung a convivial song in 1791 on the anniversary of his election (see *New CBEL* ii. 1214–15) and reports dining with him at the Old Bailey on 16 Jan. 1794 (Journ.).

next morning to him. But he did not then chuse to go. I breakfasted with him.

[London] Friday 14th.

What say you to a party tomorrow to see the Embarkation of the Cavalry for Flanders.[1]

The papers say, that they are to embark at 9, but where, is not mentioned.[2]—If you will inform yourself, I will be ready to attend you. Yours etc.

W. WINDHAM

From Thomas Barnard, Tuesday 25 March 1794

MS. Yale (C 99).

ADDRESS: James Boswell Esqr., 47 Great Portland Street, London.

POSTMARKS: IRELAND, MR ?26, ?MR 94.

Dublin, March 25th 1794

MY DEAR BOSWELL: Your Proverb of Better Late than Never, is perhaps one of the Most Comprehensive ones that we are in Possession of; as I believe, it will suit with every Case that can be stated; But Especially, as applied to your Kind Letter of Congratulation on my Sons Marriage, which Late, as it came, was Better in every sense of the Word, (Not only than *Never*, but Even) than if it reach'd me *Sooner*; as it would Then have only claim'd a *share* of my Attention, among a multitude of others, on the same Subject, whereas it has now, all the merit and Value, of a Fine Fruit, after the ordinary Season is past, which, tho' equally

---

[1] After occupying the Austrian Netherlands, France opened hostilities against Holland and England on 1 Feb. 1793. Although England took small part in military operations, mainly subsidizing the allies, she sent a contingent to aid the Austrians and Prussians in the Netherlands.

[2] *The London Chronicle* for 11–13 Mar. (lxxv. 248) announced, "The drafts of cavalry for foreign service are to embark immediately. The draft from the 11th, 15th, and 16th, embark on Friday at Mr. Perry's Dock, Blackwall." The embarkation was apparently delayed, for the next issue of the *Chronicle* (13–15 Mar., p. 256) reported, "The first division of troops ordered for the Continent ... embarked this morning [Saturday the 15th] at 9 o'clock."

delicious Before, is infinitely more Precious on that account, as it is more unexpected. The Amen of the Clerk, always makes a more Distinct Impression on our Ears, Than the Joint Responses of a whole Congregation: and to Conclude my Comparisons, He that comes last into a Company (Especially if they have almost done their Dinner,) is always more attended to by the Rest, than any other of the guests, and often the most Welcome. However that be, I sincerely Thank you for this Token of your Remembrance, and Confess that I should have been rather Mortified, if you had totally omitted it. I have made your Compliments to Mr. Barnard and Lady Anne, and they are very Kindly accepted. I do not Intend that they shall have an opportunity of thanking you in Person as long as I can Keep them Here; especially, as their House in Berkely Square is not yet ready for their Reception, and they do not seem to be Tired of Ireland.[1]

I think our Royal Academy has acted very Discreetly in abandoning their First Idea of a general Exhibition of our Labours of 25 years, for the Excellent Reasons you have assign'd. A Handsome Medal will certainly be acceptable to their Members, and a good dinner Equally so, to their guests. And Neither can possibly give offence; except to such, as have the misfortune to be excluded. I am glad however that they do not mean to Drop their annual exhibition, as They would be as much Sufferers in Profit, as in Fame, besides incurring the Resentment of the Publick, for Dissappointing Them of an annual Amusement, They have so long been taught to Expect, as a Matter of Course.

I shall be very Impatient for the Publication of Gibbons Private Memoirs, as I hope it will be full of Interesting anecdote; But if it be only a Dry apology for his own Life and opinions, I have no Curiosity to Read it; for His Motives, as well as his Private History, are Equally Indifferent to me, even if they were *Sincerely* display'd, which we have no Reason to Expect. I should like such a Book much better, if his Executors could find a Second Boswell to do it for Him, and Embellish the Work with the History of the Age he Lived in, and the Learned at Home and abroad with whom he Conversed: I always thought his Familiar Conversation the

---

[1] Lady Anne and Andrew Barnard went to Dublin after their marriage and remained there a year. On their return to England, they lived with Lady Anne's sister, Lady Margaret Fordyce, in Berkeley Square (Dorothea Fairbridge, *Lady Anne Barnard at the Cape of Good Hope*, 1924, p. 10).

most Valuable Part of his Character, as well as the most agreeable *Feature* about him. His affected Stile I never admired.

You ask my opinion, who is most Worthy, to be Elected by the R. Academy as his Successor, and I feel *no Choice of Difficulties*, in Answering your Quære: as I think there is no Competitor with William Mitford Author of the *History of Greece*,[2] among all the Surviving Compilers of Antient History, Resident in England: and I presu⟨me⟩ you are not to go Abroad for a Professor.

With Respect to the Two New Members to fill up o⟨ur⟩ Literary Club, the Election is not So Easy; even if your opinion could Ensure the Success of your Candidates. We have already Peers and Bishops full enough;[3] The Qualifications for our Members ought not, to be, those that would Entitle a Candidate to a Fellowship of All Souls; who according to their Statutes, Should be, *Bene Natus*, Bene moratus, Bene Vestitus, *Mediocriter Doctus*.[4] Find me Two Men of *Known* abilities, Unblemished Character, Polite and Easy Manners, whose conversation is at the Same Time Pleasant, and Improving, and who are already no Strangers to the Majority of the Club: Such Men, I say, will be a real Acquisition to your Society, and you will do it an Essential Service, by Introducing them among us, If you can find 'em. But

[2] *The History of Greece, from the Earliest Accounts to the Death of Philip, King of Macedonia*, 5 vols., 1784–1810. Only two volumes had been published by 1794. Mitford (1744–1827) undertook his history of Greece at Gibbon's suggestion. JB wrote to the members of the Academy on 24 Apr., recommending Mitford and quoting Barnard's praise. There was considerable opposition to Mitford, perhaps because of his strongly anti-democratic views, and JB wrote from Auchinleck to Joseph Farington, treasurer of the Royal Academy Club, on 29 Dec., "In case a certain election [that of John Gillies (1747–1836), author of a rival *History of Greece*, 1786, 2 vols.] be made, which besides other considerations I should think so disrespectfull to the Bishop of Killaloe and myself that (though I should be very sorry indeed) it would oblige me to withdraw you will put the inclosed [another letter to Farington of the same date, stating his intention of attending the last meeting of the Royal Academy Club in Jan., but earnestly requesting that the date be changed from 30 Jan., King Charles Martyr's day, to 31 Jan.] in the fire, if not you will be pleased to read it to the Club." No one was elected at this time, because the King was determined not to sanction any election that was not unanimous. Mitford was finally elected in 1818 (*Farington Diary* i. 48–49).

[3] At the time Barnard wrote, there were in The Club four bishops (Dromore, Killaloe, Clonfert, and Salisbury) and eight peers (Earl of Charlemont, Earl of Upper Ossory, Earl Spencer, Baron Eliot, Earl of Lucan, Viscount Palmerston, Earl Macartney, Duke of Leeds).

[4] "Well born, well mannered, well dressed, moderately learned." C. Grant Robertson thought that this statement of the alleged qualifications of the College was "first found perhaps in Fuller's Church History. . . . Like most academic *bon mots*, much of its virtue lies in the complete absence of solid fact" (*All Souls College*, 1899, p. 188).

I do not think that the Red Book[5] will be the best place to Search for them.

Yesterday I had the Honor of Entertaining Your old Patron Lord Lonsdale and Sir Michael le Fleming.[6] His Lordship was very free and Communicative, and seemd Pleas'd with his Fare and his Company. Your name was mention'd with Esteem, and affection, and wishes Express'd by the whole Company, (which was numerous,) to see more of your works. Don't grow Idle, my very good Freind, now your Name is up.—I am just come home from the House of Lords after concluding a short but very unanimous Session of Parliament, in which all our Patriots have join'd the government to save their Estates.[7] It is Happily over; and if the French come Hither, we are prepared to receive them. Adieu my Dear Boswell, my Paper Fails; Remember me to our Worthy President, and to all that do me the Favor to Enquire for me. Mrs. B., Mr. B., and Lady Anne, Salute you Kindly. I am affectionately yours

THOS. KILLALOE

To Bennet Langton, Wednesday 26 March 1794[1]

MS. Yale (*L 849.9).

ADDRESS: To Bennet Langton Esq.

[5] A popular name for the *Royal Kalendar, or, Complete Annual Register* (see OED, Red book, 3).

[6] Fleming, who died in 1806, was M.P. for Westmorland from 1774 until his death (*Comp. Bar.* iv. 193). Since he was one of Lonsdale's "nine-pins", JB had seen him frequently in Lonsdale's company and liked him.

[7] The fear of French invasion and the passing of the Catholic Relief Bill in 1793, granting Catholics the franchise, the right to serve on grand juries, and other privileges they had been seeking for many years, resulted in the relatively quiet session of 1794. In the latter year, only three major subjects were discussed: a motion to oppose the war, which was soundly defeated; Grattan's motion for a commercial understanding, which was withdrawn at the request of the Government; and a reform bill, defeated the year before, which was again rejected. Grattan, who ordinarily opposed the Government, set the tone of the session on 21 Jan., when he stated that the function of the Irish Parliament was to influence Great Britain into correcting abuses, "but that these measures, this general plan of conduct, should be pursued by Ireland with a fixed, steady, and unalterable resolution to stand and fall with Great Britain" (*London Chronicle*, 30 Jan.–1 Feb. 1794, lxxv. 106).

[1] On Wednesday 19 Mar. 1794, Langton called at JB's house, having apparently just arrived in London. On Tuesday 25 Mar. Langton and JB dined

[London] Wednesday

MY DEAR LANGTON: You did not mention at my house where you were to be found. You were equally neglectful at Marquis George's.[2] We are both vowing vengeance. I should have gone amongst the Stage Waggons in Piccadilly to look for you, had not Malone directed me to this Linnen shop.[3] Pray come tomorrow at five to my family dinner *"not a dinner to ask a man to"*[4]—and go in the evening to Widow Francis's Dr. Burneys daughter.[5] Yours most cordially

JA. BOSWELL

From John Douglas, Saturday 3 May 1794

MS. Yale (C 1106).

ADDRESS: To James Boswell Esq., No. 46. or 47.[1] Great Portland Street

ENDORSEMENT: Bishop of Salisbury, 3 May 1794.

[London] Saturday Afternoon

DEAR SIR: I find that my Wife has engaged Company to dine with me on Wednesday; which will put it out of my Power to wait upon you. She was not at home when I gave the verbal Answer to

at Lord Townshend's (Journ.). The present letter was therefore probably written on Wednesday 26 Mar. If so, Langton was unable to accept, for JB dined at home alone on Thursday 27 Mar. (Journ.).

[2] Townshend was created a marquess on 31 Oct. 1787 (*Comp. Peer.* xii. pt. 1. 809). JB told Joseph Farington on 28 Mar. 1794 that Townshend was "very proud and fond of his Marquisate, yet affecting to under-value titles" (*Farington Diary* i. 44).

[3] Langton probably had taken lodgings in a house containing a linen shop.

[4] MS. "JOHNSON" deleted. JB, in *Life* i. 470, related how SJ, even when invited to dine with an intimate friend, "was not pleased if something better than a plain dinner was not prepared for him. I have

heard him say on such an occasion, 'This was a good dinner enough, to be sure; but it was not a dinner to *ask* a man to.'"

[5] Charlotte, fourth daughter of Dr. Charles Burney, in 1786 married Clement Francis, surgeon and former secretary to Warren Hastings in India (Joyce Hemlow, *The History of Fanny Burney*, 1958, p. 193). Francis died in Oct. 1792 (*ibid.* p. 228). After his solitary dinner on 27 Mar., JB went to the Haymarket Theatre to see Cumberland's *Box Lobby Challenge* (Journ.). He may have gone to Mrs. Francis's afterwards, but it is perhaps more likely that he changed his plans on learning that Langton could not go with him.

---

[1] JB lived at 47 Great Portland Street.

your Card, and I lose no time to rectify the Mistake. I am Dear Sir Your's etc.

J. SARUM

From William Windham, Wednesday 7 May 1794

MS. Yale (C 3141).

ADDRESS: James Boswell Esqr., Portland Street.

ENDORSEMENT: Right Hon. W. Windham 7 May 1794.

[London]

DEAR BOSWELL: I fear, that I shall be detained so late to day,[1] as hardly to be able to be of your party.—Pray let me know, what it consists of, and whether it is necessary to make any extraordinary efforts, beyond what would be inspired by the general desire of your company.[2] Yours Ever

W. W.

To Sir William Scott, late December 1794

Not reported. Sent from Auchinleck. Referred to in next letter.

[1] Windham was active as usual in business connected with the trial of Hastings, of which he was one of the Managers, and was also at just about this time being solicited to take office under Pitt. On 11 July 1794 he entered the Cabinet as Secretary at War (Windham's Diary, pp. 308, 314).

[2] JB wrote of this gathering to his son Sandy on 10 May: "Very rarely do I give a dinner. I had however a good one last Wednesday. The Company Lord Eliot who had treated me superbly in Cornwall, Lord Sunderlin and his brother Mr. Malone, Mr. Windham, Jack Courtenay Jack Wilkes and Uncle David.—Wilkes was as pleasant as ever and entertained most of us highly, though the Commentator [Malone] did not relish him. Upon the whole it was a rich day."

From Sir William Scott, Tuesday 13 January 1795

MS. Yale (C 2446).

ADDRESS: James Boswell Esq., Auchinleck, Mauchline.[1]

FRANK: London, January thirteenth 1795, Wm. Scott.

POSTMARKS: AIR, FREE JA 13 95.

[London] Jany. 13. 95

MY DEAR SIR: I received your obliging Letter, and I need not tell you that you thought justly in supposing me to be ready to lend a Hand to stave off from every Society I am connected with any Communication with that accursed Leaven which is doing so much mischief in the World at present and with so little successful Resistance to it. But I received your Letter only on the Morning of the Club-day,[2] and You know enough of a Family-Man in this Town at this Season of the year to know that I am not likely to stand clear of other Engagements which it was impossible to extricate myself from, with[ou]t being amenable in my domestick forum. It was therefore not in my Power to attend, and I have not heard what passed. But I take for granted that if it was the Cause of bad Principles, it was successful there as it is every where else.[3] I long to see you to talk over the dire Misfortunes of this last Summer and the present Winter;[4] I am afraid We shall not

[1] "Ayrshire" struck through by Scott and "Mauchline" substituted. Auchinleck was not a post-office.

[2] Surely the day of meeting of The Club, the date in question being presumably 6 Jan. Scott was offered membership in the Essex Head Club, but never attended (*Lit. Anec.* ii. 553).

[3] The Club minutes show that on 9 Dec. 1794 Major James Rennell (1742–1830), the geographer; Dr. Richard Farmer (1735–97), Master of Emmanuel College, Cambridge; and "Mr. Adam" were proposed for membership. "Mr. Adam" was presumably William Adam (1751–1839), politician and intimate friend of Fox. JB and Scott would undoubtedly have considered Adam's political principles "that accursed Leaven which is doing so much mischief in the

World at present", for Adam had supported Fox's unpopular position towards the French Revolution after everyone else had deserted him. JB had shown strong dislike of Adam for years, calling him "low . . . vulgar and impudent and the Bravo of a party" (his comments on "a certain *Mason* in parlmt.", Journ. 12 May 1783). Nothing of note happened at the meeting of 6 Jan. Major Rennell was elected on 20 Jan. and Dr. Farmer on 3 Feb., JB being present at both elections. Adam was not elected.

[4] The allies had been unsuccessful on the Continent during the summer and autumn of 1794, and the British, in Jan. 1795, abandoned the province of Utrecht. The coalition against France was crumbling.

want for Conversation of that Kind for some time to come, as all present Appearances are unfavourable enough.—Yours very faithfully

W. Scott

From William Windham, n.d.

MS. Yale (C 3142).[1]

ADDRESS: James Boswell Esqr.

[London]

I wish very much that it was in my power to join you But I am engaged in a way not to get off. My inclinations will be with you. Yours truly

W. W.

From Thomas Barnard to Sir William Forbes, Sunday 27 March 1796

MS. Fettercairn Papers, National Library of Scotland.

Dublin, March 27th. 1796

DEAR SIR: My Conscience has Smitten me severely for some time Past, for having so Long Delayd to acknowledge the Honor of your very obliging Letter, which I found Lying on my Table in Dublin, on my Return from Limerick, about a Fortnight Since, But the Inexcusable Spirit of Procrastination, (So incident to Old Men) has kept me, from Day to Day, under Pretence of waiting for a Frank, from paying a Debt, which I ought to have discharged Long Since. Will you still have the goodness to accept so Lame an apology? accompanied with my Very sincere Thanks, for the Kind part you have taken in my Favor, on so affecting an occasion?

The Freindly Remembrance of my Freind Mr. Boswell in his Last Moments,[1] is very Flattering to me who Sincerely Lov'd him,

---

[1] Undated and undatable. It has been arbitrarily placed here in the latest possible position. JB died on 19 May 1795.

[1] Forbes, the executor of JB's personal estate, had probably just got around to implementing the small legacies of JB's will, which included a mourning ring for Barnard. (JB died deeply in debt, and Forbes could not have been sure for some

and was sensible of all his good Qualities, as well as Truly Concern'd at Loosing him. Many Pleasant, and many Serious Hours, have we pass'd together (our Tete's a Téte, were generally of the Latter Sort,) for several Years Past: and the Last time I saw him, in the Year 1793,[2] My Forebodings told me that we should never meet more, in this Life. I hope we shall hereafter; as I have good Reason to be assured that his Principles were those of a Christian, and *not Lightly* taken up. I should be most happy to pay my Respects to you at your own House in Edinburgh, if it ever Lies in my Power to take such an Excursion: To which I have also a second Motive; from my Present Connexion with Lady Dowager Balcarras,[3] whose Daughter Lady Anne Lindsay is now married to my Son; and her mother Honors me sometimes with her Correspondence. But my Time is so much occupied here, as seldom to give me Leisure for a Longer Absence from Ireland than about Six Weeks in Two Years; and London soon Consumes that short Period. However I do not Despair of carrying my wish of Visiting Scotland into execution once more before I die; When the Tranquillity of the British Empire is again Restored, which I think we have now; some Prospect of Living to see.

The Traitors and Malcontents of this Country are now pretty well Subdued. They find by Experience that their Crime really amounts to Treason, and that there are juries not afraid to do their Duty; Neither of which they Believ'd some months ago. The Army and Militia, whom they hoped to Corrupt, have on all occasions behaved as they ought, and the opposition have join'd the Government to Preserve the Peace of the Kingdom, and their own Estates. So that I hope, all the nonsense of Reform in Parliament, and such Plausible Pretexts to Destroy the Constitution, under Pretence of Improving it, are at Last at an End.[4] In the

time that money for the legacies would be forthcoming.) This, however, will not explain JB's "Freindly Remembrance . . . in his Last Moments", for the codicil to the will that affected Barnard had been drawn as far back as 1785, and JB had told Barnard about it at the time (*ante* To Barnard, 1 July 1785; From Barnard, c. 17 July 1785). Presumably, in sending the legacy, Forbes also transmitted some remark of JB's made in his last illness and reported to Forbes by T. D. Boswell or one of JB's children.

[2] JB's journal lapses from 10 Jan. to 1 Aug. 1793, the period during which this meeting must have taken place.

[3] Anne (1727–1820), daughter of Sir Robert Dalrymple of Castleton by his second wife, widow of James Lindsay (1691–1768), fifth Earl of Balcarres.

[4] Barnard refers to the Defender movement, an organization of Roman Catholic peasants originally organized to defend themselves from the Protestants. Gradually, however, the members of the group adopted the view that a French invasion

mean time the Commerce and Prosperity of the Kingdom has been so far from being injured by this French War, that it has Encreased beyond all former Periods; and the Revenue is so much risen Last Season, as to become more than adequate to the Expenditure of the last half year. All things, in Short, wear a much more Smiling Aspect than they have done for several years Past.

Mrs. Barnard begs Leave to join in best Respects and Compliments to you and Lady Forbes. I have the Honor to be with very Sincere Esteem and Regard, Dear Sir, your obedient and obliged humble Servant

THOS. LIMERICK

From George Steevens to Edmond Malone, Friday 1 April 1796

MS. Yale (C 2548). A copy in Lord Sunderlin's hand, on second page of From Sunderlin to James Boswell the younger, 14 June 1813, which also contains a copy of From Edmund Burke to Malone, 8 Apr. 1796.[1]

Hampstead Heath, April 1st. 1796

Mr. Stephens presents his best Compliments to Mr. Malone and most sincerely thanks him for his very elegant present, which exhibits one of the most decisive pieces of criticism, that ever was produced.[2]

would best serve its interests, and some worked actively for that end. A party of Dissenters, the Orangemen, further complicated matters by carrying out acts of terror against the Catholics. As a result of these acts, the Irish Parliament in the winter and early spring of 1796 passed an act of indemnity for the victims of persons who had exceeded their legal powers in the preservation of order. It also passed an extremely severe insurrection act.

---

[1] The texts of both letters were printed in Sir James Prior's *Life of Edmond Malone*, 1860, pp. 224 (From Steevens), 226–27 (From Burke).

[2] Steevens refers to Malone's recently published *Inquiry into the Authenticity of*

Certain Miscellaneous Papers and Legal Instruments Published [by S. and W. H. Ireland], *Dec. 24, 1795, and Attributed to Shakespeare*, 1796, in which he proved from "orthography, phraseology, dates given, or deducible by inference, and dissimilitude of handwriting, that not a single paper or deed in this extraordinary volume was written or executed by the person to whom it was ascribed" (quoted by Prior, *Life of Edmond Malone*, p. 224). William Henry Ireland (1777–1835), the possibly illegitimate son of the author and engraver Samuel Ireland (d. 1800), began, at the age of 17, to forge Elizabethan documents on bits of parchment cut from old deeds stored in the chambers of the solicitor for whom he worked, which he passed off to his father as genuine. Subsequently, he provided his father with further documents and signatures supposedly written by Shakespeare, Queen Elizabeth, and the Earl of Southampton. In Feb. 1795 the elder Ireland exhibited the documents at his house, to which he invited the leading literary men of the time. Samuel Parr and Joseph Warton were among the many who accepted the display as genuine, and JB was reported to have "kissed the supposed relics on his knees" (DNB; W. H. Ireland, *Confessions*, 1805, pp. 75, 80). The collection continued to grow, and in Dec. 1795, apparently without the assent of his son, Samuel Ireland published the documents in facsimile. Both Steevens and Malone were among those who recognized the forgeries and who were active in exposing the fraud to the public. William Ireland later confessed to forgery and absolved his father, who never admitted his son's guilt, of any responsibility.

APPENDICES

Introductory Note

With the exception of Boswell's *Prologue for the Opening of the Theatre Royal* in Edinburgh, all the verses and letters contained in the following appendices were found among the deposits of Boswell's papers at Malahide and Fettercairn. How, when, and why the letters to Langton printed *ante* and in Appendix 2 came into Boswell's possession appears to be matter of pure speculation. He may have solicited some of them for use in the lives of Reynolds, Oglethorpe, and Young which we know he planned to write.[1] He may even have planned to write a life of Langton, either as an independent work or as part of that history of The Club which Dr. Burney urged him to undertake.[2] Perhaps we should look no farther for a motive than his strong passion of collecting: the wish to stock his archives at Auchinleck with original letters from well-known men. It is just possible that Langton was an unwitting donor. ("One sometimes gets the feeling," says Professor Pottle, "that [Boswell] was not above walking off with other people's papers when he found them lying about and thought they were not likely to be preserved."[3]) It is much more likely, however, that some time when he was at Langton's he asked permission to sort a mass of papers and take any he wanted. Langton, one thinks, would have made no objection. He was astonishingly unjealous of his personal privacy, and he lacked all interest in archives.

[1] *Lit. Car.* pp. 302, 308; Journ. 24 Apr. 1779, 9 May 1781; Yale MS. M 208.
[2] See *ante* From Burney, 16 July 1791.
[3] *London Journal*, limited ed., 1951, p. xii.

APPENDIX 1

Verses

Boswell's Prologue to The Earl of Essex, Written for the Opening of the Theatre Royal, Edinburgh, 9 December 1767

MS. BM Add. MSS. 38150, f. 55v. Copied on a blank side of *ante* To Langton, 10 Apr. 1774.[1]

Scotland for learning and for arms renownd
In ancient annals is with lustre crown'd,
And still she shares whate'er the world can yield
Of letterd fame, or glory in the field:
In ev'ry distant land Great Britain knows
The Thistle springs promiscuous with the Rose.

While in all points with other lands she vied,
The Stage alone to Scotland was denied.
Mistaken Zeal in times of darkness bred
O'er the best minds it's gloomy vapours spread;
Taste and Religion were suppos'd at strife,
And twas a sin—to view this glass of life!

When the Muse ventur'd the ungracious task
To play elusive with unlicens'd mask,
Mirth was restraind by Statutory awe
And Tragick Greatness fear'd the scourge of Law.
Illustrious Heroes arrant vagrants seem'd,
And gentlest Nymphs were sturdy beggars deem'd.

[1] These verses were widely printed in newspapers and magazines of Dec. 1767 and Jan. 1768 (see *New CBEL* ii. 1218–19), but the present appears to be the only known autograph manuscript of the piece. It shows no substantive differences from the version in *The European Magazine* (June 1791) xix. 326, which was probably also printed from a manuscript in JB's hand, though the printer was no doubt largely responsible for the accidentals.

This night lov'd GEORGE's free enlighten'd age
Bids Royal Favour shield the Scottish Stage;
His Royal Favour ev'ry bosom cheers,
The Drama now with dignity appears.
Hard is my fate if murmurings there be
Because the favour is announc'd by me.

Anxious, alarm'd, and awed by ev'ry frown,
May I intreat the candour of the Town?
You see me here by no unworthy art.
My All I venture where I've fix'd my heart.
Fondly ambitious of an honest fame
My humble labours your indulgence claim.
I wish to hold no Right but by your choice;
I'll risk my Patent on the Publick Voice.

Verses on Thomas Barnard's Promotion to the See of Killaloe

MS. Yale (M 303). A draft, stanzas 11 and 12 on a separate scrap of paper; stanzas 13 and 14 on the verso of "Extempore [on Bishop Lowth] in Gen. Paolis Chariot 2 May 1781" (M 304). Barnard, Dean of Derry, was consecrated Bishop of Killaloe on 29 Feb. 1780. JB was not in London that year, but in 1781 he and Barnard were in London at the same time. JB "made out Verses on Bishop of Killaloe", probably stanzas 1–10 only, at Richmond on 26 Apr. 1781 (Journ.); stanzas 11 and 12, mentioning Paoli, were probably written somewhat later, as were also stanzas 13 and 14. On 10 May, at a dinner given by Barnard, JB sang or recited the verses (Journ.; To Barnard, 14 Feb. 1783). No fair copy has been reported. Besides the copy sent to Barnard in 1783, JB is known to have given a copy to Mary Palmer (Journ. 30 May 1781). As is usual in JB's verse drafts, the MS. contains a good many uncancelled alternative readings, written above the line. The reading on the line has been taken for the text except when an alternative reading was clearly written later or when JB has appended a foot-note to it. Deleted and alternative readings are collected at the end of the text (pp. 416–17). Deleted readings are enclosed in full brackets.

1

Brisk Barnard was a jovial Blade
When he was Dean of Derry.
For cordial freinds the cloth was laid
And O how we were merry.

2

But now raisd high bove me and you   5
His merit has such savour
Lord Bishop He's of Killaloe
By Buckingham's[1] just favour.

3

But lets not think weve Barnard lost
It were a cruel Notion   10
By his good fortune to be crost
And sink[2] on his promotion.

4

No no we yet shall with him live
His fancy shall be brighter
And lordly dinners he shall give   15
With sanction of the Mitre.

5

With this good Prelate you shall find
The choicest literati
The wondrous powers of Johnsons mind
And Boswells honest gayety.   20

6

Reynolds genius and fine taste
Burke's knowledge and Allusion
Where language almost runs to waste,
There's such a rich profusion.

---

[1] John Hobart, second Earl of Buckinghamshire (1723–93), was Lord Lieutenant of Ireland from 1777 to 1780 (ante
p. xxxi; To Barnard, 19 Feb. 1794, n.
13).

[2] Become depressed or dejected.

7

Earl Charlemont with pleasing smile   25
At once shall entertain us
With Egypts pyramids and Nile
And inimica manus.[3]

8

Gratton with brilliancy shall speak
And learned Thomas Leland   30
With the great soul of ancient Greek
Rejoice that Ireland's Free land.[4]

9

Freindship and wit and wine shall flow
Sound s⟨ense⟩ and wholesome Claret
Nor shall we mad or muddy grow   35
For all of us can bear it.

[3] "Earl Charlemont: His Lordship travelled in Egypt and is General of the Volunteers of Ireland" (JB's note). Charlemont had spent a short time in Egypt in 1749 (M. J. Craig, *The Volunteer Earl*, 1948, pp. 66–67) and for the rest of his life seems to have enjoyed telling his listeners of the large serpent he had seen in one of the pyramids (*Life* iii. 352–53, Journ. 12 May 1778). With "Brave Charlemont" (the first cast of the line) compare JB's "boldness of a General of Irish Volunteers" (*Life* iv. 79). When JB was writing these verses, Charlemont was a national hero, commander-in-chief of the Volunteer Army which had been formed to protect Ireland from French invasion, but was now spiriting up the Irish Parliament to resist domination by the Crown and the Parliament of Great Britain. The slogan "Manus haec inimica tyrannis" ("This hand unfriendly to tyrants") had been used by Algernon Sidney, and was the motto of several armigerous families, including that of Charlemont's friend John Joshua Proby,

Baron (later Earl of) Carysfort. Just how JB came to think of it as standing for the Volunteers generally is not known, but it is clear that some of the Volunteers were fond of it. It was painted on the colours of the Knappagh company, and appears on a medal presented to a member of the Carrickfergus company for skill in arms (T. G. F. Paterson, "The County Armagh Volunteers of 1778–1793", *Ulster Journal of Archaeology*, 3rd ser. vi, 1943, 73 and n. 17; see plate facing p. 76).

[4] Henry Grattan (1746–1820), the fiery orator, had been given a seat in the Irish Parliament by Charlemont. Dr. Leland (1722–85), a fellow of Trinity College, Dublin, from 1746 to 1781, had been persuaded by Charlemont to publish an English translation of the orations of Demosthenes, which appeared in parts from 1756 to 1770; he was also author of, among other works, *The History of the Life and Reign of Philip, King of Macedon* (2 vols., 1758).

10

From sin presumptuous[5] lets refrain
Our virtues be increasing
And may we at Armagh obtain
Old Bishop Barnard's blessing.[6]   40

11

Paoli this Prelate's board shall grace
On an Hibernian visit
While Liberty so fills the place
Himself shall scarcely miss it.

12

His Country's wrongs he shall forget   45
In a more happy island
Moments shall easy pass but yet
His Grief returns tho' silent.

13

True to his trust in every way
He fills his sacred function   50
With dignity instructs to pray
And preaches with an unction.

14

Vers'd in divine and human lore
(All else is but vain glory)
He is (I cannot praise him more)   55
A Christian and a Tory.[7]

---

[5] JB's usual spelling, indicating that to him it was a three-syllable word.

[6] That is, "May Barnard finally rise to be Archbishop of Armagh, Primate of the Church of Ireland."

[7] "I honestly acknowledge that I am guilty of the atrocious charge of being both a Christian and a Tory" (From Barnard, 2 Mar. 1783).

Deleted and alternative readings: 3 cordial] hearty   lively   honest   5 But high[er far than] me and you   But high [a]bove [both] me and you   6 such] [a]   8 Buckingham's] Hobart's w (*probably for* worthy)   9 Lets not suppose   Let us not fear   13 [O] no   14 His wit shall ev'n   Our days shall ev'n   15 lordly] [noble]   princely   17 With this good Prelate] At Barnard's table   19 A Johnson's wondrous powers of mind   20 honest] various   varied   21 genius and

fine] [elegance of]   22 knowledge and] [masterly]   23 language] [genius]
25 Brave Charlemont   And Charlemont   with pleasing smile] the while   28
inimica manus] by his manner gain us   31 great] pure   34 Sound sense and
wholesome] Sound [light] well flavoured   39 may we at Armagh] late at Killaloe
41 this Prelate's] Hibernia's   42 On an Hibernian] With Boswell on a   next
summer on a   44 scarcely] hardly   50 He fills his sacred] His Lordship fills his

Verses to Bishop Barnard on Lady Anne Lindsay

MS. Yale (M *336*). Written on the verso of a wrapper addressed,
"Miss Boswell, Portland Street"; notations by JB on the recto, "Bishop
of Killaloe" and "Dund[a]s of Convicts", suggest a date in Aug. 1792.[1]
See *ante* From Barnard, 25 Feb. 1792, n. 7. The verses, which may
never have been sent, show JB attempting to joke Barnard out of opposition to his son's marriage to Lady Anne.

> Bishop Barnard ist a sin, say
> To be in love with Anna Lindsay
> Is there Statesman out or in say
> Who admires not Anna Lindsay
> Gainst Prelacy more zeal shew'd Prynne say
> Than I in praising Anna Lindsay
> Would your Revrence care a pin say
> Censure to bear[2] for Anna Lindsay
> Would not you claret change for gin say
> To change old spouse for Anna Lindsay
> Would you at play a million win say
> Or win the heart of Anna Lindsay
> Is there wing or is there fin say
> To fly or swim from Anna Lindsay

[1] JB wrote to Barnard on 16 Aug. 1792; he wrote to Dundas on 10 Aug., requesting a brief interview, "only for five minutes, to mention the Case of the five persons who made a wonderful escape from New South Wales, and are now in Newgate". On 28 Mar. 1791, eleven prisoners, including one woman and two children, escaped from the penal colony at Botany Bay, Australia, in an open cutter. They arrived safely on 5 June at Kupang, in Timor, where they were arrested by English authorities and sent back to England. Before they reached England, six of them died. The five survivors were imprisoned. JB took an interest in them and was apparently their only counsel. They were eventually freed (F. A. Pottle, *Boswell and the Girl from Botany Bay*, 1936; Journ. 19 Aug. and 2 Nov. 1793).

[2] The first cast was, "Would not your Revrence censure [*line uncompleted*]/For the Sake of".

Ah no! then how shall I begin say
To court the charming Anna Lindsay
To pity is not love akin say
Thus I'll touch dear Anna Lindsay.

John Courtenay's Verses for No Abolition of Slavery, between Monday 11 and Saturday 16 April 1791 [1]

MS. Yale (C 842). Written on verso of wrapper addressed in Joseph Warton's hand: John Courtenay Esqr., M.P., London; postmarked: Winchester, FREE AP ?11 91.

Note in JB's hand: The above lines in Courtenay's handwriting were of his own composition, and given by him to me to introduce into my Poem "No Abolition of Slavery" etc. He did not advert that *idle* is not a good rhime to *bible*. I inserted them with this alteration of one line which I made "I'd have the rogue beware of libel". [2]

> Let Courtenay—sneer and gibe and hack
> We know Ham's Sons are always black
> On sceptic themes he wildly raves
> Yet Afric's Sons were always slaves
> I wish he'd check this scoffing idle
> And spare a jest—when on the bible.

Deleted and discarded readings: 1 Let] Tho'   *Following* 2 And always were 5 If thus he writes hes better idle   6 Let him laugh less and read the bible—. *Following* 6 Their Colour given them for a Curse.—/And happy they it is no worse.

[1] *No Abolition of Slavery* was entered at Stationers' Hall on 16 Apr. 1791, and was advertised in *The St. James's Chronicle*, 14–16 Apr., p. 4, as "This day was published".

[2] JB's poem was an attack on Wilberforce's bill to abolish the slave trade, which was introduced in the House of Commons on 18 Apr. 1791. On 19 Apr. Courtenay spoke in favour of the bill, with sarcastic references to the supposed Biblical authority for Negro slavery: "[He] ridiculed the observations made upon the supposed use to which the pulpit was applied, to favour the improving the morals of the negroes, by Bishops having given premiums to their inferior clergy for preaching to the world the good, christian, charitable doctrine, that the negroes were designed by Providence to be slaves to the end of time, and making the planters and slave dealers a species of scriptural Aristocrates" (*London Chronicle*, 18–20 Apr. 1791, lxix. 379). The rejoinder which he furnished JB was in short written several days before he made the speech.

APPENDIX 2

Miscellaneous Letters to Bennet Langton

From Edward Young to Bennet Langton, Sunday 6 July 1755[1]

MS. Yale (C 3162).

ADDRESS: To Mr. Benet Langton, near Spilsby in Lincolnshire.

POSTMARKS: WELWYN, 7 JY.

[Welwyn] July 6 1755

MY DEAR SIR: You greatly oblige me by your kind Present,[2] and your kinder Letter. They are Both the peculiar Natives of Lincolnshire. Both of exquisite Tast. Proceed, Dear Sir, in your litterary Pursuits: Heaven bless you in them. And if your Progress is equall to your Setting out, I will venture to prophecy that the Name of a Langton will be frequent in the mouth of late Posterity.

It is therefore with Ambition, as well as with great Sinserity, and the truest Affection that I Subscribe myself, Dear, and Uncommon Sir, Your most Obedient and humble Servant

E. YOUNG

Pray my best Respect to your Father, Mother, Unckle,[3] Mr. and Mrs. Battel.[4]

---

[1] See *ante* p.lvi.

[2] Probably game of some kind. In 1759, SJ thanked Langton for the "game which you were pleased to send me" (*Letters SJ* i. 114).

[3] Either his uncle Peregrine, who lived at Partney, or Samuel.

[4] Possibly the Rev. Ralph Battell, M.A. (d. 9 Feb. 1780, aged 83), rector of Somerby and Bag Enderby, Lincs.

(*Gent. Mag.* l. 153; *Lincolnshire Notes & Queries* xi. 88). Bag Enderby is only two or three miles from Langton, and Young may have met Battell while at Langton, if he had not known him before. A "Mr. Battle" accompanied Langton, his father, and his uncle Peregrine to London and back in Dec. 1754 (diary of Bennet Langton the elder, 1754—in the possession of J. C. P. Langton, Esq.).

From Joseph Spence to Bennet Langton, Saturday 6 November 1756[1]

MS. Yale (C 2527).

ADDRESS: To Bennet Langton Esqr.

Sedgfield, Nov. 6, 1756

DEAR SIR, I bar all Apologies, and Professions of writing in the very opposite manner to what you really use, after the first Letter: I beg your Friendship; and that when you favour me with a Letter, that you wou'd write to me only as a Friend, of you and all the good Family.

I am not a fair person to speak of Guthrie's *History*:[2] I allways dislik'd the man; and as much dislike the very little I have read of his Work.

Neither of my Associates at the time mention'd a word of Mr. Carte.[3] I have since read more of him. He reads heavily, in general; but has taken so much pains in consulting Records and Papers, that he may be of service sometimes, to clear up points in which all the rest may be deficient.

The *Parliamentary History*[4] is absolutely necessary to be in a Gentleman's Library, that wou'd look thoroughly into our affairs; but I shou'd think is fitter to be consulted, as Doubts and Occassions may offer; than to be read over, like a current History.

A particular friend of mine, Mr. Herbert,[5] (who has often been

---

[1] See *ante* p. lvi.

[2] William Guthrie (1708–70), miscellaneous writer and compiler, *A General History of England, from the Invasion of the Romans under Julius Caesar, to the late Revolution in 1688; including the Histories of the Neighbouring People and States, so far as they are connected with that of England*, 3 vols., 1744–51. Guthrie also translated some works of Cicero and Quintilian into English, and compiled *A Complete History of English Peerage*, 2 vols., 1763. He appears afterwards to have been conductor of *The Critical Review* (Journ. 25 Mar. 1768).

[3] Thomas Carte (1686–1754) was the author of, among other works, *A General History of England*, 4 vols., 1747–55; and *A Collection of Original Letters and Papers*, concerning the Affairs of England from the year 1641 to 1660. Found among the Duke of Ormonde's Papers, 2 vols., 1739.

[4] *The Parliamentary or Constitutional History of England; being a faithful account of all the most remarkable transactions in Parliament, from the earliest times*. By several hands, 23 vols. plus index, 1751–61. Thirteen volumes had been published by 1753 and twenty by 1757 (*Monthly Review*, Mar. 1754, I. x. 176; *ibid*. Nov. 1757, I. xvii. 432).

[5] Nicholas Herbert of Suffolk, whom Spence had visited in the late summer of 1754 (Austin Wright, *Joseph Spence*, 1950, p. 120), and whom he planned to accompany in May of 1756 to Suffolk, where Herbert had built a new house (N & Q, 1945, clxxxviii. 271–72).

himself an Actor,) on my mentioning in a Letter to him how highly I had been entertain'd at Ashford,[6] desired me to send him the Dramatis Personæ. I have one of the most unhappy Memories in the world; it is either worn out, or (rather) has not been enough usd for many years. If it would not be too troublesome, I should be much oblig'd to you for those to *Mackbeth* and *Lethé*:[7] and if you could be so good as to add what ⟨I⟩ heard Shakespear speak at your own house,[8] it wou'd ⟨com⟩pleat the favor.

The Wildnesses of Finkall[9] are undiscribable; the best way wou'd be, to come and see it.

I heartily wish Blakeney[10] on such a Pedestal, as you mention; and those higher, who may deserve it.

With my best Services and Wishes to all the good family, I am Yours, affectionately,

Jo. SPENCE

Dr. Lowth[11] desires his compliments to you.

---

[6] Presumably by private theatricals in which Langton had taken part. Ashford is a small village a few miles north-west of Hampton. Neither Spence's journals in the possession of Dr. James M. Osborn nor his letters in the possession of Professor Austin Wright mention the entertainment.

[7] *Lethe*, a dramatic satire by Garrick, was first performed at Drury Lane in 1740. It was printed in 1745 under the title *Lethe; or Aesop in the Shades.*

[8] Probably a prologue in the character of Shakespeare, written by Langton and spoken by him or another at private theatricals in the Langton house in London. Spence frequently drove the twenty miles from Byfleet to London, and the Langtons were among the persons with whom he associated (Wright, pp. 119–20). On a separate sheet at the beginning of a diary for 1754, in the hand of the elder Bennet Langton, is the following note: "Jan. 15 Paid for Musick at our Play 3-3-0/To Adams the Playr. 1/0."

[9] The ruins of Finchale (pronounced "Finkle") Abbey, three and a half miles north-east of Durham.

[10] William Blakeney, Lord Blakeney (1672–1761), at the outbreak of the Seven Years War in the spring of 1756 had defended the almost indefensible island of Minorca against a French expedition for seventy days. The 84-year-old general was widely welcomed back to England as a hero, particularly since he had managed to negotiate terms with the French which allowed his garrison to be transported to Gibraltar and not taken as prisoners. But Spence surely means, "I heartily wish with you that Blakeney were mounted on the pillory [or gallows], together with all his superiors who condoned his surrender."

[11] Robert Lowth, or Louth (1710–87), at this time a fellow prebendary of Spence's in Durham and rector of Sedgefield, where Spence was apparently staying. He was later (1766) Bishop of St. David's and (1777) Bishop of London. One of Spence's executors, he composed the inscription of his monument.

APPENDIX 2

From Joseph Spence to Bennet Langton, Saturday 24 July 1762

MS. Yale (C 2528).

[?Byfleet] July 24 62

DEAR SIR: I heartily thank You for your last Visit to Bifleet,[1] tho' it was but a very short one; and yet, short as it was, I think I discover'd in it two or three symptoms of his being a Crow-Pelter,[2] in a certain Gentleman that I love, and esteem, very much. On my mentioning the British Musæum, he was for returning to London, and studying the Curiosities there, for two or three weeks; and on my showing Mr. Porter's *Proposals*,[3] he was (as immediately) for going thorough a Course of Mathematics. Now as I wish as well to the said Gentleman, as I do to any man in the world; I can't help wishing, and that most earnestly, That he wou'd fix some settled Aim (or Aims) for so much Industry, and such an extream Desire to excell; and add a regular Method of pursuing those Aims, to the uncommon Abilities that Heaven has blest him with. I have usd Aims in the Plural, (tho' it rather sounds

---

[1] Byfleet, Surrey, where Spence had a house, given to him in 1748 by his former pupil Lord Lincoln (Henry Fiennes Pelham-Clinton, ninth Earl of Lincoln and second Duke of Newcastle). It was "within two miles of Oatlands [Lord Lincoln's seat] with about an acre of Garden Ground, and five of Meadow laying all around the Garden ... as rural as anything in Yorkshire" (From Spence to William Burrell Massingberd, 14 Apr. 1748—Austin Wright, *Joseph Spence*, 1950, p. 114). According to his diary, Langton visited Spence on Sunday 9 May 1762. He very likely was in the neighbourhood on some kind of family business, possibly the Wey Navigation. He also had visited Spence twice during Oct. 1761, apparently on his way down to and on his way back from the Isle of Wight.

[2] Since the OED records no occurrence of the noun "pelter" before Webster's *Dictionary*, 1828–32, the allusion here was probably private to Spence and Langton. Spence seems to be comparing Langton's diffusion of energies to that of a man who lets himself be diverted from a useful task of cultivation by hopeless pursuit of crows. An animal fable may be involved, though there is none just like this in Aesop.

[3] Unidentified. BM *Cat.* lists no eighteenth-century work in mathematics by an author named Porter; it does record John Potter, *A System of Practical Mathematics*, 1753, second edition 1757. This work (for the extremely long full title of which see *Monthly Review* I. ix. 447–48) covered in a non-theoretical manner arithmetic (with logarithms), geometry, and trigonometry, with sections on surveying, astronomy, and "dialling". The author is said to have been vicar of Cloford, Somerset (DNB under John Potter, miscellaneous writer, fl. 1754–1804). In any case, the book for which the proposals were issued may never have appeared.

as if it clash'd with my Doctrine,) because I had two, in particular, in my thoughts: the excelling in the knowledge of History, and in the Practice of Painting;[4] one for Business, and the other for Diversion. But whatever the Aim be, I can't help thinking, That a man of a Moderate Genius with Method, will excell the greatest Genius that ever was, without it; when they come to cast up the Sum of their Acquisitions, in the end. *Lucidus Ordo*, a Motto to one of Mr. Addison's Papers,[5] was as much the occasion of that Writer's excelling so greatly in his charming way of writing, as his Humour, or his Elegance; and both of them, without the former, wou'd have lost at least half their force. Without it, they must have been like Diamonds ill sorted, and ill set; a confusion of Spangles, that wou'd rather distract than please the Eye: "a meer Milky-way of Wit," as somebody has said of Cowley; or Cowley, of somebody.[6] I really imagine that a regular Method is as necessary in our Studies, as Discipline is for an Army: and what multitudes of brave Irregulars wou'd be overcome, by a handfull of well-disciplin'd Soldiers, you wou'd easily allow; without my quoting Alexander of old, or Cortez in later times. Was a Painter to begin a History-Piece without any Plan previously settled in his mind, what good effect cou'd there be expected from the Wanderings of his Thought and Pencil? Or was a Tragic Poet to write a Play, without aiming at any fixt Moral in it, what Doctrine can he be expected to impress upon the Minds of his Audience, thoroughout the whole course of it, as he ought to do? The former I suppose is too wild, ever to have been practis'd; but the latter, tho' as entirely wrong, has been no uncommon practise.

[4] See *ante* To Langton, 14 Aug. 1773, n. 4.

[5] *The Spectator*, No. 476, Friday 5 Sept. 1712. The phrase is taken from Horace, *Ars Poetica*, 41: "nec facundia deseret hunc, nec lucidus ordo": "[Whoever shall choose a theme within his range] neither speech will fail him nor clearness of order" (H. R. Fairclough's translation in Loeb ed.).

[6] Spence refers to Addison's "An Account of the Greatest English Poets" (lines 32–41):

Great *Cowley* then (a mighty genius) wrote,
O'er-run with wit, and lavish of his thought:

His turns too closely on the reader press:
He more had pleas'd us, had he pleas'd us less.
One glittering thought no sooner strikes our eyes
With silent wonder, but new wonders rise.
As in the milky-way a shining white
O'er-flows the heav'ns with one continu'd light;
That not a single star can shew his rays,
Whilst jointly all promote the common blaze.

But comon as it may have been, I am sure you will join with me in condemning it, most heartily; and I beg we may join in going one step farther together; in Sacrificing at the Altars of Design and Method, before we enter on any sort of Study whatever. Have not I half talkd you to death, in my irregular way of preaching up Order to you? If you can forgive me for it, you will very much oblige, your most Affectionate Humble Servant

J. SPENCE

P.S. I beg my best Compliments to my Worthy Patron,[7] and all the good Family at Langton.

From Robert Orme to Bennet Langton, Thursday 16 January 1772[1]

MS. Yale (C 2144).

ADDRESS: To Benjamin Langton Esqr., at Langton, near Spilsby, Lincolnshire [Benjamin *underlined by JB, who added above the line after the name*:] should be Bennet.

POSTMARK: 16 JA.

Harley Street, Jany. 16. 1772

DEAR SIR: I am so very much in your debt, that I am ashamed to appear in your sight. But at the time I received your Letter and your present of the translation of Aristotle's *Politics* by Regius,[2]

[7] Undoubtedly Bennet Langton (1696–1769), Langton's father, who seems to have offered Spence some kind of advancement several years earlier. In a letter to Massingberd, 14 Sept. 1753, Spence wrote: "You judg'd very rightly, as to my opinion of Mr. Langton's kind Proposal: I am very much oblig'd to that Gentleman, for his good thoughts of me; but I live now in so easy and so satisfy'd a way, that I dont care to have any thing . . . to disturb it: so that my Answer must be the same as I have giv'n upon other occasions, of the same kind, since my Retirement; a great many Thanks, and an absolute Declining of the Favour" (Wright, p. 140). Professor Wright assumes that all references to Mr.

Langton are to Bennet the younger; but in this case, it seems most unlikely, since in 1753 Bennet the younger was only 16. It is not impossible that the elder Langton offered Spence a living at or near Langton as he did SJ in 1756 (*Life* i. 320). Since JB places the offer merely at "about this period", it may have been that the same living was offered to both Spence and SJ.

[1] See *ante* p. lix.

[2] *Les Politiques d'Aristote . . . traduictes de grec en françois, avec expositions prises des meilleurs aucteurs, specialement d'Aristote mesme, & de Platon . . .* Par Loys le Roy, dict Regius, 1568. An English translation of the French work

ORME TO LANGTON, 16 JANUARY 1772

I was full of Indian Affairs, and scarcely ever out of the company of those who were occupied concerning them. Indeed the Intricacy of the national Interests in India, the continuation of my *History*,[3] my beloved Greek, my friends and some business, have continually made me these 6 months the most occupied man in London to the least purpose—I have been but once off the pavement[3a] since I received your Letter.

Five books of the *History of Animals* [by] Aristotle,[4] some Orations of Lysias,[5] Some Greek Epigrams, is all I have been able to add to my Store of Greek reading since August—Add Taylors *Elements of Civil Law*[6] in which there are many excellent greek quotations, but I have read only half of this. Mcgowen[7] I have not resumed.—

My other readings have been concerning the Indies in Ramusio, Purchas, Barros, Castelneda[8] and other Incogniti, with much

appeared in 1597. Le Roy, or Regius, a professor of Greek at the College Royal, Paris, died in 1577. Regius also translated into French some of the works of Plato and Demosthenes.

[3] *A History of the Military Transactions of the British Nation in Indostan, from the year MDCCXLV. To which is prefixed, a Dissertation on the Establishment made by Mahomedan Conquerors in Indostan*, 2 vols., 1763–78. Only vol. i had appeared at this time; vol. ii was published in two parts in 1778.

[3a] Presumably "in the country". See the last paragraph of the letter.

[4] *Historia Animalium*, "Researches on Animals", a collection of facts regarding animal life, probably consisted of ten books in the edition that Orme read. The tenth book is now generally held to be spurious.

[5] Lysias (c. 458–c. 378 B.C.), great Attic orator, wrote over two hundred speeches, of which thirty-four have survived.

[6] *Elements of the Civil Law*, 1755, by John Taylor (1704–66), critic and philologist.

[7] Probably *The Life of Joseph, the Son of Isræl*, 1771, by John Macgowan (1726–80), Baptist minister and controversialist. His *Infernal Conference: or*

Dialogues of Devils, "By the Listener", 2 vols. 12mo, 1772, might seem a more plausible nominee, but it was probably not yet published (in "Catalogue of New Publications", *Gent. Mag.* Sept. 1772, xlii. 429).

[8] Giovanni Battista Ramusio (1485–1557), a collector of voyages and travels, whose principal work was *Delle navigationi et viaggi*, 3 vols., 1550–59.—Samuel Purchas (c. 1577–1626), English divine, had published two collections of voyages: *Purchas his Pilgrimage. Or Relations of the World and the Religions Observed in all Ages and Places Discovered, from the Creation to this Present*, 1613, and *Hakluytus Posthumus or Purchas his Pilgrimes. Contayning a History of the World, in Sea Voyages, & Lande Travells, by Englishmen & Others*, 4 vols., 1625. The fourth edition of *Pilgrimage* (1626) is often grouped with *Pilgrimes* as a fifth or supplementary volume.—João de Barros (1496–1570), Portuguese historian, wrote about the early history of Portuguese exploration and government in Asia in *Décadas da Ásia* (4 vols., 1552–1615).—Fernão Lopes de Castanheda (d. 1559), *Historia do descobrimento e conquista da India pelos Portugueses*, 8 vols., 1551–61. The work was translated into English by Nicholas Lichefield in 1582.

425

extract from them. I have even taken a history of the Conquest of the Canary islands and wrote it over again my own way in 40 pages—it is Curious because short.[9]—I have made the most copious Index possible to two Volumns in Quarto, in which I dare say there are 5000 proper names. It is the translation of Feritsha[10]—This is my confession to gain your indulgence for my apparent neglect of Yourself.—

You my Good Sir will cultivate in your retreat with out interuption the Studies which I can only attend to by intervals; and with health I can not wish you more happiness. I am with very much esteem, Dear Sir, Your very faithful Servant

R. ORME

Benjamin Langton Esqr.

From Sir William Blackstone to Bennet Langton, Wednesday 13 September 1775[1]

MS. Yale (C 153).

ADDRESS: To Bennet Langton Esqr., at Langton near Boston, Lincolnshire.

POSTMARKS: 14 SE, WA⟨LLI⟩N⟨GFOR⟩D.

Wallingford,[2] 13 Sept. 1775

SIR: As it never was my Intention, by the Fines which I imposed at

[9] This digest is now in the Library of the India Office, Orme having left his MSS. to the East India Company. See S. C. Hill, *Catalogue of Manuscripts in European Languages belonging to the Library of the India Office*, ii. pt. 1 (Orme Collection), No. 176. The work in question was a translation by George Glas (*The History of the Discovery and Conquest of the Canary Islands*, 1764) of the then unpublished *Historia de la conquista de las sietas islas de Gran Canaria*, 1632, by Juan de Abreu de Galindo.

[10] Muhammed Kasim ibn Hindu Shah of Astarabad (c. 1552–c. 1623), Persian historian known as Ferishta(h), or Firishta(h), wrote an account of Moslem rule in India, including some Indian history before the arrival of Islam. It was translated into English by Alexander Dow in 1768 as the *History of Dekkan from the first Mahummedan Conquests*. This index appears not to be among the Orme MSS. in the Library of the India Office. See n. 9.

[1] See *ante* p. lix.
[2] Wallingford, Berkshire, was Blackstone's home. He had been elected Recorder of Wallingford in 1749 and remained in that position for twenty-one years. In 1753, he purchased an estate, Castle Priory, just outside the town, and, after his death, was buried in the vault of St. Peter's Church (L. C. Warden, *The Life of Blackstone*, 1938, pp. 109, 198, 205).

Lincoln,[3] to bear hard upon any Individuals; but only to awaken Gentlemen in general to a Sense of the Necessity of their Attendance; I have therefore the more easily allowed such Excuses as have been made on behalf of particular Jurymen. This indeed has reduced the Number of Defaulters remaining on the List into so small a Compass, that to continue their Fines might have the Appearance of Partiality. I shall therefore give Directions to the Clerk of Assise to remit not only Your Fine, but those of the Rest of the Grand Jurymen; and am, Sir, Your most obedient Servant

W. BLACKSTONE

[3] As a Puisne Justice of the Common Pleas, Blackstone was a member of the Commission of Oyer and Terminer for the Midland Circuit (of which Lincoln formed a part) for the Summer Assizes (Circuit Fiats, 1772–1782, C.189/6, Public Record Office, London). It is not possible to determine, however, whether or not he presided over the Assizes at Lincoln, since the Assize Records for the Midland Circuit do not survive for any period earlier than 1818. The day appointed for the hearings at Lincoln was Saturday 29 July 1775 (letter from Public Record Office, 8 Feb. 1954). Lists of men eligible for jury duty were posted every year before Michaelmas, and those eligible were required to be present at the drawings for juries at the time of the assizes. Any person not appearing "after three times calling" was "liable to a fine between 40s. and 5l. at the discretion of the judge" (William Cobbett, ed., *Cobbett's Parliamentary History of England*, 1806–20, viii. 802 n.).

Index

The following abbreviations are used: D. (Duke), M. (Marquess), E. (Earl), V. (Viscount), B. (Baron), Bt. (Baronet), JB (James Boswell), SJ (Samuel Johnson). *Life* refers to *Boswell's Life of Johnson*; *Tour* refers to his *Journal of a Tour of the Hebrides*. Page numbers for foot-notes refer to pages on which the foot-notes begin, although the item which is indexed may be on a following page. Sources and authorities cited are usually omitted from the index. Boswell's relationships with his correspondents are indexed under their names.

INDEX

Edwards, Edward, painter, 1738–1806, 279 *n.* 7

Eldon, John Scott, 1st E. of, Lord Chancellor, 1751–1838, lxxxix

Elibank, Patrick Murray, 5th Lord, 1703–1778, lix

Eliot of St. Germans, Edward Craggs-Eliot, 1st B., 1727–1804; correspondence with JB, xiv (table), 339–40, 376–77; [missing], 376; biographical account of, xlvii–xlviii; in Club, xix, 150 *n.* 2; Mahogany, drink made by, xlviii, 149 *n.* 1, 150 *and n.* 6; created Baron, 150 *and n.* 6; JB and Temple visit, 376, 377 *and n.* 2; mentioned, xcv, 127 *and n.* 4, 131 *n.* 8, 403 *n.* 2

Elizabeth I, Queen of England and Ireland, 1533–1603, 10 *n.* 4

Elliott, Sir John, M.D., 1736–86, 117 *n.* 1, 120 *n.* 1

Ellis, William, Master of Alford Grammar School, Lincolnshire, 1730–1801, 58 *and n.* 3, 59

Ely, Henry Loftus, 3rd E. of, 1709–83, 202 *n.* 5, 241 *n.* 13

Ely, Mary (Hume), Lady, wife of 1st E. of Ely, 202 *n.* 5

Ely, Nicholas Hume-Loftus, 2nd V. and 1st E. of, d. 1766, 202 *n.* 5

Ely, Nicholas Hume-Loftus, 2nd E. of, 1738–69, 202 *and n.* 5, 203–04, 241 *n.* 13

Ely Cause, 157, 159, 189, 196 *and n.* 5, 202 *and n.* 5, 211 *and n.* 11, 241 *n.* 13; Barnard's summary, 202–05, 207

Enborne, Berkshire, 231, 232 *n.* 11

Englefield, Sir Henry Charles, Bt., 1752–1822, 354 *n.* 4

Éon de Beaumont, Charles-Geneviève-Louis-Auguste-André-Timothée d', 1728–1810, 342 *and n.* 3

Erasmus, Desiderius, c. 1466–1536, *Adagia*, 26 *n.* 1

Erskine, Hon. Andrew, 1740–93: letters to, from JB, 3, 371 *n.* 4; *Letters between the Honourable Andrew Erskine and James Boswell, Esq.*, 3 *n.* 2

Erskine, Sir Charles, of Alva, Kt., d. 1663, li

Erskine, Henry, *later* Lord Advocate, 1746–1817, 53 *n.* 4

Erskine, Col. James Francis, 1743–1806, 192 *n.* 2

Erskine, Thomas, *later* 1st B. Erskine *and* Lord Chancellor, 1750–1823, 347 *n.* 2

Esher, Surrey, xxix

Essex, Robert Devereux, 2nd E. of, 1566–1601, 10 *n.* 4

Essex Head Club, xciii, 404 *n.* 2

Eton College: Alexander Boswell at, 273 *and n.* 4, 301 *and n.* 3; mentioned, xlviii, xcii, xcviii, 313

Eumelian Club, 397 *and nn.* 1–2

Euripides, 5th century B.C., *Alcestis*, 286 *n.* 8

European Magazine, 43 *n.* 7, 310 *n.* 8

Evans, Thomas, publisher, 1739–1803, 26 *n.* 2

Farington, Joseph, painter and diarist, 1747–1821, xli, 279 *n.* 7, 395 *n.* 4, 400 *n.* 2, 402 *n.* 2

Farmer, Richard, D.D., Master of Emmanuel College, Cambridge, 1735–97, in Club, xx, 404 *n.* 3

Farquhar, George, 1678–1707, *The Recruiting Officer*, 231 *n.* 8

Farquhar, Rev. John, 1732–68, *Sermons on Various Subjects*, 23 *and n.* 20

Faulder, Robert, bookseller, action against Courtenay, 376 *and n.* 2

Favras, Thomas de Mahy, Marquis de, 1745–90, 295 *n.* 1

Feilding, Augusta: letters to: from Bennet Langton, lxiii–lxv; from Elizabeth Langton, lxvi; mentioned, lxvii *n.* 52

Felixmarte of Hircania. See Ortega, Melchior

Ferdinand IV, King of Naples (Ferdinand III of Sicily), 1751–1825, 262 *and n.* 13

Ferguson, Adam, Professor of Philosophy, Edinburgh University, 1723–1816, in Ossian (*Fingal*) controversy, lxxxiii, 117 *and n.* 1, 119 *n.* 1, 120 *n.* 1, 139 *n.* 1

Ferishta(h) or Firishta(h), c. 1552–c. 1623, 426 *and n.* 10

Fettercairn House, Kincardineshire, papers, liii, 411

Fielding, Henry, 1707–54: *Amelia*, 280; *Joseph Andrews*, 280; *Tom Jones*, 234, 280

fiery cross (burnt stick), 132 *and n.* 3

Fife, James Duff, 2nd E., 1729–1809, 34 *n.* 9, 53 *n.* 4

Finch-Hatton, George, M.P., 1747–1823, 372 *n.* 10

441

vasion of Ireland feared, 401 and *n*. 7, 406 *n*. 4. *See also* French Revolution

Francis, Charlotte Ann (Burney), dau. of Dr. Charles Burney, 1761–1838, 84 *n*. 2, 402 *and n*. 5

Francis, Clement, surgeon, d. 1792, 402 *n*. 5

Franklin, Benjamin, 1706–90, 92 *n*. 1, 344 *n*. 5

Frederick Augustus, D. of York and Albany, 1763–1827, 365

Freire, Cipriano Ribeiro de, Secretary of Portuguese Legation, 281 *second n*. 2

French Academy, *Dictionnaire*, lvii

French Revolution: Burke's speech on, lxxxiv, 279 *and n*. 5, 282; British opinions on, 279 *n*. 6, 283 *n*. 2, 404 *n*. 3; Burke's *Reflections* on, 321 *and n*. 1; Bastille Day commemorated, 341 *n*. 2, 342 *n*. 3, 368 *n*. 4; stone from Bastille, 342 *and n*. 3; in 1792, 374 *and nn*. 14–15; Irish rebellion connected with, 380 *n*. 5, *n*. 7; mentioned, xxxv, xlv, xcviii

Fréron, Élie-Catherine, journalist, 1719–1776, 391 *and n*. 17

Front, Count St. Martin de, Sardinian Envoy Extraordinary, 281 *second n*. 2

Fullarton, William, of Rosemount, ?1737–1805, 21 *n*. 11

Fuseli, Henry, artist, 1742–1825, 279 *n*. 7

Galindo. *See* Abreu de Galindo

Galloway, 135 *and n*. 14

Gardner (Gardiner), Capt. (? Richard), in North Lincolnshire Militia, 385 *and n*. 3

Garforth, John Baynes. *See* Baynes Garforth, John

Garrick, David, actor, 1717–79: letter from, to Langton, xvii (table), 11–12; letter to, from Beauclerk, xviii (table), 75–76; in Club, xx, lix, 81, 344; biographical account of, 1; wants copy of Percy's list of SJ's works, 14, 16; Beauclerk entertains him, 68; relationship with Le Texier, 75 *nn*. 3–4; misunderstanding with Beauclerk, 75–76; death and funeral, 88 *and nn*. 3–4, 265; portrait by Reynolds, 99, 102 *and n*. 8; life of, by Davies, 107 *and n*. 24; SJ's observation on his death, 299 *n*. 2; mentioned, xxxii, xxxviii, lv, lxxxii, 8 *n*. 2, 12 *n*. 3, *nn*. 5–6, 26, 67 *n*. 2, 298

n. 5, 386; *The Clandestine Marriage* (with Colman), 8 *n*. 2; *Lethe*, 421 *and n*. 7; *Letters*, 12 *n*. 3; *She Stoops to Conquer*, prologue, 24

Garrick, Eva Maria (Violetti), wife of preceding, ?1725–1822: letter from, to JB, xiv (table), 115 *n*. 4; mentioned, 12, 67 *n*. 2, 68, 114, 298 *n*. 5

Gay, John, 1685–1732, "The Elephant and the Bookseller", 324 *n*. 5

General Assembly. *See* Church of Scotland

Gentleman's Magazine, lxvi–lxvii, 120 *n*. 1, 131 *n*. 11, 199 *n*. 2, 361 *n*. 6

George II, King of Great Britain and Ireland, 1683–1760, xxix *n*. 4, 55 *n*. 8, 80 *n*. 6

George III, King of Great Britain and Ireland, 1738–1820: Langton's relations with, lxv, lxvii *n*. 52; Beattie's audience with, 38 *and nn*. 5–6; and government changes after American Revolution, 129 *n*. 2, 138 *n*. 5; East India Bill, opposed, 149 *n*. 3; JB composes address to, 149 *n*. 3, 153 *and n*. 6, 372 *n*. 9; request for funds from him for SJ's Italian journey, 169 *n*. 2, 171 *n*. 1, 172, 176 *n*. 6; JB's interview with, 208 *and n*. 4; SJ's conversation with, 254 *and n*. 3, 296 *n*. 5; and Barnard's appointment as Chaplain of Royal Academy, 352 *and n*. 4; Langton's conversation with, lvii *n*. 52, 363; at Salisbury and Weymouth, 370 *and n*. 1; and Irish reform, 380 *and n*. 6; and twenty-fifth anniversary of Royal Academy, 395; mentioned, xxix *n*. 4, lxii, lxiii, 5, 42 *n*. 6, 131 *n*. 10, 313, 400 *n*. 2

George IV, King of Great Britain and Ireland, 1762–1830, as Prince of Wales, lxvii *n*. 52, 395

"George star" (Uranus), 363 *n*. 4

Germany, French war in, 375 *n*. 1

Ghent, 375 *and n*. 1

Gibbon, Edward, historian, 1737–94: in Club, xx, xxi, 50 *n*. 6, 68 *and n*. 1; in Parliament, 150 *n*. 2; Professor of Ancient History in Royal Academy, 391, 396; death, 396 *and n*. 8; Barnard's comment on, 399–400; mentioned, xlvii, lxxviii *n*. 16, 69, 77, 400 *n*. 2; *Miscellaneous Works*, 396 *and n*. 9, 399–400

INDEX

Innes, Mr. (?John), of Edingight, 53 n. 4

Ireland, Samuel, engraver, d. 1800, 407 n. 2

Ireland, William Henry, forger, 1777–1835, 407 n. 2

Ireland: Barnard's opinion of, xxxvi, 351; Barnard's life in, xxxvii, 133 and n. 4; Scotland compared with, 131 n. 11; politics, Barnard's accounts of, 134, 157–58, 182–83, 210–11, 214, 261, 304, 369, 380–81, 401, 406–07; British reforms in, 155 n. 3; commercial union with Britain, 182 and n. 3, 206 and n. 13, 210 and nn. 9–10, 211, 241 and n. 12; copyright laws, 187, 188 and nn. 2–3, 196 n. 4; postal services, franking repealed, 189, 190 n. 8; slow transportation of mail from England, 282, 294; Scots as emigrants to, 293; Malone in, 310 and n. 11, 324 and n. 7, 334 and n. 2; Catholics in, 358 and n. 4, 359 and n. 5, 369 n. 8, 380 and nn. 5–6, 381, 401 n. 7, 406 n. 4; Volunteer Movement, 369 n. 8, 380 and n. 7, 415 n. 3; National Guards, 380 and n. 7; French invasion feared, 401 and n. 7, 406 n. 4; Defender movement, 406 n. 4; Orangemen, 406 n. 4; mentioned, 152, 197

Ireland, Parliament: fails to protect manufactures, 160 n. 8; and commercial union with Britain, 182 and n. 3, 206 n. 13, 210 and nn. 9–10, 211; reform proposed, 182 and n. 4, 406; Relief Bill for Catholics, 358 and n. 4, 359, 401 n. 7; indemnity and insurrection acts, 406 n. 4; mentioned, 243–44, 415 n. 3

House of Commons, 261 and n. 8, 358

House of Lords: Ely Cause in, 157, 159, 189, 196 and n. 5, 204, 241 n. 13; Barnard's efforts for copyright bill, 187, 188 and nn. 2–3, 196; mentioned, 211, 243, 261 and n. 9, 304 n. 4, 401

iron crown, Goldsmith's allusion to, 137, 141, 153 and n. 9

Isle of Wight, lxiii, lxiv

Italy: Beauclerk in, lvii; JB in, 33 and n. 5; SJ plans trip to, 125, 169 and n. 2, 171 and n. 1, 172–73, 176 and n. 7; Andrew Barnard in, 262–63; Forbes in, 374 and n. 13

Ivemay, John, malefactor, d. 1785, 199 n. 2

Jackson, Cyril, Dean of Christ Church, Oxford, 1746–1819, 277 and n. 6

Jackson, Robert, malefactor, d. 1785, 199 n. 2

James I, King of Scotland, 1394–1437, 141 n. 5

James, Lady Jane (Pratt), wife of Sir Walter James, 1761–1825, 309 and n. 5

James, Dr. Robert, 1705–76: James's powder, 95 n. 2; Medical Dictionary, 56 n. 11

James, Sir Walter James, Bt., 1759–1829, 308 and n. 4, 309

Jenkinson, Charles. See Hawkesbury

Jenner, Robert, proctor, 1743–1810, 349 and n. 7

Jenyns, Soame, 1704–87, View of the Internal Evidence of the Christian Religion, 70 and n. 9.

Jephson, Robert, dramatist and poet, 1736–1803, xcv, 267, 268 and n. 3

Johnson, Elizabeth (Porter), wife of SJ, 1689–1752, 176 n. 8

Johnson, Michael, father of SJ, 1656–1731, 247

JOHNSON, SAMUEL, LL.D., 1709–1784.

Letters from: to JB, 35 n. 2, 63 n. 2, 64 n. 7, 77 n. 1, 81 and n. 1, 83 n. 3, 98 n. 5, 113 n. 4, 130 and n. 6, 149 n. 2, 152 n. 5, 169 n. 3, 171 n. 2; to Chambers, 3 second n. 1; to Langton, 4 n. 4; to Reynolds, 251 and n. 2; to Steevens, 235 n. 3, n. 5; to Taylor, 72 n. 6; to Mrs. Thrale, 40 n. 11, 101 n. 2; to J. Warton, 245, 253–54; to T. Warton, xix n. 2, 222–23, 228, 229, 232, 235–236

Letters to: from JB, 49 n. 4, 71 n. 3, 72, 79 n. 2, 80 and n. 3, 95 n. 5, 357, 367; from Langton [missing], 37 and n. 2

Barnard's acquaintance with, xxxii, xxxvi, 130 and n. 5, 137, 184 and n. 6; Barnard's verses on, 184 n. 6; in Club, see Club; relationship with Club members, xxxiv, xl, xlii, xliii, xliv, xlvii, l, li, lxxviii; Beauclerk's acquaintance with, xxxviii–xxxix; Round Robin addressed to, xlviii, 127, 211 and n. 11, 216 and n. 4, 217, 322, 325; Goldsmith's relationship with, l–li; Langton's relationship with, lii, lvii, lviii, lx, lxvii, lxix–lxxii, 41, 44–45, 49 n. 4, 50, 71–72, 77 n. 1, 111 n. 10; Dictionnaire

447

INDEX

INDEX

INDEX

Lonsdale, James Lowther, 1st E. of, 1736–1802: editorial account of, 239 *n.* 3; JB with him in Carlisle election, 239 *and n.* 3, 242 *and n.* 1, *n.* 3; recommends JB as Recorder of Carlisle, 259, 260, 263, 300 *second n.* 1; quarrel with JB, 300 *second n.* 1, 301; mentioned, xxxv, xlvii, xlix, lxxxiv, 255 *and second n.* 1, 256 *first n.* 2, 269 *n.* 2, 273 *n.* 5, 297 *n.* 1, 401 *and n.* 6

Lord Advocate. *See* Montgomery, James William

Lorn, Argyll, 135 *and n.* 14

Lothian, William John Kerr, 5th M. of, 1737–1815, lxvii *n.* 52, 100 *n.* 1a

Louis XV, King of France, 1710–74, 66

Louis XVI, King of France, 1754–93, 304 *n.* 8, 374 *n.* 14

Lowth (Louth), Robert, *later* Bishop of London, 1710–87, 421 *and n.* 11

Luc, Jean-André de, the elder, Swiss physician and geologist, 1727–1817: *Lettres physiques et morales,* 124 *n.* 9; *Recherches sur les modifications de l'atmosphere,* 124 *n.* 9

Lucan, 39–65 A.D., *Pharsalia,* 50 *and n.* 7

Lucan, Charles Bingham, 1st B., *later* E. of, 1735–99, in Club, xx, 150 *n.* 2, 356; mentioned, lxxviii, 104 *n.* 18, 105

Lucan, Margaret (Smith), Lady, d. 1814, 104 *and n.* 18

Luke. *See* Dósza, Gregory

Lukin, Catherine (Doughty), wife of following, 339 *and n.* 3, 378 *n.* 4

Lukin, Rev. George William, *later* Dean of Wells, 1740–1812, 339 *n.* 3, 378 *n.* 4

Lukin, Kitty, dau. of George Lukin, 339 *and n.* 4

Lukin, Mary, dau. of George Lukin, d. 1800, 339 *and n.* 4

Lukin, Robert, son of George Lukin, b. c. 1772, 378 *and n.* 4

Lumm, Sir Francis, Bt., c. 1732–97, 296 *n.* 5

Lunardi, Vincenzo, 1759–1806, 192–93; balloon ascension, 192 *n.* 3

Luther, Martin, 1483–1546, 167 *n.* 12

Lutherans, 167

Lysias, c. 458–c. 378 B.C., 425 *and n.* 5

Macartney, George Macartney, 1st E., 1737–1806: letter from, to Douglas, xviii (table), 361 *n.* 1; letters to: from

Bonar, xviii (table), 280-81; from Douglas, xviii (table), 361–62; biographical account of, lxxvi–lxxvii, 105 *n.* 19; in Club, xx, lxiii, 281 *first n.* 3; ambassador to China, 372 *and n.* 8; mentioned, xix, 104, 280 *n.* 1, 281 *second n.* 2, 295 *n.* 1

Macaulay, Kenneth, 1723–79, 209 *and n.* 4

Macdonald, Sir Alexander, of Sleat, Bt., *later* 1st B., ?1745–95: letter to JB through Courtenay, 224; JB's quarrel with, xxii, xlvi, 42 *and n.* 5, 223–27; JB challenges him to a duel, 225 *and n.* 2, 226, 227 *n.* 3; SJ's opinion of, 42 *and n.* 5; in *Tour,* 209 *and n.* 6, 212 *and second nn.* 1–2, 223 *second n.* 1

Macdonald, Archibald, M.P., *later* Lord Chief Baron of Exchequer (England) *and* Bt., 1747–1826, 138 *n.* 5

Macdonald, William, *Select Works of John Douglas,* memoir, 255

Macgowan, John, 1726–80, *The Life of Joseph,* 425 *and n.* 7

Mackenzie, Henry, novelist, 1745–1831, 124 *and n.* 7; *Julia de Roubigné,* 124 *n.* 7; *The Man of Feeling,* 124 *and n.* 7; *The Man of the World,* 124 *n.* 7; *see also Mirror*

Macklin, Charles, actor and playwright, ?1697–1797, 284 *n.* 2

Mackye, John Ross, 1707–97, lxxxvii *n.* 19

Maclaurin, John, *later* Lord Dreghorn, 1734–96, 21 *n.* 11

MacLeod, John, of Raasay, d. 1786, 62, 64 *and n.* 6

MacLeod, Norman, of MacLeod, 1754–1801, 45 *and n.* 3, 62

Macpherson, James, 1736–96: controversy on his Ossianic poetry, xxiii, lxxxiii, 117 *and n.* 1, 119, 120 *and n.* 1, 138 *and n.* 3, 139 *n.* 1, 221 *n.* 1; controversy on origin of the Scots, 130 *n.* 7, 135; *Fingal,* 117 *n.* 1, 120 *n.* 1, 221 *n.* 1; *Introduction to the History of Great Britain and Ireland,* 130 *n.* 7, 135; *Temora,* 117 *n.* 1, 120 *n.* 1

Macpherson, John, *later* Governor General of India *and* Bt., 1745–1821, 117 *n.* 1, 120 *n.* 1

Macqueen, Robert, *later* Lord Braxfield, 1722–99, 21 *n.* 11

Macredie, Jean, 21 *n. 9*
Madden, Samuel, D.D., 1686–1765, 198 *and n. 9*
Madras, 396
Maetae, 136 *and n. 16*
Magnus, Olaus, Archbishop of Uppsala, 1490–1558, 132 *n. 3*
Mahogany (drink), 48, 149 *n. 1*, 150 *and n. 6*
Maidstone, Kent, Assizes, 349 *and n. 6*, 354 *first n. 2*
Mairobert, M.-F. Pidansat de, 1707–1779, *Anecdotes sur Me. la Comtesse Du Barri*, 65 *n. 3*, 66 *n. 4*
Majendie, Dr. John James, tutor of Prince of Wales, 1709–83, 38 *n. 5*
Major (Mair), John, historian, 1469–1550, 136 *and n. 15*, 141 *n. 6*
Malahide Castle, Co. Dublin, papers, liii, 156 *n. 10*, 208 *n. 3*, 411
Malone, Edmond, 1741–1812: correspondence with JB, xx, xxv *n. 5*, 325, 326 *n. 2*, 331 *n. 2*, 332 *n. 2*, 346 *n. 1*; letter from, to Windham, lxxxi *n. 9*; letters to: from Forbes, lxxxvi; from Langton, lxi; from Scott, xix *n. 2*; from Steevens, xviii (table), 314, 407; James Boswell the younger as his executor, xix *n. 2*; in Club, xx, xxi *n. 2*, 106, 107 *and n. 23*, 356, 361 *n. 1*; *Tour* revised by, xxiv–xxv, 196, 211, 212 *second n. 1*, 213 *n. 3*; JB's literary executor, lxi; on JB's character, lxxxi *and n. 9*; Forbes asks him to censor *Life*, lxxxvi; and Percy's objections to material in *Life*, lxxxvi, 327, 330, 331 *n. 2*, 373 *n. 12*; and Macdonald's correspondence with JB, 224 *n. 1*; Courtenay visits, 268 *and n. 2*; and SJ's monument, 273 *n. 1*, 274 *and n. 2*; advice on payment for *Life*, 289 *n. 6*; and publication of *Life*, 300, 301 *and n. 2*, 310, 324 *n. 5*; in Ireland, 310 *and n. 11*, 324 *and n. 7*, 334 *and n. 2*; advises JB against publishing private conversations, 346 *n. 1*; on death of Reynolds, 361; exposes Ireland's Shakespeare forgeries, 407 *n. 2*; mentioned, xlv, li, lxxvii, xcii, xciv, xcviii *n. 3*, 155 *nn. 5–6*, 191 *n. 5*, 208 *n. 3*, 221 *n. 1*, 223 *second n. 1*, 237, 240 *and n. 9*, 251 *second n. 1*, 253, 255 *n. 1*, 256 *and n. 1*, 258, 268 *first n. 1*, *nn. 2–3*, 274 *n. 1*,

284 *n. 5*, 339, 347 *n. 2*, 354 *n. 4*, 371, 382 *n. 3*, 392 *and n. 4*, 394 *and first n. 1*, 396, 397, 402, 403 *n. 2*; *Inquiry into the Authenticity of Certain Miscellaneous Papers . . . Attributed to Shakespeare*, 407 *n. 2*; *The Plays and Poems of Shakespeare*, ed., xciv, 259 *and n. 4*, 284, 310 *n. 11*, 314 *and n. 1*; *The Works of Sir Joshua Reynolds*, ed., 371 *and n. 2*
Mannucci, C., Count, 72, 73 *and n. 9*
Mansfield, William Murray, 1st E. of, 1705–93: praises JB's *Prologue*, 42, 43 *and n. 7*; biographical account of, 43 *n. 7*; and Donaldson *v.* Becket, 47 *and n. 8*; mentioned, xxxi *and nn. 13–14*, 55 *n. 8*, 205 *and nn. 10–11*
Margate, Kent, 366, General Sea-bathing Infirmary, 366 *n. 4*
Maria Carolina, Queen of Naples, 1752–1814, 262 *and n. 13*
Marlay, Richard, Bishop of Waterford, c. 1728–1802: letter from, to JB, xv, (table), 251; biographical account of, lxvii–lxviii; in Club, xix; mentioned, 251 *second n. 1*
Marlborough, Caroline (Russell), Duchess of, wife of 4th D. of, 1743–1811, 4 *n. 6*
Marlborough, Charles Spencer, 3rd D. of, 1706–58, xxxviii
Marlborough, George Spencer, 4th D. of, 1739–1817, 4 *n. 6*
Marra, John, gunner's mate, 65 *n. 2*
Martial, 1st century A.D., *Epigrams*, 18 *n. 2*
Mary, Queen of Scots, 1542–87, painting of, by Hamilton, 56 *and n. 1*, 57 *and first n. 2*
Massingberd, William Burrell, 1719–1802, lv
Memis, John, M.D., c. 1720–after 1776, cause, lxxiii, 62 *and n. 8*, 63 *and n. 5*, 64
Menteith, Malise Graham, E. of, c. 1407–c. 90, 141 *and n. 5*
Metcalfe, Philip, 1733–1818, 207 *and n. 3*, 240, 273 *n. 1*, 274 *n. 1*, 289, 354 *first n. 3*
Middleton, Adm. Sir Charles, Bt., M.P., *later* 1st B. Barham, 1726–1813, xix *n. 1*
Millar, Rev. Alexander, JB's "chaplain", d. 1804, 183 *n. 1*

INDEX

Ramsay, Allan, painter, 1713–84; party described by Langton, 101–02; death, 173 and n. 2; mentioned, 99 n. 9

Ramusio, Giovanni Battista, 1485–1557, 425 n. 8

Rankin, Robert, clerk to Robert Boswell, 153 n. 6

Raphael (Raffaello Sanzio), 1483–1520, 349 n. 1

Raye, Rev. William, of Weldon, 372 n. 10

Reading Grammar School, Berkshire, lv and n. 14

Reid, John, sheep-stealer, d. 1774, 44 n. 12

Reid, Thomas, D.D., Professor of Moral Philosophy at Glasgow University, 1710–96, 30; *An Inquiry into the Human Mind*, 30 and n. 8

Rennell, Maj. James, geographer, 1742–1830, in Club, xx, 404 n. 3

Rennell, Thomas, D.D., Dean of Winchester, 1754–1840, lxi and n. 40

Respublica et Status Regni Hungariae, 153 and n. 8

Revolution Society, 279 n. 6

Reynolds, Frances, sister of Sir Joshua, 1729–1807, lxii, 30 n. 5, 57 n. 3, 126, 328 n. 3

Reynolds, Sir Joshua, 1723–92: correspondence with JB, xv (table), xxiii, 56–57, 112–15, 127–28, 148–51, 171–173, 174–177, 194–95, 199–200, 238, 270, 274; [missing], 52–53, 86, 92, 122, 198, 199; letters from: to Douglas (with others), xviii (table), 273–74; to Langton, xvii (table), 125–26; to Percy, 279 n. 5, 282; to Rutland, 173 n. 3; to Sheridan, 323 n. 3; letters to: from Barnard, 352 n. 5; from SJ, 251 n. 2; biographical account of, lxxxvii–lxxxviii; in Club, xix, xxi n. 2, 107, 151 n. 3, 265, 368 and n. 5; portraits of Thomas and Anne Barnard, xxxii; relationship with Club members, xxxiii, xxxviii, xlv, xlvii, xlviii, l; with SJ, founds Club, lxxxvii, 298 and n. 6; *Life* dedicated to, lxxxviii; portrait of SJ given to JB, lxxxviii, 194 n. 3; JB meets, lxxxvii–lxxxviii, 8 and n. 2; Beattie meets, 29, 30 and n. 5, 32, 33 n. 6; portrait of Beattie, 30 n. 5; Langton copies painting for, 33 n. 4; portrait of Garrick, 99, 102 and n. 8;

portrait of SJ given to Langton by Lady Diana Beauclerk, 99, 102 and n. 8; at Ramsay's party, 101 and n. 3; portrait of Mary Beauclerk, 112 and n. 3; makes notes for essays, 126; dislikes writing, 127, 189 and n. 7, 197 and n. 7; proposes Round Robin to invite JB to London, 127; and plans for SJ's Italian journey, 169 n. 2, 171 and nn. 1–2, 172–73; as King's Principal Painter, 173 and n. 3; SJ's executor, 175 and n. 2; Barnard's comments on, 189 and n. 7, 323–24; portrait of JB, 194 and n. 3, 195, 198; in Brussels, 197 n. 7, 207 and n. 3; JB takes him to see an execution, 199 and n. 2, 200 and nn. 3–4; and Round Robin to SJ, 216–17, 322; dines with Company of Painters, 238 and nn. 1–4; JB dines with, visits, 13 n. 1, 131 n. 8, 240, 274 and n. 1, 340 and n. 2; loss of sight, 270 n. 1, 323 and n. 3, 356; and SJ's monument, 273 and n. 1, 274, 333; disagreement with Academy, 279 and n. 7, 287 and n. 9; sends Burke's speech to Percy, 279 and n. 5; painting for Catherine the Great and her gift of a snuffbox, 290, 291 and n. 4; and Barnard's appointment as chaplain of Academy, 352 and n. 4; last illness and death, 356 and n. 5, 357–58, 361, 371; Barnard's concern for his spiritual life, 357–58; funeral, 361 and n. 6; "The Death of Cardinal Beaufort", 357 and n. 2; JB considers writing biography of, 371 and n. 4, 411; mentioned, li, lix, lxx, lxxxviii, 26, 27 and n. 2, 70 second n. 2, 77, 82 n. 1 and second n. 2, 86 n. 1, 104, 115, 125, 140, 180, 183, 186 n. 2, 192 n. 2, 236 and n. 1, 244, 253, 256 n. 5, 262, 290 n. 3, 294, 295 n. 1, 347 n. 2, 354 first n. 3, n. 4; *Discourses*, lxxxvii, 30 and nn. 6–7, 32–33, 189 n. 7, 291 n. 4; *The Idler*, three numbers, lxxxvii; *Works*, ed. by Malone, 371 and n. 2

Richardson, Jonathan, the younger, painter, 1694–1771, 186 n. 2, 247

Richardson, Samuel, 1689–1761, 4 n. 2

Richardson, William, Professor of Humanity (Latin), Glasgow University, 1743–1814, 124 and n. 7, *A Poetical Address in Favour of the Corsicans* (mistakenly attrib. to JB), 124 n. 7

INDEX

Russia: Paradise as agent of, 14 *n.* 2; English books translated into Russian, 280–81

Rutland, Charles Manners, 4th D. of, 1754–87; letter to, from Reynolds, 173 *n.* 3; Lord Lieutenant of Ireland, 157 *and n.* 5, 158, 160, 206 *n.* 13, 214 *and n.* 3

Sacramentarians, 167 *and n.* 12

St. Albans, Charles Beauclerk, 1st D. of, 1670–1726, xxxviii

St. Andrews, 344 *n.* 5

St. Gluvias, Cornwall, 371 *n.* 3

St. James's Chronicle, xciii, xciv, 8 *n.* 2, 117 *n.* 1, 120 *n.* 1, 128 *n.* 5, 175 *n.* 3

St. Kitts, West Indies, 327 *n.* 1

St. Martin de Front. *See* Front, Count St. Martin de

St. Petersburg, 280 *n.* 1, 281

Salisbury, Wiltshire, xlvii, 370

Salkeld, Elizabeth (Palmer), d. ?1784, 172 *and n.* 4

Sandys, George, 1578–1644, Ovid's *Metamorphoses*, translation, 328 *n.* 5

Scarron, Paul, 1610–60, *Le Roman comique*, 12 *n.* 6

Scotland: Privy Council of, 18 *and n.* 5; emigration from, 39 *and n.* 8, 42 *and n.* 4, 45 *n.* 3; controversy on origin of Scots, 130 *and n.* 7, 135–36; Ireland compared with, 131 *n.* 11; Scots said to love Scotland better than truth, 135 *and n.* 13; Scots in Ireland, 293; motto, *Nemo me impune lacesset*, 354 *and second n.* 3

Scots Magazine, 20 *n.* 3, 39 *n.* 8

Scott, Francis, of Johnston, d. 1761, 7 *and n.* 2

Scott, Hew Campbell, brother of 3rd D. of Buccleuch, 1747–66, 7 *n.* 3

Scott, Isabella (Woodhouse), widow of Francis Scott, 7 *and n.* 2, *n.* 4

Scott, Sarah (Robinson), sister of Mrs. Montagu, d. 1795, 252 *n.* 2

Scott, Sir Walter, 1771–1832, 124 *n.* 7, 213 *n.* 3; *The Lady of the Lake*, 132 *n.* 3; *Marmion*, xlviii, 71 *n.* 2

Scott, Sir William, *later* B. Stowell, 1745–1836: correspondence with JB, xv (table), 332, 345–50, 354, 392, 404–405; [missing], 345, 403; letters from: to James Boswell the younger, xix *n.*

2; to Malone, xix *n.* 2; biographical account of, lxxxviii–xc; in Club, xix, lxxxix, 88 *n.* 5; JB's relationship with, lxxxix–xc; SJ's executor, 175 *n.* 2; criticizes JB for publishing private conversations, 346 *and n.* 1, 348; JB replies to criticism, 347–48, 349–50; anecdote of Blackstone in *Life*, 348 *n.* 1; mentioned, lxii, lxxvi, 273 *n.* 1, 354 *first n.* 3, 356, 394

Selden, John, 1584–1654, *Table Talk*, 155 *and n.* 9, 186

Senhouse, Sir Joseph, mayor of Carlisle, 1743–1829, 242 *n.* 3

Session, Court of: plan to reduce number of Lords, 194 *n.* 2, 195, 201; mentioned, 34 *n.* 9, 35 *n.* 4, 47 *n.* 8, 53 *n.* 4, 63

Seward, Anna, poetess, 1742–1809: letter to, from JB, 160 *n.* 7; mentioned, 252 *n.* 2

Shakespeare, William, 1564–1616: SJ and Steevens as editors, xcii; Malone's edition, xciv, 259 *and n.* 4, 284, 310 *n.* 11, 314 *and n.* 1; Hanmer's edition, edited by Hawkins, 23 *n.* 19; Ireland's forgeries, 407 *n.* 2; *Antony and Cleopatra*, 6 *n.* 12; *As You Like It*, 137 *n.* 19; *Hamlet*, 364 *and n.* 9; *Henry V*, 380 *and n.* 8; *2 Henry VI*, 357 *and n.* 2, 358 *n.* 3; *Love's Labour's Lost*, 102 *n.* 8; *Macbeth*, 12 *and n.* 3, 421; *Merchant of Venice*, 24 *and n.* 2; *Merry Wives of Windsor*, 137 *n.* 19; *Much Ado about Nothing*, 157 *and n.* 3; *Othello*, 137 *n.* 19; *Richard III*, 12 *and n.* 3; *Taming of the Shrew*, 137 *n.* 19

Sharp, Richard ("Conversation"), 1759–1835, 376 *and n.* 3

Sharp (Sharpe), William, Regius Professor of Greek, Oxford, d. 1782, 10 *and n.* 5

Shaw, Peter, malefactor, d. 1785, 199 *and n.* 2, 200 *n.* 4

Shaw, William, Gaelic scholar, 1749–1831: in Ossian (*Fingal*) controversy, 117 *and n.* 1, 119 *and n.* 1, 120 *n.* 1, 138 *and n.* 3; *Rejoinder to an Answer from Mr. Clarke*, 139 *n.* 2; *Reply to Mr. Clarke's Answer*, 138 *n.* 3

Sheffield, John Baker Holroyd, 1st B., *later* E. of, 1735–1821, 396 *and n.* 9

461

INDEX

Shelburne, William Petty, 2nd E. of, later M. of Lansdowne, 1737–1805, government of, 129 *n.* 2, 133 *and nn.* 6–7, 134 *and nn.* 8, 10, 137 *n.* 1, 138 *n.* 5

Sheridan, Richard Brinsley, 1751–1816: in Club, xx, 150 *n.* 2; mentioned, 323 *n.* 3; *The Rivals,* xlvi

Shield, William, composer, 1748–1829, 395 *and n.* 6

Shipley, Jonathan, Bishop of St. Asaph, 1714–88: in Club, xx, 344 *and n.* 5; mentioned, 114 *and n.* 3

Shrewsbury, 231 *and n.* 8

Sidney, Algernon, 1622–83, 415 *n.* 3

Sitwell, Susan (Tait), Lady, 1797–1880, 122 *n.* 1

Skegness, Lincolnshire, lxii

Skynner, Sir John, Chief Baron of the Court of Exchequer, Ireland, 1724–1805, 205 *and n.* 10

slavery, abolition of, 418 *and n.* 2

Smellie, William, printer, 1740–95, *Account of . . . the Society of Antiquaries of Scotland,* 191 *n.* 4

Smith, Adam, 1723–90: letter from, to JB [missing], xv (table), 7; 3, letters to, from JB, xv (table), 7; biographical account of, xc–xcii; in Club, xix, xxi, xci; JB's opinion of, xc–xcii; Reynolds consults him about writing, 126; mentioned, 7 *n.* 3, 101 *n.* 3; "Of Imitation", 126 *and n.* 5; *The Theory of Moral Sentiments,* xc; *The Wealth of Nations,* xc

Smith, Rev. John, 1747–1807, 117 *n.* 1

Smith, Capt. (Lieut.) Robert, of South Lincolnshire Regiment, 319 *and n.* 13

Smollett, Tobias, 1721-71, *Compleat History of England,* 229 *n.* 1

Society of Antiquaries of Scotland, 191 *and n.* 4

Southampton, lxiii, lxvi

South Sea Company, liv

Spa, mineral waters, 115 *n.* 4

Spectator, The, 237 *and n.* 2, 423 *and n.* 5

Spence, Joseph, 1699–1768: letters from, to Langton, xvii (table), lv–lvi, 420–424; biographical account of, xcii; Langton's friendship with, lv, lvi, lxviii; notes on conversations with literary and learned men, xcii; men-

tioned, lix; *Essay on Pope's Odyssey,* xcii; *Observations,* lv; *Polymetis,* xcii

Spencer, George John Spencer, 2nd E. (styled V. Althorp) 1758–1834; in Club, xx, 88 *n.* 5, 104 *and n.* 14a, 150 *n.* 2; mentioned, xix *n.* 2, 103 *and n.* 14, 382 *n.* 2

Spencer, Lord Robert, M.P., 1747–1831, 99 *n.* 1

Spenser, Edmund, ?1552–99, 233 *and n.* 4

Stamford, Lincolnshire, 255 *and second n.* 1

Stanes, William, Chelmsford bookseller, 383 *and n.* 3

Stanhope, Charles Stanhope, 3rd E., 1753–1816: answer to Burke's speech on French Revolution, 279 *and n.* 6, 282; mentioned, 342 *n.* 3

Stanhope, Edwin Francis, 199 *n.* 2

Stanhope, Philip, son of Lord Chesterfield, 1732–68, xlvii

Stanyard, prize-fighter, 377 *second n.* 2, 378 *n.* 3

Stedman, Rev. Thomas, c. 1747–1825, letter to, from Percy, lxxxvi, lxxxvii *and n.* 17

Steele, Sir Richard, 1672–1729, 394 *n.* 2; *see also Guardian; Tatler*

Steevens, George, 1736–1800: correspondence with JB, xv (table), 234–35, 250–51, 251–52, 312, 313–14; letters from, to Malone, xviii (table), 314, 407; letters to, from SJ, 235 *nn.* 3, 5; biographical account of, xcii–xciv; in Club, xix, xciii, xciv, 50 *n.* 6, 235 *n.* 5; Shakespeare edited by, xcii; SJ's opinion of, xciii; hoax on JB and Hackman's execution, xciii–xciv; and *Life,* xciv; contributions to *Life,* 234–235, 251 *and n.* 2; mentioned, 86 *n.* 1, 273 *n.* 3

Stephenson, Roland, candidate in Carlisle election, ?1728–1807, 242 *n.* 3

Stewart, Dugald, Professor of Moral Philosophy, Edinburgh, 1753–1828, 221 *n.* 1

Stilton, Huntingdonshire, 19 *n.* 1

Stirling (Sterling), Rev. Joseph, 333 *and n.* 4

Stockdale, John, publisher, ?1749–1814, xciv, 290 *and n.* 1a, 293

Stone, Andrew, 1703–73, xxix *and n.* 4

462

INDEX

Stone, George, Archbishop of Armagh, ?1708-64, xxix, xxxi

Stopford, Gen. Edward, b. 1732, 251 second n. 1

Stourbridge Grammar School, Worcestershire, 247 and n. 13

Strahan, William, M.P., printer, 1715–1785, 79 n. 2, 123 n. 5, 215 n. 1

Strathbogie, Presbytery of, 53 n. 4

Streatham, 71 and n. 4

Stuart, Andrew, M.P., 1725–1801, 192 first n. 2

Stuart, Lieut.-Col. the Hon. James Archibald (Stuart Wortley-Mackenzie), 1747-1818: JB visits his regiment, 92, 94 and n. 2; mentioned, 108 n. 6, 192 first n. 1

Stuart, Margaret (Cunynghame), wife of preceding, d. 1808, 114 n. 7

Stuart, Hon. William, Bishop of St. Davids, later Archbishop of Armagh, 1755–1822, lxxxvii n. 19

Sully, Maximilien de Béthune, Duc de, 1560–1641, Memoirs, 13 n. 4

Sumner, Robert Carey, D.D. Master of Harrow, 1729–71, 246 and n. 4

Sunderlin, Philippa (Rooper), Lady, d. 1831, 268 n. 1

Sunderlin, Richard Malone, 1st B., Malone's brother, c. 1738–1816, 324 n. 7, 403 n. 2, 407

Surrey, Henry Howard, styled E. of, ?1517–47, poems, ed. by Percy, xciii

Sussex, Hester (Hall), Countess of, wife of 3rd E. of, ?1736–77, lxxix

Sussex, George Augustus Yelverton, 2nd E. of, 1727–58, 17 n. 4

Sussex, Henry Yelverton, 3rd E. of, 1728–99, 17 n. 4

Swift, Jonathan, 1667–1745, xxxvi, Description of a City Shower, 353 n. 5a

Symons (originally Peers), Sir Richard, Bt., c. 1744–96, 338 and second n. 1

Syrus, Publilius, 1st century B.C., 392 n. 3

Tait, Archibald Campbell, Archbishop of Canterbury, 1811–82, 122 second n. 1

Tait, Craufurd, son of John Tait, 1765–1832, 122 second n. 1

Tait, John, W. S., d. 1802, 122 and second n. 1, 123

Tandy, James Napper, Irish patriot, 1740–1803, 369 and n. 8, 380 n. 7

Tatler, The, Percy's project for edition of, 237 and n. 2

Taylor, John, oculist, 1703–72, 80 and n. 6

Taylor, Rev. John, LL.D., 1711–88, SJ visits at Ashbourne, 72 and n. 6, 74 n. 4

Taylor, Rev. John, LL.D., 1704–66, Elements of the Civil Law, 425 and n. 6

Temple, George Nugent-Temple-Grenville, 2nd E., later M. of Buckingham, Lord Lieutenant of Ireland, 1753–1813, 129 n. 2, 134 and n. 10

Temple, Rev. William Johnson, 1739–1796: letters from: to JB, 149 n. 1, 172 n. 4; to Langton, lxi; letters to, from JB, 33 n. 5, 53 n. 4, 63 n. 2, 138 n. 5, 176 n. 8, 180 n. 9, 332 n. 2; JB's executor, lxi; visits JB, 297 n. 1, 300 second n. 1; JB and daughters visit, 371 n. 3; visits Lord Eliot, 376, 377 and n. 2; mentioned, 74 n. 3, 148–49, 172, 383 n. 6; Diaries, lxi and n. 36, n. 38

Terrie (Terry), Thomas, landlord in London, lvii n. 23

Terry, Mrs., landlady in London, lvii and n. 23

Test Act, Debates, 283 and n. 2, 290 and n. 1a, 293

Texier. See Le Texier

Thanet, Sackville Tufton, 9th E. of, 1769–1825, 326

Themistocles, c. 528–c. 462 B.C., 260 and n. 2

Thessalonica, 55

Thomas, Charles, fruiterer in London, 28

Thornton, Bonnell, author, 1724–68, lvi, 8 n. 2, 286 n. 2; Adventurer papers, 286 and n. 4; Connoisseur (with Colman), lvi, 286 and n. 6

Thrale, Henry, c. 1728–81; in Paris with SJ, 60 and n. 2, 305 n. 1, 306 n. 1; death, 251 n. 2; mentioned, 29 and n. 3, 71 nn. 3–4, 72, 73 n. 9, 102 n. 8, 104, 349 n. 5

Thrale, Hester Lynch (Salusbury), wife of preceding, later Mrs. Piozzi, 1741–1821: letters to, from SJ, 40 n. 11, 101 n. 2; on Langton, lii and n. 3, liii, lxxv, 77 n. 1; on Lady Rothes, lviii; Langton visits, 29 and n. 1; in Paris with SJ, 60 and n. 2, 305 n. 1, 306 n. 1; in Brighton with SJ, 125 and n. 1; SJ's Sapphic Ode addressed to her, 209 n.